DHARMA 2021
© 2021 Hari Venu Singh
First Edition 2021

Chakra Foundation
info@chakra-foundation.org

Print and Publishing: BoD – Books on Demand Norderstedt
ISBN 978-3-7543-1525-5

For Jonah, Mira, Arjun, You & Me

"For the accomodation of these travellers principally, the Chetrums (Kshetra) have been established, and to each of them pagodas, choultries, and schools are annexed. I will now explain to you the nature and extent of the charities dispensed by them. All travellers from the Bramin to the Pariar inclusive, pilgrims of every description including jogues (Yogīs), jungums (ascetics?), ateets (Atithi) and byragies (Vairāgī) are fed with boiled rice. Those who do not choose to eat the boiled rice receive it unboiled with spices &c. These distributions continue till midnight when a bell is rung and proclamation made requiring all those who have not been fed to appear and take the rice prepared for them. The travellers who may be unable to proceed in their journey are fed as long as they remain at the Chetrum. In each chetrum a teacher to each of the four vedums (Veda) is appointed, and a school-master and doctors, skillful in the care of diseases, swellings, and the poison of reptiles; all the orphans of strangers who may come to the chetrum are placed under the care of the school-master. They are also fed three times a day, and once in four days they are annointed with oil. They receive medicine when they require it; cloths also are given to them and the utmost attention paid to them. They are instructed in the sciences to which they may express a preference, and after having obtained a competent knowledge of them the expences of their marriage are defrayed. Travellers who fall sick at the chetrum or before their arrival, receive medicine, and the diet proper for them, and are attended with respect and kindness untill their recovery. The obsequies of those who die during their residence at the chetrum are performed according to the rites of their cast. Milk is provided for infants; pregnant women are entertained with kindness, and if they happen to be delivered at the chetrum, their expenses are defrayed, medicines are given to them and they are permitted to remain in the chetrum three months after their delivery. Those who apply to the chetrum and state their inability to defray the expence of receiving the Braminical thread, of their marriage, or of the performance of the ceremonies, subsequent to their father's death, receive a sum of money proportionate to the occasion. As the lands annexed to the chetrums is in general very poor, it happens frequently from a deficiency of rain, that they do not produce sufficient for the expences. When this is the case my anxiety to prevent any diminution of these excellent charities, which I consider as the most honourable appendage of my dignity, has always induced me to send to them from the circuar both grain and money sufficient to make up the deficiency. ... The superintendence of them has always descended from the older to the younger queen. It has remained in the hands of the senior until her death and then descended to the wife of the reigning Rajah. I have a perfect confidence that this custom of my ancestors will not be deviated from, and that I shall not suffer the disgrace of seeing it abolished in my reign." (His Excellency Serfojee Rajah of Tanjore to the British Government, 1801)

DHARMA 2021

NOTES

Arab. _ Arabic	Ital. _ Italian	Pers. _ Persian	= _ same as
Chin. _ Chinese	Jap. _ Japanese	Pl. _ Plural	→ _ see also
comp. _ compound	Lat. _ Latin	Russ. _ Russian	» « _ compare
esp. _ especially	^M _ Muslim Chronicle		' ' _ literally
f. _ feminine	m. _ masculine	(1), (2), ... _ from	" " _ quote
Germ. _ German	mod. _ modern	different roots	/translation
Gr. _ Greek	n. _ neuter	[ ] _ implied	(?) _ doubt/guess
ind. _ indeclinable	opp. _ opposed to	{ } _ derived from	√ _ Dhatu

ऽ _ अवग्रह of an initial *a*, as in ऽर्जुनः. Sometimes hinting at सन्धि, as in अम्बाऽसक्त (*ā-a*), अम्बाऽऽसक्त (*ā-ā*).

ॄ _ Consonant ending हल्-अन्त, as in त्वम्

। _ विराम, as in सत्यमेव जयते ।

॥ _ पूर्ण-विराम, ending a verse, as in ... किमकुर्वत सञ्जय ॥ Often with the verse number, as in ... किमकुर्वत सञ्जय ॥१॥

° _ Abbrev., as in गी° (गीता); also in repeating, as in भूपति °तल (for भूतल)

INTRODUCTION

समाप्तिकामो मङ्गलमाचरेत् ।[1] मङ्गलमिष्टदेवतानमस्कारः ।[2]
विनायकं गुरुं भानुं ब्रह्माविष्णुमहेश्वरान् । सरस्वतीं प्रणम्यादौ सर्वकार्यार्थ-
सिद्धये ॥[3]

"The Europeans are apt to imagine that before the great Greek thinkers, Socrates, Plato, and Aristotle, there was a crude confusion of thought, a sort of chaos without form and void. Such a view becomes almost a provincialism when we realize that systems of thought which influenced countless millions of human beings had been elaborated by people who never heard the names of the Greek thinkers." (Sir Sarvepalli Radhakrishnan, Indian Prof. at Oxford University and President of India, 1888-1975)

"I will omit all discussion of the science of the Hindus, a people not the same as Syrians, their subtle discoveries in the science of astronomy, discoveries more ingenious than those of the Greeks and the Babylonians; their valuable method of calculation; their computing that surpasses description. I wish only to say that this computation is done by means of nine signs. If those who believe because they speak Greek, that they have reached the limits of science should know these things, they would be convinced that there are also others who know something." (Severus Sebokht, Syrian scholar and bishop, c. 575-666)

"The land where books were first written and from where wisdom and knowledge sprang is India." (Ali, c. 594-661)

"The Hindus excel in astrology, mathematics, medicine and in various other sciences. They have developed to a perfection, arts like sculpture, painting, and architecture. They have collections of poetry, philosophy, literature and science of morals. From India we received the book called Kalilah wa Dimnah. These people have judgment and are brave. They possess the virtues of cleanliness and purity. Contemplation has originated with them." (Al-Jahiz; Muslim historian, 776-868)

"The Hindus are superior to all other nations in intelligence and thoughtfulness. They are more exact in astronomy and astrology than any other people. The Siddhanta is a good proof of their intellectual powers; by this book the Greeks and Persians have also profited. In medicine their opinion ranks first." (Ahmad ibn Ya'qubi, Muslim geographer and historian, ?-897)

"The Indians among all nations, through many centuries and since antiquity, have been the source of wisdom, fairness and moderation. They are creators of sublime thoughts, universal apologues, rare inventions and remarkable concepts." "To their credit, the Indians have made great strides in the study of numbers and of geometry. They have acquired immense information and reached the zenith in their knowledge of the movements of the stars (astronomy) and the secrets of the skies (astrology) as well as other mathematical studies. After all that, they have surpassed all the other peoples in their knowledge of medical science and the strengths of various drugs, the characteristics of compounds and the peculiarities of substances [chemistry]." (Said Al-Andalusi, Muslim historian and judge, 1029-1070)

"Hindus had made considerable advances in astronomy, algebra, arithmetic, botany and medicine, not to mention their superiority in grammar, long before some of these sciences were cultivated by the most ancient nations of Europe." (Sir Monier Monier-Williams, British Indologist and head of the Oxford's Boden Chair, 1819-1899)

"Many of the advances in the sciences that we consider today to have been made in Europe were in fact made in India centuries ago." (Sir Montstuart Elphinstone Grant Duff, British historian and Governor of Madras, 1829-1906)

"If [modern Indian] teachers were not so ignorant, as a rule, of their own culture, they would have no difficulty in showing their students that the much vaunted 'scientific temper' is nothing new to India." (Michel Danino, French-Indian historian)

1. Foreword[4]

"Were an Asiatic to ask me for a definition of Europe, I should be forced to answer him: It is that part of the world which is haunted by the incredible delusion that man was created out of nothing, and that his present birth is his first entrance into life." (Arthur Schopenhauer, German philosopher and writer, 1788-1860)

All beings are eternal, conscious आत्मा, perpetually undergoing संसार in this जगत् among all species, following the universal law of कर्म. Both, आत्मा and जगत्, have their origin in the Absolute ब्रह्म, represented in sound by the syllable ॐ. On factually realizing its divine nature, purified through धर्म, the आत्मा achieves माक्ष.

ओंकारमूलमन्त्राध्यः पुनर्जन्मदृढाशयः। गोभक्तो भारतगुरुर् हिन्दुर् हिंसन-दूषकः॥[5]

Because a majority of Hindu scriptures and 70% of Hindus are वैष्णव in character (*Britannica Book of the Year 1996*), popular believe and culture follows intrinsically द्वैत-/द्वैताद्वैत-वाद (not अद्वैत) and ब्रह्म-/परिणाम-वाद of व्यासदेव (not माया-वाद of शङ्कराचार्य), which certainly reflects in this book.

अनन्तशास्त्रं बहुलाश्च विद्याः स्वल्पश्च कालो बहुविघ्नता च।
यत्सारभूतं तदुपासनीयं हंसो यथा क्षीरमिवाम्बुमध्यात्॥[6]

"The three books which are most common in all the schools, and which are used indiscriminately by the several castes, are the Ramayanum, Maha Bharata, and Bhagvata ..." (The Collector of Bellary, 1823)

प्रातर्द्यूतप्रसङ्गेन मध्याह्ने स्त्रीप्रसङ्गतः। रात्रौ चौरप्रसङ्गेन कालो गच्छति धीमताम्॥[7]

Rituals are based either on वेद or पुराण; if the latter is more complex, we present them here in the light of the original Vedic (वैदिक) version, according to Pandurang Vaman Kane's famous *History Of Dharmashastra*.

The use of Sanskrit words in an English sentence is ruled by the principles of लोक-प्रमाण. In translations, Sanskrit words in brackets are in their प्रकृति form, as in: "An unable person (अशक्त) becomes साधु, a poor person ब्रह्मचारी (ब्रह्मचारिन्), a sick person देव-भक्त, and an old woman पति-व्रता."[8] Sometimes, a modern name or wrong version is also explained in brackets, as with Sanskrit (संस्कृत), Benares (वाराणसी), Agarbatti (अगरुवर्ती), and 'Vasudeva Kutumbakam' (वसुधैव कुटुम्बकम्)[9]. Because verses are presented out of their original context (सत्यमेव जयते ।[10] एकं सन्तं बहुधा कल्पयन्ति ।[11]), references are given, wherever available. मूर्खो वदति विष्णाय बुधो वदति विष्णवे। नम इत्येवमर्थं च द्वयोरेव समं फलम् ॥ यस्मै दत्तं च यज्ज्ञानं ज्ञानदाता हरिः स्वयम्। ज्ञानेन तेन स स्तौति भावग्राही जनार्दनः ॥[12]

2. Space

Distances (मात्रा):

अङ्गुल	1.9 cm	वितस्ति	22,5 cm	पद	30 cm	दण्ड	1.80 m
मुष्टि	8 cm	हस्त	45 cm	प्रक्रम	60 cm	रज्जु	18 m
धनुर्मुष्टि	16 cm						

The directions are presided by different देव, as depicted in the ideal pattern of a house, known as वास्तु-पुरुष-मण्डल of 81 squares:

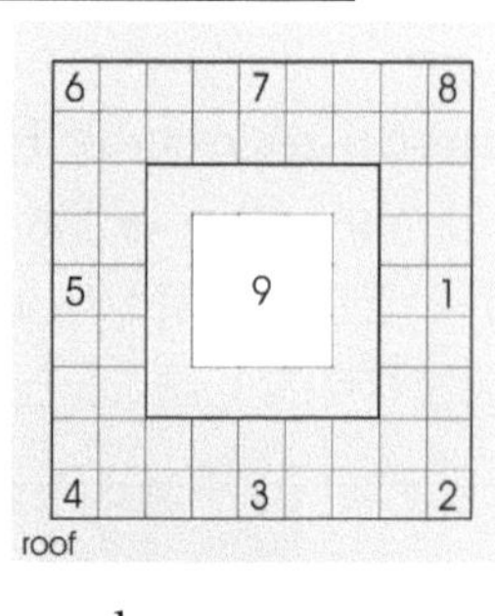

	direction		देव	element	and purpose
1	पूर्व		सूर्य/मित्र		entrance hall
2	दक्षिण-पूर्व	आग्नेय	अग्नि	अग्नि	kitchen
3	दक्षिण		यम		bedroom
4	दक्षिण-पश्चिम	नैर्ऋत्य	निर्ऋति	भूमि	bedroom, store
5	पश्चिम		वरुण		dining room
6	उत्तर-पश्चिम	वायव्य	वायु	वायु	cattle, grains
7	उत्तर		कुवेर		treasury, library
8	उत्तर-पूर्व	ऐशान	ईशन/शिव	जल	well, meditation
9	center		ब्रह्मा	आकाश	empty

Sole basis of all Vedic observations were the 27 नक्षत्र (plus अभिजित्, now only a placeholder without sector) and the tool of analyzing them was the सर्वतोभद्र-चक्र :

1 कृत्तिका 2 रोहिणी/ब्राह्मी 3 मृगशीर्षा/आग्रहायणी
4 आर्द्रा 5 पुनर्वसु/यामकौ 6 पुष्य/पुण्य 7 आश्लेषा
8 मघा 9 पूर्व-फाल्गुनी 10 उत्तर-फाल्गुनी 11 हस्त
12 चित्रा 13 स्वाति 14 विशाखा/राधा 15 अनुराधा
16 ज्येष्ठा 17 मूल 18 पुर्वाषाढा 19 उत्तराषाढा
20 अभिजित् 21 श्रवण 22 श्रविष्ठा/धनिष्ठा 23 शतभिषा
24 पूर्व-भाद्रपद 25 उत्तर-भाद्रपद 26 रेवती 27 अश्विनी
28 भरणी

	1	2	3	4	5	6	7	
28								8
27								9
26								10
25								11
24								12
23								13
22								14
	21	20	19	18	17	16	15	

"The motion of the stars calculated by the Hindus before some 4500 years vary not even a single minute from the tables of Cassine and Meyer (used in the 19th century). The Indian tables give the same annual variation of the moon as the discovered by Tycho Brahe – a variation unknown to the school of Alexandria and also to the Arabs who followed the calculations of the school... The Hindu systems of astronomy are by far the oldest and that from which the Egyptians, Greek, Romans and – even the Jews derived from the Hindus their knowledge." (Jean-Sylvaine Bailly, French astronomer, 1736-1793)

The modern Hindu calendar is called पञ्चाङ्ग, treating 5 astronomical aspects – तिथि, नक्षत्र, राशि, योग and करण. The popular राशि charts evolved from the Greek 12-Sign Zodiac (with Vedic gods), mixed with the नक्षत्र system and other methods to make predictions. It became prevalent in India only after 149 CE when the first Yavana astrological text was translated into Sanskrit by Yavaneshvara.

3. Time					
निमेष	0.5 s	दण्ड	24 min	प्रहर	3 h
क्षण	1.5 s	मुहूर्त	48 min	अहर्	12 h
लघु	2 min			वासर	24 h

अहोरात्रे विभजते सूर्यो मानुषलौकिके। रात्रिः स्वप्नाय भूतानां चेष्टायै कर्मणामहः ॥13 अनायुष्यं दिवा स्वप्नं तथाभ्युदितशायिता ।14 नक्तचर्या दिवा-स्वप्नम् आलस्यं पैशुनं मदम् । अतियोगमयोगं च श्रेयसो ऽर्थी परित्यजेत् ॥15

Humans are diurnal, i.e., most active during day. Dawn and dusk are not considered auspicious for any work, but the famous ब्रह्म-मुहूर्त is esp. suited for meditation.

	biological rhythm, दोष	best for ...
05:00	low body temperature, वात	getting up, meditation
06:00	rise in blood pressure	सन्ध्या, अष्टाङ्ग-योग
08:00	greatest bowel movement, कफ	evacuation, light breakfast
10:00 ±2h	highest alertness	study, स्वाध्याय
noon	पित्त	lunch
16:00 ±2h	best reaction/strength, वात	physical work, exercises
18:00		सन्ध्या
19:00	कफ	light dinner
02:00 ±3h		sleep

Factors that disturb our biorhythm are artificial light (esp. LED), radiation (5G), shift-work, irregular eating times and drugs.

उत्थाय नेत्रे प्रक्षाल्य शुचिर्भूत्वा समाहितः। परिजप्य च मन्त्राणि भक्षयेद्दन्तधावनम् ॥[16] ब्राह्मे मुहूर्ते उत्थाय चिन्तयेदात्मनो हितम्। गुरुं विष्णुं नमस्कृत्य मातरं पितरं तथा ॥[17]

गेयं गीता नामसहस्रं ध्येयं श्रीपतिरूपमजस्त्रम्।
नेयं सज्जनसङ्गे चित्तं देयं दीनजनाय च वित्तम् ॥[18]

Sandhya:

विप्रो वृक्षस्तस्य मूलं च सन्ध्या वेदः शाखा धर्मकर्माणि पत्रम्।
तस्मान्मूलं यत्नतो रक्षणीयं छिन्ने मूले नैव शाखा न पत्रम् ॥[19]

Food:[20] Taste is of six kinds – मधुर-अम्ल-लवण-कटु-तिक्त-कषाय – and all should ideally be represented in a meal. Traditionally, all food cooked (or a small sample) is offered with पूजा to God – before tasting it. It is thereafter accepted and disributed as प्रसाद, mercy of God. Many festivals are observed with व्रत like उपवास (till noon, moon-rise, etc.), but later प्रसाद, दक्षिण and दान is distributed. One can always remember:

हरिर्दाता हरिर्भोक्ता हरिरन्नं प्रजापतिः। हरिः सर्वशरीरस्थो भुङ्क्ते भोजयते हरिः ॥[21]

The evening is celebrated with दीप and आरात्रिक.

Days (वार/वासर) are nowadays grouped into the imported सप्ताह, where each day is said to be dedicated to a Vedic ग्रह.

आदित्याय च सोमाय मङ्गलाय बुधाय च। गुरुशुक्रशनिभ्यश्च राहवे केतवे नमः ॥[22]

The worship of सूर्य every रवि-वार spread as martial मित्र/Mithras cult from Persia to Rome, where Sunday became a holiday in 321 CE.: "On the venerable day of the Sun let the magistrate and people residing in cities rest, and let all workshops be closed." Later, it was declared the new Christian Sabbat or 'resting day', entering official India under British rule as Sunday-off.

---

4. Calendar

Lunar Day & Month:

1. प्रतिपद्	अग्नि	ceremonies, चन्द्र-दर्शन in शुक्ल-पक्ष
2. द्वितीया	ब्रह्मा	laying of any foundation
3. तृतीया	गौरी	shaving, etc.
4. चतुर्थी	गणेश	struggle, गणेश-पूजा with उपवास (till moonrise)
5. पञ्चमी	नाग	medical treatment
6. षष्ठी	कार्तिकेय	meeting
7. सप्तमी	सूर्य	journey
8. अष्टमी	रुद्र	fortification and struggle, अनध्याय
9. नवमी	अम्बिका	struggle
10. दशमी	धर्म/यम	acts of virtue
11. एकादशी	रुद्र	हरि-वासर with उपवास
12. द्वादशी	विष्णु	ceremonies
13. त्रयोदशी	कामदेव	festivities
14. चतुर्दशी	कलि	शिव-रात्रि, गायत्री-व्रत in शुक्ल-पक्ष, अनध्याय
15. पूर्णिमा	सोम	सत्य-नारायण-व्रत, यज्ञ, अनध्याय
/अमावास्या	पितृ	day-off, अनध्याय
		श्राद्ध (esp. in आश्विन-कृष्ण, called पितृ-पक्ष)

एकादशी-सङ्कल्प (in the morning, after सन्ध्या):
एकादश्यां निराहारः स्थित्वा चाहं परेऽहनि । भोक्ष्ये ऽहं पुण्डरीकाक्ष शरणं मे भवाच्युत ॥[23]

अमावास्या is considered to be inauspicious (except for दीपावलि) and it was observed as a day off, until British rule brought Sunday-off to India.

Since Āryabhatta, the calculation of a lunar day (तिथि) is based on incremental differences of 12° between the longitudes of Moon and Sun. But, such तिथि may start at any time of the day, and if the Moon doesn't progress that much, the previous तिथि

is considered to exist on that day as well. Better to return to the practical Vedic system, in which a तिथि is the time from sunrise to sunrise:

अहः पूर्वं ततो रात्रिर् मासाः शुक्क्लादयः स्मृताः । श्रविष्ठादीनि ऋक्षाणि ऋतवः शिशिरादयः ॥[24]

The lunisolar year (संवत्सर /वर्ष) should start after उत्तरायण (~21.12.) with शुक्ल-पक्ष and end with अमावास्या, an order called अमान्त, still in use in South-India. About every third year, an अधिक-मास (intercalary month) resynchronizes it with उत्तरायण. Memory of उत्तरायण is preserved in the festival of मकर-सङ्क्रान्ति (~14.01.), which coincided in 285 CE, but occurs about 24 days later at the present time, showing the need of a reform.

In the present official (North-Indian) calendar, the year starts late with चैत्र कृष्ण-पक्ष (पूर्णिमान्त).

उत्तरायण			
शिशिर Jan/Feb	पौष	शुक्ल	15 पौष-पूर्णिमा
		कृष्ण	माघ-मास North-India
	माघ	शुक्ल	5 वसन्त-पञ्चमी with सरस्वती-पूजा 8 भीष्माष्टमी
		कृष्ण	फाल्गुन-मास North-India 13 त्रयोदशी-चतुर्दशी with महा-शिवरात्रि
वसन्त Mar/Apr	फाल्गुन	शुक्ल	15 सत्यव्रत-/होलिका-पूर्णिमा with होलिका-दहन
		कृष्ण	1 प्रतिपद् with होली /Hola Mohalla नव-वर्ष (चैत्र-मास) North-India
	चैत्र	शुक्ल	5 श्री-/लक्ष्मी-पञ्चमी (noon) 8 अन्नपूर्णा-पूजा 9 राम-नवमी (noon) 10 धर्मराज-दशमी 13 महावीर-जयन्ती 15 पूर्णिमा with हनुमज्जयन्ती
		कृष्ण	वैशाख-मास North-India
ग्रीष्म May/Jun	वैशाख	शुक्ल	3 अक्षय-तृतीया 9 सीता-नवमी 14 नृसिंह-चतुर्दशी 15 बुद्ध-पूर्णिमा
		कृष्ण	ज्यैष्ठ-मास North-India
	ज्यैष्ठ	शुक्ल	10 गङ्गा-दशमी with दशहरा and सेतु-बन्ध 11 निर्जल-एकादशी 15 वट-पूर्णिमा with सावित्री-व्रत
		कृष्ण	आषाढ-मास North-India

दक्षिणायन			
वर्षा Jul/Aug	आषाढ	शुक्ल	2 द्वितीया with जगन्नाथ-रथयात्रा
			11 एकादशी with चातुर्मास्य-व्रत-प्रारम्भ
			15 गुरु-पूर्णिमा
		कृष्ण	श्रावण-मास North-India
	श्रावण	शुक्ल	5 नाग-पञ्चमी
			12 पवित्रारोपण
			15 पूर्णिमा with रक्षा-बन्धन /Rakhi
		कृष्ण	भाद्रपद-मास North-India
			8 जन्माष्टमी (midnight)
शरद् Sep/Okt	भाद्रपद	शुक्ल	4 गणेश-चतुर्थी (noon)
			8 राधाष्टमी
		कृष्ण	आश्विन-मास North-India
	आश्विन	शुक्ल	1 प्रतिपद् with नवरात्र-प्रारम्भ
			10 विजया-दशमी with Dussehra[25] and सरस्वती-पूजा
			15 शरद्-/मित्र-पूर्णिमा
		कृष्ण	कार्तिक-मास North-India
			15 अमावास्या with दीपावलि / दीपाली /Diwali
हेमन्त Nov/Dec	कार्तिक	शुक्ल	1 बलि-प्रतिपद् with गोवर्धन-पूजा
			2 भ्रातृ-द्वितीया
			11 एकादशी with भीष्म-पञ्चक-प्रारम्भ
			15 कार्तिक-पूर्णिमा, Guru Nanak Gurpurab
		कृष्ण	मार्गशीर्ष-मास North-India
	मार्ग-शीर्ष	शुक्ल	11 एकादशी with गीता-जयन्ती
		कृष्ण	पौष-मास North-India

Timeline[26]: Kings of भारत[27] (synchronized in generations), रामायण[28], महाभारत[29]

निषेकगर्भजन्मानि बाल्यकौमारयौवनम् । वयोमध्यं जरा मृत्युर् इत्यवस्थास्तनोर्नव ॥30 लालयेत्पञ्चवर्षाणि दशवर्षाणि ताडयेत् । प्राप्ते तु षोडशे वर्षे पुत्रे मित्रवदाचरेत् ॥31

To form man as human being there is a series of ceremonies, each introducing a new stage of purification and education. There are lists of 48 (अग्नि-पुराण 166.9ff.) and 40 संस्कार (गौतम-स्मृति ch.8).

गर्भाधानं तु प्रथमं ततः पुंसवनं स्मृतम् । सीमन्तोन्नयनं जात-कर्म नामानुशासनम् । चूडाकृतिं व्रतबन्धं वेदव्रतान्यशेषतः ॥32

Stage	Age	Sacraments
1. Conception (निषेक)		गर्भाधान
2. Embryo (गर्भ)		पुंसवन, सीमन्त-उन्नयन
3. Birth (जन्मन्)		जात-कर्म, नाम-करण
4. Infancy (बाल्य)	0-5	निष्क्रमण, अन्न-प्राशन, मुण्डन/चौल
5. Childhood (कौमार)	5-15	
a) Boyhood (पौगण्ड)	5-10	विद्यारम्भ, school
b) Teenage (कैशोर)	10-15	दीक्षा/उपनयन, profession
6. Youth (यौवन)	15-45	university, (boys:) केशान्त, विवाह
7. Middle Age (वयो-मध्य)	45-60	
8. Old Age (जरा)	60+	वानप्रस्थ
9. Death (मृत्यु)		अन्त्येष्टि, श्राद्ध

1. गर्भाधान before impregnation; the mother is blessed with appropriate verses: विष्णुर्योनिं कल्पयतु त्वष्टा रूपाणि पिंशतु । आसिञ्चतु प्रजापतिर् धाता गर्भ दधातु ते । गर्भं धेहि सिनीवालि गर्भं धेहि सरस्वति ॥33

2. पुंसवन (after the third month) and सीमन्त-उन्नयन (in the eighth month), to cheer and bless the mother-to-be दौहृदस्याप्रदानेन गर्भो दोषमवाप्नुयात् । वैरूप्यं मरणं वापि तस्मात्कार्यं प्रियं स्त्रिया: ॥34

3. जात-कर्म and नाम-करण स्त्रीणां सुखोद्यमक्रूरं विस्पष्टार्थं मनोहरम् । मङ्गल्यं दीर्घवर्णान्तम् आशीर्वादाभिधानवत् ॥35

4. निष्क्रमण in the 4th month

5. अन्न-प्राशन after 6-7 months

6. मुण्डन/चौल in the 3rd year

The tonsure leaves a चूडा/शिखा. As hairstyle, it is an indication of cleanliness and personal sacrifice to God. The शिखा is always tied or knotted, except for sleeping, funerals and death anniversaries. In North-India it is max. 4 cm in diameter, in the South larger. Today it is seen mainly among ब्राह्मण and priests, but until around 1900, the शिखा was one of the few external signs of all male Hindus, transcending caste and region.[36]

7. कर्ण-वेध at the time of मुण्डन or उपनयन

8. विद्यारम्भ with 5 years

9. दीक्षा either as उपनयन (from 8 to 24 years) or पञ्च-संस्कार

10. (girls) ऋतु-काल-संस्कार after first menstruation (Menarche)

11. (boys) केशान्त with 16 years

12. विवाह (Marriage). Preliminary ceremonies: 1. वधू-वर-गुण-परीक्षा, 2. वर-प्रेषण, 3. मण्डप-करण (if the ceremony is performed outside the house), 4. गौरी-हर-पूजा, 5. तैल-हरिद्रा-आरोपण, 6. वधू-गृह-आगमन, 7. मधुपर्क, 8. समञ्जन (both), 9. वधू-वर-निष्क्रमण, 10. परस्पर-समीक्षण; Essential: 11. कन्या-दान, 12. होम, 13. पाणि-ग्रहण, 14. लाज-होम, 15. अग्नि-परिणयन, 16. अश्म-आरोहन, 17. सप्त-पदी, 18. मूर्ध-अभिषेक, 19. हृदय-स्पर्श, 20. मङ्गलसूत्र-बन्धन, 21. आर्द्र-अक्षत-आरोपण; Subsequent: 23. प्रेक्षक-अनुमन्त्रण, 24. दक्षिणा-दान, 25. गृह-प्रवेश, 26. ध्रुव-अरुन्धती-दर्शन, 27. त्रिरात्र-व्रत, 28. चतुर्थी-कर्म

स्वगोत्राद् भ्रश्यते नारी उद्वाहात्सप्तमे पदे। भर्तृगोत्रेण कर्तव्यं दानपिण्डोदकक्रिया ॥[37]

13. Retirement as वानप्रस्थ

14. अन्त्येष्टि (Last Rite).

काव्यशास्त्रविनोदेन कालो गच्छति धीमताम् । व्यसनेन तु मूर्खाणां निद्रया कलहेन वा ॥³⁸ गन्धेन गावः पश्यन्ति वेदैः पश्यन्ति ब्राह्मणाः । चारैः पश्यन्ति राजानश् चक्षुभ्यामितरे जनाः ॥³⁹ धृत्या शिश्नोदरं रक्षेत् पाणिपादं च चक्षुषा । चक्षुःश्रोत्रे च मनसा मनो वाचं च विद्यया ॥⁴⁰

सर्वद्रव्येषु विद्यैव द्रव्यमाहुरनुत्तमम् । अहार्यत्वादनर्घत्वाद् अक्षय्यत्वाच्च सर्वदा ॥⁴¹ कामधेनुगुणा विद्या ह्यकाले फलदायिनी । प्रवासे मातृसदृशी विद्या गुप्तं धनं स्मृतम् ॥⁴² विद्वान्प्रशस्यते लोके विद्वान्सर्वत्र पूज्यते । विद्यया लभते सर्वं विद्या सर्वत्र पूज्यते ॥⁴³

अजातमृतमूर्खाणां वरमाद्यौ न चान्तिमः । सकृद्दुःखकरावाद्याव् अन्तिमस्तु पदे पदे ॥⁴⁴ वरमेको गुणी पुत्रो न च मूर्खशतान्यपि । एकश्चन्द्रस्तमो हन्ति न च तारागणो ऽपि च ॥⁴⁵ एकेनापि सुवृक्षेण पुष्पितेन सुगन्धिना । वासितं तद्वनं सर्वं सुपुत्रेण कुलं यथा ॥ एकेन शुष्कवृक्षेण दह्यमानेन वह्निना । दह्यते तद्वनं सर्वं कुपुत्रेण कुलं यथा ॥⁴⁶ रूपयौवनसम्पन्ना विशालकुलसम्भवाः । विद्याहीना न शोभन्ते निर्गन्धाः किंशुका यथा ॥⁴⁷ किं कुलेन विशालेन विद्याहीनेन देहिनाम् । दुष्कुलं चापि विदुषो देवैरपि स पूज्यते ॥⁴⁸ शुनः पुच्छमिव व्यर्थं जीवितं विद्यया विना । न गुह्यगोपने शक्तं न च दंशनिवारणे ॥⁴⁹

मणिर्लुण्ठति पादाग्रे काचः शिरसि धार्यते । क्रयविक्रयवेलायां काचः काचो मणिर्मणिः ॥⁵⁰ विषादप्यमृतं ग्राह्यं बालादपि सुभाषितम् । अमित्रादपि सद्वृत्तम् अमेध्यादपि काञ्चनम् ॥⁵¹ श्रेष्ठो हि पण्डितः शत्रुर् न च मित्रमपण्डितः ।⁵² सर्वत्र ब्राह्मणाः सन्ति सन्ति सर्वत्र क्षत्रियाः । वैश्याः शूद्रास्तथा कर्ण स्त्रियः साध्व्यश्च सुव्रताः ॥⁵³ दाने तपसि शौर्ये वा विज्ञाने विनये नये । विस्मयो न हि कर्तव्यो बहुरत्ना वसुन्धरा ॥⁵⁴

पुस्तकस्था तु या विद्या परहस्तगतं धनं । कार्यकाले समुत्पन्ने न सा विद्या न तद्धनम् ॥⁵⁵ जले तैलं खले गुह्यं पात्रे दानं मनागपि । प्राज्ञे शास्त्रं स्वयं याति विस्तारं वस्तुशक्तितः ॥⁵⁶ यस्य नास्ति स्वयं प्रज्ञा शास्त्रं तस्य करोति किम् । लोचनाभ्यां विहीनस्य दर्पणः किं करिष्यति ॥⁵⁷

विद्यारम्भ ('beginning of education'), also called अक्षर-स्वीकरण, a संस्कार after बाल्य, is performed on an auspicious day, like विजयादशमी or वसन्तपञ्चमी. After the worship of गणेश, हरि, लक्ष्मी and सरस्वती, the child prays:

सरस्वति नमस्तुभ्यं वरदे कामरूपिणि। विद्यारम्भं करिष्यामि सिद्धिर्भवतु मे सदा ॥[58]

"The education of the Hindoo youth generally commences when they are five years old. On reaching this age, the master and scholars of the school to which the boy is to be sent, are invited to the house of his parents. The whole are seated in a circle round an image of Gunasee, and the child to be initiated is placed exactly opposite to it. The school master, sitting by his side, after having burnt incense and presented offerings, causes the child to repeat a prayer to Gunasee entreating wisdom. He then guides the child to write with its finger in rice the mystic name of the deity, and is dismissed with a present from the parents, according to their ability. The child, next morning commences the great work of his education." (The Collector of Bellary, 1823)

"The education of youth in India is much simpler, and not near so expensive as in Europe. The children assemble half naked under the shade of a coconut tree; place themselves in rows on the ground, and trace out on the sand, with the fore finger of the right hand, the elements of their alphabet, and then smooth it with the left when they wish to trace out other characters. The writing master, called Agian, or Eluttacien, who stations himself opposite to his pupils, examines what they have done; points out their faults, and shows them how to correct them. At first, he attends them standing; but when the young people have acquired some readiness in writing, he places himself cross-legged on a tiger's or deer's skin, or even on a mat made of the leaves of the coconut-tree, or wild ananas, which is called Kaida, plaited together. This method of teaching writing was introduced into India two hundred years before the birth of Christ, according to the testimony of Magasthenes, and still continues to be practised. No people, perhaps, on earth have adhered so much to their ancient usages and customs as the Indians. A schoolmaster in Malabar receives every two months, from each of his pupils, for the instruction given them, two Fanon or Panam. Some do not pay in money, but give him a certain quantity of rice, so that this expense becomes very easy to the parents. There are some teachers who instruct children without any fee, and are paid by the overseers of the temple, or by the chief of the caste. ... When the Guru, or teacher, enters the school, he is always received with the utmost reverence and respect. His pupils must throw themselves down at full length before him; place their right hand on their mouth, and not venture to speak a single word until he gives them express permission. Those who talk and prate contrary to the prohibition of their master are expelled from the school, as boys who cannot restrain their tongue, and who are consequently unfit for the study of philosophy. By these means the preceptor always receives that respect which is due to him: the pupils are obedient, and seldom offend against rules which are so carefully inculcated." (Paulinus of St. Bartholomew, Austrian Carmelite missionary and Orientalist, 1748-1806)

"Besides their regular stipends, school masters generally receive presents, from the parents of their pupils, at the Dassarah and other great feasts; a fee is also given when the pupil begins a new book." (The Collector of Coimbatore, 1822)

"... besides the allowance mentioned in the preceding paragraph each scholar gives him about one seer rice once every fortnight, at the new and full moons. They also pay him some presents when they are first put in the school, and after they finish the reading of any of their introductory books, such as Baularamayanum, Amarum, etc., and also pay a present to him when they complete their education, and leave the school." (The Collector of Nellore, 1823)

"Accounts of education in India do often state, that the absence of girls in schools was explained, however, by the fact that most of their education took place in the home. ... It may not be too erroneous to assume that the number of those 'privately' studying Theology, Law, Astronomy, Metaphysics, Ethics, Poetry and Literature, Medical Science, Music, and Dance (all of which existed in this period) was perhaps several times the number of those who were receiving such education institutionally. ... In comparison to those being educated in schools in Madras, this number is 4.73 times." (Dharampal, *The Beautiful Tree*; Indian historian, 1922-2006)

"The school at Dharail affords a good specimen of the mode in which a small native community unite to support a school. At that place there are four families of Chaudhuris, the principal persons in the village; but they are not so wealthy as to be able to support a teacher for their children without the cooperation of others. They give the teacher an apartment in which his scholars may meet, one of the outer apartments of their own house in which business is sometimes transacted, and at other times worship performed and strangers entertained. One of those families further pays four annas a month, a second an equal sum, a third eight annas, and a fourth twelve annas, which include the whole of their disbursements on this account, no presents or perquisites of any kind being received from them, and for the sums mentioned their five children receive a Bengali education. The amount thus obtained, however, is not sufficient for the support of the teacher, and he, therefore, receives other scholars belonging to other families – of whom one gives one anna, another gives three annas, and five give each four annas a month, to which they add voluntary presents amounting per month to about four annas, and consisting of vegetable, rice, fish and occasionally a piece of cloth, such as a handkerchief or an upper or under garment. Five boys of Kagbariya, the children of two families, attend the Dharail school, the distance being about a mile, which, in the rainy season, can be travelled only by water. Of the five, two belonging to one family give together two annas, and the three others belonging to the other family give together four annas a month, and thus the whole income of the master is made up. This case shows by what pinched and stinted contributions the class just below the wealthy and the class just above the indigent unite to support a school; and it constitutes a proof of the very limited means of those who are anxious to give a Bengali education to their children, and of the sacrifices which they make to accomplish that object." (William Adam's State of Education in Bengal 1835-38)

8. Public Schools

"Every village had its schoolmaster, supported out of the public funds; in Bengal alone, before the coming of the British, there were some 80,000 native schools – one to every four hundred population. Instruction was given to him in the 'Five Shastras' or sciences: grammar, arts and crafts, medicine, logic and philosophy. Finally, the child was sent out into the world with the wise admonition that education came only one-fourth from the teacher, one-fourth from private study, one-fourth from one's fellows, and one-fourth from life." (Will Durant, American historian and philosopher, 1885-1981)

Dharampal (The Beautiful Tree) has effectively debunked the myth that Dalits had no place in the indigenous system of education. When Sir Thomas Munro, Governor of Madras, ordered a mammoth survey in June 1822, the district collectors furnished the caste-wise division of students. Shudras (plus other castes and Muslims) comprised between 53 and 84% of all students.

"Around 1780, 'Popular education was still approached as a missionary enterprise (in Europe).' The maxim was 'that every child should learn to read the Bible.' 'The hope of securing a decent observance of Sunday' led to a concentrated effort on the promotion of Sunday schools. After some years, this attention focussed on the necessity of day schools. From then on, school education grew apace. Nevertheless, even as late as 1834, 'the curriculum in the better class of national schools was limited in the main to religious instruction, reading, writing and arithmetic: in some country schools writing was excluded for fear of evil consequences.' ... Dobbs writes that 'allowing for irregularity of attendance, the average length of school life rises on a favourable estimate from about one year in 1835 to about two years in 1851.' It was not till 1851 that Mathematics became a part of the regular school work. ... According to this hard data ... in many respects Indian schooling seems to have been much more extensive (and, it should be remembered, that it is a greatly damaged and disorganised India that one is referring to). The content of studies was better than what was then studied in England. The duration of study was more prolonged. The method of school teaching was superior and it is this very method which is said to have greatly helped the introduction of popular education in England but which had prevailed in India for centuries. School attendance, ... even in the decayed state of the period 1822-25, was proportionately far higher than the numbers in all variety of schools in England in 1800. The conditions under which teaching took place in the Indian schools were less dingy and more natural; and, it was observed, the teachers in the Indian schools were generally more dedicated and sober than in the English versions." (Dharampal, *The Beautiful Tree*; Indian historian, 1922-2006)

"I have to observe that the scholars generally assemble in the morning at 6 o'clock and stay until nine and then go to their houses to take their morning meal and return again to school within 11 o'clock and continue until 2 or 3 o'clock in the evening, and again to their respective houses to eat their rice and return by 4 o'clock and continue until 7 o'clock in the evening. The morning and evening generally are the times for reading and afternoon for writing. (The Collector of Guntur, 1823)

"If the boys are of Vydeea Bramins, they are, so soon as they can read properly, removed direct from schools to colleges of Vadums and Sastrums." (The Collector of Masulipatam, 1823)

"As instruction amongst the natives here, is encouraged and promoted solely in proportion to the personal profit obtainable by it, the course of education is considered complete when the scholar becomes a proficient in writing and arithmetic. He is then taken from school, all other accomplishments are learned at home, and he arrives at experience, and attains improvement in what he has already acquired, only by attending his father's shop and writing his accounts, or by being permitted to qualify himself for employment by volunteering his services in our public Cutcherries. The period during which each scholar receives instruction at school (and after the expiration of which he is usually considered to have completed his education) is about 2 years." (The collector of Cuddapah 1825)

"These children are sent to school when they are above five years old and their continuance in it depends in a great measure on their mental faculties, but it is generally admitted that before they attain their thirteenth year of age, their acquirement in the various branches of learning are uncommonly great, a circumstance very justly ascribed to an emulation and perseverance peculiar only to the Hindoo castes." (The Collector of Madras, 1822)

9. Peer Teaching

"In the mean time, while the burthens were getting in order, I entertain'd myself in the Porch of the Temple, beholding little boys learning Arithmetick after a strange manner, which I will here relate. They were four, and having all taken the same lesson from the Master, in order to get that same by heart and repeat likewise their former lessons and not forget them, one of them singing musically with a certain continu'd tone, (which hath the force of making deep impression in the memory) recited part of the lesson; as, for example, "One by its self makes one"; and whilst he was thus speaking he writ down the same number, not with any kind of Pen, nor on Paper, but (not to spend Paper in vain) with his finger on the ground, the pavement being for that purpose strew'd all over with very fine sand; after the first had writ what he sung, all the rest sung and writ down the same thing together. Then the first boy sung and writ down another part of the lesson, ... which all the rest repeated in the same manner, and so forward in order. When the pavement was full of figures, they put them out with the hand, and, if need were, strew'd it with new sand from a little heap' which they had before them wherewith to write further. And thus, they did as long as the exercise continu'd; in which manner likewise, they told me, they learnt to read and write without spoiling Paper, Pens, or Ink, which certainly is a pretty way. I ask'd them, if they happen'd to forget, or be mistaken in any part of the lesson, who corrected and taught them? they being all Scholars without the assistance of any Master; they answer'd me and said true, that it was not possible for all four of them to forget, or mistake in the same part, and that thus they exercis'd together, to the end that if one happen'd to be out the others might correct him. Indeed, a pretty, easie and secure way of learning." (Pietro Della Valle, Italian musicologist and traveller, 1586-1652)

One morning around 1787, in the course of his early ride along the shore of Madras, the British Rev. Dr. Andrew Bell "happened to pass a school, which, as usual with Indian schools, was held in the open air. He saw the little children writing with their fingers on sand, which, after the fashion of such schools, had been strewn before them for that purpose." He also saw them peer teaching, children learning from one another rather than from their masters.

"When the whole are assembled, the scholars according to their number and attainments, are divided into several classes. The lower ones of which are placed partly under the care of monitors, whilst the higher ones are more immediately under the superintendence of the master, who at the same time has his eye upon the whole school. The number of classes is generally four; and a scholar rises from one to the other, according to his capacity and progress. ... The economy with which children are taught to write in the native schools, and the system by which the more advanced scholars are caused to teach the less advanced and at the same time to confirm their own knowledge is certainly admirable, and well deserved the imitation it has received in England." (The Collector of Bellary, 1823)

Bell returned to London in 1797 and published the description of his own version as "Madras Method", having a dispute with Joseph Lancaster about who really invented the system. By 1821, 300,000 children were being educated under Bell's principles. The system allowed the learning of reading and writing in two years instead of the five to six years previously required, and transformed Western education.

"They are particularly anxious and attentive to instruct their children to read and to write. Education with them is an early and an important business in every family. Many of their women are taught to read and write. The Bramans are generally the school masters, but any of the respectable castes may, and often do, practice teaching. The children are instructed without violence, and by a process peculiarly simple. It is the same system which has caused so much heat and controversy, as to the inventors of it, in this country, and the merit of which was due to neither of the claimants. The system was borrowed from the Bramans and brought from India to Europe. It has been made the foundation of National schools in every enlightened country. Some gratitude is due to a people from whom we have learnt to diffuse among the lower ranks of society instruction by one of the most unerring and economical methods which has ever been invented. The pupils are the monitors of each other, and the characters are traced with a rod, or the finger on the sand. Reading and writing are acquired at the same time, and by the same process. This mode of teaching however is only initial. If the pupil is meant to study the higher branches of learning, he is removed from these primary schools, where the arts of reading, writing and accounts are acquired, and placed under more scientific masters. It is to these elementary schools that the labouring classes in India owe their education. It gives them an access, from the introduction of the system into this part of the world; advantage which the same classes in Europe, only now partially conferred on them a superior share of intelligence and placed them in a situation to perform better all the duties of life. … We are continually reproaching the natives of India with the slow advances they have made in knowledge and their neglect of opportunities to acquire it. There we have an instance of the same neglect in Europeans, who have allowed two centuries to pass after they were acquainted with this invention, before they applied it to any practical use. It was at length introduced into this country without any acknowledgement and it was even claimed as an invention by two individuals who disputed upon the priority of discovery." (Alexander Walker, British Brigadier-General and explorer, 1764-1831)

In France, fear caused the method to be decried:

"Firstly, it questioned the idea that the permanent authority of a teacher is necessary to guarantee the good morality of students and to watch over their development of intellect and knowledge. Secondly, from an economic viewpoint, the monitoring system allowed the low-cost instruction of the extremely poor and in record time. Also, some statistics of the time showed that this teaching method had allowed a 750% increase in the number of children being educated (Journal d'éducation, October 1828, p. 378). This method represented the possibility of educating the masses and a chance for individuals to progress from the lowly position of student to that of the teacher: a way of rising to another social rank." (Canadian Centre for Home Education)

10. Crafts

"The boys, in the ninth year of their age, are initiated with great ceremony into the calling or occupation of the caste to which their father belongs, and which they can never abandon. This law, mention of which occurs in Diodorous Siculus, Strabo, Arrian, and other Greek writers, is indeed exceedingly hard; but, at the same time, it is of great benefit to civil order, the arts and sciences, and even to religion. According to a like regulation, no one is allowed to marry from one caste into another. Hence it happens that the Indians do not follow that general and superficial method of education by which children are treated as if they were all intended for the same condition and for discharging the same duties; but those of each caste are from their infancy formed for what they are to be during their whole lives. A future Brahman, for example, is obliged, from his earliest years, to employ himself in reading and writing, and to be present at the presentation of offerings, to calculate eclipses of the sun and moon; to study the laws and religious practices; to cast nativities; in short to learn every thing, which, according to the injunction of the Veda, or sacred books of the Indians, it is necessary he should know. The Vayshya on the other hand, instruct youth in agriculture; the Kshetria, in the science of government and the military arts, the Shudra, in mechanics, the Mucaver, in fishing; the Ciana, in gardening and the Banyen, in commerce. By this establishment the knowledge of a great many things necessary for the public good is not only widely diffused, but transmitted to posterity; who are thereby enabled still farther to improve them, and bring them nearer to perfection. In the time of Alexander the Great, the Indians had acquired such skill in the mechanical arts, that Nearchus, the commander of his fleet, was much amazed at the dexterity with which they imitated the accoutrements of the Grecian soldiers. I once found myself in a similar situation. Having entrusted to an Indian artist a lamp made in Portugal, the workmanship of which was exceedingly pretty, some days after he brought me another so like my own that I could scarcely distinguish any difference. It, however, cannot be denied, that the arts and sciences in India have greatly declined since foreign conquerors expelled the native kings; by which several provinces have been laid entirely waste, and the castes confounded with each other. Before that period, the different kingdoms were in a flourishing condition; the laws were respected, and justice and civil order prevailed; but, unfortunately, at present everything in many of the provinces must give way to absolute authority and despotic sway." (Paulinus of St. Bartholomew, Austrian Carmelite missionary and Orientalist, 1748-1806)

"Some 45 years after Adam, Dr G. W. Leitner, (one time Principal of Government College, Lahore, and for some time acting Director of Public Instruction in the Panjab) prepared an even more voluminous survey of indigenous education there. The survey is very similar to that of W. Adam. Leitner's language and conclusions, however, were more direct and much less complementary to British rule. Incidentally, as time passed, the inability of the British rulers to face any criticism grew correspondingly. They had really begun to believe in their 'divinely ordained' mission in India, and other conquered areas. In the documents reproduced in this work, or in those others of the eighteenth, or early nineteenth century on the subject of education in India, while there is much on the question of higher learning, especially of Theology, Law, Medicine, Astronomy, and Astrology, there is scarcely any reference to the teaching and training in the scores of technologies, and crafts which had then existed in India. There is also little mention of training in Music, and Dance. These latter two, it may be presumed, were largely taken care of by the complex temple organisations. The major cause of the lack of reference about the former, however, is obviously because those who wrote on education – whether as government administrators, travellers, Christian missionaries, or scholars – were themselves uninterested in how such crafts were taught, or passed from one generation to another. Some of them were evidently interested in a particular technology, or craft: as indicated by the writings on their manufacture of iron and steel, the fashioning of agricultural tools, the cotton and silk textiles, the materials used in architecture, and buildings, the materials used in the building of ships, the manufacture of ice, paper, etc. But even in such writings, the interest lay in the particular method and technology and its technological and scientific details; and, not in how these were learnt. Yet another cause for the lack of information on the teaching of techniques and crafts may possibly lie in the fact that ordinarily in India most crafts were basically learnt in the home. What was termed apprenticeship in Britain (one could not practise any craft, profession, etc., in England without a long and arduous period under a master craftsman, or technologist) was more informal in India, the parents usually being the teachers and the children the learners. Another reason might have been that particular technologies or crafts, even like the profession of the digging of tanks, or the transportation of commodities were the function of particular specialist groups, some of them operating in most parts of India, while others in particular regions, and therefore any formal teaching and training in them must have been a function of such groups themselves. Remarks available to the effect that, 'it is extremely difficult to learn the arts of the Indians, for the same caste, from father to son, exercises the same trade and the punishment of being excluded from the caste on doing anything injurious to its interests is so dreadful that it is often impossible to find an inducement to make them communicate anything', appear to indicate some organisation of individual technologies at group levels. However, to know anything regarding their teaching, the innovations and improvisations in them, (there must have been innumerable such instances even if these were on a decline), it is essential to have much more detailed information on such groups, the nature of these technologies, and what in essence constituted a formal, or informal apprenticeship in the different crafts." (Dharampal, *The Beautiful Tree*; Indian historian, 1922-2006)

---

11. Higher Education

The गुरुकुल, a small domestic school run by a teacher who admitted resident pupils, was the original, Vedic educational system, still observed in the 19th century. Other teachers, the चारक, were wandering.

"At the age of from 10 to 16 years, if he has not the means of obtaining instruction otherwise, a young Brahmin leaves his home, and proceeds to the residence of a man of his own caste who is willing to afford instruction without recompense to all those resorting to him for the purpose. They do not, however, derive subsistence from him for as he is generally poor himself, his means could not of course give support to others, and even if he has the means his giving food and clothing to his pupils would attract so many as to defeat that object itself which is professed. The Board would naturally enquire how these children who are so destitute as not to be able to procure instruction in their own villages, could subsist in those to which they are strangers, and to which they travel from 10 to 100 miles, with no intention of returning for several years. They are supported entirely by charity, daily repeated, not received from the instructor for the reasons above mentioned, but from the inhabitants of the villages generally. They receive some portion of alms daily at the door of every Brahmin in the village, and this is conceded to them with a cheerfulness which considering the object in view must be esteemed as a most honourable trait in the native character, and its unobtrusiveness ought to enhance the value of it. We are undoubtedly indebted to this benevolent custom for the general spread of education amongst a class of persons whose poverty would otherwise be an insurmountable obstacle to advancement in knowledge, and it will be easily inferred that it requires only the liberal and fostering care of Government to bring it to perfection." (The collector of Cuddapah 1825)

Study meant, learning 5 months from a teacher and 7 months at home, through स्वाध्याय (repetition through loud recitation) of वेदाङ्ग, especially during शुक्ल-पक्ष. Except for स्वाध्याय, study was stopped on the days of अनध्याय: "Teaching on अमावास्या destroys the गुरु, चतुर्दशी the शिष्य, and अष्टमी and पूर्णिमा (पौर्णमास्य) destroy [remembrance of] the वेद (ब्रह्म) – therefore one should avoid them [for studying]." (मनु-संहिता 4.114)

"When a person has obtained all the knowledge possessed by one teacher, he makes some respectful excuse to his guide and avails himself of the instructions of another." (William Adam's State of Education in Bengal 1835-38)

Higher education sprung from the आश्रम, or 'hermitage' of a famous teacher: 49 गोत्र (families of teachers) are especially famous, like शौनक at नैमिष, भरद्वाज at प्रयाग, and व्यास at बदरी. Colleges were either brahminical मठ or buddhist विहार.

"The school opens early every morning by the teacher and pupils assembling in the open reading-room, when the different classes read in turns. Study is continued till towards mid-day, after which three hours are devoted to bathing, worship, eating and sleep; and at three they resume their studies which are continued till twilight. Nearly two hours are then devoted to evening-worship, eating, smoking and relaxation, and the studies are again resumed and continued till ten or eleven at night. The evening studies consist of a revision of the lessons already learned, in order that what the pupils have read may be impressed more distinctly on the memory. ... In the first class of colleges, the pupils repeat assigned lessons from the grammar used in each college, and the teacher communicates the meaning of the lessons after they have been committed to memory. In the others the pupils are divided into classes according to their progress. The pupils of each class having one or more books before them seat themselves in the presence of the teacher, when the best reader of the class reads aloud, and the teacher gives the meaning as often as asked, and thus they proceed from day to day till the work is completed. ... As soon as a student has obtained such a knowledge of grammar as to be able to read and understand a poem, a law book, or a work on philosophy, he may commence this course of reading also, and carry on at the same time the remainder of his grammar-studies." (William Adam's State of Education in Bengal 1835-38)

Famous universities with each about 10,000 students were तक्षशिला (Taxila, with पाणिनि, चारक and चाणक्य), वाराणसी (Benares), विक्रमशील and नालन्दा.

"From the Guru the student would pass, about the age of sixteen, to one of the great universities that were the glory of ancient and medieval India. Benares, Taxila, Vidarbha, Ajanta, Ujjain or Nalanda. Benares was the stronghold of learning in Buddha's days. Taxila was known at the time of Alexander's invasion, was known to all of Asia as the leading seat of Hindu scholarship, renowned above all for its medical school; Ujjain was held in high repute for astronomy, Ajanta for the teaching of art. The facade of one of the ruined buildings at Ajanta suggests the magnificence of these old universities." (Dr. Ernest Binfield Havell, principal to the Madras College of Art, 1861-1934)

"The day is not sufficient for asking and answering profound questions. From morning till night, they engage in discussion; the old and the young mutually help one another." (Hieun /Xuanzang Tsang, Chinese scholar and pilgrim to India, 602-664)

"Hiuen Tsang, the Chinese traveler, stayed (in the 7th century) five years at Nalanda University, where more than seven thousand monks lived. He mentions a very considerable literature in Sanskrit and other works on history, statistics and geography, none of which have survived. He also writes of officials whose job it was to write records of all important events. At Nalanda, studies included the Vedas, the Upanishads, cosmology (Sankhya), realist or scientific philosophy (Vaisheshika), logic (Nyaya), to which great importance was attached, and Jain and Buddhist philosophy. Studies also included grammar, mechanics, medicine, and physics. Medicine was highly effective, and surgery was quite developed. The pharmacopoeia was enormous, and astronomy was very advanced. The earth's diameter had been calculated very precisely. In physics, Brahmagupta had discovered the law of gravity." (Alain Danielou, French ethnomusicologist, head of the UNESCO Institute for Comparative Musicology, 1907-1994)

"Attached to the university was a kind of post-graduate department, a group of learned Brahmins known collectively as a Parishad. A Parishad seems usually to have consisted of ten men; four 'walking encyclopedias' each of whom had learnt all the four Vedas by heart, three who had specialized in one of the Sūtras, and representative of the three orders of Brahmacārī, Grihastha and Vānaprastha – student, householder and hermit. The Parishad gave decisions on disputed points of religion of learning. I-Tsing reports that at the end of their course of studies, 'to try the sharpness of their wit' some men 'proceed to the king's court to lay down before it the sharp weapon of their abilities: there they present their schemes and show their talent, seeking to be appointed in the practical government...'" (Padmini Sengupta, Indian author of Everyday Life in Ancient India)

National Gatherings were promoted by kings. The first mentioned (in बृहद्-आरण्यक-उपनिषद्) is that of Janaka Videha. Their best discussions are recorded in the Upanishads.

12. Subjects

Already at home the child is taught लिपि (अ-आ-इ-ई), सङ्ख्या, the specific विद्या cultivated by the family, and playing a musical instrument.

"The chief branches taught by the Guru are: 1st, the principles of writing and accounts; 2nd, ... the art of speaking with elegance; 3rd, ... the book Vyagarna; 4th, the Amarasinha, or Brahmanic dictionary." (Paulinus of St. Bartholomew, Austrian Carmelite missionary and Orientalist, 1748-1806)

"Having attained a thorough knowledge of the letters, the scholar next learns to write the compounds, ... then the names of men, villages, animals, etc., and finally arithmetical signs. He then commits to memory an addition table, and counts from one to a hundred; he afterwards writes easy sums in addition, and subtraction of money; multiplication and the reduction of money, measures, etc. ... The other parts of a native education consist in deciphering various kinds of hand writing, in public and other letters, which the school master collects from the different sources; writing common letters, drawing up forms of agreement; reading; fables and legendary tales; and committing various kinds of poetry to memory, chiefly with a view to attain distinctness and clearness in pronunciation, together with readiness and correctness in reading any kind of composition. The lighter kind of stories which are read for amusement, are generally the Punchatantra, Bhatalapunchavansatee, Punklee Soopooktahuller, Mahantarungenee. The books on the principles of the vernacular languages themselves, are the several dictionaries and grammars, such as the Nighantoo, Umara, Subdamumbured, Shubdeemunee Durpana, Vyacurna Andradeepeca, Andhranamasungraha, etc." (The Collector of Bellary, 1823)

"About the same time the scholar is taught the rules of arithmetic, beginning with addition and subtraction, but multiplication and division are not taught as separate rules—all the arithmetical processes hereafter mentioned being effected by addition and subtraction with the aid of a multiplication table which extends to the number 20, and which is repeated aloud once every morning by the whole school and is thus acquired not as a separate task by each boy, but by the mere force of joint repetition and mutual imitation. After addition and subtraction, the arithmetical rules taught divide themselves into two classes, agricultural and commercial, in one or both of which instruction is given more or less fully according to the capacity of the teacher and the wishes of the parents. ... With the exception of the Multiplication Table, the rhyming arithmetical rules of Subhankar, and the form of address to Saraswati, all which the younger scholars learn by mere imitation of sounds incessantly repeated by the elder boys, without for a long time understanding what those sounds convey – with these exceptions, native school-boys learn everything that they do learn not merely by reading but by writing it. They read to the master or to one of the oldest scholars what they have previously written, and thus the hand, the eye, and the ear are equally called into requisition. This appears preferable to the mode of early instruction current amongst ourselves, according to which the elements of language are first taught only with the aid of the eye and the ear, and writing is left to be subsequently acquired." (William Adam's State of Education in Bengal 1835-38)

Sixty-four कला are listed in काम-सूत्र 1.3.15, रामायण 1.9.5, भागवत-पुराण 10.45.36, महाभाष्य 1.1.57, and दशकुमार-चरित 2.21. Summary:

(1) स्वरगत – the seven notes; गीत – singing; (2) वाद्य – playing on musical instruments: वीणा, डमरु, मुरज, कांस्यताल, दर्दुरपुत; उदक-वाद्य – ringing waterpots; अनेक-वाद्य-विकृतौ तद्वादन – playing that (music) on many instruments (in orchestre); (3) समताल – beating time to music; (4) नृत्य, नर्तन – dancing; हाव-भावादि-संयुक्त – with gesture and heart; (5) नाट्य – drama; (6) आलेख्य – painting; चित्रादि-आलेखन – drawing, painting and calligraphy; (7) रङ्गावली – Rangoli, Kolam; तण्डुल-कुसुम-बली-विकार – preparing auspicious designs on the floor with rice and flowers, पुष्प-आस्तरण – strewing flowers; (8) मेन्धी – Mehandi; विशेषक-च्छेद्य – painting figures of various designs on the body; दशन-अङ्ग-राग – coloring one's teeth and limbs; (9) अनेक-रूपाविर्भाव-कृति-ज्ञान – forming, sculpturing: making various forms or figures out of stone, wood, etc.; मधूच्छिष्ट-कृत – wax-modelling; (10) उत्सादन – anointing; सुगन्ध-युक्ति, गन्ध-युक्ति – applying aromatics; (12) केश-

मार्जन / -मर्दन – hairdressing (with ornaments and flowers); क्षुर-कर्म – shaving; (13) वस्त्रालङ्कार-सन्धान – decorating with dress and ornaments, भूषण-योजन – decorating with jewelry; (14) माल्य-ग्रथन, पुष्पादि-ग्रथन – binding garlands with flowers; (15) वस्त्र-गोपन – disguise with a dress; (16) गृह-भाण्डादि-मर्जन – cleansing houses and furniture; (17) सूद-कर्म – culinary art; आस्वाद्य-विधान – preparing savouries; हीनादि-रस-संयोग-अन्नदि-सम्पाचन, अन्न-विधि – cooking rice etc. by combining different tasts; चित्र-शाकापूप-भक्ष्य-विकार-क्रिया – preparing varieties of salad, cake and other food; (18) पान-विधि, पानक-रस-राग-आसव-योजन – preparing drinks and juices with red color; (19) मनोनुकूल-सेवा-कृति-ज्ञान – the art of serving another to his heart's content; (20) लिपि-ज्ञान – writing the alphabet; (21) पुस्तक-वाचन – reciting books easily and quickly; (22) संवाच्य – conversation; (23) हास्य – humor; दुर्वचक-योग – tongue twisters; प्रहेलिका – riddles (making and solving); (24) आख्यात – story telling; नाटिकाख्यायिका-दर्शन – enacting short plays and writing anecdotes, dramaturgy and story writing; ग्रन्थ-रचित – book writing; (25) देश-भाषा-ज्ञान – knowledge of provincial dialects; म्लोच्छित-कुतर्क-विकल्प – fabricating foreign sophistry; नाना-देशीय-वर्ण-लेखन-ज्ञान – writing the alphabets of various countries (ब्राह्मी, यवनलिपि, खरोष्ठी, पाहारि, गन्धर्वलिपि, महेश्वरी, द्राविडी); (26) इतिहास, पुराण – history; सर्वाणि अपदानानि – all ancient chronicles; (27) व्याकरण – Sanskrit grammar; (28) निरुक्त – etymology; (29) गणित – arithmetics; सङ्ख्या – numbers; (30) ज्योतिष – astrology; ग्रह-गणित – astronomy; (31) सामुद्रिक – palmistry; निमित्त-ज्ञान – omens; धारण-मातृका – amulets; यन्त्र-मातृका – magic squares; (32) वास्तु-विद्या – architecture; नगर-निवेश – town-planning; नगर-मान – measurement of cities; (33) वैनयिकी विद्या – 'science of conduct', education, pedagogics; शिशु-संरक्षण-धारण-क्रीडन-ज्ञान – protecting, bringing up and playing with children; (34) बालक-क्रीडनक – playing with children's toys; (35) सूत्र-क्रीडा – making puppets dance by manipulating thin threads; (36) हस्त-लाघव – lightness of hand, cleverness; द्यूत-विशेष – gambling with dice (पाशा, अक्ष), etc.; ऐन्द्रजाल – jugglery; (37) अक्षर-मुष्टिका-कथन – telling what is written in a book or hidden in another's fist without seeing it; मध्यमाङ्गुलि-ग्रहण – middle finger catching; (38) सुनिमीलितक – hide-and-seek; (39) शकुन-रूय, शकुन-विद्या, शकुन – the cries of birds; शुक-प्रलापन – making parrots to speak and answer; (40) मुद्रा-देवता-तोषण – pleasing deities by different मुद्रा; (41) योगासन – Yoga postures; (11) संवाहन – massage; (42) व्यायाम-विद्या – physical science; (43) जले बाह्वादिभिः तरणम् – swimming with hands; (44) मल्ल-युद्ध – wrestling; four kinds: बाहु (arms), दण्ड (lathis), मुष्टि (fists), अस्थि (bones); (45) अस्त्र-निपातन – hurling weapons and missiles: चाप (bow and arrow), चक्र (disc), तोमर (spear); शब्द-वेधित्व – hitting (the mark or game) by its sound; (46) शस्त्र – other weapons: वर्म (armor), क्रिपाण (sword), परशु (axe), गदा (club); (47) रथ-चर्या, सारथ्य – charioteering; गजाश्वादि-गति-शिक्षा – training the movement of elephants, horses, etc.; (48) तिर्यक्-योनि-चिकित्सा – veterinary science; (49) दुग्ध-दोहादि-घृतान्त-विज्ञान – the process of milking upto making ghee; (50) शीराद्या-कर्षण-ज्ञान – ploughing, hoeing; (51) जल-संसेचन-संहरण – distributing and collecting water, irrigation; (52) वृक्षायुर्वेद – nursing and treating plants; वृक्षादि-प्रसव-आरोप-पालनादि-कृति – the art of grafting, planting and culture of plants; भूरुहाण-दोहन – grafting trees (making them small or big), and make them produce all sorts of abnormal fruits; वृक्षादि-आरोहन-ज्ञान – climbing trees and the like; (53) तिलादि-स्नेह-निष्कासन-कृति – extracting oil out of seeds; (54) तर्कु-कर्म – spindle work; सूत्रादि-रज्जु-करण-विज्ञान – the art of making yarns, ropes, etc.; (55) अनेक-तन्तु-संयोग-पट-बन्ध – weaving cloth out of a variety of yarns; सूची-वाय-कर्म – needlework and weaving; (56) वस्त्र-राग – dyeing cloth; वस्त्र-सम्मर्जन – cleaning cloth, laundry; (57) मृत्-क्रिया – work in clay; (58) वेणु-क्रिया – work in bamboo; वेणु-तृणादि-पत्र-कृति-ज्ञान – art of making cups out of bamboo, reeds, etc. (59) दारु-क्रिया – work in wood; तक्षण – carpentry; (60) चर्म-क्रिया – work in leather; (61) अश्म-क्रिया – work in stones; (62) रत्न-शास्त्र – jewels; रौप्य-रत्न-परीक्षा – testing silver and jewels; कृत्रिम-स्वर्ण-रत्नादि-क्रिया-ज्ञान – manufacturing artificial gold and precious stones; मणि-राग-ज्ञान – coloring jewels; मणि-भूमिका-कर्म – inlaying a floor with jewels; लेपादि-सत्कृति – enamelling, polishing, varnishing, etc.; (63) लोह-क्रिया – work in metals; धातु-वाद, धातु-पाक – metallurgy; आकर-ज्ञान – mineralogy, mining; (64) नौका-रथादि-यान-कृति-ज्ञान – the science of constructing ships, chariots and other vehicles.

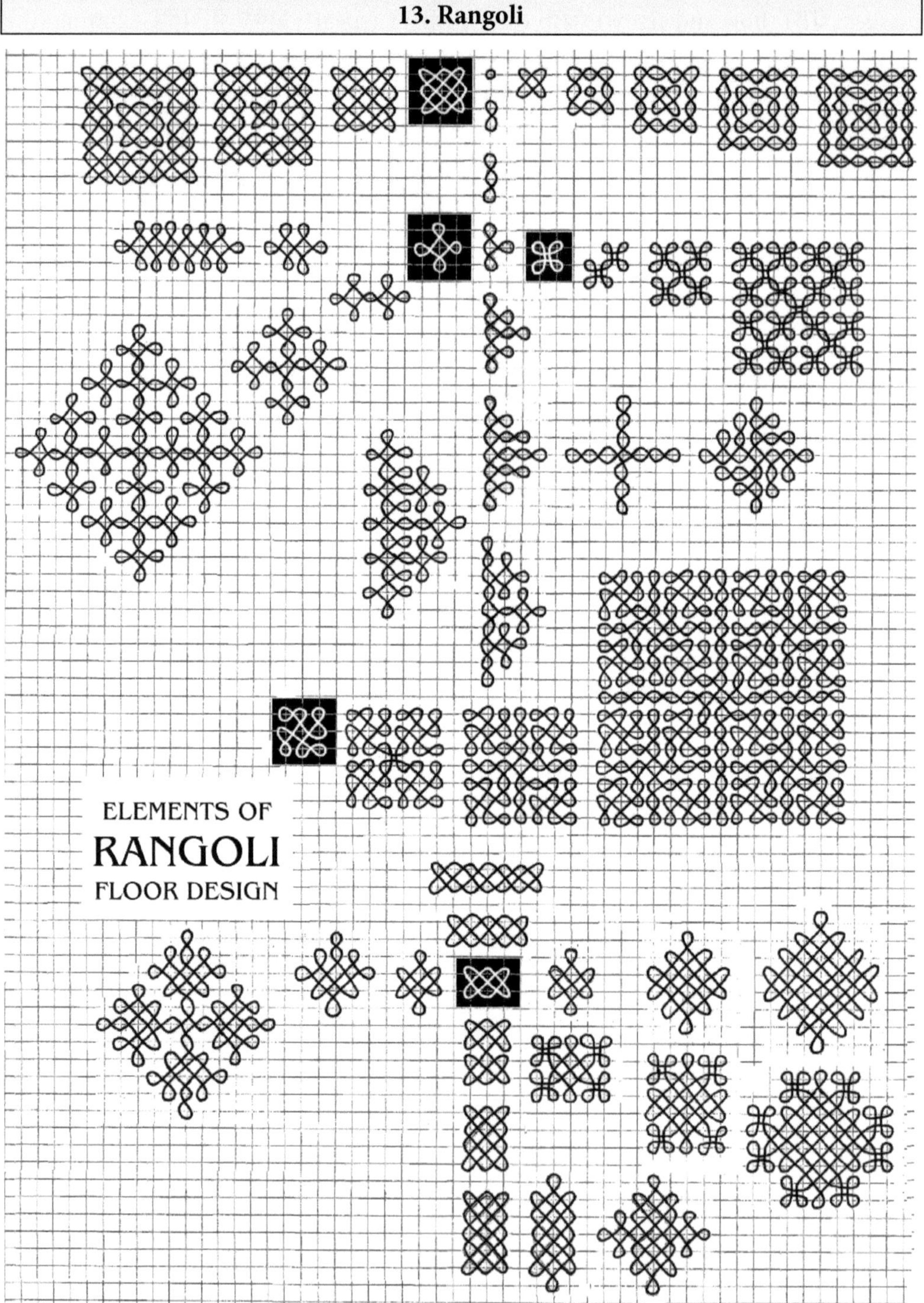

Design[59]

वीणावादनतत्त्वज्ञः श्रुतिजातिविशारदः । तालज्ञश्चाप्रयासेन मोक्षमार्गं नियच्छति ॥[60]

"Some of the Greeks attribute to that country (India) the invention of nearly all the science of music." (Strabo; Greek scholar, 63 BCE-24 AD)

"What has reached us from the work of the Indians in music is the book that contains the fundamentals of modes and the basics in the construction of melodies." (Said Al-Andalusi, Muslim historian and judge, 1029-1070)

"Indian music, the fire that burns heart and soul, is superior to the music of any other country." (Amir Khusrow, Indian scholar and musician, 1234-1325)

"O holy land (India), I salute thee, thou source of all music, thou voice of the heart." (Johann Gottfried von Herder, German philosopher and poet, 1744-1803)

"Despite predisposition in India's favor, I have to acknowledge that Indian music took me by surprise. I knew neither its nature nor its richness, but here, if anywhere, I found vindication of my conviction that India was the original source." "We would find all, or most, strands (raga) beginning in India; for only in India have all possible modes been investigated, tabulated, and each assigned a particular place and purpose. Of these many hundreds, some found their way to Greece; others were adopted by nomadic tribes such as the Gypsies; others became the mainstay of Arabic music. Indian classical music, compared with our Western music, is like a pure crystal. It forms a complete perfected world of its own, which any admixture could only debase. It has, quite logically and rightly, rejected those innovations which have led the development of Western music into the multiple channels which have enabled our art to absorb every influence under the sun. Freedom of development in Indian music is accorded the performer, the individual, who, within fixed limits, is free to improvise without any restraint imposed externally by other voices, whether concordance or discordant – but not to the basic style, which exclude polyphony and modulation." (Sir Yehudi Menuhin, Russian-born American violinist, 1916-1999)

	(1)	(2)	(3)	(4)	(5)	(6)	(7)
India	षड्ज	ऋषभ	गान्धार	मध्यम	पञ्चम	धैवत	निषाद
modern	सा /Sa	रे /Re	ग /Ga	म /Ma	प /Pa	ध /Da	नि /Ni
Persia	do	re	ma	fa	so	le	ci
Europe	do	re	mi	fa	sol	la	si

... plus soft (कोमल) Re, Ga, Da, Ni, and hard (तीव्र) Ma

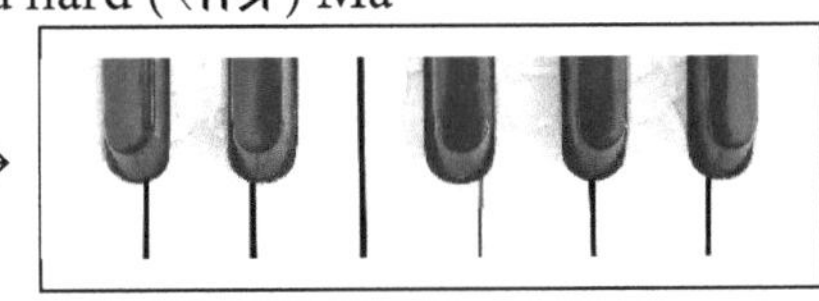

"A regular system of notation was worked out before the age of Panini, and seven notes were designated by their initial letters [now Sa, Re, Ga, Ma, Pa, Dha, Ni]. This notation passed from the Brahmins through the Persians to Arabia [as do, re, ma, fa, so, le, ci], and was thence

introduced into European music by Guido d'Arezzo at the beginning of the eleventh century [as do, re, mi, fa, sol, la, ti]." "Not content with the tones and semi-tones, the Indian musicians employed a more minute sub-division, together with a number of sonal modifications which the Western ear neither recognizes or enjoys. Thus, they divide the octave into 22 sub-tones instead of 12 semi-tones of the European scales. The Indian musician declines altogether to be judged by the new simple Hindu airs which the English ear can appreciate." (Sir William Wilson Hunter, Scottish historian, 1840-1900) "Jazz musicians like to think of themselves as masters of rhythm (and in comparison to European music, they are in the forefront) but ... how crude and primitive the conventional jazz musician's grasp of rhythm is in comparison with Indian music. ... And jazz musicians who desire to really acquire a grasp of rhythm should, if at all possible, study Indian music." (Don /Donald Johnson Ellis, American musician and composer, 1934-1978)

"The Hindu music will provide Western musicians with fresh resources of expression and with colors hitherto unknown to the palate of the musicians." (Prof. Louis-Albert Bourgalt-Ducoudray, French pianist and musicologist, 1840-1910)

"It is impossible to divorce Indian music from the whole structure of Indian culture and philosophy with which it is interwoven in a number of ways from the earliest times of which we have records." (Dr. Arnold Adriaan Bake, Dutch sanskritist and musicologist, 1899-1963)

"Nada Brahma is a primal word in Indian spirituality, a primal word that also refers to India's great classical music. Nada is a Sanskrit word meaning 'sound.' The term nadi is also used to mean 'stream of consciousness,' a meaning that goes back 4,000 years to the oldest of India's four sacred Vedic scriptures, the Rig Veda. Thus, the relationship between sound and consciousness has long been documented in language." (Joachim-Ernst Berendt, German music journalist and author, 1922-2000)

"Our tradition teaches us that sound is God – Nada Brahma. That is, music of sound and the musical experience are steps to the realization of the self. We view music as a kind of spiritual discipline that raises one's inner being to divine peacefulness and bliss. We are taught that one of the fundamental goals a Hindu works toward in his lifetime is a knowledge of the true meaning of the universe – its unchanging, eternal essence – and this is realized first by a complete knowledge of one's self and one's own nature. The highest aim of our music is to reveal the essence of the universe it reflects, and the ragas are among the means by which this essence can be apprehended. Thus, through music, one can reach God." (Ravi Shankar, Indian musician and composer, 1920-2012)

Dance:

आङ्गिकं भुवनं यस्य वाचिकं सर्ववाङ्मयम् । आहार्यं चन्द्रतारादि तं नुमः सात्त्विकं शिवम् ॥[61] पताकस्त्रिपताको ऽर्ध-पताकः कर्तरीमुखः । मयूराख्यो ऽर्धचन्द्रश्च अरालः शुकतुण्डकः ॥ मुष्टिश्च शिखराख्यश्च कपित्थः कटकामुखः । सूची चन्द्रकला पद्म-कोशः सर्पशिरस्तथा ॥ मृगशीर्षः सिंहमुखः काङ्गुलश्चालपद्मकः । चतुरो भ्रमरश्चैव हंसास्यो हंसपक्षकः ॥ शन्दंशो मुकुलश्चैव ताम्रचूडस्त्रिशूलकः । इत्यसंयुतहस्तानाम् अष्टाविंशतिरीरिता ॥[62] अञ्जलिश्च कपोतश्च कर्कटः स्वस्तिकस्तथा । दोलाहस्तः पुष्पपुट उत्सङ्गः शिवलिङ्गकः ॥ कटकावर्धनश्चैव कर्तरीस्वस्तिकस्तथा । शकटं शङ्खचक्रे च सम्पुटः

पाशकीलकौ ॥ मत्स्यः कूर्मो वराहश्च गरुडो नागबन्धकः । खड्वा भेरुण्ड इत्येते सङ्ख्याताः संयुताः कराः ॥[63]

"That which has reached us from the discoveries of their clear thinking and the marvels of their inventions is the (game) of chess [Caturanga]. The Indians have, in the construction of its cells, its double numbers, its symbols and secrets, reached the forefront of knowledge. They have extracted its mysteries from supernatural forces. While the game is being played and its pieces are being maneuvered, there appear the beauty of structure and the greatness of harmony. It demonstrates the manifestation of high intentions and noble deeds, as it provides various forms of warnings from enemies and points out ruses as well as ways to avoid dangers. And in this, there is considerable gain and useful profit." (Said Al-Andalusi, Muslim historian and judge, 1029-1070)

Indian Games:

Mokshapat, **Ashta Changa** (below left)[64], Pachisi, Chaupar, **Aadu Huli** (right)[65]

Gitta[66], **Lagori**[67], **Surr** (below)[68], Kho Kho

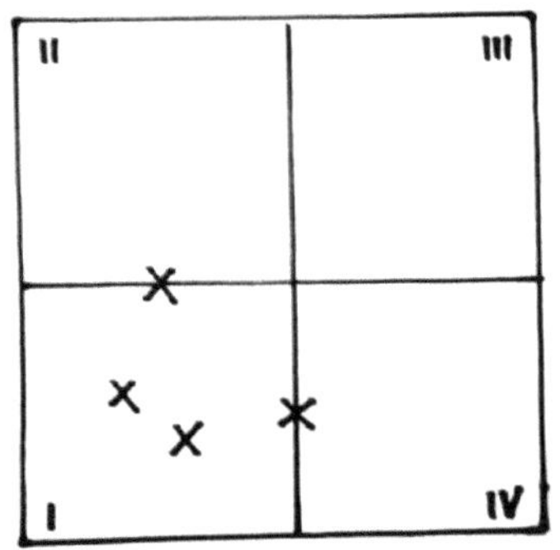 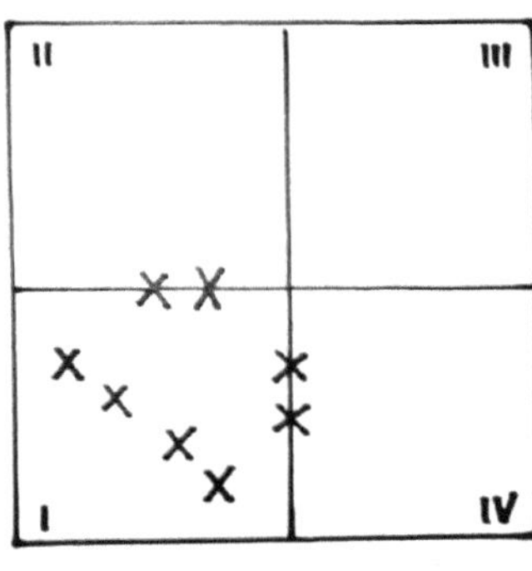

In Hindu-India wrestling was practiced by women also. Although under Mughal rule the Persian Pehlwani style was favoured, it kept most of the ancient मल्ल-युद्ध traditions and is now known as Kushti. मल्ल-पुराण describes preliminary व्यायाम, Mallakhamb, exercises with stones and clubs, traditional massage and wrestling itself.

Martial Arts: Silambam, Kalaripayat

"All the Grecian historians represent the Indians as people of greater size, and much more robust than those of other nations. Though this is not true in general, it is certain that the purity of the air, wholesome nourishment, temperance and education contribute, in an uncommon degree, to the bodily conformation, and to the increase of these people. Their newborn children lie always on the ground, as if they were thrown away or neglected; and they are never wrapped up with bandages, or confined in any other manner, as is done in Europe. Their limbs, therefore, can expand themselves without the least restraint; their nerves and bones become more solid; and when these children attain the period of youth, they acquire not only a beautiful figure, but a sound, well turned, and robust bodily conformation. The frequent use of the cold bath, repeated rubbing the body with coconut oil and the juice of the Ingia plant, as well as their exercises, which have a great resemblance to the Juvenilia, and which I have often seen in Malabar, all contribute to increase their strength and agility. ... In a word, I seldom saw in India a person either lame, crooked, or otherwise deformed." ... "The other sciences and branches of learning taught to the Indian youth are: Poetry, Gavya; Fencing, Payatta; Botany and medicine, Vaydyasastra, or Bheszagiashastra: Navigation, Naushastra: The use of the spear on foot (Hastiludium), Cundera: The art of playing at ball, Pandacali: Chess, Ciudarangam: Tennis, Coladi: Logic, Tarkashastra: Astrology, Giodisha: Law, Svadhyaya: Silence, Mauna. ... The management of the lance, fencing, playing at ball and tennis, have been introduced into their education on good grounds, to render their youth active and robust, and that they may not want dexterity to distinguish themselves in battles and engagements where cannons are not used." (Paulinus of St. Bartholomew, Austrian Carmelite missionary and Orientalist, 1748-1806)

16. Permaculture[69]

Checklist India:

1. Water[70]: Watershed[71], Check Dam[72], Trench[73], Catchment[74], Pond[75], Recharge Well[76], Drinking Well[77], Purification[78]
2. Infrastructure: Dry Stone[79], Wall, Gate, Road, Shed[80], Bio Fence[81], Hedge, Thorns[82], Espalier[83], Bamboo
3. Soil: Fast Trees[84], Cover Crop[85], Compost[86], Pit Toilet[87], Sealing[88]
4. Forest: Wood[89], Fruit Trees[90], Flower Trees[91], Others[92], Palms[93] & Banana[94]
5. Crop: No-Till[95], Seedballs[96], Grains[97], Grasses[98]
6. Garden: Nursery, Pandal, Vines[99], Flowers[100], Herbs[101]
7. Processing: Energy, Food, Storage, Preservation, Medicine
8. Animals: Insects, Bees, Birds, Goshala, Dung[102]

About 140 plants of Northern India:

In brackets: [Use, Max. Hight] Left out are all poisenous plants and (almost) all from the Americas. We recommend *Religious & Useful Plants of Nepal & India* by Dr. Rohit Kumar Majupuria.

Thorns: **Kabra** [max. 1m], **Karanda** [3], **Guggul** [4], **Kair** [5], **Shikakai** [climbing,10], **Ber** [15], Khair [15], Babul [20].

Espalier: All trees, but esp. fruit trees like Aadu [max. 4], Seb [4], Galgal [5], Anjir [8], Nimbu [15], Santara [10], Paiyaun [30].

Fast Growing: **Amrud, Arjun, Baint, Bans, Ber, Chitvan, Gamhar, Kadam, Mahua, Neem,** Nimbu, **Palash,** Lal Chandan, Rajbriksha, Safeda, **Sagaun, Sahajan,** Shirish, **Shisham.** Planted also as future Pandal (plus legume trees **Karaunda, Padauk**).

Shade: Ashok [9], Devdar [10], Bhilava [15], Kapur [15], **Shalmali** [20], **Karnikara** [25], Pakhad [25], Banyan [30], Pipal [30], **Badam** [35].

Wood: **Khejri** [5], **Rohida** [5], **Lal Chandan** [8], Chandan [10], Shirish [10], Bakul [16], Mandara [20], Pakar [20], **Arjun** [25], Shisham [25], Nag-Champa [30], **Padauk** [30], Sagaun [30], **Sal** [30], Vijaya Shal [30], Nagalinga [35], Agaru [40], Kadam [45], **Tun** [50].

Wood Plus: Jaal [leaves,6], Paras [bark,10], Putranjiva [leaves,seed,12], Kath Champa [nut,15], Palash [flower,15], Akash Neem ['cork',20], Jarul [leaves,20], Kathal [fruit,20], Mahuva [flower,seed,20], Neem [leaves,20], Peela Gulmohar [flower,20], Rajbriksha [flower,20], **Rudraksh** [beads,20], Tamal [leaves,20], **Asan** [water,25], Okhar [nut,30], Hollong [resin,40], Champa [flower,50].

Fruti Trees: **Karanda** [3], **Kair** [5], Papita [5], Galgal [5], Lasoda [5], Amrud [7], Amla [8], Phalsa [8], Kaith [9], **Anar** [10], **Gular** [10], Santara [10] Bael [13], Ber [15], Bilimbi [15], Chiku [15], Kokum [15], Nimbu [15], Shehtut [15], Imli [18], Chakka [20], Jatiphal [20], Lichi [20], **Aam** [40], Haritaki [30], Jamun [30], Paiyaun [30], Sabera [45].

Palms: Khajur, Nariyal, Salak, Taal.

Flower Trees: Chameli [4], Sthalkamal [5], Kachnar [10], Parijat [10], Buransh [15].

Others: Kapas [cotton,2], Tejpatta [leaf,5], Kadi [food,6], Henna [color,8], Long [spice,10], Sahajan [food,10], Reetha [nut,15], Shalmali [cotton,20].

Cover Crop: **Alfalfa**, **Bhang**, **Kans**, Kudzu, Matar, Mung, **Patsan**, San, Senji, Urad (in rainy season).

Other Legumes: **Arhar**, Gulmohar, Kabra, Kacchnar, **Karaunda**, Padauk.

TRADE NAME [Use, Max. Hight] Sanskrit, Local, English, Latin

Aadu[103] [fruit,4] Satalu, Peach, Prunus persica (var. Indian Blood Peach). **Aam**[104] [fruit,40] आम्र, Mango, Mangifera indica. **Agaru**[105] [wood,40] अगुरु, Agar, Agarwood, Aloeswood, Aquilaria agallocha. **Akash Neem**[106] [wood,'cork',20] Neem Chameli, Indian Cork Tree, Millingtonia hortensis. **Alfalfa**[107] [crop] मरुन्माला, Lusan Ghas, Sinjhi, Lucerne, Medicago sativa. **Amla**[108] [fruit,8] अमला, आमलकी, Amlaki, Amalak, Indian Gooseberry, Phyllanthus emblica. **Amrud**[109] [fruit,7] बीजपूर, Amba, Peru, Guava, Psidium guajava. **Anar**[110] [fruit,10] दाडिम, Darim, Dalim, Bedana, Pomegranate, Punica granatum. **Angur**[111] [fruit] द्राक्षा, Vine, Grapes, Vitis. **Anjir**[112] [fruit,8] अञ्जीर, Common Fig, Ficus carica. **Arhar**[113] [Dal] काक्षी, आढकी, Tuvar, Tori, Tur, Pigeon Pea, Red Gram, Cajanus cajan. **Arjun**[114] [wood,25] अर्जुन, Kauha, Koha, Kahn, Sadad, Arjun Tree, Terminalia arjuna (var. Asan, Badam, Baheda, Haritaki). **Asan**[115] [water,25] आसन, Matti, Rakta Arjun, Sadan, Sadar, Saj, Marda, Indian Laurel, Terminalia elliptica (see Tejpatta; var. Arjun, Badam, Baheda, Haritaki). **Ashok**[116] [9] अशोक, Saraca asoca (see Devdar).

Ashwagandha[117] [herb,1] अश्वगन्ध, Winter Cherry, Indian Ginsen, Withania somnifera.   **Babul**[118] [wood,20] शैलेन्द्र, Shailendra, Gum Arabic Tree, Vachellia nilotica.   **Badam**[119] [shade,wood,fruit,nut,35] बादाम, Indian Almond, Terminalia catappa (var. Arjun, Asan, Baheda, Haritaki).   **Bael**[120] [fruit,13] बिल्व, Bili, Shri-Vriksha, Bengal Quince, Aegle marmelos.   **Baint**[121] [rope] वञ्जुल, Narkul, Vetas, Rattan, Salix tetrasperma.   **Bajra**[122] [crop] Kambu, Pearl Millet, Pennisetum glaucum (var. Ragi).   **Bakul**[123] [wood,16] बकुल, Maulshri, Maulsar, Bullet Wood, Spanish Cherry, Mimosa Tree, Mimusops elengi.   **Bans**[124] [grass,12] वंश, Bamboo, Bambusa (var. वेणु, thin Bamboo).   **Banyan**[125] [30] वट, न्यग्रोध, Bat, Bar, Bargad, Banyan, Ficus benghalensis (var. Gular, Pakar, Pipal).   **Ber**[126] [fruit,15] बदरी, Bor, Indian Jujube, Zizyphus mauritiana (var. Thai Apple Ber).   **Bhang**[127] [fiber,seeds,5] भङ्गा, Katutiktaka, Ganja, Indian Hemp, Cannabis sativa.   **Brahmi**[128] [herb] ब्राह्मी, Herb of Grace, Bacopa monnieri.   **Chakka**[129] [fruit,20] पनसनालिका, Nirpanas, Kadapila, Breadfruit, Artocarpus altilis (var. Kathal).   **Chameli**[130] [flower,4] मालती, Malti, Tree Jasmine, Jasminum.   **Champa**[131] [wood,flower,50] चम्पक, Michelia champaca.   **Chana**[132] [crop] चणक, Gram, Chole, Chickpea, Cicer arietinum.   **Chandan**[133] [wood,10] चन्दन, Srikhand, Sandalwood, Santalum album.   **Chiku**[134] [fruit,15] सपीतक, Sapota, Sapodilla, Manilkara zapota.   **Chinar**[135] [wood,30] भवानी, Buin, Oriental Plane, Platanus orientalis.   **Chitvan**[136] [wood,bark,40] सप्तपर्ण, Chatian, Shaitan, Blackboard Tree, Alstonia, Alstonia scholaris.   **Devdar**[137] [10] देवदारु, False Ashoka, Polylathia longifolia.   **Dhan**[138] [crop] धान्य, Rice, Oryza sativa.   **Durva**[139] [grass] दूर्वा, Dubo, Bermuda Grass, Cynodon dactylon.   **Galgal**[140] [fruit,5] मातुलुङ्ग, Citron, Citrus medica (the origin of Mausambi, Nimbu and Santara).   **Gamhar**[141] [wood,30] गम्भारी, Gamari, Gumar, White Teak, Gmelina arborea.   **Ganna**[142] [sugar,4] इक्षु, Ukhu, Sugarcane, Saccharum officinarum (var. Kans).   **Genda**[143] [flower,2] Marigold, Tagetes erecta.   **Guggul**[144] [resin,4] गुग्गुलु, Gugal, Mukul Myrrh, Commiphora wightii.   **Gular**[145] [fruit,10] उदुम्बर, Dumari, Atti, Umaraa, Goolar Fig, Indian Fig Tree, Ficus racemosa (var. Banyan, Pakar, Pipal).   **Gulmohar**[146] [flower,5] Flamboyant, Flame Tree, Delonix regia (var. Bean).   **Guma**[147] [herb] द्रोणपुष्पी, Gumpati, Leucas cephalotes.   **Gwarpatha**[148] [leaf] कुमारी, Aloe, Aloe vera.   **Haldi**[149] [root] हलदी, Curcuma, Besar, Turmeric, Curcuma longa.   **Haritaki**[150] [fruit,30] हरीतकी, Harro, Black Myrobalan, Terminalia chebula (var. Arjun, Asan, Badam, Baheda).   **Henna**[151] [color,8] मेन्धिका, Mehandi, Mehari, Henna Tree, Lawsonia inermis.   **Hollong**[152] [wood,resin,40] Hulunga, Dipterocarpus retusus.   **Imli**[153] [fruit,18] अम्लक,

Tamarind, Tamarindus indica. **Jaal**[154] [wood,leaves,6] पीलु, Meswak, Arak, Digaru, Toothbrush Tree, Salvadora persica. **Jamun**[155] [fruit,30] जम्बु, जाम्बुल, Jambuka, Neredu, Java Plum, Syzygium cumini (var. Long). **Jatiphal**[156] [fruit,nut,20] जातिफल, जयफल, Nutmeg, Myristica fragrans. **Kabra**[157] [fruit,1] हिंस्र, Caper Bush, Capparis spinosa. **Kachnar**[158] [flower,buds,10] काञ्चनार, Orchid Tree, Mountain Ebony, Bauhinia variegata. **Kadam**[159] [wood,45] कदम्ब, Burflower Tree, Neolamarckia cadamba. **Kadi**[160] [food,6] गिरिनिम्ब, Mithi Neem, Kadi Patta, Curry Tree, Murraya koenigii. **Kaith**[161] [fruit,9] कपित्थ, Kaitho, Kenth, Wood Apple, Limonia acidissima, Feronia limonia. **Kair**[162] [fruit,5] करीर, Karira, Ker, Capparis decidua. **Kamal**[163] [flower] कमल, (Indian) Lotus, Nelumbo nucifera. **Kamrakh**[164] [fruit,7] कर्मर, कर्मरङ्ग, Carambola, Starfruit, Averrhoa carambola. **Kankro**[165] [vegetable] Khira, Cucumber, Cucumis sativus. **Kans**[166] [sugar,3] काश, Kas, Thatch Grass, Wild Sugarcane, Sacchharum spontaneum (var. Ganna). **Kapas**[167] [cotton,2] कर्पास, Roee, Tree Cotton, Gossypium arboreum. **Kapur**[168] [camphor,15] कर्पूर, Camphor Tree, Cinnamomum camphora (var. Tamal). **Karanda**[169] [fruit,3] करमर्द, Bengal Currant, Corinda Tree, Carissa carandas. **Karaunda**[170] [shade,seed,20] करञ्ज, Indian Beech, Pongamia pinnata. **Karnikara**[171] [shade,25] कर्णिकार, Bayur Tree, Pterospermum acerifolium (var. Lal Chandan, Padauk, Vijaya Shal). **Kathal**[172] [wood,fruit,20] पनस, Kathar, Jackfruit, Artocarpus integrifolius (var. Chakka). **Kath Champa**[173] [wood,nut,15] पुन्नग, Surpan, Alexandrian Laurel, Calophyllum inophyllum. **Kela**[174] [fruit,5] कदली, Kera, Banana, Plantain, Musa paradisiaca. **Khair**[175] [wood,15] खदिर, Kattha, Catechu Tree, Senegalia catechu. **Khajur**[176] [fruit,10] खर्जूर, Indian Date, Sugar Date Palm, Phoenix sylvestris. **Khejri**[177] [wood,5] शमी, Jammi, Khijro, Jant, Prosopis cineraria. **Kokum**[178] [fruit,seed,15] वृक्षामला, Biran, Bheranda, Red Mango, Butter Tree, Garcinia indica. **Kovidar**[179] [flower] कोविदार (var. of Kachnar). **Kudzu**[180] [crop] Pueraria phaseoloides /javanica. **Kusha**[181] [grass] कुश, Kush, Halfa Grass, Desmotachya bipinnata. **Langsat**[182] [fruit,20] Duku, Lanzones, Lansium parasiticum. **Lal Chandan**[183] [wood,8] रक्तचन्दन, कृष्णागरु, Red Sandalwood, Pterocarpus santalinus (var. Karnikara, Padauk, Vijaya Shal). **Lasoda**[184] [fruit,5] Gunda, Booch, Indian Cherry, Cordia dichotoma. **Lichi**[185] [fruit,20] Lychee, Sapindaceae. **Long**[186] [spice,10] लवङ्ग, Clove, Syzygium aromaticum (var. Jamun). **Louki**[187] [vegetable] Bottle Gourd, Lagenaria siceraria. **Mahua**[188] [wood,flower,seed,20] मधुक, Ellopa Tree, Madhuca longifolia. **Makhan**[189] [seeds] Euryale ferox. **Mandar**[190] [wood,20] मन्दार, Panjira, Coral Tree, Erythrina.

Matar[191] [crop] कलाय, Kerao, Pea, Pisum sativum. **Mausambi**[192] [fruit,8] Mausam, Mita Nimbu, Sweet Lemon, Citrus Limetta (var. Galgal, Nimbu, Santara) **Mung**[193] [crop] मुद्र, माष, Mungi, Golden Gram, Vigna radiata (var. Urad). **Nag Champa**[194] [wood,30] नागकेसर, Nageshwari, Iron Wood, Indian Rose Chestnut, Mesua ferrea. **Nariyal**[195] [nut,20] नारिकेल, Coconut, Cocos nucifera. **Nashpati**[196] [fruit,9] आरुक, Indian Pear, Pyrus pyrifolia. **Neem**[197] [wood,leaves,20] निम्ब, पिचुमर्द, Picuman, Indian Lilak, Azadirachta indica. **Nimbu**[198] [fruit,15] निम्बू, निम्बूक, Dhauranjo, Lime, Lemon, Citrus (var. Galgal, Santara, Mausambi). **Okhar**[199] [wood,nut,30] आखोट, अक्षोट, Akharot, Walnut, Juglans regia. **Padauk**[200] [wood,30] Mukwa, Amboyna, Andaman Redwood, East Indian Mahogony, Pterocarpus dalbergioides (var. Karnikara, Lal Chandan, Vijaya Shal). **Paiyaun**[201] [fruit,gum,30] पद्मक, Himalayan Cherry, Prunus cerasoides. **Pakar**[202] [wood,20] प्लक्ष, Pilkhan, Ficus lacor (var. Banyan, Gular, Pipal). **Pakhad**[203] [leaves,25] प्लक्ष, Pilkhan, Bassari, White Fig, Ficus virens (a strangling fig). **Palash**[204] [wood,flower,15] पलाश, Kimshuka, Kankrai, Dhak, Bastard Teak, Flame of the Forest, Parrot Tree, Butea monosperma. **Papita**[205] [fruit,5] Papaya, Carica papaya. **Paras**[206] [wood,bark,10] पारिश, पार्श्वपिप्पल, Portia Tree, Thespesia populnea. **Parijat**[207] [flower,10] परिजात, घुतरु, Harsinghar, Night Jasmine, Nyctanthes arbror-tristis. **Patsan**[208] [fiber,seed,3] Ambari, Pat, Kenaf, Java Jute, Deccan Hemp, Hibiscus cannabinus (also called San and thus often confused with San). **Peela Gulmohar**[209] [wood,flower,20] Tamraparni, Copperpod, Peltophorum pterocarpum. **Petha**[210] [gourd] Kubhindo, Kumbala, Kushmanda, Kolu, White Gourd, Benincasa hispida. **Phalsa**[211] [fruit,8] पारुषक, Falsa, Grewia asiatica. **Pipal**[212] [30] पिप्पल, अश्वत्थ, Bodhidruma, Holy Fig, Ficus religiosa (var. Banyan, Gular, Pakar). **Putranjiva**[213] [wood,leaves,seed,12] पुत्रजीवक, Putijia, Lucky Bean Tree, Putranjiva roxburghii. **Ragi**[214] [crop] रागी, Kodo, Finger Millet, Eleusine coracana (var. Bajra). **Rajbriksha**[215] [wood,flower,20] राजवृक्ष, Amaltash, Golden Shower, Purging Cassia, Indian Laburnum, Cassia fistula. **Reetha**[216] [nut,15] अरिष्ट, Soapnut, Indian Soapberry, Sapindus. **Rohida**[217] [wood,5] Desert Teak, Marwar Teak, Tecomella undulata. **Rudraksh**[218] [beads,20] रुद्राक्ष, Utrasum Bead Tree, Elaeocarpus. **Sabera**[219] [fruit,45] विभीतक, Baheda, Beleric, Myrabolan, Terminalia bellirica (var. Arjun, Asan, Badam, Haritaki). **Sagaun**[220] [wood,30] शाक, Saigun, Teku, Teak, Tectona grandis. **Sahajan**[221] [food,10] शिग्र, Sehjan, Drumstick, Moringa, Moringa oleifera. **Sal**[222] [wood,30] शाल, सर्ज, अश्वकर्ण, Shal, Sakhuwa, Ajakarna, Shorea robusta. **Salak**[223] [fruit,6] Snake Fruit, Salacca zalacca. **San**[224] [fiber] दीर्घफल,

Shon, Jhunjhunia, Masina, Taag, Sunn Hemp, Crotalaria juncea (see Patsan). **Santara**[225] [fruit,10] नारङ्ग, Narangi, Orange, Citrus x (var. Nimbu, Galgal; other var. are Kinnu-Mandarin and Mausambi). **Sarso**[226] [crop] सर्षप, राजिका, Rai, Oriental /Indian /Brown Mustard, Brassica juncea (var. White Mustard, Sinapis alba). **Seb**[227] [fruit,4] सेव, Apple, Malus domestica (var. in Punjab: Anna variety and Dorsette Golden variety). **Senji**[228] [cover crop] Indian Sweet Clover, Melilot, Melilotus indicus. **Shahtut**[229] [fruit,15] तूत, Tuti, Mulberry, Morus indica. **Shalmali**[230] [20] शल्मलि, Veshta, Sevar, Semal, Silk-Cotton Tree, Bombax ceiba. **Shikakai**[231] [leaves,10] श्रीवल्ली, Soap-Pod, Acacia concinna. **Shirish**[232] [wood,10] शिरीष, Siris, Parrot Tree, East Indian Walnut, Albizia. **Shisham**[233] [wood,25] शिंशपा, पिच्छिल, Sisu, Tali, Indian Rosewood, Dalbergia sissoo. **Singhara**[234] [vegetable] शृङ्गाटक, Singhada, Paniphal, Water Caltrop, Trapa bispinosa. **Sonapatha**[235] [wood,leaves,15] स्योनाक, Indian Caper, Oroxylum indicum (see Kabra). **Sthalkamal**[236] [flower,5] स्थलपद्म, Confederate Rose, Hibiscus mutabilis. **Taal**[237] [fruit,leaves,30] ताल, Taad, Karpaha, Nungu, Palmyra Tree, Borassus. **Tamal**[238] [wood,leaves,20] तमालपत्र, Tejpat, Indian Bay Leaf, Indian Bark, Cinnamomum tamala (var. Kapur). **Tejpatta**[239] [leaf,5] Bay Tree, Laurel, Laurus nobilis (see Asan). **Til**[240] [crop] तिल, Sesame, Sesamum indicum. **Tulsi**[241] [herb] तुलसी, Holy Basil, Ocimum tenuiflorum. **Tun**[242] [wood,50] नन्दिक, नन्दिवृक्ष, Toon, Red Cedar, Indian Mahogany, Toona ciliata. **Urad**[243] [crop] उडिद, Mans, Black Gram, Vigna mungo (var. Mung). **Vijay Shal**[244] [wood,30] विजयसार, Bandhuk Pushpa, Indian Kino Tree, Pterocarpus marsupium (var. Karnikara, Lal Chandan, Padauk).

---

17. Roman Letters

Teaching in India Roman letters with Hindi names, new letters introduced in bold:

RAM Ram (m) AMAR Amar (m) MIRA … (f) MANI (m/f) MINA (f) **HARI** (m) AMBA (f) **ABHA** (f) BHIMA (m) DINA (m/f) NANDA (m/f) ANAND (m) ANANDA (f) ANANDI (f) NIDRA (f) INDRA (m) INDIRA (f) BRINDA (f) **DHARMA** (m) **CHANDA** (f) CHANDI (f) MANU (m/f) ARUN (m) ARUNA (f) URMILA (f) BUDDHA (m) DITI (f) ADITI (f) AMIT (m) AMITA (f) AMRIT (m) AMRITA (f) NITIN (m) ANANT (m) BHARAT (m) CHITRA (f) SITA (f) HAMSA (f) **ASHA** (f) ANISH (m) MANISH (m) MANISHA (f) HARISH (m) HARSHA (m/f) **KUSH** (m) KANTA (f) KANTI (f) KUNTI (f) KASHI (f) AKASH (m) KIRTI (f) ADHIK (m) SHUKA (m) ANKUR (m) ANKIT (m) ANKITA (f) KUMAR (m) KUMARI (f) KAMINI (f)

NITIKA (f)   KARUNA (f)   KISHAN (m)   ILA (f)   LILA (f)   NILA (f)   NALA (m)
MALA (f)   LATA (f)   BALA (m/f)   ANIL (m)   ANILA (f)   NAKUL (m)
AMALA (f)   AKHIL (m)   NIKHIL (m)   LALITA (f)   NALINI (f)   MURALI (m)
MALINI (f)   MALATI (f)   KAMALA (f)   NILIMA (f)   NIRMAL (m)   OM (m)
ASHOK (m)   MOHAN (m)   MOHINI (f)   KISHOR (m)   LOCHAN (m)   DIPA (f)
DIPAK (m)   DIPTI (f)   DIPALI (f)   DIPIKA (f)   DILIP (m)   KAPIL (m)
ANUPAM (m/f)   VASU (m)   KAVI (m)   KAVITA (f)   DHRUV (m)   NAVIN (m)
NAVINA (f)   NIRAV (m)   AVANI (f)   AVANTI (f)   ISHVAR (m)   UDDHAV (m)
MADHAV (m)   GITA (f)   AGNI (m)   GAURI (f)   GOTAM (m)   GAUTAM (m)
GOVIND (m)   GOMATI (f)   GOPI (f)   GOPIKA (f)   GOPAL (m)   GIRISH (m)
DURGA (f)   JIVA (m)   JIVAN (m)   AJIT (m)   ANUJ (m)   ARJUN (m)   NIRAJ (m)
NIRJA (f)   ANJALI (f)   JAGJIT (m)   DEV (m)   DEVI (f)   DEVAKI (f)   DEVIKA (f)
DEVDAN (m)   DEVDAS (m)   DEVRAJ (m)   ADESH (m)   MAHESH (m)
MUKESH (m)   GANESH (m)   DINESH (m)   KEVALA (f)   KAVERI (f)
CHETAN (m)   ARYA (f)   DAYA (m/f)   MAYA (f)   MAYUR (m)   JAYA (f)
AJAY (m)   VIJAY (m)   NITYA (m/f)   ABHAY (m)   DIVYA (f)   JYOTI (f)
YAMUNA (f)   ADITYA (m)   KALYAN (m)

Sometimes W is used for V, as in: ALWAR   GWALIOR   GUWAHATI
HARIDWAR   AISHWARYA (m/f)   VIJAYAWADA

More Words: ANUPAM (m)   ANUPAMA (f)   ARAVIND (m)   ARCHANA (f)
AVINASH (m)   AYODHYA   BALADEV (m)   BHASKAR (m)   BHAVANA (f)
BHAVANI (m/f)   BHISHMA (m)   BIJAPUR   BIKANER   BRIJESH (m)
CHANDAN (m)   CHANDRA (m)   CHENNAI   CHETANA (f)   DAMODAR (m)
DARSHAN (m)   DAYARAM (m)   DRISHTI (f)   DVARAKA   GAYATRI (f)
INDRANI (f)   JAUNPUR   JAYANTI (f)   JODHPUR   JYOTSNA (f)   KAILASH (m)
KALIDAS (m)   KALINDA (f)   KALPANA (f)   KALYANI (f)   KISHORI (f)
KOLKATA   KRISHNA (m)   LAKSHMI (f)   LAVANYA (f)   LOCHANA (f)
MADHAVI (f)   MADHURI (f)   MADURAI   MAHAVIR (m)   MANISHA (f)
MANJULA (f)   MATHURA   NANDINI (f)   NANDITA (f)   NARAYAN (m)
NATARAJ (m)   NIRMALA (f)   PANIPAT   PATIALA   PRAHLAD (m)   RAIGANJ
RAMGARH   RUKMINI (f)   SAHADEV (m)   SHIMOGA   SOLAPUR   SONIPAT
UDAIPUR   VASUDEV (m)

SANSKRIT

"This is the most perfect and logical language in the world, the only one that is not named after the people who speak it. Indeed, the word itself means perfected language." (Warwick Jessup, Head Sanskrit Department St. James School London)

"Sanskrit means 'complete', 'perfect' and 'definitive'. In fact, this language is extremely elaborate, almost artificial, and is capable of describing multiple levels of meditation, states of consciousness and psychic, spiritual and even intellectual processes. As for vocabulary, its richness is considerable and highly diversified. Sanskrit has for centuries lent itself admirably to the diverse rules of prosody and versification. Thus, we can see why poetry has played such a preponderant role in all of Indian culture and Sanskrit literature." (Georges Ifrah, French historian)

"The whole of their original works are composed in Sanscrite, a language of great antiquity, but which is no longer spoken, though its history is intimately connected with several of the present languages of Europe, with those of Greece and Rome, and with the whole of the numerous family of cognate Gothic tongues. Sancrite holds the same place in India, that Latin and Greek do in Europe; but as it would require an amazing period of time, and many political changes in society before a language could fall into disuse and be unemployed in speech, this circumstance without any further proof, would carry us, back to the first ages. It is natural to suppose that the sciences would first prosper where men were not exposed to excessive labour in order to procure the necessaries of life; plenty and tranquility would leave them at liberty to cultivate knowledge, to apply their minds to books, and learning." (Alexander Walker, British Brigadier-General and explorer, 1764-1831)

"The Pānini grammar reflects the wondrous capacity of the human brain, which till today no other country has been able to produce except India." (Sir Monier Monier-Williams, British Indologist and head of the Oxford's Boden Chair, 1819-1899)

"The grammar of Panini stands supreme among the grammars of the world, alike for its precision of statement, and for its thorough analysis of the roots of the language and of the formative principles of words. By employing an algebraic terminology, it attains a sharp succinctness unrivalled in brevity, but at times enigmatical. It arranges, in logical harmony, the whole phenomena which the Sanskrit language presents, and stands forth as one of the most splendid achievements of human invention and industry. So elaborate is the structure, that doubts have arisen whether its complex rules of formation and phonetic change, its polysyllabic derivatives, its ten conjugations with their multiform aorists and long array of tenses, could ever have been the spoken language of a people." (Sir William Wilson Hunter, Scottish historian, 1840-1900)

"The great grammarian Panini is now being called the first software man, without the hardware. And the focus is on the roughly 4,000 rules of Sanskrit grammar that he evolved. Rules that are so scientific and logical in manner that they closely resemble structures used by computer scientists throughout the world."   "In India's long history, Sanskrit has been the greatest integrating force, the source of cultural continuum, the medium of literary creativity, the voice of the sages and the languages of the most sublime thoughts and the profoundest of the philosophies of life. Sanskrit had its impact in many countries outside. It became the language of the learned even in the South-East Asia and to some extent parts of Central Asia.

Most interestingly, many of the ancient Sanskrit plays that exist were found not in India but in Turfan on the edge of the Great Gobi Desert in China." (Dr. Subramanian Swamy, Indian economist and politician)

"It took only 200 years for us to Christianise the whole of Africa, but even after 400 years India eludes us, I have come to realize that it is Sanskrit which has enabled India to do so. And to break it I have decided to learn Sanskrit." (Friedrich Max Müller, German-born orientalist, 1823-1900)

"Language is the distillation of hundreds, if not thousands of years of experience of a collective. ... So, when the language disappears, you're really throwing away that whole library of knowledge." (Rachel Nez, Navajo speaker)

"A dead language, you say! Impossible to revive? But that's what they argued about Hebrew. And did not the Jewish people, when they got back their land in 1948, revive their 'dead' language, so that it is spoken today by all Jewish people and has become alive again? The same thing ought to be done with Sanskrit. Let the scholars begin now to revive and modernize the Sanskrit language, it would be a sure sign of the dawning of the Renaissance of India. In a few years it should be taught as the second language in schools throughout the country, with the regional language as the first and English as the third. Then will India again have its own unifying language." (Francois Gautier, French journalist based in India)

18. Devanagari

u	ū	a	ā	o	au	ma
bha	ga	na	ta	la	va	ba
ka	ca	ja	ña	pa	pha	ṣa
ṇa	ya	tha	gha	dha	ra	sa
kha	e	ai	ḍa	ṅa	i	ī
jha	ṭa	ṭha	ḍha	da	cha	ha
śa	ṛ	ki	kī	ku	kū	kṛ
ke	kai	ko	kau	ru	rū	hṛ
kta	kṣa	jña	śva	tta	rka	kra
tra	śra	1	2	3	4	5
6	7	8	9		oṁ

The first vowels are अ (as in 'mother') and आ (as in 'father'). Please practice writing the letters and use the dotted line as a guide where to place the uppermost horizontal line of each letter. Thus the letter will be below the line:

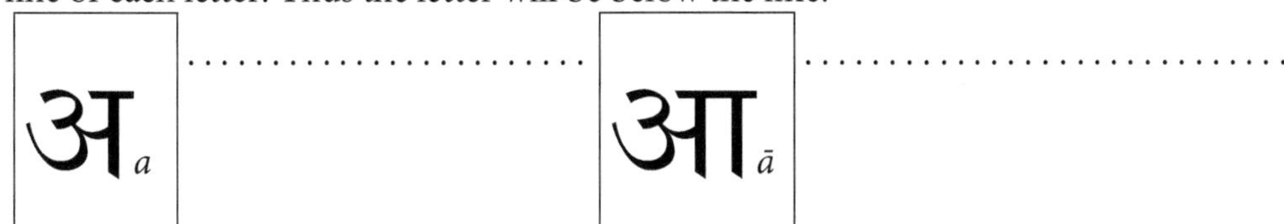

The first consonant we all learn is म *ma* and our first word is मम *mama* (my):

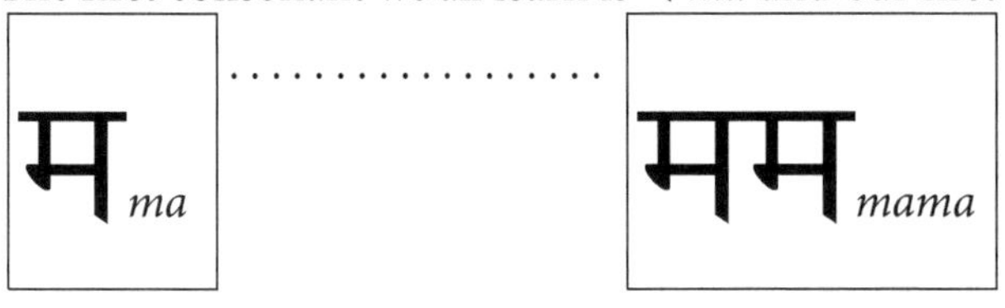

The upper horizontal line is written at the end over both letters at once, and not over each letter separately. Since every consonant is already pronounced with an inherent *a*, the letter अ *a* is only written at the beginning of a word. The inherent *a* can be cut with हल्-अन्त (consonant ending), so that म *ma* becomes म्*m*, आम*āma* becomes आम्*ām*, etc. For a long *ā* after consonants, a vertical line is added: मा*mā*, अमा*amā*.

Reading Exercises 1-9:

1	अ	म	मम	म्	आ	मा
	अम	अमा	आम	आमा	ममा	माम्

भ*bha*	भाम आभा

ग*ga*	अग आगम भाग

न*na*	अन् नाना नाम मान नाग गगन

2	ग	ना	न	गा	न	ग
	अग	अन्	नाना	नाग	नाम	गगन
	अमा	मान	भाग	भाम	आभा	आगम

| व *va* | वन नव भव वाम वामन भगवान् |

| क *ka* | काक काम कानन |

| ब *ba* | बक |

| र *ra* | नर नगर वर वार भार राम राका आकर |

| स *sa* | सम साम सार रस मास वास नासा सभा सनक सागर समास आसन अवसर |

A vowel can be followed by विसर्ग ('echo' *ḥ*), marked with a colon

| कः *kaḥ* | (say 'kaha') नमः मनः सरः भाः

... or by अनुस्वार , the pure nasal (marked with a dot):

| कं *kaṁ* | कंस संसार

3

न	कः	मा	नर	मम	माम्
भाग	रस	नाग	नाम	वर	भाम
वन	सम	काम	मनः	आम्	मास
नव	भव	बक	वाम	नाना	मान
राम	काक	साम	वार	सार	वास
भार	नगर	सरः	कंस	नमः	सभा
राका	गगन	समास	कानन	नासा	सनक
सागर	आकर	वामन	आगम	आसन	संसार

As we saw before, the letter अ *a* is written only in the beginning of a word, because every consonant is pronounced with an inherent *a*. When the inherent *a* is to be replaced by another vowel, the corresponding Vowel Sign is added. The Vowel Sign for a long *ā* is a vertical line and क *ka* becomes का *kā*, etc.

अ *a*	आ *ā*	इ *i*	ई *ī*	उ *u*	ऊ *ū*	ऋ *ṛ*	ए *e*	ऐ *ai*	ओ *o*	औ *au*
Sign: ा		ि	ी	◌ु	◌ू	◌ृ	े	ै	ो	ौ
क	का	कि	की	कु	कू	कृ	के	कै	को	कौ
न	ना	नि	नी	नु	नू	नृ	ने	नै	नो	नौ
ब	बा	बि	बी	बु	बू	बृ	बे	बै	बो	बौ
भ	भा	भि	भी	भु	भू	भृ	भे	भै	भो	भौ
म	मा	मि	मी	मु	मू	मृ	मे	मै	मो	मौ
र	रा	रि	री	रु	रू		रे	रै	रो	रौ
व	वा	वि	वी	वु	वू	वृ	वे	वै	वो	वौ
स	सा	सि	सी	सु	सू	सृ	से	सै	सो	सौ

4

कु	वी	म	का	न	कौ	रै	भौ	नृ	कृ
मी	रा	कै	सौ	वो	बे	नू	र	वे	को
वि	से	भ	गा	मो	ने	क	बि	मौ	बृ
बै	नि	वा	सी	रू	रौ	कू	भी	सि	भृ
भु	वै	के	मे	भे	रे	सृ	वृ	बौ	मृ
भा	नै	सै	व	मै	भू	ब	रो	बू	भि
नी	बी	नौ	कि	बा	मू	भो	सो	री	वू
वु	बो	भै	स	रि	की	वौ	सू	नो	मि
ना	नु	बु	मा	मु	रु	सा	सु	भे	नि

There are three ways of forming Ligatures between consonants.

(1) dropping the vertical line of the first component:

म् *m* + ब *ba* → म्‍ + ब → म्ब *mba*   अम्बा अम्बर

म् *m* + भ *bha* → म्‍ + भ → म्भ *mbha*   आरम्भ

स् *s* + म *ma* → स्‍ + म → स्म *sma*   भस्म

स् *s* + न *na* → स्‍ + न → स्न / स्न *sna*   स्नान

स् *s* + व *va* → स्‍ + व → स्व *sva*   स्वर

<table>
<tr><td rowspan="4">5</td><td>सभा</td><td>अम्बर</td><td>भस्म</td><td>कंस</td><td>स्व</td><td>गगन</td></tr>
<tr><td>स्नान</td><td>काक</td><td>संसार</td><td>नगर</td><td>समास</td><td>नमः</td></tr>
<tr><td>सरः</td><td>आकर</td><td>आरम्भ</td><td>आगम</td><td>सागर</td><td>अम्बा</td></tr>
<tr><td>मनः</td><td>स्वर</td><td>वामन</td><td>कानन</td><td>आसन</td><td>सनक</td></tr>
</table>

कि *ki*   गिर् गिरि कवि रवि नाभि वारि विराम अवनि आविस् निम्ब बिम्ब अग्नि विवस्वान्

की *kī*   नीर मीन मीरा वीर सीमा गम्भीर

ऋ *r* is another Sanskrit vowel, pronounced similar to the syllable रि *ri*. But one has to remember that ऋ is a vowel, while र *ra* in रि is a consonant.

कृ *kr*   नृ मृग वृक कृमि

त *ta*   तमः तात वात तारा तीर माता सत् सीता रीति भारत अवतार समिति
In Ligature: न्त अन्त अन्तर् प्त तृप्त ल्त रत्न स्त स्तन स्तम्भ अस्ति विस्तार त्म आत्मा त्स वत्स कृत्स्न

6					
अम्बा	अम्बर	अग्नि	बिम्ब	विराम	गिरि्
भारत	गिरि	निम्ब	वीर	सीमा	नीर
भस्म	मीन	मीरा	तमः	तात	नृ
स्नान	मृग	वृक	समिति	कृमि	वारि
स्व	स्वर	अवनि	कवि	आगम	नाभि
आरम्भ	तारा	तीर	माता	सत्	सीता
अन्त	तृप्त	रत्न	स्तन	स्तम्भ	रीति
अस्ति	आत्मा	वत्स	आकर	वात	रवि

ल *la*	लता लम्ब लाभ तल तिल नल नील लीला बल बाल बलि बिल काल कला माला अमल कमल कम्बल सरल विरल मालती विलास म्ल अम्ल ल्म वल्मी ल्व बिल्व ल्क कल्कि
प *pa*	पर पान पाल पवन पति पिता पीत अप् तपः कपि लिपि वापी समीप विपिन पिपासा ल्प अल्प प्ल प्लव प्त सप्त आप्त प्न स्वप्न प्प पिप्पल पिप्पलि
फ *pha*	फल कफ
य *ya*	यम अयः अयन वयः पयः आय काय माया स्मय आलय अन्वय नयन समय त्य त्याग नित्य नृत्य न्य अन्य न्याय न्यास कन्या स्य स्याल सस्य व्य व्यास व्यापार भ्य अभ्यास ल्य लाल्य त्स्य मत्स्य
थ *tha*	अथ रथ नाथ कथा पथ तिथि मिथः न्थ कन्था स्थ अस्थि थ्य मिथ्या

7					
लता	लम्ब	लाभ	तल	तिल	नल
नील	लीला	बल	बाल	बलि	बिल

काल	कला	माला	अमल	कमल	कम्बल
सरल	विरल	मालती	कफ	अम्ल	कल्कि
वल्मी	लाल्य	बिल्व	यम	अयः	अयन
वयः	आय	काय	माया	स्मय	आलय
अन्वय	नयन	समय	त्याग	नित्य	नृत्य
अन्य	न्याय	न्यास	कन्या	स्याल	सस्य
व्यास	फल	आप्त	अथ	रथ	नाथ
कथा	तिथि	मिथः	कन्था	सप्त	स्वप्न
पर	पयः	पथ	पान	पाल	पवन
पति	पिता	पीत	अप्	तपः	कपि
लिपि	वापी	समीप	विपिन	अल्प	प्लव

कु *ku* — कुल नु युग युव सुर तुला पुर पुरः मुनि वसु वपुः पुंस् पुनर् कुमार कुम्भ कुसुम अम्बु आयुर् गुप्त तुलसी पुस्तक पृथु मथुरा मुरली विपुल यमुना सुरभि स्तुति

कू *kū* — कूप कूल मूल भू मयूर सूनु स्तूप स्थूल निम्बू

Note the combinations:

रु *ru* — तरु कुरु पुरु गुरु अगुरु मरुत्   and **रू** *rū* — रूप

ख *kha* — नख मुख सुख सखि अ-खिल ख्य ख्याति

द *da* — दल दम दाम दान दास दया वाद दिन दीप पद यदु नाद नदी
दिव् विद् तद् आदर सदन नारद कदली कुमुद सदस्य आदित्य न्त
दन्त न्द नन्द बिन्दु मन्दिर वृन्दा सुन्दर सिन्दूर स्कन्द अरविन्द

| ह *ha* | हय हर हल हस हंस सह हनु रह: वाह हित हिम हीरा गृह बहु बाहु महत् बृहत् हलदी हविर् हस्त महिला विहार संहित सिंह स्वाहा अहिंसा व्यवहार हृद् हृदय सुहृद् |

| के *ke* | वेद देव देह हेतु हेम भेद सेतु सेना सेवा मेरु मेला रेखा कुवेर केदार केलि केवल केसर निकेत विवेक स्नेह नारिकेल |

| कै *kai* | तैल दैव वैर कैलास दैनिक वैदिक |

8

भेद	अप्	बहु	दाम	देव	दया
हेतु	हय	भू	अथ	बलि	दान
दैव	फल	हल	बिल	आय	अय:
बल	दास	दल	गृह	हनु	दिन
रूप	बाहु	सिंह	देह	दम	गुरु
हीरा	दिव्	पिता	बाल	तिथि	मिथ:
दीप	हंस	हर	गिरि	गिर्	तिल
काय	कला	कुल	लता	माया	मीरा
हिम	विद्	कफ	कथा	कूप	मृग
मेरु	मुख	हित	कृमि	कपि	कुरु
लाभ	माला	मेला	मुनि	लिपि	काल
कवि	कूल	लीला	माता	मीन	मूल
नृ	नाथ	नीर	पान	पीत	पुर
रह:	सेना	नख	नदी	नु	पद

पर	पुरः	रवि	सेतु	नाद	नल
पृथु	पति	युव	पयः	रथ	सेवा
नाभि	नील	पाल	पथ	पुरु	रेखा
रीति	सह	सखि	सुख	तारा	तल
तुला	वारि	वैर	वयः	सीमा	सूनु
तात	तमः	वृक	वापी	वपुः	यदु
सीता	सुर	तद्	तपः	वाद	वात
वीर	यम	सत्	तरु	तैल	तीर
वाह	वेद	वसु	युग	व्यास	आप्त
आत्मा	अग्नि	अल्प	अन्वय	भारत	आदर

9

अमल	अम्ल	अन्य	अस्ति	अस्थि	आलय
अम्बु	निम्ब	बिम्ब	अन्त	हविर्	आयुर्
अवनि	दैनिक	विपिन	प्लव	बृहत्	गुप्त
अगुरु	दन्त	वैदिक	विरल	कल्कि	कन्या
अयन	गम्भीर	विहार	स्मय	कमल	केदार
सरल	स्कन्द	स्तुति	स्याल	कम्बल	केलि
हल्दी	बिन्दु	निम्बू	पिप्पल	कन्था	कैलास
हस्त	मिथ्या	नित्य	सिन्दूर	पुस्तक	सप्त

बिल्व	निकेत	लम्ब	महिला	विराम	कदली
केसर	कुमुद	मालती	मन्दिर	मयूर	नयन
केवल	कुसुम	नारद	न्याय	नृत्य	न्यास
विपुल	विवेक	पवन	सदन	कुम्भ	कुवेर
संहित	समिति	रत्न	सदस्य	कुमार	लाल्य
मरुत्	मथुरा	वृन्दा	सस्य	समीप	सुन्दर
महत्	मुरली	नन्द	आत्मा	स्थूल	भारत
त्याग	वत्स	वल्मी	यमुना	समय	सुरभि
स्तन	स्वप्न	स्तूप	तुलसी	पुनर्	स्वाहा

Before another consonant, *r* is written as a hook on top of that letter:

| कर्*rka* |

अर्क तर्क वर्ग सर्ग मार्ग मर्म नर्म वर्म कर्म अर्थ सर्प गर्भ आर्य पर्व सर्व दुर्ग मूर्ख कूर्म पूर्व सूर्य स्वर्ग तीर्थ अथर्व पर्वत कीर्तन मुहूर्त विवर्त सम्पर्क सन्दर्भ तिर्यक् स्थैर्य

It has to be read before the complete syllable: दुर्गा वर्त्म सर्पिः मूर्ति कर्पूर

After another consonant, *r* is written as a small stroke:

| क्र*kra* |

क्रम क्रतु तक्र ग्रह ग्राम ग्रन्थ ग्रीव ग्रसन भ्रम भ्राता भ्रू व्रत प्रभा प्राय समग्र क्रिया आम्र प्रकार प्रथम प्रहर प्रिय विप्र तीव्र प्रभव प्रसाद प्रातर् प्रकृति व्रीहि प्रवाला प्रसभम्

Special combinations:

| द्र*dra* | द्रव्य द्रुम द्रुत भद्र रुद्र दरिद्र समुद्र निद्रा मुद्रा |

| स्र*sra* | सहस्र |

त् + र → त्र → | त्र*tra* | अत्र पत्र पात्र यात्रा पुत्र सूत्र नेत्र मित्र त्रि रात्रि अमुत्र खनित्र कृत्रिम गायत्री सावित्री यन्त्र तन्त्र मन्त्र स्त्री

घ *gha*	घन अघ अर्घ मेघ घृत लघु दीर्घ व्याघ्र
ध *dha*	धी धन धाम धर्म धूप धेनु अधः अधि दधि मधु वधू राधा बुध सुधा मेधः विध विधि धनुर् अधुना समाधि अधिकार अन्ध गन्ध बन्ध दुग्ध ध्यान अध्याय मध्य ध्वनि अर्ध मूर्ध ध्रुव रन्ध्र गन्धर्व मेन्धी सन्धि सिन्धु स्कन्ध
को *ko*	नो गो गोल तोय दोला लोक लोभ लोह मोह रोम सोम होम योनि होली स्रोतः आरोह कोमल अयोध्या कोकिल कपोत मोदक रोहित विनोद व्योम सम्बोधन
कौ *kau*	नौ मौन गौर कौपीन कौन्तेय
च *ca*	चर चाप चिर चीन चित् चेल चोर चोल चरु चमर चपल चापल चतुर् चक्र चुम्ब चमत्- चन्द्र चातुरी वच रुचि रचन रेचक कवच लोचन विचार सूचना चर्च अर्चन आचार चिकित्सा आचमन परिचय प्राचीन
छ *cha*	छत्र छन्दः छिद्र अच्छ स्वच्छ तुच्छ पुच्छ पृच्छा यदृच्छया
ज *ja*	जप जय जर जल जाल अज गज राजा जीर जीव तेजः पूजा बीज जगत् जातु जानु जम्बू जल्प जागर भोजन राजीव समाज व्रज वज्र अर्जन अर्जुन आर्जव खर्जूर ज्योतिः
श *śa*	शय शर शम् शाक शाखा शाला शनि शब्द शीत शील शुभ शुक शुक्रशुचि शुल्क शूर शूल शून्य शंसन शतम् शरद् शरीर शर्म शर्करा शस्त्र शावक शासन दश दशा दिशा निशा आशा आशु शिव शिरः शिला अंश वंश यशः कुश केश कोश क्रोश पशु परशु शिशु शिखा शिखर शिग्रु शिल्प शिशिर शीघ्रम् काशी कलश आकाश किशोर विंशति विशाल
ष *ṣa*	विष मेष वेष मूष् घोष भाषा वर्ष हर्ष शीर्ष विषय वृषभ निमिष भेषज पुरुष प्रदोष अभिलाषा अम्बरीष ग्रीष्म पुष्कर पुष्कल
ण *ṇa*	कण चण गण गुण अणु बाण पाणि प्राण कोण तृण मणि रेणु वेणु वीणा लवण शरण अरुण करुण तरुण वरुण तर्पण वणिक् प्रमाण भूषण स्मरण कल्याण रोहिणी परिणाम नारायण वाराणसी व्याकरण

कर्ण पर्ण वर्ण चूर्ण पूर्ण विष्णु कृष्ण तृष्णा अरण्य पुण्य हिरण्य

There are three ways of forming ligatures between consonants. We have already shown (1) dropping the vertical line: न + त → ‍्‍ + त → न्त. Another way is, (2) to put the first on top of the second component, and two letters occur only in such ligature – ङ and ञ:

ङ् + क → ङ्क *ṅka* | अङ्क पङ्क लङ्का शङ्का शङ्कर सङ्केत सङ्कोच शशाङ्क अलङ्कार अहङ्कार सङ्कल्प सङ्कर्षण पल्यङ्क

ङ् + ख → ङ्ख *ṅkha* | शङ्ख

ङ् + ग → ङ्ग *ṅga* | अङ्ग रङ्ग सङ्ग गङ्गा लिङ्ग पङ्गु हिङ्गु अङ्गार जङ्गल मङ्गल तरङ्ग पतङ्ग पिङ्गल सङ्गीत नारङ्ग भुजङ्ग मृदङ्ग शृङ्ग शृङ्गार अङ्गुली   Further Ligature: सङ्ग्रह

ङ् + घ → ङ्घ *ṅgha* | सङ्घ सङ्घर्ष

ञ् + च → ञ्च *ñca* | पञ्च अञ्चल चञ्चल सञ्चय काञ्चन किञ्चिद्
Or as in वाञ्छा

ञ् + ज → ञ्ज *ñja* | कुञ्ज अञ्जन रञ्जन सञ्जय अञ्जलि मञ्जरी पतञ्जलि सञ्जीवन

Similarly:

च् + च → च्च *cca* | खिच्ची सच्चिदानन्द

ज् + ज → ज्ज *jja* | कज्जल मज्जन सज्जन लज्जा रज्जु

ल् + ल → ल्ल/ल्ल *lla* | मल्ल फुल्ल पल्लव वल्लभ

क् + क → क्क *kka* | कुक्कुट कुक्कुर ठक्कुर   and क्ल *kla* as in शुक्ल

न् + न → न्न *nna* | अन्न

द् + द → द्द *dda* | उद्देश

द् + ध → द्ध *ddha* | बद्ध बुद्ध बुद्धि युद्ध शुद्ध वृद्ध सिद्ध पद्धति निरुद्ध निषिद्ध

द् + ग → द्ग *dga* सद्गमय भगवद्गीता

द् + ब → द्ब *dba* बुद्बुद

द् + भ → द्भ *dbha* अद्भुत

द् + व → द्व *dva* द्वार द्वन्द्व तद्वत् विद्वान्

Important Ligatures:

क	क्य	क्क	र्क	क्र	क्ष	क्त	कृ	
ग	ग्य	ग्ग	र्ग	ग्र				
ङ					ङ्क	ङ्क्ष	ङ्ख	ङ्ग	ङ्घ
ज	ज्य	ज्ज	र्ज	ज्ञ				
ञ				श्च	अ			
ट		ट्ट		ट्र				
ण	ण्य		र्ण					
त	त्य	त्त	र्त	त्र				
द	द्य	द्द	र्द	द्र	द्र	द्ध	द्ब	द्व	ध	द्ध
न	न्य	न्न	र्न					
ल	ल्य	ल्ल	र्ल					
श	श्य	र्श	श्र	श्र	श्च			
ष	ष्य	र्ष	ष्ट	ष्ट्र	ष्ठ			
स	स्य	स्स	स्त्र	स्त्र				
ह	ह्य	र्ह	ह्ल	ह्ळ	ह्न	ह्म	ह्ल	ह्व

ट *ṭa* घट तट नट वट षट् कटु पटु कीट कूट त्रुटि कोटि रोटी शाटी कण्ट
घण्टा किरीट किलाट जटिल कुटिल कुटीर कुटुम्ब चर्पटी पर्पट प्रकट
मुकुट विराट् वेङ्कट

In Ligature:

ट् + ट → [ट्ट *ṭṭa*] घट्ट भट्ट

ष् + ट → [ष्/ष्ट *ṣṭa*] अष्ट चेष्टा जुष्ट दृष्ट पृष्ठ सृष्ट शिष्ट तुष्टि पुष्टि स्पष्ट स्पृष्ट
स्वादिष्ट

Note the change of ⌄ to ⌃ under round letters: राष्ट्र दंष्ट्र.

[ठ *ṭha*] मठ हठ पठन कठिन कण्ठ वैकुण्ठ

ष् + ठ → [ष्/ष्ठ *ṣṭha*] षष्ठ काष्ठ निष्ठा कनिष्ठ ज्येष्ठ युधिष्ठिर

[ड *ḍa*] षड् जड गुड नाडी चूडा क्रीडा गरुड डुकृञ् अण्ड खण्ड दण्ड काण्ड
पिण्ड कुण्ड कुण्डल गण्डकी गाण्डीव पाण्डव पण्डित पोगण्ड मण्डप
मण्डल मुण्डन मण्डूक पुण्डरीक

[ढ *ḍha*] दृढ मूढ

Now the third way of forming Ligatures:

(3) The two characters 'merge' into a new one.

क् + ष → [क्ष *kṣa*] क्षण क्षय क्षर क्षमा क्षेम क्षोभ अक्ष कक्ष दक्ष पक्ष रक्ष लक्ष
यक्षः चक्षु मोक्ष शिक्षा भिक्षा दीक्षा प्लक्ष क्षीर क्षिति क्षुद्र क्षेत्र
सूक्ष्म क्षत्रिय क्षेपण क्षिप्रम् तक्षक भक्षण मक्षिका

ङ् + क्ष → [ङ्क्ष *ṅkṣa*] काङ्क्षा

क् + त → [क्त *kta*] नक्त रक्त तिक्त युक्त त्यक्त वक्ता शक्ति भक्ति व्यक्ति भुक्ति
मुक्ति विविक्त

Sometimes, *ka* in ligature is written क *k* : क्व पक्व रुक्म शक्य वाक्य त्रैलोक्य
आस्तिक्य पृथक्त्व.

The double consonant ज्ञ is nowadays widely pronounced and even written as 'gya',
which is wrong. The nasal 'ñ' should not be dropped completely – better say 'gnya'.

ज् + ञ → [ज्ञ *jña*] ज्ञान आज्ञा यज्ञ

The letter श *śa* often makes Ligature with other letters in the first way: अश्म कश्मल
श्मशान प्रश्न श्लोक श्याम वैश्य दृश्य कश्यप अवश्यम्

But with certain letters श *śa* becomes श्, as in:

श् + र → श्र *śra*   श्री श्रम श्रद्धा श्रवण श्रेणि अश्रु आश्रम आश्रय मिश्र श्रीमद्भागवतम्

श् + व → श्व *śva*   श्वः श्वास श्वेत श्वशुर अश्व विश्व पार्श्व शश्वत् रामेश्वर

श् + च → श्च *śca*   पश्च निश्चय आश्चर्य वृश्चिक

त् + त → त्त *tta*   दत्त मत्त मत्तः चित्त वित्त पित्त वृत्ति निमित्त तत्त्व सत्त्व कार्त्तिक

द् + य → द्य *dya*   अद्य आद्य वाद्य विद्या वैद्य हृद्य द्युति यद्यपि प्रद्युम्न वन्द्य

द् + म → द्म *dma*   छद्म पद्म विद्महे

ह् + म → ह्म *hma*   ब्रह्म ब्राह्मण

ह् + न → ह्न *hna*   वह्नि चिह्न आह्निक

ह् + य → ह्य *hya*   ह्यः गुह्य दाह्य बाह्य

ह् + र → ह्र *hra*   ह्री ह्रस्व

ह् + ल → ह्ल *hla*   ह्लाद

ह् + व → ह्व *hva*   जिह्वा

Sometimes, in Ligature, य *ya* is written य *y*, as in: नाट्य आढ्य अग्र्य सङ्ख्य

Now the remaining letters, mainly vowels in the beginning of a word:

इ *i*   इव इह इति इष्ट इक्षु इच्छा इज्या इतर इदम् इदानीम् इन्दु इन्द्र इन्धन इन्दिरा

ई *ī*   ईश ईक्षण ईदृश

झ *jha*   झष

उ*u*	उद्. उप. उभ उमा उदर उचित उपाय उलूक उपाधि उपवीत उपनिषद् उष्ण उत्तम उत्सव उत्साह उक्त उल्लास उद्यान उद्वेग उद्भव उच्चारण उज्जयिनी उज्ज्वल
ऊ*ū*	ऊन ऊध्दः ऊर्जः ऊर्णा ऊर्ध्व
ऋ*r*	ऋक् ऋक्ष ऋण ऋत ऋद्ध ऋषि ऋषभ
ए*e*	एक एकोन एव एवम् एतद् एधः एला
ऐ*ai*	ऐक्य ऐश्वर्य ऐतिहासिक
ओ*o*	ओम् ओजः ओष्ठ ओदन
औ*au*	औम् औषध औदार्य औपम्य

---

19. Proverbs

पृथिव्यां त्रीणि रत्नानि जलमन्नं सुभाषितम् । मूढैः पाषाणखण्डेषु रत्नसञ्ज्ञा विधीयते ॥245

Proverbs from न्यायावलि

अन्धपङ्गु-न्यायः ।246 अन्धदर्पण-न्यायः ।247 अन्धगज-... ।248 अन्धचटक-... ।249

अन्धपरम्परा- ।250 अरण्यरोदन- ।251 अर्धकुक्कुटी- ।252 रज्जुसर्प- ।253 आयुर्घृत- ।254

कूपमण्डूक- ।255 वातादि- ।256 स्वप्नमन्त्रलाभ- ।257 वनव्याघ्र- ।258 स्वप्नव्याघ्र- ।259

कृत्वाचिन्ता- ।260 व्रीहिबीज- ।261 जलमन्थन- ।262 कूर्माङ्ग- ।263 आम्रवन- ।264

घटप्रदीप- ।265 बहुछिद्रघट- ।266 मक्षिका- ।267 भ्रमर- ।268 बीजवृक्ष- ।269 विषभक्षण- ।270 भिक्षुपादप्रसारण- ।271 भिक्षुभियःस्थाल्यनधिश्रयण- ।272 अश्वभृत्य- ।273

विषकृमि- ।274 मृगतृष्णा- ।275 पद्मपत्र- ।276 आढाराणामपि बहूनामिति न्यायः ।277

राजशून्यप्रजा- ।278 बहुराजकपुर- ।279 इक्षुरस- ।280 इक्षुविकार- ।281

कुशकाशावलम्बन- ।282 उष्ट्रलगुड- ।283 उष्ट्रकण्टकभक्षण- ।284 उत्पाटदंष्ट्रोरग- ।285

अजातपुत्र-नामोत्कीर्तन- ।286 कण्टक- ।287 कण्ठचमीकर- ।288 कफोणिगुड- ।289

उभयतः पाशारज्जुरिति न्यायः ।290

20. Pronunciation

According to शिक्षा, traditional phonetics, the self formulates intentions by means of intelligence and inspires the mind to speak. The mind impulses the nerves, which sets in motion breath; that, moving in the chest, generates a humming sound. That, again, rising to the palate and the crown of head, and rebounding thence, is articulated when passing through the mouth.

"The Devanagari script and spoken Sanskrit are two of the best ways for a child to overcome stiffness of fingers and the tongue. Today's European languages do not use many parts of the tongue and mouth while speaking or many finger movements while writing, whereas Sanskrit helps immensely to develop cerebral dexterity through its phonetics." (Moss – London School Makes Sanskrit Compulsory)

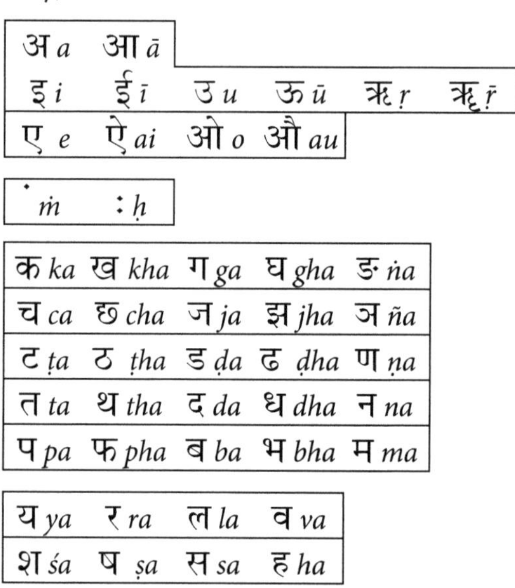

In Sanskrit, for every sound there is only one letter and for every letter there is only one sound. This principle is hardly seen in any other language, what to speak of English – far, fat, fare, fate, fall. A single वर्ण (letter) is called -कार (as in अ-कार), a pair of वर्ण is called -द्वय (as in अ-द्वय), and the whole alphabet वर्ण-क्रम.

वर्ण are divided into स्वर (पाणिनि अच्) and व्यञ्जन (हल्). स्वर are pronounced with an open, unobstructed mouth, and therefore 'shine' by themselves, whereas व्यञ्जन involve various kinds of obstruction of the air, and need to be joined to a vowel. This is shown in the English words vowel ('pronounceable') and consonant ('sounding together'). In the Sanskrit वर्णक्रम all the स्वर are listed first. This is different from the alphabets used for Western languages, which are mostly based on Egyptian hieroglyphics and the old Phoenician alphabet. The order *a, b, c, d, e...* mixes vowels and consonants indiscriminately and is unsystematic.

"We [Europeans] are still behind making even our alphabet a perfect one." (Arthur Macdonall, British Indologist, 1854-1930)

Since व्यञ्जन require a स्वर for pronunciation, the *a* is used for all the consonants by default, unless noted otherwise (क *ka*, ख *kha*, ग *ga*, etc.).

The first 5 स्वर have two forms, ह्रस्व and दीर्घ. स्वर can be followed by अनुस्वार or विसर्ग. Rarely the स्वर itself is nasalized, marked with चन्द्र-बिन्दु ँ. अनुस्वार (the pure nasal) is differentiated from the other nasals – the guttural ङ, palatal ञ, retroflex ण and dental न – because it is articulated without intervention of the tongue. Visarga is a sound similar to ह *ha*, but unvoiced/hard, and followed by a short echo of the preceding sound – मनः (say 'manaha'), अग्निः ('agnihi'), बन्धुः ('bandhuhu'), कामैः ('kāmaihi'), गौः ('gauhu'). If विसर्ग is followed by another consonant, it is heard only as a scratching guttural sound, as in 'Lo**ch** Ness'. This occurs when it is inside a word (दुःख), compound word (मनः-प्रसाद), a sentence, or a line of a verse.

Classifications of letters according to:

1. प्रयत्न

The प्रयत्न in the pronunciation of स्वर is अ-स्पर्श. The first 25 व्यञ्जन are स्पर्श, involving the complete stoppage of the path of air. They are further divided into 5 वर्ग, named after the first member of each group:

क-वर्ग क *ka* ख *kha* ग *ga* घ *gha* ङ *ṅa*

        etc.

The प्रयत्न with the next 4 व्यञ्जन is neither स्पर्श nor अस्पर्श (as with the स्वर), but अन्तःस्थ. The last 4 व्यञ्जन are sibilants.

2. प्राण (table below left)

The व्यञ्जन in bold are pronounced with महा-प्राण. The difference between त *ta* and थ *tha*, for example, is just less or more प्राण, otherwise they are the same sounds. Thus, थ – as in पथ (path) or जगन्नाथ – is not pronounced as in the English 'path'!

क	**ख**	ग	**घ**	ङ
च	**छ**	ज	**झ**	ञ
ट	**ठ**	ड	**ढ**	ण
त	**थ**	द	**ध**	न
प	**फ**	ब	**भ**	म
य	र	ल	व	
श	**ष**	**स**	**ह**	

अ	आ						
इ	ई	उ	ऊ	ऋ	ॠ	लृ	ॡ
ए	ऐ	ओ	औ				

क	ख	**ग**	घ	**ङ**
च	छ	**ज**	झ	**ञ**
ट	ठ	**ड**	ढ	**ण**
त	थ	**द**	ध	**न**
प	फ	**ब**	भ	**म**
य	**र**	**ल**	**व**	
श	ष	स	ह	

3. According to घोष (table above right)

The letters in bold, including all स्वर, are स-घोष, the others अ-घोष.

4. According to the place of articulation

वर्ण		व्यञ्जन						
(1)	अ आ	क	ख	ग	घ	ङ		ह
(2)	इ ई	च	छ	ज	झ	ञ	य	श
(3)	ऋ ॠ	ट	ठ	ड	ढ	ण	र	ष
(4)		त	थ	द	ध	न	ल	स
(5)	उ ऊ	प	फ	ब	भ	म		

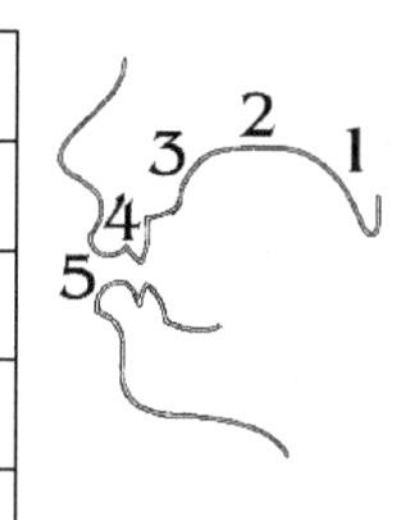

(1) कण्ठ्य

For अ (as in 'm**o**ther'), आ (as in 'f**a**ther') and ह the tongue remains relaxed at the bottom of the mouth. For the consonants from क to the nasal ङ (as in 'lo**ng**') the back of tongue raises to block and release the air.

(2) तालव्य (picture below left)

For the स्वर of this group (इ-ई) the tongue approaches the palate, without touching it. Put the tongue in the position to pronounce इ (as in 'k**i**ss'), which means you have to smile ☺, and say ई (as in 'p**ea**ce'). For pronouncing य and श, keep the tongue in this position (keep smiling).

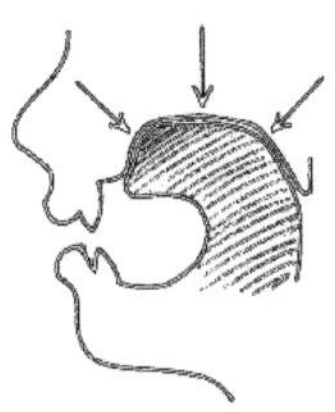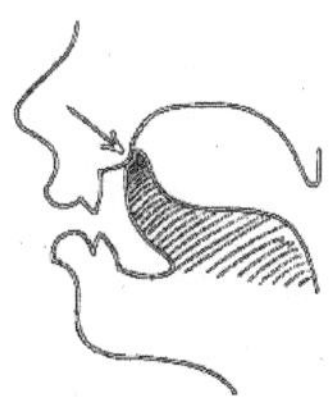

(3) मूर्धन्य (picture above right)

Except for र, all मूर्धन्य are transliterated with a dot below. You may imagine this dot to be the tip of the tongue which bents upwards, touching the palate. Therefore, these letters are also called retroflex. For the vowels of this group (ऋ-ॠ), the tongue does not touch the roof. For the consonants, the tongue touches the roof of the mouth. Say: ट, कोण, कण्ठ, पाण्डव.

(4) दन्त्य

The tip of the tongue touches slightly the root and back of the upper teeth. Mark the difference in pronunciation between तालव्य श *śa* ☺, मूर्धन्य ष *ṣa*, and दन्त्य स *sa* – as in शिव ☺, विष्णु, सेवा, and शीर्षासन.

(5) ओष्ठ्य

For all letters of this group the tongue is completely passive. The vowels of this group (उ-ऊ) are pronounced with a projection of the lips. For the consonants, put the lips together and let them spring slightly apart. The फ is pronounced as in 'she**ph**erd', as there is no *f* in Sanskrit.

---

21. Chandas

Sanskrit composition may be in the form of prose or verse. A standard verse has four पाद, arranged in two lines. Each पाद is regulated by its meter, defined in छन्द:.

| आत्ममाता गुरो: पत्नी | ब्राह्मणी राजपत्निका | । |
| धेनुर्धात्री तथा पृथ्वी | सप्तैता मातर: स्मृता: | ॥ |

The core of an अक्षर is its स्वर,

	अ *a*	इ *i*
with or without व्यञ्जय	क *ka*	मि *mi*
अनुस्वार	कं *kaṁ*	मिं *miṁ*
विसर्ग	क: *kaḥ*	मि: *miḥ*
or हलन्त.	कम् *kam*	मित् *mit*

Each अक्षर is given 1 or 2 मात्रा, to pronounce, rarely 3 मात्रा. An अक्षर with 1 मात्रा is called लघु and with 2 मात्रा is called गुरु. In the following we have marked them with a dot ('•') and a line ('–'), respectively.

The अक्षर is गुरु, when it fulfills one of the following conditions:

(1) its स्वर is दीर्घ (आ *ā*, ई *ī*, ऊ *ū*, ऋ *r̥*)	– • रा-म
or ए *e*, ऐ *ai*, ओ *o*, औ *au*	– • दे-व
(2) it has अनुस्वार or विसर्ग	– – हं-सः
(3) it is followed by a double consonant	– • ब्र-ह्म

The number of अक्षर in each पाद of a regular meter can theoretically vary from 1 to 999. Each of these classes comprehends a great number of possible meters according to the different modes in which लघु and गुरु अक्षर may be distributed. Exceptions are always possible, and are called आर्ष-प्रयोग.

The most prominent meter is called अनुष्टुप्, and has 8 अक्षर in each पाद. In it, the 5th अक्षर should be लघु ('•'), the 6th गुरु ('–'), the 7th गुरु in the 1st and 3rd पाद, and लघु in the 2nd and 4th पाद. The other अक्षर are free ('x'), either लघु or गुरु.

(1,3)		(1)	(1)		(1,2)	(3)	(1)	(1,3)		(1)	(1)		(3)		(1)
–	•	–	–	•	–	–	–	–	•	–	–	•	–	•	–
आ	त्म	मा	ता	गु	रो:	प	त्नी	ब्रा	ह्म	णी	रा	ज	प	त्नि	का

(1)	(3)	(1,3)	(1)		(1)	(3)	(1)	(3)	(1)	(1)	(1)		(2,3)		(1,2)
–	–	–	–	•	–	–	–	–	–	–	–	•	–	•	–
धे	नु	र्धा	त्री	त	था	पृ	थ्वी	स	प्तै	ता	मा	त	र:	स्मृ	ता:

<table>
<tr><th>अक्षर</th><th>मात्रा (Vertical lines mark a possible short pause)</th><th>Name</th></tr>
<tr><td>8</td><td>x x x x · — — x
x x x x · — · x</td><td>अनुष्टुप्</td></tr>
<tr><td>8</td><td>· — · — | · — · —</td><td>प्रमाणिका</td></tr>
<tr><td>8</td><td>— · · — | — · · —</td><td>माणवक</td></tr>
<tr><td>9</td><td>· · — | · — · — · —</td><td>भुजङ्ग-सङ्गता</td></tr>
<tr><td>9</td><td>— · · · — | — · · —</td><td>मणि-मध्य</td></tr>
<tr><td>10</td><td>— · · — — | — · · — —</td><td>रुक्मवती</td></tr>
<tr><td>10
+11</td><td>· · — · · — · — · —
· · — — · · — · — · —</td><td>वियोगिनी</td></tr>
<tr><td>11</td><td>· · · — · — | — · — · —</td><td>इन्दिरा</td></tr>
<tr><td>11</td><td>· — · — — | · · — · — —</td><td>उपेन्द्र-वज्रा</td></tr>
<tr><td>11</td><td>— · — | · · · — · · — —</td><td>स्वागता</td></tr>
<tr><td>11</td><td>— — · — — | · · — · — —</td><td>इन्द्र-वज्रा (a family of similar meters)</td></tr>
<tr><td>11</td><td>x — · — — | · · — · — —</td><td>उपजाति</td></tr>
<tr><td>11</td><td>— — — — | · · — — · — —</td><td>वातोर्मी</td></tr>
<tr><td>11</td><td>— — — — | — · — — · — —</td><td>शालिनी</td></tr>
<tr><td>11
+12</td><td>· · — · · — · · — · —
· · — · · — · · — · — —</td><td>हरिण-प्लुता</td></tr>
<tr><td>12</td><td>· · · · — | · · — · · — —</td><td>ताम-रस</td></tr>
<tr><td>12</td><td>· · · — · · — · · — · —</td><td>द्रुत-विलम्बित</td></tr>
<tr><td>12</td><td>· · — · | · — · · | — · · — </td><td>तोटक</td></tr>
<tr><td>12</td><td>· · — · — | · · · — · · —</td><td>प्रमिताक्षरा</td></tr>
<tr><td>12</td><td>· — · · · — | · — · · · —</td><td>जलोद्धत-गति</td></tr>
<tr><td>12</td><td>· — · — — | · · — · — · —</td><td>वंश-स्थ</td></tr>
<tr><td>12</td><td>· — — · — — | · — — · — —</td><td>भुजङ्ग-प्रयात</td></tr>
<tr><td>12</td><td>— · · — · | · — · · · — —</td><td>चन्द्र-वर्म</td></tr>
<tr><td>12</td><td>— · — — · — | — · — — · —</td><td>स्रग्विणी</td></tr>
<tr><td>12</td><td>— — · — — | · · — · — · —</td><td>इन्द्र-वंशा</td></tr>
<tr><td>12</td><td>— — · · — — | · · — — · —</td><td>मणि-माला</td></tr>
<tr><td>12</td><td>— — — — | · · · · — — — —</td><td>जलधर-माला</td></tr>
<tr><td>12</td><td>— — — — | · · · — — · — —</td><td>वैश्व-देवी</td></tr>
<tr><td>12
+13</td><td>· · · · · · — · — · — —
· · · · — · · — · — · — —</td><td>पुष्पिताग्रा</td></tr>
<tr><td>13</td><td>· · · · · · · — | — · — — · —</td><td>क्षमा</td></tr>
</table>

Syllables	Pattern	Name
13	· · — · — · · · — · · — —	कलहंस
13	· · — · — · · · — · — · —	मञ्जु-भाषिणी
13	· — — · · · · · — · · — —	रुचिरा
13	— — — · · · · · · — · — —	प्रहर्षिणी
13	— · — · · · — · · · — · —	मत्त-मयूरी
14	· · · · · — · · · · · · · —	अपराजिता
14	· · — · · · · — · · — · · —	प्रमदा
14	· · · · · · — · · · · · · —	पथ्या
14	— — · — · · · — · · — · — —	वसन्त-तिलका
14	— — — — · · · · · · · — · —	मध्य-क्षामा
15	· · · · · · · — · · · · · · —	मालिनी
15	— · — · · · — · — · — · · · —	तूणक
15	— · — · · — · — · · — · · —	लीला-खेल
16	· · · · · · · · · · · · · · — —	वाणिनी
16	· — · — · — · · — · — · — · — —	पञ्च-चामर
16	— · — · · · · · — · — · — · — —	चित्र
17	· · · · · — — · · · · · · · · · —	हरिणी
17	· · · · · · · · · · · · · — · · —	नर्दटक
17	· — · · · — · · · · — · · — · —	पृथ्वी-गुरु
17	· — · · · — · · · · · — — · — · —	शिखरिणी
17	— — — — · · · · · · — — · — — · —	मन्दाक्रान्ता
18	· · · · · · — · — · · — · — · — · —	नाराच
18	· · · · · · · · — · — · — · — · —	नन्दन
18	— · — · · · · · — · — · · · · — · —	शार्दूल-ललित
19	· · · · · — · · · — · · · — · · — —	मेघ-विस्फूर्जिता
19	— — — · · — · — · · · — — — · — — · —	शार्दूल-विक्रीडित
19	— · — · · — · — · · · — · — · — · —	सुरसा
19	— · — · · — · — · · · — · — · — · —	सुमधुरा
21	— — — · · — · — · · · — — · — · — · — — —	स्रग्धरा

Examples:

8 प्रमाणिका

धनस्य यस्य राजतो भयं न चास्ति चोरतः ।
मृतं च यन्न मुञ्चति समर्जयस्व तद्धनम् ॥

10+11 वियोगिनी

न धनं न जनं न सुन्दरीं कवितां वा जगदीश कामये ।
मम जन्मनि जन्मनीश्वरे भवताद्भक्तिरहैतुकी त्वयि ॥

11 इन्द्र-वज्रा

स्वस्ति प्रजाभ्यः परिपालयन्तां न्यायेन मार्गेण महीं महीशाः ।
गोब्राह्मणेभ्यः शुभमस्तु नित्यं लोकाः समस्ताः सुखिनो भवन्तु ॥

12 तोटक

अधरं मधुरं वदनं मधुरं नयनं मधुरं हसितं मधुरम् ।
हृदयं मधुरं गमनं मधुरं मधुराधिपतेरखिलं मधुरम् ॥

14 वसन्त-तिलका

श्रीराम राम रघुनन्दन राम राम श्रीराम राम भरताग्रज राम राम ।
श्रीराम राम रणकर्कश राम राम श्रीराम राम शरणं भव राम राम ॥

15 मालिनी

यदपसरति मेषः कारणं तत्प्रहर्तुं मृगपतिरपि कोपात्सङ्कुचत्युत्पतिष्णुः ।
हृदयनिहितभावा गूढमन्त्रप्रचाराः किमपि विगणयन्तो बुद्धिमन्तः सहन्ते ॥[291]

17 शिखरिणी

श्रियः कान्ताः कान्तः परमपुरुषः कल्पतरवो
द्रुमा भूमिश्चिन्तामणिगणमयी तोयममृतम् ।
कथा गानं नाट्यं गमनमपि वंशी प्रियसखी
चिदानन्दं ज्योतिः परमपि तदास्वाद्यमपि च ॥

17 मन्दाक्रान्ता

शान्ताकारं भुजगशयनं पद्मनाभं सुरेशं
विश्वाधारं गगनसदृशं मेघवर्णं शुभाङ्गम् ।
लक्ष्मीकान्तं कमलनयनं योगिभिर्ध्यानगम्यं
वन्दे विष्णुं भवभयहरं सर्वलोकैकनाथम् ॥

19 शार्दूल-विक्रीडित

यं ब्रह्मा वरुणेन्द्ररुद्रमरुतः स्तुन्वन्ति दिव्यैः स्तवैर्
वेदैः साङ्गपदक्रमोपनिषदैर्गायन्ति यं सामगाः ।
ध्यानावस्थिततद्गतेन मनसा पश्यन्ति यं योगिनो
यस्यान्तं न विदुः सुरासुरगणा देवाय तस्मै नमः ॥

Immediate sounds and words can be joined, 'making सन्धि', which has given Sanskrit a great fluidity. It is obligatory within नाम, समास, and between उपसर्ग and धातु. It is optional in a सूत्र, in sentences and conversation. Rules reflect the natural change of sounds when joined. In English too, 'in-pure' and 'in-regular' became 'impure' and 'irregular'.

(1) *-a/ā*	+ *a/ā-*	महा-आत्मा → महात्मा
(2)	+ *i/ī-*	गण-ईश → गणेश
(3)	+ *u/ū-*	पुरुष-उत्तम → पुरुषोत्तम
(4)	+ *ṛ/ṝ-*	देव-ऋषि → देवर्षि
(5)	+ *e/ai-*	न एव → नैव
(6)	+ *o/au-*	उत्तम-ओजस् → उत्तमौजस्
(7) *-i/ī*	+ *i/ī-*	रवि-इन्द्र → रवीन्द्र
(8)	+ other स्वर	यदि अपि → यद्यपि
(9) द्वि-वचन *-ī*	+ स्वर	मुनी अत्र → Ø (no सन्धि)
(10) *-u/ū*	+ *u/ū-*	बाहु-उदर → बाहूदर
(11)	+ other स्वर	मनु-अन्तर → मन्वन्तर
(12) द्वि-वचन *-ū*	+ स्वर	गुरू अत्र → Ø
(13) अव्यय अ आ	+ स्वर	अ अनन्त → Ø
(14) *-ṛ/ṝ*	+ *ṛ-*	पितृ-ऋण → पितॄण
(15)	+ other स्वर	पितृ-उदय → पित्रुदय
(16) *-e*	+ *a-*	वन्दे अहम् → वन्दे ऽहम्
(17)	+ other स्वर	अग्रे आसीत् → अग्रय् ... → अग्र ...
(18) द्वि-वचन *-e*	+ स्वर	गझे अत्र → Ø
		भजेते (verb) अजितम् → Ø
(19) *-ai*	+ स्वर	गोप्यै आसनम् → गोप्याय् ... → गोप्या ...
(20) *-o*	+ *a-*	नमो अस्तु → नमो ऽस्तु
(21)	+ other स्वर	विष्णो इह → विष्णव् ... → विष्ण ...
(22) अव्यय *-o*	+ स्वर	नो अच्युत → Ø
(23) सम्बोधन *-o*	+ इति	विष्णो इति → विष्णव् ... / Ø

(24)	*-au*	+ स्वर	द्वौ इमौ → द्वाविमौ
(25)	all स्वर	+ *ch-*	न छिन्द्यात् → न च्छिन्द्यात्
	(optional after दीर्घ)		

(26)	*-k*	+ *m-*	वाक्.मय → वाङ्मय
(27)		+ *ś-*	सुवाक् शौरिः → सुवाक् छौरिः
(28)		+ other सघोष	सम्यक् उभयोः → सम्यगुभयोः
			ऋक्-वेद → ऋग्वेद
(29)		+ *h-*	वाक् हरेः → वाग्घरेः

(30)	*-t*	+ *c-, ch-*	सत्-चित् → सच्चित्
(31)		+ *j-*	सत्-जन → सज्जन
(32)		+ *n-*	जगत्-नाथ → जगन्नाथ
(33)		+ *m-*	सत्-मन्त्री → सन्मन्त्री
(34)		+ *l-*	भुवनात् लोकाः → भुवनाल्लोकाः
(35)		+ *ś-*	भगवत्-शास्त्र → भगवच्छास्त्र
(36)		+ *h-*	साक्षात् हरिः → साक्षाद्धरिः
(37)		+ other सघोष	जगत्-ईश → जगदीश
			भगवत्-गीता → भगवद्गीता

(38)	*-d*	+ *c-, ch-*	मद्-चित्तः → मच्चित्तः
(39)		+ *j-*	यद् ज्ञात्वा → यज्ज्ञात्वा
(40)		+ *n-*	तद्-निष्ठ → तन्निष्ठ
(41)		+ *m-*	मद्-मनः → मन्मनः
(42)		+ *ś-*	यद् श्रेयः → यच्छ्रेयः
(43)		+ other अघोष	सुहृद् सताम् → सुहृत्सताम्
(44)		at the end of a line:	तत्त्वविद् → तत्त्ववित् ।

(45)	*-n*	+ *c-/ch-*	गतासून् च → गतासूंश्च
(46)		+ *j-/jh-*	भगवान् जयति → ∅
(47)		+ *ṭ-/ṭh-*	भगवान् टीकते → भगवांष्टीकते
(48)		+ *t-/th-*	तान् तितिक्षस्व → तांस्तितिक्षस्व
(49)		+ *l-*	श्रद्धावान् लभते → श्रद्धावाँल्लभते

(50)		+ *ś-*	भगवान् शूरः → ∅
(51)	*-an, -in, -un*	+ स्वर	प्रहसन् इव → प्रहसन्निव
(52)	*-m*	+ व्यञ्जन	अहम् भजामि → अहं भजामि
(53)	सम् .	+ क-वर्ग	सम् .कीर्तन → संकीर्तन → सङ्कीर्तन
(54)		+ च-वर्ग	सम् .जीवन → संजीवन → सञ्जीवन
(55)		+ त-वर्ग	सम् .तोष → संतोष → सन्तोष
(56)		+ प-वर्ग	सम् .मोह → संमोह → सम्मोह

The following rules also apply, where *-r* and *-s* become *-ḥ*:

	as with	अहर् → अहः → ...
		ततस् → ततः → ...
(57)	all *-ḥ*	+ *k-, kh-, p-, ph-, ś-, s-* → ∅
		शान्तिः शान्तिः → ∅
(58)		+ *c-*	वेदैः च → वेदैश्च
(59)		+ *ṭ-*	कृष्णः टीकते → कृष्णष्टीकते
(60)		+ *t-*	नमः ते → नमस्ते

(61)	esp. *-aḥ*	+ *a-*	नमः अस्तु → (61) नमो अस्तु
			→ (20) नमो ऽस्तु
(62)		+ other स्वर	अर्जुनः उवाच → अर्जुन उवाच
(63)		+ सघोष व्यञ्जन	नमः नमः → नमो नमः
(64)	सः, एषः	normally	सः कौन्तेयः → स कौन्तेयः
(65)	but:	+ *a-*	सः अपि → (61) सो अपि → (20) सो ऽपि

(66)	*-āḥ*	+ सघोष	गणाः इव → गणा इव
			नराः जानन्ति → नरा जानन्ति
(67)	*-iḥ* to *-auḥ*	+ सघोष	अग्निः ज्योतिः → अग्निर्ज्योतिः
			आयुः-वेद → आयुर्वेद
(68)	but: *-r*	+ *r-*	बहुभिः रणः → बहुभी रणः
(69)	भोः, भगोः	+ सघोष	भोः अनन्त → भो अनन्त
			भगोः राम → भगो राम

Internal Sandhi:

(70) र-ष-ऋ-द्वयेभ्यो नस्य णः सर्वेश्वर-ह-य-व-कवर्ग-पवर्ग-व्यवधानेऽपि समान-विष्णुपदे न तु विष्णुपदान्तस्य । *-n-* becomes *ṇ* after *r, ṣ, ṛ* and *ṝ*, even if other स्वर, *h, y, v*, क-वर्ग and प-वर्ग come in between in the same word; except at the end of a word. (हरिनामामृत-व्याकरण 2.26)

r-ṣ-ṛ-ṝ + *n*　　राम + .इन → रामोण

　　　　　　　　　राम-अयन → रामायण

(71) *-s-* becomes *ṣ* after all स्वर (except for *a/ā*) and after *y, r, l, v, k* and *ṅ*.

i/ī to *au, y-r-l-v-k-ṅ* + *s*　　देवे + .सु → देवेषु

　　　　　　　　　　　　　युधि-स्थिर → युधिष्ठिर

Further rules:

(72) *-aḥ (-ar, -as)*　　+ *k-, kh-, p-, ph-*　　नमः.कार → नमस्कार

(73) *-āḥ (-ās)*　　　　+ व्यञ्जन　　　　　भाः.कर → भास्कर

(74) *-iḥ (-ir, -is)*　　 + व्यञ्जन　　　　　निर्.पाप → निष्पाप

(75) *-uḥ (-ur, -us)*　　+ व्यञ्जन　　　　　दुर्.कृत → दुष्कृत

An optional rule which we do not apply:

(76) *-r-*　　　　　　+ व्यञ्जन　　　　doubling: कर्त्ता, कर्म्म, कार्य्य

23. Declension

A few नाम, like conjunctions and interjections, are अव्यय. Some combinations, like चैव and नैव, are very common. नाम other than अव्यय have a लिङ्ग, which is either पुल्लिङ्ग (पुम्, m.), नपुंसक-लिङ्ग (n.), or स्त्री-लिङ्ग (f.) – and are declined in eight विभक्ति. प्रकृति forms are listed in a dictionary.

In a sentence, words need a grammatical value. Thus, in the process of declension, specific प्रत्यय are fixed to the प्रकृति. For example, the declension of the word देव, in एक-वचन, द्वि-व°, and बहु-व°. The word देव represents not only पुल्लिङ्ग words ending in -a (the majority of all words), but also many विभक्ति of other लिङ्ग and ending.

विभक्ति	Latin	for	एक-वचन	द्वि-व°	बहु-व°
1. प्रथमा	Nomin.	कर्ता	देवः *1.1	देवौ *1.2	देवाः *1.3
2. द्वितीया	Accusat.	कर्म 'to'	देवम् *2.1	देवौ *2.2	देवान् *2.3
3. तृतीया	Instrum.	करण 'with/by'	देवेन *3.1	देवाभ्याम् *3.2	देवैः *3.3
4. चतुर्थी	Dative	सम्प्रदान 'for'	देवाय *4.1	देवाभ्याम् *4.2	देवेभ्यः *4.3
5. पञ्चमी	Ablative	अपादान 'from'	देवात् *5.1	देवाभ्याम् *5.2	देवेभ्यः *5.3
6. षष्ठी	Genitive	सम्बन्ध 'of'	देवस्य *6.1	देवयोः *6.2	देवानाम् *6.3
7. सप्तमी	Locative	अधिकरण 'in/at'	देवे *7.1	देवयोः *7.2	देवेषु *7.3
8. सम्बोधन	Vocative	सम्बोधन 'oh!'	[हे] देव *8.1	देवौ *8.2	देवाः *8.3

1. प्रथमा for उक्त (subject) of a sentence

In कर्तृ-वाच्य (active voice), the कर्ता (agent) is also the उक्त and thus called उक्त-कर्ता.

    देवः *1.1 रक्षति _ देव protects

In कर्म-वाच्य (passive voice), the कर्म (object) of the sentence is the उक्त of the sentence and thus called उक्त-कर्म:

    नरः *1.1 रक्ष्यते _ man is protected

2. द्वितीया for कर्म (object) of a sentence

    देवः *1.1 नरम् *2.1 रक्षति _ देव protects man

It is connected to the verb in 5 ways:

(1) creation: सः मालां करोति _ he makes a garland

(2) transformation: सः अन्नं पचति _ he cooks rice

(3) improvement: सः जलं वासयति _ he perfumes water

(4) attainment: सः ग्रामं गच्छति _ he goes to the village

सः जलं स्पृशति / पश्यति / शृणोति _ he touches /sees /hears water

(5) giving up: नरः देहं त्यजति _ man gives up the body

For a कर्ता which is not the subject (अनुक्त-कर्ता) of the sentence:

देवः *1.1 मालां कुर्वन्तं नरम् *2.1 रक्षति _ देव protects the man, who is making a garland

Although नर is also कर्ता (of कुर्वन्तम् _ making), the main कर्ता (of रक्षति) prevents it from taking प्रथमा.

Number of कर्म:

(1) अ-कर्मक धातु take no कर्म

देवः भवति _ देव exists

(2) स-कर्मक धातु take 1 कर्म

देवः अर्जुनं पश्यति _ देव sees अर्जुन

(3) 17 द्वि-कर्मक धातु (√दुह to √कृष) take 2 कर्म, both in द्वितीया when अनुक्त. The मुख्य-कर्म (direct कर्म) is the 'what', the गौण-कर्म (indirect कर्म) is the 'to whom' or 'where'.

देवः गां *2.1 दुग्धं *2.1 दोग्धि _ देव milks the cow (गौण) milk (मुख्य)

देवः अर्जुनं *2.1 गीतां *2.1 वदति _ देव speaks the गीता (मुख्य) to अर्जुन (गौण)

3. तृतीया for करण (instrument)

देवः हस्तेन *3.1 रक्षति _ देव protects with [his] hand

In कर्म-वाच्य, the कर्म becomes उक्त (उक्त-कर्म, see 1. प्रथमा) and the कर्ता becomes अनुक्त-कर्ता in तृतीया:

नरः *1.1 देवेन *3.1 रक्ष्यते _ man is protected by देव

4. चतुर्थी for सम्प्रदान (beneficiary or purpose)

तदनुग्रहाय *4.1 _ for its benefit

सः देवाय *4.1 सर्वस्वं ददाति _ he gives everything to देव

देवः कंसाय *4.1 भयं ददाति _ देव gives fear to कंस

If there is not transference of ownership, there is no सम्प्रदान :

सः रजकं *2.1 वस्त्रं ददाति _ he gives to the washer the garment

For worship:

देवाय *4.1 नमः _ obeisance to देव

For feelings:

सः देवाय *4.1 स्पृहयति _ he hankers for देव

सः देवाय *4.1 क्रुध्यते _ he is angry at देव

The कर्म of motions takes चतुर्थी optionally:

सः ग्रामं *2.1 / ग्रामाय *4.1 गच्छति _ he goes to the village

But not, if the motion is purely mental:

सः मनसा देवं *2.1 गच्छति _ he goes with the mind to देव

5. पञ्चमी for अपादान (source)

गङ्गा हिमालयात् *5.1 प्रभवति _ गङ्गा flows from the हिमालय

सः ग्रामात् *5.1 आगच्छति _ he comes from the village

सः रथात् *5.1 अवतरति _ he descents from the chariot

अर्जुनः देवात् *5.1 शृणोति _ अर्जुन hears from देव

For the cause:

भयात् *5.1 _ from danger, out of fear

सः असुरात् *5.1 अन्तर्धत्ते _ he hides from the असुर

कंसः देवात् *5.1 बिभेति _ कंस fears from देव

सः मार्गात् *5.1 विरमति _ he diverts from the path

For time:

मास-द्वयात् *5.1 _ 'from two months', two months ago

For comparison:

देवात् *5.1 बलवत्तरः _ stronger than देव

6. षष्ठी for सम्बन्ध (relationship)

Four kinds of सम्बन्ध :

(1) स्व-स्वामी (property-proprietor)

देवस्य *6.1 दासः _ the servant of देव

(2) जन्य-जनक (generated-generator, son-father)

देवस्य *6.1 पुत्रः _ the son of देव

(3) अवयव-अवयवी (part-whole)

देवस्य *6.1 पदम् _ the foot of देव

(4) स्थानि-आदेश (original-substitution)

स्थानिनः *6.1 आदेशः _ the substitution of the original

For a selection:

इन्द्रियानां *6.3 मनः अस्मि _ among the senses I am the mind

Compare this to the standard 'सम्बन्ध-षष्ठी':

भूतानां *6.3 चेतना अस्मि _ of living beings I am consciousness

For अनुक्त-कर्ता:

देवस्य *6.1 कृतिः _ the creation of देव

For अनुक्त-कर्म:

कर्मणः *6.1 कर्ता _ the doer of action

Two अनुक्त-कर्म of a द्वि-कर्मक:

गवाम् *6.3 दुग्धस्य *6.1 दोग्धा _ the milker of the milk of cows

7. सप्तमी for अधिकरण / आधार (basis)

In space and time:

देशे *7.1 _ in the country

काले *7.1 _ in time

As reference, with the word सति ('being') implied (सति-सप्तमी):

धर्मे *7.1 नष्टे *7.1 [सति] _ धर्म [being] lost

Selection:

सहस्रेषु *7.3 कश्चिद् _ someone among thousands

8. Vocative for सम्बोधन (address)

[हे] देव *8.1 _ Oh देव!

According to लोक-प्रमाण (established usage) one can determine rules for quoting Sanskrit words in a text or conversation:

(1) The प्रकृति form is used with words ending in a स्वर :

धर्म → your धर्म, दुर्गा → goddess दुर्गा, हरि → the name हरि, etc.

... and (against theory) also with words ending in -*r* :

कर्तृ → the कर्तृ; पितृ → the पितृ

(2) The प्रथमा form is used with words ending in व्यञ्जन :

भगवत् → the भगवान् feature; हनुमत् → Lord हनुमान्

आत्मन् → the आत्मा; कर्मन् → bad कर्म

ब्रह्मन् → the [Absolute] ब्रह्म (n.), the [person] ब्रह्मा (m.)

स्वामिन् → a स्वामी; सन्न्यासिन् → a सन्न्यासी

(3) Both forms (प्रकृति/प्रथमा) are possible with words ending in -*s*, (though we prefer प्रथमा):

the मनस्/मनः, the रजस्/रजः, the तेजस्/तेजः

... and titles of works:

महाभारत → the महाभारत (प्रकृति)

भागवत → the भागवतम् (प्रथमा)

(4) In word lists, in order to teach the gender of words, all words are listed in प्रथमा :

काल → कालः (points at m.), पत्र → पत्रम् (n.), गोपी → गोपी (f.)

25. Tables

(1) Words ending in स्वर (अच् → अजन्त)

देव (m.)			राम (m.)		
देवः	देवौ	देवाः	like देव + सन्धि (70)		
देवम्	देवौ	देवान्			
देवेन	देवाभ्याम्	देवैः	रामेण		
देवाय	देवाभ्याम्	देवेभ्यः			
देवात्	देवाभ्याम्	देवेभ्यः			
देवस्य	देवयोः	देवानाम्	रामाणाम्		
देवे	देवयोः	देवेषु			
हे देव	देवौ	देवाः			

कुल (n.)			हृदय (n.)		
कुलम्	कुले	कुलानि	like कुल + options		
कुलम्	कुले	कुलानि			/हृन्दि
			/हृदा	/हृद्द्याम्	/हृद्दिः
like देव			/हृदे	/हृद्द्याम्	/हृद्द्यः
			/हृदः	/हृद्द्याम्	/हृद्द्यः
			/हृदः	/हृदोः	/हृदाम्
			/हृदि	/हृदोः	/हृत्सु
हे कुल	कुले	कुलानि			

राधा (f.)			जरा (f.)		
राधा	राधे	राधाः		/जरसौ	/जरसः
राधाम्	राधे	राधाः	/जरसम्	/जरसौ	/जरसः
राधया	राधाभ्याम्	राधाभिः	/जरसा		
राधायै	राधाभ्याम्	राधाभ्यः	/जरसे		
राधायाः	राधाभ्याम्	राधाभ्यः	/जरसः		
राधायाः	राधयोः	राधानाम्	/जरसः	/जरसोः	/जरसाम्
राधायाम्	राधयोः	राधासु	/जरसि	/जरसोः	
हे राधे	राधे	राधाः		/जरसौ	/जरसः

हरि (m.)			पति (m.)		सखि (m.)		
हरिः	हरी	हरयः			सखा	सखायौ	सखायः
हरिम्	हरी	हरीन्			सखायम्	सखायौ	
हरिणा	हरिभ्याम्	हरिभिः	पत्या		सख्या		
हरये	हरिभ्याम्	हरिभ्यः	पत्ये		सख्ये		
हरेः	हरिभ्याम्	हरिभ्यः	पत्युः		सख्युः		
हरेः	हर्योः	हरीणाम्	पत्युः	पत्योः	सख्युः	सख्योः	
हरौ	हर्योः	हरिषु	पत्यौ	पत्योः	सख्यौ	सख्योः	
हे हरे	हरी	हरयः				सखायौ	सखायः

वारि (n.)			दधि (n.)		
वारि	वारिणी	वारीणि			
वारि	वारिणी	वारीणि			
वारिणा			दध्ना		
वारिणे			दध्ने		
वारिणः			दध्नः		
वारिणः	वारिणोः		दध्नः	दध्नोः	दध्नाम्
वारिणि	वारिणोः		/दधि	दध्नोः	
हे वारि/वारे	वारिणी	वारीणि			

एक-व°

भक्ति (f.)			कोटि (f.)
भक्तिः	भक्ती	भक्तयः	कोटिः
भक्तिम्	भक्ती	भक्तीः	कोटिम्
भक्त्या	भक्तिभ्याम्	भक्तिभिः	कोट्या
भक्त्यै/भक्तये	भक्तिभ्याम्	भक्तिभ्यः	कोट्यै
भक्त्याः/भक्तेः	भक्तिभ्याम्	भक्तिभ्यः	कोट्याः
भक्त्याः/भक्तेः	भक्त्योः	भक्तीनाम्	कोट्याः
भक्त्याम्/भक्तौ	भक्त्योः	भक्तिषु	कोट्याम्
हे भक्ते	भक्ती	भक्तयः	हे कोटे

बहु-व°   द्वि-व°   बहु-व°

कति (m.n.f.)	द्वि (m.)	(n.f.)	त्रि (m.)	(n.)	(f.)
कति	द्वौ	द्वे	त्रयः	त्रीणि	तिस्रः
कति	द्वौ	द्वे	त्रीन्	त्रीणि	तिस्रः
कतिभिः	द्वाभ्याम्	द्वाभ्याम्	त्रिभिः	त्रिभिः	तिसृभिः
कतिभ्यः	द्वाभ्याम्	द्वाभ्याम्	त्रिभ्यः	त्रिभ्यः	तिसृभ्यः
कतिभ्यः	द्वाभ्याम्	द्वाभ्याम्	त्रिभ्यः	त्रिभ्यः	तिसृभ्यः
कतीनाम्	द्वयोः	द्वयोः	त्रयाणाम्	त्रयाणाम्	तिसृणाम्
कतिषु	द्वयोः	द्वयोः	त्रिषु	त्रिषु	तिसृषु
	हे द्वौ	हे द्वे	हे त्रयः	हे त्रीणि	हे तिस्रः

in समास: -श्री (m.)			-नी (m.)		
-श्रीः	-श्रियौ	-श्रियः		/-न्यौ	/-न्यः
-श्रियम्	-श्रियौ	-श्रियः	-न्यम्	/-न्यौ	/-न्यः
-श्रिया	-श्रीभ्याम्	-श्रीभिः	-न्या		
-श्रिये	-श्रीभ्याम्	-श्रीभ्यः	-न्ये		
-श्रियः	-श्रीभ्याम्	-श्रीभ्यः	-न्यः		
-श्रियः	-श्रियोः	-श्रियाम्	-न्यः	/-न्योः	/-न्याम्
-श्रियि	-श्रियोः	-श्रीषु	-न्याम्	/-न्योः	
हे -श्रीः	-श्रियौ	-श्रियः		/-न्यौ	/-न्यः

गोपी (f.)			स्त्री (f.)		
गोपी	गोप्यौ	गोप्यः	स्त्री	स्त्रियौ	स्त्रियः
गोपीम्	गोप्यौ	गोपीः	स्त्रीम्/स्त्रियम्	स्त्रियौ	स्त्रीः/स्त्रियः
गोप्या	गोपीभ्याम्	गोपीभिः	स्त्रिया	स्त्रीभ्याम्	स्त्रीभिः
गोप्यै	गोपीभ्याम्	गोपीभ्यः	स्त्रियै	स्त्रीभ्याम्	स्त्रीभ्यः
गोप्याः	गोपीभ्याम्	गोपीभ्यः	स्त्रियाः	स्त्रीभ्याम्	स्त्रीभ्यः
गोप्याः	गोप्योः	गोपीनाम्	स्त्रियाः	स्त्रियोः	स्त्रीणाम्
गोप्याम्	गोप्योः	गोपीषु	स्त्रियाम्	स्त्रियोः	स्त्रीषु
हे गोपि	गोप्यौ	गोप्यः	हे स्त्रि	स्त्रियौ	स्त्रियः

विष्णु (m.)			क्रोष्टु (m.)		
विष्णुः	विष्णू	विष्णवः	क्रोष्टा	क्रोष्टारौ	क्रोष्टारः
विष्णुम्	विष्णू	विष्णून्	क्रोष्टारम्/क्रोष्ट्रा	क्रोष्टारौ	
विष्णुना	विष्णुभ्याम्	विष्णुभिः	/क्रोष्ट्रे		
विष्णवे	विष्णुभ्याम्	विष्णुभ्यः	/क्रोष्टुः		
विष्णोः	विष्णुभ्याम्	विष्णुभ्यः	/क्रोष्टुः	क्रोष्ट्वोः/क्रोष्ट्रोः	
विष्णोः	विष्णुवोः	विष्णूनाम्	/क्रोष्टारि	क्रोष्ट्वोः/क्रोष्ट्रोः	
विष्णौ	विष्णुवोः	विष्णुषु	क्रोष्टारौ		क्रोष्टारः
हे विष्णो	विष्णू	विष्णवः			

वस्तु (n.)			धेनु (f.)		
वस्तु	वस्तुनी	वस्तूनि	धेनुः	धेनू	धेनवः
वस्तु	वस्तुनी	वस्तूनि	धेनुम्	धेनू	धेनूः
वस्तुना	वस्तुभ्याम्	वस्तुभिः	धेन्वा	धेनुभ्याम्	धेनुभिः
वस्तुने	वस्तुभ्याम्	वस्तुभ्यः	धेन्वै/धेनवे	धेनुभ्याम्	धेनुभ्यः
वस्तुनः	वस्तुभ्याम्	वस्तुभ्यः	धेन्वाः/धेनोः	धेनुभ्याम्	धेनुभ्यः
वस्तुनः	वस्तुनोः	वस्तूनाम्	धेन्वाः/धेनोः	धेन्वोः	धेनूनाम्
वस्तुनि	वस्तुनोः	वस्तुषु	धेन्वाम्/धेनौ	धेन्वोः	धेनुषु
हे वस्तु/वस्तो	वस्तुनी	वस्तूनि	हे धेनो	धेनू	धेनवः

-भू (m.)			वधू (f.)		
-भूः	-भुवौ	-भुवः	वधूः	वध्वौ	वध्वः
-भुवम्	-भुवौ	-भुवः	वधूम	वध्वौ	वधूः
-भुवा	-भूभ्याम्	-भूभिः	वध्वा	वधूभ्याम्	वधूभिः
-भुवे	-भूभ्याम्	-भूभ्यः	वध्वै	वधूभ्याम्	वधूभ्यः
-भुवः	-भूभ्याम्	-भूभ्यः	वध्वाः	वधूभ्याम्	वधूभ्यः
-भुवः	-भुवोः	-भुवाम्	वध्वाः	वध्वोः	वधूनाम्
-भुवि	-भुवोः	-भूषु	वध्वाम्	वध्वोः	वधूषु
हे -भूः	-भुवौ	-भुवः	हे वधु	वध्वौ	वध्वः

कर्तृ (m.)			पितृ (m.)		
कर्ता	कर्तारौ	कर्तारः	पिता	पितरौ	पितरः
कर्तारम्	कर्तारौ	कर्तॄन्	पितरम्	पितरौ	पितॄन्
कर्त्रा	कर्तृभ्याम्	कर्तृभिः	पित्रा	पितृभ्याम्	पितृभिः
कर्त्रे	कर्तृभ्याम्	कर्तृभ्यः	पित्रे	पितृभ्याम्	पितृभ्यः
कर्तुः	कर्तृभ्याम्	कर्तृभ्यः	पितुः	पितृभ्याम्	पितृभ्यः
कर्तुः	कर्त्रोः	कर्तॄणाम्	पितुः	पित्रोः	पितॄणाम्
कर्तरि	कर्त्रोः	कर्तृषु	पितरि	पित्रोः	पितृषु
हे कर्तः	कर्तारौ	कर्तारः	हे पितः	पितरौ	पितरः

कर्तृ (n.)			मातृ (f.)		
कर्तृ	कर्तृणी	कर्तॄणि	माता	मातरौ	मातरः
कर्तृ	कर्तृणी	कर्तॄणि	मातरम्	मातरौ	मातॄः
/कर्तृणा	कर्तृभ्याम्	कर्तृभिः	मात्रा		
/कर्तृणे	कर्तृभ्याम्	कर्तृभ्यः	मात्रे		
/कर्तृणः	कर्तृभ्याम्	कर्तृभ्यः	मातुः		
/कर्तृणः	/कर्तृणोः	कर्तॄणाम्	मातुः	मात्रोः	
/कर्तृणि	/कर्तृणोः	कर्तृषु	मातरि	मात्रोः	
हे /कर्तृ	कर्तृणी	कर्तॄणि	हे मातः	मातरौ	मातरः

-रै (m.)			(n.)		
-राः	-रायौ	-रायः	-रि	-रिणी	-रीणि
-रायम्	-रायौ	-रायः	-रि	-रिणी	-रीणि
-राया	-राभ्याम्	-राभिः	/-रिणा		
-राये	-राभ्याम्	-राभ्यः	/-रिणे		
-रायः	-राभ्याम्	-राभ्यः	/-रिणः		
-रायः	-रायोः	-रायाम्	/-रिणः	/-रिणोः	/-रीणाम्
-रायि	-रायोः	-रासु	/-रिणि	/-रिणोः	
हे -राः	-रायौ	-रायः	हे -रे/रि	-रिणी	-रीणि

गो (m.f.)			नौ (m.)		
गौः	गावौ	गावः	नौः	नावौ	नावः
गाम्	गावौ	गाः	नावम्	नावौ	नावः
गवा	गोभ्याम्	गोभिः	नावा	नौभ्याम्	नौभिः
गवे	गोभ्याम्	गोभ्यः	नावे	नौभ्याम्	नौभ्यः
गोः	गोभ्याम्	गोभ्यः	नावः	नौभ्याम्	नौभ्यः
गोः	गवोः	गवाम्	नावः	नावोः	नावाम्
गवि	गवोः	गोषु	नावि	नावोः	नौषु
हे गौः	गावौ	गावः	हे नौः	नावौ	नावः

(2) Words ending in व्यञ्जन (हल् → हलन्त)

प्रत्यञ्च् (m.)			-मुच् (m.)		
प्रत्यङ्	प्रत्यञ्चौ	प्रत्यञ्चः	-मुक्	-मुचौ	-मुचः
प्रत्यञ्चम्	प्रत्यञ्चौ	प्रतीचः	-मुचम्	-मुचौ	-मुचः
प्रतीचा	प्रत्यग्भ्याम्	प्रत्यग्भिः	-मुचा	-मुग्भ्याम्	-मुग्भिः
प्रतीचे	प्रत्यग्भ्याम्	प्रत्यग्भ्यः	-मुचे	-मुग्भ्याम्	-मुग्भ्यः
प्रतीचः	प्रत्यग्भ्याम्	प्रत्यग्भ्यः	-मुचः	-मुग्भ्याम्	-मुग्भ्यः
प्रतीचः	प्रतीचोः	प्रतीचाम्	-मुचः	-मुचोः	-मुचाम्
प्रतीचि	प्रतीचोः	प्रत्यक्षु	-मुचि	-मुचोः	-मुक्षु
हे प्रत्यङ्	प्रत्यञ्चौ	प्रत्यञ्चः	हे -मुक्	-मुचौ	-मुचः

वाच् (f.)			स्रज् (f.)		
वाक्/वाग्	वाचौ	वाचः	स्रक्/ग्	स्रजौ	स्रजः
वाचम्	वाचौ	वाचः	स्रजम्	स्रजौ	स्रजः
वाचा	वाग्भ्याम्	वाग्भिः	स्रजा	स्रग्भ्याम्	स्रग्भिः
वाचे	वाग्भ्याम्	वाग्भ्यः	स्रजे	स्रग्भ्याम्	स्रग्भ्यः
वाचः	वाग्भ्याम्	वाग्भ्यः	स्रजः	स्रग्भ्याम्	स्रग्भ्यः
वाचः	वाचोः	वाचाम्	स्रजः	स्रजोः	स्रजाम्
वाचि	वाचोः	वाक्षु	स्रजि	स्रजोः	स्रक्षु
हे वाक्/ग्	वाचौ	वाचः	हे स्रक्/ग्	स्रजौ	स्रजः

मरुत् (m.=f.)			जगत् (n.)		
मरुत्	मरुतौ	मरुतः	जगत्	जगती	जगन्ति
मरुतम्	मरुतौ	मरुतः	जगत्	जगती	जगन्ति
मरुता	मरुद्भ्याम्	मरुद्भिः			
मरुते	मरुद्भ्याम्	मरुद्भ्यः			
मरुतः	मरुद्भ्याम्	मरुद्भ्यः			
मरुतः	मरुतोः	मरुताम्			
मरुति	मरुतोः	मरुत्सु			
हे मरुत्	मरुतौ	मरुतः	हे जगत्	जगती	जगन्ति

भवत् [u] (.vat[u]) (m.)			महत् [u] (m.)			(n.)		
भवान्	भवन्तौ	भवन्तः	महान्	महान्तौ	महान्तः	महत्	महती	महान्ति
भवन्तम्	भवन्तौ		महान्तम्	महान्तौ		महत्	महती	महान्ति
Words formed with [ś]at[ṛ] are declined like कुर्वत् → कुर्वन् *1.1 सत् → सन् *1.1								
हे भवन्	भवन्तौ	भवन्तः	हे महन्	महान्तौ	महान्तः	हे महत्	महती	महान्ति

सुहृद् (m.)		
सुहृद्/त्	सुहृदौ	सुहृदः
सुहृदम्	सुहृदौ	सुहृदः
सुहृदा	सुहृद्भ्याम्	सुहृद्भिः
सुहृदे	सुहृद्भ्याम्	सुहृद्भ्यः
सुहृदः	सुहृद्भ्याम्	सुहृद्भ्यः
सुहृदः	सुहृदोः	सुहृदाम्
सुहृदि	सुहृदोः	सुहृत्सु
हे सुहृद्/त्	सुहृदौ	सुहृदः

आत्मन् (m.)			राजन् (m.)		
आत्मा	आत्मानौ	आत्मानः			राज्ञः
आत्मानम्	आत्मानौ	आत्मनः			
आत्मना	आत्मभ्याम्	आत्मभिः	राज्ञा		
आत्मने	आत्मभ्याम्	आत्मभ्यः	राज्ञे		
आत्मनः	आत्मभ्याम्	आत्मभ्यः	राज्ञः		
आत्मनः	आत्मनोः	आत्मनाम्	राज्ञः	राज्ञोः	राज्ञाम्
आत्मनि	आत्मनोः	आत्मसु	/राजि	राज्ञोः	
हे आत्मन्	आत्मानौ	आत्मानः			

कर्मन् (n.)			नामन् (n.)		
कर्म	कर्मणी	कर्माणि			/नाम्नी
कर्म	कर्मणी	कर्माणि			/नाम्नी
कर्मणा			नाम्ना		
			नाम्ने		
			नाम्नः		
			नाम्नः	नाम्नोः	नाम्नाम्
			/नाम्नि	नाम्नोः	
हे /कर्म	कर्मणी	कर्माणि	/नाम		/नाम्नी

श्वन् (m.)			-दिवन् (m.)			-हन् (m.)		
श्वा	श्वानौ	श्वानः						-हनौ
श्वानम्	श्वानौ	शुनः			-दीव्यः		-हनौ	-घ्नः
शुना	श्वभ्याम्	श्वभिः	-दीव्ना			-घ्ना		
शुने	श्वभ्याम्	श्वभ्यः	-दीव्ने			-घ्ने		
शुनः	श्वभ्याम्	श्वभ्यः	-दीव्न			-घ्नः		
शुनः	शुनोः	शुनाम्	-दीव्नः	-दीव्नोः	-दीव्नाम्	-घ्नः	-घ्नोः	-घ्नाम्
शुनि	शुनोः	श्वसु	/-दीव्नि	-दीव्नोः		/-घ्नि	-घ्नोः	
हे श्वन्	श्वानौ	श्वानः				हे -हन्	-हनौ	-हनः

पञ्चन् (m.n.f.)	अष्टन् (m.n.f.)	सीमन् (f.)		
पञ्च	अष्ट/अष्टौ	सीमा	सीमानौ	सीमानः
पञ्च	अष्ट/अष्टौ	सीमानम्	सीमानौ	सीम्नः
पञ्चभिः	अष्टभिः/अष्टाभिः	सीम्ना	सीमभ्याम्	सीमभिः
पञ्चभ्यः	अष्टभ्यः/अष्टाभ्यः	सीम्ने	सीमभ्याम्	सीमभ्यः
पञ्चभ्यः	अष्टभ्यः/अष्टाभ्यः	सीम्नः	सीमभ्याम्	सीमभ्यः
पञ्चानाम्	अष्टानाम्	सीम्नः	सीम्नोः	सीम्नाम्
पञ्चसु	अष्टसु	सीम्नि	सीम्नोः	सीमसु
हे पञ्च	हे अष्ट/अष्टौ	हे सीमन्	सीमानौ	सीमानः

योगिन् (m.)			पथिन् (m.)		
योगी	योगिनौ	योगिनः	पन्थाः	पन्थानौ	पन्थानः
योगिनम्	योगिनौ	योगिनः	पन्थानम्	पन्थानौ	पथः
योगिना	योगिभ्याम्	योगिभिः	पथा		
योगिने	योगिभ्याम्	योगिभ्यः	पथे		
योगिनः	योगिभ्याम्	योगिभ्यः	पथः		
योगिनः	योगिनोः	योगिनाम्	पथः	पथोः	पथाम्
योगिनि	योगिनोः	योगिषु	पथि	पथोः	पथिषु
हे योगिन्	योगिनौ	योगिनः	हे पन्थाः	पन्थानौ	पन्थानः

बहु-व॰

अप् (f.)	गिर् (f.)			चतुर् (m.)	(n.)	(f.)
आपः	गीः	गिरौ	गिरः	चत्वारः	चत्वारि	चतस्रः
अपः	गिरम्	गिरौ	गिरः	चतुरः	चत्वारि	चतस्रः
अद्भिः	गिरा	गीर्भ्याम्	गीर्भिः	चतुर्भिः	चतुर्भिः	चतसृभिः
अद्भ्यः	गिरे	गीर्भ्याम्	गीर्भ्यः	चतुर्भ्यः	चतुर्भ्यः	चतसृभ्यः
अद्भ्यः	गिरः	गीर्भ्याम्	गीर्भ्यः	चतुर्भ्यः	चतुर्भ्यः	चतसृभ्यः
अपाम्	गिरः	गिरोः	गिराम्	चतुर्णाम्	चतुर्णाम्	चतसृणाम्
अप्सु	गिरि	गिरोः	गीर्षु	चतुर्षु	चतुर्षु	चतसृषु
हे अपः	हे गीः	गिरौ	गिरः	हे चत्वरः	चत्वरि	चतस्रः

-विश् (m.)			दिश् (f.)	
-विड्/ट्	-विशौ	-विशः	दिग्/क्	
-विशम्	-विशौ	-विशः		
-विशा	-विड्भ्याम्	-विड्भिः	दिग्भ्याम्	दिग्भिः
-विशे	-विड्भ्याम्	-विड्भ्यः	दिग्भ्याम्	दिग्भ्यः
-विशः	-विड्भ्याम्	-विड्भ्यः	दिग्भ्याम्	दिग्भ्यः
-विशः	-विशोः	-विशाम्		
-विशि	-विशोः	विट्सु		दिक्षु
हे -विड्/ट्	-विशौ	-विशः	हे दिग्/क्	

-द्विष् (m.)	-दधृष् (m.)		षष् (m.n.f.)
-द्विड्/ट्	-दधृग्/क्		षड्/ट्
			षड्/ट्
	-दधृग्भ्याम्	-दधृग्भि	षड्भिः
	-दधृग्भ्याम्	-दधृग्भ्यः	षड्भ्यः
	-दधृग्भ्याम्	-दधृग्भ्यः	षड्भ्यः
			षण्णाम्
	-दधृक्षु		षट्सु
हे -द्विड्/ट्	हे -दधृग्/क्		हे षड्/ट्

-मनस् (m.)			(n.)		
-मनाः	-मनसौ	-मनसः	मनः	मनसी	मनांसि
-मनसम्	-मनसौ	-मनसः	मनः	मनसी	मनांसि
-मनसा	-मनोभ्याम्	-मनोभिः			
-मनसे	-मनोभ्याम्	-मनोभ्यः			
-मनसः	-मनोभ्याम्	-मनोभ्यः			
-मनसः	-मनसोः	-मनसाम्			
-मनसि	-मनसोः	-मनःसु			
हे -मनः	-मनसौ	-मनसः	हे मनः	मनसी	मनांसि

But: उशनस् → उशना *m.1.1

विद्वस् *[u]* (m.)			पुंस् (m.)		
विद्वान्	विद्वांसौ	विद्वांसः	पुमान्	पुमांसौ	पुमांसः
विद्वांसम्	विद्वांसौ	विदुषः	पुमांसम्	पुमांसौ	पुंसः
विदुषा	विद्वद्भ्याम्	विद्वद्भिः	पुंसा	पुम्भ्याम्	पुम्भिः
विदुषे	विद्वद्भ्याम्	विद्वद्भ्यः	पुंसे	पुम्भ्याम्	पुम्भ्यः
विदुषः	विद्वद्भ्याम्	विद्वद्भ्यः	पुंसः	पुम्भ्याम्	पुम्भ्यः
विदुषः	विदुषोः	विदुषाम्	पुंसः	पुंसोः	पुंसाम्
विदुषि	विदुषोः	विद्वत्सु	पुंसि	पुंसोः	पुंषु
हे विद्वन्	विद्वांसौ	विद्वांसः	हे पुमन्	पुमांसौ	पुमांसः

दोस् (m.)			धनुस् (n.)		
दोः	दोषौ	दोषः	धनुः	धनुषी	धनूंषि
दोषम्	दोषौ	दोषः	धनुः	धनुषी	धनूंषि
दोषा	दोर्भ्याम्	दोर्भिः			
दोषे	दोर्भ्याम्	दोर्भ्यः			
दोषः	दोर्भ्याम्	दोर्भ्यः			
दोषः	दोषोः	दोषाम्			
दोषि	दोषोः	दोःषु			
हे दो	दोषौ	दोषः	हे धनुः	धनुषी	धनुः

अनडुह् (m.)			-द्रुह् (m.)		
अनड्वान्	अनड्वाहौ	अनड्वाहः	-ध्रुड्/ट्	-द्रुहौ	-द्रुहः
अनड्वाहम्	अनड्वाहौ	अनडुहः	-द्रुहम्	-द्रुहौ	-द्रुहः
अनडुहा	अनडुद्ध्याम्	अनडुद्भिः	-द्रुहा	-ध्रुड्भ्याम्	-ध्रुड्भिः
अनडुहे	अनडुद्ध्याम्	अनडुद्भ्यः	-द्रुहे	-ध्रुड्भ्याम्	-ध्रुड्भ्यः
अनडुहः	अनडुद्ध्याम्	अनडुद्भ्यः	-द्रुहः	-ध्रुड्भ्याम्	-ध्रुड्भ्यः
अनडुहः	अनडुहोः	अनडुहाम्	-द्रुहः	-द्रुहोः	-द्रुहाम्
अनडुहि	अनडुहोः	अनडुत्सु	-द्रुहि	-द्रुहोः	-द्रुट्सु
हे अनड्वन्	अनड्वाहौ	अनड्वाहः	हे -ध्रुड्/ट्	-द्रुहौ	-द्रुहः

(3) सर्व-नाम (pronouns)

41 words, beginning with सर्व-विश्व-उभ-…, mainly pronouns, characterized by a particular pattern of declension (marked in bold type).

सर्व (m.)			(n.)			सर्वा (f.)		
सर्वः	सर्वौ	**सर्वे**	सर्वम्	सर्वे	सर्वाणि	सर्वा	सर्वे	सर्वाः
सर्वम्	सर्वौ	सर्वान्	सर्वम्	सर्वे	सर्वाणि	सर्वाम्	सर्वे	सर्वाः
सर्वेण	सर्वाभ्याम्	सर्वैः				सर्वया	सर्वाभ्याम्	सर्वाभिः
सर्व**स्मै**	सर्वाभ्याम्	सर्वेभ्यः				सर्वस्यै	सर्वाभ्याम्	सर्वाभ्यः
सर्व**स्मात्**	सर्वाभ्याम्	सर्वेभ्यः				सर्वस्याः	सर्वाभ्याम्	सर्वाभ्यः
सर्वस्य	सर्वयोः	सर्वेषाम्				सर्वस्याः	सर्वयोः	सर्वासाम्
सर्व**स्मिन्**	सर्वयोः	सर्वेषु				सर्वस्याम्	सर्वयोः	सर्वासु
हे सर्व	सर्वौ	**सर्वे**	हे सर्व	सर्वे	सर्वाणि	हे सर्वे	सर्वे	सर्वाः

उभय	उभ	उभय (m.)	पूर्व (m.)
उभयः	उभौ	उभये	/पूर्वाः
उभयम्	उभौ	उभयान्	
उभयेन	उभाभ्याम्	उभयैः	
उभयस्मै	उभाभ्याम्	उभयेभ्यः	
उभयस्मात्	उभाभ्याम्	उभयेभ्यः	/पूर्वात्
उभयस्य	उभयोः	उभयेषाम्	
उभयस्मिन्	उभयोः	उभयेषु	/पूर्वे

तद् (m.)			(n.)			(f.)		
सः	तौ	ते	तद्	ते	तानि	सा	ते	ताः
तम्	तौ	तान्	तद्	ते	तानि	ताम्	ते	ताः
तेन	ताभ्याम्	तैः				तया	ताभ्याम्	ताभिः
तस्मै	ताभ्याम्	तेभ्यः				तस्यै	ताभ्याम्	ताभ्यः
तस्मात्	ताभ्याम्	तेभ्यः				तस्याः	ताभ्याम्	ताभ्यः
तस्य	तयोः	तेषाम्				तस्याः	तयोः	तासाम्
तस्मिन्	तयोः	तेषु				तस्याम्	तयोः	तासु

यद् (m.)			(n.)			(f.)		
यः	यौ	ये	यद्	ये	यानि	या	ये	याः
यम्	यौ	यान्	यद्	ये	यानि	याम्	ये	याः
येन	याभ्याम्	यैः				यया	याभ्याम्	याभिः
यस्मै	याभ्याम्	येभ्यः				यस्यै	याभ्याम्	याभ्यः
यस्मात्	याभ्याम्	येभ्यः				यस्याः	याभ्याम्	याभ्यः
यस्य	ययोः	येषाम्				यस्याः	ययोः	यासाम्
यस्मिन्	ययोः	येषु				यस्याम्	ययोः	यासु

एतद् (m.)			(n.)=(m.)			(f.)		
एषः	एतौ	एते				एषा	एते	एताः
एतम्/एनम्	एतौ	एतान्				एताम्	एते	एताः
एतेन	एताभ्याम्	एतैः				एतया	एताभ्याम्	एताभिः
एतस्मै	एताभ्याम्	एतेभ्यः				एतस्यै	एताभ्याम्	एताभ्यः
एतस्मात्	एताभ्याम्	एतेभ्यः				एतस्याः	एताभ्याम्	एताभ्यः
एतस्य	एतयोः	एतेषाम्				एतस्याः	एतयोः	एतासाम्
एतस्मिन्	एतयोः	एतेषु				एतस्याम्	एतयोः	एतासु

युष्मद् (m.n.f.)			अस्मद् (m.n.f.)		
त्वम्	युवाम्	यूयम्	अहम्	आवाम्	वयम्
त्वाम्/त्वा	युवाम्/वाम्	युष्मान्/वः	माम्/मा	आवाम्/नौ	अस्मान्/नः
त्वया	युवाभ्याम्	युष्माभिः	मया	आवाभ्याम्	अस्माभिः
तुभ्यम्/ते	युवाभ्याम्/वाम्	युष्मभ्यम्/वः	मह्यम्/मे	आवाभ्याम्/नौ	अस्मभ्यम्/नः
त्वद्	युवाभ्याम्	युष्मद्	मद्	आवाभ्याम्	अस्मद्
तव/ते	युवयोः/वाम्	युष्माकम्/वः	मम/मे	आवयोः/नौ	अस्माकम्/नः
त्वयि	युवयोः	युष्मासु	मयि	आवयोः	अस्मासु

किम् (m.)			(n.)			(f.)		
कः	कौ	के	किम्	के	कानि	का	के	काः
कम्	कौ	कान्	किम्	के	कानि	काम्	के	काः
केन	काभ्याम्	कैः				कया	काभ्याम्	काभिः
कस्मै	काभ्याम्	केभ्यः				कस्यै	काभ्याम्	काभ्यः
कस्मात्	काभ्याम्	केभ्यः				कस्याः	काभ्याम्	काभ्यः
कस्य	कयोः	केषाम्				कस्याः	कयोः	कासाम्
कस्मिन्	कयोः	केषु				कस्याम्	कयोः	कासु

इदम् (m.)			(n.)			(f.)		
अयम्	इमौ	इमे	इदम्	इमे	इमानि	इयम्	इमे	इमाः
इमम्	इमौ	इमान्	इदम्	इमे	इमानि	इमाम्	इमे	इमाः
अनेन	आभ्याम्	एभिः				अनया	आभ्याम्	आभिः
अस्मै	आभ्याम्	एभ्यः				अस्यै	आभ्याम्	आभ्यः
अस्मात्	आभ्याम्	एभ्यः				अस्याः	आभ्याम्	आभ्यः
अस्य	अनयोः	एषाम्				अस्याः	अनयोः	आसाम्
अस्मिन्	अनयोः	एषु				अस्याम्	अनयोः	आसु

अदस् (m.)			(n.)			(f.)		
असौ	अमू	अमी	अदः	अमू	अमूनि	असौ	द्वि-व°	अमूः
अमुम्	अमू	अमून्	अदः	अमू	अमूनि	अमूम्	like	अमूः
अमुना	अमूभ्याम्	अमीभिः				अमुया	(m.)	अमूभिः
अमुष्मै	अमूभ्याम्	अमीभ्यः				अमुष्यै		अमूभ्यः
अमुष्मात्	अमूभ्याम्	अमीभ्यः				अमुष्याः		अमूभ्यः
अमुष्य	अमुयोः	अमीषाम्				अमुष्याः		अमूषाम्
अमुष्मिन्	अमुयोः	अमीषु				अमुष्याम्		अमूषु

26. Numbers

	सङ्ख्या-वाचक (cardinals)				क्रम-वाचक (ordinals)		
	m.	n.	f.		m.	n.	f.
९ 1	एकः	एकम्	एका	1st	प्रथमः	प्रथमम्	प्रथमा
२ 2	द्वौ	द्वे	द्वे	2nd	द्वितीयः	etc.	etc.
३ 3	त्रयः	त्रीणि	तिस्रः	3rd	तृतीयः		
४ 4	चत्वारः	चत्वारि	चतस्रः	4th	चतुर्थः		चतुर्थी
५ 5	पञ्च	From 5 onwards the numbers are the same in all three genders.		5th	पञ्चमः		etc.
६ 6	षट्			6th	षष्ठः		
७ 7	सप्त			7th	सप्तमः		
८ 8	अष्ट			8th	अष्टमः		
९ 9	नव			9th	नवमः		
९० 10	दश			10th	दशमः		

Naturally, एक is declined only in एक-वचन, द्वि only in द्वि-वचन, and the numbers from three onwards are declined only in बहु-वचन. Numbers will follow the gender of the object. When counting without mentioning any object, the neuter forms are used.

	एक (एक-व°)	द्वि (द्वि-व°)	त्रि (बहु-व°)
m.	एकः गोपः	द्वौ गोपौ	त्रयः गोपाः
f.	एका गोपी	द्वे गोप्यौ	तिस्रः गोप्यः
n.	एकम् पुष्पम्	द्वे पुष्पे	त्रीणि पुष्पाणि

११	एका-दश	२१	एक-विंशति	३१	एक-त्रिंशत्
१२	द्वा-दश	२२	द्वा-विंशति	३२	द्वा-त्रिंशत्
१३	त्रयो-दश	२३	त्रयो-विंशति	३३	त्रयस्त्रिंशत्
१४	वतुर्दश	२४	चतुर्विंशति	३४	चतुस्त्रिंशत्
१५	पञ्च-दश	२५	पञ्च-विंशति	३५	पञ्च-त्रिंशत्
१६	षोडश	२६	षड्-विंशति	३६	षट्-त्रिंशत्
१७	सप्त-दश	२७	सप्त-विंशति	३७	सप्त-त्रिंशत्
१८	अष्टा-दश	२८	अष्टा-विंशति	३८	अष्टा-त्रिंशत्
१९	एकोन-विंशति	२९	एकोन-त्रिंशत्	३९	एकोन-चत्वारिंशत्
२०	विंशति	३०	त्रिंशत्	४०	चत्वारिंशत्

४१	एक-चत्वारिंशत्	५१	एक-पञ्चाशत्	६१	एक-षष्टि
४२	द्वि-चत्वारिंशत्	५२	द्वि-पञ्चाशत्	६२	द्वि-षष्टि
४३	त्रि-चत्वारिंशत्	५३	त्रि-पञ्चाशत्	६३	त्रि-षष्टि
४४	चतुश्चत्वारिंशत्	५४	चतुः-पञ्चाशत्	६४	चतुः-षष्टि
४५	पञ्च-चत्वारिंशत्	५५	पञ्च-पञ्चाशत्	६५	पञ्च-षष्टि
४६	षट्-चत्वारिंशत्	५६	षट्-पञ्चाशत्	६६	षट्-षष्टि
४७	सप्त-चत्वारिंशत्	५७	सप्त-पञ्चाशत्	६७	सप्त-षष्टि
४८	अष्ट-चत्वारिंशत्	५८	अष्ट-पञ्चाशत्	६८	अष्ट-षष्टि
४९	एकोन-पञ्चाशत्	५९	एकोन-षष्टि	६९	एकोन-सप्तति
५०	पञ्चाशत्	६०	षष्टि	७०	सप्तति

७१	एक-सप्तति	८१	एकाशीति	९१	एक नवति
७२	द्वि-सप्तति	८२	द्व्यशीति	९२	द्वि-नवति
७३	त्रि-सप्तति	८३	त्र्यशीति	९३	त्रि-नवति
७४	चातुः-सप्तति	८४	चतुरशीति	९४	चतुर्नवति
७५	पञ्च-सप्तति	८५	पञ्चाशीति	९५	पञ्च-नवति
७६	षट्-सप्तति	८६	षडशीति	९६	षण्णवति
७७	सप्त-सप्तति	८७	सप्ताशीति	९७	सप्त-नवति
७८	अष्ट-सप्तति	८८	अष्टाशीति	९८	अष्ट-नवति
७९	एकोनाशीति	८९	एकोन-नवति	९९	एकोन-शत
८०	अशीति	९०	नवति	१००	शत

एकोन (एक-ऊन) means 'one less', as in एकोन-विंशति _ 'one less than twenty', nineteen.

Higher numbers: ۹୦୦୦ सहस्र

               ۹୦,୦୦୦ अयुत

              ۹୦୦,୦୦୦ लक्ष, 'Lakh'

            ۹,୦୦୦.୦୦୦ नियुत

           ۹୦,୦୦୦.୦୦୦ कोटि, 'Crore'

Numbers are expressed by adding अधिक (more, plus) to the lower number:

۹୦۹   एकाधिक-शत (एक-अधिक-) '1 plus 100'

२୦୦   द्वि-शत

۹۹୦۹ एकाधिक-शताधिक-सहस्र

२୦୦୦ द्वि-सहस्र

Options:

1. उत्तर instead of अधिक → अष्टोत्तर-शत _ 108

2. without अधिक/उत्तर → एकादश-शत _ 111

3. flexible expressions in poetry: द्व्यष्ट (द्वि-अष्ट) _ '2 x 8', 16

Times:

   सकृत्, एकवारम् _ once

   द्विः, द्विवारम् _ twice

   त्रिः, त्रिवारम् _ thrice

   चतुः _ four times

   पञ्चकृत्वः, पञ्चवारम् _ five times

   सहस्रकृत्वः, सहस्रवारम् _ thousand times

27. Dhatu

"Sanskrit is constructed like geometry and follows a rigorous logic. It is theoretically possible to explain the meaning of the words according to the combined sense of the relative letters, syllables and roots. Sanskrit has no meanings by connotations and consequently does not age." (Alain Danielou, French ethnomusicologist, head of the UNESCO Institute for Comparative Musicology, 1907-1994)

The essentials of Sanskrit language are its धातु and पाणिनि listed about 2,300. Most of them have one or more अनुबन्ध, which are removed in the process of grammatical operations.

All Sanskrit words with their etymological meaning are [theoretically] derived from some धातु. E.g., from √मत्रि गुप्तभाषणे (speaking confidentially) comes the word मन्त्र (advice), which specifically refers to prayers. There are also instructive ways to explain word meanings, f.e., as if मन्त्र was derived from मनः plus त्रायते ('by which the mind is delivered').

Words may also acquire a conventional meaning, different from their etymological meaning. E.g., अब्ज, अम्बुज, अम्भोज, उदज, नीरज, etc., mean 'born in mud/water'. By convention these names are reserved for the lotus, although many other plants and animals are born in the same environment.

उपसर्ग are applied to धातु and नाम, by which the meaning is either

    followed: गच्छति _ he goes → निर्गच्छति _ he goes

    qualified: धावति _ he runs → प्रधावति _ he runs fast

    or altered: गच्छति _ he goes → आगच्छति _ he comes.

अति.   very →अतिसुन्दर; beyond →अतीत; by सन्धि अत्य्. →अत्यन्त.

अधि.   Vedic »at«, Lat. »ad«; over →अधिदेव; by सन्धि अध्य्. →अध्यक्ष.

अनु.   after, along →अनुगामी; by सन्धि अन्व्. →अन्वय.

अप.   down, away, »off«, Gr. »apo-«, Lat. »ab-« →अपराध.

अभि.   towards →अभिगम; intense →अभिज्ञ.

अव.   under /down →अवतार; away →अवज्ञा.

आ.   fully →आनन्द; towards →आकर्ष; up to →आब्रह्म; with words of motion it reverses the action →आगम, आदान.

उद्.   up →उदय; »out« →उद्भव; by सन्धि उच्. →उच्छ्वास, उज्. →उज्ज्वल, उत्. →उत्तम, उन्. →उन्मूलन.

उप.   near →उपासन; »sub-«, Gr. »hypo« →उपवेद.

दुर्.   hard, →दुर्ग; bad, »dys-« →दुर्बुद्धि; by सन्धि दुः. →दुःख, दुष्. →दुष्कृत.

नि.   down, »nether« →निग्रह.

निर्.   out →निरस्त; without →निर्जल; by सन्धि निः. →निःस्पृह, निश्. →निश्चल, निष्. →निष्फल.

परि.   around, »peri-« →परिक्रम; fully →परित्याग.

प्र.   before, »pre-« →प्राक्; forth, »pro-« →प्राण; full →प्रसाद.

प्रति.   towards →प्रतीक्षा; against →प्रतिकार; each, »per« →प्रतिदिनम्; by सन्धि प्रत्य्. →प्रत्यक्ष.

वि.   away, without →विगुण; distinct, different →विज्ञान; reverse, bad →विकर्म; by सन्धि व्य्. →व्यर्थ.

सम्.   together →समवेत; complete, perfect →समर्चा; by सन्धि सं. →संस्कृत, सङ्. →सङ्ग्छा, सञ्. →सञ्जय, सन्. →सन्धि.

सु.   well →सुकृति; beautiful →सुकन्या; very →सुसुखम्; by सन्धि स्व्. →स्वल्प.

नाम are derived from धातु by adding कृत्-प्रत्यय, then called कृदन्त. There are different types, of which we give a few examples.

(1) करण

With the प्रत्यय .ana and .[t]ana भाव-प्रयोग (Abstract Nouns) and करण-प्रयोग (Instrumental Nouns) are formed:

√[डु]कृ[ञ्] → करण _ doing

(2) कर्तुम्

With .tum[u], the Infinitive is formed:

√[डु]कृ[ञ्] → कर्तुम् _ to do (अव्यय)

(3) कृत कृतवत्

In कर्म-वाच्य (Passive Voice), .[k]ta is applied:

√[डु]कृ[ञ्] → कृत _ done

Sometimes, .i. is inserted:

√स्था → स्थित _ situated

But in कर्तृ-वाच्य (Active Voice), .[k]tavat[u] is applied:

√[डु]कृ[ञ्] → कृतवत् _ 'someone who did', he did; declined like भवत् (.vat[u])

(4) कृत्वा अनुकार्य

For a preceeding action, .[k]tvā is applied:

√[डु]कृ[ञ्] → कृत्वा _ [after] doing (अव्यय)

But when उपसर्ग is applied to a धातु, .ya[p] is used instead. Such words should not be confused with (6), which are not अव्यय.

अनु.√[डु]कृ[ञ्] → अनुकार्य _ [after] imitating

(5) कुर्वत् करिष्यत् कुर्वाण करिष्यमान क्रियमान

The प्रत्यय .[ś]at[r] is used to describe an action, simultaneous to the main activity of the sentence:

√[डु]कृ[ञ्] → कुर्वत्[r] _ 'who is doing', [while] doing; declension like भवत्[r], except for कुर्वन् *1.1.

A similar प्रत्यय is .[ś]āna:

√[डु]कृ[ञ्] → कुर्वाण _ [while] doing

The Passive is formed by inserting .ya.:

√[डु]कृ[ञ्] → क्रियमान _ [while] being done
For Future, .sya. (.sya. by सन्धि) is inserted:

  √[डु]कृ[ञ्] + .[ś]at[ṛ] → करिष्यत् _ who will be doing
  √[डु]कृ[ञ्] + .[ś]āna → करिष्यमान _ who will be doing

(6) कार्य कर्तव्य करणीय

.ya (for .ya[t], .[k]ya[p] and .[ṇ]ya[t]), .tavya, and .anīya are used to point out Duty. Compare with (4).

  √[डु]कृ[ञ्] → कार्य, कर्तव्य, करणीय _ 'which has to be done', duty

(7) कर्तृ

.tṛ[n] for doership:

  √[डु]कृ[ञ्] + .tṛ[n] → कर्तृ _ doer; कर्ता *1.1
Similarly:

  √मन्त्रि + .[ṇ]in[i] → मन्त्रिन् _ advisor; मन्त्री *1.1
  √वस + .tra → वस्त्र _ 'which covers', garment
  √जनी + .tu → जन्तु _ living entity
  √नम + .ra → नम्र _ humble
  √भज + .[k]ti → भक्ति _ devotion
  √भू + .[gh]a[ṇ] → भाव _ state of being
  √यज + .na → यज्ञ _ sacrifice
  √साध + .u[ṇ] → साधु _ saintly person
Sometimes in the sense of future:

  √गम्लृ → गामिन् _ who will go; गामी *1.1

(8) -कृत्

Some कृदन्त can only be used in समास with a preceding object:

  √[डु]कृ[ञ्] → -कृत् _ doer; as in कर्म-कृत् _ doer of work
Similarly:

  √[डु]कृ[ञ्] → -द _ giving; सुख-दः _ giving happiness
  √स्था → -स्थ _ standing; योग-स्थ _ situated in योग
  √विद → -विद् _ knowing; वेद-विद् _ knowing वेद
  √ज्ञा → -ज्ञ _ knowing; क्षेत्र-ज्ञः _ knowing the field (body)
  √पा → -प _ drinking; सोम-पः _ drinking सोम
  √गम्लृ → -ग _ going; सर्वत्र-गः _ going everywhere
  √जनी → -ज _ being born; अ-जः _ unborn

तद्धित प्रत्यय are added to words to derive उपपद ('subwords').

(1) श्रीमत्

.*mat[u]*, indicates possession:

श्री → श्रीमत् _ 'with श्री (fortune)';   श्रीमान् *1.1

.*mat[u]* changes to .*vat[u]* after words ending in *a* :

भग → भगवत् _ 'with भग (opulence)';   भगवान् *1.1

.*vat[i]* looks similar, but means 'like' or 'as', and forms अव्यय :

दण्ड → दण्डवत् _ like a rod

(2) समत्व

.*tva* (n.) and .*tā[p]* (f.) are used to form Abstract Nouns.

सम → समत्व *n., समता *f. _ 'sameness', equality

(3) गुह्यतम

.*tara* makes the Comparative and .*tama* the Superlative.

गुह्य → गुह्यतर _ more secret; गुह्यतम _ most secret

Similarly, with .*īyas[u]* and .*īṣṭha*:

श्री → श्रेयस् _ 'more श्री', better; श्रेष्ठ _ 'most श्री', best

(4) मङ्गलमय

.*maya* conveys 'full/made of':

मङ्गल → मङ्गलमय _ full of fortune

A similar प्रत्यय is .*mātra* ('just this much').

निमित्त → निमित्तमात्र _ the cause only

(5) सर्वत्र

Words formed with .*tas[i]* are अव्यय and mainly interpreted like पञ्चमी :

सर्व → सर्वतस् _ from /than all;   (by सन्धि) सर्वतः

मद् → मत्तः _ from me, than me

Similarly:

सर्व + .*tra* (indicating place) → सर्वत्र _ everywhere

सर्व + .*dā* (indicating time) → सर्वदा _ always

सर्व + .*thā* (indicating manner) → सर्वथा _ in every way

Important अव्यय are formed in this way:

	+ .tas[i]	+ .tra	+ .dā	+ .thā
सर्व	सर्वतः	सर्वत्र	सर्वदा	सर्वथा
अन्य	अन्यतः	अन्यत्र	अन्यदा	अन्यथा
एक	एकतः	एकत्र	एकदा	
किम्	कुतः	कुत्र (क्व)	कदा	(कथम्)
यद्	यतः	यत्र	यदा	यथा
तद्	ततः	तत्र	तदा	तथा

For repetition:

एक + .dhā → एकधा _ one time

सहस्र + .kṛtvas[u] → सहस्रकृत्वः _ thousand times

(6) कदाचिद्

Interrogatives are made indefinite by adding .cid or .cana.

कदा → कदाचिद् and कदाचन _ sometimes

Similarly, with अपि:

कुत्र → कुत्रचिद्, कुत्रापि _ somewhere

क्व → क्वचिद्, क्वापि _ somewhere

कुतः → कुतश्चिद्/कुतश्चन, कुतोपि _ from somewhere

कः *m.1.1 → कश्चिद्/कश्चन, कोपि _ someone

का *f.1.1 → काचिद्/काचन, कापि _ someone

के *m.1.3 → केचिद्/केचन, केपि _ someone

किम् *s.1.1 → किंश्चिद्/किंश्चन, किमपि _ something

कथम् → कथंश्चिद्/कथंश्चन, कथमपि _ somehow

(7) देवी

.ī[p] forms the Feminine Gender:

m. देव god → f. देवी _ goddess

योगिन् → (m. योगी) → f. योगिनी

Less frequently .ā[p] is used:

कृष्ण → कृष्णा _ name of द्रौपदी

(8) दैव

प्रत्यय in this group express relationships or moods, causing certain transformations inside the word:

देव god → दैव _ godly

ईश्वर lord → ऐश्वर्य _ lordship
वसुदेव → वासुदेव _ son or descendent of वसुदेव
यदु → यादव _ son of यदु
मुनि → मौन _ 'the mood of a मुनि', silence, gravity

31. Visheshana

विशेषण ('qualifier') qualify विशेष्य ('qualified') either as
    Adjektive: श्यामः रामः _ dark राम
    Epithet: एकपत्निः रामः _ one-wife राम
    Participle: सङ्कीर्तितः रामः _ glorified राम
    Pronoun: सः रामः _ that राम, (or:) he is राम
    Number: त्रयः रामाः _ three राम
    or Noun: राजा रामः _ King राम

They may describe a
    Class: क्षौमं वसनम् _ silk fabric
    Quality: श्यामः रामः _ dark राम
    or Activity: विहारी देवः _ sporting देव

Gender: विशेषण have either नियत-लिङ्ग (fixed gender)
    अयोध्यायाः *f.6.1 (remains fem.) रामः *m.1.1 _ राम of अयोध्या
or वाच्य-लिङ्ग (changeable gender), taking लिङ्ग, विभक्ति and वचन of the विशेष्य:
    सुन्दरः नरः *m.1.1 _ beautiful man; सुन्दरौ नरौ *m.1.2 _ two beautiful men
    सुन्दरी स्त्री *f.1.1 _ beautiful woman
    सुन्दरम् कुलम् *n.1.1 _ beautiful family
When the विशेष्य is अव्यय, the विशेषण takes नपुंसकलिङ्ग:
    महत् *n.1.1 स्वः _ the great sky (स्वर्)

One विशेषण can have more than one विशेष्य. The following rules apply:

(1) Regarding वचन
Considering many विशेष्य individually:
    रामः च कृष्णः च सुन्दरः *m.1.1 _ राम [is beautiful] und कृष्ण ist beautiful
Considering many विशेष्य together:
    रामः च कृष्णः च सुन्दरौ *m.1.2 _ राम and कृष्ण are [both] beautiful
Sometimes a विशेषण remains in एकवचन, although the विशेष्य is in बहुवचन:
    वेदाः *m.1.3 प्रमाणम् *n.1.1 _ the [many] वेद are the [one] standard

(2) Regarding लिङ्ग

(m.) over (f.):

श्री *f. च विष्णुः *m. च सुन्दरौ *m.1.2 _ लक्ष्मी and विष्णु are beautiful

(n.) over (m.) and (f.):

कृष्णः *m. यमुना *f. वृन्दावनम् *n. श्यामानि *n.1.3 _ कृष्ण, यमुना and वृन्दावन are dark

---

32. Samasa

There are four main types of समास, explained by विग्रह ('separating' their components into a simple expression) _ रागद्वेष देवदास श्यामराम पीताम्बर.

(1) राग-द्वेष

The first type is called द्वन्द्व ('pair'), where two or more components have the same value.

रागः च द्वेषः च इति राग-द्वेषौ *m.1.2 _ राग-द्वेष means attachment and aversion

सुखम् च दुःखम् च इति सुख-दुःखे *n.1.2 _ happiness and distress

सिद्धिः च असिद्धिः च इति सिद्ध्यसिद्धी *f.1.2 _ success and failure

With more than two components, the समास is declined in बहुवचन:

चन्द्रः च अर्कः च अनिलः च इति चन्द्राकानिलाः *m.1.3 _ moon, sun and wind

But when all components are seen in समाहार (as a unit), the समास is declined in एकवचन:

रागः च द्वेषः च इति राग-द्वेषः *m.1.1 _ attachment and aversion

(2) देव-दास

The characteristic of तत्पुरुष ('his servant') is that the components are related by one of the cases. In English this relationship is shown by a preposition (by, for, from, ...).

योगम् *2.1 आरूढः इति योगारूढः _ ascended to योग

योगेन *3.1 युक्तः इति योग-युक्तः _ endowed with योग

देवाय *4.1 देयम् इति देव-देयम् _ given to god

योगात् *5.1 भ्रष्टः इति योग-भ्रष्टः _ fallen from योग

देवस्य *6.1 दासः इति देव-दासः _ servant of god

कर्मणाम् *6.3 इन्द्रियम् इति कर्मेन्द्रियम् _ sense of activities

योगे *7.1 युक्तः इति योग-युक्तः _ connected in योग

द्विजेषु *7.3 उत्तमः इति द्विजोत्तमः _ best among twice-born

With pronouns:

मम *6.1 भक्तिः इति मद्धक्तः _ my भक्ति

तस्य *6.1 अर्थम् इति तदर्थम् _ its purpose

The word order can be changed:

गुह्यानाम् *6.3 राजा इति गुह्य-राजा / राज-गुह्यम् _ the king /best of secrets

In the sense of identity:

धर्मस्य अमृतम् इति धर्मामृतम् _ the nectar of धर्म

or धर्मः एव अमृतम् इति धर्मामृतम् _ the Nectar that is धर्म

(3) श्याम-राम

When a word is qualified – usually a विशेष्य by a विशेषण , the समास is called कर्म-धारय (supporting activity). Both components are in the same case.

विशेषण + विशेष्य :

श्यामः *m.1.1 रामः *m.1.1 इति श्याम-रामः _ dark राम

पीतम् *n.1.1 अम्बरम् *n.1.1 इति पीताम्बरम् _ yellow garment

श्रीमती *f.1.1 भगवद्गीता *f.1.1 इति श्रीमद्भगवद्गीता _ blessed गीता

विशेषण + विशेषण :

श्यामः सुन्दरः इति श्यामसुन्दरः _ dark and beautiful

विशेषण as interrogative:

किम् नरः इति किन्नरः _ a human?

Special forms:

कुत्सितः योगी इति कुयोगी _ 'criticised', or bad योगी

देवेन सह इति सह-देवः _ together with God

समानम् रूपम् इति स-रूपम् _ of the same form

Often the beauty in something is compared to a lotus (which is broad, beautiful and with reddish corners) or the moon:

पद्मस्य इव लोचनम् इति पद्म-लोचनम् _ lotus(like) eye(s)

The word order can be reversed:

पद्मस्य इव मुखम् इति पद्म-मुखम् → मुख-पद्मम् _ lotus(like) mouth

चन्द्रस्य इव रामः इति चन्द्र-रामः → राम-चन्द्रः _ moon(like) राम

The negation is made in समास with the particle *na[ñ]*, of which only अ- remains:

न मलः इति अ-मलः _ 'no dirt', pure

न दृष्टम् पूर्वम् इति अ-दृष्ट-पूर्वम् _ not seen before

If the word begins with a vowel, अ- becomes अन् :

न अन्तः इति अनन्तः _ 'no end', endless

(4) पीताम्बर

When the समास refers to something which is not mentioned in it, it is called बहु-व्रीहि (who has 'much rice').

Compare (4) with the interpretation as (3):

(3) पीतम् अम्बरम् इति पीताम्बरम् *n. _ yellow garment

(4) पीतम् अम्बरम् यस्य सः पीताम्बरः *m. _ whose garment is yellow

(3) पद्मस्य इव लोचनम् इति पद्म-लोचनम् *n. _ lotus eye

(4) पद्मम् इव लोचनम् यस्य सः पद्म-लोचनः *m. _ who has lotus eyes

प्रसन्नः आत्मा यस्य सः प्रसन्नात्मा _ whose mind is satisfied

अनन्ताः बाहवः यस्य सः अनन्त-बाहुः _ whose arms (बाहु) are unlimited

दृढम् व्रतम् यस्य सः दृढ-व्रतः _ he whose vow is strict

---

33. Conjugation

धातु are conjugated into आख्यात (verb) by different processes, according to which specific process the धातु are listed in 10 गण (class) as:

1. भ्वादि-गण (भू-आदि, धातु list 'beginning with √भू'), 2. अदादि-, 3. ह्वादि-, 4. दिवादि-, 5. स्वादि-, 6. तुदादि-, 7. रुधादि-, 8. तनादि-, 9. क्र्यादि- and 10. चुरादि-गण. The number of this गण is always mentioned after the धातु – √अन प्राणने 2P. Verbs are differentiated according to पुरुष (पु॰, person) and वचन (व॰, number: Sing.-Dual-Pl.). We are using the following number code:

person		Western	एक-व॰	द्वि-व॰	बहु-व॰
प्रथम-पुरुष	first p. (he/she/it)	'third p.'	*1.1 he	*1.2 they both	*1.3 they all
मध्यम-पु॰	middle p. (you)	'second p.'	*2.1 you	*2.2 you both	*2.3 you all
उत्तम-पु॰	ultimate p. (I)	'first p.'	*3.1 I	*3.2 we both	*3.3 we all

The conjugation uses specific प्रत्यय, beginning with .ti[p] (.ti[p]-आदि, hence called तिबादि) and other विकरण ('transforming' particles). There are two sets of प्रत्यय – परस्मै-पद ('word for another', A) and आत्मने-पद ('word for one's self', P), originally used when the result of the action is intended for another, or for the doer, respectively.

P			A		
.ti[p]	.tas	.anti	.te	.āte	.ante
.si[p]	.thas	.tha	.se	.āthe	.dhve
.mi[p]	.vas	.mas	.e	.vahe	.mahe

In Active Voice, some धातु take only परस्मै-पद प्रत्यय, like *.ti[p]*, and are marked with 'P' (after the गण):

√रक्ष 1P + *.ti[p]* → रक्षति he protects

Some धातु take only आत्मने-पद प्रत्यय, like *.te*, and are marked with 'A':

√त्रैङ् 1A + *.te* → त्रायते he protects

Others can take both, are called उभय-पद ('word for both', 'U'):

√[डु]पचष् 1U + *.ti[p]* → पचति he cooks; + *.te* → पचते he cooks

Passive Voice is always formed with the A प्रत्यय, and the particle *.ya.* is inserted.

Active with P		
पचति	पचतः	पचन्ति
पचसि	पचथः	पचथ
पचामि	पचावः	पचामः

Active with A		
पचते	पचेते	पचन्ते
पचसे	पचेथे	पचध्वे
पचे	पचावहे	पचामहे

Passive with A		
पच्यते	पच्येते	पच्यन्ते
पच्यसे	पच्येथे	पच्यध्वे
पच्ये	पच्यावहे	पच्यामहे

(1) Rules regarding वचन

Verbs can indicate subjects collectively:

भीमः च अर्जुनः च पचतः *1.2 _ भीम and अर्जुन are [both] cooking

युधिष्ठिरः च भीमः च अर्जुनः च पचन्ति *1.3 _ ... are [all] cooking

... or individually:

भीमः च अर्जुनः च पचति *1.1 _ भीम [is] and अर्जुन is cooking.

युधिष्ठिरः च भीमः च अर्जुनः च पचति *1.1 _ ... 'is' cooking.

If the subjects are not named individually, this rule is not applicable:

ते पचन्ति *1.3 _ they are cooking

(2) regarding पुरुष

When there is more than one subject, the धातु is conjugated according to the highest पुरुष, i.e., उत्तम- over मध्यम- over प्रथम-पुरुष.

सः *1.1 च त्वं *2.1 च पचथः *2.2 _ he and you are cooking

सः *1.1 च त्वं *2.1 च अहं *3.1 च पचामः *3.3 _ he and you and I 'am' cooking

There are six Tenses indicating काल (time), and four moods indicating अर्थ (purpose):

1	लट्	वर्तमान-काल (present) he does
2	विधि-लिङ्	विधि (duty) and सम्भावन (possibility) he should/could
3	लोट्	प्रेरणा (command) he must
4	लङ्	अनद्यतन-भूतकाल (non-present-day past) he did
5	लुङ्	भूत-काल ([general] past) he did
6	लिट्	परोक्ष-भूतकाल (not witnessed past) he did
7	आशीर्-लिङ्	आशीर्वाद (blessing) let him
8	लुट्	अनद्यतन-भविष्यत्काल (non-present-day fut.) he will
9	लृट्	भविष्यत्-काल ([general] future) he will
10	लृङ्	कार्य-कारण (cause and effect) if he would ... he could

	P	√(डु)पचष् पाके 1U		A		
1 लट् वर्तमान- काल	पचति*1.1.1	पचतः	पचन्ति	पचते	पचेते	पचन्ते
	पचसि	पचथः	पचथ	पचसे	पचेथे	पचध्वे
	पचामि	पचावः	पचामः	पचे	पचावहे	पचामहे
2 विधि-लिङ् विधि /सम्भावन	पचेत्*2.1.1	पचेताम्	पचेयुः	पचेत	पचेयाताम्	पचेरन्
	पचेः	पचेतम्	पचेत	पचेथाः	पचेयाथाम्	पचेध्वम्
	पचेयम्	पचेव	पचेम	पचेय	पचेवहि	पचेमहि
3 लोट् प्रेरणा	पचतु*3.1.1	पचताम्	पचन्तु	पचताम्	पचेताम्	पचन्ताम्
	पच	पचतम्	पचत	पचस्व	पचेथाम्	पचध्वम्
	पचानि	पचाव	पचाम	पचै	पचावहै	पचामहै
4 लङ् अनद्यतन- भूतकाल	अपचत्	अपचताम्	अपचन्	अपचत	अपचेताम्	अपचन्त
	अपचः	अपचतम्	अपचत	अपचथाः	अपचेथाम्	अपचध्वम्
	अपचम्	अपचाव	अपचाम	अपचे	अपचावहि	अपचामहि
5 लुङ् भूत-काल	अपाक्षीत्	अपाक्ताम्	अपाक्षुः	अपक्त	अपक्षाताम्	अपक्षत
	अपाक्षीः	अपाक्तम्	अपाक्त	अपक्थाः	अपक्षाथाम्	अपग्ध्वम्
	अपाक्षम्	अपाक्ष्व	अपाक्ष्म	अपक्षि	अपक्ष्वहि	अपक्ष्महि
6 लिट् परोक्ष- भूतकाल	पपाच	पेचतुः	पेचुः	पेचे	पेचाते	पेचिरे
	पेचिथ	पेचतुः	पेच	पेचिषे	पेचाथे	पेचिध्वे
	पपाच	पेचिव	पेचिम	पेचे	पेचिवहे	पेचिमहे
7 आशीर्- लिङ् आशीर्वाद	पच्यात्	पच्यास्ताम्	पच्यासुः	पक्षीष्ट	पक्षीयास्ताम्	पक्षीरन्
	पच्याः	पच्यास्तम्	पच्यास्त	पक्षीष्ठाः	पक्षीयास्थाम्	पक्षीध्वम्
	पच्यासम्	पच्यास्व	पच्यास्म	पक्षीय	पक्षीवहि	पक्षीमहि
8 लुट् अनद्यतन- भविष्यत्काल	पक्ता	पक्तारौ	पक्तारः	पक्ता	पक्तारौ	पक्तारः
	पक्तासि	पक्तास्थः	पक्तास्थ	पक्तासे	पक्तासाथे	पक्ताध्वे
	पक्तास्मि	पक्तास्वः	पक्तास्मः	पक्ताहे	पक्तास्वहे	पक्तास्महे
9 लृट् भविष्यत्- काल	पक्ष्यति	पक्ष्यतः	पक्ष्यन्ति	पक्ष्यते	पक्ष्येते	पक्ष्यन्ते
	पक्ष्यसि	पक्ष्यथः	पक्ष्यथ	पक्ष्यसे	पक्ष्येथे	पक्ष्यध्वे
	पक्ष्यामि	पक्ष्यावः	पक्ष्यामः	पक्ष्ये	पक्ष्यावहे	पक्ष्यामहे
10 लृङ् कार्य-कारण	अपक्ष्यत्	अपक्ष्यताम्	अपक्ष्यन्	अपक्ष्यत	अपक्ष्येताम्	अपक्ष्यन्त
	अपक्ष्यः	अपक्ष्यतम्	अपक्ष्यत	अपक्ष्यथाः	अपक्ष्येथाम्	अपक्ष्यध्वम्
	अपक्ष्यम्	अपक्ष्याव	अपक्ष्याम	अपक्ष्ये	अपक्ष्यावहि	अपक्ष्यामहि

Important cases and verbs:

√भू सत्तायाम् 1P · √अस भुवि 2P

	√भू सत्तायाम् 1P			√अस भुवि 2P		
1 लट् वर्तमान-काल	भवति	भवतः	भवन्ति	अस्ति	स्तः	सन्ति
	भवसि	भवथः	भवथ	असि	स्थः	स्थ
	भवामि	भवावः	भवामः	अस्मि	स्वः	स्मः
2 विधि-लिङ् विधि /सम्भावन	भवेत्	भवेताम्	भवेयुः	स्यात्	स्याताम्	स्युः
	भवेः	भवेतम्	भवेत	स्याः	स्यातम्	स्यात
	भवेयम्	भवेव	भवेम	स्याम्	स्याव	स्याम
3 लोट् प्रेरणा	भवतु	भवताम्	भवन्तु	अस्तु	स्ताम्	सन्तु
	भव	भवतम्	भवत	एधि	स्तम्	स्त
	भवानि	भवाव	भवाम	असानि	असाव	असाम
4 लङ् अनद्यतन-भूतकाल	अभवत्	अभवताम्	अभवन्	आसीत्	आस्ताम्	आसन्
	अभवः	अभवतम्	अभवत	आसीः	आस्तम्	आस्त
	अभवम्	अभवाव	अभवाम	आसम्	आस्व	आस्म
9 लृट् भविष्यत्-काल	भविष्यति	भविष्यतः	भविष्यन्ति	भविष्यति	भविष्यतः	भविष्यन्ति
	भविष्यसि	भविष्यथः	भविष्यथ	भविष्यसि	भविष्यथः	भविष्यथ
	भविष्यामि	भविष्यावः	भविष्यामः	भविष्यामि	भविष्यावः	भविष्यामः

√ज्ञा अवबोधने 9P · √स्था गति-निवृत्तौ 1P

	√ज्ञा अवबोधने 9P			√स्था गति-निवृत्तौ 1P		
1 लट् वर्तमान-काल	जानाति	जानीतः	जानन्ति	तिष्ठति	तिष्ठतः	तिष्ठन्ति
	जानासि	जानीथः	जानीथ	तिष्ठसि	तिष्ठथः	तिष्ठथ
	जानामि	जानीवः	जानीमः	तिष्ठामि	तिष्ठावः	तिष्ठामः
2 विधि-लिङ् विधि /सम्भावन	जानीयात्	जानीयाताम्	जानीयुः	तिष्ठेत्	तिष्ठेताम्	तिष्ठेयुः
	जानीयाः	जानीयातम्	जानीयात	तिष्ठेः	तिष्ठेतम्	तिष्ठेत
	जानीयाम्	जानीयाव	जानीयाम	तिष्ठेयम्	तिष्ठेव	तिष्ठेम
3 लोट् प्रेरणा	जानातु	जानीताम्	जानन्तु	तिष्ठतु	तिष्ठताम्	तिष्ठन्तु
	जानीहि	जानीतम्	जानीत	तिष्ठ	तिष्ठतम्	तिष्ठत
	जानानि	जानाव	जानाम	तिष्ठानि	तिष्ठाव	तिष्ठाम
4 लङ् अनद्यतन-भूतकाल	अजानात्	अजानीताम्	अजानन्	अतिष्ठत्	अतिष्ठताम्	अतिष्ठन्
	अजानाः	अजानीतम्	अजानीत	अतिष्ठः	अतिष्ठतम्	अतिष्ठत
	अजानाम्	अजानीव	अजानीम	अतिष्ठम्	अतिष्ठाव	अतिष्ठाम
9 लृट् भविष्यत्-काल	ज्ञास्यति	ज्ञास्यतः	ज्ञास्यन्ति	स्थास्यति	स्थास्यतः	स्थास्यन्ति
	ज्ञास्यसि	ज्ञास्यथः	ज्ञास्यथ	स्थास्यसि	स्थास्यथः	स्थास्यथ
	ज्ञास्यामि	ज्ञास्यावः	ज्ञास्यामः	स्थास्यामि	स्थास्यावः	स्थास्यामः

	√गम्लृ गतौ 1P			√इषु इच्छायाम् 6P		
1 लट् वर्तमान- काल	गच्छति	गच्छतः	गच्छन्ति	इच्छति	इच्छतः	इच्छन्ति
	गच्छसि	गच्छथः	गच्छथ	इच्छसि	इच्छथः	इच्छथ
	गच्छामि	गच्छावः	गच्छामः	इच्छामि	इच्छावः	इच्छामः
2 विधि-लिङ् विधि /सम्भावन	गच्छेत्	गच्छेताम्	गच्छेयुः	इच्छेत्	इच्छेताम्	इच्छेयुः
	गच्छेः	गच्छेतम्	गच्छेत	इच्छेः	इच्छेतम्	इच्छेत
	गच्छेयम्	गच्छेव	गच्छेम	इच्छेयम्	इच्छेव	इच्छेम
3 लोट् प्रेरणा	गच्छतु	गच्छताम्	गच्छन्तु	इच्छतु	इच्छताम्	इच्छन्तु
	गच्छ	गच्छतम्	गच्छत	इच्छ	इच्छतम्	इच्छत
	गच्छानि	गच्छाव	गच्छाम	इच्छानि	इच्छाव	इच्छाम
4 लङ् अनद्यतन- भूतकाल	अगच्छत्	अगच्छताम्	अगच्छन्	ऐच्छत्	ऐच्छताम्	ऐच्छन्
	अगच्छः	अगच्छतम्	अगच्छत	ऐच्छः	ऐच्छतम्	ऐच्छत
	अगच्छम्	अगच्छाव	अगच्छाम	ऐच्छम्	ऐच्छाव	ऐच्छाम
9 लृट् भविष्यत्- काल	गमिष्यति	गमिष्यतः	गमिष्यन्ति	एषिष्यति	एषिष्यतः	एषिष्यन्ति
	गमिष्यसि	गमिष्यथः	गमिष्यथ	एषिष्यसि	एषिष्यथः	एषिष्यथ
	गमिष्यामि	गमिष्यावः	गमिष्यामः	एषिष्यामि	एषिष्यावः	एषिष्यामः

	√स्मृ आध्याने 1P			√दृशिर् प्रेक्षणे 1P		
1 लट् वर्तमान- काल	स्मरति	स्मरतः	स्मरन्ति	पश्यति	पश्यतः	पश्यन्ति
	स्मरसि	स्मरथः	स्मरथ	पश्यसि	पश्यथः	पश्यथ
	स्मरामि	स्मरावः	स्मरामः	पश्यामि	पश्यावः	पश्यामः
2 विधि-लिङ् विधि /सम्भावन	स्मरेत्	स्मरेताम्	स्मरेयुः	पश्येत्	पश्येताम्	पश्येयुः
	स्मरेः	स्मरेतम्	स्मरेत	पश्येः	पश्येतम्	पश्येत
	स्मरेयम्	स्मरेव	स्मरेम	पश्येयम्	पश्येव	पश्येम
3 लोट् प्रेरणा	स्मरतु	स्मरताम्	स्मरन्तु	पश्यतु	पश्यताम्	पश्यन्तु
	स्मर	स्मरतम्	स्मरत	पश्य	पश्यतम्	पश्यत
	स्मराणि	स्मराव	स्मराम	पश्यानि	पश्याव	पश्याम
4 लङ् अनद्यतन- भूतकाल	अस्मरत्	अस्मरताम्	अस्मरन्	अपश्यत्	अपश्यताम्	अपश्यन्
	अस्मरः	अस्मरतम्	अस्मरत	अपश्यः	अपश्यतम्	अपश्यत
	अस्मरम्	अस्मराव	अस्मराम	अपश्यम्	अपश्याव	अपश्याम
9 लृट् भविष्यत्- काल	स्मरिष्यति	स्मरिष्यतः	स्मरिष्यन्ति	द्रक्ष्यति	द्रक्ष्यतः	द्रक्ष्यन्ति
	स्मरिष्यसि	स्मरिष्यथः	स्मरिष्यथ	द्रक्ष्यसि	द्रक्ष्यथः	द्रक्ष्यथ
	स्मरिष्यामि	स्मरिष्यावः	स्मरिष्यामः	द्रक्ष्यामि	द्रक्ष्यावः	द्रक्ष्यामः

√डुकृञ् करणे 8U

1 लट् वर्तमान-काल	करोति	कुरुतः	कुर्वन्ति
	करोषि	कुरुथः	कुरुथ
	करोमि	कुर्वः	कुर्मः
2 विधि-लिङ् विधि /सम्भावन	कुर्यात्	कुर्याताम्	कुर्युः
	कुर्यः	कुर्यातम्	कुर्यात
	कुर्याम्	कुर्याव	कुर्याम
3 लोट् प्रेरणा	करोतु	कुरुताम्	कुर्वन्तु
	करु	कुरुतम्	कुरुत
	करवाणि	करवाव	करवाम
4 लङ् अनद्यतन-भूतकाल	अकरोत्	अकुरुताम्	अकुर्वन्
	अकरोः	अकुरुतम्	अकुरुत
	अकरवम्	अकुर्व	अकुर्म
9 लृट् भविष्यत्-काल	करिष्यति	करिष्यतः	करिष्यन्ति
	करिष्यसि	करिष्यथः	करिष्यथ
	करिष्यामि	करिष्यावः	करिष्यामः

√शक्लृ शक्तौ 5P

1 लट् वर्तमान-काल	शक्नोति	शक्नुतः	शक्नुवन्ति
	शक्नोषि	शक्नुथः	शक्नुथ
	शक्नोमि	शक्नुवः	शक्नुमः
2 विधि-लिङ् विधि /सम्भावन	शक्नुयात्	शक्नुयाताम्	शक्नुयुः
	शक्नुयाः	शक्नुयातम्	शक्नुयात
	शक्नुयाम्	शक्नुयाव	शक्नुयाम
3 लोट् प्रेरणा	शक्नोतु	शक्नुताम्	शक्नुवन्तु
	शक्नुहि	शक्नुतम्	शक्नुत
	शक्नवानि	शक्नवाव	शक्नवाम
4 लङ् अनद्यतन-भूतकाल	अशक्नोत्	अशक्नुताम्	अशक्नुवन्
	अशक्नोः	अशक्नुतम्	अशक्नुत
	अशक्नवम्	अशक्नुव	अशक्नुम
9 लृट् भविष्यत्-काल	शक्ष्यति	शक्ष्यतः	शक्ष्यन्ति
	शक्ष्यसि	शक्ष्यथः	शक्ष्यथ
	शक्ष्यामि	शक्ष्यावः	शक्ष्यामः

√सेवृ सेवने 1A

1 लट् वर्तमान-काल	सेवते	सेवेते	सेवन्ते
	सेवसे	सेवेथे	सेवध्वे
	सेवे	सेवावहे	सेवामहे
2 विधि-लिङ् विधि /सम्भावन	सेवेत	सेवेयाताम्	सेवेरन्
	सेवेथाः	सेवेयाथाम्	सेवेध्वम्
	सेवेय	सेवेवहि	सेवेमहि
3 लोट् प्रेरणा	सेवताम्	सेवेताम्	सेवन्ताम्
	सेवस्व	सेवेथाम्	सेवध्वम्
	सेवै	सेवावहै	सेवामहै
4 लङ् अनद्यतन-भूतकाल	असेवत	असेवेताम्	असेवन्त
	असेवथाः	असेवेथाम्	असेवध्वम्
	असेवे	असेवावहि	असेवामहि
9 लृट् भविष्यत्-काल	सेविष्यते	सेविष्येते	सेविष्यन्ते
	सेविष्यसे	सेविष्येथे	सेविष्यध्वे
	सेविष्ये	सेविष्यावहे	सेविष्यामहे

√डुलभष् प्राप्तौ 1A

1 लट् वर्तमान-काल	लभते	लभेते	लभन्ते
	लभसे	लभेथे	लभध्वे
	लभे	लभावहे	लभामहे
2 विधि-लिङ् विधि /सम्भावन	लभेत	लभेयाताम्	लभेरन्
	लभेथाः	लभेयाथाम्	लभेध्वम्
	लभेय	लभेवहि	लभेमहि
3 लोट् प्रेरणा	लभताम्	लभेताम्	लभन्ताम्
	लभस्व	लभेथाम्	लभध्वम्
	लभै	लभावहै	लभामहै
4 लङ् अनद्यतन-भूतकाल	अलभत	अलभेताम्	अलभन्त
	अलभथाः	अलभेथाम्	अलभध्वम्
	अलभे	अलभावहि	अलभामहि
9 लृट् भविष्यत्-काल	लप्स्यते	लप्स्येते	लप्स्यन्ते
	लप्स्यसे	लप्स्येथे	लप्स्यध्वे
	लप्स्ये	लप्स्यावहे	लप्स्यामहे

35. Anvaya

The अन्वय (regular word 'order', syntax) in an Active sentence:

कर्ता (subject)	कर्म (object)	क्रिया (verb)
देव: *1.1	नरम् *2.1	रक्षति ।
God	man	protects.

Other words can be placed wherever they fit the intention best:

अर्जुन *8.1 लोके *7.1 देव: हस्तेन *3.1 नरम् तदनुग्रहाय *4.1 भयात् *5.1 रक्षति ।

Oh Arjuna! In the world God with [his] hand man to favor him, from danger protects.

विशेषण come before their respective विशेष्य .

भक्त *8.1   अर्जुन *8.1 अस्मिन् *7.1 लोके *7.1 दयालु: *1.1 देव: *1.1 ...

Oh Bhakta Arjuna!   In this   world   the merciful God   etc.

Since the grammatical value of a word is fixed in the case ending, one can rearrange the words of a Sanskrit sentence in any order and the meaning does not change.

36. Pronouns

The Pronouns यद् and तद् can be used as correlatives in any of their forms. किम् (what?) is the original Interrogative from which अव्यय like कुत्र are derived.

क: *m.1.1 के *m.1.3	य:...स: ये...ते
का *f.1.1 का: *f.1.3 who	या...सा या:...ता: who...he
किम् *n.1.1 कानि *n.1.3 what	यद्...तद् यानि...तानि which...that
केन *3.1 with whom /what	येन...तेन with which... with that
कस्मात् *5.1 why	यस्मात्...तस्मात् because...therefore
कुत्र/क्व where	यत्र...तत्र where...there
कुत: wherefrom /why	यत:...तत: wherefrom...therefrom
कथम् how	यथा...तथा as...so
कदा when	यदा...तदा when...then
	यदि...तर्हि if...then
किम् ind.	यद्...तद्
किमर्थम् ind. why	यदर्थम्...तदर्थम् because...therefore
कति how many	यति...तति how many...so many
कीयत् how much	यावत्...तावत् how much...so much
कीदृक् what kind of	यादृक्...तादृक् as...so

किम् as question marker:

    ग्रामं गच्छसि किम् ? Are you going to the village?

वा, indicating option and question:

    गीता भागवतं वा ? गीता or भागवतम्?

    ग्रामं गच्छसि वा ? Are you going to the village?

Conditional:

    यदि ग्रामं गच्छसि or ग्रामं गच्छसि चेद् _ if you go to the village, ...

Distributive:

When the relative pronoun यद् (in any of its forms) is doubled, it acquires a distributive sense. The double relative is used along with a double correlative.

    यद् यद् श्रेष्ठः आचरति ... तद् तद् जनः _ whatever a great man does ... that very same thing people [also do]

Emphatic:

When the relative pronoun यद् is used in combination with the interrogative किम्, in any of their forms, they denote emphasis and indefiniteness.

    येन केन प्रकारेण _ by whatever (any) means

In the following cases a word is द्विरुक्ति ('said twice'):

Repetition

    संस्मृत्य संस्मृत्य ('पुनः पुनः' संस्मृत्य) _ repeatedly remembering

Generalisation

    यद् यद् _ whatever

    गृहे गृहे _ in each house

Criticism, Honor (with सम्बोधन)

    अर्जुन अर्जुन _ oh अर्जुन, अर्जुन!

Abundance

    अहो भाग्यम् [अहो] भाग्यम् _ what immense fortune!

Excitement

    पश्य पश्य पश्य _ look, look, look!

"Whenever I look around me, in the vast region of Hindoo Mythology, I discover piety in the garb of allegory: and I see Morality, at every turn, blended with every tale; and, as far as I can rely on my own judgment, it appears the most complete and ample system of Moral Allegory that the world has ever produced." (Charles Stuart, Irish-born British Army General in India, 1758-1828)

"If the attainment of the middle path consisted in a mere surrender to instinct, as the bewailers of 'naturalism' suppose, the profoundest philosophical speculation that the human mind has ever known would have no raison d'être. But, as we study the philosophy of the Upanishads, the impression grows on us that the attainment of this path is not exactly the simplest of tasks. Our Western superciliousness in the face of these Indian insights is a mark of our barbarian nature, which has not the remotest inkling of their extraordinary depth and astonishing psychological accuracy. We are still so uneducated that we actually need laws from without, and a task-master or Father above, to show us what is good and the right thing to do. And because we are still such barbarians, any trust in human nature seems to us a dangerous and unethical naturalism. Why is this? Because under the barbarian's thin veneer of culture the wild beast lurks in readiness, amply justifying his fear. But the beast is not tamed by locking it up in cage. There is no morality without freedom. When the barbarian lets loose the beast within him, that is not freedom but bondage. Barbarism must first be vanquished before freedom can be won. This happens, in principle, when the basic root and driving force of morality are felt by the individual as constituents of his own nature and not as external restrictions." (Carl Gustav Jung, Swiss psychotherapist, 1875-1961)

"The Hindu creed is monotheistic and of very high ethical value; and when I look back on my life in India and the thousands of good friends I have left there among all classes of the native community, when I remember those honorable, industrious, orderly, law-abiding, sober, manly men, I look over England and wonder whether there is anything in Christianity which can give a higher ethical creed than that which is now professed by the large majority of the people of India. I do not see it in London society, I do not see it in the slums of the East End, I do not see it on the London Stock Exchange. I think that the morality of India will compare very favorably with the morality of any country in Western Europe." (Sir Lepel Henry Griffin, British diplomat and writer, 1840-1908)

---

37. Mushika

मुनि-मूषिक-कथा ।[292]

पुरातन-काले तपोवने कश्चिद् मुनिः आसीत्। तस्य नाम महातपाः। कदाचिद् सः मुनिः आश्रमस्य समीपे काक-मुखात् परिभ्रष्टम् एकम् मूषिक-शावकम् दृष्टवान् ।[293]

करुणया तम् मूषिक-शावकम् आश्रमम् आनीतवान्। प्रतिदिनम् धान्य-कणान् दत्त्वा तम् प्रीत्या पोषितवान्। अल्पेन एव कालेन मूषिकः सम्यक् प्रवृद्धः।[294]

अथ कदाचिद् कश्चन मार्जालः तत्र आगतवान्। मार्जालात् भीतः मुषिकः मुनेः समीपम् आगत्य उक्तवान्। पूज्य ! एषः मार्जालः माम् खादितुम् आगच्छति। कृपया मार्जालात् माम् रक्षतु भवान् इति। मुनिः - भीतिः मा अस्तु। भवन्तम् अपि अहम् मार्जालम् करोमि। इति उक्त्वा स्व-तपः-प्रभावेण तम् मूषिकम् मार्जालम् कृतवान्।[295]

पुनः कदाचिद् कश्चन शुनकः तत्र आगतवान्। शुनकात् भीतः मार्जालः मुनेः समीपम् आगत्य उक्तवान्। पूज्य ! एतम् दुष्ट-शुनकम् पश्यतु। सः माम् खादितुम् इच्छति। कृपया शुनकात् माम् रक्षतु भवान् इति। मुनिः - चिन्ता मा अस्तु। भवन्तम् अपि अहम् शुनकम् करोमि।[296]

पुनः कदाचिद् कश्चन व्याघ्रः तत्र आगतवान्। व्याघ्रात् भीतः शुनकः पुनः अपि मुनेः समीपम् एव शरणम् गतवान्। मुनिम् उक्तवान् च - पूज्य ! एतस्मात् भयङ्करात् व्याघ्रात् माम् रक्षतु भवान् इति। मुनिः यथा-पूर्वम् चिन्ताम् मा करोतु भवान्। भवन्तम् अपि अहम् व्याघ्रम् करोमि।[297]

अन्तरम् च सः व्याघ्रः निर्भयेन आश्रमे सर्वत्र अटति। मुनिः तु तम् व्याघ्रम् मूषिकम् इव पश्यति स्म। तस्मात् व्याघ्रात् तस्य तु किञ्चिद् अपि भयम् न आसीत् एव।[298]

आश्रमे अन्ये अपि जनाः वासम् कुर्वन्ति स्म। तम् व्याघ्रम् दृष्ट्वा ते सर्वे वदन्ति स्म। एषः व्याघ्रः वास्तविकः व्याघ्रः न अस्ति। सः तु कश्चन मूषिकः। एषः मुनिः तपः-प्रभावेण तम् मूषिकम् व्याघ्रम् कृतवान् अस्ति। अतः एषः व्याघ्र-रूपः मूषिकः एव इति।[299]

तद् श्रुत्वा व्याघ्रः चिन्तितवान्। यावत्-पर्यन्तम् एषः मुनिः जीवति तावत्-पर्यन्तम् जनाः एवम् एव वदन्ति। ते माम् मूषिकम् एव मन्यन्ते न तु व्याघ्रम्। एषा अपकीर्तिः दूरी-करणीया चेद् मया मुनिः मारणीयः एव। अतः तम् इदानीम् एव मारयामि।[300]

इति चिन्तयित्वा मुनेः समीपम् गतवान्। परन्तु मुनिः व्याघ्रस्य दुरालोचनम् ज्ञातवान्। कोपेन व्याघ्रम् दृष्ट्वा पुनः मूषिकः भव इति उक्त्वा तम् व्याघ्रम् पुनः अपि मूषिकम् कृतवान्। मूषिकः लज्जया ततः पलायनम् कृतवान्।[301]

प्रणम्य शिरसा विष्णुं त्रैलोक्याधिपतिं प्रभुम् । नानाशास्त्रोद्धृतं वक्ष्ये राजनीतिसमुच्चयम् ॥ अधीत्येदं यथाशास्त्रं नरो जानाति सत्तमः । धर्मोपदेशविख्यातं कार्याकार्यं शुभाशुभम् ॥302 अधीते य इदं नित्यं नीतिशास्त्रं शृणोति च । न पराभवमाप्नोति शक्रादपि कदाचन ॥303 श्रुतो हितोपदेशो ऽयं पाटवं संस्कृतोक्तिषु । वाचां सर्वत्र वैचित्र्यं नीतिविद्यां ददाति च ॥304

"To render the construction of the Samscred language, and its emphatic mode of expression, more familiar to their pupils, the Guru employs various short sentences clothed in Samscred verse, which are called Shloga. These verses serve not only as examples of the manner in which the words must be combined with each other, but contain, at the same time, most excellent moral maxims, which are thus imprinted in the minds of the young people as if in play; so that, while learning the language, they are taught rules proper for forming their character, and directing their future conduct in life. That the reader may be better enabled to conceive some idea of the morality of the Brahmans, I shall here subjoin a specimen of these sentences. ... The wounds occasioned by a slanderous tongue occasion far more pain, and are much more difficult to be healed, than those which proceed from fire and the sword. ... He who revenges an injury enjoys a pleasure which endures only a day; but he who forgives receives a satisfaction which will accompany him through life." (Paulinus of St. Bartholomew, Austrian Carmelite missionary and Orientalist, 1748-1806)

श्लोकेन वा तदर्धेन तदर्धार्धाक्षरेण वा । अबन्ध्यं दिवसं कुर्याद् दानाध्ययनकर्मभिः ॥305

Story 1 – Raja

अस्ति भागीरथी-तीरे पाटलिपुत्र-नाम-धेयम् नगरम् । तत्र सुदर्शनः नाम नर-पतिः आसीत् । सः भू-पतिः एकदा श्लोक-द्वयम् शुश्राव ।306

अनेकसंशयोच्छेदि परोक्षार्थस्य दर्शकम् । सर्वस्य लोचनं शास्त्रं यस्य नास्त्यन्ध एव सः ॥307 यौवनं धनसम्पत्तिः प्रभुत्वमविवेकिता । एकैकमप्यनर्थाय किमु यत्र चतुष्टयम् ॥308

इति आकर्ण्य सः राजा उवाच । अस्ति कश्चिद् विद्वान् यः मम पुत्राणाम् नीति-शास्त्र-उपदेशेन पुनर्जन्म कारयितुम् समर्थः ।309 विष्णु-शर्मा-नामा महा-पण्डितः अब्रवीत् । षड्-मास-अभ्यन्तरे भवत्-पुत्रान् अहम् नीति-शास्त्र-अभिज्ञान् करिष्यामि ।310

तस्य विष्णु-शर्मणः करे पुत्रान् समर्पितवान् । अथ प्रासाद-पृष्ठे राज-पुत्राणाम् पुरस्तात् पण्डितः अब्रवीत् । भो राज-पुत्राः शृणुत ।311

वित्त-हीनाः सुहृन्मताः बुद्धिमन्तः काक-कूर्म-मृग-आखुवत् आशु कार्याणि साधयन्ति ।312 राज-पुत्राः ऊचुः । कथम् एतद् । सः अब्रवीत् ।313

2 – Kaka

अस्ति गोदावरी-तीरे विशालः शाल्मली-तरुः। तत्र रात्रौ पक्षिणः निवसन्ति।[314] अथ कदाचिद् रात्रौ लघुपतनक-नामा वायसः व्याधम् अपश्यत्।[315] तेन व्याधेन तण्डुल-कणान् विकीर्य जालम् विस्तीर्णम्। सः च तत्र प्रच्छन्नः भूत्वा स्थितः।[316]

अस्मिन् एव काले चित्रग्रीव-नामा कपोत-राजः स-परिवारः तान् तण्डुल-कणान् अवलोकयामास।[317] कपोत-राजः तण्डुल-कण-लुब्धान् कपोतान् प्रति आह। कुतः अत्र निर्जने वने तण्डुल-कणानाम् सम्भवः।[318] भद्रम् इदम् न पश्यामि। कङ्कणस्य तु लोभेन यथा पथिकः सम्मृतः।[319] कपोताः ऊचुः - कथम् एतद्। सः अब्रवीत्। एकदा दक्षिण-अरण्ये चरन् अहम् अपश्यम्।[320]

3 – Vyaghra

एकः वृद्धः व्याघ्रः सरः-तीरे ब्रूते। भो भो पन्थाः। इदम् सुवर्ण-कङ्कणम् गृह्यताम्।[321] ततः केनचिद् पान्थेन आलोचितम्। भाग्येन एतद् सम्भवति।[322] किन्तु सर्वत्र अर्थ-अर्जन-प्रवृत्तौ सन्देहः एव। प्रकाशम् ब्रूते। कुत्र तव कङ्कणम्। व्याघ्रः हस्तम् प्रसार्य दर्शयति।[323] पान्थः अवदत्। मार-आत्मके त्वयि कथम् विश्वासः।[324]

व्याघ्रः उवाच। शृणु रे पान्थ। मे पुत्राः दाराः च मृताः अहम् वंश-हीनः च।[325] ततः केनचिद् धार्मिकेण अहम् उपदिष्टः। दान-धर्म-आदिकम् चरतु भवान् इति।[326] तद्-उपदेशात् इदानीम् अहम् स्नान-शीलः दाता। वृद्धः गलित-नख-दन्तः कथम् न विश्वास-भूमिः। तद् अत्र सरसि स्नात्वा सुवर्ण-कङ्कणम् इदम् गृहाण।[327]

ततः यावत् असौ सरः स्नातुम् प्रविष्टः तावत् महा-पङ्के निमग्नः।[328] तम् पङ्के पतितम् दृष्ट्वा व्याघ्रः अवदत्। अहह महा-पङ्के पतितः असि। अतः त्वाम् अहम् उत्थापयामि।[329] सः पान्थः अचिन्तयत्। तद् मया भद्रम् न कृतम् यद् अत्र मार-आत्मके विश्वासः कृतः।[330] इति चिन्तयन् असौ व्याघ्रेण खादितः।[331]

2 – cont.

अतः अहम् ब्रवीमि। कङ्कणस्य तु लोभेन इत्यादि।[332] एतद् वचनम् श्रुत्वा कश्चिद् कपोतः स-दर्पम् आह। सर्वत्र एवम् विचारे तु भोजने अपि अ-प्रवर्तताम्।[333] एतद् श्रुत्वा तण्डुल-कण-लोभेन सर्वे कपोताः तत्र उपविष्टाः। अन्तरम् ते सर्वे जाल-निबद्धाः बभूवुः।[334] ततः यस्य वचनात् तत्र अवलम्बिताः तम् सर्वे तिरस्कुर्वन्ति स्म।[335]

तिरस्कारम् श्रुत्वा चित्रग्रीवः उवाच। न अयम् अस्य दोषः। यतः। आपदाम् हितः अपि हेतुताम् आयाति।[336] इदानीम् अपि एवम् क्रियताम्। जालम् आदाय उड्डीयताम्। सर्वे पक्षिणः जालम् आदाय उत्पतिताः।[337]

अथ लुब्धकम् निवृत्तम् दृष्ट्वा कपोताः ऊचुः। स्वामिन्। किम् इदानीम् कर्तुम् उचितम्।[338] चित्रग्रीवः उवाच। अस्माकम् मित्रम् हिरण्यकः नाम मूषिक-राजः गण्डकी-तीरे चित्रवने निवसति। सः अस्माकम् पाशान् छेत्स्यति।[339]

इति आलोच्य सर्वे हिरण्यक-समीपम् गताः। पाश-बद्धान् च एतान् दृष्ट्वा हिरण्यकः उवाच।[340] सखे किम् एतद्। चित्रग्रीवः उवाच - अस्माकम् प्राक्तन-जन्म-कर्मणः फलम् एतद्।[341] इति आकर्ण्य कपोतानाम् बन्धनानि तेन छिन्नानि।[342]

अथ लघुपतनक-नामा काकः सर्व-वृत्तान्त-दर्शी स-आश्चर्यम् इदम् आह।[343] अहम् अपि त्वया सह मैत्रीम् कर्तुम् इच्छामि। हिरण्यकः विहस्य आह। का त्वया सह मैत्री। यतः।[344] भक्ष्य-भक्षकयोः प्रीतिः विपत्तेः कारणम् मतम्। शृगालात् पाश-बद्धः मृगः काकेन रक्षितः।[345] वायसः अब्रवीत् - कथम् एतद्। हिरण्यकः कथयति।[346]

4 – Mriga

अस्ति मगध-देशे चम्पकवती नाम अरण्यानी। तस्याम् महता स्नेहेन मृग-काकौ निवसतः।[347] सः च मृगः केनचिद् शृगालेन अवलोकितः। तम् दृष्ट्वा शृगालः अचिन्तयत्।[348] अः एतद् मांसम् कथम् भक्षयामि। इति आलोच्य उपसृत्य अब्रवीत्। मित्र कुशलम् ते।

मृगेण उक्तम् - कः त्वम्।[349] सः ब्रूते। क्षुद्रबुद्धि-नामा जम्बुकः अहम्। अत्र अरण्ये बन्धु-हीनः एकाकी निवसामि।[350] ततः पश्चात् तौ मृगस्य वास-भूमिम् गतौ। तत्र सुबुद्धि-नामा काकः निवसति मृगस्य चिर-मित्रम्।[351]

तौ दृष्ट्वा काकः अवदत्। सखे चित्राङ्ग कः अयम् द्वितीयः।[352] मृगः ब्रूते। अस्मद्-सख्यम् इच्छन् अयम् जम्बुकः आगतः। काकः ब्रूते।[353] कस्यचिद् अ-ज्ञात-कुल-शीलस्य वासः न देयः। मार्जारस्य हि दोषेण गृध्रः जरद्रवः हतः।[354] तौ आहतुः - कथम् एतद्। काकः कथयति।[355]

5 – Marjara

अस्ति भागीरथी-तीरे गृध्रकूट-नाम्नि पर्वते महान् पर्कटी-वृक्षः। तस्य कोटरे गलित-नख-नयनः जरद्रव-नामा गृध्रः प्रतिवसति।[356] अथ कृपया तद्-वृक्ष-वासिनः पक्षिणः स्व-आहारात् किञ्चिद् तस्मै ददति। तेन असौ जीवति तेषाम् शावक-रक्षाम् च करोति।[357]

अथ कदाचिद् दीर्घकर्ण-नामा मार्जारः पक्षि-शावकान् भक्षयितुम् तत्र आगतः। ततः तम् आयान्तम् दृष्ट्वा भय-आर्तैः पक्षि-शावकैः कोलाहलः कृतः।[358] तद् श्रुत्वा जरद्रवेन उक्तम्। कः अयम् आयाति। गृध्रम् अवलोक्य दीर्घकर्णः स-भयम् आह। हा हतः अस्मि। अथवा।[359]

तावद्भयस्य भेतव्यं यावद्भयमनागतम्। आगतं तु भयं वीक्ष्य नरः
कुर्याद्यथोचितम् ॥360

इति आलोच्य तम् उपसृत्य अब्रवीत्। आर्य त्वाम् अभिवन्दे।361 गृध्रः
अवदत् - कः त्वम्। सः अवदत् - मार्जारः अहम्। गृध्रः ब्रूते - दूरम् अपसर।
नो चेद् हन्तव्यः असि मया।362 मार्जारः अवदत्। श्रूयताम् तावत् मद्-वचनम्।

अत्र गङ्गा-तीरे चान्द्रायण-व्रतम् आचरन् अहम् तिष्ठामि।363 यूयम् धर्म-ज्ञान-
रताः इति पक्षिणः सर्वे सर्वदा प्रस्तुवन्ति। अतः भवद्भयः धर्मम् श्रोतुम् इह
आगतः।364 भवन्तः च माम् अतिथिम् हन्तुम् उद्यताः।365

गृध्रः अवदत्। मार्जारः हि मांस-रुचिः। पक्षि-शावकाः च अत्र निवसन्ति। तेन
अहम् एवम् ब्रवीमि।366 तद् श्रुत्वा मार्जारः भूमिम् स्पृष्ट्वा कर्णौ स्पृशति। एवम्
विश्वास्य सः मार्जारः तरु-कोटरे स्थितः।367

ततः दिनेषु गच्छत्सु पक्षि-शावकान् स्व-कोटरम् आनीय असौ प्रत्यहम्
खादति।368 ततः जिज्ञासा समारब्धा। मार्जारः तद् परिज्ञाय पलायितः।
पश्चात् तत्र तरु-कोटरे पक्षिभिः शावक-अस्थीनि प्राप्तानि।369 अनेन एव
शावकाः खादिताः इति पक्षिभिः निश्चित्य सः गृध्रः व्यापादितः।370

4 – cont.

अतः अहम् ब्रवीमि। अज्ञात-कुल-शीलस्य इत्यादि।371 इति आकर्ण्य सः
जम्बुकः स-कोपम् आह। भवान् अपि अज्ञात-कुल-शीलः एव आसीत्।372

अयं निजः परो वेति गणना लघुचेतसाम्। उदारचरितानां तु वसुधैव
कुटुम्बकम् ॥373

यथा च अयम् मृगः मम बन्धुः तथा भवान् अपि।374 मृगः अब्रवीत्। किम्
अनेन उत्तरोत्तरेण। सर्वैः एकत्र सुखम् स्थीयताम्। काकेन उक्तम् - एवम्
अस्तु।375

एकदा शृगालः ब्रूते। सखे मृग एतस्मिन् एव वने क्षेत्रम् अस्ति।
तद् दर्शयामि।376 तथा कृते सति मृगः प्रत्यहम् तत्र गत्वा सस्यम् खादति।
ततः क्षेत्र-पतिना पाशाः तत्र योजिताः।377 तत्र चरन् पाशैः बद्धः मृगः
अचिन्तयत्। व्याध-पाशात् मित्रात् अन्यः कः माम् त्रातुम् समर्थः।378

अत्र अन्तरे जम्बुकः तत्र आगत्य अचिन्तयत्। अस्थीनि मम भोजनानि
भविष्यन्ति।379 मृगः तम् दृष्ट्वा उल्लासितः ब्रूते। सखे छिन्धि तावत् मम
बन्धनम्। यतः।380

आपत्सु मित्रं जानीयाद्रणे शूरमृणे शुचिम्। भार्यां क्षीणेषु वित्तेषु व्यसनेषु च
बान्धवान् ॥381

जम्बुकः आह - सखे स्नायु-निर्मिताः पाशाः कथम् एतान् दन्तैः स्पृशामि ।[382]
अनन्तरम् सः काकः मृगम् अन्विष्यन् तथा-विधम् तम् दृष्ट्वा उवाच - उक्तम्
एव मया पूर्वम् ।[383]

दुर्जनेन समं सख्यं वैरं चापि न कारयेत् । उष्णो दहति चाङ्गारः शीतः कृष्णायते
करम् ॥[384]

सखे मृग त्वम् आत्मानम् मृतवत् सन्दर्श्य तिष्ठ । यदा अहम् शब्दम् करोमि
तदा उत्थाय त्वम् सत्वरम् पलायिष्यसे ।[385] मृगः तथा एव काक-वचनेन
स्थितः । ततः क्षेत्र-पतिना तथा-विधः मृगः आलोकितः ।[386] आः स्वयम् मृतः
असि । इति उक्त्वा मृगम् बन्धनात् मोचयित्वा सयत्नः बभूव ।[387] मृगः काकस्य
शब्दम् श्रुत्वा सत्वरम् उत्थाय पलायितः ।[388] तम् उद्दिश्य तेन क्षेत्र-पतिना
प्रकोपात् क्षिप्तेन लगुडेन शृगालः व्यापादितः ।[389]

2 – cont.

अतः अहम् ब्रवीमि । भक्ष्य-भक्षकयोः प्रीतिः इत्यादि । लघुपतनकः ब्रूते । तव
द्वारि आत्मानम् व्यापादयिष्यामि इति ।[390] तद्-वचनम् आकर्ण्य हिरण्यकः आह ।
आप्यायितः अहम् भवताम् एतेन वचन-अमृतेन ।[391] ततः प्रभृति कुशल-प्रश्नैः
कियत् कालः अतिवर्तते । एकदा लघुपतनकः हिरण्यकम् आह ।[392]

सखे । वायसस्य इदम् स्थानम् कष्टतर-लभ्य-आहारम् । तद् एतद् परित्यज्य
स्थान-अन्तरम् गन्तुम् इच्छामि । हिरण्यकः ब्रूते ।[393]

स्थानभ्रष्टा न शोभन्ते दन्ताः केशा नखा नराः । इति विज्ञाय मतिमान् स्वस्थानं
न परित्यजेत् ॥[394]

काकः ब्रूते - मित्र कापुरुषस्य वचनम् एतद् । यतः ।[395]

स्थानमुत्सृज्य गच्छन्ति सिंहाः सत्पुरुषा गजा । तत्रैव निधनं यान्ति काकाः
कापुरुषा मृगाः ॥[396]

हिरण्यकः ब्रूते - मित्र क्व गन्तव्यम् ।[397]

चलत्येकेन पादेन तिष्ठत्येकेन बुद्धिमान् । नासमीक्ष्य परं स्थानं पूर्वमायतनं
त्यजेत् ॥[398]

वायसः ब्रूते - मित्र अस्ति दण्डिक-अरण्ये कर्पूर-गौर-अभिधानम् सरः । तत्र मे
प्रिय-सुहृद् मन्थर-अभिधानः कूर्मः प्रतिवसति ।[399] अथ वायसः तेन मित्रेण सह
तस्य सरसः समीपम् ययौ । ततः मन्थरः आह ।[400]

उपार्जितानां वित्तानां त्याग एव हि रक्षणम् । तडागोदरसंस्थानां परिवाह
इवाम्भसाम् ॥[401]

अतिसञ्चय-शीलः अयम् जम्बुकः धनुषा हतः। तौ आहतुः - कथम् एतद्।
मन्थरः कथयति।⁴⁰²

6 – Jambuka

आसीत् भैरवः नाम व्याधः। सः च एकदा धनुः आदाय विन्ध्या-अटवी-
मध्यम् गतः। तत्र तेन एकः मृगः व्यापादितः।⁴⁰³ ततः तेन शूकरः दृष्टः। मृगम्
भूमौ निधाय तेन शूकरः शरेण हतः। शूकरेण अपि हतः सः व्याधः पपात।
अथ तयोः पाद-आस्फालनेन एकः सर्पः अपि मृतः।⁴⁰⁴

अत्र अन्तरे दीर्घरावः नाम जम्बुकः तान् मृतान् मृग-व्याध-सर्प-शूकरान्
अपश्यत्। आलोक्य अचिन्तयत् च।⁴⁰⁵ प्रथम-बुभुक्षायाम् इदम् निःस्वादु स्नायु-
बन्धनम् कोदण्ड-लग्नम् खादामि। इति उक्त्वा तथा अकरोत्।⁴⁰⁶ ततः छिन्ने
स्नायु-बन्धने द्रुतम् उत्पतितेन धनुषा हृदि निर्भिन्नः सः दीर्घरावः पञ्चत्वम्
गतः।⁴⁰⁷

2 – cont.

अतः अहम् ब्रवीमि।⁴⁰⁸ सुखमापतितं सेव्यं दुःखमापतितं तथा।
चक्रवत्परिवर्तन्ते दुःखानि च सुखानि च॥⁴⁰⁹

1 – cont.

अथ राज-पुत्रैः स-आनन्दम् उक्तम्। सर्वे श्रुतवन्तः सुखिनः वयम्। सिद्धम् नः
समीहितम्।⁴¹⁰

39. Association

यादृशैः सन्निवसति यादृशांश्रोपसेवते। यादृगिच्छेच्च भवितुं तादृग्भवति
पूरुषः॥⁴¹¹

Indicators:

आचारः कुलमाख्याति देशमाख्याति भाषणम्। सम्भ्रमः स्नेहमाख्याति
वपुराख्याति भोजनम्॥⁴¹² तुष्यन्ति भोजने विप्रा मयूरा घनगर्जिते। साधवः
परसम्पत्तौ खलाः परविपत्तिषु॥⁴¹³ मूर्खाणां पण्डिता द्वेष्या निर्धनानां महाधनाः।
व्रतिनः पापशीलानाम् असतीनां कुलस्त्रियः॥⁴¹⁴ लुब्धानां याचकः शत्रुर् मूर्खाणां
बोधको रिपुः। जारस्त्रीणां पतिः शत्रुश् चौराणां चन्द्रमा रिपुः॥⁴¹⁵

यथा चतुर्भिः कनकं परीक्ष्यते निघर्षणच्छेदनतापताडनैः।

तथा चतुर्भिः पुरुषः परीक्ष्यते त्यागेन शीलेन गुणेन कर्मणा॥⁴¹⁶

स्वर्गस्थितानामिह जीवलोके चत्वारि चिह्नानि वसन्ति देहे।

दानप्रसङ्गो मधुरा च वाणी देवार्चनं ब्राह्मणतर्पणं च॥⁴¹⁷

तितिक्षवः कारुणिकाः सुहृदः सर्वदेहिनाम्। अजातशत्रवः शान्ताः साधवः
साधुभूषणाः॥⁴¹⁸

दरिद्रता धीरतया विराजते कुवस्त्रता शुभ्रतया विराजते ।

कदन्नता चोष्णतया विराजते कुरूपता शीलतया विराजते ॥419

गुणो भूषयते रूपं शीलं भूषयते कुलम् । सिद्धिर्भूषयते विद्यां भोगो भूषयते धनम् ॥ निर्गुणस्य हतं रूपं दुःशीलस्य हतं कुलम् । असिद्धस्य हता विद्या ह्यभोगेन हतं धनम् ॥420

Sva-Bhava:

सर्वस्य हि परीक्ष्यन्ते स्वभावा नेतरे गुणाः । अतीत्य हि गुणान्सर्वान् स्वभावो मूर्ध्नि वर्तते ॥421 दातृत्वं प्रियवक्तृत्वं धीरत्वमुचितज्ञता । अभ्यासेन न लभ्यन्ते चत्वारः सहजा गुणाः ॥422 पूर्वे वयसि यः शान्तः स शान्त इति मे मतिः । धातुषु क्षीयमाणेषु शमः कस्य न जायते ॥423

To be avoided:

सिंहो व्याकरणस्य कर्तुरहरत् प्राणान्प्रियान्पाणिनेर्

मीमांसाकृतमुन्ममाथ सहसा हस्ती मुनिं जैमिनिम् ।

छन्दोज्ञाननिधिं जघान मकरो वेलातटे पिङ्गलम्

अज्ञानावृतचेतसामतिरुषां को ऽर्थस्तिरश्चां गुणैः ॥424

उपसर्गे ऽन्यचक्रे च दुर्भिक्षे च भयावहे । असाधुजनसम्पर्के यः पलायेत्स जीवति ॥425 रोहते सायकैर्विद्धं छिन्नं रोहति चासिना । वचो दुरुक्तं बीभत्सं न प्ररोहति वाक्क्षतम् ॥426 अहो खलभुजङ्गस्य विपरीतो वधक्रमः । कर्णे लगति चान्यस्य प्राणैरन्यो वियुज्यते ॥427 दुर्जनस्य च सर्पस्य वरं सर्पो न दुर्जनः । सर्पो दंशति काले तु दुर्जनस्तु पदे पदे ॥428 दुर्जनैरुच्यमानानि सम्मतानि प्रियाण्यपि । अकालकुसुमानीव भयं सञ्जनयन्ति हि ॥429 प्रणयादुपकाराद्धा यो विश्वसिति शत्रुषु । स सुप्त इव वृक्षाग्रात् पतितः प्रतिबुध्यते ॥430 स्तोकेनोन्नतिमायाति स्तोकेनायात्यधोगतिम् । अहो सुसदृशी चेष्टा तुलायष्टेः खलस्य च ॥431 परोक्षे कार्यहन्तारं प्रत्यक्षे प्रियवादिनम् । वर्जयेत्तादृशं मित्रं विषकुम्भं पयोमुखम् ॥432

वरं न राज्यं न कुराजराज्यं वरं न मित्रं न कुमित्रमित्रम् ।

वरं न शिष्यो न कुशिष्यशिष्यो वरं न दारा न कुदारदारः ॥433

शकटं पञ्चहस्तेन दशहस्तेन वाजिनम् । हस्ती हस्तसहस्रेण देशत्यागेन दुर्जनम् ॥434 हस्ती अङ्कुशमात्रेण वाजी हस्तेन ताड्यते । शृङ्गी लगुडहस्तेन खड्गहस्तेन दुर्जनः ॥435

Friends:

आतुरे व्यसने प्राप्ते दुर्भिक्षे शत्रुसङ्कटे । राजद्वारे श्मशाने च यस्तिष्ठति स बान्धवः ॥436 ददाति प्रतिगृह्णाति गुह्यमाख्याति पृच्छति । भुङ्क्ते भोजायते चैव षड्विधं प्रीतिलक्षणम् ॥437

"They (Indians) are remarkably brave, and superior in war to all Asiatics; they are remarkable for integrity; they are so reasonable as seldom to have recourse to law suits, and so honest as to require neither locks to their doors nor writings to bind their agreements. They are in the highest degree truthful." (Lucius Flavius Arrian, Greek historian and military commander, c. 87-150)

धर्म is derived from √धृ, 'that which supports', maintains, holds up – a 'natural duty' to uphold society for the overall and ultimate best of all.

धारणाद्धर्ममित्याहुर् धर्मेण विधृताः प्रजाः। यः स्याद्धारणसंयुक्तः स धर्म इति निश्चयः ॥[438]

धर्म or duties can be grouped into:

(1) **Virtues**, described as four legs of धर्म

	(1)	(2)	(3)	(4)
	सत्य	दम, शौच	दान, दया	तपः, विद्या
regulated by		विवाह	यज्ञ	सुरा

वेदस्योपनिषत्सत्यं सत्यस्योपनिषद्दमः। दमस्योपनिषद्दानं दानस्योपनिषत्तपः। तपसोपनिषत्त्यागस् त्यागस्योपनिषत्सुखम् ॥[439] मुक्तिमिच्छसि चेत्तात विषयान्विषवत्त्यज। क्षमार्जवदयाशौचं सत्यं पीयूषवत्पिब ॥[440] सत्यं माता पिता ज्ञानं धर्मो भ्राता दया सखा। शान्तिः पत्नी क्षमा पुत्रः षडेते मम बान्धवाः ॥[441]

(2) स्व-धर्म in society acc. to गुण/स्व-भाव

(3) Tradition – esp. **Sacraments** (संस्कार) in different stages of life

(4) Law and **Government**

(5) Religion – Worship (भगवद्धर्म) for **Liberation** (मोक्ष)

There is a concept, that धर्म repays five **Debts** (ऋण). महाभारत divides धर्म into 4 external and 4 internal rules. In **Yoga** or अष्टाङ्ग-योग there is a similar division into यम and नियम. In स्मृति-शास्त्र, धर्म is divided into public welfare (पूर्त) and rites (इष्ट).

Although duties are eternal (सनातन-धर्म) for men, they are not the same for everyone; and because of changing circumstances in human society, certainly not a set of doctrines, but liable to change.

कारणाद्धर्ममन्विच्छेन् न लोकचरितं चरेत् ।[442] स एव धर्मः सो ऽधर्मो देशकाले प्रतिष्ठितः ।[443]

"O sage! भीष्म, the knower of eternal principles, duly described – through many stories and histories, according to वर्ण and आश्रम, and according to the स्वभाव of a man, characterizing both in terms of what is mentioned as वैराग्य and राग, with their subdivisions, in summary and explicit, together with their means – the following: धर्म for charity, for kings, for liberation, for women, towards God, and also the four धर्म-अर्थ-काम-मोक्ष."444

आहारनिद्राभयमैथुनं च सामान्यमेतत्पशुभिर्नराणाम्।
धर्मो हि तेषामधिको विशेषो धर्मेण हीनाः पशुभिः समानाः ॥445
येषां न विद्या न तपो न दानं ज्ञानं न शीलं न गुणो न धर्मः।
ते मर्त्यलोके भुवि भारभूता मनुष्यरूपेण मृगाश्चरन्ति ॥446

एतावज्जन्मसाफल्यं देहिनामिह देहिषु। प्राणैरर्थैर्धिया वाचा श्रेय आचरणं सदा ॥447 त्यज दुर्जनसंसर्गं भज साधुसमागमम्। कुरु पुण्यमहोरात्रं स्मर नित्यमनित्यतः ॥448 धनस्य यस्य राजतो भयं न चास्ति चोरतः। मृतं च यन्न मुञ्चति समर्जयस्व तद्धनम् ॥449 अकृतेष्वेव कार्येषु मृत्युर्वै सम्प्रकर्षति। युवैव धर्मशीलः स्याद् अनिमित्तं हि जीवितम। कृते धर्मे भवेत्प्रीतिर इह प्रेत्य च शाश्वती ॥450 अजरामरवत्प्राज्ञो विद्यामर्थं च चिन्तयेत्। गृहीत इव केशेषु मृत्युना धर्ममाचरेत् ॥451 विद्या मित्रं प्रवासेषु भार्या मित्रं गृहेषु च। व्याधितस्यौषधं मित्रं धर्मो मित्रं मृतस्य च ॥452 एक एव सुहृद्धर्मो निधने ऽप्यनुयाति यः। शरीरेण समं नाशं सर्वमन्यदिह गच्छति ॥453 चला लक्ष्मीश्चलाः प्राणाश् चले जीवितमन्दिरे। चलाचले च संसारे धर्म एको हि निश्चलः ॥454

जलबिन्दुनिपातेन क्रमशः पूर्यते घटः। स हेतुः सर्वविद्यानां धर्मस्य च धनस्य च ॥455 एक एव चरेद्धर्मं न धर्मध्वजिको भवेत्। धर्मवाणिजका ह्येते ये धर्ममुपभुञ्जते ॥456 दाने तपसि शौर्ये वा विज्ञाने विनये नये। विस्मयो न हि कर्तव्यो बहुरत्ना वसुन्धरा ॥457 धर्मेणापिहितो धर्मो धर्ममेवानुवर्तते ।458

---

41. Self-Preservation

शरीरं धर्मसर्वस्वं रक्षणीयं प्रयत्नतः। शरीराच्च्यवते धर्मः पर्वतात्सलिलं यथा ॥459

सिंहादेकं बकादेकं शिक्षेच्चत्वारि कुक्कुटात्। वायसात्पञ्च शिक्षेच्च षट् शुनस्त्रीणि गर्दभात् ॥460 प्रभूतं कार्यमल्पं वा यन्नरः कर्तुमिच्छति। सर्वारम्भेण तत्कार्यं सिंहादेकं प्रचक्षते ॥461 इन्द्रियाणि च संयम्य बकवत्पण्डितो नरः। देशकालबलं ज्ञात्वा सर्वकार्याणि साधयेत् ॥462 प्रत्युत्थानं च युद्धं च संविभागं च बन्धुषु। स्वयमाक्रम्य भुक्तं च शिक्षेच्चत्वारि कुक्कुटात् ॥463 गूढमैथुनं चारित्वं काले काले च सङ्ग्रहम्। अप्रमत्तमविश्वासं पञ्च शिक्षेच्च वायसात् ॥464 बह्वाशी स्वल्पसन्तुष्ट: सनिद्रो लघुचेतनः। स्वामिभक्तश्च शूरश्च षड् एते श्वानतो गुणाः ॥465

सुश्रान्तो ऽपि वहेद्द्वारं शीतोष्णं न च पश्यति । सन्तुष्टश्चरते नित्यं त्रीणि शिक्षेच्च गर्दभात् ॥४६६ य एतान्विंशतिगुणान् आचरिष्यति मानवः । कार्यावस्थासु सर्वासु अजेयः स भविष्यति ॥४६७

Duty in times of emergency:

आहारो मैथुनं निद्रा सेव्या नाति हि रुग्भवेत् ।४६८ देशभङ्गे प्रवासे वा व्याधिषु व्यसनेष्वपि । रक्षेदेव स्वदेहादि पश्चाद्धर्मं समाचरेत् ॥ आपत्काले तु सम्प्राप्ते शौचाचारं न चिन्तयेत् । स्वयं समुद्धरेत्पश्चात् स्वस्थो धर्मं समाचरेत् ॥४६९ जीवितात्ययमापन्नो यो ऽन्नमत्ति ततस्ततः । आकाशमिव पङ्केन न स पापेन लिप्यते ॥४७०

Suicide discouraged:

यदि त्वं भजमानां मां प्रत्याख्यास्यसि मानद । विषमग्निं जलं रज्जुमास्थास्ये तव कारणात् ॥४७१ अतिमानादतिक्रोधात् स्नेहाद्वा यदि वा भयात् । उद्बध्नीयात्स्त्री पुमान्वा गतिरेषा विधीयते । पूयशोणितसम्पूर्णे अन्धे तमसि मज्जति ॥४७२

Sorrow:

शब्दे स्पर्शे रसे रूपे गन्धे च रमते मनः । तेषु भोगेषु सर्वेषु न भीतो लभते सुखम् ॥४७३ मानसेन हि दुःखेन शरीरमुपताप्यते । अयःपिण्डेन तप्तेन कुम्भसंस्थमिवोदकम् ॥४७४ सन्तापाद् भ्रश्यते रूपं सन्तापाद् भ्रश्यते बलम् । सन्तापाद् भ्रश्यते ज्ञानं सन्तापाद् व्याधिमृच्छति ॥४७५ निरुत्साहस्य दीनस्य शोकपर्याकुलात्मनः । सर्वार्था व्यवसीदन्ति व्यसनं चाधिगच्छति ॥४७६

द्विविधे जायते व्याधिः शारीरो मानसस्तथा । परस्परं तयोर्जन्म निर्द्वन्द्वं नोपपद्यते ॥४७७ प्रज्ञया मानसं दुःखं हन्याच्छारीरमौषधैः ।४७८ मतिमन्तो ह्यतो वैद्याः शमं प्रागेव कुर्वते । मानसस्य प्रियाख्यानैः सम्भोगोपनयैर्नृणाम् ॥४७९

मृतं वा यदि वा नष्टं यो ऽतीतमनुशोचति । दुःखेन लभते दुःखं द्वावनर्थौ प्रपद्यते ॥ भैषज्यमेतद् दुःखस्य यदेतन्नानुचिन्तयेत् । चिन्त्यमानं हि न व्येति भूयश्चापि प्रवर्धते ॥४८० गते शोको न कर्तव्यो भविष्यं नैव चिन्तयेत् । वर्तमानेन कालेन वर्तयन्ति विचक्षणाः ॥४८१ यत्र नैव शरैः कार्यं न भृत्यैर्न च बन्धुभिः । आत्मनैकेन योद्धव्यं तत्ते युद्धमुपस्थितम् ॥४८२

दुःखमेवास्ति न सुखं यस्मात्तदुपलक्ष्यते । दुःखार्तस्य प्रतीकारे सुखसज्ञा विधीयते ॥४८३ सर्वाः सम्पत्तयस्तस्य सन्तुष्टं यस्य मानसम् । उपानद्गूढपादस्य ननु चर्मावृतेव भूः ॥४८४

The objects of human life (पुरुषार्थ), धर्म-अर्थ-काम plus मोक्ष, called त्रि-/चतुर्-वर्ग, are rooted in धर्म.

धर्मार्थकाममोक्षाणां यस्यैको ऽपि न विद्यते । जन्मजन्मनि मर्त्येषु मरणं तस्य केवलम् ॥485 धर्ममूलो ऽर्थविटपस् तथा कामफलो महान् । त्रिवर्गपादपस्तत्र रक्षया फलभाग्भवेत् ॥486 उपायं धर्ममेवाहुस् त्रिवर्गस्य विशाम्पते । लिप्समानो हि तेनाशु कक्षे ऽग्निरिव वर्धते ॥487

Be active:

अग्निहोत्रफला वेदाः शीलवृत्तफलं श्रुतम् । रतिपुत्रफला दारा दत्तभुक्तफलं धनम् ॥488 आश्रितानां भृतौ स्वामि-सेवायां धर्मसेवने । पुत्रस्योत्पादने चैव न सन्ति प्रतिहस्तकाः ॥489 उद्योगे नास्ति दारिद्र्यं जपतो नास्ति पातकम् । मौनेन कलहो नास्ति नास्ति जागरिते भयम् ॥490 पश्य कर्मवशात्प्राप्तं भोज्यकाले ऽपि भोजनम् । हस्तोद्यमं विना वक्त्रे प्रविशेन्न कथञ्चन ॥491

सुखं दुःखान्तमालस्यं दाक्ष्यं दुःखं सुखोदयम् । भूतिः श्रीर्ह्रीर्धृतिः कीर्तिर् दक्षे वसति नालसे ॥492 आलस्यापगता विद्या परहस्तगतं धनम् । अल्पबीजं हतं क्षेत्रं हतं सैन्यमनायकम् ॥493 दोषभीतेरनारम्भस् तत्कापुरुषलक्षणम् । कैरजीर्णभयाद् भ्रातर् भोजनं परिहीयते ॥494 षड् दोषाः पुरुषेणेह हातव्या भूतिमिच्छता । निद्रा तन्द्रा भयं क्रोध आलस्यं दीर्घसूत्रता ॥495

धनधान्यप्रयोगेषु विद्यासङ्ग्रहणेषु च । आहारे व्यवहारे च त्यक्तलज्जः सुखी भवेत् ॥496 श्वःकार्यमद्य कुर्वीत पूर्वाह्णे चापराह्णिकम् । न हि प्रतीक्षते मृत्युः कृतं वास्य न वा कृतम् ॥497 दिवसेनैव तत्कुर्याद् येन रात्रौ सुखं वसेत् । अष्टमासेन तत्कुर्याद् येन वर्षाः सुखं वसेत् ॥ पूर्वे वयसि तत्कुर्याद् येन वृद्धः सुखं वसेत् । यावज्जीवेन तत्कुर्याद् येन प्रेत्य सुखं वसेत् ॥498

Destiny and own activity:

क्षेत्रं पुरुषकारस्तु दैवं बीजमुदाहृतम् । क्षेत्रबीजसमायोगात् ततः रारयं समृद्ध्यते ॥499 यथा ह्येकेन चक्रेण न रथस्य गतिर्भवेत् । तथा पुरुषकारेण विना दैवं न सिद्ध्यति ॥500 उद्यमेन हि सिद्ध्यन्ति कार्याणि न मनोरथैः । न हि सुप्तस्य सिंहस्य प्रविशन्ति मुखे मृगाः ॥501 यथाग्निः पवनोद्धूतः सुसूक्ष्मो ऽपि महान्भवेत् । तथा कर्मसमायुक्तं दैवं साधु विवर्धते ॥ यथा तैलक्षयाद्दीपः प्रह्रासमुपगच्छति । तथा कर्मक्षयाद्दैवं प्रह्रासमुपगच्छति ॥502

Poverty:

धनमार्जय काकुत्स्थ धनमूलमिदं जगत् । अन्तरं नाभिजानामि निर्धनस्य मृतस्य च ॥503 उपासते ये गृहस्थाः परपाकमबुद्धयः । तेन ते प्रेत्य पशुतां

व्रजन्त्यन्नादिदायिनः ॥504 कष्टं च खलु मूर्खत्वं कष्टं च खलु यौवनम्।
कष्टात्कष्टतरं चैव परगेहनिवासनम् ॥505 अपुत्रस्य गृहं शून्यं सन्मित्ररहितस्य च।
मूर्खस्य च दिशः शून्याः सर्वशून्या दरिद्रता ॥506 शुष्कस्य कीटखातस्य
वह्निदग्धस्य सर्वतः। तरोरप्यूषरस्थस्य वरं जन्म न चार्थिनः ॥507 न तथा बाध्यते
लोके प्रकृत्या निर्धनो जनः। यथा द्रव्याणि सम्प्राप्य तैर्विहीनो ऽसुखे स्थितः ॥508

Respect:

यस्यार्थास्तस्य मित्राणि यस्यार्थास्तस्य बान्धवाः। यस्यार्थाः स पुमाँल्लोके
यस्यार्थाः स च पण्डितः ॥509 ब्रह्महापि नरः पूज्यो यस्यास्ति विपुलं धनम्।
शशिनस्तुल्यवंशो ऽपि निर्धनः परिभूयते ॥510 निर्धनं पुरुषं वेश्या प्रजा भग्नं नृपं
त्यजेत्। खगा वीतफलं वृक्षं भुक्त्वा चाभ्यागतो गृहम् ॥511 तावत्प्रीतिर्भवेल्लोके
यावद्दानं प्रदीयते। वत्सः क्षीरक्षयं दृष्ट्वा परित्यजति मातरम् ॥512

वरं वनं व्याघ्रगजेन्द्रसेवितं द्रुमालयं पत्रफलाम्बुसेवनम्।

तृणेषु शय्या शतजीर्णवल्कलं न बन्धुमध्ये धनहीनजीवनम् ॥513

त्यजन्ति मित्राणि धनैर्विहीनं पुत्राश्च दाराश्च सुहृज्जनाश्च।

तमर्थवन्तं पुनराश्रयन्ति अर्थो हि लोके मनुषस्य बन्धुः ॥514

तानीन्द्रियाण्यविकलानि तदेव नाम सा बुद्धिरप्रतिहता वचनं तदेव।

अर्थोष्मणा विरहितः पुरुषः स एव अन्यः क्षणेन भवतीति विचित्रमेतत् ॥515

Service:

एहि गच्छ पतोत्तिष्ठ वद मौनं समाचर। एवमाशाग्रहग्रस्तैः क्रीडन्ति
धनिनो ऽर्थिभिः ॥516 सेवकः स्वामिनं द्वेष्टि कृपणं परुषाक्षरम्। आत्मानं किं स
न द्वेष्टि सेव्यासेव्यं न वेत्ति यः ॥517 भूशय्या ब्रह्मचर्यं च कृशत्वं लघुभोजनम्।
सेवकस्य यतेर्यद्वद् विशेषः पापधर्मजः ॥518 शीतातपादिकष्टानि सहते यानि
सेवकः। धनाय तानि चाल्पानि यदि धर्माय मुच्यते ॥519

कान्ताविवियोगः स्वजनापमानो रणस्य शेषः कुनृपस्य सेवा।

दारिद्रभावो विषमा सभा च विनाग्निनैते प्रदहन्ति कायम् ॥520

But:

त्रिवर्गं नातिकृच्छ्रेण भजेत गृहमेध्यपि। यथादेशं यथाकालं
यावद्दैवोपपादितम् ॥521 कः कालः कानि मित्राणि को देशः कौ व्यायागमौ।
कश्चाहं का च मे शक्तिर् इति चिन्त्यं मुहुर्मुहुः ॥522 दृष्टिपूतं न्यसेत्पादं वस्त्रपूतं
जलं पिबेत्। सत्यपूतां वदेद्वाक्यं मनःपूतं समाचरेत् ॥523 अनालोक्य व्ययं कर्ता
अनाथः कलहप्रियः। आतुरः सर्वक्षेत्रेषु नरः शीघ्रं विनश्यति ॥524 एकः स्वादु न
भुञ्जीत नैकः सुप्तेषु जागृयात्। एको न गच्छेदध्वानं नैकश्चार्थान्प्रचिन्तयेत् ॥525
यो ध्रुवाणि परित्यज्य अध्रुवं परिषेवते। ध्रुवाणि तस्य नश्यन्ति अध्रुवं नष्टमेव
हि ॥526 चिरकारिक भद्रं ते भद्रं ते चिरकारिक। चिरकारी हि मेधावी

नापराध्यति कर्मसु ॥527 अतिक्लेशेन ये चार्था धर्मस्यातिक्रमेण तु। शत्रूणां प्रणिपातेन ते ह्यर्था मा भवन्तु मे ॥528

43. Ahimsa

हिंसा defined:

उद्वेगजननं हिंसा सन्तापकरणं तथा। रुक्कृतिः शोणितकृतिः पैशुण्यकरणं तथा॥ हितस्यातिनिषेधश्च मर्मोद्घाटनमेव च। सुखापह्नुतिः संरोधो वधो दशविधा च सा ॥529

धर्म is measured in अ-हिंसा :

"The first limb of Yoga is Yama (prohibitions), and Ahimsā is its first item. Without Ahimsā the other limbs of Yoga are, as it were, not performed. Abstinence from injury means not causing pain to any living creature at any time. The Yamas and Niyamas that follow have their origin in it. They are meant to achieve it. They are taught with the object of teaching it. They are taken up with the object of rendering the light of its appearance purer. And so it has been said: As the Brāhmana goes on undertaking many of a vow of restraint and observance, he goes on turning away from the sins committed on account of forgetfulness, and having their origin in injury caused to others; and by so doing he goes on rendering the Ahimsā itself purer and purer." (Yoga-Sūtra-Bhāshya 2.30)

When श्री-कृष्ण declares that, "Even a rogue, if he worships Me exclusively, is to be considered साधु ...", He immediately clarifies, that a true भक्त "will quickly become धर्मात्मा " also. (भगवद्गीता 9.30-31)

न चक्षुषा न मनसा न वाचा दूषयेदपि। न प्रत्यक्षं परोक्षं वा दूषणं व्याहरेत्क्वचित् ॥ न हिंस्यात्सर्वभूतानि मैत्रायणगतश्चरेत्। नेदं जीवितमासाद्य वैरं कुर्वीत केनचित् ॥530

हिंसा as an insult to the Creator:

ईशावास्यमिदं सर्वं यत्किञ्च जगत्यां जगत्। तेन त्यक्तेन भुञ्जीथा मा गृधः कस्यस्विद्धनम् ॥531

अभ्यर्चयित्वा प्रतिमासु विष्णुं निन्दन् जने सर्वगतं तमेव।
अभ्यर्च्य पादौ हि द्विजस्य मूर्ध्नि द्रुह्यन्निवाज्ञो नरकं प्रयाति ॥532

How to judge it?

आत्मौपम्येन मन्तव्यं बुद्धिमद्भिः कृतात्मभिः ।533 यदन्यैर्विहितं नेच्छेद् आत्मनः कर्म पूरुषः। न तत्परेषु कुर्वीत जानन्नप्रिययात्मनः ॥534

As धर्म is the basis of त्रि-वर्ग, अहिंसा is the basis of all धर्म:

न भूतानामहिंसाया ज्यायान्धर्मो ऽस्ति कश्चन ।535 अहिंसा परमं मित्रमहिंसा परमं सुखम् ।536

अहिंसा defines all other virtues, and even सत्य, which is otherwise praised as the highest virtue:

नास्ति सत्यात्परो धर्मो नानृतात्पातकं परम् । स्थितिर्हि सत्यं धर्मस्य तस्मात्सत्यं न लोपयेत् ॥ सत्यस्य वचनं श्रेयः सत्यादपि हितं वदेत् । यद्भूतहितमत्यन्तम् एतत्सत्यं मतं मम ॥537 सर्वस्वस्यापहारे तु वक्तव्यमनृतं भवेत् । तत्रानृतं भवेत्सत्यं सत्यं चाप्यनृतं भवेत् ॥ तस्माद्धर्मार्थमनृतम् उक्त्वा नानृतभाग्भवेत् ।538

Once some robbers, in search of fleeing travellers, reached the hut of a hermit. After reminding him of his vow of सत्य, the hermit pointed out the path the travellers had taken. His सत्य became falsehood.

कृते प्रतिकृतिं कुर्याद् धिंसने प्रतिहिंसनम् । तत्र दोषो न पतति दुष्टे दुष्टं समाचरेत् ॥539

44. Meat-Eating

अन्नाद्दशगुणं पिष्टं पिष्टाद्दशगुणं पयः । पयसो ऽष्टगुणं मांसं मांसाद्दशगुणं घृतम् ॥540 न मांसात्परमं किञ्चिद् रसतो विद्यते भुवि । क्षतक्षीणाभितप्तानां ग्राम्यधर्मरतात्मनाम् । अध्वना कर्शितानां च न मांसाद्विद्यते परम् ॥541

But:

स्वमांसं परमांसेन यो वर्धयितुमिच्छति । नास्ति क्षुद्रतरस्तस्मान् न नृशंसतरो नरः ॥542 रसवीर्यविपाका हि श्रमांसस्यापि वैद्यके । कीर्तिता इति तत्किं स्याद् भक्षणीयं विचक्षणैः ॥543

For many Hindus, अहिंसा includes a vegetarian diet:

नो दया मांसभोजिनः ।544 राजपुत्र चिरं जीव मा जीव मुनिपुत्रक । जीव वा मर वा साधो व्याध मा जीव मा मर ॥545 अनुमन्ता विशसिता निहन्ता क्रयविक्रयी । संस्कर्ता चोपहर्ता च खादकश्चेति घातकाः ॥546

And the very word for meat (मांस) is said to support this:

मां स भक्षयितामुत्र यस्य मांसमिहाद्म्यहम् । एतन्मांसस्य मांसत्वं प्रवदन्ति मनीषिणः ॥547 ये त्वनेवंविदो ऽसन्तः स्तब्धाः सदभिमानिनः । पशून्द्रुह्यन्ति विश्रब्धाः प्रेत्य खादन्ति ते च तान् ॥548

Meat-eating, and even garlic and onions, are forbidden for ब्राह्मण:

गृहे गुरावरण्ये वा निवसन्नात्मवान्द्विजः। नावेदविहितां हिंसाम् आपद्यपि समाचरेत्॥ समुत्पत्तिं च मांसस्य वधबन्धौ च देहिनाम्। प्रसमीक्ष्य निवर्तेत सर्वमांसस्य भक्षणात्॥549 छत्राकं विड्वराहं च लशुनं ग्रामकुक्कुटम्। पलाण्डुं गृञ्जनं चैव मत्या जग्ध्वा पतेद् द्विजः॥550 चतुष्पात्सकलो धर्मो ब्राह्मणस्य विधीयते। पादावकृष्टो राजन्ये तथा धर्मो विधीयते॥551

Concession for यज्ञ:

यज्ञाय जग्धिर्मांसस्येत्येष दैवो विधिः स्मृतः। अतोऽन्यथा प्रवृत्तिस्तु राक्षसो विधिरुच्यते॥ यावन्ति पशुरोमाणि तावत्कृत्वो ह मारणम्। वृथापशुघ्नः प्राप्नोति प्रेत्य जन्मनि जन्मनि॥ ओषध्यः पशवो वृक्षास् तिर्यञ्चः पक्षिणस्तथा। यज्ञार्थं निधनं प्राप्ताः प्राप्नुवन्त्युत्सृतीः पुनः॥552

श्रुति declared that अश्वमेध can counteract even ब्रह्महत्या, which was always disputed:

यथा पङ्केन पङ्काम्भः सुरया वा सुराकृतम्। भूतहत्यां तथैवैकां न यज्ञैर्मार्ष्टुमर्हति॥553

हिंसा is a law of nature:

अहस्तानि सहस्तानाम् अपदानि चतुष्पदाम्। फल्गूनि तत्र महतां जीवो जीवस्य जीवनम्॥554 ततस्ताभ्यो ददावन्नम् ओषधीः स्थावराणि च। जङ्गमानि च भूतानि दुर्बलानि बलीयसाम्॥555

It cannot be avoided:

ओषध्यो वीरुधश्चैव पशवो मृगपक्षिणः। अन्नादिभूता भूतानाम् इत्यपि श्रूयते श्रुतिः॥ कृषिं साध्विति मन्यन्ते तत्र हिंसा परा स्मृता। कर्षन्तो लाङ्गलैः पुंसो घ्नन्ति भूमिशयान्बहून्। जीवानन्यांश्च बहुशस् तत्र किं प्रतिभाति ते॥ जीवा हि बहवो ब्रह्मन् वृक्षेषु च फलेषु च। उदके बहवश्चापि तत्र किं प्रतिभाति ते॥556 पञ्च सूना गृहस्थस्य चुल्ली पेषण्युपस्करः। कण्डनी चोदकुम्भश्च बध्यते यास्तु वाहयन्॥557

Concession for hunting:

नात्मानमपरित्यज्य मृगया नाम विद्यते। समतामुपसङ्गम्य भूतं हन्यन्ति हन्ति वा॥ अतो राजर्षयः सर्वे मृगयां यान्ति भारत। न हि लिप्यन्ति पापेन न चैतत्पातकं विदुः॥558

But:

सर्वे वेदा न तत्कुर्युः सर्वे यज्ञाश्च भारत। यो भक्षयित्वा मांसानि पश्चादपि निवर्तते॥ दुष्करं च रसज्ञाने मांसस्य परिवर्जनम्। चर्तुं व्रतमिदं श्रेष्ठं

सर्वप्राण्यभयप्रदम् ॥559 अद्रोहेणैव भूतानाम् अल्पद्रोहेण वा पुनः । या वृत्तिः स परो धर्मस् तेन जीवामि जाजले ॥560

45. Mother Cow

"Others, the most ignoble and largest of all, though they kill not, nevertheless eat, all sorts of Animals good for food, except Cows; to kill and eat which all in general abhor, saying that the Cow is their Mother, for the Milke she gives and the Oxen she breeds, which plough the Earth and do a thousand other services ..." (Pietro Della Valle, Italian musicologist and traveller, 1586-1652)

The cow is लक्ष्मी personified:

पयसा हविषा दध्ना शकृता चाथ चर्मणा । अस्थिभिश्चोपकुर्वन्ति शृङ्गैर्वालैश्च भारत । नासां शीतातपौ स्यातां सदैताः कर्म कुर्वते ॥561 गावो लक्ष्म्यास्तथा मूलं गोषु दत्तं न नश्यति ।562 सर्वे देवा गवामङ्गे तीर्थानि तत्पदेषु च । तद्दुग्धेषु स्वयं लक्ष्मीस् तिष्ठत्येव सदा पितः ॥ गावस्तिष्ठन्ति यत्रैव तत्तीर्थं परिकीर्तितम् ।563 मातरः सर्वभूतानां गावः सर्वसुखप्रदाः । वृद्धिमाकाङ्क्षता नित्यं गावः कार्याः प्रदक्षिणाः ॥564 कीर्तनं श्रवणं दानं दर्शनं चापि पार्थिव । गवां प्रशस्यते वीर सर्वपापहरं शिवम् ॥565 सुरूपा बहुरूपाश्च विश्वरूपाश्च मातरः । गावो मामुपतिष्ठन्ताम् इति नित्यं प्रकीर्तयेत् ॥566 गा वै पश्याम्यहं नित्यं गावः पश्यन्तु मां सदा । गावो ऽस्माकं वयं तासां यतो गावस्ततो वयम् ॥567

"Cow-protection is an article of faith in Hinduism. Apart from its religious sanctity, it is an ennobling creed. Cow protection is the dearest possession of the Hindu heart. It is the one concrete belief common to all Hindus. No one who does not believe in cow-protection can possibly be called a Hindu. ... For me the cow is the personification of innocence. Cow protection means the protection of the weak and helpless." (Mohandas Gandhi, Indian politician, 1869-1948)

अङ्गुष्ठमात्रः स्थूलो वा बाहुमात्रः प्रमाणतः । आर्द्रस्तु सपलाशश्च दण्ड इत्यभिधीयते ॥568 गवाशनेषु विक्रीणंस् ततः प्राप्नोति गोवधम् । गोवृषाणां विपत्तौ च यावन्तः प्रेक्षका जनाः । न वारयन्ति तां तेषां सर्वेषां पातकं भवेत् ॥569

From about 1750 onwards a very large number of cows were daily slaughtered by the British for their army and civilian personnel in India. The Muslim community was encouraged by the British to take up the slaughter of cattle, as the large number of slaughterhouses set up by the British required professional butchers. In 1880-1894 there was a movement against cow killing in which many prominent Muslims actively participated, because a majority of Muslims in India did not eat the flesh of cow.

"I doubt whether, since the Mutiny, any movement containing in it a greater amount of potential mischief has engaged the attention of the Government of India." (Henry Petty-Fitzmaurice Lansdowne, Viceroy of India, 1845-1927)

The British tried their best, and largely succeeded in projecting this movement as a conflict between Hindus and Muslims.

"The British Origin of Cow-Slaughter in India (Dharampal 2002) – besides providing historical evidence about the genesis of mass cow-slaughter under British auspices, presents extensive documentary material about one of the most significant resistance movements in India against kine-killing by the British during the years 1880-1894. By highlighting the support given by some prominent Muslims during phases of this mass protest as well as by emphasising the crucial fact that it was the British and not the Muslims who were the main consumers of beef, Dharampal is able to dispel one of the deep-seated myths perpetuated in the interest of reinforcing divisive colonial strategies." (Wikipedia)

"Though the Muhammadan's cow killing is made the pretext for the agitation, it is, in fact, directed against us, who kill far more cows for our army, etc., than the Muhammadans." (Queen Victoria, 1819-1901)

---

46. Satya

नित्यं क्रोधात्तपो रक्षेच् छ्रियं रक्षेच्च मत्सरात् । विद्यां मानावमानाभ्याम् आत्मानं तु प्रमादतः ॥ आनृशंस्यं परो धर्मः क्षमा च परमं बलम् । आत्मज्ञानं परं ज्ञानं न सत्याद्विद्यते परम् ॥570 सत्यस्य वचनं साधु न सत्याद्विद्यते परम् । सत्येन विधृतं सर्वं सर्वं सत्ये प्रतिष्ठितम् ॥ अपि पापकृतो रौद्राः सत्यं कृत्वा पृथक्पृथक् । अद्रोहमविसंवादं प्रवर्तन्ते तदाश्रयाः ॥571 न ह्यसत्यात्परो ऽधर्म इति होवाच भूरियम् । सर्वं सोढुमलं मन्ये ऋते ऽलीकपरं नरम् ॥572

The last instruction of a teacher to his graduated student:

सत्यं वद । धर्मं चर । स्वाध्यायान्मा प्रमदः । मातृदेवो भव । पितृदेवो भव । आचार्यदेवो भव । अतिथिदेवो भव ।573

How to speak:

प्रियवाक्यप्रदानेन सर्वे तुष्यन्ति जन्तवः । तस्मात्तदेव वक्तव्यं वचने का दरिद्रता ॥574 अहिंसयैव भूतानां कार्यं श्रेयो ऽनुशासनम् । वाक्चैव मधुरा श्लक्ष्णा प्रयोज्या धर्ममिच्छता ॥575 सत्यं ब्रूयात्प्रियं ब्रूयान् न ब्रूयात्सत्यमप्रियम् । प्रियं च नानृतं ब्रूयाद् एष धर्मः सनातनः ॥576

On the other hand:

लुब्धमर्थेन गृह्णीयात् स्तब्धमञ्जलिकर्मणा । मूर्खं छन्दोऽनुवृत्या च यथार्थत्वेन पण्डितम् ॥577 सुलभाः पुरुषा राजन् सततं प्रियवादिनः । अप्रियस्य च पथ्यस्य वक्ता श्रोता च दुर्लभः ॥578 पृष्टः प्रियहितं ब्रूयान् न ब्रूयादहितं प्रियम् । अप्रियं वा हितं ब्रूयाच् छृण्वतो ऽनुमतो मिथः ॥579

Secrets:

आयुर्वित्तं गृहच्छिद्रं मन्त्रमैथुनभेषजम्। तपो दानावमानौ च नव गोप्यानि यत्नतः ॥580 आत्मनो मुखदोषेण बध्यन्ते शुकसारिकाः। बकास्तत्र न बध्यन्ते मौनं सर्वार्थसाधनम् ॥581 मनसा चिन्तितं कार्यं वाचा नैव प्रकाशयेत्। मन्त्रेण रक्षयेद्दृढं कार्ये चापि नियोजयेत् ॥582

When not to speak:

वाच्यं श्रद्धासमेतस्य पृच्छतश्च विशेषतः। प्रोक्तं श्रद्धाविहीनस्य अरण्यरुदितोपमम् ॥583 नापृष्टः कस्यचिद् ब्रूयान् नाप्यन्यायेन पृच्छतः। ज्ञानवानपि मेधावी जडवत्समुपाविशेत् ॥584 न विश्वसेत्कुमित्रे च मित्रे चापि न विश्वसेत्। कदाचित्कुपितं मित्रं सर्वं गुह्यं प्रकाशयेत् ॥585 पयःपानं भुजङ्गानां केवलं विषवर्धनम्। उपदेशो हि मूर्खाणां प्रकोपाय न शान्तये ॥586

47. Shauca

शौचं च द्विविधं प्रोक्तं बाह्यमाभ्यन्तरं तथा। मृज्जलाभ्यां स्मृतं बाह्यं भावशुद्धिस्तथान्तरम्॥ आशौचाद्धि वरं बाह्यं तस्मादाभ्यन्तरं वरम्। उभाभ्यां च शुचिर्यस्तु स शुचिर्नेतरः शुचिः ॥587

External purity:

अद्भिस्तु प्रोक्षणं शौचं बहूनां धान्यवाससाम्। प्रक्षालनेन त्वल्पानाम् अद्भिः शौचं विधीयते॥ मार्जारमक्षिकाकीट-पतङ्गकृमिदर्दुराः। मेध्यामेध्यं स्पृशन्त्येन नोच्छिष्टन्मनुरब्रवीत्॥ अदुष्टाः सन्तता धारा वातोद्धूताश्च रेणवः। स्त्रियो वृद्धाश्च बालाश्च न दुष्यन्ति कदाचन ॥588 मृदा जलेन शुद्धिः स्यान् न क्लेशो न धनव्ययः ।589 खननाद्दहनाद्घर्षाद् गोभिराक्रमणादपि। चतुर्भिः शुध्यते भूमिः पञ्चमाच्चोपलेपनात्॥ रजसा शुध्यते नारी नदी वेगेन शुध्यति। भस्मना शुध्यते कांस्यं ताम्रमम्लेन शुध्यति ॥590

उत्थाय नेत्रे प्रक्षाल्य शुचिर्भूत्वा समाहितः। परिजप्य च मन्त्राणि भक्षयेद्दन्तधावनम्॥ आयुर्बलं यशो वर्चः प्रजाः पशून्वसूनि च। ब्रह्म प्रज्ञां च मेधां च त्वं नो धेहि वनस्पते ॥591 अन्नं बुभुक्षमाणस्तु त्रिमुखेन स्पृशेदपः। भुक्त्वा चान्नं तथैव त्रिर् द्विः पुनः परिमार्जयेत् ॥592 वालेन तु न भुञ्जीत ।593

"A surprising spirit of cleanliness is to be observed among the Hindoos; the streets of their villages are commonly swept and watered, and sand is frequently strewed before the doors of the houses. The simplicity, and perfectly modest character, of the Hindoo women, cannot but arrest the attention of a stranger. With downcast eye, and equal step, they proceed along, and scarcely turn to the right or to the left to observe a foreigner as he passes, however new or singular his appearance. The men are no less remarkable for their hospitality, and are constantly attentive to accommodate the traveller in his wants." (William Hodges, British painter and traveller, 1744-1797)

जिह्वैकतो ऽच्युत विकर्षति मावितृप्ता
शिश्नो ऽन्यतस्त्वगुदरं श्रवणं कुतश्चित् ।
घ्राणो ऽन्यतश्चपलदृक्क्व च कर्मशक्तिर्
बह्वयः सपत्न्य इव गेहपतिं लुनन्ति ॥594

अदान्तः पुरुषः क्लेशम् अभीक्ष्णं प्रतिपद्यते । अनर्थांश्च बहूनन्यान्
प्रसृजत्यात्मदोषजान् ॥595 न यमं यममित्याहुर् आत्मा वै यम उच्यते । आत्मा
संयमितो येन तं यमः किं करिष्यति ॥ न तथासिस्तथा तीक्ष्णः सर्पो वा
दुरधिष्ठितः । यथा क्रोधो हि जन्तूनां शरीरस्थो विनाशकः ॥596

इन्द्रियाणि प्रमाथीनि बुद्धचा संयम्य यत्नतः । सर्वतो निष्पतिष्णूनि पिता
बालानिवात्मजान् ॥597 तावज्जितेन्द्रियो न स्याद् विजितान्येन्द्रियः पुमान् । न
जयेद्रसनं यावज् जितं सर्वं जिते रसे ॥598 निषण्णश्चापि खादेत न तु
गच्छन्कदाचन ।599 दीपो भक्षयते ध्वान्तं कज्जलं च प्रसूयते । यदन्नं भक्ष्यते नित्यं
जायते तादृशी प्रजा ॥600

नास्ति कामसमो व्याधिर् नास्ति मोहसमो रिपुः । नास्ति कोपसमो वह्निर् नास्ति
ज्ञानात्परं सुखम् ॥601 दममेव प्रशंसन्ति वृद्धाः श्रुतिसमाधयः । सर्वेषामेव वर्णानां
ब्राह्मणस्य विशेषतः ॥602 आत्मा जेयः सदा राज्ञा ततो जेयाश्च शत्रवः ।603 बलेन
परराष्ट्राणि गृह्णन् शूरस्तु नोच्यते । जितो येनेन्द्रियग्रामः स शूरः कथ्यते
बुधैः ॥604

धनेन किं यो न ददाति नाश्नुते बलेन किं यश्च रिपून्न बाधते ।
श्रुतेन किं यो न च धर्ममाचरेत् किमात्मना यो न जितेन्द्रियो भवेत् ॥605

अग्निहोत्रफला वेदाः शीलवृत्तफलं श्रुतम् । रतिपुत्रफला दारा दत्तभुक्तफलं
धनम् ॥606 यद्ददाति विशिष्टेभ्यो यजुहोति दिने दिने । तत्तु वित्तमहं मन्ये शेषं
कस्यापि रक्षति ॥607 अलब्धं चैव लिप्सेत लब्धं रक्षेत्प्रयत्नतः । रक्षितं वर्धयेद्चैव
वृद्धं पात्रेषु निक्षिपेत् ॥608 अहन्यहनि दातव्यम् अदीनेनान्तरात्मना । स्तोकादपि
प्रयत्नेन दानमित्यभिधीयते ॥609 सन्तोषस्त्रिषु कर्तव्यः स्वदारे भोजने धने । त्रिषु
चैव न कर्तव्यो ऽध्ययने जपदानयोः ॥610

Most difficult:
कः कस्य चोपकुरुते कश्च कस्मै प्रयच्छति । प्राणी करोत्ययं कर्म
सर्वमात्मार्थमात्मना ॥611 दातव्यमित्ययं धर्म उक्तो भूतहिते रतैः । तं मन्यन्ते

धनयुताः कृपणैः सम्प्रवर्तितम्। यदा नियतिकार्पण्यम् अथैषामेव रोचते ॥612
दानान्न दुष्करं तात पृथिव्यामस्ति किञ्चन। अर्थे च महती तृष्णा स च दुःखेन
लभ्यते ॥ परित्यज्य प्रियान्प्राणान् धनार्थं हि महामते। प्रविशन्ति नरा वीराः
समुद्रमटवीं तथा ॥ कृषिगोरक्ष्यमित्येके प्रतिपद्यन्ति मानवाः। पुरुषाः प्रेष्यतामेके
निर्गच्छन्ति धनार्थिनः ॥613

5 motivations: Charity is given ...

धर्मादर्थाद्व्दयात्कामात्कारुण्यादिति ।614

3 kinds of charity:

अभिगम्योत्तमं दानम् आहूतं चैव मध्यमम्। अधमं वाचमानं स्यात् सेवादानं च
निष्फलम् ॥615 परस्परस्य दानानि लोकयात्रा न धर्मतः ।616

शतेषु जायते शूरः सहस्रेषु च पण्डितः। वक्ता शतसहस्रेषु दाता भवति वा न
वा ॥ न रणे विजयाच्छूरो ऽध्ययनान्न च पण्डितः। न वक्ता वाक्पटुत्वेन न दाता
चार्थदानतः ॥ इन्द्रियाणां जये शूरो धर्मं चरति पण्डितः। हितप्रियोक्तिभिर्वक्ता
दाता सम्मानदानतः ॥617

According to ability:

एकां गां दशगुर्दद्याद् दश दद्याच्च गोशती। शतं सहस्रगुर्दद्यात् सर्वे तुल्यफला हि
ते ॥618

To whom:

वृथा वृष्टिः समुद्रेषु वृथा तृप्तेषु भोजनम्। वृथा दानं धनाढ्येषु वृथा दीपो
दिवापि च ॥619 न तेभ्यो ऽपि धनं देयं शक्ये सति कथञ्चन। पापेभ्यो हि धनं
दत्तं दातारमपि पीडयेत् ॥620

A क्षत्रिय does not accept दान, while a ब्राह्मण should accept (and quickly distribute),
but never ask for it:

क्षत्रियो ऽहं न जानामि देहीति वचनं क्वचित्। प्रयच्छ युद्धमित्येवं-वादिनः स्मो
द्विजोत्तम ॥621 ब्राह्मणो ऽनर्थनाधृतिः ।622 न तु पापकृतां राज्ञां प्रतिगृह्णन्ति
साधवः। एतस्मात्कारणाद्यज्ञैर् यजेद्राजाप्तदक्षिणैः ॥623 य उद्धतमनादृत्य
कीनाशमभियाचते। क्षीयते तद्यशः स्फीतं मानश्चावज्ञया हतः ॥624

दान can be classified according to importance:

(**1**) Protection (fearlessness):
हिरण्यदानैर्गोदानैर् भूमिदानैश्च सर्वशः। मांसस्याभक्षणे धर्मो विशिष्ट इति नः
श्रुतिः ॥625 अभयस्य हि यो दाता तस्यैव सुमहत्फलम्। न हि प्राणसमं दानं
त्रिषु लोकेषु विद्यते ॥626

(2) Livelihood (land, gold, kine and education):

भूमिर्भूतिर्महादेवी दातारं कुरुते प्रियम्। मामेवादत्त मां दत्त मां दत्त्वा मामवाप्स्यथ ॥627 यथाप्सु पतितः सद्यस् तैलबिन्दुः प्रसर्पति। एवं भूमिकृतं दानं शस्ये शस्ये प्ररोहति ॥628 सर्वान्कामान्प्रयच्छन्ति ये प्रयच्छन्ति काञ्चनम्।629

अग्नेरपत्यं प्रथमं सुवर्णो भूर्वैष्णवी सूर्यसुताश्च गावः।

लोकास्त्रयस्तेन भवन्ति दत्ता यः काञ्चनं गां च महीं च दद्यात् ॥630

येन जीवति तद् दत्त्वा फलस्यान्तो न विद्यते।631 यो ब्रूयाच्चापि शिष्याय धर्म्यां ब्राह्मीं सरस्वतीम्। पृथिवीगोप्रदानाभ्यां तुल्यं स फलमश्नुते ॥632 एकमप्यक्षरं यस्तु गुरुः शिष्यं प्रबोधयेत्। पृथिव्यां नास्ति तद् द्रव्यं यद्दत्त्वा सोऽनृणी भवेत् ॥633

(3) Help (food, water, ghee, trees, etc.):

अन्नेन सदृशं दानं न भूतं न भविष्यति।634 औषधं पथ्यमाहारं स्नेहाभ्यङ्गं प्रतिश्रयम्। यः प्रयच्छति रोगिभ्यः सर्वव्याधिविवर्जितः ॥ दानान्येतानि देयानि ह्यन्यानि च विशेषतः। दीनान्धकृपणादिभ्यः श्रेयस्कामेन धीमता ॥635 पानीयं परमं दानं दानानां मनुरब्रवीत्। तस्मात्कूपांश्च वापीश्च तडागानि च खानयेत् ॥636 तस्य पुत्रा भवन्त्येते पादपा नात्र संशयः। पुष्पिताः फलवन्तश्च तर्पयन्तीह मानवान्। वृक्षदं पुत्रवद् वृक्षास् तारयन्ति परत्र तु ॥637 पुन्नाम्नो नरकाद्यस्मात् त्रायते पितरं सुतः। तस्मात्पुत्र इति प्रोक्तः स्वयमेव स्वयम्भुवा ॥638

The best (pious) trees to plant are Peepal (पिप्पल), Neem (निम्ब), Banyan (वट), Arjun (अर्जुन), Kadamb (कदम्ब), Indian Rosewood (अगुरु), Teak (शाक), Ashok (अशोक), Anjeer (प्लक्ष), Sandal (चन्दन), Bakul (बकुल), Bamboo (वंश), Bel (बिल्व), Mango (आम्र), Chiku (सपीतक), Jackfruit (पनस), Jamun (जम्बू), Amla (अमला), Tamarind (अम्लक), Lemon (निम्बू), Guava (बीजपूर), Cocos (नारिकेल), Banana (कदली), Pomegranate (दाडिम), and Drumstick (शिग्रु). Other important plants are Tulsi (तुलसी), Brahmi (ब्रह्मी), Turmeric (हलदी), Ashwagandha (अश्वगन्ध), and Soapnut (अरिष्ट). See **Permaculture**.

---

50. Adharma

अज्ञानेनावृतो लोको मात्सर्यान्न प्रकाशते। लोभात्त्यजति मित्राणि सङ्गात्स्वर्गं न गच्छति ॥639 एकस्य कर्म संवीक्ष्य करोत्यन्यो ऽपि गर्हितम्। गतानुगतिको लोको न लोकः पारमार्थिकः ॥640

परद्रव्येष्वभिध्यानं मनसानिष्टचिन्तनम्। वितथाभिनिवेशश्च त्रिविधं कर्म मानसम् ॥ पारुष्यमनृतं चैव पैशुन्यं चापि सर्वशः। असम्बद्धप्रलापश्च वाङ्मयं

स्याच्चतुर्विधम् ॥ अदत्तानामुपादानं हिंसा चैवाविधानतः । परदारोपसेवा च शारीरं त्रिविधं स्मृतम् ॥641

<table>
<tr><td></td><td>(1)</td><td>(2)</td><td>(3)</td><td>(4)</td></tr>
<tr><td>धर्म</td><td>सत्य</td><td>शौच, दम</td><td>दया, दान</td><td>तपः, विद्या</td></tr>
<tr><td rowspan="2">अधर्म
because of</td><td>द्यूत/अक्ष</td><td>सङ्ग/स्त्रिय
काम</td><td>सूना/मृगया, स्मय
क्रोध</td><td>मद/पान
लोभ</td></tr>
</table>

गृहासक्तस्य नो विद्या नो दया मांसभोजिनः । द्रव्यलुब्धस्य नो सत्यं स्त्रैणस्य न पवित्रता ॥642 तपः शौचं दया सत्यम् इति पादाः कृते कृताः । अधर्मांशैस्त्रयो भग्नाः स्मयसङ्गमदैस्तव ॥643 अभ्यर्थितस्तदा तस्मै स्थानानि कलये ददौ । द्यूतं पानं स्त्रियः सूना यत्राधर्मश्चतुर्विधः ॥ पुनश्च याचमानाय जातरूपमदात्प्रभुः । ततोऽनृतं मदं कामं रजो वैरं च पञ्चमम् ॥644 पानमक्षाः स्त्रियश्चैव मृगया च यथाक्रमम् । एतत्कष्टतमं विद्याच्चतुष्कं कामजे गणे ॥645 द्यूतमेतत्पुरा कल्पे दृष्टं वैरकरं महत् । तस्माद् द्यूतं न सेवेत हास्यार्थमपि बुद्धिमान् ॥646

वार्द्धुषिं भ्रूणहत्यां च तुलया समतोलयत् । अतिष्ठद् भ्रूणहा कोट्यां वार्द्धुषिर्न्यक्पपात ह ॥ द्विकं त्रिकं चतुष्कं च पञ्चकं च शतं स्मृतम् । मासस्य वृद्धिं गृह्णीयाद् वर्णानामनुपूर्वशः ॥647

Conclusions:

कलहान्तानि हर्म्याणि कुवाक्यान्तं च सौहृदम् । कुराजान्तानि राष्ट्राणि कुकर्मान्तं यशो नृणाम् ॥648 धनेनाधर्मलब्धेन यच्छिद्रमपिधीयते । असंवृतं तद्भवति ततोऽन्यदवदीर्यते ॥649 वर्धत्यधर्मेण नरस् ततो भद्राणि पश्यति । ततः सपत्नान् जयति समूलस्तु विनश्यति ॥650 सर्वतः शङ्कते स्तेनो मृगो ग्राममिवेयिवान् । बहुधाचरितं पापम् अन्यत्रैवानुपश्यति ॥651 समानकर्माचरणं पतितानां न पातकम् ।652 न मांसभक्षणे दोषो न मद्ये न च मैथुने । प्रवृत्तिरेषा भूतानां निवृत्तिस्तु महाफला ॥653

---

51. Karma

कर्म-वाद (the theory of reaction of work, or responsibility):

मानुषेषु महाराजन् धर्माधर्मौ प्रवर्ततः । न तथान्येषु भूतेषु मनुष्यरहितेष्विह ॥654

यस्माच्च येन च यथा च यदा च यच्च यावच्च यत्र च शुभाशुभमात्मकर्म ।
तस्माच्च तेन च तथा च तदा च तच्च तावच्च तत्र च विधातृवशादुपैति ॥655

बालो युवा च वृद्धश्च यत्करोति शुभाशुभम् । तस्यां तस्यामवस्थायां तत्फलं प्रतिपद्यते ॥656 रोगशोकपरीताप-बन्धनव्यसनानि च । आत्मापराधवृक्षाणां फलान्येतानि देहिनाम् ॥657

Witnesses:

ज्ञानपूर्वकृतं पापं छादयत्यबहुश्रुतः । नैनं मनुष्याः पश्यन्ति पश्यन्त्येव दिवौकसः ॥658 द्यौर्भूमिरापो हृदयं चन्द्रार्कग्नियमानिलाः । रात्रिः सन्ध्ये च धर्मश्च वृत्तज्ञाः सर्वदेहिनाम् ॥659 यथा धेनुसहस्रेषु वत्सो विन्दति मातरम् । तथा पूर्वकृतं कर्म कर्तारमनुगच्छति ॥

"The law of Karma postulates that in this world there are no rewards or punishments; it is simply a case of inevitable consequences. As you sow, so shall you reap." (Nanabhoy /Nani Ardeshir Palkhivala; Indian lawyer and Ambassador to the USA, 1920-2002)

Own and shared कर्म /responsibility:

एकः प्रजायते जन्तुर् एक एव प्रलीयते । एको ऽनुभुङ्क्ते सुकृतम् एक एव च दुष्कृतम् ॥660 स्वयं कर्म करोत्यात्मा स्वयं तत्फलमश्नुते । स्वयं भ्रमति संसारे स्वयं तस्माद्विमुच्यते ॥661 आरोप्यते शिला शैले यत्नेन महता यथा । निपात्यते क्षणेनाधस् तथात्मा गुणदोषयोः ॥662 यात्यधो ऽधः व्रजत्युच्चैर् नरः स्वैरेव कर्मभिः । कूपस्य खनिता यद्वत् प्राकारस्येव कारकः ॥663

अनिष्टादिष्टलाभे ऽपि न गतिर्जायते शुभा । यत्रास्ते विषसंसर्गो ऽमृतं तदपि मृत्यवे ॥664 पुण्यात्षड्भागमादत्ते न्यायेन परिपालयन् । सर्वदानाधिकं यस्मात् प्रजानां परिपालनम् ॥ अरक्ष्यमाणाः कुर्वन्ति यत्किञ्चित्किल्बिषं प्रजाः । तस्मात्तु नृपतेरर्धं यस्माद् गृह्णात्यसौ करान् ॥665 अन्नादे भ्रूणहा मार्ष्टि पत्यौ भार्यापचारिणी । गुरौ शिष्यश्च याज्यश्च स्तेनो राजनि किल्बिषम् ॥666 पतत्यर्धं शरीरस्य यस्य भार्या सुरां पिबेत् ॥667 यतये काञ्चनं दत्त्वा ताम्बुलं ब्रह्मचारिणे । चोरेभ्यो ऽप्यभयं दत्त्वा दातापि नरकं व्रजेत् ॥668

Provision in कलि-युग :

धर्मकार्यं यतन् शक्त्या नो चेत्प्राप्नोति मानवः । प्राप्तो भवति तत्पुण्यम् अत्र मे नास्ति संशयः ॥ मनसा चिन्तयन्पापं कर्मणा नातिरोचयन् । न प्राप्नोति फलं तस्येत्येवं धर्मविदो विदुः ॥669 नानुद्वेष्टि कलिं सम्राट् सारङ्ग इव सारभुक् । कुशलान्याशु सिध्यन्ति नेतराणि कृतानि यत् ॥670

"I am no Hindu, but I hold the doctrine of the Hindus concerning a future state to be incomparably more rational, more pious, and more likely to deter men from vice, than the horrid opinions, inculcated on punishments without end." (Sir William Jones, British judge of the Supreme Court at Calcutta, 1746-1794)

Two stages of कर्म:

1. अ-प्रारब्ध-फल ('whose result has not yet come'), or आगामि (which is 'coming' later): Sometimes subdivided into कूट ('heap', subtle total stock), बीज (seed), and फल-उन्मुख ('awaiting the fruit', ripening).

2. प्रारब्ध-फल ('whose result has come'), that which has fructified in the form of our present body

कर्मणा दैवनेत्रेण जन्तुर्देहोपपत्तये । स्त्रियाः प्रविष्ट उदरं पुंसो रेतःकणाश्रयः ॥[671]

The effects of कर्म are जन्म/जाति (good or bad birth), आयुः (lifespan), भोग (सुख from past सुकृति and दुःख/क्लेश from past पाप), ऐश्वर्य (lordship), श्रुति/विद्या (education), and श्री (beauty).

आयुः कर्म च वित्तं च विद्या निधनमेव च । पञ्चैतानि हि सृज्यन्ते गर्भस्थस्यैव देहिनः ॥[672]

दैव, destiny:

आपदामापतन्तीनां हितो ऽप्यायाति हेतुताम् । मातृजङ्घा हि वत्सस्य स्तम्भीभवति बन्धने ॥[673] नाप्राप्तकालो म्रियते विद्धः शरशतैरपि । कुशाग्रेणापि संस्पृष्टः प्राप्तकालो न जीवति ॥[674] यो ऽधिकाद्योजनशतात् पश्यतीहामिषं खगः । स एव प्राप्तकालस्तु पाशबन्धं न पश्यति ॥[675]

अरक्षितं तिष्ठति देवरक्षितं सुरक्षितं देवहतं विनश्यति ।
जीवत्यनाथो ऽपि वने विसर्जितः कृतप्रयत्नो ऽपि गृहे विनश्यति ॥[676]

छित्त्वा पाशमपास्य कूटरचनां भङ्क्त्वा बलाद्धागुरां
पर्यन्ताग्निशिखाकलापजटिलान्निर्गत्य दूरं वनात् ।
व्याधानां शरगोचरादपि जवेनोत्पत्य धावन्मृगः
कूपान्तःपतितः करोतु विधुरे किं वा विधौ पौरुषम् ॥[677]

दुःखेष्वेकतरेणापि दैवभूतात्महेतुषु । जीवस्य न व्यवच्छेदः स्याच्चेत् तत्तत्प्रतिक्रिया ॥ यथा हि पुरुषो भारं शिरसा गुरुमुद्वहन् । तं स्कन्धेन स आधत्ते तथा सर्वाः प्रतिक्रियाः ॥[678]

But, दैव itself is the result of previous activities:

दैवे पुरुषकारे च कर्मसिद्धिर्व्यवस्थिता । तत्र दैवमभिव्यक्तं पौरुषं पौर्वदेहिकम् ॥[679]

न पश्यति च जन्मान्धः कामान्धो नैव पश्यति । मदोन्मत्ता न पश्यन्ति अर्थी दोषं न पश्यति ॥680

"After reading and considering the works of Babhravya and other ancient authors, and thinking over the meaning of the rules given by them, this treatise (Kāma-Sūtra) was composed, according to the precepts of the sacred law, for the benefit of the world, by Vatsyayana, while leading the life of a religious student at Benares, and wholly engaged in the contemplation of the Deity. This work is not to be used merely as an instrument for satisfying our desires. A person acquainted with the true principles of this science, who preserves his Dharma-Artha-Kāma, and who has regard to the customs of the people, is sure to obtain the mastery over his senses. In short, an intelligent and knowing person attending to Dharma-Artha-Kāma, without becoming the slave of his passions, will obtain success in everything that he may do." (Vatsyayana; Indian philosopher, 2nd century)

The root of कर्म is काम /desire:

"काम, क्रोध and लोभ – this threefold gate to hell is the destruction of awareness of the self. Therefore, this triple one should give up." (भगवद्गीता 16.21)

क्षमया क्रोधमुच्छिन्द्यात् कामं सङ्कल्पवर्जनात् । सत्त्वसंसेवनाद्धीरो निद्रां च च्छेत्तुमर्हति ॥681 एकया द्वे विनिश्चित्य त्रींश्चतुर्भिर्वशे कुरु । पञ्च जित्वा विदित्वा षट् सप्त हित्वा सुखी भव ॥682

यद्यदेव हि वाञ्छेत ततो वाञ्छा प्रवर्तते । प्राप्त एवार्थतः सो ऽर्थो यतो वाञ्छा निवर्तते ॥683

And the root of काम is ignorance of the soul:

उपद्रवांस्तथा रोगान् हितजीर्णमिताशनात् । लोभं मोहं च सन्तोषाद् विषयांस्तत्त्वदर्शनात् ॥ उत्थानेन जयेत्तन्द्रीं वितर्कं निश्चयाज्जयेत् । मौनेन बहुभाष्यं च शौर्येण च भयं त्यजेत् ॥ यच्छेद् वाङ्मनसी बुद्ध्या तां यच्छेज्ज्ञानचक्षुषा । ज्ञानमात्मावबोधेन यच्छेदात्मानमात्मना ॥684

<hr>

54. Tapa

The following chapters cover topics concerning inner purification, like तप:, प्रायश्चित्त, पञ्च-यज्ञ, क्षमा and punishment.
व्रतं हि कर्तृसन्तापात् तप इत्यभिधीयते ।685 सर्वमेतत्तपोमूलं कवयः परिचक्षते । न ह्यतप्ततपा मूढः क्रियाफलमवाप्नुते ॥686 ईहमानः समारम्भान् यदि नासादयेद्धनम् । उग्रं तपः समारोहेन् न ह्यनुप्तं प्ररोहति ॥687

कालेन स्नानशौचाभ्यां संस्कारैस्तपसेज्यया । शुध्यन्ति दानैः सन्तुष्ट्या द्रव्याण्यात्मात्मविद्यया ॥688 कालो ऽग्निः कर्म मृद्वायुर् मनो ज्ञानं तपो जलम् । पश्चात्तापो निराहारः सर्वे ऽमी शुद्धिहेतवः ॥689 एकाकिना तपो द्वाभ्यां पठनं गायनं त्रिभिः । चतुर्भिर्गमनं क्षेत्रं पञ्चभिर्बहुभी रणः ॥690

As atonement:

शरीरपातनाच्चैव तपसाध्ययनेन च । मुच्यते पापकृत्पापाद् दानाच्चापि प्रमुच्यते ॥691 शक्यते विधिना पापं यथोक्तेन व्यपोहितुम् । आस्तिके श्रद्दधाने च विधिरेष विधीयते ॥692 तपसा कर्मणा चैव प्रदानेन च भारत । पुनाति पापं पुरुषः पुनश्चेन्न प्रवर्तते ॥693

द्वितीयमपराधं न कस्यचित्क्षमेत् ।694

Methods:

(1) cutting hair

यत्किञ्चित्क्रियते पापं सर्वं केशेषु तिष्ठति । सर्वान्केशान्समुद्धृत्य च्छेदयेदङ्गुलिद्वयम् ॥695

(2) ब्रह्म-कूर्च ('spiritual bundle' of कुश grass), a process of taking पञ्च-गव्य

(3) उपवास, also called कृच्छ्र ('hardship')

समुन्नमग्रतो वस्त्रं पश्चाच्छुध्यति कर्मणा । उपवासैः प्रतप्तानां दीर्घं सुखमनन्तकम् ॥696

"Eating in the evening and in the morning is prescribed in the वेद for men. If food is not taken in between sunrise and sunset one is also as if fasting."697 ... called नक्त-व्रत ('night penance', eating only at night) in अत्रि-स्मृति 131.

"For three days one eats in the evening, three days in the early morning, three days only what is unsolicited, and the last three days one should fast – this is described as प्राजापत्य rule." 698

"During कृष्ण-पक्ष one should reduce the food every day by one morsel, and during शुक्ल-पक्ष one should increase it. On अमावास्या / अमावस्या one should not eat. This is the चान्द्रायण rule."699 Thus one starts and ends with fourteen morsels. According to other sources the व्रत starts with शुक्ल-पक्ष, first increasing the food.

But:

मासपक्षोपवासेन मन्यन्ते यत्तपो जनाः । आत्मतन्त्रोपघातस्तु न तपस्तत्सतां मतम् ॥ त्यागश्च सर्वतश्चैव शिष्यते तप उत्तमम् । सदोपवासी च भवेद् ब्रह्मचारी सदा भवेत् ॥700 अहिंसा सत्यवचनम् आनृशंस्यं दमो घृणा । एतत्तपो विदुर्धीरा न शरीरस्य शोषणम् ॥701

क्षमा (forgiveness):

अपमानात्तपोवृद्धिः सम्मानात्तपसः क्षयः ।[702] आक्रोशपरिवादाभ्यां विहिंसन्त्यबुधा बुधान् । वक्ता पापमुपादत्ते क्षममाणो विमुच्यते ॥[703] एकः क्षमावतां दोषो द्वितीयो नोपपद्यते । यदेनं क्षमया युक्तम् अशक्तं मन्यते जनः ॥ द्वाविमौ पुरुषौ राजन् स्वर्गस्योपरि तिष्ठतः । प्रभुश्च क्षमया युक्तो दरिद्रश्च प्रदानवान् ॥[704]

When राम was forced into exile He said to लक्ष्मण :

बुद्धिः प्रणीता येनेयं मनश्च सुसमाहितम् । तं तु नार्हामि सङ्क्लेष्टुं प्रव्रजिष्यामि मा चिरम् ॥[705] परवाच्येषु निपुणः सर्वो भवति सर्वदा । आत्मवाच्यं न जानीते जानन्नपि न मुह्यति ॥[706]

55. Debt

Every human being has five debts:

	(1)	(2)	(3)	(4)	(5)	
debt to	देव	ऋषि	पितृ	नृ/भृत्य	भूत/देवता	
for	light, water	knowledge	inheritance	service	protection	
repaid as	देव-	ब्रह्म-	पितृ-	नृ-	भूत-	यज्ञ
through	होम	अध्ययन /अध्यापन	श्राद्ध /तर्पण	अभ्यर्चन /आतिथ्य	बलि	

देवतार्तिथिभृत्येभ्यः पितृभ्यश्चात्मनस्तथा । ऋणवान् जायते मर्त्यस् तस्मादनृणतां व्रजेत् ॥ स्वाध्यायेन महर्षिभ्यो देवेभ्यो यज्ञकर्मणा । पितृभ्यः श्राद्धदानेन नृणामभ्यर्चनेन च ॥[707] अध्यापनं ब्रह्मयज्ञः पितृयज्ञस्तु तर्पणम् । होमो दैवो बलिर्भौतो नृयज्ञो ऽतिथिपूजनम् ॥[708]

Especially a गृहस्थ should perform पञ्च-यज्ञ to repay those debts.
वैवाहिके ऽग्नौ कुर्वीत गृह्यं कर्म यथाविधि । पञ्चयज्ञविधानं च पक्तिं चान्वाहिकीं गृही ॥ देवानृषीन्मनुष्यांश्च पितॄन्गृह्याश्च देवताः । पूजयित्वा ततः पश्चाद् गृहस्थः शेषभुग्भवेत् ॥[709]

He should eat only what is left after such offerings, after everyone has eaten, including servants. "Saints who eat food which is left after यज्ञ are freed from all sin, but those who cook just for their own sake, eat verily sin." (भगवद्गीता 3.13)

अभ्यर्चन (reverence):

नास्ति मातृसमं दैवं नास्ति पितृसमो गुरुः ।710

भृतो वृद्धो यो न बिभर्ति पुत्रः स्वयोनिजः पितरं मातरं च ।
तद्वै पापं भ्रूणहत्याविशिष्टं तस्मान्नान्यः पापकृदस्ति लोके ।।711

आत्ममाता गुरोः पत्नी ब्राह्मणी राजपत्निका । धेनुर्धात्री तथा पृथ्वी सप्तैता
मातरः स्मृताः ।।712 यश्चैनमुत्पादयते यश्चैनं त्रायते भयात् । यश्चास्य कुरुते वृत्तिं
सर्वे ते पितरस्त्रयः ।।713

आतिथ्य (hospitality):

अध्वनीनो ऽतिथिर्ज्ञेयः श्रोत्रियो वेदपारगः । मान्यावेतौ गृहस्थस्य
ब्रह्मलोकमभीप्सतः ।।714 अराववप्युचितं कार्यम् आतिथ्यं गृहमागते । छेत्तुमप्यागते
छायां नोपसंहरते द्रुमः ।।715 अतिथिर्यस्य भग्नाशो गृहात्प्रतिनिवर्तते । स दत्त्वा
दुष्कृतं तस्मै पुण्यमादाय गच्छति ।।716

---

56. Punishment

सर्पाणां च खलानां च परद्रव्यापहारिणाम् । अभिप्राया न सिध्यन्ति तेनेदं वर्तते
जगत् ।।717 गुरुरात्मवतां शास्ता राजा शास्ता दुरात्मनाम् । इह प्रच्छन्नपापानां
शास्ता वैवस्वतो यमः ।।718

According to महाभारत 1.108.13, there is no punishment for a person below 14 years
of age, and ...

वानस्पत्यं मूलफलं दार्वग्न्यर्थं तथैव च । तृणं च गोभ्यो ग्रासार्थम् अस्तेयं
मनुरब्रवीत् ।।719 कर्मभ्यो विप्रमुच्यन्ते यत्ताः संवत्सरं स्त्रियः । स्त्रियस्त्वाशङ्किताः
पापा नोपगम्या विजानता । रजसा ता विशुध्यन्ते भस्मना भाजनं यथा ।।720

"The doctrines of the Hindoo religion have been singularly careful to protect the female sex and
infants from violence; and it is unlawful to put a woman to death for any offense whatever."
(James Peggs, English missionary in India, 1793-1850)

गृहीतान्समाहर्ता पौरजानपदानां दर्शयेत् । चोरग्रहणीं विद्यामधीते राजा ।
तस्योपदेशादिमे चोरा गृहीताः ।721

Different punishments:

पुरा धिग्दण्ड एवासीद् वाग्दण्डस्तदनन्तरम् । आसीदादानदण्डो ऽपि वधदण्डो ऽद्य
वर्तते ।।722 मनुष्याणां पशूनां च दुःखाय प्रहृते सति । यथा यथा महद्दुःखं दण्डं
कुर्यात्तथा तथा ।।723 धनं तु यस्यापहरेत् तस्मै दद्यात्समं वसु । विविधेनाभ्युपायेन
तदा मुच्येत किल्बिषात् ।।724 अपराधानुरूपं च दण्डं पापेषु धारयेत् । वियोजयेद्
धनैर्ऋद्धान् अधनानथ बन्धनैः ।।725

"In the code of Hindu laws and customs, it is said: 'If the property of a dancing woman should by any circumstance become subject to seizure, the magistrate shall except her clothes, jewels, and dwelling. In the same manner, to a soldier shall be left his arms; and to a man exercising any profession, the implements of that profession; but the rest of his property may be confiscated.'" (Quintin Craufurd, British author, 1743-1819)

Capital punishment:

अग्निदो गरदश्चैव शस्त्रपाणिर्धनापहः । क्षेत्रदारहरश्चैव षडेत आततायिनः ॥[726] नाततायिवधे दोषो हन्तुर्भवति कश्चन ।[727] निकृत्या निकृतिप्रज्ञा हन्तव्या इति निश्चयः । न हि नैकृतिकं हत्वा निकृत्या पापमुच्यते ॥[728] स्वप्राणान् यः परप्राणैः प्रपुष्णात्यघृणः खलः । तद्वधस्तस्य हि श्रेयो यद्दोषाद्यात्यधः पुमान् ॥[729] शरीरस्य विमोक्षेण मुच्यते कर्मणोऽशुभात् ।[730] राजभिः कृतदण्डास्तु कृत्वा पापानि मानवाः । निर्मलाः स्वर्गमायान्ति सन्तः सुकृतिनो यथा ॥[731]

But:

दस्यून्निहन्ति वै राजा भूयसो वाप्यनागसः । भार्या माता पिता पुत्रो हन्यन्ते पुरुषेण ते ॥ असाधुश्चैव पुरुषो लभते शीलगोकदा । साधोश्चापि ह्यसाधुभ्यः शोभना जायते प्रजा ॥ यदा पुरोहितं वा ते पर्येयुः शरणैषिणः । करिष्यामः पुनर्ब्रह्मन् न पापमिति वादिनः । तदा विसर्गमर्हाः स्युर् इतीदं धातृशासनम् ॥[732]

"This singular passage, dealing with an abnormally high punishment for a minor offence, is evidently an interpolation, as it is inconsistent not only with the authors principle of gradation in punishments proportional to crimes, but also with his intention to get rid of mutilation of limbs by fines levied in lieu thereof." (Note by R. Shamasastry on a passage in Kautiliya-Artha-Shastra, ch.76)

---

57. Society

विप्रक्षत्रियविट्शूद्रा मुखबाहूरुपादजाः । गृहाश्रमो जघनतो ब्रह्मचर्यं हृदो मम । वक्षःस्थलाद्वनेवासः सन्यासः शिरसि स्थितः ॥[733]

"Since its origin, Hindu society has been built on rational bases by sages who sought to comprehend man's nature and role in creation as a whole. They organized the society in such a way as to facilitate the development of each human being, taking into account his inner nature and the reasons for his existence, since for the Hindus the world is not merely the result of a series of chances but the realization of a divine plan in which all aspects are interconnected. Thus, Hindu society is the result of an attempt to situate man in the plan of creation." "The Hindus assert that their social formula meets the requirements of man's individual and collective nature. The fact that the Hindu civilization has been able to survive over thousands of years, despite disorders caused by invasions, schisms, and internal wars, and has been capable of constant renewal, as demonstrated by one brilliant period after another, merits all our attention in the study of a social system whose longevity is unique in history." (Alain Danielou, French ethnomusicologist, head of the UNESCO Institute for Comparative Musicology, 1907-1994)

"The fundamental needs of society are the moral and the spiritual, the military and the economic. In Indo-European society these three functions are assigned to three different groups, the men of learning and virtue, the men of courage and fight, and the men who provide the economic needs, the Brahmana, the Kshatriya and the Vaishya. Below them are the Shudras devoted to service. These distinctions are found in the Rig-Veda, though they are not crystallised into castes. Ancient Iranian society was constituted on a similar pattern." (Sir Sarvepalli Radhakrishnan, Indian Prof. at Oxford University and President of India, 1888-1975)

Castes in India are not economically structured. Each caste has its own rich and its own poor. There are rich Brahmins and poor Brahmins. As a general rule, Brahmins were among the poorest section of society. This observation runs counter to the prevalent view that Indian society is Brahmin dominated and Brahmin exploited. Different castes in India are like different ethnic groups within the United States. There are rich Italians and poor Italians, rich Irish and poor Irish. Also, like caste groups in India, till recently the ethnic groups in America married in their own community, i.e., Jews would marry other Jews, the Polish would marry other Polish, and so on.

"Caste systems in India evolved, just as they have done in the US, as a labor group by the kind of work. This is why each of India's castes corresponds to a category of labor, much like the modern guild of American workers of a given profession, with its own procedures for membership and strategies to compete with outsiders. In India, this segmentation got perpetuated because training was done through work apprenticeship under one's parents, thereby turning family lineages into specialized labor." (Rajiv Malhotra, Indian scientist and writer)

"Westerners tend to be perplexed and scandalized by the caste system but they forget that the aristocracy which ruled over Europe for a thousand years was a caste of sorts. The guilds of the Ancient Regime resembled Indian castes as they had existed initially, each caste corresponding to a particular trade." (Guy Sorman, French-American economist and philosopher)

"It would lead to a greater respect for India's culture, and indeed a better understanding of it, if it were recognized that the caste system has never been totally static, that it is adapting itself to today's changing circumstances and that it has positive as well as negative aspects. The caste system provides security and a community for millions of Indians. It gives them an identity that neither Western Science nor Western thought has yet provided, because caste is not just a matter of being a Brahmin or a Harijan: it is also a kinship system. The system provides a wider support group than a family: a group which has a social life in which all its members participate." (Prof. Ronald B. Inden, American historian)

"The caste system provides for relatively greater stability and dignity to the individuals than they would have as atomized individuals. This in part explains why the Indian poor retain a strong sense of self-respect. It is that self-respect which the thoughtless insistence on egalitarianism destroys." (Prof. Madhu Purnima Kishwar, Indian academic and writer)

"Caste has created and maintained an infinite capacity for toleration and assimilation. Caste made it possible for the Persians, Greeks, Scythians, Huns, Malays, Christians, Jews and Parsees to be slowly fitted into Hindu society and made it, with the least conflict, into the most diverse community of races in the world. It is this marvelous diversity of man in India which has made that country both a museum and a laboratory for the study of man. For this reason, the most profound lessons in the study of society have come from India." (Prof. Cyril Dean Darlington, English biologist and geneticist, 1903-1981)

Louis Dumont, who had seen both class and race wars in the West, argues that castes inhere in human nature. And this explains the indifference to caste of the earlier European travelers who came to India.

"Indians are as attached to their caste as our gentlemen to theirs." (N.J. Desvaulx, 1745-1825)

It was only later with modernity that a reaction set in. The hostility of the West to castes may well have something to do with the zeal of Christian missionaries to convert. As Islam had shown, the untouchables were the easiest to proselytize and that is why they aroused the most compassion.

As a political category, caste is a British invention. The British introduced the category of caste for purposes of counting population in the census that began in 1871, ranking them by status and economics. Many petitions were filed by new resurgent groups to seek higher ranking. Caste began to be organized as political movement – in a similar fashion, as the counting of people by tribal identity in Africa led to tribalism. Sikhism was defined as a separate religion by the British, and it became so. These points are elaborated in an excellent book by Nicholas Dirks, *Castes of Mind: Colonialism and the Making of Modern India*, 2001.

"In modern popularizing writings, one often reads that 'egalitarian' Buddhism was essentially a 'protest movement' against the Brahminical caste system. ... But neither the Buddha himself, nor any pre-modern Buddhist teacher after him has combated the caste system. Buddhism's non-interest in social reform is also demonstrated by its career outside India. After centuries of profound impact of Buddhism, Tibetan society was in such a state that the Chinese Communists could claim in 1950 that 95% of the Tibetans were living in slavery; ... the fact remains that Buddhism had not rendered Tibet's traditional feudalism any more egalitarian than it had been in the pre-Buddhist past. Outside India, a number of independent sources confirm that Buddhist monasteries employed slaves." (Prof. Erik Zürcher, Dutch sinologist, 1928-2008)

"The Buddha never said: 'Down with the Brahmins! Break Brahmin tyranny!' On the contrary, he taught about how to be a true Brahmin, as against having the outer attributes but not the inner qualities of the Brahmin. Many of his disciples were Brahmins. The myth of Buddhist social revolution against Brahmin tyranny can be disproven on many counts with the Buddha's own words." (Dr. Koenraad Elst, Dutch historian)

Degradation:

The caste system in ancient times was not static. Castes rose and fell. Castes became static and rigid during extended foreign rule.

Under Muslim rule, some caste groups that fought against domination were pushed to the outer edges of the social system. Among the sweeper castes in India, one finds many Rajput Gotras (royal families).

राक्षसाः कलिमाश्रित्य जायन्ते ब्रह्मयोनिषु । उत्पन्ना ब्राह्मणकुले बाधन्ते श्रोत्रियान्कृशान् ॥734

When there is too much attachment to sense gratification, human society is utilized by selfish men to pose an artificial predominance over the weaker section. Exploitation of the weaker living being by the stronger is a natural tendency. There is no possibility of checking it by any artificial means.

"The present static Caste system is a dark spot on Hinduism. It goes against the principles and lofty philosophy of Hinduism which considers each soul as potentially divine and eternal. Hindu philosophy insists on an attitude of tolerance. Universal brotherhood is the chief message of Hindu religious tradition. The goal is to manifest this divinity within. It is simply remarkable that in a country of diversities, people belonging to different castes and creed cut across all barriers to converge for the great festival of Kumbh mela. "Whereas the caste system based on birth as at present existing is manifestly contrary to universal truth and morals: whereas it is the very antithesis of the fundamental spirit of the Hindu religion: whereas it flouts the elementary rights of human equality, this all India Hindu Mahasabha declares its uncompromising opposition to the system and calls upon the Hindu society to put a speedy end to it." (Hindu Mahasabha)

It is said that राम-राज्य (the just kingdom of God) is impossible without राम (God), and वर्णाश्रम-धर्म is stable only when it is दैव (for the worship of the Lord).

वर्णाश्रमाचारवता पुरुषेण परः पुमान् । विष्णुराराध्यते पन्था नान्यत् तत्तोषकारणम् ॥735 अतः पुम्भिर्द्विजश्रेष्ठा वर्णाश्रमविभागशः । स्वनुष्ठितस्य धर्मस्य संसिद्धिर्हरितोषणम् ॥736

"From whom comes the manifestation or activity of all beings, and by whom all this world is pervaded, by worshiping Him with one's duty, a man attains perfection." (Bhagavad-Gita 18.46)

"At the pagoda of jaggernaut, people of all casts and ranks eat together, without distinction or pre-eminence. This is peculiar to that place, being nowhere else allowed; and the permission, or rather order, for the pilgrims of different casts to do so, is said to be in commemoration of their hero and philosopher Krishna, who always recommended complacency and affection for each other." (Quintin Craufurd, British author, 1743-1819)

58. Varna

आदौ कृतयुगे वर्णो नृणां हंस इति स्मृतः । कृतकृत्याः प्रजा जात्या तस्मात्कृतयुगं विदुः ॥737 न वै राज्यं न राजासीन् न च दण्डो न दाण्डिकः । धर्मेणैव प्रजाः सर्वा रक्षन्ति स्म परस्परम् ॥738

वर्ण means 'color', occupation, guild, social class, and वर्ण-धर्म occupational or social duty. The social status, which is connected to वर्ण, is called जाति ('birth', rank, lineage).

Society requires wisdom, power, wealth, and service. Wisdom conceives the order, power sanctions and enforces it, wealth and production provide the means for carrying out the order, and service carries out. At the same time, some men are inclined to wisdom, some to power, some to wealth, and some to none of these specifically. Thus, people can be divided into different groups according to social needs and individual action.

(1)	(2)	(3)	(4)
ब्राह्मण	क्षत्रिय	वैश्य	शूद्र
scholar, teacher, priest	nobility, warrior, administrator	entrepreneur, farmer, merchant	employee

"According to one's nature (गुण) and actual work (कर्मन्) the system of four वर्ण was created by Me." (भगवद्गीता 4.13)

बलं विद्या च विप्राणां राज्ञां सैन्यं बलं तथा । बलं वित्तं च वैश्यानां शूद्राणां पारिचर्यकम् ॥739 बलज्येष्ठं स्मृतं क्षत्रं मन्त्रज्येष्ठा द्विजातयः । धनज्येष्ठाः स्मृता वैश्याः शूद्रास्तु वयसाधिकाः ॥740 शर्मवद् ब्राह्मणस्य स्याद् राज्ञो रक्षासमन्वितम् । वैश्यस्य पुष्टिसंयुक्तं शूद्रस्य प्रेष्यसंयुतम् ॥741

Changing वर्ण

यस्य यल्लक्षणं प्रोक्तं पुंसो वर्णाभिव्यञ्जकम् । यदन्यत्रापि दृश्येत तत्तेनैव विनिर्दिशेत् ॥742 शूद्रे चैतद्भवेल्लक्ष्यं द्विजे तच्च न विद्यते । न वै शूद्रो भवेच्छूद्रो ब्राह्मणो न च ब्राह्मणः ॥743 न योनिर्नापि संस्कारो न श्रुतं न च सन्ततिः । कारणानि द्विजत्वस्य वृत्तमेव तु कारणम् ॥ सर्वोऽयं ब्राह्मणो लोके वृत्तेन तु विधीयते । वृत्ते स्थितस्तु शूद्रोऽपि ब्राह्मणत्वं नियच्छति ॥744 अपारे यो भवेत्पारम् अप्लवे यः प्लवो भवेत् । शूद्रो वा यदि वाप्यन्यः सर्वथा मानमर्हति ॥ नित्यं यस्तु सतो रक्षेद् असतश्च निवर्तयेत् । स एव राजा कर्तव्यस् तेन सर्वमिदं धृतम् ॥745

सूत गोस्वामी, the great authority on पुराण, was from the सूत class. (भागवत-पुराण 1.18.18-19) शौनक was a descendent of King वीतहव्य who became a ब्राह्मण. (महाभारत) Among the 100 sons of King ऋषभ, 81 became ब्राह्मण. (भागवत-पुराण 5.4.13) In the dynasty of King पूरु were many ब्राह्मण lines started. (भागवत-पुराण 9.20.1) In the dynasty of भरद्वाज some became ब्राह्मण. (भागवत-पुराण 9.21.19-21) Sage ऐतरेय also had a 'low birth'.

"If one is born in a family of ब्राह्मण who are absorbed in hearing divine sound, but has bad character and behaviour, he is not worshipable as a ब्राह्मण. On the other hand, व्यास and वैभाण्डक were born in unclean circumstances, but they are worshipable. In the same way, विश्वामित्र was born a क्षत्रिय, but he became equal to me by his qualities and activities. वसिष्ठ was born as a son of a prostitute. Many other great souls who manifested the qualities of first-class ब्राह्मण also took birth in similar humble circumstances, but they are called perfect. The place where one takes birth is of no importance in determining whether one is a ब्राह्मण. Those who have the qualities of ब्राह्मण are recognized everywhere as such, and those who have such qualities are worshipable by everyone." (पद्म-पुराण 43.321-22)

---

59. Brahmana

Who is a ब्राह्मण?

1. The embodiment of virtue

"शम, दम, तपः, शौच, क्षान्ति and आर्जव, ज्ञान, विज्ञान and आस्तिक्य – this is the natural behavior of a ब्राह्मण." (भगवद्गीता 18.42) In essence:

मैत्रो ब्राह्मण उच्यते ।[746] शूद्रयोनौ हि जातस्य सद्गुणानुपतिष्ठतः । वैश्यत्वं लभते ब्रह्मन् क्षत्रियत्वं तथैव च । आर्जवे वर्तमानस्य ब्राह्मण्यमभिजायते ॥[747] आर्जवं धर्ममित्याहुर् अधर्मो जिह्म उच्यते । आर्जवेनेह संयुक्तो नरो धर्मेण युज्यते ॥[748]

There is the story of सत्यकाम, whose father died early, and who was brought up by his single mother जबलि. When the teacher गौतम asked the boy for his वर्ण, the boy asked his mother, but she did not know the वर्ण of the father. The boy conveyed the fact unhesitatingly to गौतम, who immediately accepted the boy as a ब्राह्मण because of the symptom of आर्जव (honesty). गौतम said: "A non-ब्राह्मण is not able to explain this. O gentle one, bring wood, I will initiate you."[749]

2. Who has वैराग्य

अहेरिव गणाद्भीतः सौहित्यान्नरकादिव । कुणपादिव च स्त्रीभ्यस् तं देवा ब्राह्मणं विदुः ॥[750]

3. Who knows ब्रह्म

जन्मना जायते शूद्रः संस्काराद्धि भवेद् द्विजः । वेदपाठाद्भवेद्विप्रो ब्रह्म जानातीति ब्राह्मणः ॥[751] स्पृहयामि द्विजातिभ्यो येषां ब्रह्म परं धनम् । येषां स्वप्रत्ययः स्वर्गस् तपः स्वाध्यायसाधनम् ॥[752]

"When India was invaded by foreign powers, the Brahmins proved to be a great obstacle, particularly against religious conversion. Muslim rulers made special efforts to convert or even kill Brahmins. They destroyed Hindu temples in order to deprive the Brahmins, who were mainly temple priests, of their influence and their income. The British rulers of colonial India targeted the Brahmins and dismantled the traditional educational system that the Brahmins upheld. ... Somehow this oppressed group has been stereotyped as the ruling oppressors! As Brahmins are vilified as the oppressive ruling elite one would expect that the Brahmins routinely ruled the country. Not only was this not true in the period of foreign rule, it wasn't true in the period of classical India either. In this regard it is important to look at the social role traditionally held by Brahmins. In traditional India Brahmins served as the priestly class, providing teachers of all types as well performing religious sacraments and temple worship. The traditional Brahmin was given to a life of poverty, social service, and spiritual practice. Brahmin families usually gave one of their sons to become a monk and led lives of religious austerity. The Brahmins therefore had neither economic nor political advantage. Their status was on a religious and intellectual level. They were praised as religious leaders, not as a political or economic elite. ... The Brahmins as the priestly class did not control the military or economy of the country except when individual Brahmins stepped beyond the traditional limits of their class, which was rare." (David Frawley, American Indologist)

"But how to convert them? One would persecute resistance and opposition. How to respond to indifference? The attitude of these heathens towards Christianity, it is this: indifference." (Prof. S. N. Balagangadhara, Indian philosopher)

"The British were not wrong in their distrust of educated Brahmins in whom they saw a potential threat to their supremacy in India. For instance, in 1879 the Collector of Tanjore in a communication to Sir James Caird, member of the Famine Commission, stated that 'there was no class (except Brahmins) which was so hostile to the English.' The predominance of the Brahmins in the freedom movement confirmed the worst British suspicions of the community. Innumerable reports of the period commented on Brahmin participation at all levels of the nationalist movement. In the words of an observer, 'If any community could claim credit for driving the British out of the country, it was the Brahmin community. Seventy per cent of those who were felled by British bullets were Brahmins.' ... In the attempt to rewrite Indian history, Brahmins began to be portrayed as oppressors and tyrants who willfully kept down the rest of the populace. ... As a result of their machinations non-Brahmins turned on the Brahmins with a ferocity that has few parallels in Indian history. This was all the more surprising in that for centuries Brahmins and non-Brahmins had been active partners and collaborators in the task of political and social management." (Meenakshi Jain, Indian historian)

"The Brahmans are always ready to receive all who will submit to them. The process of manufacturing Rajputs (Kshatriya) from ambitious aborigines (tribals) goes on before our eyes." (Sir John Campbell, British army officer in India, 1802-1878)

"More persons in India become every year Brahmanists than all the converts to all the other religions in India put together. ... These teachers address themselves to every one without distinction of caste or of creed ..." (Sir Alfred Comyn Lyall, British civil servant and historian, 1835-1911)

Duties:

अध्ययन-यजन-दान-तपस् are his कर्म (duty) and अध्यापन-याजन-प्रतिग्रह are his वृत्ति (livelihood).

अध्यापनमध्ययनं यजनं याजनं तथा। दानं प्रतिग्रहं चैव ब्राह्मणानामकल्पयत् ॥753 कर्म विप्रस्य यजनं दानमध्ययनं तपः। प्रतिग्रहो ऽध्यापनं च याजनं चेति वृत्तयः ॥754 अधीयीरंस्त्रयो वर्णाः स्वकर्मस्था द्विजातयः। प्रब्रूयाद् ब्राह्मणस्त्वेषां नेतराविति निश्चयः ॥755 सदोपवीती चैव स्यात् सदा बद्धशिखो द्विजः ।756

विद्या ह वै ब्राह्मणमाजगाम गोपाय मा शेवधिस्ते ऽहमस्मि।

असूयकायानृजवे ऽव्रताय न मा ब्रूया वीर्यवती तथा स्याम् ॥757

अशक्तः क्षत्रधर्मेण वैश्यधर्मेण वर्तयेत्। कृषिगोरक्ष्यमास्थाय व्यसने वृत्तिसङ्क्षये ॥ शूद्रधर्मा यदा तु स्यात् तदा पतति वै द्विजः ।758 ब्राह्मणः क्षत्रियत्वं हि याति शस्त्रसमुद्यमात् ।759

"These castes were under the direction of their Pundits and the Punchayats, or General Assembly of the caste, and used to examine the conduct of the members of their society, and the consequence of their censure was sometimes a total exclusion of the guilty individual from the community. No Brahmin was supported by the public who was unlearned or who did not contribute his assistence in forming the minds of the lower classes, and teach them morality, and the duties enjoined by laws. Under such an establishment for the instruction of the lower classes it was not difficult to form an efficient Police. But the cruel reverse, which the invasion of the unprincipled and bigoted Musalmans introduced, may account for the wide torrent of corruption that has overflooded this country. They considered the conquered Hindus as infidels, and treated them with unrelenting persecution and cruelty. They thought that every insult and injury upon them were acts pleasing to God and the Prophet. Their destructive bigotry attacked the books and learning of the Hindus, and the Brahmins, persecuted with incessant atrocities, ceased to exercise their functions. ... Their learning fell into neglect, and in course of time the Brahmins came to want that instruction themselves which it was their duty to afford to others. Missing in all the selfish squabble of common life, they gradually lost, by their own example, in the eyes of the Hindus, that respect which was so necessary to give force and energy to instruction." (Papers Relating to East India Company Affairs 1813)

"The Brahmins attached to knowledge and learning is what has helped the Indian civilization endure and allowed the arts to flourish. If comparisons have to be made, it may be said that the endurance of the Brahmins in India has kept her elite intact, whereas in neighboring China the anti-intellectualism of communist peasants has completely wiped out the intelligentsia of that country. The Brahmins kept knowledge and art alive in India, preserving not only their savant but also their popular forms. The Brahmin elite is perhaps egoistical and domineering, nonetheless it has preserved a sense of dignity and beauty that has disappeared from China where all that remains is vulgarity and crass ignorance." (Guy Sorman, French-American economist and philosopher)

The world belongs to saints:

नारी तु पत्यभावे वै देवरं कुरुते पतिम् । पृथिवी ब्राह्मणालाभे क्षत्रियं कुरुते पतिम् ॥760 स्वमेव ब्राह्मणो भुङ्क्ते स्वं वस्ते स्वं ददाति च । गुरुर्हि सर्ववर्णानां ज्येष्ठः श्रेष्ठश्च वै द्विजः ॥761 श्रुतवृत्ते विदित्वास्य वृत्तिं धर्म्या प्रकल्पयेत् । संरक्षेत्सर्वतश्चैनं पिता पुत्रमिवोरसम् ॥762

ब्राह्मणेभ्यः करादानं न कुर्यात् । ते हि राज्ञो धर्मकरदाः ।763 अकरः श्रोत्रियो राजपुमानथ प्रव्रजितः ।764 सर्वत्रास्खलितादेशः सप्तद्वीपैक-दण्डधृक् । अन्यत्र ब्राह्मणकुलाद् अन्यत्राच्युतगोत्रतः ॥765 ब्राह्मणार्थं हि सर्वेषां शस्त्रग्रहणमिष्यते ।766

But:

अब्राह्मणानां वित्तस्य स्वामी राजेति वैदिकम् । ब्राह्मणानां च ये केचिद् विकर्मस्था भवन्त्युत ॥767 अश्रोत्रियाः सर्व एव सर्वे चानाहिताग्नयः । तान्सर्वान्धार्मिको राजा बलिं विष्टिं च कारयेत् ॥768 अव्रता ह्यनधीयाना यत्र भैक्षचरा द्विजाः । तं ग्रामं दण्डयेद्राजा चौरभुक्तपदो हि सः ॥ यश्च काष्ठमयो हस्ती यश्च चर्ममयो मृगः । यश्च विप्रो ऽनधीयानस् त्रयस्ते नामधारकाः ॥769

अवृत्तिर्भयमन्त्यानां मध्यानां मरणाद्भयम् । उत्तमानां तु मर्त्यानाम् अवमानात्परं भयम् ॥770 वरं प्राणपरित्यागो मानभङ्गेन जीवनात् । प्राणत्यागे क्षणं दुःखं मानभङ्गे दिने दिने ॥771 वपनं द्रविणादानं स्थानान्नियार्पणं तथा । एष हि ब्रह्मबन्धूनां वधो नान्यो ऽस्ति दैहिकः ॥772 अर्जुनः सहसाज्ञाय हरेर्हर्दमथासिना । मणिं जहार मूर्धन्यं द्विजस्य सहमूर्धजम् ॥

<hr>

60. Kshatriya

क्रव्याद्श्च इव भूतानाम् अदान्तेभ्यः सदा भयम् । तेषां विप्रतिषेधार्थं राजा सृष्टः स्वयम्भुवा ॥773 यस्मिन्भयार्दितः सम्यक् क्षेमं विन्दत्यपि क्षणम् । स स्वर्गजित्तमो ऽस्माकं सत्यमेतद् ब्रवीमि ते ॥774 नाभिषेको न संस्कारः सिंहस्य क्रियते मृगैः । विक्रमार्जितराज्यस्य स्वयमेव मृगेन्द्रता ॥775 एकेनापि सुधीरेण सोत्साहेन रणं प्रति । सोत्साहं जायते सैन्यं भग्ने भङ्गमवाप्नुयात् ॥776

"Heroism, vigor, determination, expertness, courage in battle, generosity, and leadership – this is the natural behavior of a क्षत्रिय." (भगवद्गीता 18.43)

Duty:

प्रजानां रक्षणं दानम् इज्याध्ययनमेव च । विषयेष्वप्रसक्तिश्च क्षत्रियस्य समादिशत् ॥777 तस्करेभ्यो नियुक्तेभ्यः शत्रुभ्यो नृपवल्लभात् । नृपतिर्निजलोभाच्च

प्रजा रक्षेत्पितेव हि ॥778 सामान्यतो हृतं चौरैस् तद्वै दद्यात्स्वयं नृपः।
चौररक्षाधिकारिभ्यो राजापि हृतमाप्नुयात् ॥779

गवार्थे ब्राह्मणार्थे च स्त्रीवित्तहरणे तथा। प्राणांस्त्यजति यो युद्धे तस्य लोकाः
सनातनाः ॥780 धनानि जीवितं चैव परार्थे प्राज्ञ उत्सृजेत्। सन्निमित्ते वरं त्यागो
विनाशे नियते सति ॥781 यदि नित्यमनित्येन निर्मलं मलवाहिना। यशः कायेन
लभ्येत तन्न लब्धं भवेन्तु किम् ॥782

Income:
बलिषष्ठेन शुल्केन दण्डेनाथापराधिनाम्। शास्त्रनीतेन लिप्सेथा वेतनेन
धनागमम् ॥783 कारुकान् शिल्पिनश्चैव शूद्रांश्चात्मोपजीविनः। एकैकं कारयेत्कर्म
मासि मासि महीपतिः ॥784 ऊर्ध्वश्छिन्द्यात्तु यो धेन्वाः क्षीरार्थी न लभेत्पयः। एवं
राष्ट्रमयोगेन पीडितं न विवर्धते ॥785

The king makes the age:
यत्रादृष्टं भयं ब्रह्म प्रजानां शमयत्युत। दृष्टं च राजा बाहुभ्यां तद्राज्यं
सुखमेधते ॥786 सर्ववेदमयो विप्रः सर्वदेवमयो नृपः ।787 कालो वा कारणं राज्ञो
राजा वा कालकारणम्। इति ते संशयो मा भूद् राजा कालस्य कारणम् ॥788
अधर्मः क्षत्रियस्यैष यद् व्याधिमरणं गृहे ।789 भूमिरेतौ निगिरति सर्पो
बिलशयानिव। राजानं चाविरोद्धारं ब्राह्मणं चाप्रवासिनम् ॥790

Training:
त्रैविद्येभ्यस्त्रयीं विद्यां दण्डनीतिं च शाश्वतीम्। आन्वीक्षिकीं चात्मविद्यां
वार्तारम्भांश्च लोकतः ॥791 युक्तिशास्त्रं च ते ज्ञेयं शब्दशास्त्रं च भारत।
गान्धर्वशास्त्रं च कलाः परिज्ञेया नराधिप ॥792

"The forenoon he should undergo training in the sciences of fighting with elephants,
horses, and chariots, the afternoon in hearing history." (कौटिलीय-अर्थ-शास्त्र 2.6)

Daily routine of a king according to अग्नि-पुराण 235.1 ff.: The king should rise 90
minutes before sunrise with music, hear a financial report, visit the bathroom, do the
morning सन्ध्या and worship the Lord, perform यज्ञ, make gifts to the ब्राह्मण and
receive their blessings, put on ornaments, hear about the nature of the day, take his
medicines, touch auspicious items, see his elders, visit the council to see important
men, hear the daily report, determine the business of the day, consult his ministers,
then do exercises with cars or weapons, take bath again, see the worship of the Lord
and the sacrifice, take his meal (lunch), rest for a while, study books, see the parade of
his soldiers, do the evening सन्ध्या, do consultations, direct his spies, take a meal
(dinner), enter his private quarter and hear music.

स्वाम्यमात्यौ पुरं राष्ट्रं कोशदण्डौ सुहृत्तथा । सप्त प्रकृतयो ह्येताः सप्ताङ्गं राज्यमुच्यते ॥ सप्तानां प्रकृतीनां तु राज्यस्यासां यथाक्रमम् । पूर्वं पूर्वं गुरुतरं जानीयाद् व्यसनं महत् ॥793

Counsel:

मन्त्रमूलं च विजयम् ।794 एतदर्थं कुलीनानां नृपाः कुर्वन्ति सङ्ग्रहम् । आदिमध्यावसानेषु न त्यजन्ति च ते नृपम् ॥795 गुणालयो ऽप्यसन्मन्त्री नृपतिर्नाधिगम्यते । प्रसन्नस्वादुसलिलो दुष्टग्राहो यथा ह्रदः ॥796 पञ्चोपधाव्यतीतांश्च कुर्याद्राजार्थकारिणः ।797

ततः सम्प्रेषयेद्राष्ट्रे राष्ट्रीयाय च दर्शयेत् ।798 अतीतदिवसे वृत्तं प्रशंसन्ति न वा पुनः । गुप्तैश्चारैरनुमतैः पृथिवीमनुसारयेत् ॥799 अनुरागकरं कर्म चरेज्जह्याद्विरागजम् । जनानुरागया लक्ष्म्या राजा स्याज्जनरञ्जनात् ॥800 रञ्जिताश्च प्रजाः सर्वास् तेन राजेति शब्द्यते ।801

Settlements:

"He should settle villages of 100-500 families of mainly शूद्र and agriculturists, the boundery extending up to 1 or 2 क्रोश, and capable of self-defence." (कौटिलीय-अर्थ-शास्त्र 17.2) "A headman of each village is to be appointed, and above him headmen of 10, 20, 100, and 1,000 villages." (महाभारत 12.87.3) Ten headmen of single villages should maintain the one of 10 villages, two of those the one of 20. The headman of 100 villages should receive a large village and all honors from the king. The one of 1,000 should receive a small town and manage all affairs. In every town should be an officer of the king, supervising through agents the affairs and taxes to the king.

Immigration:

"When people have arrived from another country with the desire to live under his protection, the king should shelter them, not considering whether they may be wicked or honest." (अग्नि-पुराण 220.18)802 The text further explains that, if they are wicked, the king should employ detectives and honor only those who are deserving.

Hindus have surrendered all varieties of community धर्म (incl. all privileges) to the constitution of the country in which they live. Special provisions in India are still: (1) Village councils (consisting of five, or more, members), called Panchayat (from पञ्च-आयत्ति?) Modern Indian Panchayati Raj consists of 250,000 Gram-Panchayats (or -Sabhas). In addition, there are Khap-Panchayats (representing a clan/class), which are not affiliated with government bodies. The system was reintroduced in Nepal 1962:

"At the local level, there were 4,000 village assemblies (Gram Sabha) electing nine members of the village Panchayat, who in turn elected a mayor (Sabhapati). Each village Panchayat sent a member to sit on one of 75 district (Zilla) Panchayats, representing from 40 to 70 villages; one-third of the members of these assemblies were chosen by the town Panchayat. Members of the district Panchayat elected representatives to fourteen zone assemblies (Anchal Sabha), functioning as electoral colleges for the National Panchayat, or Rastriya Panchayat, in Kathmandu. In addition, there were class organizations at village, district, and zonal levels for peasants, youth, women, elders, laborers, and ex-soldiers, who elected their own representatives to assemblies." (Wikipedia 2018)

(2) A certain leniency towards all forms of non-cooperation, like Bandh /strike

"In India the nation at large has generally used passive resistance in all departments of life. We cease to cooperate with our rulers when they displease us." (Mohandas Gandhi, Indian politician, 1869-1948)

"Whenever this traditional pattern of relationship [between ruler and ruled] was disturbed by an autocratic ruler, the people were entitled to offer resistance in the customary manner, that is, by peaceful non-cooperation and civil disobedience. It also appears that in the event of such action, the response of the ruling authority was not to treat it as unlawful defiance, rebellion or disloyalty that had to be put down at any cost before the issue in dispute could be taken up, but as rightful action that called for speedy negotiated settlement." (Jayaprakash Narayan, Indian politician, 1902-1979)

उन्मर्यादे प्रवृत्ते तु दस्युभिः सङ्करे कृते । सर्वे वर्णा न दुष्येयुः शस्त्रवन्तो युधिष्ठिर ॥[803] अरक्षितारं हर्तारं विलोप्तारमनायकम् । तं वै राजकलिं हन्युः प्रजाः सन्नह्य निर्घृणम् ॥[804]

62. Policy

विद्यार्थी सेवकः पान्थः क्षुधार्तो भयकातरः । भाण्डारी प्रतिहारी च सप्त सुप्तान्प्रबोधयेत् ॥ अहिं नृपं च शार्दूलं वृद्धं च बालकं तथा । परश्रानं च मूर्खं च सप्त सुप्तान्न बोधयेत् ॥[805]

"The source of peace and industry is the sixfold policy (षाड्गुण्य)."[806] "Truce (सन्धि), war (विग्रह), maintaining a position, preparing for an attack, alliance, and dividing one's force is the sixfold policy, the teachers say."[807] Other lists include उपेक्षा (indifference). अग्नि-पुराण (226.6) includes stratagems to frighten and harm an enemy by tricks, propaganda and substances (like certain incense).

Most important are the 'four policies' साम-दान-भेद-विग्रह to deal with मित्र, उदासीन (neither मित्र nor शत्रु), मध्यम (who might become शत्रु), and शत्रु, respectively.

साम्ना दानेन भेदेन समस्तैरथवा पृथक् । विजेतुं प्रयतेतारीन् न युद्धेन कदाचन ॥808

The respective chapters of हितोपदेश are (2) मित्र-लाभ, (3) सुहृद्-भेद, (4) विग्रह and (1) सन्धि.

Most effective:
पश्य दानस्य माहात्म्यं सद्यः प्रत्ययकारकम् । यत्प्रभावादपि द्वेषो मित्रतां याति तत्क्षणात् ॥809 न सोऽस्ति नाम दानेन वशगो यो न जायते । दानवानेव शक्नोति संहतान्भेदितुं परान् ॥810

War as last means:
द्वावुपायाविह प्रोक्तौ विमुक्तौ शत्रुदर्शने । हस्तयोश्चालनादेको द्वितीयः पादवेगजः ॥811 युद्धमुत्तरमुच्यते ।812 दण्डस्त्ववगतिका गतिः ।813 यत्रायुद्धे ध्रुवो नाशो युद्धे जीवितसंशयः । तं कालमेकं युद्धस्य प्रवदन्ति मनीषिणः ॥814 न गणस्याग्रतो गच्छेत् सिद्धे कार्ये समं फलम् । यदि कार्यविपत्तिः स्यान् मुखरस्तत्र हन्यते ॥815

"The Hindu laws of war are very chivalrous and humane, and prohibit the slaying of the unarmed, of women, of the old, and of the conquered." (Prof. Horace Hayman Wilson, British surgeon and orientalist, 1786-1860)

मत्तं प्रमत्तमुन्मत्तं सुप्तं बालं स्त्रियं जडम् । प्रपन्नं विरथं भीतं न रिपुं हन्ति धर्मवित् ॥816 राजा प्राप्य विदेशं तु देशाचारं हि पालयेत् । देवानां पूजनं कुर्यान् न च्छिन्द्याद् आयमत्र तु । नावमन्येत तद्देश्यान् आगत्य स्वपुरं पुनः ॥817

"Whereas among other nations it is usual, in the contests of war, to ravage the soil and thus to reduce it to an uncultivated waste, among the Indians, on the contrary, by whom husbandmen are regarded as a class that is sacred and inviolable, the tillers of the soil, even when battle is raging in their neighborhood, are undisturbed by any sense of danger, for the combatants on either side in waging the conflict make carnage of each other, but allow those engaged in husbandry to remain quite unmolested. Besides, they never ravage an enemy's land with fire, nor cut down its trees." (Megasthenes, Greek historian and diplomat, c. 350-290 BCE)

63. Others

पशूनां रक्षणं दानम् इज्याध्ययनमेव च । वणिक्पथं कुसीदं च वैश्यस्य कृषिमेव च ॥818 वैश्यः शूद्रः सदा कुर्यात् कृषिवाणिज्यशिल्पकान् ।819 वाणिज्यं पाशुपाल्यं च तथा शिल्पोपजीवनम् । शूद्रस्यापि विधीयन्ते यदा वृत्तिर्न जायते ॥820

Two persons are called शूद्र. (1) One who is inclined to do payed service: "Payed service is the natural work of a शूद्र." (भगवद्गीता 18.44)   (2) A कृपण, or low-class person: "He who is always fond of all kinds of food, does all sorts of work, is impure, has given up the वेद, and has no good conduct, he alone is called शूद्र."[821]

Mixed वर्ण:

सूत – son of ब्राह्मण and क्षत्रिय (both ways), chariot driver, royal herold; reciter of histories; मागध – वैश्य father and क्षत्रिय mother, king's messenger, professional bard; reciter of genealogies; वन्दी/बन्दी – क्षत्रिय father and शूद्र mother, 'praiser', bard, accompanies a prince or army; reciter of prayers; करण/कायस्थ – different mixed castes are called so, among them lawyers and politicians.

Peonage (debt bondage):

दण्डप्रणीतः कर्मणा दण्डमुपनयेत् ।[822]
स्वामिनः स्वस्यां दास्यां जातं समातृकमदासं विद्यात् ।[823]
आत्मविक्रयिणः प्रजामार्यां विद्यात् । आत्माधिगतं स्वामिकर्मादिरुद्धं लभेत् । पित्र्यं च दायम् । मूल्येन चार्यत्वं गच्छेत् ।[824]

India was admired for being prosperous without slavery:

बलाद्दासीकृतश्चौरैर् विक्रीतश्चापि मुच्यते ।[825]

"As for good works and sins, they all agree with the Doctrine of Morality and the universal consent of Mankind, that there are differences of Virtue and Vice in all the world. They hold not only Adultery, but even simple Fornication, a great sin; nor do they account it lawful, as the Mahometans do, to have commerce with female slaves, or with others besides their own Wives. Yea, slaves of either sex they no-wise admit, but hold it a sin; making use of free persons for their service, and paying them wages, as we do in Europe. Which likewise was their ancient custom, as appears by Strabo, who cites Megasthenes and other Authors of those times for it."
(Pietro Della Valle, Italian musicologist and traveller, 1586-1652)

आश्रम ('hermitage') in society is a stage of life, and आश्रम-धर्म a personal (spiritual) duty in each stage, of supposedly a quarter of a man's life-span.

	(1)	(2)	(3)	(4)
आश्रम or	ब्रह्मचार्य pupilage	गार्हस्थ्य houshold life गृह-आश्रम	वानप्रस्थ्य retirement	सन्न्यास mendicancy ब्रह्म-आश्रम, भैक्ष्य-चर्य, प्रव्रज्य, पारिव्राज्य
member or	ब्रह्मचारी student	गृहस्थ householder गृही, गृह-मेधी	वानप्रस्थ hermit/monk वनी, वने-वासी, वैखानस, तपस्वी	सन्न्यासी mendicant भिक्षु, त्रि-दण्डी
			both also called यति / यती	

ब्रह्मचार्य may refer to 'practice of spiritual life (ब्रह्म)', which means first of all celibacy; 'practice of the वेद (ब्रह्म)' as a disciple/student, छात्र/शिष्य under a teacher, शिक्षक/उपाध्याय/आचार्य; or any pupilage.

ब्रह्मचारी गुरुकुले वसन्दान्तो गुरोर्हितम्। आचरन्दासवन्नीचो गुरौ सुदृढ-सौहृदः ॥826 खनित्वा हि खनित्रेण भूतले वारि विन्दति। तथा गुरुगतां विद्यां शुश्रूषुरधिगच्छति ॥827

For a ब्राह्मण stages 1-4 were obligatory, for a क्षत्रिय 1-3, for a वैश्य 1-2 and for शूद्र only stage 2. But anyone could 'escape' at any time into stage 3 (and even 4).

ब्रह्मचर्यं समाप्य गृही भवेत्। गृही भूत्वा वनी भवेत्। वनी भूत्वा प्रव्रजेत्। यदि वा इतरथा ब्रह्मचर्यादेव प्रव्रजेद् गृहाद्वा वनाद्वा। यदहरेव विरज्येत तदहरेव प्रव्रजेत्।828

"Spiritual life in India has solitary meditation as one of its essential stages. It has been the cherished ambition and pursuit of the lonely ascetic. It is assumed that those who are distracted by the cares and encumbered by the possessions of the world find it hard to secure their spiritual ends. Those emancipated from these are free to devote themselves to the highest aim. When once the end is reached, the Indian sannyasi travels at pleasure and has no fixed residence or occupation. The first Christians were homeless wanderers. The mendicant rather than the resident community of monks has been the Indian ideal. Monasteries are more temporary rest-houses or centres of learning than permanent habitations. The Hindu system of ashramas according to which every one of the twice-born towards the close of his life must renounce the world and adopt the homeless life and the ascetic's garb has had great influence on the Indian mind. Though in intention, certain classes were not eligible to become monks, in practice monks were recruited from all castes. The Jain and the Buddhist orders though based on the ancient Hindu custom have become more centralised and co-ordinated." (Sir Sarvepalli Radhakrishnan, Indian Prof. at Oxford University and President of India, 1888-1975)

65. Women

प्रजापतिः स्त्रियं चक्रे स्वदेहार्धम् ।[829]

द्विधा कृत्वात्मनो देहमर्धेन पुरुषो ऽभवत् । अर्धेन नारी ।[830]

यावन्न विन्दते जायां तावदर्धो भवेत्पुमान् । नार्धं प्रजायते सर्वं प्रजायेतेत्यपि श्रुतिः ॥[831]

"In all consultations and emergencies, they take advice of the women." (Al-Biruni /Alberuni; Persian scholar, 973-1048)

सोमः शौचं ददावासां गन्धर्वश्च शुभां गिरम् । पावकः सर्वमेध्यत्वं मेध्या वै योषितो ह्यतः ॥[832] पूज्या लालयितव्याश्च स्त्रियो नित्यं जनाधिप । स्त्रियो यत्र च पूज्यन्ते रमन्ते तत्र देवताः ॥ अपूजिताश्च यत्रैताः सर्वास्तत्राफलाः क्रियाः । तदा चैतत्कुलं नास्ति यदा शोचन्ति जामयः ॥[833]

"And it may be confidently asserted that in no nation of antiquity were women held in so much esteem as amongst the Hindus." (Prof. Horace Hayman Wilson, British surgeon and orientalist, 1786-1860)

"India of the Vedas entertained a respect for women amounting to worship; a fact which we seem little to suspect in Europe when we accuse the extreme East of having denied the dignity of woman, and of having only made her an instrument of pleasure and of passive obedience." "Here is a civilization, which you cannot deny to be older than your own, which places the woman on a level with the man and gives her an equal place in the family and in society." (Louis Francois Jacolliot, French judge in India and writer, 1837-1890)

"Indian wives often possess greater influence than wives of Europeans. He is not a true Hindu who does not regard a woman's body as sacred as the temple of God. He is an outcast who touches a woman's body with irreverence, hatred or anger." (Sir Monier Monier-Williams, British Indologist and head of the Oxford's Boden Chair, 1819-1899)

प्रजायन्ते सुतान्नार्यो दुःखेन महता विभो । पुष्णन्ति चापि महता स्नेहेन द्विजपुङ्गव ॥ याश्च क्रूरेषु सत्त्वेषु वर्तमाना जुगुप्सिताः । स्वकर्म कुर्वन्ति सदा दुष्करं तच्च मे मतम् ॥[834]

But:

उशना वेद यच्छास्त्रं यच्च वेद बृहस्पतिः । स्वभावेनैव तच्छास्त्रं स्त्रीबुद्धौ सुप्रतिष्ठितम् ॥[835]

कुर्वन्ति तावत्प्रथमं प्रियाणि यावन्न जानन्ति नरं प्रसक्तम् ।

ज्ञात्वा च तं मन्मथपाशबद्धं ग्रस्तामिषं मीनमिवोद्धरन्ति ॥[836]

चतुर्थमायुषो भागम् उषित्वाद्यं गुरौ द्विजः। द्वितीयमायुषो भागं कृतदारो गृहे वसेत् ॥837

Among the twelve great personalities in this list, seven were गृहस्थ*:
"ब्रह्मा*, नारद, शिव*, the four कुमार, कपिल, स्वायम्भुव मनु*, प्रह्लाद*, जनक*, भीष्म, बलि*, शुकदेव and यमराजा*."838

Considerations:

यस्मिन्देशे न सम्मानो न वृत्तिर्न च बान्धवः। न च विद्यागमः कश्चित् तं देशं परिवर्जयेत् ॥839 धनिकः श्रोत्रियो राजा नदी वैद्यस्तु पञ्चमः। पञ्च यत्र न विद्यन्ते तत्र वासं न कारयेत् ॥840 न तादृग्जायते सौख्यम् अपि स्वर्गे शरीरिणाम्। दारिद्र्ये ऽपि हि यादृक्स्यात् स्वदेशे स्वपुरे गृहे ॥841 यत्र वेदध्वनिध्वान्तं न च गोभिरलङ्कृतम्। यत्र बालैः परिवृतं श्मशानमिव तद् गृहम् ॥842 पुत्रपौत्रवधूभृत्यैर् आकीर्णमपि सर्वतः। भार्याहीनं गृहस्थस्य शून्यमेव गृहं भवेत्। न गृहं गृहमित्याहुर् गृहिणी गृहमुच्यते ॥843

अनभ्यासे विषं शास्त्रम् अजीर्णे भोजनं विषम्। दरिद्रस्य विषं गोष्ठी वृद्धस्य तरुणी विषम् ॥844 नोपभोक्तुं न च त्यक्तुं शक्नोति विषयान् जरी। अस्थि निर्दशनः श्वेव जिह्वया लेढि केवलम् ॥845 नामृतं न विषं किञ्चिद् एकां मुक्त्वा नितम्बिनीम्। यस्याः सङ्गेन जीव्येत म्रियते च वियोगतः ॥846 धनाशा जीविताशा च गुर्वी प्राणभृतां सदा। वृद्धस्य तरुणी भार्या प्राणेभ्यो ऽपि गरीयसी ॥847

विरोधं नोत्तमैर्गच्छेन् नाधमैश्च सदा बुधः। विवाहश्च विवादश्च तुल्यशीलैर्नृपेष्यते ॥848 दूरस्थानामविद्यानां मोक्षधर्मानुवर्तिनाम्। शूराणां निर्धनानां च न देया कन्यका बुधैः ॥849

"They have peculiar months; in which only they allow the consummation of marriages. In these months what with illuminations, singers, dancer and horrid musick, one would imagine the days and nights reversed for they never begin the entertainment before it is dark, nor conclude them while that favours the demonstration of their fireworks. All this time, the bride and bridegroom richly dres'd, are well mounted on horse back or carried in pallankeens (like a couch, in which there is a mattress and pillows) upon four or six men's shoulders thro the town, accompanied by the relations and friends of both families, preceded by the dancing girls, musicians, singers, with great mumber of massals or links attending them. Previous to this, there are machines of fire erected over against all their friends houses to whom they intend to pay respect, where always they stop, and are entertained by the dancers. And during the exhibition of the fireworks, throughout the whole procession the bride and bridegroom are incessantly employed threwing flowers at one another, of which the servants carry basketsful for that purpose. Though these ceremonies are not finished in less than six or eight days, yet in regard to their entertainments they never exceed a low sweetmeats and butlenuts, which they use as Europeans do tobacco, but the former is a fine aromatick and in every respect much preferable, at the same time promiscuously sprinkling rose-water and other perfumes amongst their guests. You would be surprised to think how great a sum the expence of one of their better sort of marriages will amount to. I saw one my last voyage at Bengall, which I was well informed could not cost less than ten or twelve thousand pounds sterling, and one since I have been in Bombay that amounted to about one third of that sum." (Alex Knox ? in 1753)

Eight kinds of marriage:

ब्राह्मो दैवस्तथैवार्षः प्राजापत्यस्तथासुरः । गान्धर्वो राक्षसश्चैव पैशाचश्चाष्टमो ऽधमः ॥850

Common principle of (1-4):

शीलवृत्ते समाज्ञाय विद्यां योनिं च कर्म च । सद्भिरेवं प्रदातव्या कन्या गुणयुते वरे ॥851

(5) गान्धर्व

आत्माभिप्रेतमुत्सृज्य कन्याभिप्रेत एव यः । अभिप्रेता च या यस्य तस्मै देया युधिष्ठिर ॥852

No marriage without consent:

वरं वरयते कन्या माता वित्तं पिता श्रुतम् । बान्धवाः कुलमिच्छन्ति मिष्टान्नमितरे जनाः ॥853 न सुवर्णं न रत्नानि न च राज्यपरिक्रियाम् । तथा वाञ्छन्ति कामिन्यो यथाभीष्टतमं वरम् ॥854 अनिष्टः कन्यकाया यो वरो रूपान्वितो ऽपि यः । यदि स्यात्तस्य नो देया कन्या श्रेयोभिवाञ्छता ॥855 न ह्यकामेन संवासं मनुरेवं प्रशंसति । यस्त्वत्र मन्त्रसमयो भार्यापत्योर्मिथः कृतः । तमेवाहुर्गरीयांसं यश्चासौ ज्ञातिभिः कृतः ॥856 अकामां कामयानस्य शरीरमुपतप्यते ।857

"Those races (the Indian viewed from a moral aspect) are perhaps the most remarkable people in the world. They breathe an atmosphere of moral purity, which cannot but excite admiration, and this is especially the case with the pioneer classes, who, notwithstanding the privations of their humble lot, appear to be happy and contented. Domestic felicity appears to be the rule among the Natives, and this is the more strange when the customs of marriage are taken into account, parents arranging all such matters. Many Indian households afford examples of the married state in its highest degree of perfection." (James Young, British officer, 1782-1848)

मूर्खा यत्र न पूज्यन्ते धान्यं यत्र सुसञ्चितम् । दाम्पत्ये कलहो नास्ति तत्र श्रीः स्वयमागता ॥858 अनुकूलकलत्रो यस् तस्य स्वर्ग इहैव हि । प्रतिकूलकलत्रस्य नरको नात्र संशयः । स्वर्गे ऽपि दुर्लभं ह्येतद् अनुरागः परस्परम् ॥859 परस्परं द्वेषान्मोक्षः ।860

नष्टे मृते प्रव्रजिते क्लीबे च पतिते पतौ । पञ्चस्वापत्सु नारीणां पतिरन्यो विधीयते ॥861

Dowry:

धनेन बहुधा क्रीत्वा सम्प्रलोभ्य च बान्धवान्। असुराणां नृपैतं वै धर्ममाहुर्मनीषिणः ॥862 यासां नाददते शुल्कं ज्ञातयो न स विक्रयः। अर्हणं तत्कुमारीणाम् आनृशंस्यं च केवलम् ॥863

"As I observed before, their marriages are all conducted by the parents during the parties infancy, the expence of this ceremoney, which is considerable according to the ranks of the persons married, is always from the bridegroom's family, nor is it customary to give any fortunes with their daughters, because it should not be said they were obliged to buy them husbands, for this custom it seems they despise the Europeans very much." (Alex Knox ? in 1753)

Then why Dahej is widely practiced in India? Its name points to the Arabic root Jahez and a custom to arrange marriages purely with profit in mind. The present dowry practice in India can be traced only to the 19th century:

"The concept of stri dhan in which gifts – usually jewelry, including often a quarter pound of gold – was given to the bride by her family, in order to secure some personal wealth for her when she married. This jewelry remained her personal property throughout the marriage, providing some security in case of her husband's death or other calamity. However, in approximately the 19th century, under the British rule, the loving practice of stri dhan was joined by the very much different concept of dowry. Dowry became first an expected, then a demanded, offering given by the bride's family to the groom's family at the time of marriage. Whereas stri dhan is considered the property only of the woman, passed matrilineally, dowry is not. ... In the pre-colonial period, dowry was an institution managed by women, for women, to enable them to establish their status and have recourse in an emergency. As a consequence of the massive economic and societal upheaval brought on by British rule, womens' entitlements to the precious resources obtained from land were erased and their control of the system diminished, ultimately resulting in a devaluing of their very lives." (Rajeev Srinivasan, Indian-born American engineer and manager)

"Atrocity literature played its part in downgrading women's right, too. Veena Oldenburg's seminal book, Dowry Murder, gives details on how the British encouraged the Indians to dish out cases of atrocities that could then be blamed on the native cultures. They systematically compiled these anecdotes, mostly unsubstantiated and often exaggerated and one-sided. This became a justification to enact laws that downgraded the rights of common citizens. The book shows how the dowry extortions that have become so common in middle-class today, were actually started when women's traditional property rights were taken away by the British through convoluted logic." (Rajiv Malhotra, Indian scientist and writer)

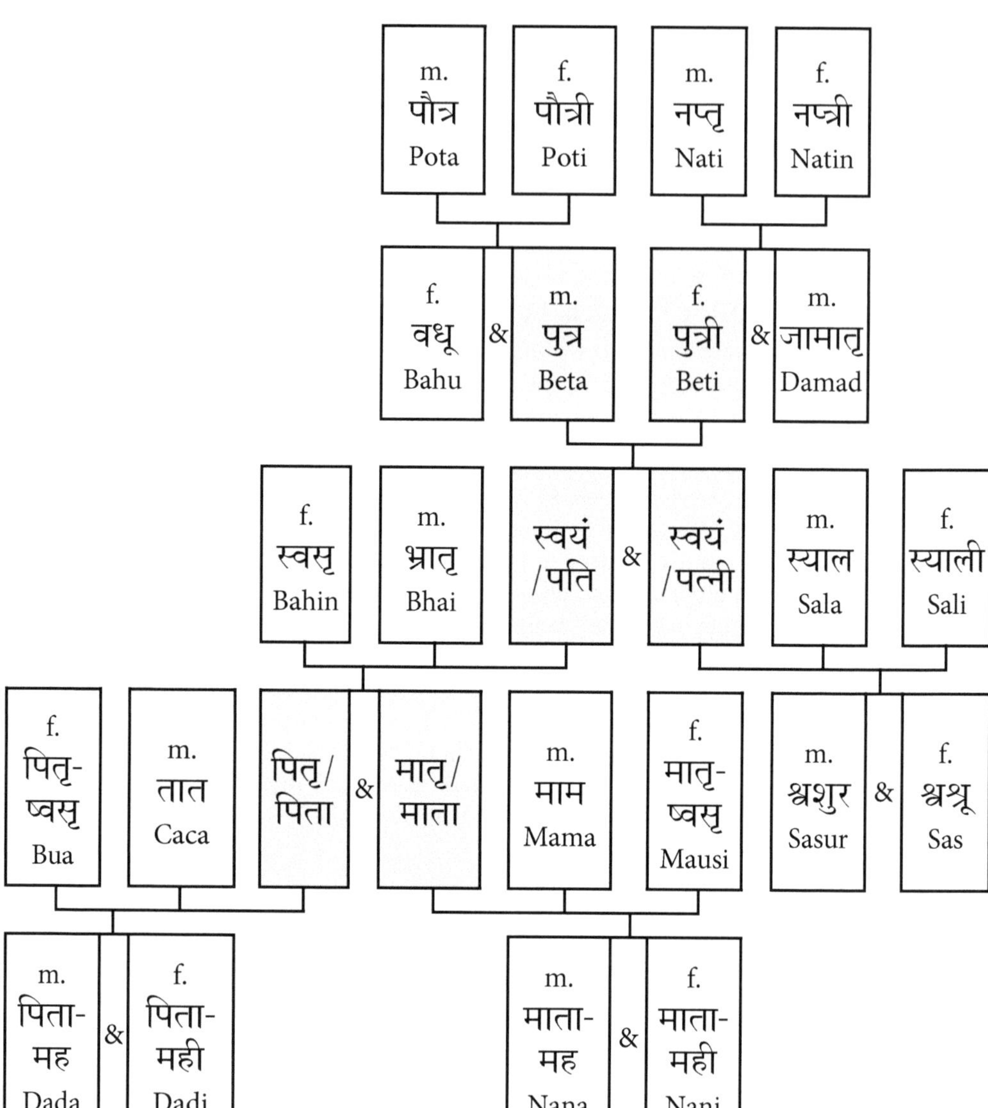

तातगु = पितृव्य, पितृ-ष्वसृ = पितृव्या, मातृ-ष्वसृ = मातुला, माम = मातुल = मातृक = मातृ-भ्रात्र, स्याल = श्याल, स्याली = श्याली

68. Hermit

पञ्चाशोर्ध्वं वनं व्रजेत् ।[865] गृहस्थस्तु यदा पश्येद् वलीपलितमात्मनः ।
अपत्यस्यैव चापत्यं वनमेव तदा श्रयेत् ॥[866] सम्भाव्य पुत्रान्कालेन यौवन-
स्थान्निवेश्य च । समर्थान् जीवने ज्ञात्वा मुक्तश्चर यथासुखम् ॥[867] वानप्रस्थाश्रम-
पदेष्वभीक्ष्णं भैक्ष्यमाचरेत् ।[868]

मुनयो वातवासना श्रमणा ऊर्ध्वमन्थिनः । ब्रह्माख्यं धाम ते यान्ति शान्ताः
सन्न्यासिनो ऽमलाः ॥[869]

"There are two divisions of philosophers, the Brahmanas (Brāhmana) and the Samanas
(Shramana). The Brahmanas form the leading sect, and succeed by right of birth to this kind of
divine wisdom as to a priesthood. They are not subjected to the authority of the king, and pay
no tribute. They subsist on fruits, cow milk and wild rice. To taste anything else, or so much as
to touch animal food, is held to be the height of impurity and impiety. They inculcate the duty
of worshipping the deity with pious reverence. ... The whole day and greater part of the night
they set apart for hymns and prayers to the gods. Each of them has a hut of his own in which he
passes as much time as possible in solitude. The Samanas, on the other hand, are collected from
the whole society, and when any one is to be enrolled in their order, he presents himself before
the magistrates of the city or of the village to which he happens to belong, and there resigns all
his possessions and his other means. The superfluous parts of his person are then shaved off,
and he puts on the mendicants robe and goes away to join the mendicants, taking no concern
either for his wife or his children, if he has any, and thinks of them no more. The king takes
charge of his children and supplies their wants, while his relatives provide for his wife. ... They
and the Brahmanas are held in such high honor by the other Indians that even the king himself
will visit them and solicit their prayers." (Porphyrios; Greek philosopher and writer, c. 233- c.
301)

69. Sannyasi

स वने ऽग्नीन्यथान्यायम् आत्मन्यारोप्य धर्मवित् । निर्द्वन्द्वो वीतरागात्मा
ब्रह्माश्रमपदे वसेत् ॥[870]

"He should not make disciples, study many books, undertake discourses (as a means of
livelihood), and attempt enterprises in any way."[871]

ध्यानं शौचं तथा भिक्षा नित्यमेकान्तशीलता । भिक्षोश्चत्वारि कर्माणि पञ्चमो
नोपपद्यते ॥[872]

Four stages:

1. कुटीचक – 'who lives in a कुटी/कुटीर' outside the village; his family supplies food
   until he is experienced how to beg.

2. बहूदक – 'who has much water (उदक)', begging food at bathing places; also called
   मधुकारी – 'like a bee'

स्तोकं स्तोकं ग्रसेद् ग्रासं देहो वर्तेत यावता । गृहानहिंसन्नतिष्ठेद् वृत्तिं माधुकरीं मुनि: ॥[873]

3. हंस – 'swan', also called परिव्राजक – 'wandering' mendicant

अनग्निरनिकेतश्च ग्राममन्नार्थमाश्रयेत् ।[874] बहूनां कलहो नित्यं द्वयो: सङ्कथनं ध्रुवम् । एकाकी विचरिष्यामि कुमारीशङ्क्को यथा ॥[875]

भ्रमन्सम्पूज्यते राजा भ्रमन्सम्पूज्यते द्विज: । भ्रमन्सम्पूज्यते योगी स्त्री भ्रमन्ती विनश्यति ॥[876]

4. परमहंस, निष्क्रिय, अवधूत, 'Babaji'; he is beyond all आश्रम, with the vows of अ-याचित-वृत्ति (mode of taking what is not begged) and अजगर-वृत्ति (mode of a python). "Abandoning त्रि-दण्ड, कमण्डलु, etc., into water with 'भू: स्वाहा', in this stage one should seek out the आत्मा."[877]

Much honored:

All आश्रम are spiritually equally important, but a सन्न्यासी is held in high esteem because of his renunciation.

देवताप्रतिमां दृष्ट्वा यतिं चैव त्रिदण्डिनम् । नमस्कारं न कुर्याच्चेद् उपवासेन शुद्ध्यति ॥[878]

It may be said, that सन्न्यास is a license for sense gratification on the mental platform – learning, honor and influence.

A fallen सन्न्यासी:

"One who leaves his home as the 'field of त्रि-वर्ग', and later again engages in those material activities, that सन्न्यासी is indeed a shameless 'eater of vomit'."[879]   "The neglect of his व्रत by a ब्रह्मचारी, the neglect of his rituals by a गृहस्थ, life in a village by a वानप्रस्थ, and sense gratification by a सन्न्यासी – these are certainly degradations and derisions of the आश्रम. Those who are thus bewildered by the Lord's माया one should neglect out of compassion."[880]   "A सन्न्यासी who wishes to come back to houshold life should perform three प्राजापत्य fasts, or one चान्द्रायण fast. And he has to perform the whole process of संस्कार beginning with जात-कर्म."[881] Or else: "One who has given up सन्न्यास shall do the king's service."[882]

जीर्णमन्नं प्रशंसन्ति भार्यां च गतयौवनाम् । शूरं विजितसङ्ग्रामं गतपारं तपस्विनम् ॥[883]

यथा काष्ठं च काष्ठं च समेयातां महोदधौ। समेत्य च व्यपेयातां तद्वद्भूतसमागमः ॥884 अनित्यं यौवनं रूपं जीवितं द्रव्यसञ्चयः। ऐश्वर्य प्रियसंवासो मुह्येत्तत्र न पण्डितः ॥885 कालः पचति भूतानि कालः संहरते प्रजाः। कालः सुप्तेषु जागर्ति कालो हि दुरतिक्रमः ॥886 आसन्नतरतामेति मृत्युर्जन्तोर्दिने दिने। आघातं नीयमानस्य वध्यस्येव पदे पदे ॥887

यामेव रात्रिं प्रथमामुपैति गर्भे निवासं नरवीर लोकः।
ततः प्रभृत्यस्खलितप्रयाणः स प्रत्यहं मृत्युसमीपमेति ॥888

External symptoms of सन्न्यास:

Out of 108 सन्न्यास names, 10 are declared to be most prestigious: तीर्थ, आश्रम, वन, अरण्य, गिरि, पर्वत, सागर, सरस्वती, भारती, and पुरी (via मुक्तिक-उपनिषद् and सात्त्वत-संहिता). "He should wear शिखा, उपवीत, त्रि-दण्ड, कमण्डलु, a cup or कुश for purifying water, and saffron cloth. And he should always chant गायत्री."889

But:

वेणुभिर्न भवेद्यतिः।890 लिङ्गान्युत्पथभूतानि न मोक्षायेति मे मतिः।891 नित्यं नैमित्तिकं काम्यं कर्म त्रिविधमुच्यते। सन्न्यासः कर्मणां न्यासो न्यासी तद्धर्ममाचरन् ॥892

"Renunciation of काम्य-कर्म the sages know as सन्न्यास." (भगवद्गीता 18.2) ... which does not necessitate to give up नित्य and नैमित्तिक duty in society. And:

सन्न्यसेत्सर्वकर्माणि वेदमेकं न सन्न्यसेत्। वेदसन्न्यासतः शूद्रस् तस्माद्वेदं न सन्न्यसेत् ॥893

The real meaning of त्रि-दण्ड is self-control, for which a सन्न्यासी is called स्वामी (master), गो-स्वामी (master of the senses), or महा-राजा (lord):

वाग्दण्डो ऽथ मनोदण्डः कायदण्डस्तथैव च। यस्यैते निहिता बुद्धौ त्रिदण्डीति स उच्यते ॥894 त्रिदण्डव्यपदेशेन जीवन्ति बहवो नराः। यो हि ब्रह्म न जानाति न त्रिदण्डार्ह एव सः ॥895

YOGA

71. Pramana

प्रमा ('measure', scale, standard, proof), प्रमाण ('measuring', proving), मात्रा/मात्र (a measure of any kind, unit, quantity, size), प्रमेय (what is to be measured out), अनुमान (inference), उपमान (comparison)

3 प्रमाण in साङ्ख्य

प्रत्यक्षानुमानागमाः प्रमाणानि ।[896]

प्रत्यक्षं चानुमानं च शास्त्रं च विविधागमम्। त्रयं सुविदितं कार्य धर्मशुद्धिमभीप्सता ॥[897]

	(1)	(2)	(3)	
	प्रत्यक्ष	अनुमान	शास्त्र	
or	स्मृति-	न्याय-	श्रुति-	प्रस्थान
also called	शास्त्र		वेद	
esp. through	इतिहास-पुराण	वेदान्त	वेद, उपनिषद्	

न्याय and वेदान्त schools also accept varieties like ऐतिह्य, आर्ष, उपमान, अर्थापत्ति, सम्भव, चेष्टा and अ-भाव.

श्रुतिस्मृती च विप्राणां चक्षुषी देवनिर्मिते। काणस्तत्रैकया हीनो द्वाभ्यामन्धः प्रकीर्तितः ॥[898]

72. Shruti

शास्त्र/श्रुति is also called वेद (knowledge), आगम ('coming', tradition), आम्नाय ('mentioned', tradition), शब्द (sound), and आप्त-वाक्य ('word of authority').

"After gradual research I have come to the conclusion that long before all heavenly books, God had revealed to the Hindus, through the Rishis of yore, of whom Brahma (Brahmā) was the Chief, His four books of knowledge, the Rig Veda, the Yajur Veda, the Sama Veda and the Atharva Veda." (Prince Muhammad Dara Shikoh, eldest son of Moghul Emperor Shah Jahan, 1615-1659)

Four kinds of Vedic मन्त्र exist eternally, each serving a different function, and the sages were competent to locate those needed. "After sorting the heap of unsorted मन्त्र

of the ऋक्, साम, यजुर्, अथर्व into four groups, व्यास made four संहिता (the actual वेद), like sorting a collection of jewels."[899] ... and gave the ऋक्-संहिता to पैल, the साम to जैमिनि, the यजुर् to वैशम्पायन, and the अथर्व to सुमन्तु (अङ्गिरा).

<table>
<tr><td></td><td colspan="4">वेद   plus</td><td></td></tr>
<tr><td rowspan="4">with</td><td>संहिता</td><td>ब्राह्मण</td><td>आरण्यक</td><td>उपनिषद्</td><td rowspan="3">काण्ड</td></tr>
<tr><td>कर्म-</td><td>उपासन-</td><td>उपासन-</td><td>ज्ञान-</td></tr>
<tr><td>मन्त्र</td><td>their application in rituals</td><td>interpretation for renunciation</td><td>and for liberation</td></tr>
<tr><td>memorized by ब्रह्मचारी</td><td>practiced by गृहस्थ</td><td>studied by वानप्रस्थ</td><td>studied by सन्न्यासी</td><td></td></tr>
</table>

उपनिषद् means 'that which is learned by sitting close to the teacher,' because words are sometimes contradictory; (or:) 'which destroys passion and ignorance'. Its teachings form the basis of वेदान्त philosophy. In मुक्तिका-उपनिषद् (30-39) there is a list of 108 उपनिषद्. 11 are considered topmost, because वेदान्त-सूत्र refers to them. The founders of religious sects have sometimes supported their teachings by calling them उपनिषद्. Even an Allah-Upanishad was composed in the sixteenth century by court-poet Shekh-bhavan in eulogy of emperor Akbar.

Examples:

संहिता	ब्राह्मण	आरण्यक	उपनिषद्
ऋग्वेद	ऐतरेय, कौषीतकि		ऐतरेय, कौषीतकि
सामवेद	छान्दोग्य		छान्दोग्य
यजुर्वेद	शतपथ, तैत्तिरीय	तैत्तिरीय	ईश, श्वेताश्वतर, बृहद्-आरण्यक, तैत्तिरीय, कठ
अथर्ववेद	गोपथ		माण्डूक्य, मुण्डक, प्रश्न

"In the whole world there is no study so beneficial and so elevating as that of the Upanishads. They are destined sooner or later to become the faith of the people." (Arthur Schopenhauer, German philosopher and writer, 1788-1860)

"For the historian, who pursues the history of human thought, the Upanishads have a yet far greater significance. From the mystical doctrines of the Upanishads, one current of thought may be traced to the mysticism of the Persian Sufism, to the mystic, theosophical logos doctrine of the Neo-Platonics and the Alexandrian Christian Mystics, Eckhart and Tauler, and finally to the philosophy of the great German mystic of the nineteenth century, Schopenhauer." (Moriz Winternitz, Austrian Indologist, 1863-1937)

"They are the oldest extant philosophy and psychology of our race; the surprisingly subtle and patient effort of man to understand the mind and the world, and their relation. The Upanishads are as old as Homer, and as modern as Kant." (Will Durant, American historian and philosopher, 1885-1981)

"When our self is illuminated with the light of love, then the negative aspect of its separateness with others loses its finality, and then our relationship with others is no longer that of competition and conflict, but of sympathy and co-operation. I feel strongly that this, for us, is the teaching of the Upanishads, and that this teaching is very much needed in the present age for those who boast of the freedom enjoyed by their nations, using that freedom for building up a dark world of spiritual blindness, where the passions of greed and hatred are allowed to roam unchecked ..." (Sir Sarvepalli Radhakrishnan, Indian Prof. at Oxford University and President of India, 1888-1975)

73. Smriti

(1) 6 वेदाङ्ग

शिक्षा कल्पो व्याकरणं निरुक्तं छन्दोविचितिज्र्योतिषमिति चाङ्गानि ।[900]

(2) 4 उपवेद

आयुर्वेद texts are चारक-संहिता (1500 BCE, by Caraka), सुश्रुत-संहिता (on surgery, by Sushruta), अष्टाङ्ग-हृदयम् (by Vāgbhatta), भाव-प्रकाश (medicinal formulas), माधव-निदान (diagnosis), शार्ङ्गधर-संहिता (pharmacy), There is a summary in अग्नि-पुराण 279.1 ff., which includes hygienic effects of different trees and how to treat plants and animals, and mantras for health.

धनुर्वेद, see अग्नि-पुराण 242 ff.

स्थापत्य-वेद, वास्तु-शास्त्र

गान्धर्व-वेद

(3) धर्म-/अर्थ-/नीति-शास्त्र like कौटिलीय-अर्थ-शास्त्र and मनु-स्मृति, पञ्चतन्त्र and हितोपदेश, dealing with आचार – 'good conduct', custom, traditional usage, general duties and rites; व्यावहार – 'practice', social intercourse, legal process, government; and प्रायश्चित्त – atonement of sins committed. कौटिल्य ('crookedness', deceit) is a name given to विष्णुगुप्त/चाणक्य (fourth century BCE), but: "Such (wicked political measure) should be applied only among wicked and lawless men, not among others."[901]

(4) तन्त्र-शास्त्र like 28 शैव-आगम, containing activities like magic and regulations for those who are grossly engaged in meat eating, intoxication and sex.

(5) पञ्चरात्र literature like नारद-पञ्चरात्र, सनत्कुमार-संहिता, सात्वत-तन्त्र, ब्रह्म-संहिता and गार्ग-संहिता. नारद is mentioned as seer in अथर्व-वेद (5.19.9), as priest in ऐतरेय-ब्राह्मण (7.13), as pupil of बृहस्पति in समविधान-ब्राह्मण (3.9), and of सनत्कुमार in the छान्दोग्य-उपनिषद् (3.3.1).

(6) इतिहास, like रामायण and महाभारत, which generally concentrate on single heroes or events, while पुराण deals with an assortment of topics. The वाल्मीकि-रामायण (24,000 verses) is said to have passed from नारद to वाल्मीकि, to कुश and लव, who narrated it to राम Himself.

The महाभारत developed from the first version जय of 8,800 verses (ततो जयमुदीरयेत्), to the enlarged भारत of 24,000 verses, to the महाभारत of वैशम्पायन of 100,000 verses.

नारायणं नमस्कृत्य नरं चैव नरोत्तमम् । देवीं सरस्वतीं व्यासं ततो जयमुदीरयेत् ॥[902]

(7) The 18 महा-पुराण[903] are विष्णु-(धर्म-)पु° (7,000 verses) plus विष्णु-धर्मोत्तर (16,000) by पराशर, (बृहन्-)नारदीय-पु° (25,000), भागवत-पु°/श्रीमद्-भागवतम् (18,000)[904], गरुड-पु° (19,000), पद्म-पु° (55,000), वराह-पु° (24,000), ब्रह्माण्ड-पु° (12,000), ब्रह्म-वैवर्त-पु° (18,000), मार्कण्डेय-पु° (9,000), भविष्य-पु° (14,500), वामन-पु° (10,000), ब्रह्म-पु° (10,000), मत्स्य-पु° (14,000), कूर्म-पु° (17,000), लिङ्ग-पु° (10,000), शिव-पु° (24,000), स्कन्द-पु° (81,000), and अग्नि-पु° (15,400).

सर्गश्च प्रतिसर्गश्च वंशो मन्वन्तराणि च । वंशानुचरितं चेति पुराणं पञ्चलक्षणम् ॥[905]

एतद्यदृग्वेदो यजुर्वेदः सामवेदो ऽथर्वाङ्गिरस इतिहासः पुराणम् । अस्यैवैतानि सर्वाणि निःश्वसितानि ।[906]

सामग्यर्जुर्वेदास्त्रयस्त्रयी । अथर्ववेदेतिहासवेदौ च वेदाः ।[907]

अथर्वणं चतुर्थमितिहासपुराणं पञ्चमम् ।[908]

इतिहासपुराणाभ्यां वेदं समुपबृंहयेत् ।[909]

---

74. Nyaya

न्याय means 'rule', system, legal proceeding, argument, logic, dialectics. It also refers to all kinds of सूत्र literature, like न्यायावली, षड्-दर्शन, and specifically to the न्याय philosophy of गौतम.

अल्पाक्षरमसन्दिग्धं सारवत्विश्वतोमुखम् । अस्तोभमनवद्यं च सूत्रं सूत्रविदो विदुः ॥[910]

षड्-दर्शन[911]:

Buddha mentions 62 different philosophies together with many subdivisions. Six of them have stood out as the most typical and representative of them all. They are distinguished as orthodox systems from the heterodox systems of the Buddhists, Jains and Carvakas, because they are somehow reconcilable with the Vedic system, though they mutually differ in their relations to the same. The sages mentioned as authors just gave the final form to older philosophies, and again, the extant works are just named after that author. The doctrine of Adhikara implies that each individual should pursue a discipline suitable to his nature.

(1) न्याय-सूत्र of गौतम (अक्षपाद) with भाष्य of वात्स्यायन

Logic sets up rules for philosophical debate and identifies basic subjects (matter, soul, God, liberation). It consists of a combination of enthymeme and syllogism, and has 5 members – प्रतिज्ञा, हेतु, उदाहरण, उपनय and निगमन.

(2) वैशेषिक-सूत्र of कणाद (कणभक्ष) with भाष्य of प्रशस्तपाद

It analyzes matter and breaks it down into invisible atoms (परमाणु-वाद); suffering comes from ignorance and liberation from knowledge.

(3) साङ्ख्य-सूत्र of कपिल (पञ्चशिख) with साङ्ख्यकारिका of ईश्वरकृष्ण

It analyses the evolution of matter, metaphysics, philosophical training of the mind. Material nature is cause of all causes; integration of material elements is cause of suffering and disintegration cause of freedom.

"The various theories of creation, arrangement and development were each elaborated, and the views of the modern physiologists at the present day are a return with new light to the evolution theory of Kapila, whose Sankhya system is the oldest of the Darsanas." (Sir William Wilson Hunter, Scottish historian, 1840-1900)

(4) योग-सूत्र of पतञ्जलि (विषाधर) with भाष्य of व्यास and महाभाष्य of पाणिनि

The योग discipline was a common practice and implied in all other systems. In post-Vedic times it developed into this formal system.

(5) पूर्व-मीमांस-सूत्र of जैमिनि (on कर्म) with भाष्य of शबर

मीमांसा means 'analysis' and is a preliminary study of वेद with a view to कर्म. Material existence is endless, without liberation. The best one can aim at, is higher birth among देव. Therefore, the whole purpose of वेद is to engage human beings in rituals for creating पुण्य. There is a mechanism of achieving अर्थ and काम by science of sound (मन्त्र) and देवता are their forms.

(6) उत्तर-मीमांसा (on ब्रह्म) of अष्टावक्र or वेदान्त-/ब्रह्म-सूत्र of व्यास with शारीरक-भाष्य of शङ्कर

वेदान्त-सूत्र is the full deliberation on ब्रह्म and accepted as the most exalted philosophical exposition in the world. It is divided into 4 अध्याय (1-2 सम्बन्ध, 3 अभिधेय/साधन, 4 प्रयोजन); each अध्याय into 4 पाद; each पाद into 5 अधिकरण (topics); each अधिकरण discusses in five steps: विषय (thesis, or statement), संशय (doubt in the statement), पूर्व-पक्ष (first objection, argument), सिद्धान्त (conclusion, by quotation from Vedic scriptures), and सङ्गति (confirmation with quotes). In India, any philosophy had to support its view with a commentary on वेदान्त-सूत्र. Important commentaries are शारीरक-भाष्य of शङ्कर, श्री-भाष्य of रामानुज, पूर्णप्रज्ञ-भाष्य of मध्वा, and पारिजात-सौरभ-भाष्य of निम्बार्क.

अथातो ब्रह्मजिज्ञासा |[912] 'Now' (अथ) that one has studied and understood वेद, followed वर्णाश्र-धर्म and observed सत्य, one can attain heaven, temporarily. Therefore, ... But in उपनिषद् the ब्रह्म is also described. What need is there to study वेदान्त-सूत्र? It will strengthen the student's understanding by clearing doubts: "The distinction between body and soul is taught, ascertained by arguments, by the words of the वेदान्त-सूत्र." (भगवद्गीता 13.5)

"Mr Ward, from whom many of the preceding details have been copied estimates that 'amongst one hundred thousand Brahmans, there may be one thousand who learn the grammar of the Sunskritu, of whom four or five hundred may read some parts of the kavyu (or poetical literature), and fifty some parts of the ulunkaru (or rhetorical) shastras. Four hundred of this thousand may read some of the smriti (or law works); but not more than ten any part of the tuntrus (or the mystical and magical treatises of modern Hinduism). Three hundred may study the nyayu (or logic), but only five or six the meemangsu, (explanatory of the ritual of the veds), the sunkhyu (a system of philosophical materialism), the vedantu (illustrative of the spiritual portions of the veds), the patunjulu (a system of philosophical asceticism), the vaisheshika (a system of philosophical anti-materialism), or the veda (the most ancient and sacred writings of Hindoos). Ten persons in this number of Brahmans may become learned in the astronomical shastras, while ten more understand these very imperfectly. Fifty of this thousand may read the shree bhaguvutu, and some of the pooranas.'" (William Adam's State of Education in Bengal 1835-38)

75. Conclusion

प्रत्यक्ष alone is inconclusive, because it is very limited:
It is theoretically possible to create a philosophy that accepts the validity only of प्रत्यक्ष-प्रमाण. Such materialism is ascribed to चार्वाक, who is said to have denied both न्याय and the law of कर्म. He is famous for teaching:
ऋणं कृत्वा घृतं पिबेद् यावज्जीवेत्सुखं जीवेत्। भस्मीभूतस्य देहस्य किं पुनरागमो भवेत् ॥[913]

A world-view without अनुमान invited ridicule from rival philosophers:

चार्वाक तव चार्वङ्गीं जारतो वीक्ष्य गर्भिणीम् । प्रत्यक्षमात्रविश्वासो घनश्वासं किमुज्झसि ॥[914]

Four human defects:

भ्रमप्रमादविप्रलिप्साकरणापाटवदोषाः ।[915]

(1) भ्रम ('whirling', confusion): An error due to mistaking something for something else. Like taking a tree at dusk for a man, or a rope for a snake.

(2) प्रमाद ('intoxication', carelessness). An error due to inattention, if our mind is not connecting with a particular perceiving sense. We may sit through a lecture but miss portions of it.

(3) विप्रलिप्सा ('cheating'): An error due to the desire to deceive even oneself. When pressured, one tends to fill in some lack of information.

(4) करण-अपाटव ('un-sharpness of the senses'). An error due to weakness of the senses (f.e., the eyes cannot see the own eye-lids).

अनुमान alone is also inconclusive:

Sometimes logic is used to 'refute' atheism. E.g., the 'theleological argument' to proof the existence of God by logic is that anything invested with intelligence (like a watch) is testimony of a creator; therefore, this world must have a creator. But according to the standard of science, a theory (like Darwin's 'Theory') should only be accepted as fact after its confirmation by any number of experiments – especially in spiritual matters.

नैषा तर्केण मतिरापनेया ।[916] तर्काप्रतिष्ठानात् ।[917]

अचिन्त्याः खलु ये भावा न तांस्तर्केण योजयेत् ।[918]

शास्त्र alone is inconclusive:

शास्त्रं यदि भवेदेकं श्रेयो व्यक्तं भवेत्तदा ।[919]

The महात्मा draws the conclusion

तर्को ऽप्रतिष्ठः श्रुतयो विभिन्ना   नासावृषिर्यस्य मतं न भिन्नम् ।
धर्मस्य तत्त्वं निहितं गुहायां   महाजनो येन गतः स पन्थाः ॥[920]

... which everyone has to see/realize for himself

उत्तिष्ठत जाग्रत प्राप्य वरान्निबोधत । क्षुरस्य धारा निशिता दुरत्यया । दुर्गं पथस्तत्कवयो वदन्ति ।[921]

... by some mercy:

नायमात्मा प्रवचनेन लभ्यो   न मेधया न बहुना श्रुतेन ।
यमेवैष वृणुते तेन लभ्यस्   तस्यैष आत्मा विवृणुते तनूं स्वाम् ॥[922]

द्वे विद्ये वेदितव्य इति ह स्म यद् ब्रह्मविदो वदन्ति परा चैव अपरा च । अथ परा यया तदक्षरमधिगम्यते ।[923]

को ऽहं कथमिदं किं वा कथं मरणजन्मनी । विचारयान्तरे वेत्थं महत्तत्फलमेष्यसि ॥[924] वेदा ब्रह्मात्मविषयास् त्रिकाण्डविषया इमे । परोक्षवादा ऋषयः परोक्षं मम च प्रियम् ॥[925]

"The Vedanta and the Sankhya hold the key to the laws of mind and thought process which are co-related to the Quantum Field, i.e., the operation and distribution of particles at atomic and molecular levels." (Prof. Brian David Josephson, Welsh physicist and Nobel Laureate)

वेदान्त deals with three तत्त्व, categories:

	(1)	(2)	(3)
	ब्रह्म	जीव	जगत्
or	अदस्		इदम्
which is		सत्	असत्

द्वैतं चैव तथाद्वैतं द्वैताद्वैतं तथैव च । न द्वैतं नापि चाद्वैतमितो तत्परमार्थिकम् ॥[926]

(1) अद्वैत-वाद

अहं ब्रह्मास्मि ।[927] अयमात्मा ब्रह्म ।[928] तत् त्वमसि श्वेतकेतो ।[929]

अहं ब्रह्म परं धाम ।[930]

पुरुषेश्वरयोरत्र न वैलक्षण्यमण्वपि ।[931] अहं भवान् न चान्यस्त्वं त्वमेवाहं विचक्ष्व भोः ।[932]

(2) द्वैत-वाद

गुहां प्रविष्टावात्मानौ हि तद्दर्शनात् । विशेषणाच्च ।[933]

यद्वै तत्सुकृतं रसो वै सः । रसं ह्येवायं लब्ध्वानन्दी भवति । को ह्येवान्यात्कः प्राण्याद्यदेष आकाश आनन्दो न स्यात् । एष ह्येवानन्दयति ।[934]

अणोरणीयान्महतो महीयान् आत्मास्य जन्तोर्निहितो गुहायाम् ।[935]
नित्यो नित्यानां चेतनश्चेतनानाम् एको बहूनां यो विदधाति कामान् ।
तमात्मस्थं ये ऽनुपश्यन्ति धीरास् तेषां शान्तिः शाश्वती नेतरेषाम् ॥[936]

द्वा सुपर्णा सयुजा सखाया समानं वृक्षं परिषस्वजाते ।
तयोरन्यः पिप्पलं स्वादु अत्ति अनश्नन्नन्यो अभिचाकशीति ॥
समाने वृक्षे पुरुषो निमग्नो अनीशया शोचति मुह्यमानः ।
जुष्टं यदा पश्यति अन्यमीशम् अस्य महिमानमेति वीतशोकः ॥937

78. Brahma & Jagat

यतो वा इमानि भूतानि जायन्ते येन जातानि जीवन्ति यत्प्रयन्त्यभिसंविशन्ति
तद् ब्रह्म ।938 आत्मैवेदमग्र आसीत्पुरुषविधः ।939 आत्मा वा इदमेक एवाग्र
आसीत् । स ऐक्षत लोकान्नु सृजा इति ।940 तदैक्षत बहु स्यां प्रजायेयेति ।941
सो ऽकामयत बहु स्यां प्रजायेय ।942

Conclusion: ब्रह्म-वाद

इदं ब्रह्म । इदं सर्वम् ।943 सर्व खल्विदं ब्रह्म ।944 आत्मैवेदं सर्वम् ।945

Vyasa:

अथातो ब्रह्मजिज्ञासा । जन्माद्यस्य यतः ।946 आत्मकृतेः परिणामात् ।947

Thus:

सन्मूलाः सौम्येमाः प्रजाः सदायतनाः सत्प्रतिष्ठाः ।948
यथोर्णनाभिः सृजते गृह्लते च यथा पृथिव्यामोषधयः सम्भवन्ति ।
यथा सतः पुरुषात्केशलोमानि तथाक्षरात्सम्भवतीह विश्वम् ॥949
ब्रह्म सत्यं तपः सत्यं सत्यं चैव प्रजापतिः । सत्याद्भूतानि जातानि सत्यं भूतमयं
जगत् ॥950

Shankara's माया-वाद of ब्रह्म सत्यं जगन्मिथ्या जीव ब्रह्मैव न परः ।951 ('जगत् is
false') is certainly not in accord with Vyāsa's परिणाम-वाद . भगवद्गीता describes such
a philosophy as 'demoniac mentality' (16.8).

Thus, whenever जगत् is called illusion (माया, मिथ्या), it must refers to its temporary,
destructable nature, or its not being our real home:

स्वशक्त्या सृष्ट्वान्विष्णुर् यथार्थं सर्वविज्जगत् । इत्युक्तेः सत्यमेवैतद्
वैराग्यार्थमसद्वचः ॥952 यदिदं मनसा वाचा चक्षुर्भ्यां श्रवणादिभिः । नश्वरं
गृह्यमानं च विद्धि मायामनोमयम् ॥953

A real illusion is called विवर्त :

सतत्त्वतो ऽन्यथाप्रथा विकार इत्युदाहितः । अतत्त्वतो ऽन्यथाप्रथा विवर्त
इत्युदाहृतः ॥954

अथ हैनं विदग्धः शाकल्यः पप्रच्छ । कति देवाः याज्ञवल्क्य इति । त्रयश्च त्री च शता त्रयश्च त्री च सहस्रेति । …त्रयश्च त्रिंशदिति । …षडिति । …त्रय इति । …द्वाविति । …अध्यर्ध इति । …एक इति ।⁹⁵⁵

यथेन्द्रियैः पृथग्द्वारैर् अर्थो बहुगुणाश्रयः । एको नानेयते तद्वद् भगवान् शास्त्रवर्त्मभिः ॥⁹⁵⁶

"The monistic emphasis led the Vedic thinkers to look upon the Vedic deities as different names of the One Universal Godhead, each representing a power of the divine being. ... Agni, Yama, etc., are symbols. They are not gods in themselves. They express different qualities of the object worshiped. The Vedic seers were not conscious of any iconoclastic mission. They did not feel called upon to denounce the worship of the various deities as disastrous error or mortal sin. They led the worshippers of the many deities to the worship of the one and only God by a process of reinterpretation and reconciliation. ... For Plutarch and Maximus of Tyre, the different gods worshipped in the third century Roman Empire were symbolic representations of a Supreme God who is unknowable in His inmost nature. 'God Himself, the father and fashioner of all ... is unnameable by any lawgiver, unutterable by any voice, not to be seen by any eye. ... But if a Greek is stirred to the remembrance of God by the art of Phidias, an Egyptian by paying worship to animals, another man by a river, another by fire, I have no anger for their divergence; only let them know, let them love, let them remember.' In the Taittiriya-samhita and Shatapatha-brahmana, it is said that Praja-pati assumed certain forms of fish (matsya), tortoise (kurma) and boar (varaha) for the attainment of certain ends. When the doctrine of avataras, incarnations, becomes established, these three become the incarnations of Vishnu." (Sir Sarvepalli Radhakrishnan, Indian Prof. at Oxford University and President of India, 1888-1975)

यं ब्रह्म वेदान्तविदो वदन्ति परे प्रधानं पुरुषं तथान्ये ।
विश्वोद्गतेः कारणमीश्वरं वा तस्मै नमो विघ्नविनाशनाय ॥⁹⁵⁷

Esp. three features:

वदन्ति तत् तत्त्वविदस् तत्त्वं यज्ज्ञानमद्वयम् । ब्रह्मेति परमात्मेति भगवानिति शब्द्यते ॥⁹⁵⁸ नमस्तुभ्यं भगवते ब्रह्मणे परमात्मने ।⁹⁵⁹

As पुरुष:

महतः परमव्यक्तम् अव्यक्तात्पुरुषः परः । पुरुषान्न परं किञ्चित् सा काष्ठा सा परा गतिः ॥⁹⁶⁰

तं त्वा औपनिषदं पुरुषं पृच्छामि ।⁹⁶¹

वेदाहमेतं पुरुषं महान्तं आदित्यवर्णं तमसः परस्तात् ।⁹⁶²

काम एव यस्यायतनं हृदयं लोको मनो ज्योतिर्यो वै तं पुरुष विद्यात्सर्वस्यात्मनः परायणं स वै वेदिता स्यात् ।⁹⁶³

क्लेशकर्मविपाकाशयैरपरामृष्टः पुरुषविशेष ईश्वरः । तत्र निरतिशयं सर्वज्ञबीजम् । स एष पूर्वेषामपि गुरुः कालेनानवच्छेदात् ।⁹⁶⁴

ॐ सहस्रशीर्षा पुरुषः सहस्राक्षः सहस्रपात्। स भूमिं विश्वतो वृत्वा अत्यतिष्ठद्दशाङ्गुलम् ॥965 ईशावास्यमिदं सर्वं यत्किञ्च जगत्यां जगत्।966 पुराण्यनेन सृष्टानि नृतिर्यग्ऋषिदेवताः। शेते जीवेन रूपेण पुरेषु पुरुषो ह्यसौ ॥967 सर्वाणि तत्र भूतानि वसन्ति परमात्मनि। भूतेषु च स सर्वात्मा वासुदेवस्ततः स्मृतः ॥968 हिरण्मयेन पात्रेण सत्यस्यापिहितं मुखम्। तत् त्वं पूषन्नपावृणु सत्यधर्माय दृष्टये। ॐ क्रतो स्मर कृतं स्मर क्रतो स्मर कृतं स्मर ॥969

एवं सर्वेषु भूतेषु भक्तिरव्यभिचारिणी। कर्तव्या पण्डितैर्ज्ञात्वा सर्वभूतमयं हरिम् ॥970 सर्वदेवमयो हरिः।971 ॐ तद्विष्णोः परमं पदं सदा पश्यन्ति सूरयः।972

यथा तरोर्मूलनिषेचनेन तृप्यन्ति तत्स्कन्धभुजोपशाखाः।
प्राणोपहाराच्च यथेन्द्रियाणां तथैव सर्वार्हणमच्युतेज्या ॥973

अर्चिते देवदेवेश अब्जशङ्खगदाधरे। अर्चिताः पितरो देवा यतः सर्वमयो हरिः ॥974 हरिरेव सदाराध्यः सर्वदेवेश्वरेश्वरः। इतरे ब्रह्मरुद्राद्या नावज्ञेया कदाचन ॥975 शृणुते सर्वधर्मांश्च सर्वान्देवान्नमस्यति। अनसूयुर्जितक्रोधस् तस्य तुष्यति केशवः ॥976

विष्णोस्तु त्रीणि रूपाणि पुरुषाख्यान्यथो विदुः। प्रथमं महतः स्रष्टृ द्वितीयं त्वण्डसंस्थितम्। तृतीयं सर्वभूतस्थं तानि ज्ञात्वा विमुच्यते ॥977

Sun & Fire:
विष्णुर्जिष्णुर्भविष्णुश्च अग्निसूर्यादिरूपवान्। अग्निरूपेण देवादेर् मुखं विष्णुः परा गतिः। वेदेषु च पुराणेषु यज्ञमूर्तिश्च गीयते ॥978
यज्ञो वै विष्णुः।979

Although exclusive सौर (worship of सूर्य) has declined worldwide, Hindus worship the sun as a representation of ब्रह्म (असावादित्यो ब्रह्म) or विष्णु (सूर्य-नारायण) daily at सन्ध्या with ब्रह्म-गायत्री, occasionally at मकर-सङ्क्रान्ति, and for protection with आदित्य-हृदयम्.

"How artistic, that there should be room for such variety – how rich the texture is, and how much more interesting than if the Almighty had decreed one antiseptically safe, exclusive, orthodox way. Although he is Unity, God finds, it seems, his recreation in variety! But beyond these differences, the same goal beckons." (Huston Smith, American religion scholar, 1919-2016)

ब्रह्मवर्चसकामस्तु यजेत ब्रह्मणः पतिम्। इन्द्रमिन्द्रियकामस्तु प्रजाकामः प्रजापतीन्॥ देवीं मायां तु श्रीकामस् तेजस्कामो विभावसुम्। वसुकामो वसून्रुद्रान् वीर्यकामोऽथ वीर्यवान्॥ अन्नाद्यकामस्त्वदितिं स्वर्गकामो अदितेः सुतान्। विश्वान्देवान्राज्यकामः साध्यान्संसाधको विशाम्॥ आयुष्कामो अश्विनौ देवौ पुष्टिकाम इलां यजेत्। प्रतिष्ठाकामः पुरुषो रोदसी लोकमातरौ॥

रूपाभिकामो गन्धर्वान् स्त्रीकामो ऽप्सर उर्वशीम् । आधिपत्यकामः सर्वेषां यजेत परमेष्ठिनम् ॥ राज्यकामो मनून्देवान् निर्ऋतिं त्वभिचरन्यजेत् । कामकामो यजेत्सोमम् अकामः पुरुषं परम् ॥⁹⁸⁰ अकामः सर्वकामो वा मोक्षकाम उदारधीः । तीव्रेण भक्तियोगेन यजेत पुरुषं परम् ॥⁹⁸¹

80. Shakti

The question then is, how the ब्रह्म (pure spirit) can turn into जगत् (matter). The answer is शक्ति-परिणाम-वाद – ब्रह्म can act through its शक्ति, remaining unchanged like a loadstone:

पूर्णमदः पूर्णमिदं पूर्णात्पूर्णम् उदच्यते । पूर्णस्य पूर्णमादाय पूर्णम् एवावशिष्यते ॥⁹⁸² एकदेशस्थितस्याग्नेर् ज्योत्स्ना विस्तारिणी यथा । परस्य ब्रह्मणः शक्तिस् तथेदमखिलं जगत् ॥⁹⁸³ विष्णुशक्तिः परा प्रोक्ता क्षेत्रज्ञाख्या तथा परा । अविद्याकर्मसञ्ज्ञान्या तृतीया शक्तिरिष्यते ॥⁹⁸⁴

For the purpose of material creation विष्णु is said to 'glance over matter', thereby impregnating it. This glance takes the form of सदा-शिव, whose contact with दुर्गा, the personification of material energy, is depicted as शिव-लिङ्ग inside a योनि.

लिङ्गयोन्यात्मिका जाता इमा माहेश्वरीप्रजाः । शक्तिमान्पुरुषः सो ऽयं लिङ्गरूपी महेश्वरः ॥⁹⁸⁵

नित्यैव सा जगन्माता विष्णोः श्रीरनपायिनी । यथा सर्वगतो विष्णुस् तथैवेयं द्विजोत्तम ॥⁹⁸⁶ एवं यथा जगत्स्वामी देवदेवो जनार्दनः । अवतारं करोत्येष तथा श्रीस्तत्सहायिनी ॥⁹⁸⁷

As दुर्गा/पार्वती She has forms like उमा, कात्यायनी, गौरी, काली, हैमवती, ईश्वरी, शिवा, भवानी, रुद्राणी, शर्वाणी, सर्वमङ्गला, अपर्णा, पार्वती, मृडानी, चण्डिका, अम्बिका, आर्या, दाक्षायणी, गिरिजा, and मेनकात्मजा (अमर-कोष 1.1.36-37). She is the mother of कार्तिकेय and गणेश. As सरस्वती She embodies inspiration, learning and arts. God is always depicted with His energy (शक्ति, देवी), as लक्ष्मी-नारायण, शिव-शक्ति, etc.

Some of this energy is in women also. Hindu wives remember पञ्च-कन्या in a morning prayer.

लक्ष्मी manifests as unlimited energies or potencies (भग, opulence):

अध्यर्हणीयासनमास्थितं परं वृतं चतुःषोडशपञ्चशक्तिभिः ।
युक्तं भगैः स्वैरितरत्र चाध्रुवैः स्व एव धामन् रममाणमीश्वरम् ॥⁹⁸⁸

Esp. six भग:

ऐश्वर्यस्य समग्रस्य वीर्यस्य यशसः श्रियः। ज्ञानवैराग्ययोश्चैव षण्णां भग इतीङ्गना ॥[989]

All those potencies are classified into three:

न तस्य कार्यं करणं च विद्यते न तत्समश्चाभ्यधिकश्च दृश्यते।
परास्य शक्तिर्विविधैव श्रूयते स्वाभाविकी ज्ञानबलक्रिया च ॥[990]

	(1)	(2)	(3)
	बल	ज्ञान	क्रिया
same as	सत्	चित्	आनन्द
or	willing	thinking	feeling

---

81. Sarga

Eight stages of सर्ग:

1. प्रधान (material potency), also called सगुण-ब्रह्म (opp. to निर्गुण-पर-ब्रह्म) or महत्-ब्रह्म: "The महत् ब्रह्म is My womb." (भगवद्गीता 14.3). When agitated by काल, it becomes …

2. प्रकृति (material energy): "When her गुण are agitated by दैव, the Supreme Person invested His energy in form of all the जीव in that womb and she then delivered the effulgent महत्-तत्त्व."[991]

3. महत् (initiated material energy, a junction between pure spirit and matter), the collective कर्म of the जीव, also called बुद्धि (cosmic 'intelligence', a portion of which is represented in everyone as intellect).

"I suspect that general relativity and quantum theory are two complimentary aspects of a deeper theory that will involve a kind of cosmic consciousness. The cosmic consciousness or the Mahat of India's Samkhya Philosophy is the basis of entire creation." (Jack Sarfatti, American theoretical physicist)

4. अहङ्कार, the binding force of material existence. शिव manifests it threefold (a-c), from which develop …

5. मनः-बुद्धि-इन्द्रिय-प्राण-तन्मात्र-महाभूत
   (a) from सात्त्विक-अहङ्कार in the वैकारिक (modifying) stage of creation → मनः
   (b) राजस-अ॰ in तैजस stage → बुद्धि, इन्द्रिय and प्राण

(c) तामस-अ° in तामस stage → तन्मात्र and महाभूत

Thus, the 1 प्रकृति is perceived through 5 ज्ञानेन्द्रिय as 5 तन्मात्र of 5 महा-भूत:

	(1)	(2)	(3)	(4)	(5)
ज्ञानेन्द्रिय	श्रोत्र	त्वक्	चक्षु	जिह्वा	घ्राण
तन्मात्र	शब्द	स्पर्श	रूप	रस	गन्ध
महाभूत	आकाश	वायु	अग्नि	जल	भूमि

(1) आकाश – space of information/शब्द; another space-time than our; (2) वायु – impulse, force, power, energy; when influencing bodies, it is called प्राण, vital force; its quality is स्पर्श /(electro-magnetic) vibration, perceived as density (hard/soft) and temperature (cold/hot); वायु creates (and is seen in) movement (fire): (3) अग्नि (light) – exhibits forms; one-dimensional process, movement, evolution of forms, sizes, individuality; fire of digestion, evaporation, hunger, thirst; its quality is form, perceived through light with eyes (broken light as colors); in its purest form from sun and moon (प्रभास्मि ...); this fire has nothing to do with heat (air), because form is independent of temperature; (4) जल – liquid aggregate, floating, condensed fire/process; moistens, makes soft, creates satisfaction; (5) भूमि – particle, solid aggregate, condensed 'water', substance of all solid manifestations. Since the cause exists in its effect as well, the characteristics of all the elements exist in भूमि alone.

In आयुर्वेद, कफ is a combination of आकाश-जल, पित्त of अग्नि-भूमि, and वात of आकाश-वायु.

6. All above (1.-5.) 'Causes' form a कारण-सागर, of which गङ्गा is one drop. In साङ्ख्य, the causes (कारण) are 24 – प्रधान, महत्, अहङ्कार, मनः, 10 इन्द्रिय, 5 तन्मात्र, 5 महा-भूत, plus काल and परमात्मा. In other systems the same elements are differently summarized as 7, 9, 13, 16 or 22 elements. For example:

अग्निर्मही गगनमम्बु मरुद्दिशश्च कालस्तथात्ममनसीति ।[992]

7. After creating unlimited universes (ब्रह्माण्ड), God enters each one as विष्णु, resting on its गर्भोदक. In His navel lake pierces an effulgent lotus bud through His abdomen, called हिरण्य-गर्भ, the form of the sum total of all the living entities' कर्म. In it, He generates the Personality of Vedic wisdom, ब्रह्मा.

8. Secondary creation by the 'Creator God' ब्रह्मा: At first, ब्रह्मा could not understand his identity and purpose, but after austerities and meditation, he was able to recreate त्रि-लोक as it was before. ब्रह्मा, as प्रजापति, is interested in good progeny. To please him, wedding invitations are still issued with his picture.

त्रि-लोक refers to 3 planes of material existence, either भूर्-भुवर्-स्वर् (physical-mental-intellectual), or, incl. hellish/materialistic existences, hell-earth-heaven, further subdivided into चतुर्दश-भुवन:

Seven higher लोक (planes): (1) भूर्/भू-मण्डल/महा-तल (=middle plane for humans), (2) भुवर् (भूत, प्रेत), (3) स्वर्/स्वर्ग/दिव्य-स्वर्ग (देव), (4) महर् (याग), (5) जन (तपस्य), (6) तपः (सन्न्यास), (7) सत्य-/ब्रह्म-लोक (ब्रह्मा).

Seven lower लोक: अतल-वितल-सुतल-तलातल-महातल-रसातल-पाताल.

वैतरणी is like a river between भूर् and lower regions.

3 regions are sometimes called स्वर्ग (heaven): दिव्य-स्वर्ग (celestial heaven), भौम-स्वर्ग (certain regions on Earth), and बिल-स्वर्ग (lower planets with material prosperity).

3761 BCE is the year of world creation in the Jewish religious calendar. 4004 BCE is Archbishop Usher's (17th century) supposed date of the creation of the world, based on genealogies in the Old Testament.

"A stone was found there in the temple of the great Budda, on which an inscription was written purporting that the temple had been founded fifty thousand years ago. The Sultan was surprised at the ignorance of these people, because those who believe in the true faith represent that only seven thousand years have elapsed since the creation of the world."[M]

"A millennium before Europeans were willing to divest themselves of the Biblical idea that the world was a few thousand years old, the Mayans were thinking of millions and the Hindus billions." "The Hindu religion is the only one of the world's great faiths dedicated to the idea that the Cosmos itself undergoes an immense, indeed an infinite, number of deaths and rebirths. It is the only religion in which the time scales correspond to those of modern scientific cosmology." (Dr. Carl Sagan, American astrophysicist and author, 1934-1996)

"The idea of a periodically expanding and contracting universe, which involves a scale of time and space of vast proportions; has arisen not only in modern cosmology, but also in ancient Indian mythology. Experiencing the universe as an organic and rhythmically moving cosmos, the Hindus were able to develop evolutionary cosmologies which come very close to our modern scientific models. The Hindu sages were not afraid to identify this rhythmic divine play with the evolution of the cosmos as a whole. They pictured the universe as periodically expanding and contracting and gave the name kalpa to the unimaginable time span between the beginning and the end of one creation. The scale of this ancient myth is indeed staggering; it has taken the human mind more than two thousand years to come up again with a similar concept." (Fritjof Capra, Austrian-born physicist and ecologist)

The essence of all beings, our true identity, is the eternal आत्मा, made of ब्रह्म.

यथाग्नेः क्षुद्रा विस्फुलिङ्गा व्युच्चरन्ति एवमेवास्मादात्मनः। सर्वे प्राणाः सर्वे लोकाः सर्वे देवाः सर्वाणि भूतानि व्युच्चरन्ति ।[993]

"I may mention here another fundamental error of Christianity, an error which cannot be explained away, and the mischievous consequences of which are obvious every day: I mean the unnatural distinction Christianity makes between man and the animal world to which he really belongs. It sets up man as all-important, and looks upon animals as merely things. Brahmanism and Buddhism, on the other hand, true to the facts, recognize in a positive way that man is related generally to the whole of nature, and specially and principally to animal nature; and in their systems man is always represented by the theory of metempsychosis and otherwise, as closely connected with the animal world. The important part played by animals all through Buddhism and Brahmanism, compared with the total disregard of them in Judaism and Christianity, puts an end to any question as to which system is nearer perfection, however much we in Europe may have become accustomed to the absurdity of the claim. Christianity contains, in fact, a great and essential imperfection in limiting its precepts to man, and in refusing rights to the entire animal world…" (Arthur Schopenhauer, German philosopher and writer, 1788-1860)

We are marginal, fragmental and atomic ब्रह्म, perpetually reborn among all species, and then called living being (जीव, जन्तु):

यत्तटस्थं तु चिद्रूपं स्वसंवेद्याद्विनिर्गतम्। रञ्जितं गुणरागेण स जीव इति कथ्यते ॥[994] आदित्यवर्णं सूक्ष्माभं अब्बिन्दुमिव पुष्करे। नक्षत्रमिव पश्यन्ति योगिनो ज्ञानचक्षुषा ॥[995] बालाग्रशतभागस्य शतधा कल्पितस्य च। भागो जीवः स विज्ञेयः स चानन्त्याय कल्पते ॥ नैव स्त्री न पुमानेष न चैवायं नपुंसकः। यद्यच्छरीरमादत्ते तेन तेन स रक्ष्यते ॥[996]

Illusioned:

जीवस्य मोहो ऽयम् अहंममेति ।[997]
क्लिश्यमानः शतं वर्षं देहे देही तमोवृतः ।[998] जन्तुर्वै भव एतस्मिन् यां यां योनिमनुव्रजेत्। तस्यां तस्यां स लभते निर्वृतिं न विरज्यते ॥[999]
यस्यात्मबुद्धिः कुणपे त्रिधातुके स्वधीः कलत्रादिषु भौम इज्यधीः।
यत्तीर्थबुद्धिः सलिले न कर्हिचिज् जनेष्वभिज्ञेषु स एव गोखरः ॥[1000]
असुर्या नाम ते लोका अन्धेन तमसावृताः। तांस्ते प्रेत्याभिगच्छन्ति ये के चात्महनो जनाः ॥[1001]

5 stages of illusion:

परेशवैमुख्यात् तेषामविद्याभिनिवेशः ।[1002]
अविद्यास्मितारागद्वेषाभिनिवेशः क्लेशाः ।[1003]

(1)	(2)	(3)	(4)	(5)
अविद्या	अस्मिता	राग	द्वेष	अभिनिवेश
forgetting identity as soul	bodily mis-identification	material enjoyment	anger upon frustration	sense of death

शरीरं पुरमित्याहुः स्वामिनी बुद्धिरिष्यते । तत्त्वबुद्धेः शरीरस्थं मनो नामाथ चिन्तकम् ॥[1004] आत्मानं रथिनं विद्धि शरीरं रथमेव तु । बुद्धिं तु सारथिं विद्धि मनः प्रग्रहमेव च ॥ इन्द्रियाणि हयानाहुर् विषयांस्तेषु गोचरान् । आत्मेन्द्रियमनोयुक्तं भोक्तेत्याहुर्मनीषिणः ॥ विज्ञानसारथिर्यस्तु मनःप्रग्रहवान्नरः । सो ऽध्वनः पारमाप्नोति तद्विष्णोः परमं पदम् ॥[1005]

<h2 style="text-align:center">83. Consciousness</h2>

Although the soul is always conscious, as जीव it witnesses and imitates बुद्धि-गुण, 3 states of awareness:

जाग्रत्स्वप्नः सुषुप्तं च गुणतो बुद्धिवृत्तयः । तासां विलक्षणो जीवः साक्षित्वेन विनिश्चितः ॥[1006] नृत्यतो गायतः पश्यन् यथैवानुकरोति तान् । एवं बुद्धिगुणान्पश्यन्न् अनीहो ऽप्यनुकार्यते ॥[1007]

(1) जाग्रत् / जागरित / बुद्ध

जागरितस्थानो बहिष्प्रज्ञः वैश्वानरः ।[1008]

In this state the same physical universe bound by uniform laws presents itself to all.

(2) स्वप्न

स्वप्नस्थानो ऽन्तःप्रज्ञः तैजसः ।[1009]

In this state everyone fashions his own world in dreams.

अत्रैष देवः स्वप्ने महिमानमनुभवति । यद् दृष्टं दृष्टमनुपश्यति । श्रुतं श्रुतमेवार्थमनुशृणोति । दृष्टं चादृष्टं च ।[1010]

तद्यथा महामत्स्य उभे कूले अनुसञ्चरति पूर्वं चापरं च एवमेवायं पुरुष एतावुभावन्तावनुसञ्चरति स्वप्नान्तं च बुद्धान्तं च ।[1011]

(3) सुषुप्त, सुषुप्ति

सुषुप्तस्थानः ... प्रज्ञानघनः ... प्राज्ञः ।[1012]

In this state there is temporary union with ब्रह्म.

सुप्तिमूर्च्छोपतापेषु प्राणायनविघाततः । नेहते ऽहमिति ज्ञानं मृत्युप्रज्वारयोरपि ॥[1013]

(4) तुर्य

चतुर्थम् ... आत्मा ।[1014]
This is where the union with ब्रह्म is permanent.

84. Bondage

Different philosophies stress the importance of different factors of bondage. The overall picture is, that the soul is dragged ...

by (**1**) निमित्त-माया (a subtle 'causal energy', instrumental or efficient cause) with its factors आत्मा (the ब्रह्म, acc. to अद्वैत-वाद, or 'oneself', acc. to नास्तिक), दैव (destiny), काल (time, acc. to व्यावहारिक), कर्म (activity, acc. to मीमांसक), स्वभाव/गुण (one's nature, acc. to चार्वाक), and काम (lust, acc. to वात्स्यायन)

through (**2**) प्रधान-/उपादान-माया ('substance energy', operative or material cause) with its factors आत्मा (which is both cause and ingredient), प्राण (life air), द्रव्य/पञ्च-भूत (matter, elements), क्षेत्र (the world), विकार (senses) or अहङ्कार, सङ्घात (the body).

Most prominent is the idea, that "By the गुण born of one's प्रकृति everyone is helplessly forced to act." (भगवद्गीता 3.5) Because ...
गुणैर्नेनीयते बुद्धिः ।[1015] परिद्रष्टा गुणानां तु संसृष्टान्मन्यते तथा ।[1016]

As the internal energy is displayed in three spiritual modes/potencies (सत्-चित्-आनन्द), the external energy is displayed in three material modes, the गुण:

	(1)	(2)	(3)
	सत्	चित्	आनन्द
गुण	तमः, तमो-गुण	सत्त्व, सत्त्व-गुण	रजः, रजो-गुण
forming	तन्मात्र and महा-भूत	मनः	बुद्धि and इन्द्रिय
	कार्य (objects)	कर्ता (desires)	कारण (senses)
for	annihilation	maintenance	creation
Deities	शिव	विष्णु	ब्रह्मा

कर्तृत्व (doership):
Thus, the जीव is not independent, but still responsible – and not the गुण, because the injunctions of scripture are meaningful only if a conscious doer exists: कर्ता शास्त्रार्थवत्त्वात् । "The soul is कर्ता, because शास्त्र has a purpose." (वेदान्त-सूत्र

2.3.31) "With the help of oneself one should elevate oneself." (भगवद्गीता 6.5) "After considering fully whatever I have explained to you, do as you like!" (भगवद्गीता 18.63)

85. Liberation

यश्च मूढतमो लोके यश्च बुद्धेः परं गतः । तावुभौ सुखमेधेते क्लिश्यत्यन्तरितो जनः ॥1017

When the जीव realizes its identity as आत्मा, it may achieve liberation.

ममेति बध्यते जन्तुर्निर्ममेति विमुच्यते ।1018 मुक्तिर्हित्वान्यथा रूपं स्वरूपेण व्यवस्थितिः ।1019 सर्वोपाधिविनिर्मुक्तम् ।1020

तदा द्रष्टुः स्वरूपे ऽवस्थानम् ।1021

घनो यदार्कप्रभवो विदीर्यते चक्षुः स्वरूपं रविमीक्षते तदा ।

यदा ह्यहङ्कार उपाधिरात्मनो जिज्ञासया नश्यति तर्ह्यनुस्मरेत् ॥1022

Liberation has different names like श्रेयः, मोक्ष, मुक्ति, विमुक्ति, निर्वाण, ब्रह्म-भूय, अमृतत्व, आत्म-साक्षात्कार, सायुज्य, कैवल्य, एकत्व, and शून्यता. The path of liberation is called निवृत्ति-मार्ग, अपवर्ग, देव-यान, and of course योग.

श्रेयश्च प्रेयश्च मनुष्यमेतस् तौ सम्परीत्य विविनक्ति धीरः ।

श्रेयो हि धीरो ऽभिप्रेयसो वृणीते प्रेयो मन्दो योगक्षेमाद् वृणीते ॥1023

लब्ध्वा सुदुर्लभमिदं बहुसम्भवान्ते मानुष्यमर्थदमनित्यमपीह धीरः ।

तूर्णं यतेत न पतेदनुमृत्यु यावन् निःश्रेयसाय विषयः खलु सर्वतः स्यात् ॥1024

पञ्चेन्द्रियजलां घोरां लोभकूलां सुदुस्तराम् । मन्युपङ्कामनाधृष्यां नदीं तरति बुद्धिमान् ॥1025

According to Bhagavad-Gita (4.9,8.16,8.21,15.6.) the spiritual world is not a place where one is thrown out, like Adam and Eva ...

ये दारागारपुत्राप्तान् प्राणान्वित्तमिमं परम् । हित्वा मां शरणं याताः कथं तांस्त्यक्तुमुत्सहे ॥1026

... or which a liberated soul wants to flee, like Lucifer.

धौतात्मा पुरुषः कृष्ण-पादमूलं न मुञ्चति । मुक्तसर्वपरिक्लेशः पान्थः स्वशरणं यथा ॥1027

न स पुनरावर्तते ।1028

"Hindu religion does not consist in struggles and attempts to believe a certain doctrine or dogma, but in realizing, not in believing, but in being and becoming." (Swami Vivekanada, Indian philosopher, 1863-1902)

दुर्जनः सज्जनो भूयात् सज्जनो शान्तिमाप्नुयात् । शान्तो मुच्येत बन्धेभ्यो मुक्तश्चान्यान्विमोचयेत् ॥1029

"Religious faith in the case of the Hindus has never been allowed to run counter to scientific laws, moreover the former is never made a condition for the knowledge they teach, but they are always scrupulously careful to take into consideration the possibility that by reason both the agnostic and atheist may attain truth in their own way." (Romain Rolland, French novelist and Nobel laureate, 1866-1944)

आत्मनो गुरुरात्मैव पुरुषस्य विशेषतः । यत्प्रत्यक्षानुमानाभ्यां श्रेयो ऽसावनुविन्दते ॥[1030]

अणुः पन्था विततः पुराणः । मां स्पृष्टो ऽनुवित्तो मयैव । तेन धीरा अपि यान्ति ब्रह्मविदः स्वर्गं लोकमित ऊर्ध्वं विमुक्ताः ।[1031]

"Hindu tradition is based on the experience of sages, sane men and women who observed the world and explored consciousness. Its approach is scientific: the Vedic truths are verifiable, universal and repeatable, not dependent on the views of privileged individuals ('prophets') but apaurusheya, 'impersonal'." (Dr. Koenraad Elst, Dutch historian)

The word योग can be derived from three युज्-धातु and has thus all these meanings: (1) 'meditation', absorption, समाधि; (2) 'restraint', mind control; (3) union (as in योग-वियोग – plus-minus, meeting-separation); engagement; gain: "Peace and industry are the source of योग and क्षेम." (कौटिलीय-अर्थ-शास्त्र 97.1); Plus (4) mysticism; as in योग-माया, योग-निद्रा, योग-सिद्धि, योगेश्वर.

योग is composed of (1) कर्म (activity with the body), (2) ज्ञान (discrimination with mind and intelligence) and (3) भक्ति (devotion with the heart or soul). According to the focus, योग is then called कर्म-, ज्ञान-, or भक्ति-योग. तपः (austerity), अष्टाङ्ग-योग, etc., are included in ज्ञान- and भक्ति-योग.

योगास्त्रयो मया प्रोक्ता नृणां श्रेयोविधित्सया। ज्ञानं कर्म च भक्तिश्च नोपायो ऽन्यो ऽस्ति कुत्रचित्॥ निर्विण्णानां ज्ञानयोगो न्यासिनामिह कर्मसु। तेष्वनिर्विण्णचित्तानां कर्मयोगस्तु कामिनाम् ॥1032

कर्म-योग is also called कर्म-अर्पण (offering one's work), or ब्रह्म-अर्पण (offering to the Absolute). It has two qualities: (a) भगवत्-प्रीणन ('pleasing the Lord'), doing all duty just to please Him; and (b) फल-न्यास, त्याग ('renunciation of the fruit'), offering at least some of the results of work to the Lord.

प्रीणातु भगवानीशः कर्मणानेन शाश्वतः। करोति सततं बुद्ध्या ब्रह्मार्पणमिदं परम्॥ यद्वा फलानां सन्न्यासं प्रकुर्यात्परमेश्वरे। कर्मणामेतदप्याहुर् ब्रह्मार्पणमनुत्तमम् ॥1033

But:

यदृच्छया मत्कथादौ जातश्रद्धस्तु यः पुमान्। न निर्विण्णो नातिसक्तो भक्तियोगो ऽस्य सिद्धिदः ॥1034 एतावानेव लोके ऽस्मिन् पुंसां धर्मः परः स्मृतः। भक्तियोगो भगवति तन्नामग्रहणादिभिः ॥1035

In उपनिषद्:

त्रिरुन्नतं स्थाप्य समं शरीरं हृदीन्द्रियाणि मनसा सन्निवेश्य।
ब्रह्मोडुपेन प्रतरेत विद्वान् स्रोतांसि सर्वाणि भयावहानि ॥1036
प्राणायामः प्रत्याहारो ध्यानं धारणा तर्कः समाधिः षडङ्गा इत्युच्यते योगः।
अनेन यदा पश्यन्पश्यति रुक्मवर्णं कर्तारमीशं पुरुषं ब्रह्मयोनिम् ।1037

In योग-सूत्र:

अथ योगानुशासनम्। योगश्चित्तवृत्तिनिरोधः ।1038

प्रमाणविपर्ययविकल्पनिद्रास्मृतयः ।1039 अभ्यासवैराग्याभ्यां तन्निरोधः ।1040
श्रद्धावीर्यस्मृतिसमाधिप्रज्ञापूर्वक इतरेषाम् । ईश्वरप्रणिधानाद्वा ।1041

Since surrender to the Lord counts here as optional category, योग is capable of assimilation even in atheistic schools of thought.

यमनियमासन-प्राणायामप्रत्याहार-धारणाध्यानसमाधयो ऽष्टावङ्गानि ।1042

1. यम (primary internal 'restraint', prohibitions, self-control)

तत्राहिंसा-सत्यास्तेय-ब्रह्मचर्यापरिग्रहा यमाः ।1043

Some may follow these prohibitions limited by time, place and circumstance – the fisherman may not kill other beings than fish, the warrior not outside a war, the general mass not during a pilgrimage – but the योगी is asked to follow them universally. व्यास describes the following effects of यम : By practicing अहिंसा, other living beings give up their mutual hostilities in one's presence; by practicing सत्य, one's blessings to others come true; by अस्तेय comes wealth; by ब्रह्मचर्य one obtains certain mental abilities (सिद्धि) like healing; by अपरिग्रह one obtains knowledge of previous and future births and events.

2. नियम (secondary external 'observance', prescriptions)

शौचसन्तोष-तपःस्वाध्यायेश्वरप्रणिधानानि नियमाः ।1044
इज्याध्ययनदानानि तपः सत्यं क्षमा घृणा । अलोभ इति मार्गो ऽयं धर्मस्याष्टविधः स्मृतः ॥ तत्र पूर्वचतुर्वर्गो दम्भार्थमपि सेव्यते । उत्तरस्तु चतुर्वर्गो नामहात्मसु तिष्ठति ॥1045

तपःस्वाध्यायेश्वरप्रणिधानानि क्रियायोगः ।1046
क्रियाक्रमेण योगो ऽपि ध्यानिनः सम्प्रवर्तते ।1047

3. आसन ('sitting', seat, posture, body-control)

स्थिरसुखमासनम् ।1048

4. प्राणायाम ('breath-control')

तस्मिन्सति श्वासप्रश्वासयोर्गतिविच्छेदः प्राणायामः ।1049
प्राणस्य शोधयेन्मार्ग पूरकुम्भकरेचकैः । प्रतिकूलेन वा चित्तं यथा स्थिरमचञ्चलम् ॥ मनो ऽचिरात्स्याद्विरजं जितश्वासस्य योगिनः । वाय्वग्निभ्यां यथा लोहं ध्मातं त्यजति वै मलम् ॥1050

Thus, one becomes fit for concentration. The primary exercises to clear the breathing are पूरक-कुम्भक-रेचक, in four stages: 1. बाह्य-वृत्ति during exhalation, 2. अभ्यन्तर-वृत्ति during inhalation, 3. refining both gross breathings, and then 4. the subtle प्राण.

5. प्रत्याहार (sensory 'withdrawel', sense-control)

स्वविषयासम्प्रयोगे चित्तस्य स्वरूपानुकार इवेन्द्रियाणां प्रत्याहारः ।[1051]

By practice, the senses should be made to imitate ('follow') the controlled mind, like bees their queen, thus bringing them under control of the mind. Otherwise, the mind is prone to follow the unrestraint senses. By withdrawing the attention from external sense objects, the scattered forces of senses and mind are recollected, and when the senses are dissolved in the mind, 6. concentration naturally takes place.

मलिनो हि यथादर्श आत्मज्ञानाय न क्षमः। तथा विपक्षकरण आत्मज्ञानाय न क्षमः ॥[1052]

Thus (1.-5.) ends the description of the external control, called साधन. Now (6.-8.) comes the description of the internal control, called संयम ('full control', concentration), which is the result of योग. No one who has not conquered the lower plane, can jump to the higher plane.

6. धारणा ('sustaining', concentration, mind-control)

देशबन्धश्चित्तस्य धारणा ।[1053]

There can be no concentration without something upon which the mind may rest, e.g., (1) parts of the body, like the sphere of the navel (नाभि-चक्र), the lotus of the heart (हृदय-पुण्डरीक), the light in the brain (मूर्ध्नि ज्योति), the fore-part of the nose (नासिकाग्र) and the fore-part of the tongue (जिह्वाग्र); (2) sacred syllables and मन्त्र; or (3) objects like certain देव or God Himself:

नास्ति विष्णुसमं ध्येयं तपो नानशनात्परम्। नास्त्यारोग्यसमं धन्यं नास्ति गङ्गासमा सरित् ॥[1054] हृदयस्थस्य योगेन देवदेवस्य दर्शनम् ।[1055]

7. ध्यान ('meditation')

तत्र प्रत्ययैकतानता ध्यानम् ।[1056]
स्थितं व्रजन्तमासीनं शयानं वा गुहाशयम् ध्यायेत् ।[1057]

"Zen is the Japanese equivalent of Sanskrit Dhyana (meditation) or Ch'an and is the name given to the sect founded in China by Bodhidharma." (Sir Charles Elliot, British linguist, botanist and diplomat, 1862-1931)

8. समाधि ('holding', absorption, trance)

तदेवार्थमात्रनिर्भासं स्वरूपशून्यमिव समाधिः ।[1058]

यदा पञ्चावतिष्ठन्ते ज्ञानानि मनसा सह। बुद्धिश्च न विचेष्टति तामाहुः परमां गतिम्। तां योगमिति मन्यन्ते स्थिरामिन्द्रियधारणाम् ॥[1059] (said to be the first ever description of Yoga)

तथोक्त्वा योगमास्थाय ज्योतिर्भूतो महातपाः । पुराणं पुरुषं विष्णुं जगाम मनसा परम् ॥[1060]

हठ-योग ('forced meditation'), propounded by स्वात्मराम in हठ-प्रदीपिका, concentrates on the withdrawel from sense objects by आसन and प्राणायाम.

Its modern forms are Shivananda Yoga by Swami Shivananda (plus singing and meditation); Kundalini Yoga by Yogi Bhajan (plus meditation and martial art); Vini Yoga by Krishnamacarya (exercises for therapeutic purposes); Iyangar Yoga by Indian Iyangar (with the help of ropes, etc.); Bikram Yoga by Bikram Choudhury (under 40 degree Celsius); Jivamukti Yoga in the US (with music and singing); Vipassana Yoga by SN Goenka (meditation).

सिद्धि is a mystic 'perfection', esp. 18:

(1) अणिमा _ 'smallness' of the body; (2) महिमा – greatness; (3) लघिमा – lightness; (4) प्राप्ति – gain, reaching far with the senses; (5) प्राकाम्य – 'enjoyment' of things seen (in this world) or just heard of (about the other world) [by magic within laws of nature]; (6) ईशिता – manipulating शक्ति; (7) वशिता – non-attachment to गुण; (8) काम-अवसायिता – getting the desired object [by magic even contradicting laws of nature]; (9) अनूर्मिमत्त्वा – 'being without the waves' of hunger, thirst, etc.; (10) दूर-श्रवण-दर्शन – hearing and seeing far; (11) मनो-जव – 'speed of the mind', moving the body quickly; (12) काम-रूप – assuming any 'form at will'; (13) पर-काय-प्रवेश – entering the bodies of others; (14) स्व-छन्द-मृत्यु – death at will, or प्राण-अपहार – 'taking life' of anybody; or प्राण-दान – 'giving life' to anybody; (15) witnessing the pastimes of the देव; (16) सङ्कल्प-संसिद्धि – executing one's determination; (17) giving orders whose fulfillment is unimpeded; (18) सृष्टि-पत्तन – creating anything; plus त्रि-काल-ज्ञत्व – knowing past, present, future; अ-द्वन्द्व – tolerance of dualities; पर-चित्तादि-अभिज्ञता – knowing the minds of others; अग्नि-अर्क-अम्बु-विषादीनां प्रतिष्टम्भ – checking the potency of fire, sun, water, poison etc.; अ-पराजय – remaining unconquered. Some सिद्ध are said to be able to produce gold by eating mercury, putting some copper coins in next morning's urin and heating it. Others are said to be able to fly on any vehicle (आकाश-यानम्).

"It is never admired by those who are expert. Since the body is subject to destruction, an endeavor for those सिद्धि is useless, like an endeavor for the fruit of a tree."[1061] The soul is compared here to a tree, the temporary body to a fruit.

GITA

"The Vedas, the Upanishads, and the Gita can be seen as the main literary supports for the great religious civilization of India, the oldest surviving culture in the world." (Thomas Merton, 1915-1968)

The Bhagavad-Gita was first translated into English in 1785 and published with an introduction by Lord Warren Hastings:

"The writers of the Indian philosophies will survive when the British Dominion in India shall long have ceased to exist, and when the sources which it yielded of wealth and power are lost to remembrance ... I hesitate not to pronounce the Gita's performance of great originality, of sublimity of conception, reasoning and diction almost unequalled; and a single exception, amongst all the known religions of mankind." (Lord Warren Hastings, Governor-General of British India, 1754-1826)

This translation, by an East India Company official, sparked translations of the Gita in various European languages and drew for it world-wide attention.

"The most beautiful, perhaps the only true philosophical song existing in any known tongue ... perhaps the deepest and loftiest thing the world has to show." (Wilhelm von Humboldt, German minister of education and linguist, 1767-1835)

भगवद्गीता describes a threefold way of action: विकर्म (forbidden work, sin) produces bad reactions and has to be given up all together. अकर्म (inactivity), trying to stop all work, is not recommended (2.47) and not even possible (3.5). कर्म (one's duty, स्व-धर्म, 2.48), further divided into a) नित्य- (regular) and b) नैमित्तिक- (occasional). Although themselves not causes of liberation, both are at least helpful, because they keep away the evil effects which would result from their non-performance. c) काम्य-कर्म (work for enjoyment). To attain freedom from the bondage of कर्म (i.e., liberation), one has to give it up (see 18.7).

About the further procedure to attain liberation there are two paths delineated:

(1) कर्म-योग – the path of duty (in the गीता also refered to as योग or बुद्धि-योग): It stresses to renounce all fruits of work (कर्म-फल-त्याग, कर्म-त्याग, त्याग) by doing one's duty. Thus, one gradually becomes purified of material desires (निष्काम), and achieves knowledge (बुद्धि). बुद्धि-योग means बुद्धि-रूपः योगः – the means (योग, उपाय) in the form of understanding.

(2) ज्ञान-योग – the path of knowledge (in the गीता also refered to as साङ्ख्य): It stresses to renounce all work meant for sense gratification (कर्म-न्यास, कर्म-सन्न्यास, सन्न्यास, सन्न्यास-योग) by cultivating detachment through spiritual knowledge (ज्ञान, साङ्ख्य).

Both paths are actually non-different, because the goal is the same – detachment from this world and attachment God. Or else, they can be seen as different stages on the same path (see 5.4). Since (2) कर्म-सन्न्यास is only possible when the mind is already purified from desires for sense gratification, to (1) work for purification is a save path for all (see 3.6,7,17,19). What गीता recommends is to perform one's duty as a service to God. This is the sum and substance of the instructions: After cutting your doubt with the sword of knowledge, stand up (4.42), always remember Me, and fight (the specific duty of Arjuna) (8.7), one who works for Me in devotion, comes to Me (11.55). Therefore, the paths refered to in the गीता as कर्म-योग, योग, नैष्कर्म, कर्म-त्याग and बुद्धि-योग refer ultimately to भक्ति-योग; and to be a योगी or योग-युक्त means to be a भक्त.

Religious texts of India were preserved with great accuracy, as the pupil had to learn the text, word by word, from the mouth of the teacher. Still, a variation in the original text can happen due to indistinct pronunciation, defective hearing or failure of memory. Alternative readings, none of which make a real difference, are found in the following verses: 1.19,43; 2.4,9,26,64; 3.42; 4.35; 5.26; 6.8,18,26; 8.7; 10.7; 11.20,28; 12.7,20; 13.13,18,21; 14.23; 16.13,23; 17.6,11; 18.25,35,44,66,68. The numbering differs in various editions and verse 13.1 is sometimes omitted.

In our translation of the seven hundred गीता verses we have added information from the commentary of श्रीधर स्वामी, an influential scholar who lived in the fourteenth century. His सुबोधिनी ('which gives a clear understanding') is indeed so beautiful, that it ruled out almost all earlier गीता commentaries. Other information was taken from the commentaries of रामानुज (1017-1137, श्री-सम्प्रदाय), विश्वनाथ (1646-1755) and बलदेव (?-1768), both belong to the गौडीय-सम्प्रदाय.

See also **Mahabharata**[1062], **Gita Wordlist** and **Dictionary**.

पार्थाय प्रतिबोधितां भगवता नारायणेन स्वयं
व्यासेन ग्रथितां पुराणमुनिना मध्येमहाभारतम् ।
अद्वैतामृतवर्षिणीं भगवतीमष्टादशाध्यायिनीम्
अम्ब त्वामनुसन्दधामि भगवद्गीते भवद्वेषिणीम् ॥[1063]

भगवद्गीता किञ्चिदधीता गङ्गाजललवकणिका पीता ।
सकृदपि येन मुरारिसमर्चा क्रियते तस्य यमेन न चर्चा ॥[1064]

गीताशास्त्रमिदं पुण्यं यः पठेत्प्रयतः पुमान् । विष्णोः पदमवाप्नोति भयशोकादिवर्जितः ॥[1065] गीताध्ययनशीलस्य प्राणायामपरस्य च । नैव सन्ति हि पापानि पूर्वजन्मकृतानि च ॥[1066] मलनिर्मोचनं पुंसां जलस्नानं दिने दिने ।

सकृद्गीताम्भसि स्नानं संसारमलनाशनम् ॥1067 सर्वोपनिषदो गावो दोग्धा गोपालनन्दनः। पार्थो वत्सः सुधीर्भोक्ता दुग्धं गीतामृतं महत् ॥1068 गीता सुगीता कर्तव्या किमन्यैः शास्त्रविस्तरैः। या स्वयं पद्मनाभस्य मुखपद्माद्विनिःसृता ॥1069 सर्वशास्त्रमयी गीता सर्वदेवमयो हरिः। सर्वतीर्थमयी गङ्गा सर्ववेदमयो मनुः ॥1070

अस्य श्रीमद्भगवद्गीतामालामन्त्रस्य भगवान्वेदव्यास ऋषिः। श्रीकृष्णः परमात्मा देवता ।1071

ॐ नमो भगवते वासुदेवाय।

श्रीमद्भगवद्गीता[1072]

---

1 – Arjuna's Despondence

King Dhritarāshtra asked his secretary Sanjaya:

धर्मक्षेत्रे कुरुक्षेत्रे समवेता युयुत्सवः। मामकाः पाण्डवाश्चैव किमकुर्वत सञ्जय ॥1.1

Sanjaya:

दृष्ट्वा तु पाण्डवानीकं व्यूढं दुर्योधनस्तदा। आचार्यमुपसङ्गम्य राजा वचनम् अब्रवीत् ॥1.2

Duryodhana to Drona:

पश्यैतां पाण्डुपुत्राणामाचार्य महतीं चमूम्। व्यूढां द्रुपदपुत्रेण तव शिष्येण धीमता ॥1.3 अत्र शूरा महेष्वासा भीमार्जुनसमा युधि। युयुधानो विराटश्च द्रुपदश्च महारथः॥ धृष्टकेतुश्चेकितानः काशिराजश्च वीर्यवान्। पुरुजित्कुन्तिभोजश्च शैब्यश्च नरपुङ्गवः॥ युधामन्युश्च विक्रान्त उत्तमौजाश्च वीर्यवान्। सौभद्रो द्रौपदेयाश्च सर्व एव महारथाः ॥1.4-6 अस्माकं तु विशिष्टा ये तान्निबोध द्विजोत्तम। नायका मम सैन्यस्य सञ्ज्ञार्थं तान्ब्रवीमि ते ॥1.7 भवान्भीष्मश्च कर्णश्च कृपश्च समितिञ्जयः। अश्वत्थामा विकर्णश्च सौमदत्तिस्तथैव च ॥1.8 अन्ये च बहवः शूरा मदर्थे त्यक्तजीविताः। नानाशस्त्रप्रहरणाः सर्वे युद्धविशारदाः ॥1.9 अपर्याप्तं तदस्माकं बलं भीष्माभिरक्षितम्। पर्याप्तं त्विदमेतेषां बलं भीमाभिरक्षितम् ॥1.10 अयनेषु च सर्वेषु यथाभागमवस्थिताः। भीष्ममेवाभिरक्षन्तु भवन्तः सर्व एव हि ॥1.11

Sanjaya continued:

तस्य सञ्जनयन्हर्षं कुरुवृद्धः पितामहः। सिंहनादं विनद्योच्चैः शङ्खं दध्मौ प्रतापवान् ॥1.12 ततः शङ्खाश्च भेर्यश्च पणवानकगोमुखाः। सहसैवाभ्यहन्यन्त स शब्दस्तुमुलोऽभवत् ॥1.13 ततः श्वेतैर्हयैर्युक्ते महति स्यन्दने स्थितौ। माधवः

पाण्डवश्चैव दिव्यौ शङ्खौ प्रदध्मतुः ॥1.14 पाञ्चजन्यं हृषीकेशो देवदत्तं धनञ्जयः ।
पौण्ड्रं दध्मौ महाशङ्खं भीमकर्मा वृकोदरः ॥1.15 अनन्तविजयं राजा कुन्तीपुत्रो
युधिष्ठिरः । नकुलः सहदेवश्च सुघोषमणिपुष्पकौ ॥1.16 काश्यश्च परमेष्वासः
शिखण्डी च महारथः । धृष्टद्युम्नो विराटश्च सात्यकिश्चापराजितः ॥ द्रुपदो
द्रौपदेयाश्च सर्वशः पृथिवीपते । सौभद्रश्च महाबाहुः शङ्खान्दध्मुः पृथक्पृथक् ॥1.17-
18 स घोषो धार्तराष्ट्राणां हृदयानि व्यदारयत् । नभश्च पृथिवीं चैव तुमुलो
ऽभ्यनुनादयन् ॥1.19 अथ व्यवस्थितान्दृष्ट्वा धार्तराष्ट्रान्कपिध्वजः । प्रवृत्ते शस्त्र-
सम्पाते धनुरुद्यम्य पाण्डवः । हृषीकेशं तदा वाक्यमिदमाह महीपते ॥1.20

Arjuna:

सेनयोरुभयोर्मध्ये रथं स्थापय मे ऽच्युत । यावदेतान्निरीक्षे ऽहं योद्धुकामान्
अवस्थितान् ॥1.21 कैर्मया सह योद्धव्यम् अस्मिन् रणसमुद्यमे ॥1.22 योत्स्यमानान्
अवेक्षे ऽहं य एते ऽत्र समागताः । धार्तराष्ट्रस्य दुर्बुद्धेर्युद्धे प्रियचिकीर्षवः ॥1.23

Sanjaya:

एवमुक्तो हृषीकेशो गुडाकेशेन भारत । सेनयोरुभयोर्मध्ये स्थापयित्वा
रथोत्तमम् ॥ भीष्मद्रोणप्रमुखतः सर्वेषां च महीक्षिताम् । उवाच पार्थ पश्यैतान्
समवेतान्कुरूनिति ॥1.24-25 तत्रापश्यत् स्थितान्पार्थः पितॄनथ पितामहान् ।
आचार्यान्मातुलान्भ्रातृन् पुत्रान्पौत्रान्सखींस्तथा । श्वशुरान्सुहृदश्चैव सेनयोरुभयोर्
अपि ॥1.26 तान्समीक्ष्य स कौन्तेयः सर्वान्बन्धूनवस्थितान् । कृपया परयाविष्टो
विषीदन्निदमब्रवीत् ॥1.27

Arjuna:

दृष्ट्वेमं स्वजनं कृष्ण युयुत्सुं समुपस्थितम् । सीदन्ति मम गात्राणि मुखं च
परिशुष्यति ॥1.28 वेपथुश्च शरीरे मे रोमहर्षश्च जायते । गाण्डीवं स्रंसते
हस्तात् त्वक्चैव परिदह्यते ॥1.29 न च शक्नोम्यवस्थातुं भ्रमतीव च मे मनः ।
निमित्तानि च पश्यामि विपरीतानि केशव ॥1.30 न च श्रेयो ऽनुपश्यामि हत्वा
स्वजनमाहवे । न काङ्क्षे विजयं कृष्ण न च राज्यं सुखानि च ॥1.31 किं नो
राज्येन गोविन्द किं भोगैर्जीवितेन वा । येषामर्थे काङ्क्षितं नो राज्यं भोगाः
सुखानि च ॥ त इमे ऽवस्थिता युद्धे प्राणांस्त्यक्त्वा धनानि च । आचार्याः पितरः
पुत्रास्तथैव च पितामहाः । मातुलाः श्वशुराः पौत्राः श्यालाः सम्बन्धिनस्
तथा ॥1.32-33 एतान्न हन्तुमिच्छामि घ्नतो ऽपि मधुसूदन । अपि त्रैलोक्यराज्यस्य
हेतोः किं नु महीकृते ॥1.34 निहत्य धार्तराष्ट्रान्नः का प्रीतिः स्याज्जनार्दन ।
पापमेवाश्रयेदस्मान् हत्वैतानाततायिनः ॥1.35 तस्मान्नार्हा वयं हन्तुं धार्तराष्ट्र
न्स्वबान्धवान् । स्वजनं हि कथं हत्वा सुखिनः स्याम माधव ॥1.36 यद्यप्येते न
पश्यन्ति लोभोपहतचेतसः । कुलक्षयकृतं दोषं मित्रद्रोहे च पातकम् ॥ कथं न
ज्ञेयमस्माभिः पापादस्मान्निवर्तितुम् । कुलक्षयकृतं दोषं प्रपश्यद्भिर्जनार्दन ॥1.37-38
कुलक्षये प्रणश्यन्ति कुलधर्माः सनातनाः । धर्मे नष्टे कुलं कृत्स्नमधर्मो

ऽभिभवत्युत ॥1.39 अधर्माभिभवात्कृष्ण प्रदुष्यन्ति कुलस्त्रियः। स्त्रीषु दुष्टासु वार्ष्णेय जायते वर्णसङ्करः ॥1.40 सङ्करो नरकायैव कुलघ्नानां कुलस्य च। पतन्ति पितरो ह्येषां लुप्तपिण्डोदकक्रियाः ॥1.41 दोषैरेतैः कुलघ्नानां वर्णसङ्करकारकैः। उत्साद्यन्ते जातिधर्माः कुलधर्माश्च शाश्वताः ॥1.42 उत्सन्नकुलधर्माणां मनुष्याणां जनार्दन। नरके नियतं वासो भवतीत्यनुशुश्रुम ॥1.43 अहो बत महत्पापं कर्तुं व्यवसिता वयम्। यद्राज्यसुखलोभेन हन्तुं स्वजनमुद्यताः ॥1.44 यदि माम् अप्रतीकारमशस्त्रं शस्त्रपाणयः। धार्तराष्ट्रा रणे हन्युस्तन्मे क्षेमतरं भवेत् ॥1.45

Sanjaya:

एवमुक्त्वार्जुनः सङ्ख्ये रथोपस्थ उपाविशत्। विसृज्य सशरं चापं शोकसंविग्न-मानसः ॥1.46

2 – Knowledge of the Soul

तं तथा कृपयाविष्टम् अश्रुपूर्णाकुलेक्षणम्। विषीदन्तमिदं वाक्यम् उवाच मधुसूदनः ॥2.1

Krishna:

कुतस्त्वा कश्मलमिदं विषमे समुपस्थितम्। अनार्यजुष्टमस्वर्ग्यम् अकीर्ति-करमर्जुन ॥2.2 क्लैब्यं मा स्म गमः पार्थ नैतत्त्वय्युपपद्यते। क्षुद्रं हृदयदौर्बल्यं त्यक्त्वोत्तिष्ठ परन्तप ॥2.3

Arjuna:

कथं भीष्ममहं सङ्ख्ये द्रोणं च मधुसूदन। इषुभिः प्रतियोत्स्यामि पूजार्हावरिसूदन ॥2.4

गुरूनहत्वा हि महानुभावान् श्रेयो भोक्तुं भैक्ष्यमपीह लोके।
हत्वार्थकामांस्तु गुरूनिहैव भुञ्जीय भोगान्रुधिरप्रदिग्धान् ॥2.5
न चैतद्विद्मः कतरन्नो गरीयो यद्वा जयेम यदि वा नो जयेयुः।
यानेव हत्वा न जिजीविषामस् तेऽवस्थिताः प्रमुखे धार्तराष्ट्राः ॥2.6
कार्पण्यदोषोपहतस्वभावः पृच्छामि त्वां धर्मसम्मूढचेताः।
यच्छ्रेयः स्यान्निश्चितं ब्रूहि तन्मे शिष्यस्तेऽहं शाधि मां त्वां प्रपन्नम् ॥2.7
न हि प्रपश्यामि ममापनुद्याद् यच्छोकमुच्छोषणमिन्द्रियाणाम्।
अवाप्य भूमावसपत्नमृद्धं राज्यं सुराणामपि चाधिपत्यम् ॥2.8

Sanjaya:

एवमुक्त्वा हृषीकेशं गुडाकेशः परन्तपः। न योत्स्य इति गोविन्दमुक्त्वा तूष्णीं बभूव ह ॥2.9 तमुवाच हृषीकेशः प्रहसन्निव भारत। सेनयोरुभयोर्मध्ये विषीदन्तमिदं वचः ॥2.10

Krishna:

अशोच्यान् अन्वशोचस्त्वं प्रज्ञावादांश्च भाषसे। गतासूनगतासूंश्च नानुशोचन्ति पण्डिताः ॥2.11 न त्वेवाहं जातु नासं न त्वं नेमे जनाधिपाः। न चैव न भविष्यामः सर्वे वयमतः परम् ॥2.12 देहिनो ऽस्मिन्यथा देहे कौमारं यौवनं जरा। तथा देहान्तरप्राप्तिर् धीरस्तत्र न मुह्यति ॥2.13 मात्रास्पर्शास्तु कौन्तेय शीतोष्णसुखदुःखदाः। आगमापायिनो ऽनित्यास् तांस्तितिक्षस्व भारत ॥2.14 यं हि न व्यथयन्त्येते पुरुषं पुरुषर्षभ। समदुःखसुखं धीरं सो ऽमृतत्वाय कल्पते ॥2.15 नासतो विद्यते भावो नाभावो विद्यते सतः। उभयोरपि दृष्टो ऽन्तस् त्वनयोस्तत्त्वदर्शिभिः ॥2.16 अविनाशि तु तद्विद्धि येन सर्वमिदं ततम्। विनाशमव्ययस्यास्य न कश्चित्कर्तुमर्हति ॥2.17 अन्तवन्त इमे देहा नित्यस्योक्ताः शरीरिणः। अनाशिनो ऽप्रमेयस्य तस्माद्युध्यस्व भारत ॥2.18 य एनं वेत्ति हन्तारं यश्चैनं मन्यते हतम्। उभौ तौ न विजानीतो नायं हन्ति न हन्यते ॥2.19

न जायते म्रियते वा कदाचिन् नायं भूत्वा भविता वा न भूयः।
अजो नित्यः शाश्वतो ऽयं पुराणो न हन्यते हन्यमाने शरीरे ॥2.20

वेदाविनाशिनं नित्यं य एनमजमव्ययम्। कथं स पुरुषः पार्थ कं घातयति हन्ति कम् ॥2.21

वासांसि जीर्णानि यथा विहाय नवानि गृह्णाति नरो ऽपराणि।
तथा शरीराणि विहाय जीर्णान्यन्यानि संयाति नवानि देही ॥2.22

नैनं छिन्दन्ति शस्त्राणि नैनं दहति पावकः। न चैनं क्लेदयन्त्यापो न शोषयति मारुतः ॥2.23 अच्छेद्यो ऽयमदाह्यो ऽयम् अक्लेद्यो ऽशोष्य एव च। नित्यः सर्वगतः स्थाणुर् अचलो ऽयं सनातनः ॥2.24 अव्यक्तो ऽयमचिन्त्यो ऽयम् अविकार्यो ऽयमुच्यते। तस्मादेवं विदित्वैनं नानुशोचितुमर्हसि ॥2.25

अथ चैनं नित्यजातं नित्यं वा मन्यसे मृतम्। तथापि त्वं महाबाहो नैनं शोचितुमर्हसि ॥2.26 जातस्य हि ध्रुवो मृत्युर् ध्रुवं जन्म मृतस्य च। तस्मादपरिहार्ये ऽर्थे न त्वं शोचितुमर्हसि ॥2.27 अव्यक्तादीनि भूतानि व्यक्तमध्यानि भारत। अव्यक्तनिधनान्येव तत्र का परिदेवना ॥2.28

आश्चर्यवत्पश्यति कश्चिदेनम् आश्चर्यवद्वदति तथैव चान्यः।
आश्चर्यवच्चैनमन्यः शृणोति श्रुत्वाप्येनं वेद न चैव कश्चित् ॥2.29

देही नित्यमवध्यो ऽयं देहे सर्वस्य भारत। तस्मात्सर्वाणि भूतानि न त्वं शोचितुमर्हसि ॥2.30

स्वधर्ममपि चावेक्ष्य न विकम्पितुमर्हसि। धर्म्याद्धि युद्धाच्छ्रेयो ऽन्यत् क्षत्रियस्य न विद्यते ॥2.31 यदृच्छया चोपपन्नं स्वर्गद्वारमपावृतम्। सुखिनः क्षत्रियाः पार्थ

लभन्ते युद्धमीदृशम् ॥2.32 अथ चेत्त्वमिमं धर्म्यं सङ्ग्रामं न करिष्यसि । ततः स्वधर्मं कीर्तिं च हित्वा पापमवाप्स्यसि ॥2.33 अकीर्तिं चापि भूतानि कथयिष्यन्ति ते ऽव्ययाम् । सम्भावितस्य चाकीर्तिर् मरणादतिरिच्यते ॥2.34 भयाद्रणादुपरतं मंस्यन्ते त्वां महारथाः । येषां च त्वं बहुमतो भूत्वा यास्यसि लाघवम् ॥2.35 अवाच्यवादांश्च बहून् वदिष्यन्ति तवाहिताः । निन्दन्तस्तव सामर्थ्यं ततो दुःखतरं नु किम् ॥2.36 हतो वा प्राप्स्यसि स्वर्गं जित्वा वा भोक्ष्यसे महीम् । तस्मादुत्तिष्ठ कौन्तेय युद्धाय कृतनिश्चयः ॥2.37 सुखदुःखे समे कृत्वा लाभालाभौ जयाजयौ । ततो युद्धाय युज्यस्व नैवं पापमवाप्स्यसि ॥2.38

एषा ते ऽभिहिता साङ्ख्ये बुद्धिर्योगे त्विमां शृणु । बुद्ध्या युक्तो यया पार्थ कर्मबन्धं प्रहास्यसि ॥2.39 नेहाभिक्रमनाशो ऽस्ति प्रत्यवायो न विद्यते । स्वल्पमप्यस्य धर्मस्य त्रायते महतो भयात् ॥2.40 व्यवसायात्मिका बुद्धिर् एकेह कुरुनन्दन । बहुशाखा ह्यनन्ताश्च बुद्धयो ऽव्यवसायिनाम् ॥2.41 यामिमां पुष्पितां वाचं प्रवदन्त्यविपश्चितः । वेदवादरताः पार्थ नान्यदस्तीति वादिनः ॥ कामात्मानः स्वर्गपरा जन्मकर्मफलप्रदाम् । क्रियाविशेषबहुलां भोगैश्वर्यगतिं प्रति ॥2.42-43 भोगैश्वर्यप्रसक्तानां तयापहृतचेतसाम् । व्यवसायात्मिका बुद्धिः समाधौ न विधीयते ॥2.44

त्रैगुण्यविषया वेदा निस्त्रैगुण्यो भवार्जुन । निर्द्वन्द्वो नित्यसत्त्वस्थो निर्योगक्षेम आत्मवान् ॥2.45 यावानर्थ उदपाने सर्वतः सम्प्लुतोदके । तावान्सर्वेषु वेदेषु ब्राह्मणस्य विजानतः ॥2.46

कर्मण्येवाधिकारस्ते मा फलेषु कदाचन । मा कर्मफलहेतुर्भूर् मा ते सङ्गो ऽस्त्वकर्मणि ॥2.47 योगस्थः कुरु कर्माणि सङ्गं त्यक्त्वा धनञ्जय । सिद्ध्यसिद्ध्योः समो भूत्वा समत्वं योग उच्यते ॥2.48 दूरेण ह्यवरं कर्म बुद्धियोगाद्धनञ्जय । बुद्धौ शरणमन्विच्छ कृपणाः फलहेतवः ॥2.49 बुद्धियुक्तो जहातीह उभे सुकृतदुष्कृते । तस्माद्योगाय युज्यस्व योगः कर्मसु कौशलम् ॥2.50 कर्मजं बुद्धियुक्ता हि फलं त्यक्त्वा मनीषिणः । जन्मबन्धविनिर्मुक्ताः पदं गच्छन्त्यनामयम् ॥2.51 यदा ते मोहकलिलं बुद्धिर्व्यतितरिष्यति । तदा गन्तासि निर्वेदं श्रोतव्यस्य श्रुतस्य च ॥2.52 श्रुतिविप्रतिपन्ना ते यदा स्थास्यति निश्चला । समाधावचला बुद्धिस् तदा योगमवाप्स्यसि ॥2.53

Arjuna:

स्थितप्रज्ञस्य का भाषा समाधिस्थस्य केशव । स्थितधीः किं प्रभाषेत किमासीत व्रजेत किम् ॥2.54

Krishna:

प्रजहाति यदा कामान् सर्वान्पार्थ मनोगतान् । आत्मन्येवात्मना तुष्टः स्थितप्रज्ञस्तदोच्यते ॥2.55 दुःखेष्वनुद्विग्नमनाः सुखेषु विगतस्पृहः । वीतरागभय-

क्रोधः स्थितधीर्मुनिरुच्यते ॥2.56 यः सर्वत्रानभिस्नेहस् तत्तत्प्राप्य शुभाशुभम्।
नाभिनन्दति न द्वेष्टि तस्य प्रज्ञा प्रतिष्ठिता ॥2.57 यदा संहरते चायं कूर्मो ऽङ्गानीव
सर्वशः। इन्द्रियाणीन्द्रियार्थेभ्यस् तस्य प्रज्ञा प्रतिष्ठिता ॥2.58 विषया विनिवर्त्तन्ते
निराहारस्य देहिनः। रसवर्जं रसो ऽप्यस्य परं दृष्ट्वा निवर्त्तते ॥2.59 यततो ह्यपि
कौन्तेय पुरुषस्य विपश्चितः। इन्द्रियाणि प्रमाथीनि हरन्ति प्रसभं मनः ॥2.60
तानि सर्वाणि संयम्य युक्त आसीत मत्परः। वशे हि यस्येन्द्रियाणि तस्य प्रज्ञा
प्रतिष्ठिता ॥2.61 ध्यायतो विषयान्पुंसः सङ्गस्तेषूपजायते। सङ्गात्सञ्जायते कामः
कामात्क्रोधो ऽभिजायते ॥2.62 क्रोधाद्भवति सम्मोहः सम्मोहात् स्मृतिविभ्रमः।
स्मृतिभ्रंशाद् बुद्धिनाशो बुद्धिनाशात्प्रणश्यति ॥2.63 रागद्वेषविमुक्तैस्तु विषयान्
इन्द्रियैश्चरन्। आत्मवश्यैर्विधेयात्मा प्रसादमधिगच्छति ॥2.64 प्रसादे सर्वदुःखानां
हानिरस्योपजायते। प्रसन्नचेतसो ह्याशु बुद्धिः पर्यवतिष्ठते ॥2.65 नास्ति
बुद्धिरयुक्तस्य न चायुक्तस्य भावना। न चाभावयतः शान्तिर् अशान्तस्य कुतः
सुखम् ॥2.66 इन्द्रियाणां हि चरतां यन्मनो ऽनुविधीयते। तदस्य हरति प्रज्ञां
वायुर्नावगिवाम्भसि ॥2.67 तस्माद्यस्य महाबाहो निगृहीतानि सर्वशः।
इन्द्रियाणीन्द्रियार्थेभ्यस् तस्य प्रज्ञा प्रतिष्ठिता ॥2.68 या निशा सर्वभूतानां तस्यां
जागर्ति संयमी। यस्यां जाग्रति भूतानि सा निशा पश्यतो मुनेः ॥2.69

आपूर्यमाणमचलप्रतिष्ठं समुद्रमापः प्रविशन्ति यद्वत्।
तद्वत्कामा यं प्रविशन्ति सर्वे स शान्तिमाप्नोति न कामकामी ॥2.70

विहाय कामान्यः सर्वान् पुमांश्चरति निःस्पृहः। निर्ममो निरहङ्कारः स
शान्तिमधिगच्छति ॥2.71 एषा ब्राह्मी स्थितिः पार्थ नैनां प्राप्य विमुह्यति।
स्थित्वास्यामन्तकाले ऽपि ब्रह्मनिर्वाणमृच्छति ॥2.72

3 – Work for Realization

Arjuna:

ज्यायसी चेत्कर्मणस्ते मता बुद्धिर्गनार्दन। तत्किं कर्मणि घोरे मां नियोजयसि
केशव ॥3.1 व्यामिश्रेणेव वाक्येन बुद्धिं मोहयसीव मे। तदेकं वद निश्चित्य येन
श्रेयो ऽहमाप्नुयाम् ॥3.2

Krishna:

लोके ऽस्मिन्द्विविधा निष्ठा पुरा प्रोक्ता मयानघ। ज्ञानयोगेन साङ्ख्यानां कर्मयोगेन
योगिनाम् ॥3.3 न कर्मणामनारम्भान् नैष्कर्म्यं पुरुषो ऽश्नुते। न च सन्न्यसनादेव
सिद्धिं समधिगच्छति ॥3.4 न हि कश्चित्क्षणमपि जातु तिष्ठत्यकर्मकृत्। कार्यते
ह्यवशः कर्म सर्वः प्रकृतिजैर्गुणैः ॥3.5 कर्मेन्द्रियाणि संयम्य य आस्ते मनसा
स्मरन्। इन्द्रियार्थान्विमूढात्मा मिथ्याचारः स उच्यते ॥3.6 यस्त्विन्द्रियाणि मनसा

नियम्यारभते ऽर्जुन । कर्मेन्द्रियैः कर्मयोगमसक्तः स विशिष्यते ॥3.7 नियतं कुरु कर्म त्वं कर्म ज्यायो ह्यकर्मणः । शरीरयात्रापि च ते न प्रसिध्येदकर्मणः ॥3.8

यज्ञार्थात्कर्मणो ऽन्यत्र लोको ऽयं कर्मबन्धनः । तदर्थं कर्म कौन्तेय मुक्तसङ्गः समाचर ॥3.9 सहयज्ञाः प्रजाः सृष्ट्वा पुरोवाच प्रजापतिः । अनेन प्रसविष्यध्वम् एष वो ऽस्त्विष्टकामधुक् ॥3.10 देवान्भावयतानेन ते देवा भावयन्तु वः । परस्परं भावयन्तः श्रेयः परमवाप्स्यथ ॥3.11 इष्टान्भोगान्हि वो देवा दास्यन्ते यज्ञ-भाविताः । तैर्दत्तानप्रदायैभ्यो यो भुङ्क्ते स्तेन एव सः ॥3.12 यज्ञशिष्टाशिनः सन्तो मुच्यन्ते सर्वकिल्बिषैः । भुञ्जते ते त्वघं पापा ये पचन्त्यात्मकारणात् ॥3.13 अन्नाद्भवन्ति भूतानि पर्जन्यादन्नसम्भवः । यज्ञाद्भवति पर्जन्यो यज्ञः कर्म-समुद्भवः ॥3.14 कर्म ब्रह्मोद्भवं विद्धि ब्रह्माक्षरसमुद्भवम् । तस्मात्सर्वगतं ब्रह्म नित्यं यज्ञे प्रतिष्ठितम् ॥3.15 एवं प्रवर्तितं चक्रं नानुवर्तयतीह यः । अघायुरिन्द्रियारामो मोघं पार्थ स जीवति ॥3.16 यस्त्वात्मरतिरेव स्याद् आत्मतृप्तश्च मानवः । आत्मन्येव च सन्तुष्टस् तस्य कार्यं न विद्यते ॥3.17 नैव तस्य कृतेनार्थो नाकृतेनेह कश्चन । न चास्य सर्वभूतेषु कश्चिदर्थव्यपाश्रयः ॥3.18

तस्मादसक्तः सततं कार्यं कर्म समाचर । असक्तो ह्याचरन्कर्म परमाप्नोति पूरुषः ॥3.19 कर्मणैव हि संसिद्धिम् आस्थिता जनकादयः । लोकसङ्ग्रहमेवापि सम्पश्यन्कर्तुमर्हसि ॥3.20 यद्यदाचरति श्रेष्ठस् तत्तदेवेतरो जनः । स यत्प्रमाणं कुरुते लोकस्तदनुवर्तते ॥3.21 न मे पार्थास्ति कर्तव्यं त्रिषु लोकेषु किञ्चन । नानवाप्तमवाप्तव्यं वर्त एव च कर्मणि ॥3.22 यदि ह्यहं न वर्तेयं जातु कर्मण्यतन्द्रितः । मम वर्त्मानुवर्तन्ते मनुष्याः पार्थ सर्वशः ॥3.23 उत्सीदेयुरिमे लोका न कुर्यां कर्म चेदहम् । सङ्करस्य च कर्ता स्याम् उपहन्यामिमाः प्रजाः ॥3.24 सक्ताः कर्मण्यविद्वांसो यथा कुर्वन्ति भारत । कुर्याद्विद्वांस् तथासक्तश् चिकीर्षुर्लोकसङ्ग्रहम् ॥3.25 न बुद्धिभेदं जनयेद् अज्ञानां कर्म-सङ्गिनाम् । जोषयेत्सर्वकर्माणि विद्वान्युक्तः समाचरन् ॥3.26 प्रकृतेः क्रियमाणानि गुणैः कर्माणि सर्वशः । अहङ्कारविमूढात्मा कर्ताहमिति मन्यते ॥3.27 तत्त्ववित्तु महाबाहो गुणकर्मविभागयोः । गुणा गुणेषु वर्तन्त इति मत्वा न सज्जते ॥3.28 प्रकृतेर्गुणसम्मूढाः सज्जन्ते गुणकर्मसु । तानकृत्स्नविदो मन्दान् कृत्स्नविन्न विचालयेत् ॥3.29 मयि सर्वाणि कर्माणि सन्न्यस्याध्यात्मचेतसा । निराशीर्निर्ममो भूत्वा युध्यस्व विगतज्वरः ॥3.30 ये मे मतमिदं नित्यम् अनुतिष्ठन्ति मानवाः । श्रद्धावन्तो ऽनसूयन्तो मुच्यन्ते ते ऽपि कर्मभिः ॥3.31 ये त्वेतदभ्यसूयन्तो नानुतिष्ठन्ति मे मतम् । सर्वज्ञानविमूढांस्तान् विद्धि नष्टानचेतसः ॥3.32

सदृशं चेष्टते स्वस्याः प्रकृतेर्ज्ञानवानपि । प्रकृतिं यान्ति भूतानि निग्रहः किं करिष्यति ॥3.33 इन्द्रियस्येन्द्रियस्यार्थे रागद्वेषौ व्यवस्थितौ । तयोर्न वशमागच्छेत्

तौ ह्यस्य परिपन्थिनौ ॥3.34 श्रेयान्स्वधर्मो विगुणः परधर्मात्स्वनुष्ठितात् । स्वधर्मे निधनं श्रेयः परधर्मो भयावहः ॥3.35

Arjuna:

अथ केन प्रयुक्तो ऽयं पापं चरति पूरुषः । अनिच्छन्नपि वार्ष्णेय बलादिव नियोजितः ॥3.36

Krishna:

काम एष क्रोध एष रजोगुणसमुद्भवः । महाशनो महापाप्मा विद्ध्येनमिह वैरिणम् ॥3.37 धूमेनाव्रियते वह्निर् यथादर्शो मलेन च । यथोल्बेनावृतो गर्भस् तथा तेनेदमावृतम् ॥3.38 आवृतं ज्ञानमेतेन ज्ञानिनो नित्यवैरिणा । कामरूपेण कौन्तेय दुष्पूरेणानलेन च ॥3.39 इन्द्रियाणि मनो बुद्धिर् अस्याधिष्ठानमुच्यते । एतैर्विमोहयत्येष ज्ञानमावृत्य देहिनम् ॥3.40 तस्मात्त्वमिन्द्रियाण्यादौ नियम्य भरतर्षभ । पाप्मानं प्रजहि ह्येनं ज्ञानविज्ञाननाशनम् ॥3.41 इन्द्रियाणि पराण्याहुर् इन्द्रियेभ्यः परं मनः । मनसस्तु परा बुद्धिर् यो बुद्धेः परतस्तु सः ॥3.42 एवं बुद्धेः परं बुद्ध्वा संस्तभ्यात्मानमात्मना । जहि शत्रुं महाबाहो कामरूपं दुरासदम् ॥3.43

---

4 – Work without Karma

Krishna:

इमं विवस्वते योगं प्रोक्तवानहमव्ययम् । विवस्वान्मनवे प्राह मनुरिक्ष्वाकवे ऽब्रवीत् ॥4.1 एवं परम्पराप्राप्तम् इमं राजर्षयो विदुः । स कालेनेह महता योगो नष्टः परन्तप ॥4.2 स एवायं मया ते ऽद्य योगः प्रोक्तः पुरातनः । भक्तो ऽसि मे सखा चेति रहस्यं ह्येतदुत्तमम् ॥4.3

Arjuna:

अपरं भवतो जन्म परं जन्म विवस्वतः । कथमेतद्विजानीयां त्वमादौ प्रोक्तवानिति ॥4.4

Krishna:

बहूनि मे व्यतीतानि जन्मानि तव चार्जुन । तान्यहं वेद सर्वाणि न त्वं वेत्थ परन्तप ॥4.5 अजो ऽपि सन्नव्ययात्मा भूतानामीश्वरो ऽपि सन् । प्रकृतिं स्वामधिष्ठाय सम्भवाम्यात्ममायया ॥4.6 यदा यदा हि धर्मस्य ग्लानिर्भवति भारत । अभ्युत्थानमधर्मस्य तदात्मानं सृजाम्यहम् ॥4.7 परित्राणाय साधूनां विनाशाय च दुष्कृताम् । धर्मसंस्थापनार्थाय सम्भवामि युगे युगे ॥4.8 जन्म कर्म च मे दिव्यम् एवं यो वेत्ति तत्त्वतः । त्यक्त्वा देहं पुनर्जन्म नैति मामेति सो ऽर्जुन ॥4.9 वीतरागभयक्रोधा मन्मया मामुपाश्रिताः । बहवो ज्ञानतपसा पूता

मद्भावमागताः ॥4.10 ये यथा मां प्रपद्यन्ते तांस्तथैव भजाम्यहम् । मम वर्त्मानुवर्तन्ते मनुष्याः पार्थ सर्वशः ॥4.11

काङ्क्षन्तः कर्मणां सिद्धिं यजन्त इह देवताः । क्षिप्रं हि मानुषे लोके सिद्धिर्भवति कर्मजा ॥4.12 चातुर्वर्ण्यं मया सृष्टं गुणकर्मविभागशः । तस्य कर्तारमपि मां विद्ध्यकर्तारमव्ययम् ॥4.13 न मां कर्माणि लिम्पन्ति न मे कर्मफले स्पृहा । इति मां यो ऽभिजानाति कर्मभिर्न स बध्यते ॥4.14 एवं ज्ञात्वा कृतं कर्म पूर्वैरपि मुमुक्षुभिः । कुरु कर्मैव तस्मात्त्वं पूर्वैः पूर्वतरं कृतम् ॥4.15 किं कर्म किमकर्मेति कवयो ऽप्यत्र मोहिताः । तत्ते कर्म प्रवक्ष्यामि यज्ज्ञात्वा मोक्ष्यसे ऽशुभात् ॥4.16 कर्मणो ह्यपि बोद्धव्यं बोद्धव्यं च विकर्मणः । अकर्मणश्च बोद्धव्यं गहना कर्मणो गतिः ॥4.17 कर्मण्यकर्म यः पश्येदकर्मणि च कर्म यः । स बुद्धिमान्मनुष्येषु स युक्तः कृत्स्नकर्मकृत् ॥4.18

यस्य सर्वे समारम्भाः कामसङ्कल्पवर्जिताः । ज्ञानाग्निदग्धकर्माणं तमाहुः पण्डितं बुधाः ॥4.19 त्यक्त्वा कर्मफलासङ्गं नित्यतृप्तो निराश्रयः । कर्मण्यभिप्रवृत्तो ऽपि नैव किञ्चित्करोति सः ॥4.20 निराशीर्यतचित्तात्मा त्यक्तसर्वपरिग्रहः । शारीरं केवलं कर्म कुर्वन्नाप्नोति किल्बिषम् ॥4.21 यदृच्छालाभसन्तुष्टो द्वन्द्वातीतो विमत्सरः । समः सिद्धावसिद्धौ च कृत्वापि न निबध्यते ॥4.22 गतसङ्गस्य मुक्तस्य ज्ञानावस्थितचेतसः । यज्ञायाचरतः कर्म समग्रं प्रविलीयते ॥4.23

ब्रह्मार्पणं ब्रह्म हविर् ब्रह्माग्नौ ब्रह्मणा हुतम् । ब्रह्मैव तेन गन्तव्यं ब्रह्मकर्म-समाधिना ॥4.24 दैवमेवापरे यज्ञं योगिनः पर्युपासते । ब्रह्माग्नावपरे यज्ञं यज्ञेनैवोपजुह्वति ॥4.25 श्रोत्रादीनीन्द्रियाण्यन्ये संयमाग्निषु जुह्वति । शब्दादीन् विषयानन्य इन्द्रियाग्निषु जुह्वति ॥4.26 सर्वाणीन्द्रियकर्माणि प्राणकर्माणि चापरे । आत्मसंयमयोगाग्नौ जुह्वति ज्ञानदीपिते ॥4.27 द्रव्ययज्ञास्तपोयज्ञा योगयज्ञास् तथापरे । स्वाध्यायज्ञानयज्ञाश्च यतयः संशितव्रताः ॥4.28 अपाने जुह्वति प्राणं प्राणे ऽपानं तथापरे । प्राणापानगती रुद्ध्वा प्राणायामपरायणाः । अपरे नियताहाराः प्राणान्प्राणेषु जुह्वति ॥4.29

सर्वे ऽप्येते यज्ञविदो यज्ञक्षपितकल्मषाः । यज्ञशिष्टामृतभुजो यान्ति ब्रह्म सनातनम् ॥4.30 नायं लोको ऽस्त्ययज्ञस्य कुतो ऽन्यः कुरुसत्तम ॥4.31 एवं बहुविधा यज्ञा वितता ब्रह्मणो मुखे । कर्मजान्विद्धि तान्सर्वान् एवं ज्ञात्वा विमोक्ष्यसे ॥4.32 श्रेयान्द्रव्यमयाद्यज्ञाज् ज्ञानयज्ञः परन्तप । सर्वं कर्माखिलं पार्थ ज्ञाने परिसमाप्यते ॥4.33 तद्विद्धि प्रणिपातेन परिप्रश्नेन सेवया । उपदेक्ष्यन्ति ते ज्ञानं ज्ञानिनस्तत्त्वदर्शिनः ॥4.34

यज्ज्ञात्वा न पुनर्मोहम् एवं यास्यसि पाण्डव । येन भूतान्यशेषाणि द्रक्ष्यस्यात्मन्यथो मयि ॥4.35 अपि चेदसि पापेभ्यः सर्वेभ्यः पापकृत्तमः । सर्व

ज्ञानप्लवेनैव वृजिनं सन्तरिष्यसि ॥4.36 यथैधांसि समिद्धो ऽग्निर् भस्मसात्कुरुते
ऽर्जुन। ज्ञानाग्निः सर्वकर्माणि भस्मसात्कुरुते तथा ॥4.37 न हि ज्ञानेन सदृशं
पवित्रमिह विद्यते। तत्स्वयं योगसंसिद्धः कालेनात्मनि विन्दति ॥4.38
श्रद्धावाँल्लभते ज्ञानं तत्परः संयतेन्द्रियः। ज्ञानं लब्ध्वा परां शान्तिम्
अचिरेणाधिगच्छति ॥4.39 अज्ञश्चाश्रद्दधानश्च संशयात्मा विनश्यति। नायं लोको
ऽस्ति न परो न सुखं संशयात्मनः ॥4.40 योगसन्न्यस्तकर्माणं ज्ञानसञ्छिन्न-
संशयम्। आत्मवन्तं न कर्माणि निबध्नन्ति धनञ्जय ॥4.41 तस्मादज्ञानसम्भूतं
हृत्स्थं ज्ञानासिनात्मनः। छित्त्वैनं संशयं योगम् आतिष्ठोत्तिष्ठ भारत ॥4.42

---

5 – Renunciation

Arjuna:

सन्न्यासं कर्मणां कृष्ण पुनर्योगं च शंससि। यच्छ्रेय एतयोरेकं तन्मे ब्रूहि
सुनिश्चितम् ॥5.1

Krishna:

सन्न्यासः कर्मयोगश्च निःश्रेयसकरावुभौ। तयोस्तु कर्मसन्न्यासात् कर्मयोगो
विशिष्यते ॥5.2 ज्ञेयः स नित्यसन्न्यासी यो न द्वेष्टि न काङ्क्षति। निर्द्वन्द्वो हि
महाबाहो सुखं बन्धात्प्रमुच्यते ॥5.3 साङ्ख्ययोगौ पृथग्बालाः प्रवदन्ति न
पण्डिताः। एकमप्यास्थितः सम्यग् उभयोर्विन्दते फलम् ॥5.4 यत्साङ्ख्यैः प्राप्यते
स्थानं तद्योगैरपि गम्यते। एकं साङ्ख्यं च योगं च यः पश्यति स पश्यति ॥5.5
सन्न्यासस्तु महाबाहो दुःखमाप्तुमयोगतः। योगयुक्तो मुनिर्ब्रह्म न
चिरेणाधिगच्छति ॥5.6 योगयुक्तो विशुद्धात्मा विजितात्मा जितेन्द्रियः।
सर्वभूतात्मभूतात्मा कुर्वन्नपि न लिप्यते ॥5.7 नैव किञ्चित्करोमीति युक्तो मन्येत
तत्त्ववित्। पश्यन् शृण्वन्स्पृशन् जिघ्रन्न् अश्नन्गच्छन्स्वपन् श्वसन् ॥
प्रलपन्निवसृजन्गृह्णन्न् उन्मिषन्निमिषन्नपि। इन्द्रियाणीन्द्रियार्थेषु वर्तन्त इति
धारयन् ॥5.8-9 ब्रह्मण्याधाय कर्माणि सङ्गं त्यक्त्वा करोति यः। लिप्यते न स
पापेन पद्मपत्रमिवाम्भसा ॥5.10 कायेन मनसा बुद्ध्या केवलैरिन्द्रियैरपि। योगिनः
कर्म कुर्वन्ति सङ्गं त्यक्त्वात्मशुद्धये ॥5.11 युक्तः कर्मफलं त्यक्त्वा शान्तिमाप्नोति
नैष्ठिकीम्। अयुक्तः कामकारेण फले सक्तो निबध्यते ॥5.12

सर्वकर्माणि मनसा सन्न्यस्यास्ते सुखं वशी। नवद्वारे पुरे देही नैव कुर्वन्
कारयन् ॥5.13 न कर्तृत्वं न कर्माणि लोकस्य सृजति प्रभुः। न कर्मफलसंयोगं
स्वभावस्तु प्रवर्तते ॥5.14 नादत्ते कस्यचित्पापं न चैव सुकृतं विभुः। अज्ञानेनावृतं
ज्ञानं तेन मुह्यन्ति जन्तवः ॥5.15 ज्ञानेन तु तदज्ञानं येषां नाशितमात्मनः।
तेषामादित्यवज्ज्ञानं प्रकाशयति तत्परम् ॥5.16 तद्बुद्धयस्तदात्मानस तन्निष्ठास
तत्परायणाः। गच्छन्त्यपुनरावृत्तिं ज्ञाननिर्धूतकल्मषाः ॥5.17 विद्याविनयसम्पन्ने

ब्राह्मणे गवि हस्तिनि। शुनि चैव श्वपाके च पण्डिताः समदर्शिनः ॥5.18 इहैव तैर्जितः सर्गो येषां साम्ये स्थितं मनः। निर्दोषं हि समं ब्रह्म तस्माद् ब्रह्मणि ते स्थिताः ॥5.19 न प्रहृष्येत्प्रियं प्राप्य नोद्विजेत्प्राप्य चाप्रियम्। स्थिरबुद्धिरसम्मूढो ब्रह्मविद् ब्रह्मणि स्थितः ॥5.20 बाह्यस्पर्शेष्वसक्तात्मा विन्दत्यात्मनि यत्सुखम्। स ब्रह्मयोगयुक्तात्मा सुखमक्षयमश्नुते ॥5.21 ये हि संस्पर्शजा भोगा दुःखयोनय एव ते। आद्यन्तवन्तः कौन्तेय न तेषु रमते बुधः ॥5.22 शक्नोतीहैव यः सोढुं प्राक्शरीरविमोक्षणात्। कामक्रोधोद्भवं वेगं स युक्तः स सुखी नरः ॥5.23 यो ऽन्तःसुखो ऽन्तरारामस् तथान्तर्ज्योतिरेव यः। स योगी ब्रह्मनिर्वाणं ब्रह्मभूतो ऽधिगच्छति ॥5.24 लभन्ते ब्रह्मनिर्वाणम् ऋषयः क्षीणकल्मषाः। छिन्नद्वैधा यतात्मानः सर्वभूतहिते रताः ॥5.25 कामक्रोधविमुक्तानां यतीनां यतचेतसाम्। अभितो ब्रह्मनिर्वाणं वर्तते विदितात्मनाम् ॥5.26 स्पर्शान्कृत्वा बहिर्बाह्यांश् चक्षुश्चैवान्तरे भ्रुवोः। प्राणापानौ समौ कृत्वा नासाभ्यन्तरचारिणौ ॥ यतेन्द्रिय-मनोबुद्धिर् मुनिर्मोक्षपरायणः। विगतेच्छाभयक्रोधो यः सदा मुक्त एव सः ॥5.27-28

भोक्तारं यज्ञतपसां सर्वलोकमहेश्वरम्। सुहृदं सर्वभूतानां ज्ञात्वा मां शान्तिमृच्छति ॥5.29

---

6 – Self-Control

Krishna:

अनाश्रितः कर्मफलं कार्यं कर्म करोति यः। स सन्न्यासी च योगी च न निरग्निर्न चाक्रियः ॥6.1॥ यं सन्न्यासमिति प्राहुर् योगं तं विद्धि पाण्डव। न ह्यसन्न्यस्त-सङ्कल्पो योगी भवति कश्चन ॥6.2 आरुरुक्षोर्मुनेर्योगं कर्म कारणमुच्यते। योगारूढस्य तस्यैव शमः कारणमुच्यते ॥6.3

यदा हि नेन्द्रियार्थेषु न कर्मस्वनुषज्जते। सर्वसङ्कल्पसन्न्यासी योगारूढस् तदोच्यते ॥6.4 उद्धरेदात्मनात्मानं नात्मानमवसादयेत्। आत्मैव ह्यात्मनो बन्धुर् आत्मैव रिपुरात्मनः ॥6.5 बन्धुरात्मात्मनस्तस्य येनात्मैवात्मना जितः। अनात्मनस्तु शत्रुत्वे वर्तेतात्मैव शत्रुवत् ॥6.6 जितात्मनः प्रशान्तस्य परमात्मा समाहितः। शीतोष्णसुखदुःखेषु तथा मानापमानयोः ॥6.7 ज्ञानविज्ञानतृप्तात्मा कूटस्थो विजितेन्द्रियः। युक्त इत्युच्यते योगी समलोष्टाश्मकाञ्चनः ॥6.8 सुहृन्मित्रार्युदासीन-मध्यस्थद्वेष्यबन्धुषु। साधुष्वपि च पापेषु समबुद्धिर् विशिष्यते ॥6.9 योगी युञ्जीत सततम् आत्मानं रहसि स्थितः। एकाकी यतचित्तात्मा निराशीरपरिग्रहः ॥6.10 शुचौ देशे प्रतिष्ठाप्य स्थिरमासनमात्मनः। नात्युच्छ्रितं नातिनीचं चैलाजिनकुशोत्तरम् ॥ तत्रैकाग्रं मनः कृत्वा यतचित्तेन्द्रिय-क्रियः। उपविश्यासने युञ्ज्याद् योगमात्मविशुद्धये ॥6.11-12

समं कायशिरोग्रीवं धारयन्नचलं स्थिरः। सम्प्रेक्ष्य नासिकाग्रं स्वं दिशश्चानवलोकयन्॥ प्रशान्तात्मा विगतभीर् ब्रह्मचारिव्रते स्थितः। मनः संयम्य मच्चित्तो युक्त आसीत मत्परः॥6.13-14 युञ्जन्नेवं सदात्मानं योगी नियतमानसः। शान्तिं निर्वाणपरमां मत्संस्थामधिगच्छति॥6.15 नात्यश्नतस्तु योगो ऽस्ति न चैकान्तमनश्नतः। न चातिस्वप्नशीलस्य जाग्रतो नैव चार्जुन॥6.16 युक्ताहारविहारस्य युक्तचेष्टस्य कर्मसु। युक्तस्वप्नावबोधस्य योगो भवति दुःखहा॥6.17 यदा विनियतं चित्तम् आत्मन्येवावतिष्ठते। निस्पृहः सर्वकामेभ्यो युक्त इत्युच्यते तदा॥6.18 यथा दीपो निवातस्थो नेङ्गते सोपमा स्मृता। योगिनो यतचित्तस्य युञ्जतो योगमात्मनः॥6.19 यत्रोपरमते चित्तं निरुद्धं योगसेवया। यत्र चैवात्मनात्मानं पश्यन्नात्मनि तुष्यति॥ सुखमात्यन्तिकं यत्तद् बुद्धिग्राह्यम् अतीन्द्रियम्। वेत्ति यत्र न चैवायं स्थितश्चलति तत्त्वतः॥ यं लब्ध्वा चापरं लाभं मन्यते नाधिकं ततः। यस्मिन्स्थितो न दुःखेन गुरुणापि विचाल्यते॥ तं विद्याद् दुःखसंयोग-वियोगं योगसञ्ज्ञितम्॥6.20-23

स निश्चयेन योक्तव्यो योगो ऽनिर्विण्णचेतसा। सङ्कल्पप्रभवान्कामांस् त्यक्त्वा सर्वानशेषतः। मनसैवेन्द्रियग्रामं विनियम्य समन्ततः॥6.24 शनैः शनैरुपरमेद् बुद्ध्या धृतिगृहीतया। आत्मसंस्थं मनः कृत्वा न किञ्चिदपि चिन्तयेत्॥6.25 यतो यतो निश्चलति मनश्चञ्चलमस्थिरम्। ततस्ततो नियम्यैतद् आत्मन्येव वशं नयेत्॥6.26 प्रशान्तमनसं ह्येनं योगिनं सुखमुत्तमम्। उपैति शान्तरजसं ब्रह्म-भूतमकल्मषम्॥6.27 युञ्जन्नेवं सदात्मानं योगी विगतकल्मषः। सुखेन ब्रह्म-संस्पर्शम् अत्यन्तं सुखमश्नुते॥6.28 सर्वभूतस्थमात्मानं सर्वभूतानि चात्मनि। ईक्षते योगयुक्तात्मा सर्वत्र समदर्शनः॥6.29 यो मां पश्यति सर्वत्र सर्वं च मयि पश्यति। तस्याहं न प्रणश्यामि स च मे न प्रणश्यति॥6.30 सर्वभूतस्थितं यो मां भजत्येकत्वमास्थितः। सर्वथा वर्तमानो ऽपि स योगी मयि वर्तते॥6.31 आत्मौपम्येन सर्वत्र समं पश्यति यो ऽर्जुन। सुखं वा यदि वा दुःखं स योगी परमो मतः॥6.32

Arjuna:

यो ऽयं योगस्त्वया प्रोक्तः साम्येन मधुसूदन। एतस्याहं न पश्यामि चञ्चलत्वात् स्थितिं स्थिराम्॥6.33 चञ्चलं हि मनः कृष्ण प्रमाथि बलवद् दृढम्। तस्याहं निग्रहं मन्ये वायोरिव सुदुष्करम्॥6.34

Krishna:

असंशयं महाबाहो मनो दुर्निग्रहं चलम्। अभ्यासेन तु कौन्तेय वैराग्येण च गृह्यते॥6.35 असंयतात्मना योगो दुष्प्राप इति मे मतिः। वश्यात्मना तु यतता शक्यो ऽवाप्तुमुपायतः॥6.36

Arjuna:

अयतिः श्रद्धयोपेतो योगाच्चलितमानसः। अप्राप्य योगसंसिद्धिं कां गतिं कृष्ण गच्छति ॥6.37 कच्चिन्नोभयविभ्रष्टश् छिन्नाभ्रमिव नश्यति। अप्रतिष्ठो महाबाहो विमूढो ब्रह्मणः पथि ॥6.38 एतन्मे संशयं कृष्ण छेत्तुमर्हस्यशेषतः। त्वदन्यः संशयस्यास्य छेत्ता न ह्युपपद्यते ॥6.39

Krishna:

पार्थ नैवेह नामुत्र विनाशस्तस्य विद्यते। न हि कल्याणकृत्कश्चिद् दुर्गतिं तात गच्छति ॥6.40 प्राप्य पुण्यकृतां लोकान् उषित्वा शाश्वतीः समाः। शुचीनां श्रीमतां गेहे योगभ्रष्टो भिजायते ॥6.41 अथवा योगिनामेव कुले भवति धीमताम्। एतद्धि दुर्लभतरं लोके जन्म यदीदृशम् ॥6.42 तत्र तं बुद्धिसंयोगं लभते पौर्वदेहिकम्। यतते च ततो भूयः संसिद्धौ कुरुनन्दन ॥6.43 पूर्वाभ्यासेन तेनैव ह्रियते ह्यवशो पि सः। जिज्ञासुरपि योगस्य शब्दब्रह्मातिवर्तते ॥6.44 प्रयत्नाद्यतमानस्तु योगी संशुद्धकिल्बिषः। अनेकजन्मसंसिद्धस् ततो याति परां गतिम् ॥6.45 तपस्विभ्यो धिको योगी ज्ञानिभ्यो पि मतो धिकः। कर्मिभ्यश्चाधिको योगी तस्माद्योगी भवार्जुन ॥6.46 योगिनामपि सर्वेषां मद्गतेनान्तरात्मना। श्रद्धावान्भजते यो मां स मे युक्ततमो मतः ॥6.47

<hr>

7 – Knowledge and Realization

Krishna:

मय्यासक्तमनाः पार्थ योगं युञ्जन्मदाश्रयः। असंशयं समग्रं मां यथा ज्ञास्यसि तच्छृणु ॥7.1 ज्ञानं ते हं सविज्ञानम् इदं वक्ष्याम्यशेषतः। यज्ज्ञात्वा नेह भूयो न्याज् ज्ञातव्यमवशिष्यते ॥7.2 मनुष्याणां सहस्रेषु कश्चिद्यतति सिद्धये। यततामपि सिद्धानां कश्चिन्मां वेत्ति तत्त्वतः ॥7.3

भूमिरापो नलो वायुः खं मनो बुद्धिरेव च। अहङ्कार इतीयं मे भिन्ना प्रकृतिरष्टधा ॥7.4 अपरेयमितस्त्वन्यां प्रकृतिं विद्धि मे पराम्। जीवभूतां महाबाहो ययेदं धार्यते जगत् ॥7.5 एतद्योनीनि भूतानि सर्वाणीत्युपधारय। अहं कृत्स्नस्य जगतः प्रभवः प्रलयस्तथा ॥7.6 मत्तः परतरं नान्यत् किञ्चिदस्ति धनञ्जय। मयि सर्वमिदं प्रोतं सूत्रे मणिगणा इव ॥7.7

रसो हमप्सु कौन्तेय प्रभास्मि शशिसूर्ययोः। प्रणवः सर्ववेदेषु शब्दः खे पौरुषं नृषु ॥7.8 पुण्यो गन्धः पृथिव्यां च तेजश्चास्मि विभावसौ। जीवनं सर्वभूतेषु तपश्चास्मि तपस्विषु ॥7.9 बीजं मां सर्वभूतानां विद्धि पार्थ सनातनम्। बुद्धिर्बुद्धिमतामस्मि तेजस्तेजस्विनामहम् ॥7.10 बलं बलवतां चाहं कामराग-विवर्जितम्। धर्माविरुद्धो भूतेषु कामो स्मि भरतर्षभ ॥7.11 ये चैव सात्त्विका भावा राजसास्तामसाश्च ये। मत्त एवेति तान्विद्धि न त्वहं तेषु ते मयि ॥7.12

त्रिभिर्गुणमयैर्भावैर् एभिः सर्वमिदं जगत्। मोहितं नाभिजानाति मामेभ्यः परमव्ययम् ॥7.13

दैवी ह्येषा गुणमयी मम माया दुरत्यया। मामेव ये प्रपद्यन्ते मायामेतां तरन्ति ते ॥7.14 न मां दुष्कृतिनो मूढाः प्रपद्यन्ते नराधमाः। माययापहृतज्ञाना आसुरं भावमाश्रिताः ॥7.15 चतुर्विधा भजन्ते मां जनाः सुकृतिनोऽर्जुन। आर्तो जिज्ञासुरर्थार्थी ज्ञानी च भरतर्षभ ॥7.16 तेषां ज्ञानी नित्ययुक्त एकभक्तिर् विशिष्यते। प्रियो हि ज्ञानिनोऽत्यर्थम् अहं स च मम प्रियः ॥7.17 उदाराः सर्व एवैते ज्ञानी त्वात्मैव मे मतम्। आस्थितः स हि युक्तात्मा मामेवानुत्तमां गतिम् ॥7.18 बहूनां जन्मनामन्ते ज्ञानवान्मां प्रपद्यते। वासुदेवः सर्वमिति स महात्मा सुदुर्लभः ॥7.19

कामैस्तैस्तैर्हृतज्ञानाः प्रपद्यन्तेऽन्यदेवताः। तं तं नियममास्थाय प्रकृत्या नियताः स्वया ॥7.20 यो यो यां यां तनुं भक्तः श्रद्धयार्चितुमिच्छति। तस्य तस्याचलां श्रद्धां तामेव विदधाम्यहम् ॥7.21 स तया श्रद्धया युक्तस् तस्याराधनमीहते। लभते च ततः कामान् मयैव विहितान्हि तान् ॥7.22 अन्तवत्तु फलं तेषां तद्भवत्यल्पमेधसाम्। देवान्देवयजो यान्ति मद्भक्ता यान्ति मामपि ॥7.23 अव्यक्तं व्यक्तिमापन्नं मन्यन्ते मामबुद्धयः। परं भावमजानन्तो ममाव्ययमनुत्तमम् ॥7.24 नाहं प्रकाशः सर्वस्य योगमायासमावृतः। मूढोऽयं नाभिजानाति लोको मामजमव्ययम् ॥7.25 वेदाहं समतीतानि वर्तमानानि चार्जुन। भविष्याणि च भूतानि मां तु वेद न कश्चन ॥7.26 इच्छाद्वेषसमुत्थेन द्वन्द्वमोहेन भारत। सर्वभूतानि सम्मोहं सर्गे यान्ति परन्तप ॥7.27

येषां त्वन्तगतं पापं जनानां पुण्यकर्मणाम्। ते द्वन्द्वमोहनिर्मुक्ता भजन्ते मां दृढव्रताः ॥7.28 जरामरणमोक्षाय मामाश्रित्य यतन्ति ये। ते ब्रह्म तद्विदुः कृत्स्नम् अध्यात्मं कर्म चाखिलम् ॥7.29 साधिभूताधिदैवं मां साधियज्ञं च ये विदुः। प्रयाणकालेऽपि च मां ते विदुर्युक्तचेतसः ॥7.30

---

8 – The Absolute

Arjuna:

किं तद् ब्रह्म किमध्यात्मं किं कर्म पुरुषोत्तम। अधिभूतं च किं प्रोक्तम् अधिदैवं किमुच्यते ॥8.1 अधियज्ञः कथं कोऽत्र देहेऽस्मिन्मधुसूदन। प्रयाणकाले च कथं ज्ञेयोऽसि नियतात्मभिः ॥8.2

Krishna:

अक्षरं ब्रह्म परमं स्वभावोऽध्यात्ममुच्यते। भूतभावोद्भवकरो विसर्गः कर्म-सञ्ज्ञितः ॥8.3 अधिभूतं क्षरो भावः पुरुषश्चाधिदैवतम्। अधियज्ञोऽहमेवात्र देहे

देहभृतां वर ॥8.4 अन्तकाले च मामेव स्मरन्मुक्त्वा कलेवरम्। यः प्रयाति स मद्भावं याति नास्त्यत्र संशयः ॥8.5 यं यं वापि स्मरन्भावं त्यजत्यन्ते कलेवरम्। तं तमेवैति कौन्तेय सदा तद्भावभावितः ॥8.6 तस्मात्सर्वेषु कालेषु मामनुस्मर युध्य च। मय्यर्पितमनोबुद्धिर् मामेवैष्यस्यसंशयः ॥8.7 अभ्यासयोगयुक्तेन चेतसा नान्यगामिना। परमं पुरुषं दिव्यं याति पार्थानुचिन्तयन् ॥8.8

कविं पुराणमनुशासितारम् अणोरणीयांसमनुस्मरेद्यः।
सर्वस्य धातारमचिन्त्यरूपम् आदित्यवर्णं तमसः परस्तात् ॥
प्रयाणकाले मनसाचलेन भक्त्या युक्तो योगबलेन चैव।
भ्रुवोर्मध्ये प्राणमावेश्य सम्यक् स तं परं पुरुषमुपैति दिव्यम् ॥8.9-10
यदक्षरं वेदविदो वदन्ति विशन्ति यद्यतयो वीतरागाः।
यदिच्छन्तो ब्रह्मचर्यं चरन्ति तत्ते पदं सङ्ग्रहेण प्रवक्ष्ये ॥8.11

सर्वद्वाराणि संयम्य मनो हृदि निरुध्य च। मूर्ध्न्याधायात्मनः प्राणम् आस्थितो योगधारणाम् ॥ ओमित्येकाक्षरं ब्रह्म व्याहरन्मामनुस्मरन्। यः प्रयाति त्यजन्देहं स याति परमां गतिम् ॥8.12-13 अनन्यचेताः सततं यो मां स्मरति नित्यशः। तस्याहं सुलभः पार्थ नित्ययुक्तस्य योगिनः ॥8.14 मामुपेत्य पुनर्जन्म दुःखालयमशाश्वतम्। नाप्नुवन्ति महात्मानः संसिद्धिं परमां गताः ॥8.15

आब्रह्मभुवनाल्लोकाः पुनरावर्तिनोऽर्जुन। मामुपेत्य तु कौन्तेय पुनर्जन्म न विद्यते ॥8.16 सहस्रयुगपर्यन्तम् अहर्यद् ब्रह्मणो विदुः। रात्रिं युगसहस्रान्तां ते ऽहोरात्रविदो जनाः ॥8.17 अव्यक्ताद् व्यक्तयः सर्वाः प्रभवन्त्यहरागमे। रात्र्यागमे प्रलीयन्ते तत्रैवाव्यक्तसञ्ज्ञके ॥8.18 भूतग्रामः स एवायं भूत्वा भूत्वा प्रलीयते। रात्र्यागमे ऽवशः पार्थ प्रभवत्यहरागमे ॥8.19

परस्तस्मात्तु भावोऽन्यो ऽव्यक्तोऽव्यक्तात्सनातनः। यः स सर्वेषु भूतेषु नश्यत्सु न विनश्यति ॥8.20 अव्यक्तोऽक्षर इत्युक्तस् तमाहुः परमां गतिम्। यं प्राप्य न निवर्तन्ते तद्धाम परमं मम ॥8.21 पुरुषः स परः पार्थ भक्त्या लभ्यस्त्वनन्यया। यस्यान्तःस्थानि भूतानि येन सर्वमिदं ततम् ॥8.22

यत्र काले त्वनावृत्तिमावृत्तिं चैव योगिनः। प्रयाता यान्ति तं कालं वक्ष्यामि भरतर्षभ ॥8.23 अग्निर्ज्योतिरहः शुक्लः षण्मासा उत्तरायणम्। तत्र प्रयाता गच्छन्ति ब्रह्म ब्रह्मविदो जनाः ॥8.24 धूमो रात्रिस्तथा कृष्णः षण्मासा दक्षिणायनम्। तत्र चान्द्रमसं ज्योतिर् योगी प्राप्य निवर्तते ॥8.25 शुक्लकृष्णे गती ह्येते जगतः शाश्वते मते। एकया यात्यनावृत्तिम् अन्ययावर्तते पुनः ॥8.26 नैते सृती पार्थ जानन्योगी मुह्यति कश्चन। तस्मात्सर्वेषु कालेषु योगयुक्तो भवार्जुन ॥8.27

वेदेषु यज्ञेषु तपःसु चैव दानेषु यत्पुण्यफलं प्रदिष्टम्।

---

9 – Knowledge of God

Krishna:

इदं तु ते गुह्यतमं प्रवक्ष्याम्यनसूयवे । ज्ञानं विज्ञानसहितं यज्ज्ञात्वा मोक्ष्यसे
ऽशुभात् ॥9.1 राजविद्या राजगुह्यं पवित्रमिदमुत्तमम् । प्रत्यक्षावगमं धर्म्यं सुसुखं
कर्तुमव्ययम् ॥9.2 अश्रद्दधानाः पुरुषा धर्मस्यास्य परन्तप । अप्राप्य मां निवर्तन्ते
मृत्युसंसारवर्त्मनि ॥9.3 मया ततमिदं सर्वं जगदव्यक्तमूर्तिना । मत्स्थानि
सर्वभूतानि न चाहं तेष्ववस्थितः ॥9.4 न च मत्स्थानि भूतानि पश्य मे
योगमैश्वरम् । भूतभृन्न च भूतस्थो ममात्मा भूतभावनः ॥9.5 यथाकाशस्थितो
नित्यं वायुः सर्वत्रगो महान् । तथा सर्वाणि भूतानि मत्स्थानीत्युपधारय ॥9.6

सर्वभूतानि कौन्तेय प्रकृतिं यान्ति मामिकाम् । कल्पक्षये पुनस्तानि कल्पादौ
विसृजाम्यहम् ॥9.7 प्रकृतिं स्वामवष्टभ्य विसृजामि पुनः पुनः । भूतग्रामगिगं
कृत्स्नम् अवशं प्रकृतेर्वशात् ॥9.8 न च मां तानि कर्माणि निबध्नन्ति धनञ्जय ।
उदासीनवदासीनम् असक्तं तेषु कर्मसु ॥9.9 मयाध्यक्षेण प्रकृतिः सूयते
सचराचरम् । हेतुनानेन कौन्तेय जगद्विपरिवर्तते ॥9.10 अवजानन्ति मां मूढा
मानुषीं तनुमाश्रितम् । परं भावमजानन्तो मम भूतमहेश्वरम् ॥ मोघाशा
मोघकर्माणो मोघज्ञाना विचेतसः । राक्षसीमासुरीं चैव प्रकृतिं मोहिनीं
श्रिताः ॥9.11-12 महात्मानस्तु मां पार्थ दैवीं प्रकृतिमाश्रिताः । भजन्त्यनन्यमनसो
ज्ञात्वा भूतादिमव्ययम् ॥9.13 सततं कीर्तयन्तो मां यतन्तश्च दृढव्रताः ।
नमस्यन्तश्च मां भक्त्या नित्ययुक्ता उपासते ॥9.14 ज्ञानयज्ञेन चाप्यन्ये यजन्तो
मामुपासते । एकत्वेन पृथक्त्वेन बहुधा विश्वतोमुखम् ॥9.15

अहं क्रतुरहं यज्ञः स्वधाहमहमौषधम् । मन्त्रो ऽहमहमेवाज्यम् अहमग्निरहं
हुतम् ॥9.16 पिताहमस्य जगतो माता धाता पितामहः । वेद्यं पवित्रमोङ्कार
ऋक्साम यजुरेव च ॥9.17 गतिर्भर्ता प्रभुः साक्षी निवासः शरणं सुहृत् । प्रभवः
प्रलयः स्थानं निधानं बीजमव्ययम् ॥9.18 तपाम्यहमहं वर्षं निगृह्णाम्युत्सृजामि
च । अमृतं चैव मृत्युश्च सदसच्चाहमर्जुन ॥9.19

त्रैविद्या मां सोमपाः पूतपापा यज्ञैरिष्ट्वा स्वर्गतिं प्रार्थयन्ते ।
ते पुण्यमासाद्य सुरेन्द्रलोकम् अश्नन्ति दिव्यान्दिवि देवभोगान् ॥9.20
ते तं भुक्त्वा स्वर्गलोकं विशालं क्षीणे पुण्ये मर्त्यलोकं विशन्ति ।
एवं त्रयीधर्ममनुप्रपन्ना गतागतं कामकामा लभन्ते ॥9.21

अनन्याश्चिन्तयन्तो मां ये जनाः पर्युपासते । तेषां नित्याभियुक्तानां योगक्षेमं
वहाम्यहम् ॥9.22 ये ऽप्यन्यदेवताभक्ता यजन्ते श्रद्धयान्विताः । ते ऽपि मामेव

कौन्तेय यजन्त्यविधिपूर्वकम् ॥9.23 अहं हि सर्वयज्ञानां भोक्ता च प्रभुरेव च। न तु मामभिजानन्ति तत्त्वेनातश्च्यवन्ति ते ॥9.24 यान्ति देवव्रता देवान् पितृन्यान्ति पितृव्रताः। भूतानि यान्ति भूतेज्या यान्ति मद्याजिनो ऽपि माम् ॥9.25 पत्रं पुष्पं फलं तोयं यो मे भक्त्या प्रयच्छति। तदहं भक्त्युपहृतम् अश्नामि प्रयतात्मनः ॥9.26 यत्करोषि यदश्नासि यज्जुहोषि ददासि यत्। यत्तपस्यसि कौन्तेय तत्कुरुष्व मदर्पणम् ॥9.27 शुभाशुभफलैरेवं मोक्ष्यसे कर्मबन्धनैः। सन्न्यासयोगयुक्तात्मा विमुक्तो मामुपैष्यसि ॥9.28 समो ऽहं सर्वभूतेषु न मे द्वेष्यो ऽस्ति न प्रियः। ये भजन्ति तु मां भक्त्या मयि ते तेषु चाप्यहम् ॥9.29

अपि चेत्सुदुराचारो भजते मामनन्यभाक्। साधुरेव स मन्तव्यः सम्यग्व्यवसितो हि सः ॥9.30 क्षिप्रं भवति धर्मात्मा शश्वच्छान्तिं निगच्छति। कौन्तेय प्रतिजानीहि न मे भक्तः प्रणश्यति ॥9.31 मां हि पार्थ व्यपाश्रित्य ये ऽपि स्युः पापयोनयः। स्त्रियो वैश्यास्तथा शूद्रास् ते ऽपि यान्ति परां गतिम् ॥9.32 किं पुनर्ब्राह्मणाः पुण्या भक्ता राजर्षयस्तथा। अनित्यमसुखं लोकमिमं प्राप्य भजस्व माम् ॥9.33 मन्मना भव मद्भक्तो मद्याजी मां नमस्कुरु। मामेवैष्यसि युक्त्वैवम् आत्मानं मत्परायणः ॥9.34

10 – Divine Glories

Krishna:

भूय एव महाबाहो शृणु मे परमं वचः। यत्ते ऽहं प्रीयमाणाय वक्ष्यामि हितकाम्यया ॥10.1 न मे विदुः सुरगणाः प्रभवं न महर्षयः। अहमादिर्हि देवानां महर्षीणां च सर्वशः ॥10.2 यो मामजमनादिं च वेत्ति लोकमहेश्वरम्। असम्मूढः स मर्त्येषु सर्वपापैः प्रमुच्यते ॥10.3 बुद्धिर्ज्ञानमसम्मोहः क्षमा सत्यं दमः शमः। सुखं दुःखं भवो ऽभावो भयं चाभयमेव च ॥ अहिंसा समता तुष्टिस् तपो दानं यशो ऽयशः। भवन्ति भावा भूतानां मत्त एव पृथग्विधाः ॥10.4-5 महर्षयः सप्त पूर्वे चत्वारो मनवस्तथा। मद्भावा मानसा जाता येषां लोक इमाः प्रजाः ॥10.6 एतां विभूतिं योगं च मम यो वेत्ति तत्त्वतः। सो ऽविकल्पेन योगेन युज्यते नात्र संशयः ॥10.7

अहं सर्वस्य प्रभवो मत्तः सर्वं प्रवर्तते। इति मत्वा भजन्ते मां बुधा भावसमन्विताः ॥10.8 मच्चित्ता मद्गतप्राणा बोधयन्तः परस्परम्। कथयन्तश्च मां नित्यं तुष्यन्ति च रमन्ति च ॥10.9 तेषां सततयुक्तानां भजतां प्रीतिपूर्वकम्। ददामि बुद्धियोगं तं येन मामुपयान्ति ते ॥10.10 तेषामेवानुकम्पार्थम् अहमज्ञानजं तमः। नाशयाम्यात्मभावस्थो ज्ञानदीपेन भास्वता ॥10.11

Arjuna:

परं ब्रह्म परं धाम पवित्रं परमं भवान्। पुरुषं शाश्वतं दिव्यम् आदिदेवमजं विभुम्॥ आहुस्त्वामृषयः सर्वे देवर्षिर्नारदस्तथा। असितो देवलो व्यासः स्वयं चैव ब्रवीषि मे॥10.12-13 सर्वमेतदृतं मन्ये यन्मां वदसि केशव। न हि ते भगवन्व्यक्तिं विदुर्देवा न दानवाः॥10.14 स्वयमेवात्मनात्मानं वेत्थ त्वं पुरुषोत्तम। भूतभावन भूतेश देवदेव जगत्पते॥10.15 वक्तुमर्हस्यशेषेण दिव्या ह्यात्मविभूतयः। याभिर्विभूतिभिर्लोकान् इमांस्त्वं व्याप्य तिष्ठसि॥10.16 कथं विद्यामहं योगिंस् त्वां सदा परिचिन्तयन्। केषु केषु च भावेषु चिन्त्यो ऽसि भगवन्मया॥10.17 विस्तरेणात्मनो योगं विभूतिं च जनार्दन। भूयः कथय तृप्तिर्हि शृण्वतो नास्ति मे ऽमृतम्॥10.18

Krishna:

हन्त ते कथयिष्यामि दिव्या ह्यात्मविभूतयः। प्राधान्यतः कुरुश्रेष्ठ नास्त्यन्तो विस्तरस्य मे॥10.19 अहमात्मा गुडाकेश सर्वभूताशयस्थितः। अहमादिश्च मध्यं च भूतानामन्त एव च॥10.20 आदित्यानामहं विष्णुर् ज्योतिषां रविरंशुमान्। मरीचिर्मरुतामस्मि नक्षत्राणामहं शशी॥10.21 वेदानां सामवेदो ऽस्मि देवानामस्मि वासवः। इन्द्रियाणां मनश्चास्मि भूतानामस्मि चेतना॥10.22 रुद्राणां शङ्करश्चास्मि वित्तेशो यक्षरक्षसाम्। वसूनां पावकश्चास्मि मेरुः शिखरिणामहम्॥10.23 पुरोधसां च मुख्यं मां विद्धि पार्थ बृहस्पतिम्। सेनानीनामहं स्कन्दः सरसामस्मि सागरः॥10.24 महर्षीणां भृगुरहं गिरामस्म्येकमक्षरम्। यज्ञानां जपयज्ञो ऽस्मि स्थावराणां हिमालयः॥10.25 अश्वत्थः सर्ववृक्षाणां देवर्षीणां च नारदः। गन्धर्वाणां चित्ररथः सिद्धानां कपिलो मुनिः॥10.26 उच्चैःश्रवसमश्वानां विद्धि माममृतोद्भवम्। ऐरावतं गजेन्द्राणां नराणां च नराधिपम्॥10.27 आयुधानामहं वज्रं धेनूनामस्मि कामधुक्। प्रजनश्चास्मि कन्दर्पः सर्पाणामस्मि वासुकिः॥10.28 अनन्तश्चास्मि नागानां वरुणो यादसामहम्। पितृणामर्यमा चास्मि यमः संयमतामहम्॥10.29 प्रह्लादश्चास्मि दैत्यानां कालः कलयतामहम्। मृगाणां च मृगेन्द्रो ऽहं वैनतेयश्च पक्षिणाम्॥10.30 पवनः पवतामस्मि रामः शस्त्रभृतामहम्। झषाणां मकरश्चास्मि स्रोतसामस्मि जाह्नवी॥10.31 सर्गाणामादिरन्तश्च मध्यं चैवाहमर्जुन। अध्यात्मविद्या विद्यानां वादः प्रवदतामहम्॥10.32 अक्षराणामकारो ऽस्मि द्वन्द्वः सामासिकस्य च। अहमेवाक्षयः कालो धाताहं विश्वतोमुखः॥10.33 मृत्युः सर्वहरश्चाहम् उद्भवश्च भविष्यताम्। कीर्तिः श्रीर्वाक्च नारीणां स्मृतिर्मेधा धृतिः क्षमा॥10.34 बृहत्साम तथा साम्नां गायत्री छन्देसामहम्। मासानां मार्गशीर्षो ऽहम् ऋतूनां कुसुमाकरः॥10.35 द्यूतं छलयतामस्मि तेजस्तेजस्विनाम् अहम्। जयो ऽस्मि व्यवसायो ऽस्मि सत्त्वं सत्त्ववतामहम्॥10.36 वृष्णीनां वासुदेवो ऽस्मि पाण्डवानां धनञ्जयः। मुनीनामप्यहं व्यासः कवीनामुशना कविः॥10.37 दण्डो दमयतामस्मि नीतिरस्मि जिगीषताम्। मौनं चैवास्मि गुह्यानां ज्ञानं ज्ञानवतामहम्॥10.38 यच्चापि सर्वभूतानां बीजं तदहमर्जुन। न तदस्ति

विना यत्स्यान् मया भूतं चराचरम् ॥10.39 नान्तो ऽस्ति मम दिव्यानां विभूतीनां परन्तप । एष तूद्देशतः प्रोक्तो विभूतेर्विस्तरो मया ॥10.40 यद्यद्विभूतिमत्सत्त्वं श्रीमदूर्जितमेव वा । तत्तदेवावगच्छ त्वं मम तेजोंशसम्भवम् ॥10.41 अथवा बहुनैतेन किं ज्ञातेन तवार्जुन । विष्टभ्याहमिदं कृत्स्नम् एकांशेन स्थितो जगत् ॥10.42

---

11 – The Universal Form

Arjuna:

मदनुग्रहाय परमं गुह्यमध्यात्मसञ्ज्ञितम् । यत्त्वयोक्तं वचस्तेन मोहो ऽयं विगतो मम ॥11.1 भवाप्ययौ हि भूतानां श्रुतौ विस्तरशो मया । त्वत्तः कमलपत्राक्ष माहात्म्यमपि चाव्ययम् ॥11.2 एवमेतद्यथात्थ त्वम् आत्मानं परमेश्वर । द्रष्टुमिच्छामि ते रूपम् ऐश्वरं पुरुषोत्तम ॥11.3 मन्यसे यदि तच्छक्यं मया द्रष्टुमिति प्रभो । योगेश्वर ततो मे त्वं दर्शयात्मानमव्ययम् ॥11.4

Krishna:

पश्य मे पार्थ रूपाणि शतशो ऽथ सहस्रशः । नानाविधानि दिव्यानि नानावर्णाकृतीनि च ॥11.5 पश्यादित्यान्वसून्रुद्रान् अश्विनौ मरुतस्तथा । बहून्यदृष्टपूर्वाणि पश्याश्चर्याणि भारत ॥11.6 इहैकस्थं जगत्कृत्स्नं पश्याद्य सचराचरम् । मम देहे गुडाकेश यच्चान्यद् द्रष्टुमिच्छसि ॥11.7 न तु मां शक्यसे द्रष्टुम् अनेनैव स्वचक्षुषा । दिव्यं ददामि ते चक्षुः पश्य मे योगमैश्वरम् ॥11.8

Sanjaya to Dhritarāshtra:

एवमुक्त्वा ततो राजन् महायोगेश्वरो हरिः । दर्शयामास पार्थाय परमं रूपमैश्वरम् ॥11.9 अनेकवक्त्रनयनम् अनेकाद्भुतदर्शनम् । अनेकदिव्याभरणं दिव्यानेकोद्यतायुधम् ॥ दिव्यमाल्याम्बरधरं दिव्यगन्धानुलेपनम् । सर्वाश्चर्यमयं देवम् अनन्तं विश्वतोमुखम् ॥11.10-11 दिवि सूर्यसहस्रस्य भवेद्युगपदुत्थिता । यदि भाः सदृशी सा स्याद् भासस्तस्य महात्मनः ॥11.12 तत्रैकस्थं जगत्कृत्स्नं प्रविभक्तमनेकधा । अपश्यद्देवदेवस्य शरीरे पाण्डवस्तदा ॥11.13 ततः स विस्मयाविष्टो हृष्टरोमा धनञ्जयः । प्रणम्य शिरसा देवं कृताञ्जलिरभाषत ॥11.14

Arjuna:

पश्यामि देवांस्तव देव देहे सर्वांस्तथा भूतविशेषसङ्घान् ।
ब्रह्माणमीशं कमलासनस्थम् ऋषींश्च सर्वानुरगांश्च दिव्यान् ॥11.15
अनेकबाहूदरवक्त्रनेत्रं पश्यामि त्वां सर्वतो ऽनन्तरूपम् ।
नान्तं न मध्यं न पुनस्तवादिं पश्यामि विश्वेश्वर विश्वरूप ॥11.16
किरीटिनं गदिनं चक्रिणं च तेजोराशिं सर्वतो दीप्तिमन्तम् ।
पश्यामि त्वां दुर्निरीक्ष्यं समन्ताद् दीप्तानलार्कद्युतिमप्रमेयम् ॥11.17

त्वमक्षरं परमं वेदितव्यं त्वमस्य विश्वस्य परं निधानम् ।
त्वमव्ययः शाश्वतधर्मगोप्ता सनातनस्त्वं पुरुषो मतो मे ॥11.18
अनादिमध्यान्तमनन्तवीर्यम् अनन्तबाहुं शशिसूर्यनेत्रम् ।
पश्यामि त्वां दीप्तहुताशवक्त्रं स्वतेजसा विश्वमिदं तपन्तम् ॥11.19
द्यावापृथिव्योरिदमन्तरं हि व्याप्तं त्वयैकेन दिशश्च सर्वाः ।
दृष्ट्वाद्भुतं रूपमुग्रं तवेदं लोकत्रयं प्रव्यथितं महात्मन् ॥11.20
अमी हि त्वां सुरसङ्घा विशन्ति केचिद्भीताः प्राञ्जलयो गृणन्ति ।
स्वस्तीत्युक्त्वा महर्षिसिद्धसङ्घाः स्तुवन्ति त्वां स्तुतिभिः पुष्कलाभिः ॥11.21
रुद्रादित्या वसवो ये च साध्या विश्वे ऽश्विनौ मरुतश्चोष्मपाश्च ।
गन्धर्वयक्षासुरसिद्धसङ्घा वीक्षन्ते त्वां विस्मिताश्चैव सर्वे ॥11.22
रूपं महत्ते बहुवक्त्रनेत्रं महाबाहो बहुबाहूरुपादम् ।
बहूदरं बहुदंष्ट्राकरालं दृष्ट्वा लोकाः प्रव्यथितास्तथाहम् ॥11.23
नभःस्पृशं दीप्तमनेकवर्णं व्यात्ताननं दीप्तविशालनेत्रम् ।
दृष्ट्वा हि त्वां प्रव्यथितान्तरात्मा धृतिं न विन्दामि शमं च विष्णो ॥11.24
दंष्ट्राकरालानि च ते मुखानि दृष्ट्वैव कालानलसन्निभानि ।
दिशो न जाने न लभे च शर्म प्रसीद देवेश जगन्निवास ॥11.25
अमी च त्वां धृतराष्ट्रस्य पुत्राः सर्वे सहैवावनिपालसङ्घैः ।
भीष्मो द्रोणः सूतपुत्रस्तथासौ सहास्मदीयैरपि योधमुख्यैः ॥
वक्त्राणि ते त्वरमाणा विशन्ति दंष्ट्राकरालानि भयानकानि ।
केचिद्विलग्ना दशनान्तरेषु सन्दृश्यन्ते चूर्णितैरुत्तमाङ्गैः ॥11.26-27
यथा नदीनां बहवो ऽम्बुवेगाः समुद्रमेवाभिमुखा द्रवन्ति ।
तथा तवामी नरलोकवीरा विशन्ति वक्त्राण्यभिविज्वलन्ति ॥11.28
यथा प्रदीप्तं ज्वलनं पतङ्गा विशन्ति नाशाय समृद्धवेगाः ।
तथैव नाशाय विशन्ति लोकास् तवापि वक्त्राणि समृद्धवेगाः ॥11.29
लेलिह्यसे ग्रसमानः समन्ताल् लोकान्समग्रान्वदनैर्ज्वलद्भिः ।
तेजोभिरापूर्य जगत्समग्रं भासस्तवोग्राः प्रतपन्ति विष्णो ॥11.30
आख्याहि मे को भवानुग्ररूपो नमो ऽस्तु ते देववर प्रसीद ।
विज्ञातुमिच्छामि भवन्तमाद्यं न हि प्रजानामि तव प्रवृत्तिम् ॥11.31

Krishna:

कालो ऽस्मि लोकक्षयकृत्प्रवृद्धो लोकान्समाहर्तुमिह प्रवृत्तः ।
ऋते ऽपि त्वां न भविष्यन्ति सर्वे ये ऽवस्थिताः प्रत्यनीकेषु योधाः ॥11.32
तस्मात्त्वमुत्तिष्ठ यशो लभस्व जित्वा शत्रून्भुङ्क्ष्व राज्यं समृद्धम् ।
मयैवैते निहताः पूर्वमेव निमित्तमात्रं भव सव्यसाचिन् ॥11.33
द्रोणं च भीष्मं च जयद्रथं च कर्णं तथान्यानपि योधवीरान् ।
मया हतांस्त्वं जहि मा व्यथिष्ठा युध्यस्व जेतासि रणे सपत्नान् ॥11.34

एतच्छ्रुत्वा वचनं केशवस्य   कृताञ्जलिर्वेपमानः किरीटी ।
नमस्कृत्वा भूय एवाह कृष्णं   सगद्गदं भीतभीतः प्रणम्य ॥11.35

Arjuna:

स्थाने हृषीकेश तव प्रकीर्त्या   जगत्प्रहृष्यत्यनुरज्यते च ।
रक्षांसि भीतानि दिशो द्रवन्ति   सर्वे नमस्यन्ति च सिद्धसङ्घाः ॥11.36
कस्माच्च ते न नमेरन्महात्मन्   गरीयसे ब्रह्मणो ऽप्यादिकर्त्रे ।
अनन्त देवेश जगन्निवास   त्वमक्षरं सदसत्तत्परं यत् ॥11.37
त्वमादिदेवः पुरुषः पुराणस्   त्वमस्य विश्वस्य परं निधानम् ।
वेत्तासि वेद्यं च परं च धाम   त्वया ततं विश्वमनन्तरूप ॥11.38
वायुर्यमो ऽग्निर्वरुणः शशाङ्कः   प्रजापतिस्त्वं प्रपितामहश्च ।
नमो नमस्ते ऽस्तु सहस्रकृत्वः   पुनश्च भूयो ऽपि नमो नमस्ते ॥11.39
नमः पुरस्तादथ पृष्ठतस्ते   नमो ऽस्तु ते सर्वत एव सर्व ।
अनन्तवीर्यामितविक्रमस्त्वं   सर्वं समाप्नोषि ततो ऽसि सर्वः ॥11.40
सखेति मत्वा प्रसभं यदुक्तं   हे कृष्ण हे यादव हे सखेति ।
अजानता महिमानं तवेदं   मया प्रमादात्प्रणयेन वापि ॥
यच्चावहासार्थमसत्कृतो ऽसि   विहारशय्यासनभोजनेषु ।
एको ऽथवाप्यच्युत तत्समक्षं   तत्क्षामये त्वामहमप्रमेयम् ॥11.41-42
पितासि लोकस्य चराचरस्य   त्वमस्य पूज्यश्च गुरुर्गरीयान् ।
न त्वत्समो ऽस्त्यभ्यधिकः कुतो ऽन्यो   लोकत्रये ऽप्यप्रतिमप्रभाव ॥11.43
तस्मात्प्रणम्य प्रणिधाय कायं   प्रसादये त्वामहमीशमीड्यम् ।
पितेव पुत्रस्य सखेव सख्युः   प्रियः प्रियायार्हसि देव सोढुम् ॥11.44
अदृष्टपूर्वं हृषितो ऽस्मि दृष्ट्वा   भयेन च प्रव्यथितं मनो मे ।
तदेव मे दर्शय देव रूपं   प्रसीद देवेश जगन्निवास ॥11.45
किरीटिनं गदिनं चक्रहस्तम्   इच्छामि त्वां द्रष्टुमहं तथैव ।
तेनैव रूपेण चतुर्भुजेन   सहस्रबाहो भव विश्वमूर्ते ॥11.46
मया प्रसन्नेन तवार्जुनेदं   रूपं परं दर्शितमात्मयोगात् ।
तेजोमयं विश्वमनन्तमाद्यं   यन्मे त्वदन्येन न दृष्टपूर्वम् ॥11.47
न वेदयज्ञाध्ययनैर्न दानैर्   न च क्रियाभिर्न तपोभिरुग्रैः ।
एवंरूपः शक्य अहं नृलोके   द्रष्टुं त्वदन्येन कुरुप्रवीर ॥11.48
मा ते व्यथा मा च विमूढभावो   दृष्ट्वा रूपं घोरमीदृङ् ममेदम् ।
व्यपेतभीः प्रीतमनाः पुनस्त्वं   तदेव मे रूपमिदं प्रपश्य ॥11.49

Sanjaya:

इत्यर्जुनं वासुदेवस्तथोक्त्वा   स्वकं रूपं दर्शयामास भूयः ।
आश्वासयामास च भीतमेनं   भूत्वा पुनः सौम्यवपुर्महात्मा ॥11.50

Arjuna:

दृष्ट्वेदं मानुषं रूपं तव सौम्यं जनार्दन। इदानीमस्मि संवृत्तः सचेताः प्रकृतिं गतः ॥11.51

Krishna:

सुदुर्दर्शमिदं रूपं दृष्ट्वानसि यन्मम। देवा अप्यस्य रूपस्य नित्यं दर्शनकाङ्क्षिणः ॥11.52 नाहं वेदैर्न तपसा न दानेन न चेज्यया। शक्य एवंविधो द्रष्टुं दृष्ट्वानसि मां यथा ॥11.53 भक्त्या त्वनन्यया शक्य अहमेवंविधो ऽर्जुन। ज्ञातुं द्रष्टुं च तत्त्वेन प्रवेष्टुं च परन्तप ॥11.54 मत्कर्मकृन्मत्परमो मद्भक्तः सङ्गवर्जितः। निर्वैरः सर्वभूतेषु यः स मामेति पाण्डव ॥11.55

<hr>

12 – Bhakti

Arjuna:

एवं सततयुक्ता ये भक्तास्त्वां पर्युपासते। ये चाप्यक्षरमव्यक्तं तेषां के योगवित्तमाः ॥12.1

Krishna:

मय्यावेश्य मनो ये मां नित्ययुक्ता उपासते। श्रद्धया परयोपेतास् ते मे युक्ततमा मताः ॥12.2 ये त्वक्षरमनिर्देश्यम् अव्यक्तं पर्युपासते। सर्वत्रगमचिन्त्यं च कूटस्थमचलं ध्रुवम्॥ सन्नियम्येन्द्रियग्रामं सर्वत्र समबुद्धयः। ते प्राप्नुवन्ति मामेव सर्वभूतहिते रताः ॥12.3-4 क्लेशो ऽधिकतरस्तेषाम् अव्यक्तासक्तचेतसाम्। अव्यक्ता हि गतिर्दुःखं देहवद्भिरवाप्यते ॥12.5 ये तु सर्वाणि कर्माणि मयि सन्न्यस्य मत्पराः। अनन्येनैव योगेन मां ध्यायन्त उपासते॥ तेषामहं समुद्धर्ता मृत्युसंसारसागरात्। भवामि न चिरात्पार्थ मय्यावेशितचेतसाम् ॥12.6-7

मय्येव मन आधत्स्व मयि बुद्धिं निवेशय। निवसिष्यसि मय्येव अत ऊर्ध्वं न संशयः ॥12.8 अथ चित्तं समाधातुं न शक्नोषि मयि स्थिरम्। अभ्यासयोगेन ततो मामिच्छाप्तुं धनञ्जय ॥12.9 अभ्यासे ऽप्यसमर्थो ऽसि मत्कर्मपरमो भव। मदर्थमपि कर्माणि कुर्वन्सिद्धिमवाप्स्यसि ॥12.10 अथैतदप्यशक्तो ऽसि कर्तुं मद्योगमाश्रितः। सर्वकर्मफलत्यागं ततः कुरु यतात्मवान् ॥12.11 श्रेयो हि ज्ञानमभ्यासाज् ज्ञानाद् ध्यानं विशिष्यते। ध्यानात्कर्मफलत्यागस् त्यागाच्छान्तिरनन्तरम् ॥12.12 अद्वेष्टा सर्वभूतानां मैत्रः करुण एव च। निर्ममो निरहङ्कारः समदुःखसुखः क्षमी॥ सन्तुष्टः सततं योगी यतात्मा दृढनिश्चयः। मय्यर्पितमनोबुद्धिर् यो मद्भक्तः स मे प्रियः ॥12.13-14 यस्मान्नोद्विजते लोको लोकान्नोद्विजते च यः। हर्षामर्षभयोद्वेगैर् मुक्तो यः स च मे प्रियः ॥12.15 अनपेक्षः शुचिर्दक्ष उदासीनो गतव्यथः। सर्वारम्भपरित्यागी यो मद्भक्तः स मे प्रियः ॥12.16 यो न हृष्यति न द्वेष्टि न शोचति न काङ्क्षति। शुभाशुभपरित्यागी भक्तिमान्यः स मे प्रियः ॥12.17 समः शत्रौ च मित्रे च तथा मानापमानयोः।

शीतोष्णसुखदुःखेषु समः सङ्गविवर्जितः ॥ तुल्यनिन्दास्तुतिर्मौनी सन्तुष्टो येन केनचित् । अनिकेतः स्थिरमतिर् भक्तिमान्मे प्रियो नरः ॥12.18-19 ये तु धर्मामृतमिदं यथोक्तं पर्युपासते । श्रद्दधाना मत्परमा भक्तास्तेऽतीव मे प्रियाः ॥12.20

13 – Body and Soul

Arjuna:

प्रकृतिं पुरुषं चैव क्षेत्रं क्षेत्रज्ञमेव च । एतद्वेदितुमिच्छामि ज्ञानं ज्ञेयं च केशव ॥13.1

Krishna:

इदं शरीरं कौन्तेय क्षेत्रमित्यभिधीयते । एतद्यो वेत्ति तं प्राहुः क्षेत्रज्ञ इति तद्विदः ॥13.2 क्षेत्रज्ञं चापि मां विद्धि सर्वक्षेत्रेषु भारत । क्षेत्रक्षेत्रज्ञयोर्ज्ञानं यत्तज्ज्ञानं मतं मम ॥13.3 तत्क्षेत्रं यच्च यादृक्च यद्विकारि यतश्च यत् । स च यो यत्प्रभावश्च तत्समासेन मे शृणु ॥13.4 ऋषिभिर्बहुधा गीतं छन्दोभिर्विविधैः पृथक् । ब्रह्मसूत्रपदैश्चैव हेतुमद्भिर्विनिश्चितैः ॥13.5

महाभूतान्यहङ्कारो बुद्धिरव्यक्तमेव च । इन्द्रियाणि दशैकं च पञ्च चेन्द्रियगोचराः ॥ इच्छा द्वेषः सुखं दुःखं सङ्घातश्चेतना धृतिः । एतत्क्षेत्रं समासेन सविकारमुदाहृतम् ॥13.6-7 अमानित्वमदम्भित्वम् अहिंसा क्षान्तिरार्जवम् । आचार्योपासनं शौचं स्थैर्यमात्मविनिग्रहः ॥ इन्द्रियार्थेषु वैराग्यम् अनहङ्कार एव च । जन्ममृत्युजराव्याधि-दुःखदोषानुदर्शनम् ॥ असक्तिरनभिष्वङ्गः पुत्रदार-गृहादिषु । नित्यं च समचित्तत्वम् इष्टानिष्टोपपत्तिषु ॥ मयि चानन्ययोगेन भक्तिरव्यभिचारिणी । विविक्तदेशसेवित्वम् अरतिर्जनसंसदि ॥ अध्यात्मज्ञान-नित्यत्वं तत्त्वज्ञानार्थदर्शनम् । एतज्ज्ञानमिति प्रोक्तमज्ञानं यदतोऽन्यथा ॥13.8-12

ज्ञेयं यत्तत्प्रवक्ष्यामि यज्ज्ञात्वामृतमश्नुते । अनादि मत्परं ब्रह्म न सत्तन्नासदुच्यते ॥13.13 सर्वतः पाणिपादं तत् सर्वतोऽक्षिशिरोमुखम् । सर्वतः श्रुतिमल्लोके सर्वमावृत्य तिष्ठति ॥13.14 सर्वेन्द्रियगुणाभासं सर्वेन्द्रियविवर्जितम् । असक्तं सर्वभृच्चैव निर्गुणं गुणभोक्तृ च ॥13.15 बहिरन्तश्च भूतानाम् अचरं चरमेव च । सूक्ष्मत्वात्तदविज्ञेयं दूरस्थं चान्तिके च तत् ॥13.16 अविभक्तं च भूतेषु विभक्तमिव च स्थितम् । भूतभर्तृ च तज्ज्ञेयं ग्रसिष्णु प्रभविष्णु च ॥13.17 ज्योतिषामपि तज्ज्योतिस् तमसः परमुच्यते । ज्ञानं ज्ञेयं ज्ञानगम्यं हृदि सर्वस्य विष्ठितम् ॥13.18

इति क्षेत्रं तथा ज्ञानं ज्ञेयं चोक्तं समासतः । मद्भक्त एतद्विज्ञाय मद्भावायोपपद्यते ॥13.19 प्रकृतिं पुरुषं चैव विद्ध्यनादी उभावपि । विकारांश्च

गुणांश्चैव विद्धि प्रकृतिसम्भवान् ॥13.20 कार्यकारणकर्तृत्वे हेतुः प्रकृतिरुच्यते। पुरुषः सुखदुःखानां भोक्तृत्वे हेतुरुच्यते ॥13.21 पुरुषः प्रकृतिस्थो हि भुङ्क्ते प्रकृतिजान्गुणान्। कारणं गुणसङ्गो ऽस्य सदसद्योनिजन्मसु ॥13.22 उपद्रष्टानुमन्ता च भर्ता भोक्ता महेश्वरः। परमात्मेति चाप्युक्तो देहे ऽस्मिन्पुरुषः परः ॥13.23 य एवं वेत्ति पुरुषं प्रकृतिं च गुणैः सह। सर्वथा वर्तमानो ऽपि न स भूयो ऽभिजायते ॥13.24

ध्यानेनात्मनि पश्यन्ति केचिदात्मानमात्मना। अन्ये साङ्ख्येन योगेन कर्मयोगेन चापरे ॥13.25 अन्ये त्वेवमजानन्तः श्रुत्वान्येभ्य उपासते। ते ऽपि चातितरन्त्येव मृत्युं श्रुतिपरायणाः ॥13.26 यावत्सञ्जायते किञ्चित् सत्त्वं स्थावरजङ्गमम्। क्षेत्रक्षेत्रज्ञसंयोगात् तद्विद्धि भरतर्षभ ॥13.27 समं सर्वेषु भूतेषु तिष्ठन्तं परमेश्वरम्। विनश्यत्स्वविनश्यन्तं यः पश्यति स पश्यति ॥13.28 समं पश्यन्हि सर्वत्र समवस्थितमीश्वरम्। न हिनस्त्यात्मनात्मानं ततो याति परां गतिम् ॥13.29 प्रकृत्यैव च कर्माणि क्रियमाणानि सर्वशः। यः पश्यति तथात्मानम् अकर्तारं स पश्यति ॥13.30 यदा भूतपृथग्भावम् एकस्थमनुपश्यति। तत एव च विस्तारं ब्रह्म सम्पद्यते तदा ॥13.31 अनादित्वान्निर्गुणत्वात् परमात्मायमव्ययः। शरीरस्थो ऽपि कौन्तेय न करोति न लिप्यते ॥13.32 यथा सर्वगतं सौक्ष्म्याद् आकाशं नोपलिप्यते। सर्वत्रावस्थितो देहे तथात्मा नोपलिप्यते ॥13.33 यथा प्रकाशयत्येकः कृत्स्नं लोकमिमं रविः। क्षेत्रं क्षेत्री तथा कृत्स्नं प्रकाशयति भारत ॥13.34 क्षेत्रक्षेत्रज्ञयोरेवम् अन्तरं ज्ञानचक्षुषा। भूतप्रकृतिमोक्षं च ये विदुर्यान्ति ते परम् ॥13.35

14 – Three Gunas

परं भूयः प्रवक्ष्यामि ज्ञानानां ज्ञानमुत्तमम्। यज्ज्ञात्वा मुनयः सर्वे परां सिद्धिमितो गताः ॥14.1 इदं ज्ञानमुपाश्रित्य मम साधर्म्यमागताः। सर्गे ऽपि नोपजायन्ते प्रलये न व्यथन्ति च ॥14.2 मम योनिर्महद् ब्रह्म तस्मिन्गर्भं दधाम्यहम्। सम्भवः सर्वभूतानां ततो भवति भारत ॥14.3 सर्वयोनिषु कौन्तेय मूर्तयः सम्भवन्ति याः। तासां ब्रह्म महद्योनिर् अहं बीजप्रदः पिता ॥14.4

सत्त्वं रजस्तम इति गुणाः प्रकृतिसम्भवाः। निबध्नन्ति महाबाहो देहे देहिनमव्ययम् ॥14.5 तत्र सत्त्वं निर्मलत्वात् प्रकाशकमनामयम्। सुखसङ्गेन बध्नाति ज्ञानसङ्गेन चानघ ॥14.6 रजो रागात्मकं विद्धि तृष्णासङ्गसमुद्भवम्। तन्निबध्नाति कौन्तेय कर्मसङ्गेन देहिनम् ॥14.7 तमस्त्वज्ञानजं विद्धि मोहनं सर्वदेहिनाम्। प्रमादालस्यनिद्राभिस् तन्निबध्नाति भारत ॥14.8 सत्त्वं सुखे सञ्जयति रजः कर्मणि भारत। ज्ञानमावृत्य तु तमः प्रमादे सञ्जयत्युत ॥14.9 रजस्तमश्चाभिभूय सत्त्वं भवति भारत। रजः सत्त्वं तमश्चैव तमः सत्त्वं

रजस्तथा ॥14.10 सर्वद्वारेषु देहे ऽस्मिन् प्रकाश उपजायते। ज्ञानं यदा तदा विद्याद् विवृद्धं सत्त्वमित्युत ॥14.11 लोभः प्रवृत्तिरारम्भः कर्मणामशमः स्पृहा रजस्येतानि जायन्ते विवृद्धे भरतर्षभ ॥14.12 अप्रकाशो ऽप्रवृत्तिश्च प्रमादो मोह एव च। तमस्येतानि जायन्ते विवृद्धे कुरुनन्दन ॥14.13

यदा सत्त्वे प्रवृद्धे तु प्रलयं याति देहभृत्। तदोत्तमविदां लोकान् अमलान्प्रतिपद्यते ॥14.14 रजसि प्रलयं गत्वा कर्मसङ्गिषु जायते। तथा प्रलीनस्तमसि मूढयोनिषु जायते ॥14.15 कर्मणः सुकृतस्याहुः सात्त्विकं निर्मलं फलम्। रजसस्तु फलं दुःखम् अज्ञानं तमसः फलम् ॥14.16 सत्त्वात्सञ्जायते ज्ञानं रजसो लोभ एव च। प्रमादमोहौ तमसो भवतो ऽज्ञानमेव च ॥14.17 ऊर्ध्वं गच्छन्ति सत्त्वस्था मध्ये तिष्ठन्ति राजसाः। जघन्यगुणवृत्तिस्था अधो गच्छन्ति तामसाः ॥14.18 नान्यं गुणेभ्यः कर्तारं यदा द्रष्टानुपश्यति। गुणेभ्यश्च परं वेत्ति मद्भावं सो ऽधिगच्छति ॥14.19 गुणानेतानतीत्य त्रीन् देही देहसमुद्भवान्। जन्म-मृत्युजरादुःखैर् विमुक्तो ऽमृतमश्नुते ॥14.20

Arjuna:

कैर्लिङ्गैस्त्रीन्गुणानेतान् अतीतो भवति प्रभो। किमाचारः कथं चैतांस् त्रीन्गुणानतिवर्त्तते ॥14.21

Krishna:

प्रकाशं च प्रवृत्तिं च मोहमेव च पाण्डव। न द्वेष्टि सम्प्रवृत्तानि न निवृत्तानि काङ्क्षति ॥14.22 उदासीनवदासीनो गुणैर्यो न विचाल्यते। गुणा वर्तन्त इत्येवं यो ऽवतिष्ठति नेङ्गते ॥ समदुःखसुखः स्वस्थः समलोष्टाश्मकाञ्चनः। तुल्यप्रियाप्रियो धीरस् तुल्यनिन्दात्मसंस्तुतिः ॥ मानापमानयोस्तुल्यस् तुल्यो मित्रारि-पक्षयोः। सर्वारम्भपरित्यागी गुणातीतः स उच्यते ॥14.23-25 मां च यो ऽव्यभिचारेण भक्तियोगेन सेवते। स गुणान्समतीत्यैतान् ब्रह्मभूयाय कल्पते ॥14.26 ब्रह्मणो हि प्रतिष्ठाहम् अमृतस्याव्ययस्य च। शाश्वतस्य च धर्मस्य सुखस्यैकान्तिकस्य च ॥14.27

---

15 – The Supreme Person

ऊर्ध्वमूलमधःशाखम् अश्वत्थं प्राहुरव्ययम्। छन्दांसि यस्य पर्णानि यस्तं वेद स वेदवित् ॥15.1

अधश्चोर्ध्वं प्रसृतास्तस्य शाखा गुणप्रवृद्धा विषयप्रवालाः।
अधश्च मूलान्यनुसन्ततानि कर्मानुबन्धीनि मनुष्यलोके ॥15.2
न रूपमस्येह तथोपलभ्यते नान्तो न चादिर्न च सम्प्रतिष्ठा।
अश्वत्थमेनं सुविरूढमूलम् असङ्गशस्त्रेण दृढेन छित्त्वा ॥

ततः पदं तत्परिमार्गितव्यं यस्मिन्गता न निवर्तन्ति भूयः ।
तमेव चाद्यं पुरुषं प्रपद्ये यतः प्रवृत्तिः प्रसृता पुराणी ॥15.3-4
निर्मानमोहा जितसङ्गदोषा अध्यात्मनित्या विनिवृत्तकामाः ।
द्वन्द्वैर्विमुक्ताः सुखदुःखसञ्ज्ञैर् गच्छन्त्यमूढाः पदमव्ययं तत् ॥15.5

न तद्भासयते सूर्यो न शशाङ्को न पावकः । यद्गत्वा न निवर्तन्ते तद्धाम परमं
मम ॥15.6 ममैवांशो जीवलोके जीवभूतः सनातनः । मनःषष्ठानीन्द्रियाणि
प्रकृतिस्थानि कर्षति ॥15.7 शरीरं यदवाप्नोति यच्चाप्युत्क्रामतीश्वरः । गृहीत्वैतानि
संयाति वायुर्गन्धानिवाशयात् ॥15.8 श्रोत्रं चक्षुः स्पर्शनं च रसनं घ्राणमेव च ।
अधिष्ठाय मनश्चायं विषयानुपसेवते ॥15.9 उत्क्रामन्तं स्थितं वापि भुञ्जानं वा
गुणान्वितम् । विमूढा नानुपश्यन्ति पश्यन्ति ज्ञानचक्षुषः ॥15.10 यतन्तो
योगिनश्चैनं पश्यन्त्यात्मन्यवस्थितम् । यतन्तो ऽप्यकृतात्मानो नैनं
पश्यन्त्यचेतसः ॥15.11

यदादित्यगतं तेजो जगद्भासयतेऽखिलम् । यच्चन्द्रमसि यच्चाग्नौ तत्तेजो विद्धि
मामकम् ॥15.12 गामाविश्य च भूतानि धारयाम्यहमोजसा । पुष्णामि चौषधीः
सर्वाः सोमो भूत्वा रसात्मकः ॥15.13 अहं वैश्वानरो भूत्वा प्राणिनां देहमाश्रितः ।
प्राणापानसमायुक्तः पचाम्यन्नं चतुर्विधम् ॥15.14

सर्वस्य चाहं हृदि सन्निविष्टो मत्तः स्मृतिर्ज्ञानमपोहनं च ।
वेदैश्च सर्वैरहमेव वेद्यो वेदान्तकृद्वेदविदेव चाहम् ॥15.15

द्वाविमौ पुरुषौ लोके क्षरश्चाक्षर एव च । क्षरः सर्वाणि भूतानि कूटस्थो ऽक्षर
उच्यते ॥15.16 उत्तमः पुरुषस्त्वन्यः परमात्मेत्युदाहृतः । यो लोकत्रयमाविश्य
बिभर्त्यव्यय ईश्वरः ॥15.17 यस्मात्क्षरमतीतो ऽहम् अक्षरादपि चोत्तमः । अतो
ऽस्मि लोके वेदे च प्रथितः पुरुषोत्तमः ॥15.18 यो मामेवमसम्मूढो जानाति
पुरुषोत्तमम् । स सर्वविद्भजति मां सर्वभावेन भारत ॥15.19 इति गुह्यतमं शास्त्रम्
इदमुक्तं मयानघ । एतद् बुद्ध्वा बुद्धिमान्स्यात् कृतकृत्यश्च भारत ॥15.20

---

16 – Demoniac Attributes

Krishna:

अभयं सत्त्वसंशुद्धिर् ज्ञानयोगव्यवस्थितिः । दानं दमश्च यज्ञश्च स्वाध्यायस्तप
आर्जवम् ॥ अहिंसा सत्यमक्रोधस् त्यागः शान्तिरपैशुनम् । दया भूतेष्वलोलुप्त्वं
मार्दवं ह्रीरचापलम् ॥ तेजः क्षमा धृतिः शौचम् अद्रोहो नातिमानिता । भवन्ति
सम्पदं दैवीम् अभिजातस्य भारत ॥16.1-3 दम्भो दर्पोऽभिमानश्च क्रोधः
पारुष्यमेव च । अज्ञानं चाभिजातस्य पार्थ सम्पदमासुरीम् ॥16.4 दैवी
सम्पद्विमोक्षाय निबन्धायासुरी मता । मा शुचः सम्पदं दैवीम् अभिजातो ऽसि

पाण्डव ॥16.5 द्वौ भूतसर्गौ लोके ऽस्मिन् दैव आसुर एव च। दैवो विस्तरशः प्रोक्त आसुरं पार्थ मे शृणु ॥16.6

प्रवृत्तिं च निवृत्तिं च जना न विदुरासुराः। न शौचं नापि चाचारो न सत्यं तेषु विद्यते ॥16.7 असत्यमप्रतिष्ठं ते जगदाहुरनीश्वरम्। अपरस्परसम्भूतं किमन्यत्कामहैतुकम् ॥16.8 एतां दृष्टिमवष्टभ्य नष्टात्मानो ऽल्पबुद्धयः। प्रभवन्त्युग्रकर्माणः क्षयाय जगतो ऽहिताः ॥16.9 काममाश्रित्य दुष्पूरं दम्भमानमदान्विताः। मोहाद् गृहीत्वासद्ग्राहान् प्रवर्तन्ते ऽशुचिव्रताः ॥16.10 चिन्तामपरिमेयां च प्रलयान्तामुपाश्रिताः। कामोपभोगपरमा एतावदिति निश्चिताः॥ आशापाशशतैर्बद्धाः कामक्रोधपरायणाः। ईहन्ते कामभोगार्थम् अन्यायेनार्थसञ्चयान् ॥16.11-12 इदमद्य मया लब्धम् इमं प्राप्स्ये मनोरथम्। इदमस्तीदमपि मे भविष्यति पुनर्धनम्॥ असौ मया हतः शत्रुर् हनिष्ये चापरानपि। ईश्वरो ऽहमहं भोगी सिद्धो ऽहं बलवान्सुखी॥ आढ्यो ऽभिजनवानस्मि को ऽन्यो ऽस्ति सदृशो मया। यक्ष्ये दास्यामि मोदिष्य इत्यज्ञानविमोहिताः॥ अनेकचित्तविभ्रान्ता मोहजालसमावृताः। प्रसक्ताः कामभोगेषु पतन्ति नरके ऽशुचौ ॥16.13-16 आत्मसम्भाविताः स्तब्धा धनमान-मदान्विताः। यजन्ते नामयज्ञैस्ते दम्भेनाविधिपूर्वकम् ॥16.17 अहङ्कारं बलं दर्प कामं क्रोधं च संश्रिताः। मामात्मपरदेहेषु प्रद्विषन्तो ऽभ्यसूयकाः॥ तानहं द्विषतः क्रूरान् संसारेषु नराधमान्। क्षिपाम्यजस्रमशुभान् आसुरीष्वेव योनिषु ॥16.18-19

आसुरीं योनिमापन्ना मूढा जन्मनि जन्मनि। मामप्राप्यैव कौन्तेय ततो यान्त्यधमां गतिम् ॥16.20 त्रिविधं नरकस्येदं द्वारं नाशनमात्मनः। कामः क्रोधस्तथा लोभस् तस्मादेतत्त्रयं त्यजेत् ॥16.21 एतैर्विमुक्तः कौन्तेय तमोद्वारैस्त्रिभिर्नरः। आचरत्यात्मनः श्रेयस् ततो याति परां गतिम् ॥16.22 यः शास्त्रविधिमुत्सृज्य वर्तते कामकारतः। न स सिद्धिमवाप्नोति न सुखं न परां गतिम् ॥16.23 तस्माच्छास्त्रं प्रमाणं ते कार्याकार्यव्यवस्थितौ। ज्ञात्वा शास्त्रविधानोक्तं कर्म कर्तुमिहार्हसि ॥16.24

17 – Three Kinds of Faith

Arjuna:

ये शास्त्रविधिमुत्सृज्य यजन्ते श्रद्धयान्विताः। तेषां निष्ठा तु का कृष्ण सत्त्वमाहो रजस्तमः ॥17.1

Krishna:

त्रिविधा भवति श्रद्धा देहिनां सा स्वभावजा। सात्त्विकी राजसी चैव तामसी चेति तां शृणु ॥17.2 सत्त्वानुरूपा सर्वस्य श्रद्धा भवति भारत। श्रद्धामयो ऽयं

पुरुषो यो यच्छ्रद्धः स एव सः ॥17.3 यजन्ते सात्त्विका देवान् यक्षरक्षांसि राजसाः। प्रेतान्भूतगणांश्चान्ये यजन्ते तामसा जनाः ॥17.4 अशास्त्रविहितं घोरं तप्यन्ते ये तपो जनाः। दम्भाहङ्कारसंयुक्ताः कामरागबलान्विताः ॥ कर्षयन्तः शरीरस्थं भूतग्राममचेतसः। मां चैवान्तःशरीरस्थं तान्विद्ध्यासुरनिश्चयान् ॥17.5-6

आहारस्त्वपि सर्वस्य त्रिविधो भवति प्रियः। यज्ञस्तपस्तथा दानं तेषां भेदमिमं शृणु ॥17.7 आयुःसत्त्वबलारोग्य-सुखप्रीतिविवर्धनाः। रस्याः स्निग्धाः स्थिरा हृद्या आहाराः सात्त्विकप्रियाः ॥17.8 कट्वम्ललवणात्युष्ण-तीक्ष्णरूक्षविदाहिनः। आहारा राजसस्येष्टा दुःखशोकामयप्रदाः ॥17.9 यातयामं गतरसं पूति पर्युषितं च यत्। उच्छिष्टमपि चामेध्यं भोजनं तामसप्रियम् ॥17.10

अफलाकाङ्क्षिभिर्यज्ञो विधिदिष्टो य इज्यते। यष्टव्यमेवेति मनः समाधाय स सात्त्विकः ॥17.11 अभिसन्धाय तु फलं दम्भार्थमपि चैव यत्। इज्यते भरतश्रेष्ठ तं यज्ञं विद्धि राजसम् ॥17.12 विधिहीनमसृष्टान्नं मन्त्रहीनमदक्षिणम्। श्रद्धा-विरहितं यज्ञं तामसं परिचक्षते ॥17.13

देवद्विजगुरुप्राज्ञ-पूजनं शौचमार्जवम्। ब्रह्मचर्यमहिंसा च शारीरं तप उच्यते ॥17.14 अनुद्वेगकरं वाक्यं सत्यं प्रियहितं च यत्। स्वाध्यायाभ्यसनं चैव वाङ्मयं तप उच्यते ॥17.15 मनःप्रसादः सौम्यत्वं मौनमात्मविनिग्रहः। भाव-संशुद्धिरित्येतत् तपो मानसमुच्यते ॥17.16 श्रद्धया परया तप्तं तपस्तत्त्रिविधं नरैः। अफलाकाङ्क्षिभिर्युक्तैः सात्त्विकं परिचक्षते ॥17.17 सत्कारमानपूजार्थं तपो दम्भेन चैव यत्। क्रियते तदिह प्रोक्तं राजसं चलमध्रुवम् ॥17.18 मूढग्राहेणात्मनो यत् पीडया क्रियते तपः। परस्योत्सादनार्थं वा तत्तामसमुदाहृतम् ॥17.19

दातव्यमिति यद्दानं दीयतेऽनुपकारिणे। देशे काले च पात्रे च तद्दानं सात्त्विकं स्मृतम् ॥17.20 यत्तु प्रत्युपकारार्थं फलमुद्दिश्य वा पुनः। दीयते च परिक्लिष्टं तद्दानं राजसं स्मृतम् ॥17.21 अदेशकाले यद्दानम् अपात्रेभ्यश्च दीयते। असत्कृतमवज्ञातं तत्तामसमुदाहृतम् ॥17.22

ओं तत्सदिति निर्देशो ब्रह्मणस्त्रिविधः स्मृतः। ब्राह्मणास्तेन वेदाश्च यज्ञाश्च विहिताः पुरा ॥17.23 तस्मादोमित्युदाहृत्य यज्ञदानतपःक्रियाः। प्रवर्तन्ते विधानोक्ताः सततं ब्रह्मवादिनाम् ॥17.24 तदित्यनभिसन्धाय फलं यज्ञतपःक्रियाः। दानक्रियाश्च विविधाः क्रियन्ते मोक्षकाङ्क्षिभिः ॥17.25 सद्भावे साधुभावे च सदित्येतत्प्रयुज्यते। प्रशस्ते कर्मणि तथा सच्छब्दः पार्थ युज्यते ॥17.26 यज्ञे तपसि दाने च स्थितिः सदिति चोच्यते। कर्म चैव तदर्थीयं सदित्येवाभिधीयते ॥17.27 अश्रद्धया हुतं दत्तं तपस्तप्तं कृतं च यत्। असदित्युच्यते पार्थ न च तत्प्रेत्य नो इह ॥17.28

Arjuna:

सन्न्यासस्य महाबाहो तत्त्वमिच्छामि वेदितुम्। त्यागस्य च हृषीकेश पृथक्केशिनिषूदन ॥18.1

Krishna:

काम्यानां कर्मणां न्यासं सन्न्यासं कवयो विदुः। सर्वकर्मफलत्यागं प्राहुस्त्यागं विचक्षणाः ॥18.2 त्याज्यं दोषवदित्येके कर्म प्राहुर्मनीषिणः। यज्ञदानतपःकर्म न त्याज्यमिति चापरे ॥18.3 निश्चयं शृणु मे तत्र त्यागे भरतसत्तम। त्यागो हि पुरुषव्याघ्र त्रिविधः सम्प्रकीर्तितः ॥18.4 यज्ञदानतपःकर्म न त्याज्यं कार्यमेव तत्। यज्ञो दानं तपश्चैव पावनानि मनीषिणाम् ॥18.5 एतान्यपि तु कर्माणि सङ्गं त्यक्त्वा फलानि च। कर्तव्यानीति मे पार्थ निश्चितं मतमुत्तमम् ॥18.6

नियतस्य तु सन्न्यासः कर्मणो नोपपद्यते। मोहात्तस्य परित्यागस् तामसः परिकीर्तितः ॥18.7 दुःखमित्येव यत्कर्म कायक्लेशभयात्त्यजेत्। स कृत्वा राजसं त्यागं नैव त्यागफलं लभेत् ॥18.8 कार्यमित्येव यत्कर्म नियतं क्रियते ऽर्जुन। सङ्गं त्यक्त्वा फलं चैव स त्यागः सात्त्विको मतः ॥18.9 न द्वेष्ट्यकुशलं कर्म कुशले नानुषज्जते। त्यागी सत्त्वसमाविष्टो मेधावी छिन्नसंशयः ॥18.10 न हि देहभृता शक्यं त्यक्तुं कर्माण्यशेषतः। यस्तु कर्मफलत्यागी स त्यागीत्यभिधीयते ॥18.11 अनिष्टमिष्टं मिश्रं च त्रिविधं कर्मणः फलम्। भवत्यत्यागिनां प्रेत्य न तु सन्न्यासिनां क्वचित् ॥18.12

पञ्चैतानि महाबाहो कारणानि निबोध मे। साङ्ख्ये कृतान्ते प्रोक्तानि सिद्धये सर्वकर्मणाम् ॥18.13 अधिष्ठानं तथा कर्ता करणं च पृथग्विधम्। विविधाश्च पृथक्चेष्टा दैवं चैवात्र पञ्चमम् ॥18.14 शरीरवाङ्मनोभिर्यत् कर्म प्रारभते नरः। न्याय्यं वा विपरीतं वा पञ्चैते तस्य हेतवः ॥18.15 तत्रैवं सति कर्तारमात्मानं केवलं तु यः। पश्यत्यकृतबुद्धित्वान् न स पश्यति दुर्मतिः ॥18.16 यस्य नाहङ्कृतो भावो बुद्धिर्यस्य न लिप्यते। हत्वापि स इमाँल्लोकान् न हन्ति न निबध्यते ॥18.17 ज्ञानं ज्ञेयं परिज्ञाता त्रिविधा कर्मचोदना। करणं कर्म कर्तेति त्रिविधः कर्मसङ्ग्रहः ॥18.18

ज्ञानं कर्म च कर्ता च त्रिधैव गुणभेदतः। प्रोच्यते गुणसङ्ख्याने यथावच्छृणु तान्यपि ॥18.19 सर्वभूतेषु येनैकं भावमव्ययमीक्षते। अविभक्तं विभक्तेषु तज्ज्ञानं विद्धि सात्त्विकम् ॥18.20 पृथक्त्वेन तु यज्ज्ञानं नानाभावान्पृथग्विधान्। वेत्ति सर्वेषु भूतेषु तज्ज्ञानं विद्धि राजसम् ॥18.21 यत्तु कृत्स्नवदेकस्मिन् कार्ये सक्तमहैतुकम्। अतत्त्वार्थवदल्पं च तत्तामसमुदाहृतम् ॥18.22 नियतं सङ्गरहितम् अरागद्वेषतः कृतम्। अफलप्रेप्सुना कर्म यत्तत्सात्त्विकमुच्यते ॥18.23 यत्तु कामेप्सुना कर्म साहङ्कारेण वा पुनः। क्रियते बहुलायासं

न्द्राजसमुदाहृतम् ॥18.24 अनुबन्धं क्षयं हिंसाम् अनपेक्ष्य च पौरुषम्। मोहादारभ्यते कर्म यत्तत्तामसमुच्यते ॥18.25 मुक्तसङ्गोऽनहंवादी धृत्युत्साह-समन्वितः। सिद्ध्यसिद्ध्योर्निर्विकारः कर्ता सात्त्विक उच्यते ॥18.26 रागी कर्मफलप्रेप्सुर्लुब्धो हिंसात्मकोऽशुचिः। हर्षशोकान्वितः कर्ता राजसः परिकीर्तितः ॥18.27 अयुक्तः प्राकृतः स्तब्धः शठो नैष्कृतिकोऽलसः। विषादी दीर्घसूत्री च कर्ता तामस उच्यते ॥18.28

बुद्धेर्भेदं धृतेश्चैव गुणतस्त्रिविधं शृणु। प्रोच्यमानमशेषेण पृथक्त्वेन धनञ्जय ॥18.29 प्रवृत्तिं च निवृत्तिं च कार्याकार्ये भयाभये। बन्धं मोक्षं च या वेत्ति बुद्धिः सा पार्थ सात्त्विकी ॥18.30 यया धर्ममधर्मं च कार्यं चाकार्यमेव च। अयथावत्प्रजानाति बुद्धिः सा पार्थ राजसी ॥18.31 अधर्मं धर्ममिति या मन्यते तमसावृता। सर्वार्थान्विपरीतांश्च बुद्धिः सा पार्थ तामसी ॥18.32 धृत्या यया धारयते मनःप्राणेन्द्रियक्रियाः। योगेनाव्यभिचारिण्या धृतिः सा पार्थ सात्त्विकी ॥18.33 यया तु धर्मकामार्थान् धृत्या धारयतेऽर्जुन। प्रसङ्गेन फलाकाङ्क्षी धृतिः सा पार्थ राजसी ॥18.34 यया स्वप्नं भयं शोकं विषादं मदमेव च। न विमुञ्चति दुर्मेधा धृतिः सा पार्थ तामसी ॥18.35

सुखं त्विदानीं त्रिविधं शृणु मे भरतर्षभ ॥18.36 अभ्यासाद्रमते यत्र दुःखान्तं च निगच्छति। यत्तदग्रे विषमिव परिणामेऽमृतोपमम्। तत्सुखं सात्त्विकं प्रोक्तम् आत्मबुद्धिप्रसादजम् ॥18.37 विषयेन्द्रियसंयोगाद् यत्तदग्रेऽमृतोपमम्। परिणामे विषमिव तत्सुखं राजसं स्मृतम् ॥18.38 यदग्रे चानुबन्धे च सुखं मोहनमात्मनः। निद्रालस्यप्रमादोत्थं तत्तामसमुदाहृतम् ॥18.39

न तदस्ति पृथिव्यां वा दिवि देवेषु वा पुनः। सत्त्वं प्रकृतिजैर्मुक्तं यदेभिः स्यात्त्रिभिर्गुणैः ॥18.40

ब्राह्मणक्षत्रियविशां शूद्राणां च परन्तप। कर्माणि प्रविभक्तानि स्वभाव-प्रभवैर्गुणैः ॥18.41 शमो दमस्तपः शौचं क्षान्तिरार्जवमेव च। ज्ञानं विज्ञानमास्तिक्यं ब्रह्मकर्म स्वभावजम् ॥18.42 शौर्यं तेजो धृतिर्दाक्ष्यं युद्धे चाप्यपलायनम्। दानमीश्वरभावश्च क्षात्रं कर्म स्वभावजम् ॥18.43 कृषिगोरक्ष्यवाणिज्यं वैश्यकर्म स्वभावजम्। परिचर्यात्मकं कर्म शूद्रस्यापि स्वभावजम् ॥18.44 स्वे स्वे कर्मण्यभिरतः संसिद्धिं लभते नरः। स्वकर्मनिरतः सिद्धिं यथा विन्दति तच्छृणु ॥18.45 यतः प्रवृत्तिर्भूतानां येन सर्वमिदं ततम्। स्वकर्मणा तमभ्यर्च्य सिद्धिं विन्दति मानवः ॥18.46 श्रेयान्स्वधर्मो विगुणः परधर्मात्स्वनुष्ठितात्। स्वभावनियतं कर्म कुर्वन्नाप्नोति किल्बिषम् ॥18.47 सहजं कर्म कौन्तेय सदोषमपि न त्यजेत्। सर्वारम्भा हि दोषेण धूमेनाग्निरिवावृताः ॥18.48

असक्तबुद्धिः सर्वत्र जितात्मा विगतस्पृहः। नैष्कर्म्यसिद्धिं परमां सन्न्यासेनाधिगच्छति ॥18.49 सिद्धिं प्राप्तो यथा ब्रह्म तथाप्नोति निबोध मे। समासेनैव कौन्तेय निष्ठा ज्ञानस्य या परा ॥18.50 बुद्ध्या विशुद्धया युक्तो धृत्यात्मानं नियम्य च। शब्दादीन्विषयांस्त्यक्त्वा रागद्वेषौ व्युदस्य च॥ विविक्तसेवी लघ्वाशी यतवाक्कायमानसः। ध्यानयोगपरो नित्यं वैराग्यं समुपाश्रितः॥ अहङ्कारं बलं दर्पं कामं क्रोधं परिग्रहम्। विमुच्य निर्ममः शान्तो ब्रह्मभूयाय कल्पते ॥18.51-53 ब्रह्मभूतः प्रसन्नात्मा न शोचति न काङ्क्षति। समः सर्वेषु भूतेषु मद्भक्तिं लभते पराम् ॥18.54 भक्त्या मामभिजानाति यावान्यश्चास्मि तत्त्वतः। ततो मां तत्त्वतो ज्ञात्वा विशते तदनन्तरम् ॥18.55 सर्वकर्माण्यपि सदा कुर्वाणो मद्व्यपाश्रयः। मत्प्रसादादवाप्नोति शाश्वतं पदमव्ययम् ॥18.56 चेतसा सर्वकर्माणि मयि सन्न्यस्य मत्परः। बुद्धियोगमुपाश्रित्य मच्चित्तः सततं भव ॥18.57

मच्चित्तः सर्वदुर्गाणि मत्प्रसादात्तरिष्यसि। अथ चेत्त्वमहङ्कारान् न श्रोष्यसि विनङ्क्ष्यसि ॥18.58 यदहङ्कारमाश्रित्य न योत्स्य इति मन्यसे। मिथ्यैष व्यवसायस्ते प्रकृतिस्त्वां नियोक्ष्यति ॥18.59 स्वभावजेन कौन्तेय निबद्धः स्वेन कर्मणा। कर्तुं नेच्छसि यन्मोहात् करिष्यस्यवशो ऽपि तत् ॥18.60

ईश्वरः सर्वभूतानां हृद्देशे ऽर्जुन तिष्ठति। भ्रामयन्सर्वभूतानि यन्त्रारूढानि मायया ॥18.61 तमेव शरणं गच्छ सर्वभावेन भारत। तत्प्रसादात्परां शान्तिं स्थानं प्राप्स्यसि शाश्वतम् ॥18.62

इति ते ज्ञानमाख्यातं गुह्याद् गुह्यतरं मया। विमृश्यैतदशेषेण यथेच्छसि तथा कुरु ॥18.63

सर्वगुह्यतमं भूयः शृणु मे परमं वचः। इष्टो ऽसि मे दृढमिति ततो वक्ष्यामि ते हितम् ॥18.64 मन्मना भव मद्भक्तो मद्याजी मां नमस्कुरु। मामेवैष्यसि सत्यं ते प्रतिजाने प्रियो ऽसि मे ॥18.65 सर्वधर्मान्परित्यज्य मामेकं शरणं व्रज। अहं त्वां सर्वपापेभ्यो मोक्षयिष्यामि मा शुचः ॥18.66

इदं ते नातपस्काय नाभक्ताय कदाचन। न चाशुश्रूषवे वाच्यं न च मां यो ऽभ्यसूयति ॥18.67 य इदं परमं गुह्यं मद्भक्तेष्वभिधास्यति। भक्तिं मयि परां कृत्वा मामेवैष्यत्यसंशयः ॥18.68 न च तस्मान्मनुष्येषु कश्चिन्मे प्रियकृत्तमः। भविता न च मे तस्मादन्यः प्रियतरो भुवि ॥18.69 अध्येष्यते च य इमं धर्म्यं संवादमावयोः। ज्ञानयज्ञेन तेनाहम् इष्टः स्यामिति मे मतिः ॥18.70 श्रद्धावाननसूयश्च शृणुयादपि यो नरः। सो ऽपि मुक्तः शुभाँल्लोकान् प्राप्नुयात्पुण्यकर्मणाम् ॥18.71

कच्चिदेतच्छ्रुतं पार्थ त्वयैकाग्रेण चेतसा। कच्चिदज्ञानसम्मोहः प्रणष्टस्ते धनञ्जय ॥18.72

Arjuna:

नष्टो मोहः स्मृतिर्लब्धा त्वत्प्रसादान्मयाच्युत । स्थितो ऽस्मि गतसन्देहः करिष्ये वचनं तव ॥18.73

Sanjaya:

इत्यहं वासुदेवस्य पार्थस्य च महात्मनः । संवादमिममश्रौषम् अद्भुतं रोमहर्षणम् ॥18.74 व्यासप्रसादाच्छुतवान् एतद् गुह्यमहं परम् । योगं योगेश्वरात्कृष्णात् साक्षात्कथयतः स्वयम् ॥18.75 राजन्संस्मृत्य संस्मृत्य संवादमिममद्भुतम् । केशवार्जुनयोः पुण्यं हृष्यामि च मुहुर्मुहुः ॥18.76 तच्च संस्मृत्य संस्मृत्य रूपमत्यद्भुतं हरेः । विस्मयो मे महान्राजन् हृष्यामि च पुनः पुनः ॥18.77 यत्र योगेश्वरः कृष्णो यत्र पार्थो धनुर्धरः । तत्र श्रीर्विजयो भूतिर् ध्रुवा नीतिर्मतिर्मम ॥18.78

ॐ तत्सदिति श्रीमहाभारते शतसाहस्त्र्यां संहितायां वैयासिक्यां भीष्मपर्वणि श्रीमद्भगवद्गीतासूपनिषत्सु ब्रह्मविद्यायां योगशास्त्रे श्रीकृष्णार्जुनसंवादे ऽष्टादशो ऽध्यायः ।[1073]

MANTRA

88. Guru

(1) Instructing teachers are called शिक्षा-/श्रवण-/भजन-गुरु.
(2) Initiating teachers are called दीक्षा-/मन्त्र-गुरु, and are often hereditary शुक्राचार्य ('seminal teacher').

They might be one, as आचार्य:

आचिनोति यः शास्त्रार्थम् आचारे स्थापयत्यपि। स्वयमाचरते यस्माद् आचार्यस्तेन कीर्तितः ॥1074

But:

न ह्येकस्माद् गुरोर्ज्ञानं सुस्थिरं स्यात्सुपुष्कलम्। ब्रह्मैतदद्वितीयं वै गीयते बहुधर्षिभिः ॥1075

गुरु glorified:

तद्विज्ञानार्थं स गुरुमेवाभिगच्छेत् ।1076 आचार्यवान्पुरुषो वेद ।1077 तस्माद् गुरुं प्रपद्येत जिज्ञासुः श्रेय उत्तमम्।1078यस्य देवे परा भक्तिर् यथा देवे तथा गुरौ। तस्यैते कथिता ह्यर्थाः प्रकाशन्ते महात्मनः ॥1079 उत्पत्तिं प्रलयं चैव भूतानामागतिं गतिम्। वेत्ति विद्यामविद्यां च स वाच्यो भगवानिति ॥1080

Beware:

वेदैर्विहीनाश्च पठन्ति शास्त्रं शास्त्रेण हीनाश्च पुराणपाठाः। पुराणहीनाः कृषिणो भवन्ति भ्रष्टास्ततो भागवता भवन्ति ॥1081 अशक्तस्तु भवेत्साधुर् ब्रह्मचारी च निर्धनः। व्याधितो देवभक्तश्च वृद्धा नारी पतिव्रता ॥1082 प्रज्ञया निश्चिता धीरास् तारयन्त्यबुधान्प्लवैः। नाबुधास् तारयन्त्यन्यान् आत्मानं वा कथञ्चन ॥1083 गुरवो बहवः सन्ति शिष्य-वित्तापहारकाः। दुर्लभः सद्गुरुर्देवि शिष्यसन्तापहारकः ॥1084

Thus:

तयोर्वत्सरवासेन ज्ञातान्योन्यस्वभावयोः। गुरुता शिष्यता चेति नान्यथैवेति निश्चयः ॥1085 ज्ञानेन क्रियया वापि गुरुः शिष्यं परीक्षयेत्। संवत्सरं तदर्धं वा तदर्धं वा प्रयत्नतः ॥1086 गुरोरप्यवलिप्तस्य कार्याकार्यमजानतः। उत्पथ-प्रतिपन्नस्य परित्यागो विधीयते ॥1087

दिव्यं ज्ञानं यतो दद्यात् कुर्यात्पापस्य सङ्क्षयम् । तस्माद्दीक्षेति सा प्रोक्ता देशिकैस्
तत्त्वकोविदैः ॥1088 यथा काञ्चनतां याति कांस्यं रसविधानतः । तथा दीक्षा-
विधानेन द्विजत्वं जायते नृणाम् ॥1089

Two processes to perform उपनयन/दैक्ष्य-संस्कार (where दीक्षा is given). उपनयन
means 'coming nearer' to the understanding of Vedic knowledge, or 'taking the child
back to the Lord', or 'entering'.

(1) वैदिक उपनयन-संस्कार, obligatory for ब्राह्मण, क्षत्रिय and वैश्य
The age is according to some 5-16 for ब्राह्मण, 6-22 for क्षत्रिय and 8-24 for वैश्य. Or:
At 7 when the objective is ब्रह्म (spirituality), at 8 for आयुः (long life), at 9 for तेजः
(physical strength), at 10 for अन्नादि (livelihood), at 11 for इन्द्रिय (vital force), and at
12 for पशु (live stock); with each year passing, the time which remains for education
shortens.

(2) पाञ्चरात्रिक पञ्च-संस्कार, possible for all others
तापः पुण्ड्रं तथा नाम मन्त्रो यागश्च पञ्चमः । अमी हि पञ्च संस्काराः
परमैकान्तिहेतवः ॥1090
1. व्रत/ताप – specific vows, like उपवास, ब्रह्मचर्य; i.e., curbing material life; 2.
तिलक/पुण्ड्र – 'marking' the body as a temple of God; 3. नाम – receiving हरिनाम as
prayer and initiated name; 4. मन्त्र – receiving specific मन्त्र for worship; 5. याग/पूजा
– using the मन्त्र, the disciple begins to worship a Deity of God.

The child should be given:
1. उपवीत ('which is put on', the sacred thread) or यज्ञोपवीत, which signifies the
acceptance of a गुरु and the qualification to study वेद. While evacuating, the उपवीत
is kept wrapped around the right ear. Since all तीर्थ are said to reside in the right ear,
the thread remains pure in that place even as the rest of the body becomes ritually
impure. 2. ब्रह्म-गायत्री, the सावित्री-मन्त्र for the worship of सविता/सूर्य. Taking 3.
a दण्ड of बिल्व or पलाश for protection, the ब्रह्मचारी should start begging – first by
going to his mother and women friends of his mother. Receiving alms, he should say:
ॐ स्वस्ति – 'May there be auspiciousness.' He should give all that he receives to the
teacher.

Through संस्कार another 'birth' is possible after the शौक्र-जन्म ('seminal birth')
through mother and father – a ब्रह्म-जन्म ('spiritual birth') as द्विज (twice-born),

symbolised by मौञ्जि-बन्धन (the ceremony of 'binding the girdle of मुञ्ज grass'), with गायत्री/सावित्री as mother and the गुरु as father.
शरीरमेतौ सृजतः पिता माता च भारत । आचार्यशास्ता या जातिः सा सत्या साजरामरा ॥[1091]

There is an additional यज्ञ-दीक्षा ('birth for ceremonies'; याग in पञ्च-संस्कार) as विप्र ('stirred', inspired, wise), initiating a qualified ब्राह्मण as priest into वेद-पाठ and the performance of यज्ञ.
मातुरग्रे ऽधिजननं द्वितीयं मौञ्जिबन्धने । तृतीयं यज्ञदीक्षायां द्विजस्य श्रुति-चोदनात् ॥[1092]

---

90. Mantra

मन्त्र means 'advice', and to understand and follow is the essence. The inspiration, however to follow with faith, comes from the antiquity and authority of its ऋषि, but also from initiation rites, like उपनयन. "Their success depends on one's faith in मन्त्र, तीर्थ, देव, astrologer (दैव-ज्ञ), medicine and गुरु."[1093] "When a मन्त्र is heard at random or as song, [obtained] by stratagem, force, or written on a paper, it will be useless."[1094] But the vibration itself, even in written form, has certain effects, and 'magic' यन्त्र, न्यास, मुद्रा and prayer flags exploit this fact.

"ॐ is the best मन्त्र, and repeating it (जप) one becomes immortal (अमर). गायत्री is the best मन्त्र, repeating it one attains enjoyment (भुक्ति) [here] and liberation (मुक्ति) [thereafter]. The मन्त्र 'ॐ नमो नारायणाय' supplies every object (अर्थ). The मन्त्र 'ॐ नमो भगवते वासुदेवाय' gives everything."[1095]

The essence of all मन्त्र, taught in उपनयन:
(1) प्रणव
   तस्य वाचकः प्रणवः । तज्जपस्तदर्थभावनम् ।[1096]
ओङ्कारं बिन्दुसंयुक्तं नित्यं ध्यायन्ति योगिनः । कामदं मोक्षदं चैव ओङ्काराय नमो नमः ॥[1097]
"By that [ॐ] the [study of] this वेद science proceeds – saying 'ॐ' one recites, saying 'ॐ' one praises, saying 'ॐ' one sings."[1098] "All मन्त्र begin with ॐ (प्रणव)."[1099]

(2) व्याहृति
"भूः, भुवः and स्वः (सुवः) – these are the [first] three व्याहृति."[1100] "The Lord extracted from the three वेद [as their essence] the letters अ-उ-म, and [the व्याहृति] भूः-भुवः-स्वः."[1101]

(3) ब्रह्म-गायत्री for सन्ध्या

"Whose देवता is सविता, at whose mouth is situated the threefold fire (?), whose ऋषि is विश्वामित्र, and whose छन्दः is गायत्री – that [ब्रह्म-गायत्री] is best."[1102] "There is no better जप than गायत्री, no [मन्त्र for] sacrifice equal to व्याहृति."[1103]

Following the idea, there are तान्त्रिक गायत्री for every divinity:

ॐ … विद्महे … धीमहि । तन्नो … प्रचोदयात् ॥[1104]

गोपयेद्देवतामिष्टां गोपयेद्गुरुमात्मनः । गोपयेच्च निजं मन्त्रं गोपयेत्रिज-मालिकाम् ॥[1105] नोच्चैर्जप्यं बुधः कुर्यात् सावित्र्यस्तु विशेषतः ।[1106]

---

91. Shri-Yantra

The श्री-यन्त्र as shown here is based on a commentary of कैवल्याश्रम on सौन्दर्य-लहरी. Corrections of a3 and a5 were found elsewhere. The units given can be transformed into any scale.

	a1	a2	a3	a4	a5	a6	a7	a8	a9	a10	a11	a12	a13
units	1	5	5,5	6	6,5	8	12	20	24	35	36	43	48

(1) बिन्दु

Using a pencil, draw a cross in the middle of a sheet of graph paper. The middle of the cross, called Bindu, symbolizes the divine origin of all creation.

(2) Circles

Take a compass and draw four circles with the radii a9, a10, a12 and a13. Now draw a square around the last circle (a13) so that this circle fits exactly into the square. This square symbolizes the gross material aspect of creation.

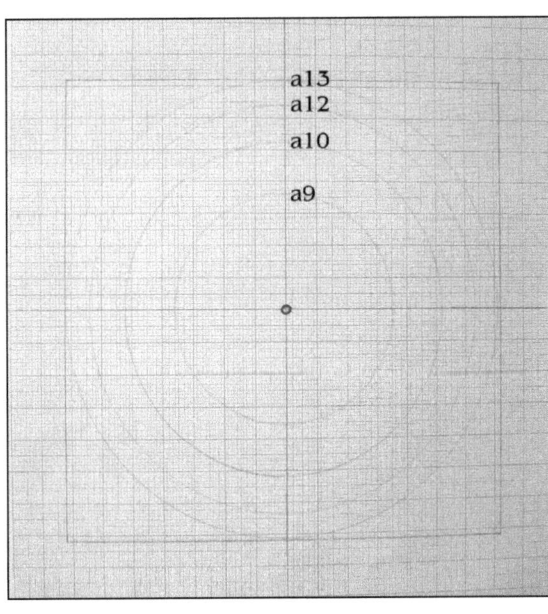

(3) Gates

Draw on top of the middle of each side a 'gate' with the width a8 and the depth a6.

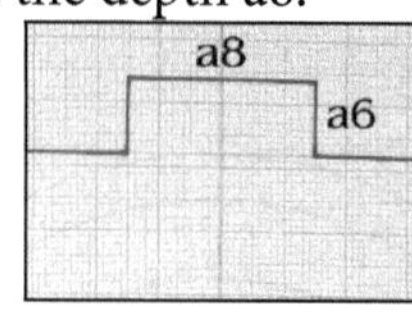

Alternatively, you can enlarge the top of each gate to a depth of a4 and a width of a11.

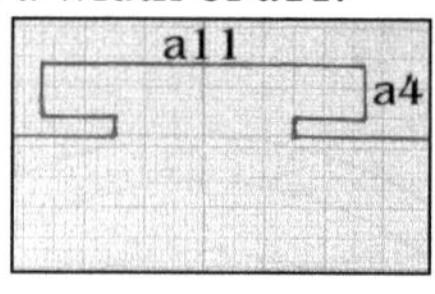

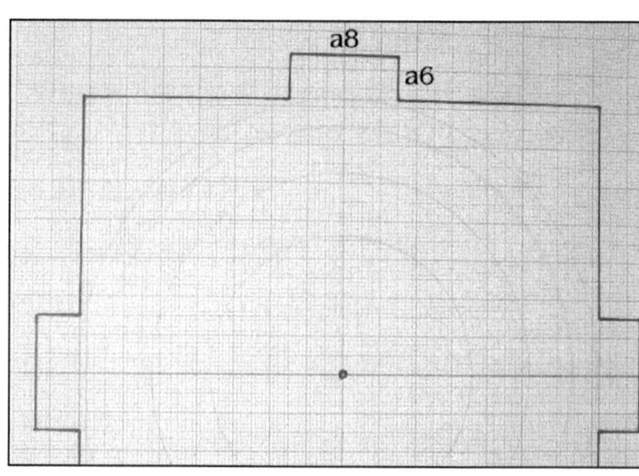

(4) Broadening

To broaden the boundary, use the outer border of the Yantra and draw two additional lines within this border with the spacing a1. The third circle (radius a12) is traced with a felt pen, and two additional circles with the radius a1 are added.

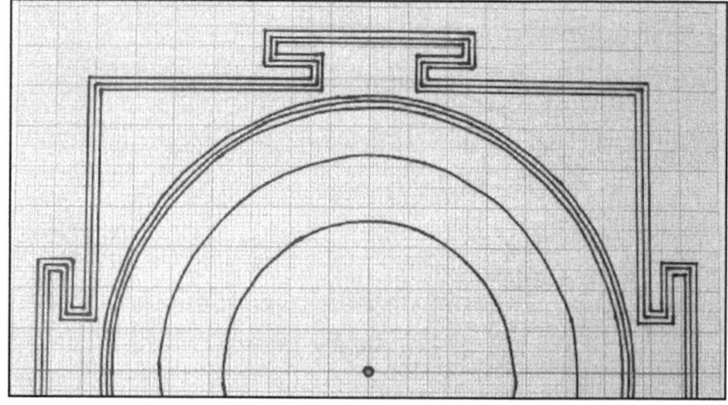

(5) Sectoring

Divide the two outer rings into sectors of 22.5 degrees.

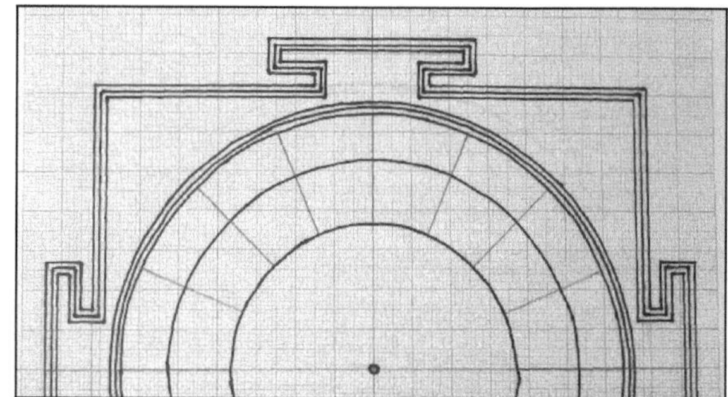

(6) Sixteen Petals
Using a compass, draw sixteen
semicircles as depicted.

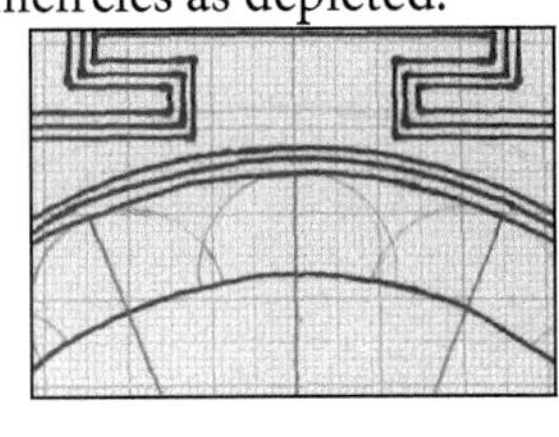

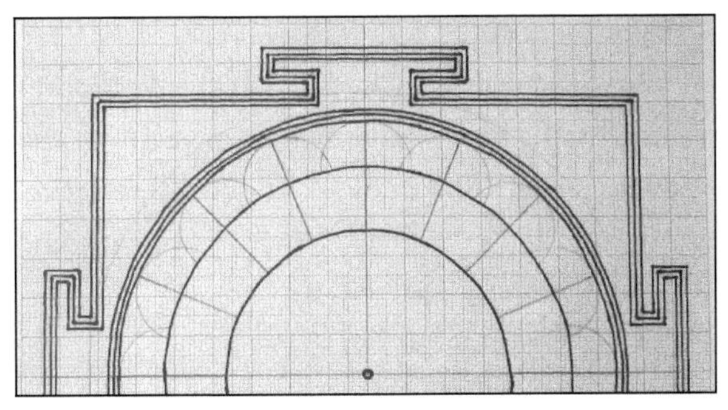

Using these semicircles as a
guide, draw the 16 petals
(षोडश-दल) of the outer lotus
according to your liking.

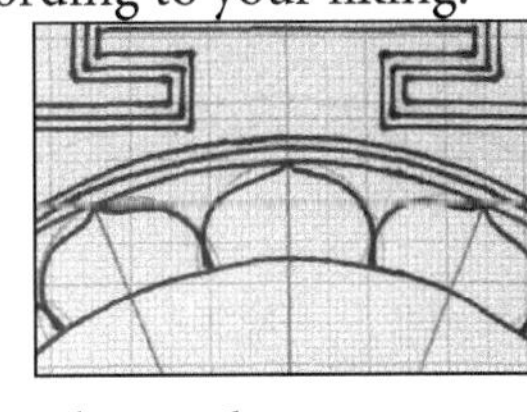

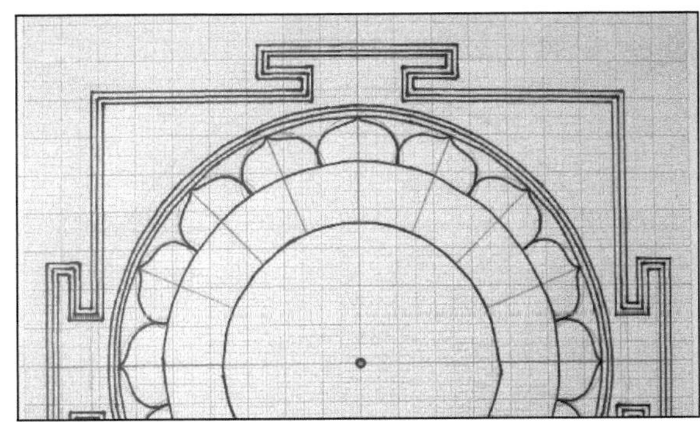

(7) Eight Petals
In the same manner, draw the
semicircle outlines of the eight
petals of the inner lotus (अष्ट-
दल-पद्म).

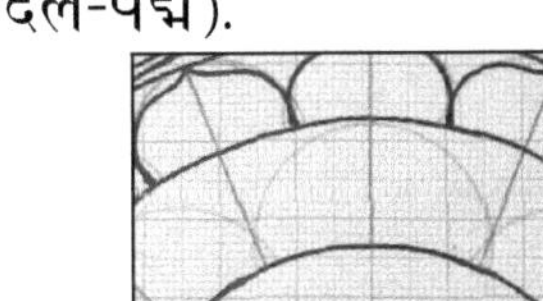

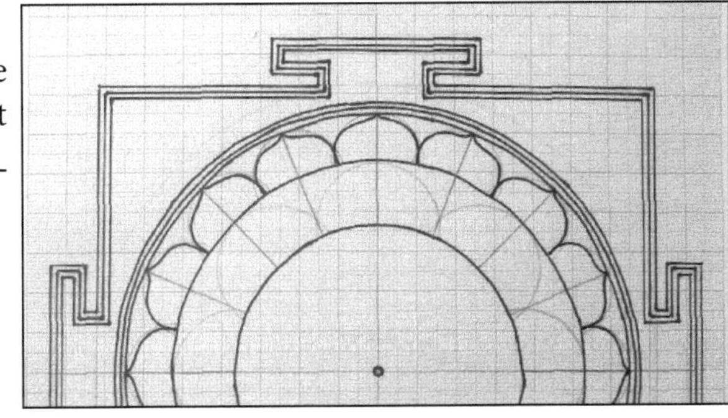

Again, draw the eight lotus
petals (अष्ट-दल) according to
your liking, using the
semicircles as guides.

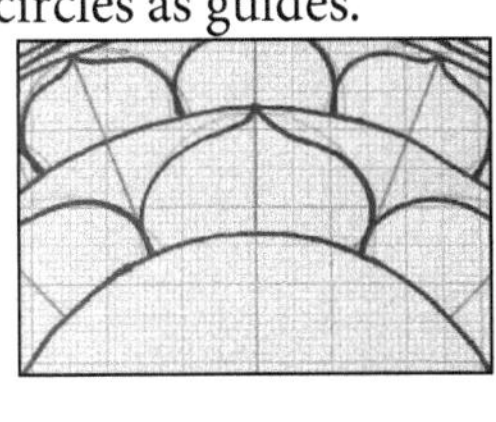

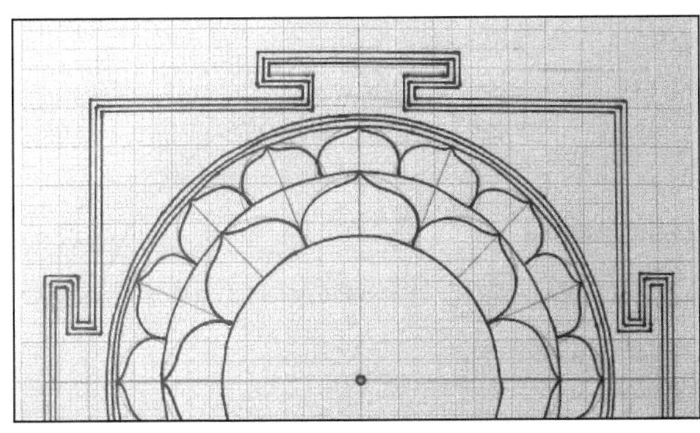

(8) Reference lines

Now we will construct the श्री-चक्र inside the inner circle, using nine triangles that indicate शक्ति. Five of them will have their apex pointing downwards, and four pointing upward. First draw six horizontal reference lines with the following distances. From the top: a4, a4 and a2, and from the bottom: a3, a5 and a4. It is very important that these measurements are exact.

(9) Triangles 1-2

Draw the first two triangles using the innermost reference lines as the base of the triangles, as depicted.

(10) Triangles 3-4

Draw triangles 3 and 4 with the apex touching the lowest and uppermost reference lines, respectively. The arms of the triangles are drawn through the intersection of the first two triangles.

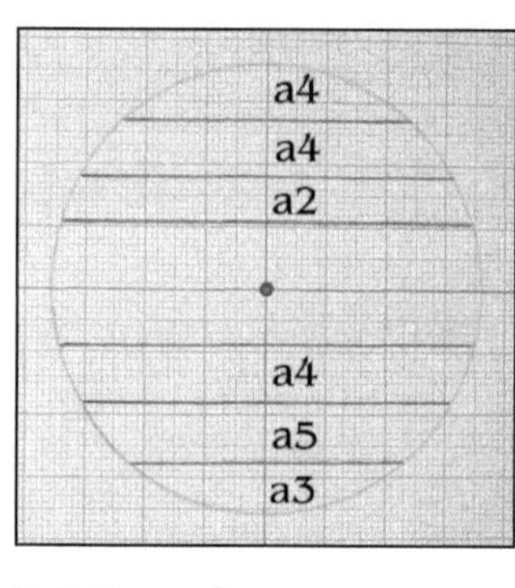
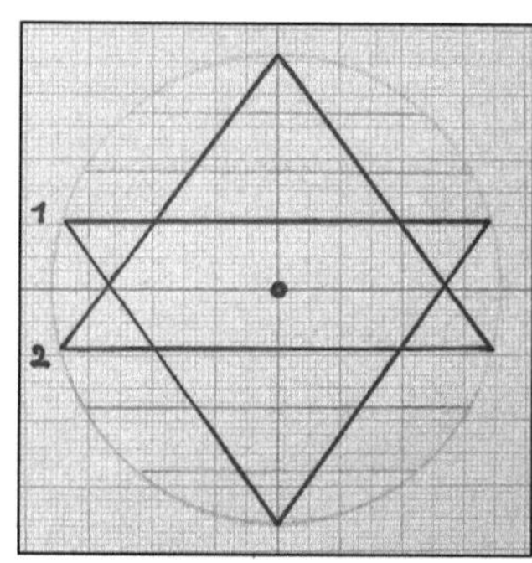
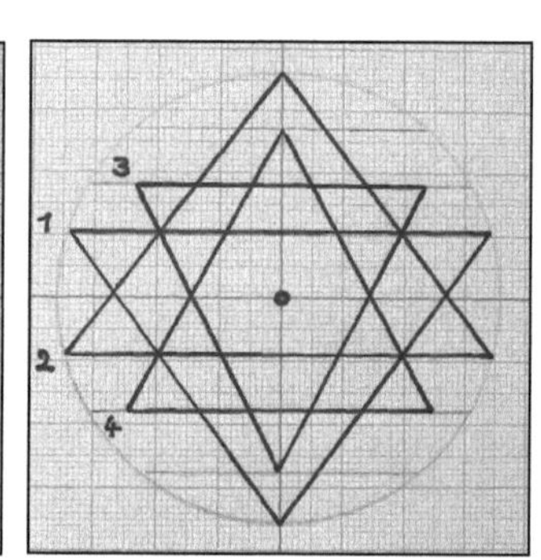

(11) Triangles 5-6

Draw a horizontal line within triangle 3. It is situated exactly between the bindu and the base of triangle 2. Now you can draw triangles 5 and 6. The apex of triangle 5 is touching the hoizontal reference line that we have just created and its arms are running through the intersections of triangles 1 and 4, and 2 and 3. The apex of triangle 6 is touching the base of triangle 1 and its arms are running through the intersections of triangles 2 and 3, and 1 and 4.

(12) Triangle 7

Now draw triangle 7. Its basis is the reference line that we created in step number (11).

(13) Triangles 8-9

The base of triangle 8 is touching the base of triangle 4 and its arms cross the intersection of triangles 6 and 7. Draw a horizontal line within triangle 7 through the intersections of triangles 5 and 6. This is the base of triangle 9. The apex of triangle 9 is touching the base of triangle 2.

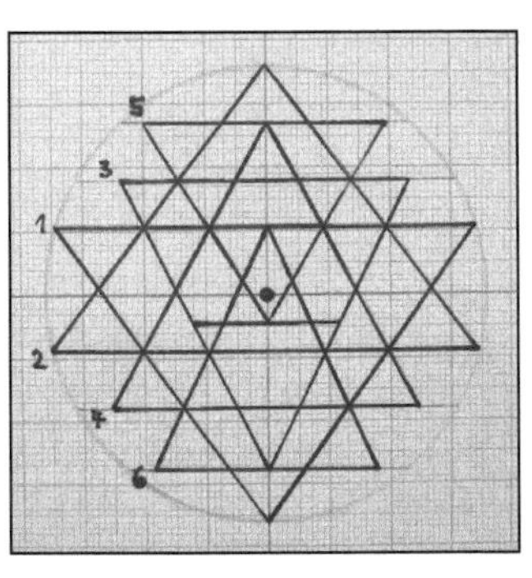
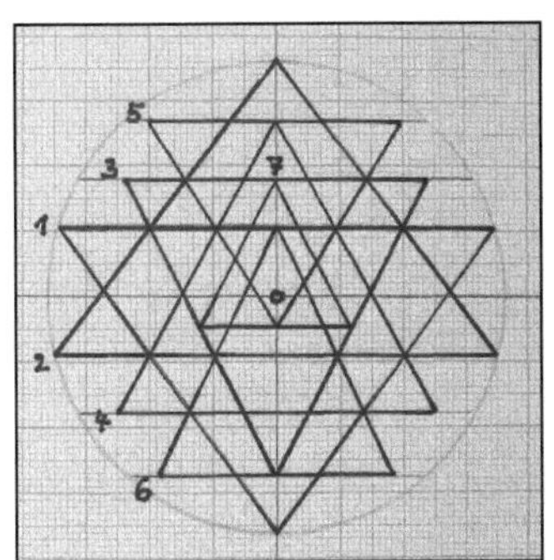
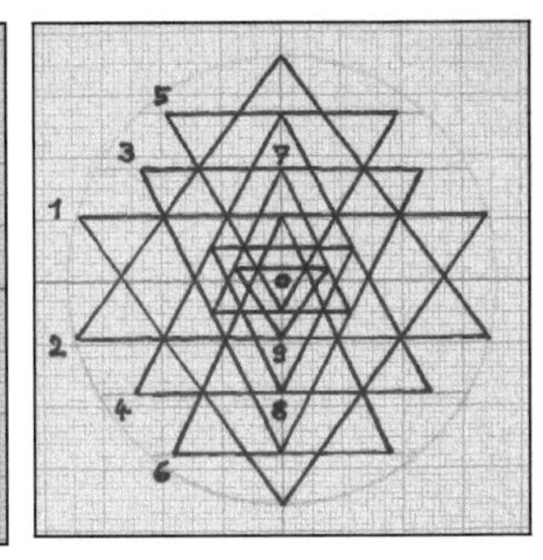

(14) Cakras

These nine triangles form fourtythree small triangles, which make up five cakras. The small triangle at the center enclosing the बिन्दु is called the त्रि-कोण-चक्र. The eight triangles surrounding it form the अष्ट-कोण-चक्र. The ten surrounding triangles form the अन्तर्दशार-चक्र, whereas the next ten surrounding triangles form the बहिर्दशार-चक्र. And finally, the outermost fourteen triangles form the चतुर्दशार-चक्र.

(15) Complete Yantra

Now you can trace all lines of the श्री-यन्त्र with a felt pen, and erase the reference lines.

(16) Simplified श्री-चक्र

Start with two reference lines with a spacing of a7 from the बिन्दु.
There are hundreds of similar यन्त्र for different deities. Below a विष्णुयन्त्र for ॐ नमो भगवते वासुदेवाय । with the outer lotus only containing twelve petals, and a simplified श्रीचक्र.

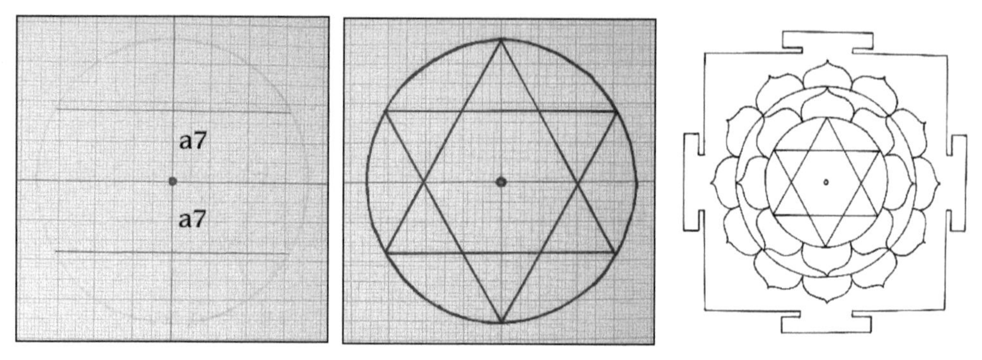

92. Bhakti

सत्सङ्गः केशवे भक्तिर् गङ्गाम्भसि निमज्जनम् । असारे खलु संसारे त्रीणि साराणि भावयेत् ॥[1107] माता च कमला देवी पिता देवो जनार्दनः । बान्धवा विष्णुभक्ताश्च स्वदेशो भुवनत्रयम् ॥[1108] भगवद्भक्तिहीनस्य जातिः शास्त्रं जपस्तपः । अप्राणस्येव देहस्य मण्डनं लोकरञ्जनम् ॥[1109]

"O sage! An activity which is prescribed in शास्त्र and aimed at हरि, that is called (साधन-) भक्ति, and by that comes परा भक्ति."[1110]

	साधन-भक्ति	प्रेम-भक्ति
also called	भजन-क्रिया	पर-, शुद्ध-, अनन्य-, उत्तम-भक्ति

आदौ श्रद्धा ततः साधु-सङ्गो ऽथ भजनक्रिया । ततो ऽनर्थनिवृत्तिः स्यात् ततो निष्ठा रुचिस्ततः ॥ अथासक्तिस्ततो भावस् ततः प्रेमाभ्युदञ्चति । साधकानामयं प्रेम्णः प्रादुर्भावे भवेत्क्रमः ॥[1111]

1. श्रद्धा, also called आस्तिक्य-बुद्धि

मन्त्रे तीर्थे द्विजे देवे दैवज्ञे भेषजे गुरौ । यादृशी भावना यस्य सिद्धिर्भवति तादृशी ॥[1112]

It is either स्वाभाविकी (natural) or aroused by the strength of convincing arguments. As the initial faith grows, that same faith is then called 5. निष्ठा, etc., and 9. प्रेम. "O भारत (Yudhiṣṭhira)! श्रद्धा saves a ceremony destroyed by wrong speech or thoughts, but correct speech and thought are not able to save a ceremony destroyed by a want of faith."[1113] Such faith in God depends on one's पुण्य:

महाप्रसादे गोविन्दे नामब्रह्मणि वैष्णवे । स्वल्पपुण्यवतां राजन् विश्वासो नैव जायते ॥[1114]

2. साधु-सङ्ग / सत्सङ्ग , '**Association** with a teacher' by hearing and initiation
सतां प्रसङ्गान्मम वीर्यसंविदो भवन्ति हृत्कर्णरसायनाः कथाः ।
तज्ज्ञोषणादाश्वपवर्गवर्त्मनि श्रद्धा रतिर्भक्तिरनुक्रमिष्यति ॥[1115]

3. भजन-क्रिया, साधन-भक्ति, **Sadhana**

4. अनर्थ-निवृत्ति ('cessation of faults')
A gradual process, passing अ-निष्ठिता (unsteadiness), where one's भक्ति is 1. उत्साहमयी ('full of enthusiasm', with the false confidence of beginners), 2. घन-तरला ('thick and thin', sporadic), 3. व्यूढ-विकल्प (with 'excessive speculation', indecision), 4. विषय-सङ्गरा (a 'struggle with विषय or sense objecs', i.e., former addictions), 5. नियम-अक्षमा ('without ability to follow rules', and 6. तरङ्ग-रङ्गिनी ('delighting in waves' of pleasure).

5. निष्ठा ('steadiness'), standard faith for the actual beginning of spiritual life
"Those who want to serve the Lord will manifest qualities like internal and external purity, austerity, and peacefulness."[1116] "When heated by fire, gold gives up its impurity (and not by other processes, like washing), and again gains its natural beauty. Similarly, by *bhakti-yoga* unto Me, the living being, removes the resultant contamination of *karma*, and then it worships Me."[1117] (... and attains Me, which is its natural position.)

6. रुचि (taste)

7. आसक्ति (attachment)

8. भाव (emotion), 54 ecstatic symptoms, beginning with अनुभाव

9. प्रेम ('love' of God)
The symptoms of भाव combine into a very individual स्थायि-भाव (steady emotion), called रस (taste, mellow), divided into 5 मुख्य-रस (शान्त-दास्य-सख्य-वात्सल्य-माधुर्य) and 7 गौण-रस. When कृष्ण returned to मथुरा, He entered the wrestling arena together with His brother बलराम and appeared thus: "For the wrestlers in रौद्र-रस as lightning, for ordinary men in अद्भुत as extraordinary person, for women in माधुर्य as incarnate Cupid, for cowherds in सख्य mixed with हास्य as their relative, for impious kings in वीर as punisher, for his parents in वात्सल्य mixed with करुण as child, for कंस in भयानक as death, for the unintelligent and worldly-minded in बीभत्स as universal form (विराट्), for the ज्ञानी in शान्त as Absolute Truth, and for the वृष्णि in दास्य as supreme worshipable Deity."[1118]
तत्ते ऽनुकम्पां सुसमीक्षमाणो भुञ्जान एवात्मकृतं विपाकम् ।
हृद्वाग्वपुर्भिर्विदधन्नमस्ते जीवेत यो मुक्तिपदे स दायभाक् ॥[1119]

साधन-भक्ति (3. above) is ruled, side by side, by external विधि (called वैधि-भक्ति) and spontaneous attraction (called राग-भक्ति).

	वैधि-भक्ति	राग-भक्ति	
or		रागानुग-, रागात्मिक-	भक्ति
also called	वैधि-	भागवत-	मार्ग
according to	पञ्चरात्रिक-	भागवत-	विधि
from	1. श्रद्धा to 7. आसक्ति	5. निष्ठा to 7. आसक्ति	
with focus on	अर्चन (worship)	स्मरण (meditation)	

वैधि-भक्ति has 64 limbs[1120], classified into nine[1121], and is thus called नव-विध-भक्ति:

(**1**) श्रवण (hearing) the Lord's नाम-रूप-गुण-लीला like परीक्षित्

(**2**) कीर्तन (chanting) like शुकदेव, esp. नाम / हरि-नाम (see **Nama**)
नाहं तिष्ठामि वैकुण्ठे योगिनां हृदयेषु वा । यत्र गायन्ति मद्भक्ताः तत्र तिष्ठामि नारद ॥[1122] कृते यद्ध्यायतो विष्णुं त्रेतायां यजतो मखैः । द्वापरे परिचर्यायां कलौ तद्धरिकीर्तनात् ॥[1123] तृणादपि सुनीचेन तरोरिव सहिष्णुना । अमानिना मानदेन कीर्तनीयः सदा हरिः ॥[1124]

(**3**) स्मरण (remembering) like प्रह्लाद
स्मर्तव्यः सततं विष्णुर् विस्मर्तव्यो न जातुचित् । सर्वे विधिनिषेधाः स्युर् एतयोरेव किङ्कराः ॥[1125] स हानिस्तन्महच्छिद्रं स मोहः स च विभ्रमः । यन्मुहूर्तं क्षणं वापि वासुदेवं न चिन्तयेत् ॥[1126]
5 stages: 1. अनुसन्धान (inquiery, research), interrupted remembrance; 2. धारणा ('sustaining' concentration), uninterrupted remembrance; 3. ध्यान ('meditation'), uninterrupted and undivided remembrance; 4. ध्रुव-अनुस्मृति ('constant remembrance'); 5. समाधि (absorption), the Lord is manifest in the heart

(**4**) सेवन (serving) like लक्ष्मी. "If there is taste and ability, one should also perform पाद-सेवा without neglecting that (स्मरण); also for the perfection of स्मरण."[1127] It includes श्री-मूर्ति-दर्शन (seeing the deity of the Lord) with परिक्रम (circumambulating it) and तीर्थ-यात्रा.
अयोध्या मथुरा माया काशी काञ्ची ह्यवन्तिका । पुरी द्वारावती चैव सप्तैता मोक्षदायिकाः ॥[1128]

(**5**) अर्चन (worshiping) like पृथु

सेवन and अर्चन constitute क्रिया-योग, practical daily duties in relation to the Lord (see **Ashtanga**). "The forest is said to be a सात्त्विक residence, the village (or city) is राजस, a gambling house तामस, but a temple ('My residence') is निर्गुण."[1129] "An image is said to be of eight kinds – made of stone (carved or as शालग्राम-शिला), wood, metal, modelled of earth, painted, made of colored sand, made in the mind, or made of jewels."[1130] "अर्चन means the offering of 64 possible articles of worship together with a मन्त्र, preceded by preliminary rituals like शुद्धि and न्यास."[1131] How to perform a simple offering: 1. recite prayers, 2. offer items like धूप-दीप-पुष्प-फल.

As परमात्मा, God is equally present in the sun, fire, etc., and even in the own body (as His tempel): "O Uddhava! The following are My places of worship: सूर्य (by Vedic hymns like the गायत्री), अग्नि (by oblations in यज्ञ), the ब्राह्मण (by hospitality), cows (गो, by feeding them), the वैष्णव (by giving honor), ether (ख, by meditation), wind (मरुत्, by understanding the importance of प्राण), water (जल, by offering water and flowers into water), earth (भू, by मन्त्र and न्यास), the own body (आत्मा, by sustaining it properly), and all beings (सर्व-भूत, by equal vision)."[1132]

"One who has performed पञ्च-संस्कार beginning with ताप, does the nine activities of worship, and knows the five objects, such a ब्राह्मण is to be known as a great devotee (महा-भागवत)." The nine activities of worship are अर्चन, मन्त्र recitation, ध्यान (योग), यज्ञ (याग), prayer (वन्दन), नाम-सङ्कीर्तन, सेवा, marking with God's symbols, and honoring (आराधन) others. The five objects are भगवान्, His abode (पद), paraphernalia (द्रव्य), and मन्त्र, and the soul (जीवात्मा).

(6) वन्दन (praising) like अक्रूर
Esp. नमस्कार/प्रणाम, which is of two types[1133]: 1. अष्टाङ्ग (also called दण्डवत्), touching the ground with arms, legs and knees, chest and head, eyes, mind and speech; 2. पञ्चाङ्ग, touching the ground with arms, legs and knees, head, mind and speech. "नमस्कार is considered यज्ञ and even the best among all यज्ञ. By a single अष्टाङ्ग नमस्कार one can reach हरि."[1134] "For those free from अहङ्कार, केशव is never far, but for those with अहङ्कार, there are ranges of mountains in between."[1135]

(7) दास्य (servitude) like हनुमान्
"'I am a servant of वासुदेव' – one who has after thousands of births this resolution, he can deliver all the worlds."[1136]

(8) सख्य (friendship) like अर्जुन, involving practices like sleeping in the temple to assist the Deity like a friend:

"In order to see the Lord like a human and to behave towards Him like a friend, some who are dedicated to attending the Deity even sleep in tempels."[1137]

(9) निवेदन/समर्पण/शरणागति (surrender) like बलि, giving up all independence: "As I am directed by a certain देव residing in the heart, so I am acting."[1138] "As one (the former owner) must not worry any more for the protection of his animal when it is sold, similarly, when offering the body unto हरि, one can/should refrain from worrying for its protection."[1139]

94. Nama

Among the items of पञ्च-संस्कार and साधन-भक्ति, नाम-कीर्तन is considered most important, by all religious schools. "Your glorification corrects all mistakes that might occur during a यज्ञ because of an improper मन्त्र, तन्त्र (ritual), देश-काल, recipient and used object."[1140]

श्रीकृष्ण गोविन्द हरे मुरारे हे नाथ नारायण वासुदेव ।
जिह्वे पिबस्वामृतमेतदेव गोविन्द दामोदर माधवेति ॥[1141]
माधवो माधवो वाचि माधवो माधवो हृदि । स्मरन्ति साधवः सर्वे सर्वकार्येषु माधवम् ॥[1142] हरेर्नाम हरेर्नाम हरेर्नामैव केवलम् । कलौ नास्त्येव नास्त्येव नास्त्येव गतिरन्यथा ॥[1143]

In the Old Testament at least twelve names are counted – God ('good'), Father (creator), etc. In some schools of Islam ninety-nine names (plus one hidden) are mentioned – Allah ('greatest'), Al-Rahman ('most merciful'), Al-Salam ('perfect'), etc. "Call upon Allah, or call upon Rahman, by *whatever name* you call upon Him (it is well). For to Him belong the most beautiful names." (Qur'an 17.110) "So chant the name of your Tremendous Lord." (Qur'an)

That names sound different in different languages does not mean that there are different Gods.

Among Sanskrit names, three are very prominent – हरि, राम and कृष्ण.
सकृदुच्चारितं येन हरिरित्यक्षरद्वयम् । बद्धः परिकरस्तेन मोक्षाय गमनं प्रति ॥[1144] रमन्ते योगिनोऽनन्ते सत्यानन्दे चिदात्मनि । इति रामपदेनासौ परं ब्रह्माभिधीयते ॥[1145] राम रामेति रामेति रमे रामे मनोरमे । सहस्रनामभिस्तुल्यं रामनाम वरानने ॥[1146] सहस्रनाम्नां पुण्यानां त्रिरावृत्त्या तु यत्फलम् । एकावृत्त्या तु कृष्णस्य नामैकं तत्प्रयच्छति ॥[1147] हरे कृष्ण हरे कृष्ण कृष्ण कृष्ण हरे हरे । हरे राम हरे राम राम राम हरे हरे ॥[1148]

Guru Granth Sahib invokes names of Krishna 10,000 times, of Rama 2,400 times, the Supersoul (Jagadish, Nirakar, Niranjan, Atma, Paramatma, Parameshwar, Antaryami, Karta) 2,600 times, personal names (Gobind, Murari, Madhav, Saligram, Vishnu, Sarangpani, Mukund, Thakur, Damodar, Vasudev, Mohan, Banwari, Madhusudan, Keshav, Chaturbhuj, etc.) 2,000 times, the Parabrahma 550 times, and Omkar 400 times.
"If you were to remove every page that contained the name of Bithal (Krishna) or Ram from the Granth, you will be left with nothing more than a few pages and the book case." (Hardyal Singh)

गणेश

शुक्लाम्बरधरं देवं शशिवर्णं चतुर्भुजम्। प्रसन्नवदनं ध्यायेत् सर्वविघ्नोपशान्तये ॥1149 वक्रतुण्ड महाकाय सूर्यकोटिसमप्रभ। निर्विघ्नं कुरु मे देव शुभकार्येषु सर्वदा ॥1150 प्रणम्य शिरसा देवं गौरीपुत्रं विनायकम्। भक्तावासं स्मरेन्नित्यम् आयुःकामार्थसिद्धये ॥1151 अभीप्सितार्थसिद्ध्यर्थं पूजितो यः सुरासुरैः। सर्वविघ्नहरस्तस्मै गणाधिपतये नमः ॥1152 गजवक्त्रं सुरश्रेष्ठं कर्ण-चामरभूषितम्। पाशाङ्कुशधरं देवं वन्दे ऽहं गणनायकम् ॥1153

ॐ महागणपतये नमो नमः। निर्विघ्नं कुरु ।1154

गुरु

अज्ञानतिमिरान्धस्य ज्ञानाञ्जनशलाकया। चक्षुरुन्मीलितं येन तस्मै श्रीगुरवे नमः ॥1155 गुरुर्ब्रह्मा गुरुर्विष्णुर् गुरुर्देवो महेश्वरः। गुरुः साक्षात्परं ब्रह्म तस्मै श्रीगुरवे नमः ॥1156 ध्यानमूलं गुरोर्मूर्तिः पूजामूलं गुरोः पदम्। मन्त्रमूलं गुरोर्वाक्यं मोक्षमूलं गुरोः कृपा ॥1157

ॐ गुरुदेवाय विद्महे परब्रह्मणे धीमहि। तन्नो गुरुः प्रचोदयात् ॥1158

ऋषि

कूजन्तं राम रामेति मधुरं मधुराक्षरम्। आरुह्य कविताशाखां वन्दे वाल्मीकि-कोकिलम् ॥1159

नमो ऽस्तु ते व्यास विशालबुद्धे फुल्लारविन्दायतपत्रनेत्र।
येन त्वया भारततैलपूर्णः प्रज्वालितो ज्ञानमयः प्रदीपः ॥1160

यं प्रव्रजन्तमनुपेतमपेतकृत्यं द्वैपायनो विरहकातर आजुहाव।
पुत्रेति तन्मयतया तरवो ऽभिनेदुस् तं सर्वभूतहृदयं मुनिमानतो ऽस्मि ॥
यः स्वानुभावमखिलश्रुतिसारमेकम् अध्यात्मदीपमतितितीर्षतां तमो ऽन्धम्।
संसारिणां करुणयाह पुराणगुह्यं तं व्याससूनुमुपयामि गुरुं मुनीनाम् ॥1161

योगेन चित्तस्य पदेन वाचां मलं शरीरस्य च वैद्यकेन।
यो ऽपाकरोत्तं प्रवरं मुनीनां पतञ्जलिं प्राञ्जलिरानतो ऽस्मि ॥1162

सूर्य

नमः सवित्रे सूर्याय भास्कराय विवस्वते। आदित्यायादिभूताय देवादीनां नमो नमः ॥1163

या देवी सर्वभूतेषु विद्यारूपेण संस्थिता। नमस्तस्यै नमस्तस्यै नमस्तस्यै नमो नमः ॥1164

96. Ashirvada

विद्यार्थी प्राप्नुयाद्विद्यां धनकामो धनं तथा। आयुष्कामस्तथैवायुः श्रीकामो महतीं श्रियम् ॥1165 सर्वे भवन्तु सुखिनः सर्वे सन्तु निरामयाः। सर्वे भद्राणि पश्यन्तु मा कश्चिद्दुःखभाग्भवेत् ॥1166

स्वस्ति प्रजाभ्यः परिपालयन्तां न्यायेन मार्गेण महीं महीशाः।
गोब्राह्मणेभ्यः शुभमस्तु नित्यं लोकाः समस्ताः सुखिनो भवन्तु ॥1167

ॐ स ह नाववतु। स ह नौ भुनक्तु। सह वीर्यं करवावहै। तेजस्वि नावधीतमस्तु। मा विद्विषावहै। ॐ शान्तिः शान्तिः शान्तिः ।1168

सं गच्छध्वं सं वदध्वं सं वो मनांसि जानताम्। देवा भागं यथा पूर्वे सञ्जानाना उपासते ॥

समानो मन्त्रः समितिः समानी समानं मनः सह चित्तमेषाम्।
समानं मन्त्रमभिमन्त्रये वः समानेन वो हविषा जुहोमि ॥

समानी व आकूतिः समाना हृदयानि वः। समानमस्तु वो मनो यथा वः सुसहासति ॥1169

ॐ असतो मा सद्गमय। तमसो मा ज्योतिर्गमय। मृत्योर्मा अमृतं गमय। ॐ शान्तिः शान्तिः शान्तिः ।1170

97. Raksha

अन्यथा शरणं नास्ति त्वमेव शरणं मम। तस्मात्कारुण्यभावेन रक्ष रक्ष जनार्दन ॥1171 वनमाली गदी शार्ङ्गी शङ्खी चक्री च नन्दकी। श्रीमान्नारायणो विष्णुर् वासुदेवो ऽभिरक्षतु ॥1172 कृष्ण कृष्ण महाबाहो भक्तानामभयङ्कर। त्वमेको दह्यमानानाम् अपवर्गो ऽसि संसृतेः ॥1173

ॐ ओजो ऽस्योजो मे दाः स्वाहा। ॐ सहो ऽसि सहो मे दाः स्वाहा। ॐ बलमसि बलं मे दाः स्वाहा। ॐ आयुरस्यायुर्मे दाः स्वाहा। ॐ श्रोत्रमसि श्रोत्रं मे दाः स्वाहा। ॐ चक्षुरसि चक्षुर्मे दाः स्वाहा। ॐ परिपाणमसि परिपाणं मे दाः स्वाहा ।1174

ॐ प्राणापानौ मृत्योर्मा पातं स्वाहा। ॐ द्यावापृथिवी उपश्रुत्या मा पातं स्वाहा। ॐ सूर्य चक्षुषा मा पाहि स्वाहा। ॐ अग्ने वैश्वानर विश्वैर्मा देवैः पाहि स्वाहा। ॐ विश्वम्भर विश्वेन मा भरसा पाहि स्वाहा ।।1175

राम-रक्षा-स्तोत्रम् 1176

शिरो मे राघवः पातु भालं दशरथात्मजः। कौसल्येयो दृशौ पातु विश्वामित्रप्रियः श्रुतौ ।।1177 घ्राणं पातु मखत्राता मुखं सौमित्रवत्सलः। जिह्वां विद्यानिधिः पातु कण्ठं भरतवन्दितः ।।1178 स्कन्धौ दिव्यायुधः पातु भुजौ भग्नेशकार्मुकः। करौ सीतापतिः पातु हृदयं जामदग्न्यजित् ।।1179 मध्यं पातु खरध्वंसी नाभिं जाम्बवदाश्रयः। सुग्रीवेशः कटी पातु सक्थिनी हनुमत्प्रभुः ।।1180 ऊरू रघूत्तमः पातु रक्षःकुलविनाशकृत्। जानुनी सेतुकृत्पातु जङ्घे दशमुखान्तकः। पादौ विभीषणश्रीदः पातु रामो ऽखिलं वपुः ।।1181

98. Ishta-Deva

विष्णु

मङ्गलं भगवान्विष्णुर् मङ्गलं गरुडध्वजः। मङ्गलं पुण्डरीकाक्षो मङ्गलायतनो हरिः ।।1182 सर्वदा सर्वकार्येषु नास्ति तेषाममङ्गलम्। येषां हृदिस्थो भगवान् मङ्गलायतनो हरिः ।।1183 लाभस्तेषां जयस्तेषां कुतस्तेषां पराजयः। येषामिन्दीवर-श्यामो हृदयस्थो जनार्दनः ।।1184 सर्ववेदेषु यत्पुण्यं सर्वतीर्थेषु यत्फलम्। तत्फलं समवाप्नोति स्तुत्वा देवं जनार्दनम् ।।1185

तदेव लग्नं सुदिनं तदेव ताराबलं चन्द्रबलं तदेव।
विद्याबलं दैवबलं तदेव लक्ष्मीपते ते ऽङ्घ्रियुगं स्मरामि ।।1186
करारविन्देन पादारविन्दं मुखारविन्दे विनिवेशयन्तम्।
वटस्य पत्रस्य पुटे शयानं बालं मुकुन्दं मनसा स्मरामि ।।1187

वासुदेवपरा वेदा वासुदेवपरा मखाः। वासुदेवपरा योगा वासुदेवपराः क्रियाः ।। वासुदेवपरं ज्ञानं वासुदेवपरं तपः। वासुदेवपरो धर्मो वासुदेवपरा गतिः ।।1188 नमः समस्तभूतानाम् आदिभूताय भूभृते। अनेकरूपरूपाय विष्णवे प्रभविष्णवे ।।1189 वासनाद्वासुदेवस्य वासितं भुवनत्रयम्। सर्वभूतनिवासो ऽसि वासुदेव नमो ऽस्तु ते ।।1190 विष्णुं जिष्णुं महाविष्णुं प्रभविष्णुं महेश्वरम्। अनेकरूपं दैत्यान्तं नमामि पुरुषोत्तमम् ।।1191

नमो ऽस्त्वनन्ताय सहस्रमूर्तये सहस्रपादाक्षिशिरोरुबाहवे।
सहस्रनाम्ने पुरुषाय शाश्वते सहस्रकोटीयुगधारिणे नमः ।।1192

शान्ताकारं भुजगशयनं पद्मनाभं सुरेशं
विश्वाधारं गगनसदृशं मेघवर्णं शुभाङ्गम् ।
लक्ष्मीकान्तं कमलनयनं योगिभिर्ध्यानगम्यं
वन्दे विष्णुं भवभयहरं सर्वलोकैकनाथम् ॥1193

यं ब्रह्मा वरुणेन्द्ररुद्रमरुतः स्तुन्वन्ति दिव्यैः स्तवैर्
वेदैः साङ्गपदक्रमोपनिषदैर्गायन्ति यं सामगाः ।
ध्यानावस्थिततद्गतेन मनसा पश्यन्ति यं योगिनो
यस्यान्तं न विदुः सुरासुरगणा देवाय तस्मै नमः ॥1194

वन्दे वन्द्यं सदानन्दं वासुदेवं निरञ्जनम् । इन्दिरापतिमाद्यादि-वरदेशवरप्रदम् ॥1195

ॐ नारायणाय विद्महे वासुदेवाय धीमहि । तन्नो विष्णुः प्रचोदयात् ॥1196

__________ राम __________

कौसल्यासुप्रजाराम पूर्वा सन्ध्या प्रवर्तते । उत्तिष्ठ नरशार्दूल कर्तव्यं
दैवमाह्निकम् ॥1197 रामाय रामभद्राय रामचन्द्राय वेधसे । रघुनाथाय नाथाय
सीतायाः पतये नमः ॥1198 आपदामपहर्तारं दातारं सर्वसम्पदाम् । लोकाभिरामं
श्रीरामं भूयो भूयो नमाम्यहम् ॥1199 दक्षिणे लक्ष्मणो यस्य वामे च जनकात्मजा ।
पुरतो मारुतिर्यस्य तं वन्दे रघुनन्दनम् ॥1200

लोकाभिरामं रणरङ्गधीरं राजीवनेत्रं रघुवंशनाथम् ।
कारुण्यरूपं करुणाकरं तं श्रीरामचन्द्रं शरणं प्रपद्ये ॥1201

श्रीराम राम रघुनन्दन राम राम श्रीराम राम भरताग्रज राम राम ।
श्रीराम राम रणकर्कश राम राम श्रीराम राम शरणं भव राम राम ॥1202

ॐ रघुवंश्याय विद्महे सीतावल्लभाय धीमहि । तन्नो रामः प्रचोदयात् ॥1203
ॐ दाशरथाय विद्महे सीतावल्लभाय धीमहि । तन्नो रामः प्रचोदयात् ॥1204

__________ कृष्ण __________

उत्तिष्ठोत्तिष्ठ गोविन्द उत्तिष्ठ गरुडध्वज । उत्तिष्ठ कमलाकान्त त्रैलोक्यं मङ्गलं
कुरु ॥1205 नमो ब्रह्मण्यदेवाय गोब्राह्मणहिताय च । जगद्धिताय कृष्णाय
गोविन्दाय नमो नमः ॥1206 वसुदेवसुतं देवं कंसचाणूरमर्दनम् । देवकीपरमानन्दं
कृष्णं वन्दे जगद्गुरुम् ॥1207 कृष्णाय वासुदेवाय देवकीनन्दनाय च ।
नन्दगोपकुमाराय गोविन्दाय नमो नमः ॥ नमः पङ्कजनाभाय नमः पङ्कजमालिने ।
नमः पङ्कजनेत्राय नमस्ते पङ्कजाङ्घ्रये ॥ जन्मैश्वर्यश्रुतश्रीभिर एधमानमदः पुमान् ।
नैवार्हत्यभिधातुं वै त्वामकिञ्चनगोचरम् ॥1208 हे कृष्ण करुणासिन्धो दीनबन्धो
जगत्पते । गोपेश गोपिकाकान्त राधाकान्त नमो ऽस्तु ते ॥1209

ॐ दामोदराय विद्महे वासुदेवाय धीमहि । तन्नः कृष्णः प्रचोदयात् ॥१२१०

शिव

मङ्गलं भगवान् शम्भुर् मङ्गलं वृषभध्वजः । मङ्गलं पार्वतीनाथो मङ्गलायतनो हरः ॥१२११ नमः शिवाय गुरवे सच्चिदानन्दमूर्तये । निष्प्रपञ्चाय शान्ताय निरालम्बाय तेजसे ॥१२१२ शिवं शिवकरं शान्तं शिवात्मानं शिवोत्तमम् । शिवमार्गप्रणेतारं प्रणतो ऽस्मि सदाशिवम् ॥१२१३ सिद्धिः साध्ये सतामस्तु प्रसादात्तस्य धूर्जटेः । जाह्नवीफेनलेखेव यन्मूर्ध्नि शशिनः कला ॥१२१४ त्रयम्बकं यजामहे सुगन्धिं पुष्टिवर्धनम् । उर्वारुकमिव बन्धनान् मृत्योर्मुक्षीय मामृतात् ॥१२१५

ॐ महादेवाय विद्महे रुद्रमूर्तये धीमहि । तन्नः शिवः प्रचोदयात् ॥१२१६

ॐ तत्पुरुषाय विद्महे महादेवाय धीमहि । तन्नो रुद्रः प्रचोदयात् ॥१२१७

ॐ सदाशिवाय विद्महे सहस्राक्ष्याय धीमहि । तन्नः साम्बः प्रचोदयात् ॥१२१८

ॐ नमः शिवाय ।

लक्ष्मी

पद्मासने स्थिते देवि परब्रह्मस्वरूपिणि । सर्वदुःखहरे देवि महालक्ष्मि नमो ऽस्तु ते ॥१२१९ नमस्ते ऽस्तु महामाये श्रीपीठे सुरपूजिते । शङ्खचक्रगदाहस्ते महालक्ष्मि नमो ऽस्तुते ॥१२२०

दुर्गा

सर्वमङ्गलमङ्गल्ये शिवे सर्वार्थसाधिके । शरण्ये त्र्यम्बके गौरि नारायणि नमो ऽस्तु ते ॥१२२१

सरस्वती-अष्टोत्तरशत-नामावलि १२२२

सरस्वत्यै _ महा-भद्रायै _ महा-मायायै _ वर-प्रदायै _ श्री-प्रदायै _ पद्म-निलयायै _ पद्माक्ष्यै _ पद्म-वक्त्रकायै _ शिवानुजायै _ पुस्तक-भृते _ ज्ञान-मुद्रायै _ रमायै _ परायै _ काम-रूपायै _ महा-विद्यायै _ महा-पातक-नाशिन्यै _ महाश्रयायै _ मालिन्यै _ महा-भोगायै _ महा-भुजायै _ महा-भागायै _ महोत्साहायै _ दिव्याङ्गायै _ सुर-वन्दितायै _ महा-काल्यै _ महा-पाशायै _ महा-कारायै _ महाङ्कुशायै _ पीतायै _ विमलायै _ विश्वायै _ विद्युन्मालायै _ वैष्णव्यै _ चन्द्रिकायै _ चन्द्र-वदनायै _ चन्द्र- लेख-विभूषितायै _ सावित्र्यै _ सुरसायै _ देव्यै _ दिव्यालङ्कार-भूषितायै _ वाग्देव्यै _ वसु-दायै _ तीव्रायै _ महा-भद्रायै _ महा-बलायै _ भोग-दायै _ भारत्यै _ भामायै _ गोविन्दायै _ गोमत्यै _ शिवायै _ जटिलायै _ विन्ध्य-वासायै _ विन्ध्याचल-विराजितायै _ चण्डिकायै _ वैष्णव्यै _ ब्राह्मयै _ ब्रह्म-ज्ञानैक-साधनायै _ सौदामिन्यै _ सुधा-मूर्त्यै _ सुभद्रायै _ सुर-पूजितायै _ सुवासिन्यै _ सुनासायै _ विनिद्रायै _ पद्म-लोचनायै _ विद्या-रूपायै _ विशालाक्ष्यै _ ब्रह्म-जायायै _ महा-फलायै _ त्रयी-मूर्त्यै _ त्रि-काल-ज्ञायै _ त्रि-गुणायै _

शास्त्र-रूपिण्यै _ शुम्भासुर-प्रमथिन्यै _ शुभ-दायै _ स्वरात्मिकायै _ रक्त-बीज-निहन्त्यै _ चामुण्डायै _ अम्बिकायै _ मुण्ड-काय-प्रहरणायै _ धूम्रलोचन-मर्दन्यै _ सर्व-देव-स्तुतायै _ सौम्यायै _ सुरासुर-नमस्कृतायै _ काल-रात्र्यै _ कला-धारायै _ रूप-सौभाग्य-दायिन्यै _ वाग्देव्यै _ वरारोहायै _ वाराह्यै _ वारिजासनायै _ चित्राम्बरायै _ चित्र-गन्धायै _ चित्र-माल्य-विभूषितायै _ कान्तायै _ काम-प्रदायै _ वन्द्यायै _ विद्या-धर-सुपूजितायै _ श्वेताननायै _ नील-भुजायै _ चतुर्वर्ग-फल-प्रदायै _ चतुरानन-साम्राज्यायै _ रक्त-मध्यायै _ निरञ्जनायै _ हंसासनायै _ नील-जङ्घायै _ ब्रह्म-विष्णु-शिवात्मिकायै

_____________ तुलसी _____________

वृन्दायै तुलसीदेव्यै प्रियायै कशवस्य च। विष्णुभक्तिप्रदे देवि सत्यवत्यै नमो नमः ॥१२२३ यानि कानि च पापानि ब्रह्महत्यादिकानि च। तानि तानि प्रणश्यन्ति प्रदक्षिणपदे पदे ॥१२२४

_____________ पञ्च-कन्या _____________

अहल्या द्रौपदी सीता तारा मन्दोदरी तथा। पञ्चकन्याः स्मरेन्नित्यं महापातकनाशिनीम् ॥१२२५

——————— स्नान ———————

——————— रुद्राक्षावली, श्री-यन्त्र ———————

——————— प्राणायाम ———————

——————— आचमन ———————

नमामि गङ्गे तव पादपङ्कजं सुरासुरैर्वन्दितदिव्यरूपम् ।
भुक्तिं च मुक्तिं च ददासि नित्यं भावानुसारेण सदा नराणाम् ॥1226

गङ्गे च यमुने चैव गोदावरि सरस्वति । नर्मदे सिन्धो कावेरि जले ऽस्मिन्सन्निधिं
कुरु ॥1227

ॐ केशवाय नमः । ॐ नारायणाय नमः । ॐ माधवाय नमः ।1228

——————— न्यास ———————

ॐ केशवाय नमः । _ नारायणाय _ माधवाय _ गोविन्दाय _ विष्णवे _ मधुसूदनाय
_ त्रिविक्रमाय _ वामनाय _ श्रीधराय _ हृषीकेशाय _ पद्मनाभाय _ दामोदराय _ plus
ॐ वासुदेवाय नमः ।1229

——————— मार्जन ———————

आपो हि ष्ठा मयोभुवस् ता न ऊर्जे दधातन । महे रणाय चक्षसे ॥
यो वः शिवतमो रसस् तस्य भाजयतेह नः । उशतीरिव मातरः ॥
तस्मा अरं गमाम वो यस्य क्षयाय जिन्वथ । आपो जनयथा च नः ॥1230

——————— अघ-मर्षण ———————

——————— मानसिक-स्नान ———————

अपवित्रः पवित्रो वा सर्वावस्थां गतो ऽपि वा । यः स्मरेत्पुण्डरीकाक्षं स
बाह्याभ्यन्तरः शुचिः ॥1231

——————— गणपति-पूजन ———————

——————— स्वस्ति-वाचन ———————

उत्थान

कराग्रे वसते लक्ष्मीः करमध्ये सरस्वती। करमूले तु गोविन्दः प्रभाते कर-
दर्शनम् ॥1232 समुद्रवसने देवि पर्वतस्तनमण्डिते। विष्णुपत्नि नमस्तुभ्यं पादस्पर्श
क्षमस्व मे ॥1233

नेत्र-प्रक्षालन, दन्त-धावन

आयुर्बलं यशो वर्चं प्रजाः पशून्वसूनि च। ब्रह्म प्रज्ञां च मेधां च त्वं नो धेहि
वनस्पते ॥1234

प्रातः-स्मरणम्

प्रातः स्मरामि हृदि संस्फुरदात्मतत्त्वं सच्चित्सुखं परमहंसगतिं तुरीयम्।
यत्स्वप्नजागरसुषुप्तिमवैति नित्यं तद् ब्रह्म निष्कलमहं न च भूतसङ्घः ॥1235
प्रातर्भजामि मनसां वचसामगम्यं वाचो विभान्ति निखिला यदनुग्रहेण।
यन्नेतिनेतिवचनैर्निगमा अवोचंस् तं देवदेवमजमच्युतमाहुरग्रयम् ॥1236
प्रातर्नमामि तमसः परमर्कवर्णं पूर्णं सनातनपदं पुरुषोत्तमाख्यम्।
यस्मिन्निदं जगदशेषमशेषमूर्तौ रज्ज्वां भुजङ्गम इव प्रतिभासितं वै ॥1237

शुद्धि

अर्घ्य

गायत्री-जप

ॐ तत्सवितुर्वरेण्यं भर्गो देवस्य धीमहि। धीयो यो नः प्रचोदयात् ॥1238
ॐ भूर्भुवः स्वः। तत्सवितुर्वरेण्यं भर्गो देवस्य धीमहि। धीयो यो नः
प्रचोदयात् ॥1239

सूर्य-अष्टकम्

आदिदेवं नमस्तुभ्यं प्रसीद मम भास्कर। दिवाकर नमस्तुभ्यं प्रभाकर नमो ऽस्तु
ते ॥1240 सप्ताश्वरथमारूढं प्रचण्डं कश्यपात्मजम्। श्वेतपद्मधरं देवं तं सूर्यं
प्रणमाम्यहम् ॥1241 लोहितं रथमारूढं सर्वलोकपितामहम्। महापापहरं देवं तं सूर्यं
प्रणमाम्यहम् ॥1242 त्रैगुण्यं च महाशूरं ब्रह्माविष्णुमहेश्वरम्। महापापहरं देवं तं
सूर्यं प्रणमाम्यहम् ॥1243 बृंहितं तेजःपुञं च वायुमाकाशमेव च। प्रभुं च
सर्वलोकानां तं सूर्यं प्रणमाम्यहम् ॥1244 बन्धूकपुष्पसङ्काशं हारकुण्डलभूषितम्।
एकचक्रधरं देवं तं सूर्यं प्रणमाम्यहम् ॥1245 तं सूर्यं जगत्कर्तारं महातेजः-

प्रदीपनम्। महापापहरं देवं तं सूर्यं प्रणमाम्यहम् ॥1246 तं सूर्यं जगतां नाथं ज्ञानविज्ञानमोक्षदम्। महापापहरं देवं तं सूर्यं प्रणमाम्यहम् ॥1247

___________ सूर्य-कवच-स्तोत्रम् 1248 ___________

शृणुष्व मुनिशार्दूल सूर्यस्य कवचं शुभम्। शरीरारोग्यदं दिव्यं सर्वसौभाग्य-दायकम् ॥1249 देदीप्यमानमुकुटं स्फुरन्मकरकुण्डलम्। ध्यात्वा सहस्रकिरणं स्तोत्रमेतदुदीरयेत् ॥1250 शिरो मे भास्करः पातु ललाटं मे जमितद्युतिः। नेत्रे दिनमणिः पातु श्रवणे वासरेश्वरः ॥1251 घ्राणं घर्मघृणिः पातु वदनं वेदवाहनः। जिह्वां मे मानदः पातु कण्ठं मे सुरवन्दितः ॥1252 स्कन्धौ प्रभाकरः पातु वक्षः पातु जनप्रियः। पातु पादौ द्वादशात्मा सर्वाङ्गं सकलेश्वरः ॥1253

___________ आदित्य-हृदयम् 1254 ___________

आदित्यहृदयं पुण्यं सर्वशत्रुविनाशनम्। जयावहं जपेन्नित्यम् अक्षय्यं परमं शिवम् ॥ सर्वमङ्गलमाङ्गल्यं सर्वपापप्रणाशनम्। चिन्ताशोकप्रशमनम् आयुर्वर्धनमुत्तमम् ॥1255 रश्मिमन्तं समुद्यन्तं देवासुरनमस्कृतम्। पूजयस्व विवस्वन्तं भास्करं भुवनेश्वरम् ॥1256 सर्वदेवात्मको ह्येष तेजस्वी रश्मिभावनः। एष देवासुरगणाँल् लोकान्पाति गभस्तिभिः ॥1257 एष ब्रह्मा च विष्णुश्च शिवः स्कन्दः प्रजापतिः। महेन्द्रो धनदः कालो यमः सोमो ह्यपां पतिः ॥ पितरो वसवः साध्या ह्यश्विनौ मरुतो मनुः। वायुर्वह्निः प्रजाप्राण ऋतुकर्ता प्रभाकरः ॥1258 आदित्यः सविता सूर्यः खगः पूषा गभस्तिमान्। सुवर्णसदृशो भानुर् हिरण्यरेता दिवाकरः ॥1259 हरिदश्वः सहस्रार्चिः सप्तसप्तिर्मरीचिमान्। तिमिरोन्मथनः शम्भुस् त्वष्टा मार्ताण्ड अंशुमान् ॥1260 हिरण्यगर्भः शिशिरस् तपनो भास्करो रविः। अग्निगर्भो अदितेः पुत्रः शङ्खः शिशिरनाशनः ॥1261 व्योमनाथस्तमोभेदी ऋग्यजुः-सामपारगः। घनवृष्टिरपां मित्रो विन्ध्यवीथीप्लवङ्गमः ॥1262 आतपी मण्डली मृत्युः पिङ्गलः सर्वतापनः। कविर्विश्वो महातेजाः रक्तः सर्वभवोद्भवः ॥1263 नक्षत्रग्रहताराणाम् अधिपो विश्वभावनः। तेजसामपि तेजस्वी द्वादशात्मन्नमो ऽस्तु ते ॥1264 नमः पूर्वाय गिरये पश्चिमायाद्रये नमः। ज्योतिर्गणानां पतये दिनाधिपतये नमः ॥1265 जयाय जयभद्राय हर्यश्वाय नमो नमः। नमो नमः सहस्रांशो आदित्याय नमो नमः ॥1266 नम उग्राय वीराय सारङ्गाय नमो नमः। नमः पद्मप्रबोधाय मार्ताण्डाय नमो नमः ॥1267 ब्रह्मेशानाच्युतेशाय सूर्यायादित्यवर्चसे। भास्वते सर्वभक्षाय रौद्राय वपुषे नमः ॥1268 तमोघ्नाय हिमघ्नाय शत्रुघ्नायामितात्मने। कृतघ्नघ्नाय देवाय ज्योतिषां पतये नमः ॥1269 तप्तचामीकराभाय वह्नये विश्वकर्मणे। नमस्तमोभिनिघ्नाय रुचये लोक-साक्षिणे ॥1270 नाशयत्येष वै भूतं तदेव सृजति प्रभुः। पायत्येष तपत्येष वर्षत्येष गभस्तिभिः ॥1271 एष सुप्तेषु जागर्ति भूतेषु परिनिष्ठितः। एष एवाग्निहोत्रं च

फलं चैवाग्निहोत्रिणाम् ॥1272 वेदाश्च क्रतवश्चैव क्रतूनां फलमेव च। यानि कृत्यानि लोकेषु सर्व एष रविः प्रभुः ॥1273

—————— सूर्य-अष्टोत्तरशत-नामावलि 1274 ——————

सूर्याय _ अर्यमणे _ भगाय _ त्वष्ट्रे _ पूष्णे _ अर्काय _ सवित्रे _ रवये _ गभस्तिमते _ अ-जाय _ कालाय _ मृत्यवे _ धात्रे _ प्रभा-कराय _ पृथिव्यै _ अद्भ्यो _ तेजसे _ खाय _ वायवे _ परायणाय _ सोमाय _ बृहस्पतये _ शुक्राय _ बुधाय _ अङ्गारकाय _ इन्द्राय _ विवस्वते _ दीप्तांशवे _ शुचये _ शौरये _ शनैश्चराय _ ब्रह्मणे _ विष्णवे _ रुद्राय _ स्कन्दाय _ वरुणाय _ यमाय _ वैद्युताग्नये _ जाठराग्नये _ ऐन्धनाग्नये _ तेजसां पतये _ धर्म-ध्वजाय _ वेद-कर्त्रे _ वेदाङ्गाय _ वेद-वाहनाय _ कृताय _ त्रेतायै _ द्वापराय _ सर्व-मलाश्रयाय _ कलये _ कलाकाष्ठा-मुहूर्तेभ्यो _ क्षपायै _ यामाय _ क्षणाय _ संवत्सर-कराय _ अश्वत्थाय _ काल-चक्राय _ विभावसवे _ शाश्वताय _ पुरुषाय _ योगिने _ व्यक्ताव्यक्ताय _ सनातनाय _ कालाध्यक्षाय _ प्रजाध्यक्षाय _ विश्व-कर्मणे _ तमो-नुदाय _ वरुणाय _ सागराय _ अंशवे _ जीमूताय _ जीवनाय _ अरि-घ्ने _ भूताश्रयाय _ भूत-पतये _ सर्व-लोक-नमस्कृताय _ स्त्रष्ट्रे _ संवर्तकाय _ वह्नये _ सर्वस्यादये _ अलोलुपाय _ अनन्ताय _ कपिलाय _ भानवे _ काम-दाय _ सर्वतो-मुखाय _ जयाय _ विशालाय _ वरदाय _ सर्व-भूत-निषेविताय _ मनः-सुपर्णाय _ भूतादये _ शीघ्र-गाय _ प्राण-धारकाय _ धन्वन्तरये _ धूम-केतवे _ आदि-देवाय _ अदितेः सुताय _ द्वादशात्मने _ अरविन्दाक्षाय _ पितृ-मातृ-पितामहेभ्यो _ स्वर्ग-द्वाराय _ प्रजा-द्वाराय _ मोक्ष-द्वाराय _ त्रिविष्टपाय _ देह-कर्त्रे _ प्रशान्तात्मने _ विश्वात्मने _ विश्वतो-मुखाय _ चराचरात्मने _ सूक्ष्मात्मने _ मैत्रेयाय _ करुणान्विताय ।

ॐ भास्कराय विद्महे महातेजाय धीमहि । तन्नः सूर्यः प्रचोदयात् ॥1275

मन्त्रहीनं क्रियाहीनं भक्तिहीनं सुरेश्वर । यत्पूजितं मया देव परिपूर्णं तदस्तु मे ॥[1277] अपराधसहस्त्राणि क्रियन्ते ऽहर्निशं मया । दासो ऽयमिति मां मत्वा क्षमस्व परमेश्वर ॥[1278]

अग्नि

अग्निं प्रज्वालितं वन्दे जातवेदं हुताशनम् । हिरण्यमनलं वन्दे समृद्धं विश्रतो-मुखम् ॥[1279] श्रद्धां मेधां यशः प्रज्ञां विद्यां बुद्धिं श्रियं बलम् । आयुष्यं तेज आरोग्यं देहि मे हव्यवाहन ॥[1280] दीपज्योतिः परब्रह्म दीपज्योतिर्जनार्दनः । दीपो हरतु मे पापं दीपज्योतिर्नमो ऽस्तु ते ॥[1281]

आरात्रिक (Hindi)

ॐ जय जगदीश हरे । स्वामी जय जगदीश हरे । भक्तजनों के संकट ।
दासजनों के संकट । क्षण में दूर करे । ॐ जय जगदीश हरे ।[1282]
जो ध्यावे फल पावे । दुख बिनसे मन का । स्वामी दुख बिनसे मन का ।
सुख सम्पत्ति घरे आवे । सुख सम्पत्ति घरे आवे । कष्ट मिटे तन का...।[1283]
माता पिता तुम मेरे । शरण गहूं किसकी । स्वामी शरण गहूं किसकी ।
तुम बिन और न दूजा । तुम बिन और न दूजा । आशा करूं जिसकी...।[1284]
तुम पूरण परमात्मा । तुम अन्तरयामी । स्वामी तुम अन्तरयामी ।
परब्रह्म परमेश्वर । परब्रह्म परमेश्वर । तुम सबके स्वामी...।[1285]
तुम करुणा के सागर । तुम पालन कर्ता । स्वामी तुम पालन कर्ता ।
मैं मूरख फल कामी । मैं सेवक तुम स्वामी । कृपा करो भर्ता...।[1286]
तुम हो एक अगोचर । सबके प्राणपति । स्वामी सबके प्राणपति ।
किस विधि मिलूं दयामय । किस विधि मिलूं दयामय । तुमको मैं कुमति...।[1287]
दीनबंधु दुखहर्ता । ठाकुर तुम मेरे । स्वामी रक्षक तुम मेरे ।
अपने हाथ उठाओ । अपने शरण लगाओ । द्वार पड़ा तेरे...।[1288]
विषय विकार मिटाओ । पाप हरो देव । स्वामी पाप हरो देव ।
श्रद्धा भक्ति बढ़ाओ । श्रद्धा भक्ति बढ़ाओ । संतन की सेवा...।[1289]

दामोदराष्टकम्

नमामीश्वरं सच्चिदानन्दरूपं लसत्कुन्दलं गोकुले भ्राजमानम् ।
यशोदाभियोलूखलाद्धावमानं परामृष्टमत्यन्ततोद्रुत्य गोप्या ॥[1290]
रुदन्तं मुहुर्नेत्रयुग्मं मृजन्तं कराम्भोजयुग्मेन सातङ्कनेत्रम् ।
मुहुः श्वासकम्पत्रिरेखाङ्ककण्ठ- स्थितग्रैवदामोदरं भक्तिबद्धम् ॥[1291]
इतीदृक्स्वलीलाभिरानन्दकुण्डे स्वघोषं निमज्जन्तमाख्यापयन्तम् ।
तदीयेशितज्ञेषु भक्तैर्जितत्वं पुनः प्रेमतस्तं शतावृत्ति वन्दे ॥[1292]

वरं देव मोक्षं न मोक्षावधिं वा न चान्यं वृणे ऽहं वरेशादपीह ।

  इदं ते वपुर्नाथ गोपालबालं सदा मे मनस्याविरास्तां किमन्यैः ॥1293

इदं ते मुखाम्भोजमत्यन्तनीलैर् वृतं कुन्तलैः स्निग्धरक्तैश्च गोप्या ।

  मुहुश्चुम्बितं बिम्बरक्ताधरं मे मनस्याविरास्तामलं लक्षलाभैः ॥1294

नमो देव दामोदरानन्त विष्णो प्रसीद प्रभो दुःखजालाब्धिमग्नम् ।

  कृपादृष्टिवृष्ट्यातिदीनं बतानुगृहाणेश मामज्ञमेध्यक्षिदृश्यः ॥1295

कुवेरात्मजौ बद्धमूर्त्यैव यद्वत् त्वया मोचितौ भक्तिभाजौ कृतौ च ।

  तथा प्रेमभक्तिं स्वकां मे प्रयच्छ न मोक्षे ग्रहो मे ऽस्ति दामोदरेह ॥1296

नमस्ते ऽस्तु दाम्ने स्फुरद्दीप्तिधाम्ने त्वदीयोदरायाथ विश्वस्य धाम्ने ।

  नमो राधिकायै त्वदीयप्रियायै नमो ऽनन्तलीलाय देवाय तुभ्यम् ॥1297

<h2 style="text-align:center">——————— मधुराष्टकम् ———————</h2>

अधरं मधुरं वदनं मधुरं नयनं मधुरं हसितं मधुरम् ।

  हृदयं मधुरं गमनं मधुरं मधुराधिपतेरखिलं मधुरम् ॥1298

वचनं मधुरं चरितं मधुरं वसनं मधुरं वलितं मधुरम् ।

  चलितं मधुरं भ्रमितं मधुरं मधुराधिपतेरखिलं मधुरम् ॥1299

वेणुर्मधुरो रेणुर्मधुरः पाणिर्मधुरः पादौ मधुरौ ।

  नृत्यं मधुरं सख्यं मधुरं मधुराधिपतेरखिलं मधुरम् ॥1300

गीतं मधुरं पीतं मधुरं भुक्तं मधुरं सुप्तं मधुरम् ।

  रूपं मधुरं तिलकं मधुरं मधुराधिपतेरखिलं मधुरम् ॥1301

करणं मधुरं तरणं मधुरं हरणं मधुरं रमणं मधुरम् ।

  वमितं मधुरं शमितं मधुरं मधुराधिपतेरखिलं मधुरम् ॥1302

गुञ्जा मधुरा माला मधुरा यमुना मधुरा वीची मधुरा ।

  सलिलं मधुरं कमलं मधुरं मधुराधिपतेरखिलं मधुरम् ॥1303

गोपी मधुरा लीला मधुरा युक्तं मधुरं मुक्तं मधुरम् ।

  दृष्टं मधुरं शिष्टं मधुरं मधुराधिपतेरखिलं मधुरम् ॥1304

गोपा मधुरा गावो मधुरा। यष्टिर्मधुरा सृष्टिर्मधुरा ।

  दलितं मधुरं फलितं मधुरं मधुराधिपतेरखिलं मधुरम् ॥1305

<h2 style="text-align:center">——————— निद्रा ———————</h2>

साधु वासाधु वा कर्म यद्यदाचरितं मया । तत्सर्वं भगवन्विष्णो गृहाणाराधनं
परम् ॥1306 रामं स्कन्दं हनुमन्तं वैनतेयं वृकोदरम् । शयने यः स्मरेन्नित्यं दुःस्वप्नं
तस्य नश्यति ॥1307

विष्णु-सहस्रनाम-स्तोत्रम् [1308]

ॐ विश्वं विष्णुर्वषट्कारो भूतभव्यभवत्प्रभुः । भूतकृद्भूतभृद्भावो भूतात्मा भूतभावनः ॥[1309] पूतात्मा परमात्मा च मुक्तानां परमा गतिः । अव्ययः पुरुषः साक्षी क्षेत्रज्ञो ऽक्षर एव च ॥[1310] योगो योगविदां नेता प्रधानपुरुषेश्वरः । नारसिंहवपुः श्रीमान् केशवः पुरुषोत्तमः ॥[1311] सर्वः शर्वः शिवः स्थाणुर् भूतादिर्निधिरव्ययः । सम्भवो भावनो भर्ता प्रभवः प्रभुरीश्वरः ॥[1312] स्वयम्भूः शम्भुरादित्यः पुष्कराक्षो महास्वनः । अनादिनिधनो धाता विधाता धातुरुत्तमः ॥[1313] अप्रमेयो हृषीकेशः पद्मनाभो ऽमरप्रभुः । विश्वकर्मा मनुस्त्वष्टा स्थविष्ठः स्थविरो ध्रुवः ॥[1314] अग्राह्यः शाश्वतः कृष्णो लोहिताक्षः प्रतर्दनः । प्रभूतस्त्रिककुब्धाम पवित्रं मङ्गलं परम् ॥[1315] ईशानः प्राणदः प्राणो ज्येष्ठः श्रेष्ठः प्रजापतिः । हिरण्यगर्भो भूगर्भो माधवो मधुसूदनः ॥[1316] ईश्वरो विक्रमी धन्वी मेधावी विक्रमः क्रमः । अनुत्तमो दुराधर्षः कृतज्ञः कृतिरात्मवान् ॥[1317] सुरेशः शरणं शर्म विश्वरेताः प्रजाभवः । अहः संवत्सरो व्यालः प्रत्ययः सर्वदर्शनः ॥[1318] अजः सर्वेश्वरः सिद्धः सिद्धिः सर्वादिरच्युतः । वृषाकपिरमेयात्मा सर्वयोग-विनिःसृतः ॥[1319] वसुर्वसुमनाः सत्यः समात्मा सम्मितः समः । अमोघः पुण्डरीकाक्षो वृषकर्मा वृषाकृतिः ॥[1320] रुद्रो बहुशिरा बभ्रुर् विश्वयोनिः शुचिश्रवाः । अमृतः शाश्वतस्थाणुर् वरारोहो महातपाः ॥[1321] सर्वगः सर्वविद्भानुर् विष्वक्सेनो जनार्दनः । वेदो वेदविदव्यङ्गो वेदाङ्गो वेदवित्कविः ॥[1322] लोकाध्यक्षः सुराध्यक्षो धर्माध्यक्षः कृताकृतः । चतुरात्मा चतुर्व्यूहश् चतुर्दंष्ट्रश्चतुर्भुजः ॥[1323] भ्राजिष्णुर्भोजनं भोक्ता सहिष्णुर्जगदादिजः । अनघो विजयो जेता विश्वयोनिः पुनर्वसुः ॥[1324] उपेन्द्रो वामनः प्रांशुर् अमोघः शुचिरूर्जितः । अतीन्द्रः सङ्ग्रहः सर्गो धृतात्मा नियमो यमः ॥[1325] वेद्यो वैद्यः सदायोगी वीरहा माधवो मधुः । अतीन्द्रियो महामायो महोत्साहो महाबलः ॥[1326] महाबुद्धिर्महावीर्यो महाशक्तिर्महाद्युतिः । अनिर्देश्यवपुः श्रीमान् अमेयात्मा महाद्रिधृक् ॥[1327] महेष्वासो महीभर्ता श्रीनिवासः सतां गतिः । अनिरुद्धः सुरानन्दो गोविन्दो गोविदां पतिः ॥[1328] मरीचिर्दमनो हंसः सुपर्णो भुजगोत्तमः । हिरण्यनाभः सुतपाः पद्मनाभः प्रजापतिः ॥[1329] अमृत्युः सर्वदृक् सिंहः सन्धाता सन्धिमान्स्थिरः । अजो दुर्मर्षणः शास्ता विश्रुतात्मा सुरारिहा ॥[1330] गुरुर्गुरुतमो धाम सत्यः सत्यपराक्रमः । निमिषो ऽनिमिषः स्रग्वी वाचस्पतिरुदारधीः ॥[1331] अग्रणीर्ग्रामणीः श्रीमान् न्यायो नेता समीरणः । सहस्रमूर्धा विश्वात्मा सहस्राक्षः सहस्रपात् ॥[1332] आवर्तनो निवृत्तात्मा संवृतः सम्प्रमर्दनः । अहःसंवर्तको वह्निर् अनिलो धरणीधरः ॥[1333] सुप्रसादः प्रसन्नात्मा विश्वधृग्विश्वभुग्विभुः । सत्कर्ता सत्कृतः साधुर् जह्नुर्नारायणो नरः ॥[1334] असङ्ख्येयो ऽप्रमेयात्मा विशिष्टः शिष्टकृच्छुचिः । सिद्धार्थः सिद्धसङ्कल्प सिद्धिदः सिद्धिसाधनः ॥[1335] वृषाही वृषभो विष्णुर् वृषपर्वा वृषोदरः । वर्धनो

वर्धमानश्च विविक्तः श्रुतिसागरः ॥1336 सुभुजो दुर्धरो वाग्मी महेन्द्रो वसुदो वसुः ।
नैकरूपो बृहद्रूपः शिपिविष्टः प्रकाशनः ॥1337 ओजस्तेजोद्युतिधरः प्रकाशात्मा
प्रतापनः । ऋद्धः स्पष्टाक्षरो मन्त्रश् चन्द्रांशुर्भास्करद्युतिः ॥1338 अमृतांशूद्भवो भानुः
शशबिन्दुः सुरेश्वरः । औषधं जगतः सेतुः सत्यधर्मपराक्रमः ॥1339 भूतभव्य-
भवन्नाथः पवनः पावनो ऽनलः । कामहा कामकृत्कान्तः कामः कामप्रदः
प्रभुः ॥1340 युगादिकृद्युगावर्तो नैकमायो महाशनः । अदृश्यो व्यक्तरूपश्च
सहस्रजिदनन्तजित् ॥1341 इष्टो ऽविशिष्टः शिष्टेष्टः शिखण्डी नहुषो वृषः । क्रोधहा
क्रोधकृत्कर्ता विश्वबाहुर्महीधरः ॥1342 अच्युतः प्रथितः प्राणः प्राणदो वासवानुजः ।
अपांनिधिरधिष्ठानम् अप्रमत्तः प्रतिष्ठितः ॥1343 स्कन्दः स्कन्दधरो धुर्यो वरदो
वायुवाहनः । वासुदेवो बृहद्भानुर् आदिदेवः पुरन्दरः ॥1344 अशोकस्तारणस्तारः
शूरः शौरिर्जनेश्वरः । अनुकूलः शतावर्तः पद्मी पद्मनिभेक्षणः ॥1345 पद्मनाभो
ऽरविन्दाक्षः पद्मगर्भः शरीरभृत् । महर्द्धिर्ऋद्धो वृद्धात्मा महाक्षो गरुडध्वजः ॥1346
अतुलः शरभो भीमः समयज्ञो हविर्हरिः । सर्वलक्षणलक्षण्यो लक्ष्मीवान्
समितिञ्जयः ॥1347 विक्षरो रोहितो मार्गो हेतुर्दामोदरः सहः । महीधरो महाभागो
वेगवानमिताशनः ॥1348 उद्भवः क्षोभणो देवः श्रीगर्भः परमेश्वरः । करणं कारणं
कर्ता विकर्ता गहनो गुहः ॥1349 व्यवसायो व्यवस्थानः संस्थानः स्थानदो ध्रुवः ।
परर्द्धिः परमस्पष्टस् तुष्टः पुष्टः शुभेक्षणः ॥1350 रामो विरामो विरजो मार्गो नेयो
नयो ऽनयः । वीरः शक्तिमतां श्रेष्ठो धर्मो धर्मविदुत्तमः ॥1351 वैकुण्ठः पुरुषः प्राणः
प्राणदः प्रणवः पृथुः । हिरण्यगर्भः शत्रुघ्नो व्याप्तो वायुरधोक्षजः ॥1352 ऋतुः
सुदर्शनः कालः परमेष्ठी परिग्रहः । उग्रः संवत्सरो दक्षो विश्रामो विश्व-
दक्षिणः ॥1353 विस्तारः स्थावरस्थाणुः प्रमाणं बीजमव्ययम् । अर्थो ऽनर्थो
महाकोशो महाभोगो महाधनः ॥1354 अनिर्विण्णः स्थविष्ठो भूर् धर्मयूपो महामखः ।
नक्षत्रनेमिर्नक्षत्री क्षमः क्षामः समीहनः ॥1355 यज्ञ इज्यो महेज्यश्च क्रतुः सत्रं सतां
गतिः । सर्वदर्शी विमुक्तात्मा सर्वज्ञो ज्ञानमुत्तमम् ॥1356 सुव्रतः सुमुखः सूक्ष्मः
सुघोषः सुखदः सुहृत् । मनोहरो जितक्रोधो वीरबाहुर्विदारणः ॥1357 स्वापनः
स्ववशो व्यापी नैकात्मा नैककर्मकृत् । वत्सरो वत्सलो वत्सी रत्नगर्भो
धनेश्वरः ॥1358 धर्मगुब्धर्मकृद्धर्मी सदसत्क्षरमक्षरम् । अविज्ञाता सहस्रांशुर् विधाता
कृतलक्षणः ॥1359 गभस्तिनेमिः सत्त्वस्थः सिंहो भूतमहेश्वरः । आदिदेवो महादेवो
देवेशो देवभृद्गुरुः ॥1360 उत्तरो गोपतिर्गोप्ता ज्ञानगम्यः पुरातनः । शरीरभूत-
भृद्भोक्ता कपीन्द्रो भूरिदक्षिणः ॥1361 सोमपो ऽमृतपः सोमः पुरुजित्पुरुसत्तमः ।
विनयो जयः सत्यसन्धो दाशार्हः सात्वतां पतिः ॥1362 जीवो विनयिता साक्षी
मुकुन्दो ऽमितविक्रमः । अम्भोनिधिरनन्तात्मा महोदधिशयो ऽन्तकः ॥1363 अजो
महार्हः स्वाभाव्यो जितामित्रः प्रमोदनः । आनन्दो नन्दनो नन्दः सत्यधर्मा
त्रिविक्रमः ॥1364 महर्षिः कपिलाचार्यः कृतज्ञो मेदिनीपतिः । त्रिपदस्त्रिदशाध्यक्षो
महाशृङ्गः कृतान्तकृत् ॥1365 महावराहो गोविन्दः सुषेणः कनकाङ्गदी । गुह्यो

गभीरो गहनो गुप्तश्चक्रगदाधरः ॥1366 वेधाः स्वाङ्गो ऽजितः कृष्णो दृढः सङ्कर्षणो ऽच्युतः । वरुणो वारुणो वृक्षः पुष्कराक्षो महामनाः ॥1367 भगवान् भगहानन्दी वनमाली हलायुधः । आदित्यो ज्योतिरादित्यः सहिष्णुर्गतिसत्तमः ॥1368 सुधन्वा खण्डपरशुर् दारुणो द्रविणप्रदः । दिविस्पृक्सर्वदृग्व्यासो वाचस्पतिरयोनिजः ॥1369 त्रिसामा सामगः साम निर्वाणं भेषजं भिषक् । सन्न्यासकृच्छमः शान्तो निष्ठा शान्तिः परायणम् ॥1370 शुभाङ्गः शान्तिदः स्रष्टा कुमुदः कुवलेशयः । गोहितो गोपतिर्गोप्ता वृषभाक्षो वृषप्रियः ॥1371 अनिवर्ती निवृत्तात्मा सङ्क्षेप्ता क्षेमकृच्छिवः । श्रीवत्सवक्षाः श्रीवासः श्रीपतिः श्रीमतां वरः ॥1372 श्रीदः श्रीशः श्रीनिवासः श्रीनिधिः श्रीविभावनः । श्रीधरः श्रीकरः श्रेयः-श्रीमाँल्लोकत्रयाश्रयः ॥1373 स्वक्षः स्वङ्गः शतानन्दो नन्दिज्योतिर्गणेश्वरः । विजितात्मा विधेयात्मा सत्कीर्तिश्छिन्नसंशयः ॥1374 उदीर्णः सर्वतश्चक्षुर् अनीशः शाश्वतस्थिरः । भूशयो भूषणो भूतिर् विशोकः शोकनाशनः ॥1375 अर्चिष्मानर्चितः कुम्भो विशुद्धात्मा विशोधनः । अनिरुद्धो ऽप्रतिरथः प्रद्युम्नो ऽमितविक्रमः ॥1376 कालनेमिनिहा वीरः शौरिः शूरजनेश्वरः । त्रिलोकात्मा त्रिलोकेशः केशवः केशिहा हरिः ॥1377 कामदेवः कामपालः कामी कान्तः कृतागमः । अनिर्देश्यवपुर्विष्णुर् वीरो ऽनन्तो धनञ्जयः ॥1378 ब्रह्मण्यो ब्रह्मकृद् ब्रह्मा ब्रह्म ब्रह्मविवर्धनः । ब्रह्मविद् ब्राह्मणो ब्रह्मी ब्रह्मज्ञो ब्राह्मणप्रियः ॥1379 महाक्रमो महाकर्मा महातेजा महोरगः । महाक्रतुर्महायज्वा महायज्ञो महाहविः ॥1380 स्तव्यः स्तवप्रियः स्तोत्रं स्तुतिः स्तोता रणप्रियः । पूर्णः पूरयिता पुण्यः पुण्यकीर्तिरनामयः ॥1381 मनोजवस्तीर्थकरो वसुरेता वसुप्रदः । वसुप्रदो वासुदेवो वसुर्वसुमना हविः ॥1382 सद्गतिः सत्कृतिः सत्ता सद्भूतिः सत्परायणः । शूरसेनो यदुश्रेष्ठः सन्निवासः सुयामुनः ॥1383 भूतावासो वासुदेवः सर्वासुनिलयो ऽनलः । दर्पहा दर्पदो दृप्तो दुर्धरो ऽथापराजितः ॥1384 विश्वमूर्तिर्महामूर्तिर् दीप्तमूर्तिरमूर्तिमान् । अनेकमूर्तिरव्यक्तः शतमूर्तिः शताननः ॥1385 एको नैकः सवः कः किं यत्तत्पदमनुत्तमम् । लोकबन्धुर्लोकनाथो माधवो भक्तवत्सलः ॥1386 सुवर्णवर्णो हेमाङ्गो वराङ्गश्चन्दनाङ्गदी । वीरहा विषमः शून्यो घृताशीरचलश्चलः ॥1387 अमानी मानदो मान्यो लोकस्वामी त्रिलोकधृक् । सुमेधा मेधजो धन्यः सत्यमेधा धराधरः ॥1388 तेजोवृषो द्युतिधरः सर्वशस्त्रभृतां वरः । प्रग्रहो निग्रहो व्यग्रो नैकशृङ्गो गदाग्रजः ॥1389 चतुर्मूर्तिश्चतुर्बाहुश् चतुर्व्यूहश्चतुर्गतिः । चतुरात्मा चतुर्भावश् चतुर्वेदविदेकपात् ॥1390 समावर्तो ऽनिवृत्तात्मा दुर्जयो दुरतिक्रमः । दुर्लभो दुर्गमो दुर्गो दुरावासो दुरारिहा ॥1391 शुभाङ्गो लोकसारङ्गः सुतन्तुस्तन्तुवर्धनः । इन्द्रकर्मा महाकर्मा कृतकर्मा कृतागमः ॥1392 उद्भवः सुन्दरः सुन्दो रत्ननाभः सुलोचनः । अर्को वाजसनः शृङ्गी जयन्तः सर्वविजयी ॥1393 सुवर्णबिन्दुरक्षोभ्यः सर्व-वागीश्वरेश्वरः । महाह्रदो महागर्तो महाभूतो महानिधिः ॥1394 कुमुदः कुन्दरः कुन्द पर्जन्यः पावनो ऽनिलः । अमृताशो ऽमृतवपुः सर्वज्ञः सर्वतोमुखः ॥1395 सुलभः

सुव्रतः सिद्धः शत्रुजिच्छत्रुतापनः । न्यग्रोधोदुम्बरो ऽश्वत्थश् चाणूरान्ध-
निषूदनः ॥1396 सहस्रार्चिः सप्तजिह्वः सप्तैधाः सप्तवाहनः । अमूर्तिरनघो
ऽचिन्त्यो भयकृद्भयनाशनः ॥1397 अणुर्बृहत्कृशः स्थूलो गुणभृन्निर्गुणो महान् ।
अधृतः स्वधृतः स्वास्यः प्राग्वंशो वंशवर्धनः ॥1398 भारभृत्कथितो योगी योगीशः
सर्वकामदः । आश्रमः श्रमणः क्षामः सुपर्णो वायुवाहनः ॥1399 धनुर्धरो धनुर्वेदो
दण्डो दमयिता दमः । अपराजितः सर्वसहो नियन्तानियमो ऽयमः ॥1400
सत्त्ववान्सात्त्विकः सत्यः सत्यधर्मपरायणः । अभिप्रायः प्रियार्हो ऽर्हः प्रिय-
कृत्प्रीतिवर्धनः ॥1401 विहायसगतिर्ज्योतिः सुरुचिर्हुतभुग्विभुः । रविर्विरोचनः सूर्यः
सविता रविलोचनः ॥1402 अनन्तो हुतभुग्भोक्ता सुखदो नैकजो ऽग्रजः ।
अनिर्विण्णः सदामर्षी लोकाधिष्ठानमद्भुतः ॥1403 सनात्सनातनतमः कपिलः
कपिरव्ययः । स्वस्तिदः स्वस्तिकृत्स्वस्ति स्वस्तिभुक्स्वस्तिदक्षिणः ॥1404 अरौद्रः
कुण्डली चक्री विक्रम्यूर्जितशासनः । शब्दातिगः शब्दसहः शिशिरः
शर्वरीकरः ॥1405 अक्रूरः पेशलो दक्षो दक्षिणः क्षमिणां वरः । विद्वत्तमो वीतभयः
पुण्यश्रवणकीर्तनः ॥1406 उत्तारणो दुष्कृतिहा पुण्यो दुःस्वप्ननाशनः । वीरहा
रक्षणः सन्तो जीवनः पर्यवस्थितः ॥1407 अनन्तरूपो ऽनन्तश्रीर् जितमन्युर्भयापहः ।
चतुरश्रो गभीरात्मा विदिशो व्यादिशो दिशः ॥1408 अनादिर्भूर्भुवो लक्ष्मीः सुवीरो
रुचिराङ्गदः । जननो जनजन्मादिर् भीमो भीमपराक्रमः ॥1409 आधारनिलयो धाता
पुष्पहासः प्रजागरः । ऊर्ध्वगः सत्पथाचारः प्राणदः प्रणवः पणः ॥1410 प्रमाणं
प्राणनिलयः प्राणभृत्प्राणजीवनः । तत्त्वं तत्त्वविदेकात्मा जन्ममृत्युजरातिगः ॥1411
भूर्भुवःस्वस्तरुस्तारः सविता प्रपितामहः । यज्ञो यज्ञपतिर्यज्वा यज्ञाङ्गो
यज्ञवाहनः ॥1412 यज्ञभृद्यज्ञकृद्यज्ञी यज्ञभुग्यज्ञसाधनः । यज्ञान्तकृद्यज्ञगुह्यम्
अन्नमन्नाद एव च ॥1413 आत्मयोनिः स्वयंजातो वैखानः सामगायनः । देवकी-
नन्दनः स्रष्टा क्षितीशः पापनाशनः ॥1414 शङ्खभृन्नन्दकी चक्री शार्ङ्गधन्वा गदाधरः ।
रथाङ्गपाणिरक्षोभ्यः सर्वप्रहरणायुधः ॥1415

    सर्वप्रहरणायुध ॐ नम इति ।1416

चिन्तामणिप्रकरसद्मसु कल्पवृक्ष- लक्षावृतेषु सुरभीरभिपालयन्तम् ।
लक्ष्मीसहस्रशतसम्भ्रमसेव्यमानं गोविन्दमादिपुरुषं तमहं भजामि ॥1418

वेणुं क्वणन्तमरविन्ददलायताक्षं बर्हावतंसमसिताम्बुदसुन्दराङ्गम् ।
कन्दर्पकोटिकमनीयविशेषशोभं गोविन्दमादिपुरुषं तमहं भजामि ॥1419

आलोलचन्द्रकलसद्वनमाल्यवंशी- रत्नाङ्गदं प्रणयकेलिकलाविलासम् ।
श्यामं त्रिभङ्गललितं नियतप्रकाशं गोविन्दमादिपुरुषं तमहं भजामि ॥1420

अङ्गानि यस्य सकलेन्द्रियवृत्तिमन्ति पश्यन्ति पान्ति कलयन्ति चिरं जगन्ति ।
आनन्दचिन्मयसदुज्ज्वलविग्रहस्य गोविन्दमादिपुरुषं तमहं भजामि ॥1421

अद्वैतमच्युतमनादिमनन्तरूपम् आद्यं पुराणपुरुषं नवयौवनं च ।
वेदेषु दुर्लभमदुर्लभमात्मभक्तौ गोविन्दमादिपुरुषं तमहं भजामि ॥1422

पन्थास्तु कोटिशतवत्सरसम्प्रगम्यो वायोरथापि मनसो मुनिपुङ्गवानाम् ।
सोऽप्यस्ति यत्प्रपदसीम्न्यविचिन्त्यतत्त्वे गोविन्दमादिपुरुषं तमहं भजामि ॥1423

एको ऽप्यसौ रचयितुं जगदण्डकोटिं यच्छक्तिरस्ति जगदण्डचया यदन्तः ।
अण्डान्तरस्थपरमाणुचयान्तरस्थं गोविन्दमादिपुरुषं तमहं भजामि ॥1424

यद्भावभावितधियो मनुजास्तथैव सम्प्राप्य रूपमहिमासनयानभूषाः ।
सूक्तैर्यमेव निगमप्रथितैः स्तुवन्ति गोविन्दमादिपुरुषं तमहं भजामि ॥1425

आनन्दचिन्मयरसप्रतिभाविताभिस् ताभिर्य एव निजरूपतया कलाभिः ।
गोलोक एव निवसत्यखिलात्मभूतो गोविन्दमादिपुरुषं तमहं भजामि ॥1426

प्रेमाञ्जनच्छुरितभक्तिविलोचनेन सन्तः सदैव हृदयेषु विलोकयन्ति ।
यं श्यामसुन्दरमचिन्त्यगुणस्वरूपं गोविन्दमादिपुरुषं तमहं भजामि ॥1427

रामादिमूर्तिषु कलानियमेन तिष्ठन् नानावतारमकरोद्भुवनेषु किन्तु ।
कृष्णः स्वयं समभवत्परमः पुमान्यो गोविन्दमादिपुरुषं तमहं भजामि ॥1428

यस्य प्रभा प्रभवतो जगदण्डकोटि- कोटिष्वशेषवसुधादिविभूतिभिन्नम् ।
तद् ब्रह्म निष्कलमनन्तमशेषभूतं गोविन्दमादिपुरुषं तमहं भजामि ॥1429

माया हि यस्य जगदण्डशतानि सूते त्रैगुण्यतद्विषयवेदवितायमाना ।
सत्त्वावलम्बिपरसत्त्वं विशुद्धसत्त्वं गोविन्दमादिपुरुषं तमहं भजामि ॥1430

आनन्दचिन्मयरसात्मतया मनःसु यः प्राणिनां प्रतिफलन्स्मरतामुपेत्य ।
लीलायितेन भुवनानि जयत्यजस्रं गोविन्दमादिपुरुषं तमहं भजामि ॥1431

गोलोकनाम्नि निजधाम्नि तले च तस्य देवीमहेशहरिधामसु तेषु तेषु ।
ते ते प्रभावनिचया विहिताश्च येन गोविन्दमादिपुरुषं तमहं भजामि ॥1432

सृष्टिस्थितिप्रलयसाधनशक्तिरेका छायेव यस्य भुवनानि बिभर्ति दुर्गा ।
इच्छानुरूपमपि यस्य च चेष्टते सा गोविन्दमादिपुरुषं तमहं भजामि ॥1433

क्षीरं यथा दधि विकारविशेषयोगात् सञ्जायते न हि ततः पृथगस्ति हेतोः ।
यः शम्भुतामपि तथा समुपैति कार्याद् गोविन्दमादिपुरुषं तमहं भजामि ॥1434

दीपार्चिरेव हि दशान्तरमभ्युपेत्य दीपायते विवृतहेतुसमानधर्मा ।
    यस्तादृगेव हि च विष्णुतया विभाति गोविन्दमादिपुरुषं तमहं भजामि ॥1435
यः कारणार्णवजले भजति स्म योग- निद्रामनन्तजगदण्डसरोमकूपः ।
    आधारशक्तिमवलम्ब्य परां स्वमूर्तिं गोविन्दमादिपुरुषं तमहं भजामि ॥1436
यस्यैकनिश्वसितकालमथावलम्ब्य जीवन्ति लोमविलजा जगदण्डनाथाः ।
    विष्णुर्महान्स इह यस्य कलाविशेषो गोविन्दमादिपुरुषं तमहं भजामि ॥1437
भास्वान्यथाश्मशकलेषु निजेषु तेजः स्वीयं कियत्प्रकटयत्यपि तद्वदत्र ।
    ब्रह्मा य एष जगदण्डविधानकर्ता गोविन्दमादिपुरुषं तमहं भजामि ॥1438
यत्पादपल्लवयुगं विनिधाय कुम्भ- द्वन्द्वे प्रणामसमये स गणाधिराजः ।
    विघ्नान्विहन्तुमलमस्य जगत्त्रयस्य गोविन्दमादिपुरुषं तमहं भजामि ॥1439
अग्निर्मही गगनमम्बु मरुद्दिशश्च कालस्तथात्ममनसीति जगत्त्रयाणि ।
    यस्माद्भवन्ति विभवन्ति विशन्ति यं च गोविन्दमादिपुरुषं तमहं भजामि ॥1440
यच्चक्षुरेष सविता सकलग्रहाणां राजा समस्तसुरमूर्तिरशेषतेजाः ।
    यस्याज्ञया भ्रगति सभृतकालचक्रो गोविन्दमादिपुरुषं तमहं भजामि ॥1441
धर्मोऽथ पापनिचयः श्रुतयस्तपांसि ब्रह्मादिकीटपतगावधयश्च जीवाः ।
    यद्दत्तमात्रविभवप्रकटप्रभावा गोविन्दमादिपुरुषं तमहं भजामि ॥1442
यस्त्विन्द्रगोपमथवेन्द्रमहो स्वकर्म- बन्धानुरूपफलभाजनमातनोति ।
    कर्माणि निर्दहति किन्तु च भक्तिभाजां गोविन्दमादिपुरुषं तमहं भजामि ॥1443
यं क्रोधकामसहजप्रणयादिभीति- वात्सल्यमोहगुरुगौरवसेव्यभावैः ।
    सञ्चिन्त्य तस्य सदृशीं तनुमापुरेते गोविन्दमादिपुरुषं तमहं भजामि ॥1444

श्रियः कान्ताः कान्तः परमपुरुषः कल्पतरवो
    द्रुमा भूमिश्चिन्तामणिगणमयी तोयममृतम् ।
कथा गानं नाट्यं गमनमपि वंशी प्रियसखी
    चिदानन्दं ज्योतिः परमपि तदास्वाद्यमपि च ॥1445
स यत्र क्षीराब्धिः स्रवति सुरभीभ्यश्च सुमहान्
    निमेषार्धाख्यो वा व्रजति न हि यत्रापि समयः ।
भजे श्वेतद्वीपं तमहमिह गोलोकमिति यं
    विदन्तस्ते सन्तः क्षितिविरलचाराः कतिपये ॥1446

चेतोदर्पणमार्जनं भवमहादावाग्निनिर्वापणं
श्रेयःकैरवचन्द्रिकावितरणं विद्यावधूजीवनम् ।
आनन्दाम्बुधिवर्धनं प्रतिपदं पूर्णामृतास्वादनं
सर्वात्मस्नपनं परं विजयते श्रीकृष्णसङ्कीर्तनम् ॥[1448]

नाम्नामकारि बहुधा निजसर्वशक्तिस् तत्रार्पिता नियमितः स्मरणे न कालः ।
एतादृशी तव कृपा भगवन्ममापि दुर्दैवमीदृशमिहाजनि नानुरागः ॥[1449]

तृणादपि सुनीचेन तरोरपि सहिष्णुना । अमानिना मानदेन कीर्तनीयः सदा हरिः ॥[1450]

न धनं न जनं न सुन्दरीं कवितां वा जगदीश कामये ।
मम जन्मनि जन्मनीश्वरे भवताद्भक्तिरहैतुकी त्वयि ॥[1451]
अयि नन्दतनुज किङ्करं पतितं मां विषमे भवाम्बुधौ ।
कृपया तव पादपङ्कज- स्थितधूलीसदृशं विचिन्तय ॥[1452]
नयनं गलदश्रुधारया वदनं गद्गदरुद्धया गिरा ।
पुलकैर्निचितं वपुः कदा तव नामग्रहणे भविष्यति ॥[1453]

युगायितं निमेषेण चक्षुषा प्रावृषायितम् । शून्यायितं जगत्सर्वं गोविन्दविरहेण मे ॥[1454]

आश्लिष्य वा पादरतां पिनष्टु माम् अदर्शनान्मर्महतां करोतु वा ।
यथा तथा वा विदधातु लम्पटो मत्प्राणनाथस्तु स एव नापरः ॥[1455]

श्रियो निवासो यस्योरः पानपात्रं मुखं दृशाम् । बाहवो लोकपालानां सारङ्गाणां पदाम्बुजम् ॥1456॥ भवे भवे यथा भक्तिः पादयोस्तव जायते । तथा कुरुष्व देवेश नाथस्त्वं नो यतः प्रभो ॥1457॥

त्वमेव माता च पिता त्वमेव त्वमेव बन्धुश्च सखा त्वमेव ।
त्वमेव विद्या द्रविणं त्वमेव त्वमेव सर्वं मम देवदेव ॥1458॥
कायेन वाचा मनसेन्द्रियैर्वा बुद्ध्यात्मना वा प्रकृतेः स्वभावात् ।
करोमि यद्यत्सकलं परस्मै नारायणायेति समर्पयामि ॥1459॥
समाश्रिता ये पदपल्लवप्लवं महत्पदं पुण्ययशो मुरारेः ।
भवाम्बुधिर्वत्सपदं परं पदं पदं पदं यद्विपदां न तेषाम् ॥1460॥
एतां स आस्थाय परात्मनिष्ठाम् अध्यासितां पूर्वतमैर्महर्षिभिः ।
अहं तरिष्यामि दुरन्तपारं तमो मुकुन्दाङ्घ्रिनिषेवयैव ॥1461॥
न वै जनो जातु कथञ्चनाव्रजेन् मुकुन्दसेव्यन्यवदङ्ग संसृतिम् ।
स्मरन्मुकुन्दाङ्घ्र्युपगूहनं पुनर् विहातुमिच्छेन्न रसग्रहो जनः ॥1462॥

कृष्ण त्वदीयपदपङ्कजपञ्जरान्तम् अद्यैव मे विशतु मानसराजहंसः ।
प्राणप्रयाणसमये कफवातपित्तैः कण्ठावरोधनविधौ स्मरणं कुतस्ते ॥1463॥
ये तु त्वदीयचरणाम्बुजकोशगन्धं जिघ्रन्ति कर्णविवरैः श्रुतिवातनीतम् ।
भक्त्या गृहीतचरणः परया च तेषां नापैषि नाथ हृदयाम्बुरुहात्स्वपुंसाम् ॥1464॥
तस्यारविन्दनयनस्य पदारविन्द- किञ्जल्कमिश्रतुलसीमकरन्दवायुः ।
अन्तर्गतः स्वविवरेण चकार तेषां सङ्क्षोभमक्षरजुषामपि चित्ततन्वोः ॥1465॥

Its history:

1. The original four verses, चतु:श्लोकी (2.9.33-36).

अहमेवासमेवाग्रे नान्यद्यत्सदसत्परम् । पश्चादहं यदेतच्च यो ऽवशिष्येत सो ऽस्म्यहम् ॥१४६६ ऋते ऽर्थं यत्प्रतीयेत न प्रतीयेत चात्मनि । तद्विद्यादात्मनो मायां यथाभासो यथा तमः ॥१४६७ यथा महान्ति भूतानि भूतेष्वच्चावचेष्वनु । प्रविष्टान्यप्रविष्टानि तथा तेषु न तेष्वहम् ॥१४६८ एतावदेव जिज्ञास्यं तत्त्व-जिज्ञासुनात्मनः । अन्वयव्यतिरेकाभ्यां यत्स्यात्सर्वत्र सर्वदा ॥१४६९

2. These were expanded by ब्रह्मा to नारद in ca. 150 verses (2.5.9-2.7.53).

3. The भागवतम् was then authored (not just compiled) by व्यास . After compiling all वेद, पुराण (including a first version of the भागवतम्) and महाभारत, व्यास was directed by नारद in 15 verses (1.5.8-22), how to revise the भागवतम् (which happened after the disappearence of कृष्ण). This version व्यास entrusted to his son शुकदेव .

तस्मिन्स्व आश्रमे व्यासो बदरीषण्डमण्डिते । आसीनो ऽप उपस्पृश्य प्रणिदध्यौ मनः स्वयम् ॥१४७० भक्तियोगेन मनसि सम्यक् प्रणिहिते ऽमले । अपश्यत्पुरुषं पूर्णं मायां च तदपाश्रयाम् ॥ यया सम्मोहितो जीव आत्मानं त्रिगुणात्मकम् । परो ऽपि मनुते ऽनर्थं तत्कृतं चाभिपद्यते ॥ अनर्थोपशमं साक्षाद् भक्तियोगमधोक्षजे । लोकस्याजानतो विद्वांश् चक्रे सात्वतसंहिताम् ॥ यस्यां वै श्रूयमाणायां कृष्णे परमपूरुषे । भक्तिरुत्पद्यते पुंसः शोकमोहभयापहा ॥१४७१ स संहितां भागवतीं कृत्वानुक्रम्य चात्मजम् । शुकमध्यापयामास निवृत्तिनिरतं मुनिः ॥१४७२ स वै निवृत्तिनिरतः सर्वत्रोपेक्षको मुनिः । कस्य वा बृहतीमेताम् आत्मारामः समभ्यसत् ॥१४७३ आत्मारामाश्च मुनयो निर्ग्रन्था अप्युरुक्रमे । कुर्वन्त्यहैतुकीं भक्तिम् इत्थम्भूतगुणो हरिः ॥१४७४

4. शुकदेव spoke to परीक्षित्, interweaving the instructions of मैत्रेय to विदुर (another भागवत line through सनत्कुमार-साङ्ख्यायन-पराशर, i.e., विष्णु-पुराण). सूत गोस्वामी, present with परीक्षित्, relates it to शौनक at नैमिषारण्य .

"It is well known that the Bhagavatam throughout, unlike other Puranas, is composed in a style which is very abstruse, antique and involved. Its syntactical construction, very often, follows that of an English sentence, rather than the usual one in Sanskrit and its derivative languages. This will be apparent to every reader who goes through the book, and it is altogether unparalleled in Sanskrit. Besides, its vocabulary is full of obsolete Vedic words and phrases, sometimes exactly reproduced from the vast Vedic literature. Its grammatical formations are very often modelled on the Vedas." (*Bhagavata Purana – A Linguistic Study*, Ashutosh Sarma Biswas)

धनञ्जये हाटकसम्परीक्षा महारणे शस्त्रभृतां परीक्षा ।
विपत्तिकाले गृहिणीपरीक्षा विद्यावतां भागवते परीक्षा ॥1475

श्रीमद्भागवतं भक्त्या पठते हरिसन्निधौ । जागरे तत्पदं याति कुलवृन्द-
समन्वितः ॥1476

It is to be read continuously to someone who is, like परीक्षित्, about to die.
Selected Verses:

जन्माद्यस्य यतो ऽन्वयादितरतश्चार्थेष्वभिज्ञः स्वराट्
   तेने ब्रह्म हृदा य आदिकवये मुह्यन्ति यत्सूरयः ।
तेजोवारिमृदां यथा विनिमयो यत्र त्रिसर्गो ऽमृषा
   धाम्ना स्वेन सदा निरस्तकुहकं सत्यं परं धीमहि ॥1477

धर्मः प्रोज्झितकैतवो ऽत्र परमो निर्मत्सराणां सतां
   वेद्यं वास्तवमत्र वस्तु शिवदं तापत्रयोन्मूलनम् ।
श्रीमद्भागवते महामुनिकृते किं वा परैरीश्वरः
   सद्यो हृद्यवरुध्यते ऽत्र कृतिभिः शुश्रूषुभिस्तत्क्षणात् ॥1478

निगमकल्पतरोर्गलितं फलं शुकमुखादमृतद्रवसंयुतम् ।
पिबत भागवतं रसमालयं मुहुरहो रसिका भुवि भावुकाः ॥1479

नैमिषे ऽनिमिषक्षेत्रे ऋषयः शौनकादयः । सत्रं स्वर्गायलोकाय सहस्र-
सममासत ॥1480 त एकदा तु मुनयः प्रातर्हुतहुताग्नयः । सत्कृतं सूतमासीनं
पप्रच्छुरिदमादरात् ॥1481 प्रायेणाल्पायुषः सभ्य कलावस्मिन्युगे जनाः । मन्दाः
सुमन्दमतयो मन्दभाग्या ह्युपद्रुताः ॥1482 भूरीणि भूरिकर्माणि श्रोतव्यानि
विभागशः । अतः साधो ऽत्र यत्सारं समुद्धृत्य मनीषया । ब्रूहि भद्राय भूतानां
येनात्मा सुप्रसीदति ॥1483 वयं तु न वितृप्याम उत्तमश्लोकविक्रमे । यच्छृण्वतां
रसज्ञानां स्वादु स्वादु पदे पदे ॥1484

स वै पुंसां परो धर्मो यतो भक्तिरधोक्षजे । अहैतुक्यप्रतिहता ययात्मा
सुप्रसीदति ॥1485 वासुदेवे भगवति भक्तियोगः प्रयोजितः । जनयत्याशु वैराग्यं
ज्ञानं च यदहैतुकम् ॥1486 धर्मः स्वनुष्ठितः पुंसां विष्वक्सेनकथासु यः ।
नोत्पादयेद्यदि रतिं श्रम एव हि केवलम् ॥1487 धर्मस्य ह्यापवर्ग्यस्य
नार्थो ऽर्थायोपकल्पते । नार्थस्य धर्मैकान्तस्य कामो लाभाय हि स्मृतः ॥1488
कामस्य नेन्द्रियप्रीतिर् लाभो जीवेत यावता । जीवस्य तत्त्वजिज्ञासा नार्थो यश्चेह
कर्मभिः ॥1489 वदन्ति तत्त्वविदस् तत्त्वं यज्ज्ञानमद्वयम् । ब्रह्मेति परमात्मेति
भगवानिति शब्द्यते ॥1490 तस्मादेकेन मनसा भगवान्सात्वतां पतिः । श्रोतव्यः
कीर्तितव्यश्च ध्येयः पूज्यश्च नित्यदा ॥1491 यदनुध्यासिना युक्ताः कर्मग्रन्थि-

निबन्धनम् । छिन्दन्ति कोविदास्तस्य को न कुर्यात्कथारतिम् ॥1492 मुमुक्षवो घोररूपान् हित्वा भूतपतीनथ । नारायणकलाः शान्ता भजन्ति ह्यनसूयवः ॥1493

तद्वाग्विसर्गो जनताघविप्लवो यस्मिन्प्रतिश्लोकमबद्धवत्यपि ।
नामान्यनन्तस्य यशो ङ्किंतानि यच्छृण्वन्ति गायन्ति गृणन्ति साधवः ॥1494
नैष्कर्म्यमप्यच्युतभाववर्जितं न शोभते ज्ञानमलं निरञ्जनम् ।
कुतः पुनः शश्वदभद्रमीश्वरे न चार्पितं कर्म यदप्यकारणम् ॥1495
त्यक्त्वा स्वधर्मं चरणाम्बुजं हरेर् भजन्नपक्वो ऽथ पतेत्ततो यदि ।
यत्र क्व वाभद्रमभूदमुष्य किं को वार्थ आप्तो ऽभजतां स्वधर्मतः ॥1496
तस्यैव हेतोः प्रयतेत कोविदो न लभ्यते यद् भ्रमतामुपर्यधः ।
तल्लभ्यते दुःखवदन्यतः सुखं कालेन सर्वत्र गभीररंहसा ॥1497
नामान्यनन्तस्य हतत्रपः पठन् गुह्यानि भद्राणि कृतानि च स्मरन् ।
गां पर्यटंस्तुष्टमना गतस्पृहः कालं प्रतीक्षन्विमदो विमत्सरः ॥1498

श्रोतव्यादीनि राजेन्द्र नृणां सन्ति सहस्रशः । अपश्यतामात्मतत्त्वं गृहेषु गृहमेधिनाम् ॥1499 निद्रया ह्रियते नक्तं व्यवायेन च वा वयः । दिवा चार्थेहया राजन् कुटुम्बभरणेन वा ॥1500 तस्माद्भारत सर्वात्मा भगवानीश्वरो हरिः । श्रोतव्यः कीर्तितव्यश्च स्मर्तव्यश्चेच्छताभयम् ॥1501 एतावान्साङ्ख्ययोगाभ्यां स्वधर्म-परिनिष्ठया । जन्मलाभः परः पुंसाम् अन्ते नारायणस्मृतिः ॥1502 एत्तन्निर्विद्यमानानाम् इच्छतामकुतोभयम् । योगिनां नृप निर्णीतं हरेर्नामानुकीर्तनम् ॥1503 किं प्रमत्तस्य बहुभिः परोक्षैर्हायनैरिह । वरं मुहूर्तं विदितं घटते श्रेयसे यतः ॥1504

केचित्स्वदेहान्तर्हृदयावकाशे प्रादेशमात्रं पुरुषं वसन्तम् ।
चतुर्भुजं कञ्जरथाङ्गशङ्ख- गदाधरं धारणया स्मरन्ति ॥
प्रसन्नवक्त्रं नलिनायतेक्षणं कदम्बकिञ्जल्कपिशङ्गवाससम् ।
लसन्महारत्नहिरण्मयाङ्गदं स्फुरन्महारत्नकिरीटकुण्डलम् ॥
उन्निद्रहृत्पङ्कजकर्णिकालये योगेश्वरास्थापितपादपल्लवम् ।
श्रीलक्षणं कौस्तुभरत्नकन्धरम् अम्लानलक्ष्म्या वनमालयाचितम् ॥
विभूषितं मेखलयाङ्गुलीयकैर् महाधनैर्नूपुरकङ्कणादिभिः ।
स्निग्धामलाकुञ्चितनीलकुन्तलैर् विरोचमानाननहासपेशलम् ॥1505

धर्मार्थकाममोक्षाख्यं य इच्छेच्छ्रेय आत्मनः । एकमेव हरेस्तत्र कारणं पादसेवनम् ॥1506 तत्तात गच्छ भद्रं ते यमुनायास्तटं शुचि । पुण्यं मधुवनं यत्र सांनिध्यं नित्यदा हरेः ॥1507 स्नात्वानुसवनं तस्मिन् कालिन्द्याः सलिले शिवे । कृत्वोचितानि निवसन्न् आत्मनः कल्पितासनः ॥ प्राणायामेन त्रिवृता प्राणेन्द्रियमनोमलम् । शनैर्व्युदस्याभिध्यायेन् मनसा गुरुणा गुरुम् ॥1508 मन्त्रेणानेन देवस्य कुर्याद् द्रव्यमयीं बुधः । सपर्यां विविधैर्द्रव्यैर् देशकालविभागवित् ॥1509

तत्साधु मन्ये ऽसुरवर्य देहिनां सदा समुद्विग्नधियामसद्ग्रहात् ।
हित्वात्मपातं गृहमन्धकूपं वनं गतो यद्धरिमाश्रयेत ॥१५१०

मतिर्न कृष्णे परतः स्वतो वा मिथो ऽभिपद्येत गृहव्रतानाम् ।
अदान्तगोभिर्विशतां तमिस्रं पुनः पुनश्चर्वितचर्वणानाम् ॥१५११

न ते विदुः स्वार्थगतिं हि विष्णुं दुराशया ये बहिरर्थमानिनः ।
अन्धा यथान्धैरुपनीयमानास् ते ऽपीशतन्त्यामुरुदाम्नि बद्धाः ॥१५१२

कौमार आचरेत्प्राज्ञो धर्मान्भागवतानिह । दुर्लभं मानुषं जन्म
तदप्यध्रुवमर्थदम् ॥१५१३ सुखमैन्द्रियकं दैत्या देहयोगेन देहिनाम् । सर्वत्र लभ्यते
दैवाद् यथा दुःखमयत्नतः ॥१५१४ पुंसो वर्षशतं ह्यायुस् तदर्धं चाजितात्मनः ।
निष्फलं यदसौ रात्र्यां शेते ऽन्धं प्रापितस्तमः ॥१५१५ मुग्धस्य बाल्ये कैशोरे क्रीडतो
याति विंशतिः । जरया ग्रस्तदेहस्य यात्यकल्पस्य विंशतिः ॥१५१६ न ह्यच्युतं
प्रीणयतो बह्वायासो ऽसुरात्मजाः । आत्मत्वात्सर्वभूतानां सिद्धत्वादिह सर्वतः ॥१५१७

शरदा नीरजोत्पत्त्या नीराणि प्रकृतिं ययुः । भ्रष्टानामिव चेतांसि
पुनर्योगनिषेवया ॥१५१८ व्योम्नो ऽब्भ्रं भूतशाबल्यं भुवः पङ्कमपां मलम् ।
शरज्जहाराश्रमिणां कृष्णे भक्तिर्यथाशुभम् ॥१५१९ सर्वस्वं जलदा हित्वा विरेजुः
शुभ्रवर्चसः । यथा त्यक्तैषणाः शान्ता मुनयो मुक्तकिल्बिषाः ॥१५२० गिरयो
मुमुचुस्तोयं क्वचिन्न मुमुचुः शिवम् । यथा ज्ञानामृतं काले ज्ञानिनो ददते न
वा ॥१५२१ नैवाविदन्क्षीयमाणं जलं गाधजलेचराः । यथायुरन्वहं क्षय्यं नरा मूढाः
कुटुम्बिनः ॥१५२२ शनैः शनैर्जहुः पङ्कं स्थलान्यामं च वीरुधः । यथाहंममतां धीराः
शरीरादिष्वनात्मसु ॥१५२३ निश्चलाम्बुरभूत्तूष्णीं समुद्रः शरदागमे । आत्मन्युपरते
सम्यङ् मुनिर्व्युपरतागमः ॥१५२४ केदारेभ्यस्त्वपो ऽगृह्णन् कर्षका दृढसेतुभिः । यथा
प्राणैः स्रवज्ज्ञानं तन्निरोधेन योगिनः ॥१५२५ खमशोभत निर्मेघं शरद्विमलतारकम् ।
सत्त्वयुक्तं यथा चित्तं शब्दब्रह्मार्थदर्शनम् ॥१५२६ गावो मृगाः खगा नार्यः पुष्पिण्यः
शरदाभवन् । अन्वीयमानाः स्ववृषैः फलैरीशक्रिया इव ॥१५२७ उदहृष्यन्वारिजानि
सूर्योत्थाने कुमुद्विना । राज्ञा तु निर्भया लोका यथा दस्यून्विना नृप ॥१५२८

कृमिविड्भस्मसञ्ज्ञान्ते राजनाम्नो ऽपि यस्य च । भूतध्रुक् तत्कृते स्वार्थं किं वेद
निरयो यतः ॥१५२९ कथं सेयमखण्डा भूः पूर्वैर्मे पुरुषैर्धृता । मत्पुत्रस्य च पौत्रस्य
मत्पूर्वा वंशजस्य वा ॥१५३० ये ये भूपतयो राजन् भुञ्जते भुवमोजसा । कालेन ते
कृताः सर्वे कथामात्राः कथासु च ॥१५३१ दृष्ट्वात्मनि जये व्यग्रान् नृपान्हसति
भूरियम् । अहो मां विजिगीषन्ति मृत्योः क्रीडनका नृपाः ॥१५३२ यां विसृज्यैव
मनवस् तत्सुताश्च कुरूद्वह । गता यथागतं युद्धे तां मां जेष्यन्त्यबुद्धयः ॥१५३३
मत्कृते पितृपुत्राणां भ्रातृणां चापि विग्रहः । जायते ह्यसतां राज्ये
ममताबद्धचेतसाम् ॥१५३४

श्रीमद्भागवतं पुराणममलं यद्वैष्णवानां प्रियं
यस्मिन्पारमहंस्यमेकममलं ज्ञानं परं गीयते ।
तत्र ज्ञानविरागभक्तिसहितं नैष्कर्म्यमाविष्कृतं
तच्छृण्वन्सुपठन्विचारणपरो भक्त्या विमुच्येन्नरः ॥1535

नामसङ्कीर्तनं यस्य सर्वपापप्रणाशनम् । प्रणामो दुःखशमनस् तं नमामि हरिं परम् ॥1536

105. Death

गतस्वार्थमिमं देहं विरक्तो मुक्तबन्धनः । अविज्ञातगतिर्जह्यात् स वै धीर उदाहृतः ॥1537 नाभिनन्देत मरणं नाभिनन्देत जीवितम् । कालमेव प्रतीक्षेत निर्वेशं भृतको यथा ॥1538 यदाकल्पः स्वक्रियायां व्याधिभिर्जरयाथवा । आन्वीक्षिक्यां वा विद्यायां कुर्यादनशनादिकम् ॥1539

मनस्वी म्रियते कामं कार्पण्यं न तु गच्छति । अपि निर्वाणमायाति नानलो याति शीतताम् ॥1540

"Both classes [of philosophers] take such a view of death that they endure life unwillingly, as being a hard duty exacted by nature, and accelerate the release of their souls from their bodies; and frequently, when their health is good and no evil forces them, they take their leave of life. They let their intention to do so be known to their friends beforehand, but no one offers to prevent them; on the contrary, all deem them happy, and charge them with messages to their dead relatives, so firm and true is the belief in their own minds, and in the minds of many others, that souls after death have intercourse with each other. When they have heard the commissions entrusted to them, they commit their body to the flames with a view to sever the soul from the body in completest purity, and then they die amid hymns resounding their praises, for their most attached friends dismiss them to death with less reluctance than it gives us to part with our fellow-citizens who set out on a distant journey. They weep, but it is for themselves, because they must continue to live, and those whose death they have witnessed they deem happy in their attainment of immortality. And neither among those Samanas nor among the Brahmanas whom I have already mentioned, has any sophist come foreward, as have so many among the Greeks, to perplex with doubts by asking where would we be if every one should copy their example." (Porphyrios; Greek philosopher and writer, c. 233- c. 301)

यदि नित्यमनित्येन निर्मलं मलवाहिना । यशः कायेन लभ्येत तन्न लब्धं भवेन्नु किम् ॥1541

Satī was the young wife of Shiva who burned herself to give up the body given by her father, when her husband was insulted by her father. To follow the dead husband into the puneral fire as 'Satī' was a great ideal, practiced by some exalted women among the nobility, and remained an exception.

"As we return'd home at night we met a Woman in the City of Ikkeri, who, her husband being dead, was resolv'd to burn herself, as it is the custom with many Indian Women. She rode on Horse-back about the City with face uncovered, holding a Looking-glass in one hand and a Lemon in the other, I know not for what purpose; and beholding herself in the Glass, with a lamentable tone sufficiently pittiful to hear, went along I know not whither, speaking, or singing, certain words, which I understood not; but they told me they were a kind of Farewell to the World and herself; and indeed, being uttered with that passionateness which the Case requir'd and might produce they mov'd pity in all that heard them, even in us who understood not the Language. She was follow'd by many other women and Men on foot, who, perhaps, were her Relations; they carry'd a great Umbrella over her, as all Persons of quality in India are wont to have, thereby to keep off the Sun, whose heat is hurtful and troublesome. Before her certain Drums were sounded, whose noise she never ceas'd to accompany with her sad Ditties, or Songs; yet with a calm and constant Countenance, without tears, evidencing more grief for her Husband's death than her own, and more desire to go to him in the other world than regret for her own departure out of this: a Custom, indeed, cruel and barbarous, but, withall, of great generosity and virtue in such Women and therefore worthy of no small praise. They said she was to pass in this manner about the City I know not how many dayes, at the end of which she was to go out of the City and be burnt, with more company and solemnity. If I can know when it will be I will not fail to go to see her and by my presence honor her Funeral with that compassionate affection which so great Conjugal Fidelity and Love seem to me to deserve. November the sixteenth. I was told that the aforemention'd Woman, who had resolv'd to burn her self for her Husband's death, was to dye this Evening. But upon further enquiry at the Woman's House I understood that it would not be till after a few dayes more, and there I saw her sitting in a Court, or Yard, and other persons beating Drums about her. She was cloth'd all in white and deck'd with many Neck-laces, Bracelets and other ornaments of Gold; on her Head she had a Garland of Flowers, spreading forth like the rayes of the Sun; in brief she was wholly in a Nuptial Dress and held a Lemon in her hand, which is the usual Ceremony. She seem'd to be pleasant enough, talking and laughing in conversation, as a Bride would do in our Countries. She and those with her took notice of my standing there to behold her, and, conjecturing by my foreign Habit who I was, some of them came towards me. I told them by an Interpreter that I was a Person of a very remote Country, where we had heard by Fame that some Women in India love their Husbands so vehemently as when they dye to resolve to dye with them; and that now, having intelligence that this Woman was such a one, I was come to see her, that so I might relate in my own Country that I had seen such a thing with my own Eyes. These people were well pleas'd with my coming, and she her self, having heard what I said, rose up from her seat and came to speak to me. We discours'd together, standing, for a good while. She told me that her name was Giaccama, of the Race Terlenga, that her Husband was a Drummer; whence I wonder'd the more; seeing that Heroical Actions, as this undoubtedly ought to be judg'd, are very rare in people of low quality. That it was about nineteen dayes since her Husband's death, that he had left two other Wives elder then she, whom he had married before her, (both which were present at this discourse) yet neither of them was willing to dye, but alledg'd for excuse that they had many Children. This argument gave me occasion to ask Giaccama, (who shew'd me a little Son of her own, about six or seven years old, besides a little Daughter she had) how she could perswade her self to leave her own little Children; and I told her, that she ought likewise to live rather than to abandon them at that age. She answer'd me that she left them well recommended to the care of an Uncle of hers there present, who also talk'd with us very cheerfully, as if rejoyeing that his Kins-woman should do such an action; and that her Husband's other two remaining Wives would also take care of them. I insisted much upon the tender age of her Children, to avert her from her purpose by moving her to compassion for them, well knowing that no argument is more prevalent with Mothers than their Love and Affection towards their Children. But all my speaking was in vain, and she still answer'd me to all my Reasons, with a Countenance not onely undismay'd and constant, but even cheerful, and spoke in such a manner as shew'd that she had not the least fear of death. She told me also, upon my asking her, that she did this of her own accord, was at her own liberty and not forc'd nor perswaded by any one. Whereupon, I inquiring whether force were at any time us'd in this matter, they told me that ordinarily it was not, but onely sometimes amongst Persons of quality, when some Widow was left young, handsome, and so in danger of marrying again (which amongst them is very ignominious), or committing a worse fault; in such Cases the Friends of the deceas'd Husband were very strict, and would constrain her to burn her self even against her own will, for preventing the disorders possible to happen in case she should live (a barbarous, indeed, and too cruel Law); but that neither force nor persuasion was used to Giaccama, and that she did it of her own free will; in which, as a magnanimous action, (as indeed it was) and amongst them of great honor, both her Relations and herself much glory'd. I ask'd concerning the Ornaments and Flowers she wore, and they told me that such was the Custom, in token of the Masti's joy (they call the Woman, who intends to burn her self for the death of her Husband, Masti) in that she was very shortly to go to him and therefore had reason to rejoyce; whereas such Widows as will not dye remain in continual sadness and lamentations, shave their Heads and live in perpetual mourning for the death of their Husbands. As last Giaccama caus'd one to tell me that she accounted my coming to see her a great fortune, and held her self much honour'd, as well by my visit and presence as by the Fame which I should carry of her to my own Country; and that before she dy'd she would come to visit me at my House, and also to ask me, as their custom is, that I would favour her with some thing by way of Alms towards the buying of fewel for the fire wherewith she was to be burnt. I answer'd her that I should esteem her visit and very willingly give her something; not for wood and fire wherein to burn her self, (for her death much displeas'd me, and I would gladly have disswaded her from it, if I could) but to do something else therewith that her self most lik'd; and I promis'd her that, so far as my weak pen could contribute, her Name should remain immortal in the World. Thus, I took leave of her, more sad for her death than she was, cursing the custom of India which is so unmerciful to Woman. Giaccama was a Woman of about thirty years of age, of a Complexion very brown for an Indian and almost black, but of a good aspect, tall of stature, well shap'd and proportion'd. My Muse could not forbear from chanting her in a Sonnet which I made upon her death, and reserve among my Poetical Papers." (Pietro Della Valle, Italian musicologist and traveller, 1586-1652)

"As they have so steadfast a belief in transmigration and their women not being permitted to marry a second husband, even the first should die in her nonage. I say from the consideration and hardships upon the tender sex, we may be enabled in some measure to account for the great fortitude and unmatched resolution of the wives burning with the bodies of their dead husbands, which instead of being obliged to, by the laws of their country, as some people have suggested, great entreaties and arguments one generally made use of, to break their resolution, but seldom to any purpose. It is certain that after they have determined to burn and the Brahmins have performed the ceremonies for that occasion, should they then attempt to retract, their friends and relations would assist to throw them into the flames. Sometimes since a young creature at Bengall embraced this resolution, she was known by many of the European ladies there, who kindly visited her, in her distress, and endeavured to move her desperate design by the most influencing reasons they could offer, as she had two very fine children, they represented to her the hardships and difficulties they would be liable to, when destitute of both parents, nor were her own relations and those of her husband less assiduous with their persuasions; however nothing could stagger her fixed determination. The day she was to burn being arrived many gentlemen attended her to the pile with several Bramins &c. The Bramins after praying with her for a considerable time, annointed her head and hair, all the while muttering some unintelligible sentences; afterwards they walked round the pile with her three times, constantly singing out their prayers. Having thus ended the ceremony, she takes off her bracelets, earrings &c and distributes them amongst her relations who attend her. Then embracing them she took her leave very pleasantly and retired to the middle of the pile, where her dead husband lay, and having placed herself at his feet, the Bramin gave a lighted match into her hand. With joy in her countenance she received it and said "this night I shall enjoy my husband's company in another form", then immediately set fire to the pile, but observing that she done it on the leeward side, she turned round and lighted it in several places to windward. The gentlemen's curiosity led them as near to the pile as the flames would admit them, yet they never heard her utter the least moan. The laws of the country do not oblige the women to this cruel custom yet in private it is certainly encouraged among them, for it is a great honour to the whole family, and the children of the woman who burns are always much regarded and very well matched." (Alex Knox, ?; written 1753)

During Moslem rule, Hindu women captured in war were forced to become sex slaves of those who just killed their husbands. Royal ladies were a great gift.

"First of all, daughters of Hindu kings captured during the course of the year come and sing and dance. Thereafter they are bestowed upon Amirs and important foreigners. After this, daughters of other Hindus dance and sing. ... Sultan gives them to brothers, sons of high officials etc. The third day also Sultan distributes girls to generals and his relatives."[M]

Many Hindu women preferred death to dishonour. In 1568, 8,000 women immolated themselves during Akbar's capture of Chittorgarh. This type of mass immolation became known as Jauhar.

The rapacity of British/Company occupation led to famines (the famine 1769-70 alone claimed the lives of one third of the population of Bengal). Under such pressure, a widow returning to her father's house was often a burden, leading to cases of forced Sati-Daha. Colonial propaganda painted a picture of Sati-Daha as another great evil of Hindu religion.

"Perhaps the most important point to which Raja Ram Mohan Roy awakened was the absence of all Vedic sanction for the self-immolation of widows (Suttee). It was principally his vehement denunciation of this practice, and the agitation against it set on foot by him, which ultimately led to the abolition of Sati throughout British India in 1819." (Sir Monier Monier-Williams, British Indologist and head of the Oxford's Boden Chair, 1819-1899)

पुत्रशोकातुराः सर्वे पाण्डवाः सह कृष्णया। स्वानां मृतानां यत्कृत्यं चक्रुर्निर्हरणादिकम्॥ ते निनीयोदकं सर्वे विलप्य च भृशं पुनः। आप्लुता हरिपादाब्ज-रजःपूतसरिज्जले ॥[1543] प्रेतदेहं शुभैः स्नानैः स्नापितं स्रग्विभूषितम्। दग्ध्वा ग्रामाद् बहिः स्नात्वा सचेलाः सलिलाशये ॥ यत्र यत्र स्थितायैतद् अमुकायेति वादिनः। दक्षिणाभिमुखा दद्युर् बान्धवाः सलिलाञ्जलिम् ॥[1544]

A dead adult Hindu is mourned with a cremation, while a dead child is typically buried. Lead mourner is the eldest son, or else a senior relative (parents, own wife, uncle, in-laws, step-parents), or a priest or teacher. He has to take bath and do the rites (an urban version):

1. Death: After the प्राण has left the body, one should note down the time and summon a doctor to obtain a death certificate, which is important for cremation permit and funeral service (cremation hall, time, car). Close relatives should be informed and asked to inform other relatives also.

गृह्णाति तत्क्षणाद्योगे शरीरं चातिवाहिकम्। आकाशवायुतेजांसि विग्रहाद् ऊर्ध्वगामिनः ॥[1545]

2. Impurity: During the first 90 minutes after death, there is no ritual impurity yet in that household, and a few spoons of गङ्गा / तुलसी / आचमन water can be poured into the mouth of the dead. ॐ नमः शिवाय is repeated three times into the right ear. But later the body should be put on a mat on the ground, and no cooking should be done in that home, incl. the preparation of tea, etc.

3. Prayer: To divert the soul's attention from family relationships to God and to remind everyone that the immortal आत्मा /self is now released from the worn-out body (which is returned to the five elements) to reach a new destination, there is constant recitation and music – भगवद्गीता (esp. 2.11-30), नारायण-सूक्त , सहस्र-नाम , Bhajans, etc. Visitors should not weep. The lead mourner performs सर्व-प्रायश्चित्त , i.e. prays for the dead and offers दान to saintly persons.

4. Rites: On the day of cremation (traditionally within a day of death), rites can be performed at the funeral parlor, or the body can be brought home. Close relatives rub oil on the head, then bath the body and dress it with new or favorite garments. The body is placed on a mat (or any spread), head facing south. Mouth and eyes are (again) closed, legs brought together, hands placed as in नमस्कार on the chest, and the two toes and thumbs are tied together. The body is covered up to the neck with a white cloth (for males and widows), or orange, yellow or red cloth (other females). A few

तुलसी leaves are put below the head next to the right ear. The forehead is decorated with विभूति or तिलक (men and widows), हल्दी and कुङ्कुम (other females), a garland, but no jewellery. An oil lamp (one wick), धूप and a photograph of the इष्ट-देव is placed at the head side. Outside the house a fire in an earthen pot with few pieces of wood, charcoal and camphor is kept alive.

5. Transport: For viewing and transport, the body is placed in the casket. Some also put a few coins and fruits tied in a new piece of cloth. Female relatives and friends pay their last respects by placing rice or rice and gram near the mouth. The casket is removed out of the house, legs first. Outside, grandsons go around the body thrice. The casket is driven to the crematorium, accompanied by two persons, the lead mourner carries the earthen pot with the fire in it. Those remaining at home will clean the house, take a bath, rinse their clothes and discard the mat.

6. Cremation: The cremation ground (श्मशान) is traditionally on the river bank. In the crematorium, enter the incineration chamber with the legs first. Prayers are continued. The body is put on the pyre, the lead mourner circumambulates it, says a eulogy or recites a hymn, places sesame seeds or rice in the dead person's mouth, sprinkles the body and the pyre with ghee, and sets the pyre ablaze. All may circumambulate the burning pyre once. All those who attend the cremation, and are exposed to the dead body or cremation smoke take a shower as soon as possible after the cremation, as the cremation ritual is considered unclean and polluting.

7. Ashes: After cremation, the mourner collects the ashes and consecrates it to the nearest river or sea. If possible, the rite of immersion of ashes into water is performed in a तीर्थ like वाराणसी on अशोकाष्टमी .

8. Mourning: Observed for 10-30 days. Sometimes the male relatives shave their head. On the tenth or twelfth day the relatives are invited for a simple meal and अन्न-दान in remembrance of the deceased. This is followed by श्राद्ध .

KOSHA

अ _ first letter of the alphabet; विष्णु.

अ- _ (a negative particle before consonants) (=अन्- before vowels) not →अमृत.

अंश _ m. part, particle.

अंशु _ m. particle, filament; sunbeam.

अंशुमान् _ m. 'with rays', sun.

अक्ष _ m. (1) »axis«, Germ. »Achse« → »axle«. (2) die for gambling. (3) organ of sense, eye, Russ. »oko« →रुद्राक्ष, प्रत्यक्ष, साक्षी.

अ-क्षय _ imperishable. अक्षय-तृतीया _ a festival on वैशाख-शुक्ल-तृतीया, also called युगादि (because कृतयुग startet on this तिथि); every endeavor on this day has अक्षय results; Celebration: उपवास, वासुदेव-पूजा, दान, स्वाध्याय.

अ-क्षर _ imperishable; n. letter, syllable, (esp.) ॐ. अक्षर-स्वीकरण _ learning the alphabet →विद्यारम्भ.

अक्षि _ (=अक्ष) n. eye.

अक्षौहिणी _ f. an army.

अ-खण्ड _ 'unbroken', entire.

अ-खिल _ 'no gap', complete, whole.

अग _ m. snake.

अगरु _ {for अगुरु}. अगरु-वर्ती _ (Agarbatti) f. 'अगुरु wick', incense.

अगुरु _ m. Agar tree (Aloeswood, Agaru, Aquilaria agallocha), wood and oil.

अग्नि _ m. fire, Lat. »ignis«, Russ. »ogon'«; sacrificial fire; digestive faculty; transformation, a महाभूत; the god of fire. अग्नि-परिणयन _ m. the groom 'leading [the bride] round the fire'. अग्नि-होत्र _ n. 'oblation to अग्नि', fire-sacrifice.

अग्र _ first, top; best; n. tip →बालाग्र. अग्र-ज _ m. 'first-born', eldest brother. अग्रम् _ ind. in front.

अग्र्य _ foremost, topmost, best.

अघ _ bad, sinful; n. sin. अघ-मर्षण _ 'enduring'/driving out sin; a ritual for purification, consisting in taking water in the right hand, holding it near one's nose, and breathing out from the nose on the water (with the idea of driving away sin from oneself); reciting the अघमर्षण hymn (ऋग्वेद 10.190).

अङ्ग _ m. curve → »angle«, Gr. »ankylos« → »English«; hook → »anchor«, Gr. »ankyra«; line, mark, ornament →शशाङ्ग; a numerical figure, a number.

अङ्कुर _ {अङ्ग} m. sprout, blade.

अङ्कुश _ {अङ्ग} m.n. hook, elephant-driver's hook.

अङ्ग _ n. limb, body part; division, department →वेदाङ्ग, उपाङ्ग; anything secondary.

अङ्गार _ m. burning »coal«.

अङ्गारक _ m. Mars, a ग्रह.

अङ्गुल _ (=अङ्गुली) m. 'finger'-width, a मात्रा (1.9 cm).

अङ्गुलि _ (=अङ्गुली).

अङ्गुली _ f. finger, the 5 fingers अङ्गुष्ठ-तर्जनी-मध्यमा-अनामिका-कनिष्ठा.

अङ्गुष्ठ _ m. thumb; great toe.

अङ्घ्रि _ m. foot; root of a tree.

अ-चल _ immovable.

अ-चित् _ f. 'unconscious', matter.

अ-चिन्त्य _ inconceivable.

अ-चिरात् _ ind. quickly.

अ-च्छ _ 'not shaded', clear.

अज _ m. goat. अज-वायन _ (Ajwain) n. 'goat's sweet'.

अजस्रम् _ ind. ever, constantly, perpetually.

अ-जित _ unconquered.

अजिन _ n. hairy skin of an antelope or tiger.

अ-जीव _ inanimate.

अ-ज्ञान _ n. ignorance.

अञ्चल _ m. border of a garment.

अञ्जन _ n. black pigment or collyrium →कज़ल.

अञ्जलि _ m. slightly hollowed joined palms, a reverent posture usually translated as 'folded hands' →पुष्पाञ्जलि.

अञ्जीर _ m. Common Fig tree (Anjir, Ficus carica) and fruit.

√अट् _ अट गतौ 1P go (wander) →अटति.

अटति _ (a verb) {√अट्} he wanders. सः ग्रामात् ग्रामम् अटति | He wanders from village to village.

अणिमन् _ {अणु} m. 'smallness', a सिद्धि.

अणिमा _ {अणिमन्}.

अणिष्ठ _ {अणु} 'most small', smallest.

अणीयः _ {अणु} 'more small', smaller.

अणु _ atomic, small, fine →परमाणु, अणिमा, (opp.) विभु; m. atom.

अण्ड _ n. egg →आण्डज, ब्रह्माण्ड.

अतः _ ind. 'from this', than this; from now; therefore.

अति. _ (a prefix, expressing:) very →अतिसुन्दर; beyond →अतीत; by सन्धि अत्य्. →अत्यन्त.

अतिक्रमण _ overstepping.

अतिथि _ m. who has 'no fixed तिथि' for coming, a chance-comer, guest →आतिथ्य. अतिथि-देवो भव | Worship an अतिथि like God!

अतिनीच _ very low.

अतिपरिचय _ {अति.} over-familiarity. अतिपरिचयादवज्ञा | From तिपरिचय comes अवज्ञा.

अतिरिक्त _ {अति.} extra, other than.

अतिसर्जन _ giving away; sending.

अतिसुन्दर _ very beautiful.

अतीत _ {अति.} 'surpassed'; gone, past.

अतीव _ ind. exceedingly.

अत्ति _ (a verb) {√अद्} he eats. अन्यः पिप्पलम् अत्ति | The other (the Jīva) eats the Pippala fruit [of fruitive work]. (श्वेताश्वतर-उपनिषद्).

अत्यन्त _ {अति.} 'beyond limit', very much.

अत्यर्थम् _ {अति.} ind. very much.

अत्र _ ind. here; in this matter.

अथ _ ind. now (for auspicious beginning); moreover. अथातो ब्रह्म-जिज्ञासा | Now (अथ) therefore (अतः) the enquiry into ब्रह्म. (वेदान्त-सूत्र)

अथवा _ ind. or else.

अथर्व _ {अथर्वन्}. अथर्व-वेद _ m. 4th वेद consisting of protective spells.

अथर्वन् _ m. a son of ब्रह्मा.

अथापि _ { अथ अपि } ind. moreover; therefore.

अथो _ (=अथ).

√अद् _ अद भक्षणे 2P »eat« → 'edible', →अत्ति-अत्सि-अद्मि-अदन्ति.

अदस् _ (a base) →असौ.

अ-दिति _ f. 'unbound', freedom; a wife of कश्यप →आदित्य, (opp.) दैत्य.

अ-दृश्य _ invisible.

अद्भुत _ wonderful; n. wonder, a गौणरस.

अद्य _ ind. now, today.

अ-द्वितीय _ 'no second', unique.

अ-द्वैत _ 'non-dual', absolute; n. 'monism' between ब्रह्म and जीव →केवलाद्वैत, (opp.) द्वैत.

अधः _ ind. down, below. अधः-पतन _ falling down.

अधम _ {अधः.तम} 'lowest', worst.

अधर _ {अधः.तर} 'lower', worse, »under«; m. lower lip, lip.

अ-धर्म _ m. 'non-virtue', sin.

अधि. _ (a prefix, expressing:) Vedic »at«, Lat. »ad«; over →अधिदेव; by सन्धि अध्य्. →अध्यक्ष.

अधिक _ much, extra. अधिक-मास _ m.
‘extra month’. The solar year of 365 days is
divided into 12 solar ‘months’ of average
30.5 days. But a मास (lunar month) takes
only about 29.5 days. The lunar year of 12
मास is therefore with 354 days 11 days
shorter than the solar year, and does not
stay synchronized with the seasons. To
synchronize the lunar year, the Vedic
calendar adds an अधिकमास about every
third year.

अधिकतम _ most.

अधिकतर _ more.

अधिकार _ m. ‘presiding’, authority, right,
qualification.

अधिकारिन् _ m. ‘who has authority’, is
entitled to or fit for.

अधिकारी _ {अधिकारिन्}.

अधिदैव _ ‘presiding destiny’ or ‘relating to
nature or destiny’.

अधिप _ m. ruler, king.

अधिपति _ (=अधिप).

अधिभूत _ ‘presiding beings’, relating to the
body or other living beings.

अधियज्ञ _ ‘presiding यज्ञ’, विष्णु.

अधिष्ठान _ {स्थान} n. basis, position.

अधीत _ {अधि.इ} ‘attained’, studied.

अधीन _ {अधि.} subordinate.

अ-धीर _ ‘not sober’, nervous.

अधुना _ ind. now, nowadays.

अधोक्ष _ {अधः-अक्ष} ‘below sight’,
transcendental, spiritual.

अध्यक्ष _ {अधि.} m. ‘presiding eye’,
supervisor.

अध्ययन _ n. reading, studying → (opp.)
अध्यापन, स्वाध्याय.

अध्यात्म _ {अधि.} ‘presiding the आत्मा’,
spiritual; ‘relating to oneself (mind and
body)’.

अध्यापक _ m. teacher.

अध्यापन _ n. teaching → (opp.) अध्ययन.

अध्याय _ m. ‘study’, lesson, chapter.

अन्- _ (a negative particle before vowels, =अ-
before consonants) no, »un-«, Lat. »in-«, Gr.
»an-« →अनन्त.

अन _ m. breath →प्राण, अपान.

अनध्याय _ {अन्-} m. a time ‘free from study’
(except for स्वाध्याय). “Teaching on
अमावास्या destroys the गुरु, चतुर्दशी the
शिष्य, and अष्टमी and पूर्णिमा (पौर्णमास्य)
destroy [remembrance of] the वेद (ब्रह्म) –
therefore one should avoid them [for
studying].” (वेदान्त-सूत्र 1.1.1)

अनन _ n. ‘breathing’, living → »animal«.

अनन्त _ {अन्-} ‘no end’, unlimited, eternal; a
नाग, also called अनन्त-शेष.

अनन्तरम् _ ind. ‘no interval’, after,
immediately.

अनन्य _ {अन्-} ‘no other’, exclusive, single-
minded.

अनर्थ _ {अन्-} ‘no value’, useless; m. a useless
object; the 6 faults काम-क्रोध-लोभ-मोह-
मद-मात्सर्य.

अनल _ m. fire.

अनादर _ {अन्-} m. disrespect.

अनादि _ {अन्-} ‘no beginning’, existing from
eternity.

अनामय _ {अन्-} ‘no disease’, healthy; pure,
transcendental.

अ-नामिका _ f. ‘nameless’, »anonymous«, the
ring-finger.

अनाहत _ {अन्-} n. ‘unbeaten’, sound which
is not produced; ॐ; a षट्चक्र in the heart.

अ-निरुद्ध _ m. ‘unopposed’, the son of प्रद्युम्न
→चतुर्व्यूह.

अनिल _ m. air, wind.

अनिष्ट _ {अन्-} ‘undesired’, unpleasant.

अनीश _ {अन्-} ‘without master’, supreme.

अनु. _ (a prefix, expressing:) after, along
→अनुगामी; by सन्धि अन्व्. →अन्वय.

अनुकम्पा _ f. 'trembling after', compassion.

अनुकरण _ n. 'acting after', imitation, similarity.

अनुकूल _ 'along the bank', favorable → (opp.) प्रतिकूल .

अनुक्त _ { अन्-} unsaid.

अनुक्रम _ m. 'going after', succession; order, method.

अनुगामिन् _ m. 'going after', follower.

अनुगामी _ { अनुगामिन् }.

अनुग्रह _ m. favor, kindness.

अनुचित _ { अन्-} 'not proper', wrong.

अनुचिन्ता _ f. 'after-thought', recollection.

अनुज _ 'after-born', younger; m. younger brother.

अनुज्ञा _ f. permission.

अनुत्तम _ { अन्-} 'no (other) highest', unsurpassed, incomparably the best.

अनुदर्शन _ n. 'after-view'; consideration.

अनुनासिक _ { नासा } 'along the nose', nasal.

अनुपम _ { अन्-} 'incomparable', best.

अनुपयुक्त _ { अन्-} 'useless'.

अनुपस्थित _ { अन्-} 'not present', absent.

अनुपस्थिति _ f. absence.

अनुबन्ध _ m. connection, result, consequence; indicatory lcttcrs 'attachcd' to धातु and प्रत्यय .

अनुभव _ m. perception, experience.

अनुभाव _ m. symptom of a feeling → भाव .

अनुमत _ 'followed in thought', approved, allowed.

अनुमन्ता _ { अनुमन्तृ }.

अनुमन्तृ _ m. who approves.

अनुमान _ m. (1) permission. (2) inference (pos. and neg.), hypothesis, a प्रमाण .

अनुमोदन _ pleasing; n. approval.

अनुयायी _ (= अनुगामी).

अनुराग _ m. affection, love.

अनुरूप _ conformable.

अनुलेपन _ n. anointing.

अनुलोम _ 'with the hair/grain', in a natural direction, conformable → (opp.) प्रतिलोम .

अनुवंश _ m. branch of a family, genealogical list.

अनुवाद _ m. translation.

अनुशासन _ n. instruction, command, discipline.

अनुशिष्टि _ f. instruction, order.

अनुशोचितुम् _ ind. to lament.

अनुष्टुप् _ f. 'following in praise' [the गायत्री meter with its 3 पाद], the standard verse meter (4 पाद , each 8 syllables).

अनुसन्धान _ n. inquiry, interrupted remembrance.

अनुसार _ following; m. accordance.

अनुरवार _ m. 'aftersound' m, nasalization after a स्वर .

अनृत _ { अन्-} 'not true', false; n. falsehood.

अनेक _ { अन्-} 'not one', many.

अनेकधा _ { अन्-} manifold.

अन्त _ m. »end«, limit; conclusion; death. - अन्त _ m. 'ending with ...' → (opp.) -आदि .

अन्तः-करण _ { अन्तर्-} n. 'internal organ', mind.

अन्ततः _ ind. finally.

अन्तर् _ ind. »intcrnal«, Lat. »intcr«, bctwccn, amongst. अन्तरङ्ग _ { अन्तर्-} 'internal limb', essential → (opp.) बहिरङ्ग . अन्तरङ्ग- शक्ति _ f. internal or spiritual energy → शक्ति , its 3 threads are सच्चिदानन्द , corresponding to त्रिगुण (सत् to तमः , चित् to सत्त्व , आनन्द to रजः). अन्तरात्मा _ { अन्तर्-} m. 'internal self', mind, heart. अन्तर्यामी _ (= परमात्मा) m. 'inner controller'.

अन्तर _ »interior«, near; n. distance.

अन्तरिक्ष _ n. space, the space between heaven and earth.

अन्तवत् _ 'with an end'; limited, temporary.

अन्तिक _ { अन्त } »until«.

अन्तिम _ {अन्त} last, final.

अन्त्य _ {अन्त} last. अन्त्य-क्रिका _
   (=अन्त्येष्टि).

अन्त्येष्टि _ {अन्त्य-इष्टि} f. 'last sacrifice', rite
   of passage with funeral, the last संस्कार.

अन्ध _ blind. अन्ध-कार _ m. 'blind-maker',
   darkness. अन्ध-कूप _ m. an over-grown
   'blind well'.

अन्न _ {अद्} n. 'eaten', food; grain, rice. अन्न-
   कूट _ m. hill of food. अन्न-पूर्णा _ f.
   'possessed of food', a form of दुर्गा,
   worshiped on चैत्र-शुक्ल-अष्टमी through
   food distribution. अन्न-प्राश/-प्राशन _ m.
   'feeding grain', first solid food, a संस्कार
   when teeth are visible in babies or after 6-7
   months; the ritual is usually celebrated with
   cooked rice, in a paste of honey, ghee and
   curd; the mother eats with the baby the
   same food; the rite includes पूजा and दान.

अन्य _ other, different.

अन्यत् _ ind. again, moreover, besides.

अन्यतः _ ind. otherwise.

अन्यत्र _ ind. elsewhere, otherwise.

अन्यथा _ ind. otherwise.

अन्यदा _ ind. at another time.

अन्योन्य _ {अन्य अन्य} mutual.

अन्वय _ {अनु.} m. succession; the natural
   order of words in a sentence, syntax.

अन्वित _ endowed with.

अन्वेषण _ seeking.

अप् _ f. water (only in Pl.) →आपः.

अप. _ (a prefix, expressing:) down, away,
   »off«, Gr. »apo-«, Lat. »ab-« →अपराध.

अपक्षय _ m. decay.

अपत्य _ n. offspring, child.

अपनयन _ taking away.

अपमान _ m. disrespect.

अपर _ {अप.} later, lower, other.

अ-पराजित _ undefeated.

अपराध _ {अप.} m. dishonor, insult; offense,
   crime.

अ-परिग्रह _ m. non-proprietorship, a यम.

अ-परिमेय _ immeasurable.

अ-परोक्ष _ 'not invisible', perceptible,
   realized.

अपवर्ग _ {अप.} m. 'leaving off', completion,
   end; final liberation.

अपहृत _ {अप.} 'carried away', stolen,
   abducted.

अपादान _ {अप.आदान} n. 'taking away',
   removal.

अपान _ {अप.अन} m. 'downward breath',
   inhalation →प्राण.

अपाय _ m. 'going away', loss.

अपावृत _ {अप.आवृत} 'uncovered', opened.

अपि _ ind. also, even, moreover.

अ-पूर्व _ 'not before', unique.

अपेक्षा _ f. 'looking round', expectation.

अपोहन _ {अप.} n. 'taking away', forgetting.

अप्यय _ m. 'entering', dissolution.

अ-प्रमेय _ immeasurable.

अ-प्रसाद _ m. displeasure.

अ-प्रारब्ध _ 'not begun'. अप्रारब्ध-कर्म _ n.
   unripe कर्मफल, in 3 stages कूट-बीज-
   फलोन्मुख.

अप्सरा _ {अप्-} f. 'going in the waters', a
   nymph inhabiting heaven (consort of
   गन्धर्व).

अब्ज _ {अप्-} n. 'water-born', lotus.

अब्द _ {अप्-} m. 'water-giver', year.

अ-भाव _ m. 'non-existence'; negative proof, a
   variety of प्रत्यक्ष.

अभि. _ (a prefix, expressing:) towards
   →अभिगम; intense →अभिज्ञ.

अभिकाङ्क्षा _ f. longing, desire.

अभिक्रम _ undertaking, beginning.

अभिगम _ approaching.

अभिजात _ born.

अभिज्ञ _ skillful, clever.

अभितः _ {अभि.} ind. 'from near', near, close by, from all sides.

अभिनिवेश _ m. 'plunging into', complete attachment; a क्लेश (clinging to the body and fear of death).

अभिप्राय _ m. purpose, intention.

अभिभव _ m. rise.

अभिमान _ m. 'self-conceit', pride.

अभिमुख _ 'facing towards', facing.

अभिरक्षित _ well-protected.

अभिलाषा _ f. keen desire.

अभिवादन _ n. salutation (of an elder) by lifting the joint hands (saying अहं अभिवादये)

अभिषेक _ m. anointment; inauguration.

अभिहित _ named.

अभ्यधिक _ {अभि.} surpassing, greater.

अभ्यन्तर _ {अभि.} inside.

अभ्यर्चन _ reverence. "No divinity (दैव) is equal to माता, no गुरु equal to पिता ." (उशना-स्मृति 1.35) "In this world there is no greater sinner than a son (पुत्र) who does not maintain his father and mother, after having been maintained and brought up by them. That पाप is worse than killing an embryo." (महाभारत 12.108.31)

अभ्यसन _ n. practicing →अभ्यास .

अभ्यसूयक _ {अभि.} m. who is envious.

अभ्यास _ {अभ्यसन} m. practice, study.

अ-गर _ 'no death', immortal →Amaranth; god.

अ-मल _ 'no dirt', pure.

अमला _ (Amla, Amlaki) f. Indian Gooseberry tree (Phyllanthus emblica) and fruit.

अमा _ ind. at home, in the house.

अमान्त _ {अमा-अन्त} m. a calender, where each month begins with शुक्लपक्ष and ends with अमावास्या .

अमात्य _ m. »mate«, »inmate«, companion; minister.

अमावास्या _ {अमा-वास्या} f. sun and moon 'dwelling in the [same] house', new moon.

अ-मित _ 'unmeasured', unlimited.

अमिताभ _ {अमित-आभा} m. 'who has unlimited splendor'.

अमुत्र _ ind. there; in the other world /life.

अ-मूल्यम् _ ind. 'invaluable', precious.

अ-मृत _ n. 'no death', immortality; nectar.

अमृतत्व _ n. the state of immortality, liberation.

अ-मेय _ immeasurable.

अम्बर _ n. garment; sky.

अम्बरीष _ m. a forefather of दशरथ celebrated for his भक्ति .

अम्बा _ (Amma) f. mother; good woman, title of respect (like देवी), Germ. »Amme« (nurse).

अम्बु _ n. water.

अम्भः _ {अम्भस्}.

अम्भस् _ n. water.

अम्ल _ sour, a रस .

अम्लक _ (Imli) m. Tamarind tree (Tamarindus indica) and fruit.

अयः _ {अयस्}.

अयन _ n. 'going', course, way; the course of the sun →उत्तरायण, दक्षिणायन .

अयम् _ {इदम्} m. he.

अयस् _ n. iron, Germ. »Eisen«; metal.

अयि _ ind. for tender calling.

अयोध्या _ f. 'not to be warred against', birthplace of राम .

अर _ m. spoke (of a wheel), radius.

अरण्य _ n. wilderness, forest.

अरविन्द _ n. a lotus.

अरि _ m. enemy.

अरिष्ट _ m. Soapnut tree (Reetha, Sapindus).

अरुण _ reddish-brown; m. dawn, personified redness of the sunlight during dawn and dusk.

अरुन्धती _ f. the constellation सप्तर्षि .

अरे _ ind. to address an inferior person.

अर्क _ m. sun.

अर्घ _ m. value.

अर्घ्य _ {अर्घ} 'valuable', respectful reception (of a guest); n. water offered to a guest; offering water to सूर्य during सन्ध्यावन्दन – taking water (or, if not possible, dust) in one's joined hands, repeating गायत्री over it, standing facing the sun and casting it up thrice.

अर्चन _ n. 'worshiping' God in a प्रतिमा by offering उपचार with मन्त्र, preceded by भूतशुद्धि and न्यास.

अर्चा _ {अर्चन} f. worship. अर्चा-विग्रह _ m. 'deity for worship', a properly installed प्रतिमा of God.

अर्जन _ earning.

अर्जुन _ white, made of silver; n. silver, Gr. »arguron«, Lat. »argentum«; m. the 3rd पाण्डव; Arjun tree (Kauha, Terminalia arjuna) and wood. अर्जुन-विषाद _ the despondency of अर्जुन.

अर्थ _ m. 'which is desired', object →इन्द्रियार्थ; aim, purpose →पुरुषार्थ; meaning →अर्थवत्; wealth, as in धर्म-अर्थ-काम-मोक्ष. अर्थस्य पुरुषो दासः। Man is the servant of wealth. अर्थ-शास्त्र _ n. economics (practically synomymous with धर्म-/नीति-शास्त्र), (esp.) कौटिलीय-अर्थशास्त्र.

-अर्थम् _ ind. for the purpose of →तदर्थम्.

अर्थवत् _ 'with meaning', significant.

अर्थात् _ ind. that means (i.e.).

अर्थीय _ meant for.

अर्ध _ half.

अर्पण _ n. offering.

अर्पित _ offered.

अर्यमन् _ m. an आदित्य (chief of पितृलोक).

अर्यमा _ {अर्यमन्}.

√अर्ह् _ अर्ह पूजायाम् 1P worship, honor →अर्हति-अर्हसि-अर्हामि-अर्हन्ति.

अर्ह _ deserving.

अर्हति _ (a verb) {√अर्ह} he deserves. सः मानम् अर्हति। He deserves respect. शोचितुं न अर्हसि। You do not deserve to lament. (भगवद्गीता).

अलङ्कार _ m. 'decorating', ornament; rhetoric.

अलम् _ ind. useless; able, competent (in both meanings 'enough').

अ-लस _ inactive.

अल्प _ little, small →स्वल्प, (opp.) प्रचुर. अल्प-मूल्य _ 'small in value', cheap.

अव. _ (a prefix, expressing:) under /down →अवतार; away →अवज्ञा.

अवकाश _ m. space, room; occasion, opportunity.

अवक्षेपण _ 'throwing down', blaming.

अवगमन _ understanding.

अवग्रह _ 'separation' ऽ of अ.

अवज्ञा _ f. disrespect.

अवज्ञात _ disrespected.

अवतार _ m. 'crossing down', descent; incarnation of विष्णु, like परमात्मा, the दशावतार, others like यज्ञ, नर-नारायण, कपिल, दत्तात्रेय, हयशीर्ष, हंस, ऋषभ, धन्वन्तरि, मोहिनी; also called अवतार are empowered (शक्त्यावेश) living beings, like ब्रह्मा, चतुःसन, नारद, पृथु and व्यास.

अवधूत _ m. who has 'shaken off' /discarded this world, a renunciant.

अवनि _ (=अवनी) f. the earth.

अवन्ति _ m. a country →उज्ज्यिनी.

अवबोधन _ waking; knowing.

अवर _ {अव.} low, inferior; posterior, younger.

अवरोध _ m. obstacle.

अवरोह _ m. descent → (opp.) आरोह .
  अवरोह-पन्थाः _ m. ‘descending path’ of
  knowledge by अधोक्ष and अपरोक्ष .
अवशिष्ट _ ‘left out’, remaining.
अ-वश्यम् _ ind. ‘unwillingly’, necessarily,
  definitely, certainly.
अवसर _ {अव.} m. descent (of water), rain;
  occasion, opportunity.
अवस्था _ f. situation, condition; stage.
अवस्थान _ staying.
अवस्थित _ situated, placed.
अ-वाच्य _ ‘not to be spoken’, improper.
अवाप्त _ {अव.} obtained.
अ-विद्या _ f. ‘no knowledge’, ignorance; a
  क्लेश (forgetfulness of one’s identity as soul).
  अविद्या-अस्मिता-राग-द्वेष-अभिनिवेश _ 5
  क्लेश .
अ-विश्वास _ disbelief.
अ-वैध _ improper, illegal.
अ-व्यक्त _ unmanifested.
अ-व्यय _ unchangable; (grammar)
  indeclinable.
√अश् _ अश भोजने 9P eat, enjoy; अति.
  →अश्नाति-अश्नासि-अश्नामि-अश्नन्ति.
अशन _ n. eating, consuming.
अ-शिक्षित _ uneducated.
अ-शेष _ ‘no remainder’, complete, all.
अशेषतः _ ind. completely.
अ-शोक _ m. no sorrow or lamentation;
  Ashok tree (Saraca asoca), scc देवदारु .
अशोकाष्टमी _ {अशोक-} a festival on चैत्र-
  शुक्ल-अष्टमी in भुवनेश्वर .
अ-शोच्य _ not lamentable.
अश्नाति _ (a verb) {√अश्} he eats. यद्
  अश्नासि तद् मद्-अर्पणं कुरुष्व । Whatever
  you eat, make that an offering to me.
  (भगवद्गीता).
अश्म _ {अश्मन्}. अश्म-सार _ m.n. ‘stone-
  core’, iron. अश्म-आरोहन _ ‘ascending a

stone’, making the bride stand on a mill-
  stone.
अश्मन् _ m. stone.
अश्रि _ f. corner, edge.
अश्रु _ n. a tear.
अश्व _ m. horse. अश्व-गन्धा _ f. ‘horse-smell’,
  Indian Ginsen (Withania somnifera).
अश्वत्थ _ m. ‘under which horses stand’, the
  पिप्पल tree.
अश्विन् _ {अश्व} m. ‘charioteer’, the twin-
  physicians of heaven.
अश्विनी _ f. mother of the two अश्विन् .
  अश्विनी-कुमार _ (=अश्विन्) m. ‘son of
  अश्विनी ’.
अष्ट _ {अष्टन्}.
अष्टक _ n. consisting of eight parts, (esp.) a
  poem.
अष्टधा _ ind. eightfold.
अष्टन् _ »eight«, Lat. »octo« → »October«;
  sacred number of लक्ष्मी .
अष्टम _ »eighth«, Lat. »octavus«.
अष्टमी _ f. ‘eighth [रात्रि]’ in both शुक्ल- and
  कृष्णपक्ष .
अष्टाङ्ग _ {अष्ट-अङ्ग} eight limbs. अष्टाङ्ग-
  प्रणाम _ m. प्रणाम with eight limbs
  (=दण्डवत्). “प्रणाम (i.e., touching thc
  ground) with chest (उरस्), head (शिरस्),
  eyes (दृष्टि), मनस् , speech (वचस्), feet
  (पद् , opt. for पाद), hands (कर) and knees
  is called अष्टाङ्ग .” अष्टाङ्ग-योग _ m.
  ‘eightfold योग ’ of पतञ्जलि – 4 साधन यम-
  नियम-आसन-प्राणायाम plus 4 संयम
  प्रत्याहार-धारणा-ध्यान-समाधि →षड्दर्शन,
  हठयोग .
अष्टादश _ eighteen (a sacred number).
अष्टोत्तर-शतम् _ {अष्ट-उत्तर-} n. ‘hundred
  higher eight’, 108, a sacred number – sun
  and moon are at a distance from the earth of
  about 108 times their own diameters, which

was paralleled by 108 steps to illumination →
108 beads on a rosary.

√अस् _ अस भुवि 2P be →अस्ति-असि-अस्मि-
सन्ति.

अ-सङ्ख्य _ innumerable.

अ-सत् _ untrue, unreal. असतो मा सद्गमय।
Lead me from असत् to सत्!

अ-सत्य _ 'untrue', false.

अ-समर्थ _ unable.

अ-सम्भव _ impossible.

अ-सामान्य _ unusual.

अ-सार _ without strength /worth /sap.

असि _ (1) {√अस्} you are. तद् त्वम् असि।
You are that [same Brahma]. (छान्दोग्य-
उपनिषद्). (2) m. sword.

अ-सित _ 'not white', black.

अ-सीम _ {सीमा} boundless.

असु _ m. breath, life.

अ-सुर _ m. demon, (esp.) दैत्य and दानव
→आसुर, (opp.) सुर.

अ-सुविधा _ f. inconvenience.

असूय _ envious.

असूया _ f. envy.

असौ _ {अदस्} m. he. असावादित्यो ब्रह्म।
{असौ आदित्यः} This sun is ब्रह्म.

अस्ति _ {√अस्} he »is«, Lat. »est«; ind.
existent →आस्तिक, नास्तिक, स्वस्तिक.
अ-मन्त्रम् अक्षरं न अस्ति। There is no letter
without meaning ('advice') (शास्त्र).

अस्तित्व _ {.त्व} n. existence.

अ-स्तेय _ n. not stealing, a यम.

अस्त्र _ n. missile weapon, arrow.

अस्थि _ n. bone, Gr. »osteon«.

अस्मद् _ (a base) →अहम्, मम.

अस्मि _ {√अस्} I »am«. अहं ब्रह्म अस्मि।I
am Brahma. (बृहद्-आरण्यक-उपनिषद्).

अस्मिता _ f. egoism; a क्लेश (self-
identification as body).

अ-स्वस्थ _ 'not healthy', ill.

अहं-ममेति _ {मम इति} thinking 'in terms of I
and mine', the bodily concept of life.

अहङ्कार _ {अहम्-} m. 'I-maker', ego;
threefold – सात्त्विक-राजस-तामस, from
सात्त्विक-अहङ्कार comes मनः, from राजस-
अहङ्कार come बुद्धि, इन्द्रिय, प्राण, and from
तामस-अहङ्कार come 5 तन्मात्र and 5
महाभूत; →प्राकृतसर्ग.

अहन् _ n. day-time (12 h, 4 प्रहर) → (opp.)
रात्रि.

अहम् _ {अस्मद्} I. अहं ब्रह्मास्मि।{ब्रह्म
अस्मि} I am ब्रह्म.

अहर् _ {अहन्}. अहर्निशम् _ ind. 'day and
night', continually.

अहह _ ind. expressing lamentation or
wonder.

अहि _ m. snake.

अ-हिंसा _ m. non-violence, a यम; →हिंसा.
अहिंसा परमो धर्मः। अहिंसा is the highest
धर्म. अहिंसा-सत्य-अस्तेय-ब्रह्मचर्य-
अपरिग्रह _ 5 यम.

अहो _ ind. expressing wonder, Ah!.

अहो-रात्र _ {अहर्-} (=अहर्निश, दिवस) m.
day and night, a मात्रा.

आ. _ (a prefix, expressing:) fully →आनन्द;
towards →आकर्ष; up to →आब्रह्म; with
words of motion it reverses the action
→आगम, आदान.

आकर _ m. abundance, a mine.

आकर्षण _ 'drawing toward'; ploughing; m.
attraction.

आकाङ्क्षा _ f. desire.

आकार _ m. form, shape → (opp.) निराकार;
gesture or expression of the face. आकार-
मौन _ m. 'silence with gesture' (avoiding
only oral speech).

आकाश _ m. space, sky; ether (space of energy
/information), a महाभूत.

आकुल _ confused, agitated.

आकृति _ f. form, shape.

आक्रम _ m. approaching, attaining, overcoming.

आक्रोश _ m. scolding, cursing.

आक्षेप _ m. blame.

आखोट _ (Okhar, Akharot) m. Walnut tree (Juglans regia) and nut.

आख्या _ f. appellation; named.

आख्यात _ n. 'told', a verb.

आख्यान _ telling.

आगत _ having come →स्वागत.

आगम _ m. »coming«, arrival; acquisition of knowledge, tradition.

आगमन _ n. »coming«, arriving.

आग्नेय _ 'relating to अग्नि'. आग्नेय-स्नान _ n. a स्नान with ashes from a sacrificial fire.

आघात _ striking, beating.

आघ्राण _ smelling.

आचमन _ n. 'sipping' water for purification, which is done before तिलक, जप, पूजा, होम, व्रत, अध्ययन, ध्यान, and after rising from bed, bathing, dressing, eating, going to an impure place, touching something impure, and returning from a journey; 1. the water for आचमन is consecrated in a small cup (of copper, wood or earthenware), calling sacred rivers with: गङ्गे च यमुने चैव ...; 2. drops of water are put thrice (before each sipping) on the palm of the right hand and sipped from the ब्राह्मतीर्थ (without touching it with the lips), each time with a मन्त्र (ॐ केशवाय नमः ...); 3. the wet fingertips of the right hand touch the following senses and limbs: mouth (with the thumb), nose (right+left), eyes (right+left), ears (right+left), navel, heart, head, and shoulders (right and left).

आचरण _ n. 'behaving'.

आचार _ m. behavior, precept.

आचार्य _ {आचार} m. preceptor, teacher. "He who collects the meaning of शास्त्र and establishes it in his behavior (आचार), because he thus behaves accordingly himself, therefore he is praised as आचार्य." आचार्यवान्पुरुषो वेद । A person with an आचार्य knows [liberation].

आच्छादन _ covering, dressing.

आज्ञा _ f. order, command; a षट्चक्र between the eyebrows (seat of मनः).

आज्य _ (=घृत) n. ghee.

आढय _ wealthy.

आण्ड-ज _ {अण्ड-} 'born from an egg', a birth → -ज.

आततायिन् _ m. aggressor, 6 kinds – who sets fire, poisons, attacks with a weapon, steals wealth, land, women.

आततायी _ {आततायिन्}.

आतिथ्य _ {अतिथि} n. 'receiving guests', hospitality. "A traveller is known as अतिथि, and one versed in वेद is known as learned (श्रोत्रिय). These two are honorable for a गृहस्थ desiring for the region of ब्रह्मा." "When an अतिथि turns back from a house (गृह) with frustrated hopes, he leaves by transferring to that [offender] all his own sin (दुष्कृत), taking all [the householder's] merit (पुण्य)."

आतिवाहिक _ {अति.वाह} (=लिङ्गशरीर) 'fleeter than wind', the subtle body.

आत्म- _ {आत्मा in comp.}. आत्म-हेतु _ 'caused by the own (body and mind)'.

-आत्मक _ of the nature of.

आत्मन् _ m. 'breath', Germ. »Atem«, movement; spirit, soul →परमात्मा; self, own →आत्म- हेतु, अध्यात्म; essence, nature →-आत्मक.

आत्मने-पद _ n. 'word for one's self', a form of conjugation (A), → (opp.) परस्मै- (P) and उभय-पद (U).

आत्मवान् _ {आत्मवत्} 'with the self', situated in the self.

आत्मा _ {आत्मन्}.

आत्यन्तिक _ {अत्यन्त} infinite, universal.

आदर _ m. regard, respect.

आदर्श _ m. 'seeing'; ideal, perfection.

आदान _ (opp. दान) taking.

आदि _ m. beginning, origin → (opp.) अनादि.
 -आदि _ m. beginning with, et cetera
 →इत्यादि , (opp.) -अन्त .

आदित्य _ m. 'son of अदिति', name of 12 देव
 (opp. दैत्य); (esp.) सूर्य , sun.

आदित्यवत् _ ind. like the sun.

आदेश _ m. 'direction', advice, order.

आद्य _ {आदि} 'at the beginning', first,
 original.

आधार _ m. support, base.

आधिपत्य _ {अधिपति} n. supremacy.

आधुनिक _ {अधुना} new, recent, modern.

आध्यात्मिक _ {अध्यात्म} spiritual.

आध्यान _ meditating, longing for.

आनक _ m. a large drum.

आनन _ {आ.अनन} n. 'breathing', mouth,
 face.

आनन्द _ {आ.} m. great pleasure, delight.

√आप् _ आप्लृ व्याप्तौ 5P pervade (obtain)
 →आप्नोति-आप्नोषि-आप्नोमि-आप्नुवन्ति;
 अव.; दुर्.प्र. obtain with difficulty; परि.;
 परि.सम् . reach, obtain; प्र. obtain; वि.
 pervade; सम् . reach, obtain, pervade.

आप: _ {अप् in Pl.} f. 'waters', water, Lat.
 »aqua«.

आपण _ m. market, shop.

आपद् _ {आ.} f. 'approaching', misfortune,
 emergency. आपत्सु मित्रं जानीयात् । In
 आपद् one can know a मित्र. आपद्धर्म _ m.
 'emergency-law', provision.

आपन्न _ {आपद्} 'approached', obtained.

आप्त _ »obtained«, Lat. »obtinere«, reached;
 m. a fit person, authority. आप्त-वाक्य _ n.
 'speech of an authority'.

आप्नोति _ (a verb) {√आप्} he obtains. कर्म
 आचरन् पूरुष: परम् आप्नोति । Performing
 duty, a person reaches the Supreme.
 (भगवद्गीता) मनुष्य: सुखं प्राप्नोति । Man
 obtains happiness.

आप्यायन _ filling, satiating.

आब्रह्म _ {आ.} upto ब्रह्म / ब्रह्मा
 (excluding/including it).

आभरण _ {आ.} n. 'decorating', ornament.

आभा _ {आ.} f. splendor.

आभास _ m. 'splendor', reflection, mere
 semblance.

आम् /ओम् _ ind. so be it, yes.

आम _ raw, uncooked; undigested.

आमय _ {आम} sickness, disease → (opp.)
 अनामय .

आमर्दन _ breaking.

आमर्शन _ touching, considering.

आमलक /आमलकी _ m./f. (=अमला).

आम्नाय _ m. sacred tradition.

आम्र _ (Aam) m. Mango tree (Mangifera
 indica) and fruit.

आम्लिका _ {अम्ल} f. tamarind (from Arab.
 tamr hindi, 'date of India').

आय _ m. 'coming', income.

आयत्ति _ {आ.} f. control, power.

आयाम _ {आ.} m. control →प्राणायाम .

आयास _ {आ.} m. effort, exertion.

आयुध _ {आ.} n. weapon.

आयुर्- _ {आयुस् in comp.}. आयुर्-धनुर्-
 गान्धर्व-स्थापत्य-वेद _ 4 उपवेद . आयुर्वेद _
 m. 'science of life', medicine, an उपवेद
 →चिकित्सा .

आयुस् _ n. life, vitality.

आरण्यक _ {अरण्य} 'relating to the forest'; n.
 उपासन-काण्ड studied by a वानप्रस्थ .

आरम्भ _ {आ.} m. 'holding firmly',
 undertaking, beginning.

आरात्रिक _ {आ.रात्रि} (Arati) n. 'nightly'
 worship by waving lights.

आराधना _ f. worship.
आराधित _ worshiped.
आराध्य _ worshipable.
आराम _ {आ.} m. delight.
आरोग्य _ {अ-रोग} n. freedom from disease, health.
आरोह _ {आ.} m. ascent → (opp.) अवरोह . आरोह-पन्थाः _ m. 'ascending path' of knowledge by प्रत्यक्ष and परोक्ष .
आर्जव _ n. 'straight', honesty.
आर्त _ 'fallen into' misfortune, afflicted.
आर्द्रक _ n. 'moist', fresh (undried) ginger →शृङ्गवेर .
आर्द्र-अक्षत-आरोपण _ mutual 'showering of wet unbroken [rice]'.
आर्य _ m. 'rising, advancing', honor, Germ. »Ehre«; nobility, misconceived by early Indology as a race. आर्यभट्ट _ m. Indian mathematician who described 100 BCE what is now known as π. आर्या-वर्त _ m. 'आर्य land', North India between हिमालय and विन्ध्याचल , सिन्धु river and प्रयाग .
आर्ष _ 'by a ऋषि', »archaic«; m. a विवाह where the father of the bride receives a pair of cows; n. another प्रमाण , but usually included in शास्त्र . आर्ष-प्रयोग _ m. 'usage by a ऋषि', an exception to the general rule.
आलय _ {आ.} m. dwelling, abode.
आलिङ्गन _ embracing.
आलु / आलुक _ n. an esculent root (in modern dialects applied to the yam, potatoe, etc.).
आलेख्य _ {आ.} n. 'to be written', writing; painting.
आलोचन _ looking, inspecting.
आवरण _ {आ.} 'covering', hiding; n. protection.
आवलि _ f. row, continuous line.
आवश्यक _ {अ-वश्य} necessary; n. necessity.
आवह _ {आ.} carrying, bringing.

आविर्- _ {आविस् in comp.}. आविर्भाव _ m. 'manifesting state', manifestation, appearance.
आविष्ट _ {आवेश} 'entered', filled with.
आविस् _ manifesting.
आवृत _ {आ.} covered.
आवृत्ति _ {आ.} f. return.
आवेश _ {आ.} m. entering, absorption →प्रवेश .
आशङ्का _ f. great doubt, fear.
आशय _ m. 'resting-place', abode; thought, intention.
आशा _ f. wish, hope.
आशिस् _ f. blessing.
आशीर्- _ {आशिस् in comp.}. आशीर्वाद _ m. 'wishing a blessing', blessing →धन्यवाद .
आशु _ ind. quickly, immediately. आशु-तोष _ m. 'who is quickly pleased', शिव .
आश्चर्य _ n. wonder, surprise.
आश्चर्यमय _ 'made of wonder', wonderful.
आश्चर्यवत् _ ind. like a wonder.
आश्रम _ {आ.} m. hermitage; गोत्र of a sage; 4 stages of life, their members are called ब्रह्मचारी , गृहस्थ , वानप्रस्थ , सन्न्यासी .
आश्रय _ {आ.} m. shelter.
आश्रित _ sheltered, surrendered; dependent.
आश्विन-पूर्णिमा _ a तिथि , celebrated as शरद्-पूर्णिमा or मित्र-पूर्णिमा .
√आस् _ आस उपवेशने विद्यमानतायां च 2A sit; be present, stay →आस्ते-आस्से-आसे-आसते ; उद्. sit above; उप."sit near", be at hand for service, attend upon, worship; परि.उप."sit near", worship, perform.
आसक्ति _ (=आसङ्ग) f.
आसङ्ग _ {आ.} m. strong attachment.
आसन _ 'sitting down', stopping, abiding; n. sitting, 3rd limb of अष्टाङ्गयोग . "Sitting without motion and pain."; sitting posture of हठयोग – like सिद्ध- पद्म-भद्र-मुक्त-वज्र-स्वस्तिक- सिंह-गोमुख-वीर-धनुर्-आसन ; a

seat, slightly raised from the ground and covered with कुश, अजिन, चैल; a high seat →सिंहासन.

आसुर _ {असुर} demoniac; m. a विवाह where dowry is asked from the groom (and the bride thus feels purchased) →शुल्क.

आसेचन _ pouring, sprinkling.

आस्तिक _ {अस्ति} m. a theist → (opp.) नास्तिक.

आस्तिक्य _ n. theism; piety.

आस्ते _ (a verb) {√आस्} he stays. सः इन्द्रिय-अर्थान् स्मरन् आस्ते । He remains contemplating sense objects. (भगवद्गीता).

आस्वादन _ tasting.

आहार _ {आ.} m. 'bringing near', taking, eating; food.

आहुति _ {आ.} f. (1) offering oblations; (2) invocation.

आह्निक _ {अहन्} daily.

आह्लाद _ {आ.} m. delight. आह्वान _ calling out.

√इ _ इण् गतौ 2P go →एति-एषि-एमि-यन्ति; अति. surpass; उप. go near, attain; अनु. go along; दुर्.अति. surpass with difficulty; प्र. depart; प्रति.अव. go down again; वि. go away; वि.अति. pass; वि.अप. go away; वि. go away; वि.परि. go round, turn; सम्.अति. surpass; सम्.अव. come together, assemble.

इ _ ind. expressing grief or anger.

इक्षु _ m. sugar-cane.

इच्छति _ (a verb) {√इष्} he desires. सः स्नानं कर्तुं इच्छति । He wants to take (do) a bath. यथा इच्छसि तथा कुरु । As you desire, so do. (भगवद्गीता) तत्त्वं वेदितुम् इच्छामि । I want to know the truth. (भगवद्गीता).

इच्छा _ f. desire.

इज्या _ f. worship.

इडा _ f. a नाडी on the left side of the body.

इतर _ another.

इति _ ind. thus (as if closing a quotation). इति उक्त्वा _ 'speaking thus'. इतिहास _ {इति-ह-आस} m. 'so indeed it was', tradition, history; a class of literature that concentrates on single heroes or events, (esp.) रामायण, महाभारत → (opp.) पुराण.

इत्यादि _ {इति-आदि} 'thus beginning', et cetera.

इदम् _ (a base) Lat. »idem« →अयम्; n. this, »it«, Lat. »id«.

इदानीम् _ ind. now.

इन्दिरा _ f. लक्ष्मी.

इन्दु _ (like बिन्दु) m. bright 'drop', moon.

इन्द्र _ m. lord; (esp.) the king of heaven. इन्द्र-प्रस्थ _ n. 'place of इन्द्र', the पाण्डव capital, (mod.) Delhi.

इन्द्रिय _ {इन्द्र} n. 'lordship', faculty of sense, sense organ – 5 ज्ञानेन्द्रिय, 5 कर्मेन्द्रिय, plus मनः (as 'inner sense').

इन्द्रियार्थ _ {इन्द्रिय-अर्थ} sense object →तन्मात्र.

इन्धन _ n. fuel.

इव _ ind. like.

√इष् _ इषु इच्छायाम् 6P desire →इच्छति-इच्छसि-इच्छामि-इच्छन्ति; अनु. search.

इषु _ m. arrow.

इष्ट _ (1) desired, pleasant, a गन्ध. (2) worshiped; n. worship, rites. "अग्निहोत्र, तपः, सत्य, protection of the वेद [through study], आतिथ्य, and worship of the gods are designated as इष्ट." इष्ट-देव _ m. one's 'desired/worshiped Lord'.

इष्वास _ {इषु-आस} m. 'arrow- throwing', bow.

इह _ ind. here; in this case; in this world /life.

√ईक्ष् _ ईक्ष दर्शने 1A see →ईक्षते-ईक्षसे-ईक्षे-ईक्षन्ते; अप. look down, watch; अव. look at, consider; दुर्.निर्. look at with difficulty; निर्. look at; वि. look at; सम्. see; सम्.प्र. stare.

ईक्षण _ n. 'looking', eye.

ईक्षते _ (a verb) {√ईक्ष्} he sees. आत्मानं सर्व-भूत-स्थम् ईक्षते । He sees the Supersoul situated in all beings. (भगवद्गीता).

ईदृश _ such.

ईप्सा _ f. desire to obtain.

ईर्ष्या _ f. envy.

ईश _ m. lord, God. ईशावास्यमिदं सर्वम् । All this [world] is pervaded (आवास्य) by ईश.

ईशान _ (=ईश).

ईश्वर _ (=ईश) →महेश्वर, ऐश्वर्य. ईश्वर-प्रणिधान _ n. surrender to God, a नियम.

ईषत् _ ind. little, slightly.

√ईह _ ईह चेष्टा-वाञ्छयो: 1A endeavor; desire →ईहते-ईहसे-ईहे-ईहन्ते.

ईहते _ (a verb) {√ईह} he desires. रा: आराधनम् ईहते । He desires the worship. (भगवद्गीता) अर्थ-सञ्चयान् ईहन्ते । They covet heaps of wealth. (भगवद्गीता).

उ _ ind. expressing conjecture, reflection.

उक्त _ 'spoken', called, designated; subject of a sentence in प्रथमा.

उक्ति _ f. speech, worthy speech or word.

उक्त्वा _ ind. 'after speaking'.

उक्षन् _ m. »ox«, Germ. »Ochse«.

उक्षा _ {उक्षन्}.

उग्र _ terrible, violent.

उचित _ correct, worthy.

उच्च _ {उद्.} high.

उच्चारण _ {उद्.} n. pronunciation.

उच्चै: _ {उच्च} ind. highly; loudly.

उच्छिष्ट _ {उद्.शिष्ट} (=अवशिष्ट).

उच्छ्रित _ {उद्.श्रित} 'lifted up', arisen.

उच्छ्वास _ {उद्.श्वास} m. 'breathing up', breath.

उज्जयिनी _ {उद्.} f. 'conquering', (mod.) Ujjain, capital of अवन्ति (with the ancient prime meridian).

उज्ज्वल _ {उद्.} 'blazing up', splendid.

उत _ (like अपि, for the sake of emphasis) ind. also, even, moreover.

उत्कण्ठा _ {उद्.} f. having the 'neck up', eagerness.

उत्क्षेपण _ throwing up/away.

उत्तम _ {उद्..तम} 'most up', highest, best → (opp.) अधम; big → (opp.) कन्य, मध्यम.

उत्तर _ {उद्..तर} 'more up', higher, better → (opp.) अधर; later; left (hand), north (when facing east); n. answer. उत्तर-मीमांसा _ f. a षड्दर्शन of अष्टवक्र.

उत्तरा _ f. north.

उत्तरायण _ {उत्तर-अयन} n. 'northern course', the progress of the sun to the north of the equator → (opp.) दक्षिणायन; formerly celebrated at winter solstice on December 21 →मकरसङ्क्रान्ति.

उत्तरोत्तर _ {उत्तर-उत्तर} n. 'more and more', 'reply on reply', conversation.

उत्थान _ {उद्.स्थ} n. 'standing up', rising.

उत्थित _ {उत्थान} 'stood up', risen.

उत्पाट _ pulled out.

उत्पाद _ {उद्.} m. product.

उत्पादन _ n. production.

उत्सन्न _ {उत्सादन} destructed.

उत्सर्ग _ m. emission, presentation.

उत्सव _ m. festival.

उत्सादन _ n. destruction.

उत्साह _ m. resolution, enthusiasm.

उत्सुक _ eager.

उद्. _ (a prefix, expressing:) up →उदय; »out« →उद्भव; by सन्धि उच्. →उच्छ्वास, उज्. →उज्ज्वल, उत्. →उत्तम, उन्. →उन्मूलन.

उद- _ (=उदक). उद-धि _ 'holding water', cloud, river, sea. उद-पान _ n. 'keeping water', a well.

उदक _ n. water.

उदय _ {उद्} m. rise.

उदर _ n. belly, stomach → »uterus«.

उदान _ m. a वात-दोष in the throat.

उदार _ {उद्} high; generous, noble →औदार्य .

उदारता _ f. generosity.

उदासीन _ {उद्} 'sitting above', indifferent, neutral.

उदाहरण _ n. 'declaring', illustration, example.

उद्गीथ _ 'chant', ओम् .

उद्देश _ {उद्} m. 'pointing out', direction, indication.

उद्धरेदात्मनात्मानम् । _ {उद्धरेत् आत्मना आत्मानम्} One should elevate oneself through the mind. (भगवद्गीता).

उद्धारण _ {उद्} n. 'drawing out', quote.

उद्भव _ m. generation, origin.

उद्भिद् _ f. a sprout.

उद्भिज्ज _ {उद्भिद्-} 'born as sprout' from a seed, a birth → -ज .

उद्यम _ m. effort, endeavor. उद्यम-शील _ active.

उद्यान _ n. garden, park.

उद्विग्न _ {उद्वेग} agitated.

उद्वेग _ {उद्.} m. 'uprising', agitation, distress.

उन्नयन _ {उद्.} 'drawing upwards', making a straight line; parting the hair.

उन्मत्त _ {उद्.मद} intoxicated, mad.

उन्मान _ n. weight, measure.

उन्मूलन _ {उद्.} n. 'uprooting', destruction.

उप. _ (a prefix, expressing:) near →उपासन ; »sub-«, Gr. »hypo« →उपवेद .

उपकार _ m. help, assistance.

उपचार _ m. 'attendance', ceremony; a present, item of worship – like पुष्प-धूप-दीप-फल ; treatment.

उपताप _ m. pain, trouble.

उपदेश _ m. 'sub-direction', advice →हितोपदेश .

उपनयन _ n. 'bringing/leading near' to spiritual knowledge, initiation from 8 to 24 years (depending on maturity, formerly caste), but before marriage; synonyms are उपायन, मौञ्जि-/मौञ्जी-बन्धन and व्रत-बन्ध ; a संस्कार for the first 3 वर्ण according to वैदिकविद्धि →ब्रह्मजन्म, द्विज ; formerly it meant to 'bring' the boy to live with the family of the teacher (गुरुकुल) for 5 months a year (the rest of the year private study). Ceremony: A simple rite, as is evident from the words of गौतम to सत्यकाम – "O gentle one, bring the wood for the fire sacrifice of initiation. I will initiate you." The disciple vows to live till समावर्तन as ब्रह्मचारी for Vedic study, and is given सावित्रीमन्त्र/ब्रह्मगायत्री (for सन्ध्यावन्दन) and उपवीत . The ceremony was done for girls also, but their study lasted [as सद्योवधू] only till puberty, or [as ब्रह्मवादिनी] they did not leave the house for study, being taught by the father, uncle or brother. Women like विश्ववारा, अपाला and घोषा काक्षीवती are stated to have been composers of ऋग्वेद hymns.

उपनिषद् _ f. 'sitting close' for instruction, secret meaning; ज्ञानकाण्ड studied by a सन्न्यासी .

उपपद _ n. 'subword', derived word.

उपमा _ f. comparison, similarity.

उपमान _ n. comparing, a variety of अनुमान .

उपयुक्त _ useful.

उपरि _ ind. »over«, above, »sur-«, »super«.

उपल _ m. stone, jewel → »opal«.

उपलभ्य _ available.

उपलेपन _ smearing, anointing.

उपवास _ m. 'abstinence', fasting till पारण ; different forms, like 'no cooked food', एकभक्त, नक्तव्रत, एकादशी, निर्जल, चान्द्रायण .

उपवीत _ n. 'put on', sacred thread (पवित्र), sometimes kept wrapped around the right ear.

उपवेद _ m. 'sub-वेद', the 4 sciences आयुर्-धनुर्-गान्धर्व-स्थापत्य-वेद .

उपवेशन _ sitting.

उपशम _ m. being/becoming pacified.

उपसर्ग _ m. 'addition', prefix.

उपसेवा _ f. service, love.

उपस्थ _ m. 'situated below', generative organ.

उपस्थान _ n. 'standing near', attendance, worship; prayers to सूर्य in सन्ध्यावन्दन.

उपस्थित _ 'situated near', present.

उपस्थिति _ f. presence.

उपाङ्ग _ {उप.अङ्ग} n. 'sub-limb', subdivision.

उपादान _ {उप.आदान} n. 'taking up', grasping; material cause, material.

उपाधि _ m. substitute, title.

उपानत् _ f. sandal, shoe.

उपाय _ m. a means, remedy, solution.

उपाश्रित _ {आश्रय} taken shelter.

उपासन _ n. 'sitting ncar', attcnding, worshiping. उपासन-काण्ड _ n. part of वेद dealing with worship → (opp.) कर्म- , ज्ञान-काण्ड .

उपासना _ f. attendance, worship.

उपेक्षा _ f. 'overlooking', disregard.

उपेत _ attained, endowed.

उभ _ both, Russ. »oba«.

उभय _ (=उभ). उभय-पद _ n. 'word for both', a form of conjugation (U), → (opp.) आत्मने- (A) and परस्मै- (P).

उमा _ (=दुर्गा, पार्वती). उमा-पति _ m. 'husband of उमा', शिव .

उर-ग _ m. 'breast-going', serpent.

उरु _ broad, great.

उलूक _ m. »owl«, Germ. »Eule«.

उल्ब _ n. cover; womb.

उल्लास _ {उद्.} m. 'coming forth', joy, happiness.

उल्लेख _ {उद्.} m. mention.

उष्ण _ hot, warm → (opp.) शीत.

उष्ट्र _ m. a camel or buffalo.

ऊधस् _ n. »udder«, Gr. »outhar«, breast.

ऊन _ less, minus →एकोन .

ऊर्जः _ {ऊर्जस्}.

ऊर्जस् _ n. strength, power.

ऊर्जित _ strong, powerful.

ऊर्णा _ f. wool; cobweb.

ऊर्ध्व _ upward, onward. ऊर्ध्व-पुण्ड्र _ n. an upward वैष्णव mark with 'U'-shape →द्वादशतिलक .

ऊर्ध्वाङ्ग _ {ऊर्ध्व-अङ्ग} n. 'upper part' of the body. ऊर्ध्वाङ्ग-चिकित्सा _ f. medicine of head and throat.

√ऋ _ ऋ गतौ प्रापणे च 1P go; get → ऋच्छति-; आ. go up, reach, fall into.

ऋक् _ {ऋच्} f. praise →ऋग्वेद .

ऋक्ष _ m. bear; a constellation; the Rickshaw (Jap. »jinrikisha«) is a 19th century Japanese invention.

ऋग्- _ {ऋक्- in comp.}. ऋग्-साग-यजुर्-वेद _ 3 वेद . ऋग्-साम-यजुर्-अथर्व-वेद _ 4 वेद . ऋग्वेद _ {ऋक्-} m. 'वेद of praise', the most ancient scripture.

ऋच्छति _ (a verb) {√ऋ} he gets. ब्रह्म-निर्वाणम् ऋच्छति । He gets liberation in Brahma. (भगवद्गीता).

ऋण _ n. debt; 5 debts of man to देव-ऋषि-पितृ-नृ-भूत for rain, knowledge, inheritance, help and service →पञ्चयज्ञ .

ऋत _ 'occured', settled, true; n. truth, promise, Russ. »rota«; sacred law. ऋतम् _ ind. rightly, truely.

ऋतु _ {ऋत} m. 'right time' (esp. for worship) → Lat. »ritus«, »rite«; →ऋत्विक्; period, season; the 6 seasons वसन्त-ग्रीष्म-वर्षा-शरद्-हेमन्त-शिशिर , see मास →चतुर्मास; the menstrual course. ऋतु-काल _ m. time of menstruation. "Flowing rivers and dust raised by the wind are not impure. Women, old and young, never become impure." ... which puts them almost beyond punishment: "Women who lead a regular life for one year are completely freed from all कर्म . ... Sinful women who are afraid [of punishment] are not to be punished by one in knowledge. They are [automatically] purified by their menstrual flow (रजस्), as a metallic plate is purified by using ashes." After ऋतुकाल, most Hindu women follow 3-5 resting days, taking a bath on the 5th day. During that time there are restrictions for performing पूजा and thus kitchen work.

ऋतुकाल-संस्कार _ mostly small and private function after the first menstruation (Menarche); the girl is welcomed into womanhood and imparted knowledge about hormonal changes, etc.; Ceremony: seclusion and turmeric bathing ceremony, wearing a half-saree for the first time, married women from the neighborhood perform her पूजा (with दीप) and देवपूजा (with भोग); प्रसाद is distributed to the girl and guests, and the girl is gifted silk Sarees; evil-eye warding off ceremony after this event.

ऋते _ ind. excepting.

ऋत्विक् _ {ऋतु-इज्} m. 'who offers at the right time', a priest; a यज्ञ involves 4 priests – होतृ-उद्गातृ- अध्वर्यु-ब्रह्म.

ऋद्ध _ 'grown', prosperous.

ऋद्धि _ f. growth, prosperity.

ऋषभ _ m. bull; the best of any kind; 2nd स्वर; the sage ऋषभदेव – after entrusting his kingdom to भरत, the eldest of his 100 sons, ऋषभदेव did तपस् at पुलहाश्रम.

ऋषि _ m. 'seer', sage →आर्ष.

ए _ ind. expressing recollection or calling.

एक _ one; alone, unique. एकं सन्तं बहुधा कल्पयन्ति। Of Him, who is but एक, they think in many ways. एक-दण्ड _ m. 'one दण्ड', the bamboo carried by a शङ्कर- सन्न्यासी. एक-भक्त _ m. who is devoted to one only; n. eating only once a day (immediately after midday), a व्रत. एक-

वचन _ n. 'speaking of one', singular number → (opp.) द्वि-, बहु-वचन.

एकता _ (=एकत्व) f. oneness.

एकत्र _ ind. 'in one place'.

एकत्व _ n. oneness.

एकदा _ ind. 'at one time', once.

एकधा _ ind. 'in one way', simply.

एकादश _ {एकादशन्}.

एकादशन् _ eleven; eleventh.

एकादशी _ f. 'eleventh [रात्रि]' in both शुक्ल- and कृष्ण-पक्ष, also called हरि-वासर. एकादशी-व्रत _ n. a vow for all (वैष्णव, शैव and सौर) with उपवास (at least in शुक्लपक्ष, at least from cooked food, or एकभक्त, or at least from grains) and जागर at night (with songs and music); पारण on द्वादशी morning; there are more considerations, because some वैष्णव observe उपवास only on शुद्ध-एकादशी, otherwise on द्वादशी (which is then called महा- द्वादशी).

एकान्त _ {एक-अन्त} 'one end', exclusive, alone, lonely.

एकोन _ {एक-ऊन} one less.

एतद् _ (a base) →एषः; n. this, Russ. »étot«.

एति _ (a verb) {√इ} he goes. सः माम् एति। He goes to me. (भगवद्गीता) सूर्यः उदेति। The sun rises. सः परं पुरुषम् उपैति। He attains the Supreme Lord. (भगवद्गीता).

एधः _ {एधस्}.

एधस् _ n. fuel, firewood.

एला _ f. cardamom.

एव _ ind. certainly, indeed.

एवम् _ ind. thus, and.

ऐ _ (=ए)

ऐतिहासिक _ {इतिहास} historical.

ऐतिह्य _ {इति-ह} n. tradition (=इतिहास); another प्रमाण, usually included in प्रत्यक्ष.

ऐश्वर्य _ {ईश्वर} n. lordship.

ओ _ (=ए)

ओं-कार _ m. 'the word ओम्'.

ओङ्कार _ {ओं-कार, different सन्धि}.

ओजः _ {ओजस्}.

ओजस् _ n. strength, energy.

ओदन _ n. grain mashed and cooked with milk, porridge.

ओम् _ the sacred syllable (related to आम्), said to be ब्रह्म in sound, also called ओंकार, प्रणव and उद्गीथ; sometimes explained as अ-उ-म् (which becomes ओम् by सन्धि); its symbol is ॐ. "The essence (रस) of all these elements (भूत) is earth (पृथिवी), of that water (अप्), of that plants (ओषधि), of that man (पुरुष), of that speech (वाच्), of that ऋग्वेद, of that सामवेद, and of that ॐ." "Speech (वाच्) is ऋग्वेद, प्राण is सामवेद. ... This pair (मिथुन) is joined into this syllable (अक्ष) ॐ. Whenever a couple comes together, both surely fulfill each other's (अन्योन्य) desire (काम). A wise man (विद्वान्) who worships the syllable (अक्षर) ॐ (उद्गीथ), becomes an obtainer (आपयितृ) of desires." ॐ is the symbol of both impersonal ब्रह्म and personal God. "ॐ is ब्रह्म. ॐ is all this [world]." "His (ईश्वर) sound-manifestation is ॐ." "The ॐ one should know to be ईश्वर, situated in the heart (हृद्) of all. Knowing ओंकार as all-pervading (सर्व- व्यापिन), a wise man (धीर) does not lament."

ओषधि _ f. 'light-containing', plant, herb.

ओष्ठ _ m. lip.

औ _ (=ए)

औदार्य _ {उदार} n. generosity, nobility.

औपम्य _ {उपमा} n. the state of similarity.

औम् _ (=ओम्).

औषध _ {ओषधि} n. 'consisting of herbs', herb, medicine.

क _ (a base) →किम्. .क _ (an affix, expressing diminution) little →बालक.

कंस _ m. metal, vessel.

कः _ {किम्} m. who?, Russ. »kto«.

कक्ष _ m. room.

कच्चिद् _ {क} ind. is it that?

कज्जल _ n. lampblack, collyrium →अञ्जन.

कटु _ 'sharp', a गन्ध; pungent, a रस.

कठिन _ hard; difficult.

कठोर _ hard; harsh.

कण _ m. grain; particle.

कणिका _ f. drop.

कण्ट _ m. thorn.

कण्टक _ m. thorn; anything pointed.

कण्ठ _ m. throat, neck.

कतर _ {क.तर} 'what more?', which of two?, Russ. »kotoryi«.

कति _ {क} ind. how many?

कथञ्चिद् _ {कथम्.चिद्} ind. somehow.

कथम् _ {क} ind. which manner?, how?, Russ. »kak«.

कथा _ f. talk, story.

कदम्ब _ m. Kadam tree (Neolamarckia cadamba) and wood.

कदली _ (Kela) f. Banana tree (Plantain, Musa paradisiaca) and fruit.

कदा _ {क} ind. when? (in time), Russ. »kogda«.

कदाचन _ (=कदाचिद्).

कदाचिद् _ ind. sometimes.

कदापि _ {कदा अपि} ind. sometimes.

कनिष्ठ _ youngest.

कनिष्ठा _ f. small finger.

कनिष्ठिका _ (=कनिष्ठा).

कन्था _ f. rag, patched garment.

कन्दर्प _ m. Cupid.

कन्दुक _ m. a ball of wood.

कन्य _ smallest → (opp.) मध्यम, उत्तम.

कन्या _ f. girl, daughter; virgin, a राशि, Lat. Virgo. कन्या-दान _ 'gift of the girl'.

कपट _ m. deceit, cheating.

कपि _ m. »ape«.

कपित्थ _ m. Kaith tree (Limonia acidissima, Feronia limonia) and fruit (Elephant Apple).

कपोत _ m. pigeon.

कफ _ m. phlegm; a दोष, said to be oily, cold, heavy, slow, smooth, slimy, and stable. कफ-पित्त-वात/वायु _ 3 दोष.

कफोणि _ m. elbow.

कमल _ m. Lotus (Kamal, Nelumbo nucifera) and its flower.

कम्पन _ moving, shaking.

कम्बल _ m. blanket.

कर _ m. (1) {√कृ} »creating«, hand; (2) tax. कर-तल _ m. palm of the hand. कर-ताल _ n. clapping the hands; m. cymbal. कर-पृष्ठ _ m. back of the hand. कर-मर्द _ m. Karanda tree (Carissa carandas) and fruit.

करञ्ज _ m. Karaunda tree (Pongamia pinnata) and seed.

करण _ {√कृ} n. »creating«, instrument; a sense.

करणापाटव _ {करण-अपाटव} n. 'non-sharpness of the senses', a दोष.

करादि _ {कर-आदि} 'hand, etc.', hands and limbs. करादि-न्यास _ see न्यास.

कराल _ gaping; dreadful.

करीर _ m. Kair tree (Capparis decidua) and fruit.

करुण _ m. 'causing compassion', pity, a गौणरस.

करुणा _ f. compassion.

करोति _ (a verb) {√कृ} he »creates«, does, makes. सन्न्यासी कार्यं कर्म करोति। A Sannyāsī does the prescribed duty. (भगवद्गीता) अग्निः एधांसि भस्मसात् कुरुते। Fire burns fuels to ashes. (भगवद्गीता) यद् करोषि तद् मद्-अर्पणं कुरुष्व। Whatever you do, make that an offering to me. (भगवद्गीता) न एव किञ्चिद् करोमि इति मन्येत। 'I [myself] am not at all doing anything', thus he should think. (भगवद्गीता) योगिनः आत्म-शुद्धये कर्म कुर्वन्ति। [Karma-] Yogīs perform work for the purification of the mind. (भगवद्गीता).

कर्क/कर्कट _ m. crab, »cancer«, Gr. »karkinos«; a राशि, Lat. Cancer.

कर्ण _ m. ear; helm or rudder of a ship. कर्ण-धार _ m. 'holding the helm', helmsman, pilot. कर्ण-वेध _ 'piercing the ears'; a संस्कार together with मुण्डन or उपनयन.

कर्णिकार _ m. Karnikara tree (Bayur, Pterospermum acerifolium).

कर्तव्य _ {√कृ} n. 'to be created /done', duty.

कर्ता _ {कर्तृ}.

कर्तृ _ {√कृ} m. »creator«, doer, worker, agent. कर्तृ-वाच्य _ n. active voice.

कर्तृत्व _ n. 'doership', agency, responsibility.

कर्पास _ (Kapas) m. Cotton tree (Gossypium arboreum).

कर्पूर _ (Kapur) m. Camphor tree (Cinnamomum camphora); n. »camphor«, Arab. »kafur«.

कर्म _ {कर्मन्, कृ} n. »creating«, making, activity, work; ritual; reaction →कर्मवाद; grammatical object.

कर्मण्येवाधिकारस्ते। {कर्मणि एव अधिकारः ते} Your अधिकार is in [your specific] duty only. कर्म-काण्ड _ n. part of वेद dealing with rituals → (opp.) ज्ञान-, उपासन-काण्ड. कर्म-कृत् _ m. who does work. कर्म-ज्ञान-भक्ति _ 3 kinds of योग practice. कर्म-धारय _ m. 'supporting activity', a समास. कर्म-फल _ n. fruit of activity; reaction, in 2 stages अप्रारब्ध- and प्रारब्ध-कर्म; it becomes destiny (दैव) and conditions every future action. कर्म-योग _ m. 'योग through कर्म', performing one's duty as worship. कर्म-वाच्य _ n. passive voice. कर्म-वाद _ m. a general thesis of how every action creates a reaction (कर्मफल) – सुकृति creates सुख,

दुष्कृति/पाप creates दुःख, the root-cause being अविद्या. कर्म-सन्न्यास _ सन्न्यास through कर्मयोग.

कर्मी _ {कर्मिन्, कर्म} m. 'performer of duty', worker, कर्मयोगी.

कर्मेन्द्रिय _ {कर्म-इन्द्रिय} n. 'sense of action' – पाणि-पाद-वाक्-उपस्थ-पायु.

कर्षति _ (a verb) {√कृष्} he draws. अ-वितृप्ता जिह्वा मा विकर्षति । The insatiable tongue pulls me. (भागवत-पुराण).

कलश _ m. water-pot.

कलह _ m. quarrel.

कला _ f. small part of anything; art. कला-कार _ m. artist.

कलि _ m. quarrel; personified as the son of क्रोध and हिंसा. कलि-युग _ n. 'युग of quarrel' (last in value).

कलिल _ n. thicket; confusion.

कलेवर _ n. body, »corpse«, Lat. »cadaver«.

कल्कि _ m. an अवतार who is to appear to destroy the wicked.

कल्प _ m. 'formation', creation; day of ब्रह्मा; notion, desire; ritual, a वेदाङ्ग. कल्प-विकल्प _ m. 'idea and doubt', functions of मनः. कल्प-वृक्ष _ (=कल्प-तरु/-द्रुम) m. 'desire-tree', a tree yielding desires; any productive or bountiful source.

कल्पते _ (a verb) {√कृप्} he is able. सः अनन्त्याय कल्पते । That [soul] is capable of infinity. (श्वेताश्वतर-उपनिषद्).

कल्पना _ f. idea, imagination.

कल्मष _ n. impure activity, sin.

कल्याण _ fortunate; n. good fortune.

कवच _ m. armor, amulet.

कवि _ (Kabir) m. 'thinker', poet →काव्य. कवि-राज _ m. 'king of poets'.

कविता _ f. poetry.

कश्मल _ n. dirt, sin; weakness, despair.

कश्यप _ m. a son of मरीचि (smt. confused with काश्यप /कण्व), father of the आदित्य, दानव, a.o.

कषाय _ astringent, a रस.

कष्ट _ n. suffering, trouble.

कस्तूरी _ f. musk →मुष्क.

कस्मात् _ {किम्} ind. 'from what?', why?

काक _ m. crow.

√काक्ष् _ काक्षि काङ्क्षायाम् 1P wish →काङ्क्षति-काङ्क्षसि-काङ्क्षामि-काङ्क्षन्ति.

काङ्क्षति _ (a verb) {√काक्ष्} he desires. सः न द्वेष्टि न काङ्क्षति । He neither hates nor desires. (भगवद्गीता).

काङ्क्षा _ f. desire.

काङ्क्षित _ desired.

काञ्चन _ n. gold.

काञ्चनार _ m. Kachnar tree (Bauhinia variegata) and flower.

काञ्ची _ f. a ornamented girdle; name of a holy town.

काण्ड _ m. »cane«, Gr. »kanna«; portion →कर्मकाण्ड; chapter (=खण्ड).

कातर _ n. timidity, despair.

कानन _ n. forest, grove.

कान्ति _ {काम} f. desire; brightness.

काम _ m. desire, pleasure; sensuality, lust; Cupid. काम-क्रोध-लोभ _ 3 'gates to hell'. काम-क्रोध-लोभ-मोह-मद-मात्सर्य _ 6 अनर्थ. काम-देव _ m. the 'god of love', Cupid. काम-धेनु _ f. 'desire-cow', a cow yielding desires. काम-सूत्र _ n. a work on sexual love by वात्स्यायन.

काम्य _ 'based on काम', desirable; optionally, for rewards (at a तीर्थ or astrological conjunction) → (opp.) नित्य, नैमित्तिक.

काय _ m. body. काय-चिकित्सा _ f. 'body /general medicine'.

-कार _ {√कृ} m. »creating«, maker; author.

कारक _ n. »creator«, maker.

कारण _ n. »creating«, making; cause, means, instrument; element →तत्त्व; reason, motive.

कारण-सागर _ m. 'ocean of elements' in their अव्यक्त form, also called कारण-उदक, विरजा-नदी, causal ocean, spiritual ocean (of which गङ्गा is but one drop) →प्राकृत-सर्ग.

कार्त्तिक _ (=कार्तिक) m. a मास. कार्त्तिक-पूर्णिमा _ a तिथि, celebrated as आविर्भाव day of मत्स्य-अवतार, वृन्दा and कार्त्तिकेय; also dedicated to the पितृ.

कार्त्तिकेय _ (=कार्तिकेय) m. a son of शिव and पार्वती.

कार्पण्य _ {कृपण} n. miserliness, weakness.

कार्य _ {√कृ} (=कर्तव्य) n. 'to be done', duty; effect.

काल _ (1) black; (2) m. 'going', 'counting', time →मात्रा; broken into भूत-वर्तमान-भविष्यत्-काल; season; destiny; death.

काल-चक्र _ n. 'wheel of time', cycle →सुदर्शनचक्र.

काली _ {काल} f. a 'black' form of दुर्गा.

काव्य _ {कवि} n. poetry.

√काश् _ काश् दीप्तौ 1A shine →काशते-काशसे-काशे-काशन्ते; प्र. shine, become visible.

काश _ (Kans) m. Wild Sugarcane (Thatch Grass, Saccharum spontaneum).

काशते _ (a verb) {√काश्} he shines. मात्सर्यात् न प्रकाशते। Because of envy one does not shine. (महाभारत).

काशी _ f. 'shining', sun; (mod.) वाराणसी (Benares).

काष्ठ _ n. wood. काष्ठ-मौन _ m. 'silence like wood' (without even a gesture).

किं पुनर् _ ind. what more?

किञ्चन _ (=किञ्चिद्).

किञ्चिद् _ {किम्} ind. whatever, somewhat, something.

किन्तु _ {किम्} ind. however, but.

किन्नर _ {किम्} m. 'is he human?', a humanlike being.

किम् _ {क →कः} (a base) n. what?; ind. what?, whether? (like a question mark) →किन्नर; frequently connected with other particles →किञ्चिद्, किञ्चन, किन्तु.

किरण _ m. ray of light.

किरीट _ n. diadem, crown.

किल _ ind. verily, indeed.

किलाट _ m. thickened milk, cheese (Paneer).

किल्बिष _ n. fault, offense, sin.

किशोर _ m. a youth, teenager →कैशोर.

कीट _ m. worm, insect.

कीर्तन _ n. 'glorifying' God's नाम-रूप-गुण-लीला; (Kirtan) a genre of devotional music, where the audience responds to the singer.

कीर्ति _ f. glory, fame.

कीलक _ m. axis.

कु. _ (a prefix, expressing deficiency) bad →कुतर्क.

कुक्कुट _ m. »cock«, Russ. »kokot«.

कुक्कुटी _ f. hen.

कुक्कुर _ m. dog.

कुङ्कुम _ n. a red powder made from केसर or हलदी, Pers. »kurkum« → »crocus«, »curcuma« (=हलदी).

कुञ्ज _ m. bower.

कुटिल _ n. bent, crooked.

कुटीर _ m. cottage.

कुटुम्ब _ n. household, family.

कुटुम्बक _ (=कुटुम्ब).

कुण्ड _ n. pit; pond, lake.

कुण्डल _ n. ring, ear-ring, bracelet; coil of a rope.

कुण्डलिनी _ f. an energy or form of दुर्गा.

कुतः _ {क} ind. 'from whom/where?', where?, why?

कुतर्क _ {कु.} m. bad argument.

कुत्र _ {क} ind. where?, Russ. »kuda«.

कुत्सा _ f. contempt.

कुबेर _ (=कुवेर).

कुमार _ m. child, boy, son →कौमार; prince; 4 sons of ब्रह्मा →चतुःसन.

कुमारी _ f. girl, daughter; miss, princess; Aloe (Gwarpatha, Aloe vera).

कुमुद _ n. white water-lily.

कुम्भ _ m. pot, Russ. »kub«; a राशि, Lat. Aquarius (waterman). कुम्भ-मेला _ a festival on कुम्भ-योग at प्रयाग (Allahabad), हरिद्वार (Haridwar), नासिक (Nashik) and उज्जयनी (Ujjain); celebrated with स्नान and सत्सङ्ग; at प्रयाग on मकरसङ्क्रान्ति, अमावास्या and वसन्तपञ्चमी. कुम्भ-योग _ a conjuncture (astron. योग) once in twelve years; celebrated as कुम्भमेला.

कुम्भक _ m. stopping the breath →प्राणायाम.

कुरण्ट／कुरब／कुरबक _ (Kuruvaka) m. different kinds of Amaranth (Barleria).

कुरु _ m. King कुरु. कुरु-क्षेत्र _ n. sacrificial 'field of King कुरु', an ancient pilgrimage and site of the महाभारत war.

कुरूप _ {कु.} 'bad form', ugly.

कुल _ n. herd, multitude; family, community. कुल-धर्म _ m. family tradition.

कुवेर _ (=कुबेर) m. the god of riches.

कुश _ m. Kusha grass (Darba, Desmotachya bipinnata) and rope, used in rites.

कुशल _ 'taking कुश' (in a ceremony), well, expert; n. well- being, happiness. कुशलम् _ ind. well, happily.

कुशिन् _ m. 'furnished with कुश', who is happy.

कुशी _ {कुशिन्}.

कुसुम _ n. flower.

√कूज् _ कूज अव्यक्ते शब्दे 1P sound →कूजति.

कूजति _ (a verb) {√कूज्} he sounds. वृक्षे खगः कूजति | In the tree the bird sounds.

कूट _ n. top; heap, stock; total stock or first stage of अप्रारब्धकर्म. कूट-बीज-फलोन्मुख _ 3 stages of अप्रारब्धकर्म. कूट-स्थ _ 'standing at the top', spiritual.

कूप _ m. a well.

कूर्च _ m. bunch, bundle of grass.

कूर्म _ m. tortoise; an अवतार; a वातदोष that helps contraction.

कूल _ n. slope; shore, bank.

√कृ _ डुकृञ् करणे 8U »creating« →करोति-करोषि-करोमि-कुर्वन्ति, Lat. »creare«, doing, making; दुर्. do bad /evil; प्र. produce; प्रति. counteract; सु. do well; सु.दुर्. do with great difficulty; →कर्म, कर्ता, कारण, कार्य, क्रिया.

कृकर _ m. a वातदोष that increases appetite.

कृच्छ्र _ difficult, painful.

-कृत् _ {√कृ} »creating«, making; m. maker →कर्मकृत्; author →वेदान्तकृत्.

कृत _ {√कृ} »created«, made; n. deed, good deed; side of a die marked with four spots (first in value). कृत-कृत्य _ 'achieved aim', accomplished. कृत-निश्चय _ 'made decision', determined. कृत-युग _ (=सत्ययुग) n. the age of good deeds (first in value).

कृताञ्जलि _ {कृत-अञ्जलि} m. 'done अञ्जलि', standing in a respectful posture.

कृतान्त _ {कृत-अन्त} m. 'causing an end', conclusion.

कृतार्थ _ {कृत-अर्थ} 'accomplished purpose', successful, satisfied.

कृत्य _ {√कृ} 'to be done', right, proper; aim.

कृत्रिम _ artificial.

कृत्वः _ ind. -fold, times, Russ. »krat« →सहस्र-कृत्वः.

कृत्वा _ {√कृ} 'after doing'.

कृत्स्न _ all, entire.

कृदन्त _ m. 'ending with a कृत्', words derived with कृत् प्रत्यय.

√कृप् _ कृपू सामर्थ्ये 1A be able →कल्पते; वि. be able.

कृपण _ poor, wretched, weak; m. a miser.

कृपया _ {कृपा} ind. 'with compassion', please!

कृपा _ f. compassion.

कृमि _ m. »worm«, Lat. »vermis«; insect.

कृश _ thin, lean.

√कृष् _ कृष विलेखने आकर्षणे च 1P draw, scratch (plow) →कर्षति; pull, attract; →कृषक, कृषि, कृष्ण.

कृषक _ m. 'plougher', farmer.

कृषि _ f. 'ploughing', farming, agriculture.

कृष्ण _ m. 'who attracts', God; (esp.) कृष्ण-अवतार, born in मथुरा on 18.07. 894 (श्रावण-कृष्ण-अष्टमी); dark, black, Russ. »cornyi« → (opp.) शुक्ल. कृष्ण-पक्ष _ m. 'dark part', dark fortnight, waning moon →चान्द्रमास.

केतकी _ m. Screw-Pine (Pandanus odorifer).

केतु _ m. comet, meteorite; dragon's tail, 9th ग्रह.

केदार _ m. field.

केन प्रकारेण _ 'by which method?', how?

केलि _ m.f. play, sport.

केवल _ exclusive, pure →कैवल्य. केवलम् _ ind. only, merely, simply.

केवलाद्वैत _ {केवल-अद्वैत} n. 'pure monism' (=मायावाद) of शङ्कराचार्य → (opp.) द्वैत, द्वैताद्वैत.

केश _ m. hair of the head, Russ. »kosa«.

केशव _ m. 'who has beautiful hair', कृष्ण.

केशाः _ {केश in Pl.} m. 'hairs', hair.

केशान्त _ cutting the 'end of the hair' (near the top of the ear) and beard (श्मश्रु) at 16 (latest before marriage); ceremony similar to चौल; on that occasion, the boy presents a cow to the teacher, for which it is also known as गो-दान.

केसर _ n. hair, filament; filament of a lotus, saffron →कुङ्कुम. केसर-चन्दन _ a mixture of चन्दन and केसर or हल्दी.

कैतव _ n. cheating.

कैलास _ m. mount »Kailash«.

कैवल्य _ {केवल} n. absolute oneness.

कैशोर _ {किशोर} n. youth, teenage, a वयः.

कोकिल _ m. »cuckoo«.

कोटि _ (Crore) f. ten million.

कोण _ m. »corner«, Gr. »gonia«, angle →त्रिकोण.

कोप _ m. passion, anger.

कोमल _ soft, gentle.

कोविदार _ m. Kovidar tree (var. of काञ्चनार) and flower.

कोश _ m. box, case; treasury.

कौटिल्य _ {कुटिल} m. name given to चाणक्य; n. crookedness.

कौन्तेय _ m. 'son of कुन्ती', अर्जुन.

कौपीन _ n. underwear.

कौमार _ {कुमार} n. youth, a वयः.

कौशल _ {कुशल} n. well-being, expertise.

क्रतु _ m. intention; sacrifice.

क्रम _ m. step, course, series, order. क्रम-पाठ _ m. 'phrase recitation' (with सन्धि) for memorization (words 1+2, 2+3, etc.) → (opp.) पदपाठ. क्रम-वाचक _ n. 'order expression', ordinal → (opp.) सङ्ख्या-वाचक.

क्रिया _ {√कृ} f. activity, verb; treatment; rite. क्रिया-योग _ m. 'ritualistic योग'. "[The three items of नियम, namely] तपः, स्वाध्याय and ईश्वरप्रणिधान are called क्रियायोग."

√क्री _ डुक्रीञ् द्रव्यविनिमये 9U exchange (buy, sell) →क्रीणाति, वि. sell.

√क्रीड् _ क्रीड् विहारे 1P play →क्रीडति.

क्रीडति _ (a verb) {√क्रीड्} he plays. सः बालकेन सह क्रीडति । He plays with the child.

क्रीडा _ f. sport, play, game.

क्रीणाति _ (a verb) {√क्री} he buyes. सः किं क्रीणाति । What does he buy? सः किं विक्रीणीते । What does he sell?

क्रुद्ध _ {क्रोध} angry.

क्रूर _ cruel.

क्रोध _ m. anger.

क्रोश _ (Kos) m. 'range of the voice', a मात्रा (22 m).

क्लीब _ impotent, weak →क्लैब्य.

क्लेदन _ making wet, moistening.

क्लेश _ m. affliction, distress; 5 [causes] – अविद्या-अस्मिता-राग-द्वेष-अभिनिवेश.

क्लेशन _ suffering.

क्लैब्य _ {क्लीब} n. impotence, weakness.

क्व _ {क} ind. where?

क्वचिद् _ {क्व} ind. anywhere; anytime, whatever.

क्षण _ m. 'instant', moment, a मात्रा (1.5 s, 3 निमेष).

क्षणन _ tolerating.

क्षत्र _ n. power, might; a क्षत्रिय (to क्षत्र or क्षेत्र the Pers. »shah« is connected).

क्षत्रिय _ {क्षत्र} m. member of the 2nd वर्ण, warrior, administrator; his prerogatives are protection and punishment.

क्षपित _ diminished, destroyed.

क्षमा _ f. tolerance, forgiveness.

क्षय _ m. destruction, decay, end.

क्षर _ 'melting away', perishable.

क्षरण _ pouring forth.

√क्षल् _ क्षल शौचे 10P wash →क्षालयति; प्र. wash.

क्षात्र _ 'relating to a क्षत्र/क्षत्रिय'.

क्षान्ति _ {क्षणन} f. patience, tolerance.

क्षालयति _ (a verb) {√क्षल्} he washes. सः हस्तौ प्रक्षालयति। He washes the hands.

क्षिति _ f. abode; the earth.

क्षिप्रम् _ ind. quickly.

क्षीण _ {क्षय} destroyed, lost.

क्षीर _ n. milk; thickened milk. क्षीर-ज _ n. a 'milk-product', cream. क्षीर-दधि-घृत-शकृत्-गोमूत्र _ 5 cow products (पञ्चगव्य).

क्षुद्र _ tiny; mean.

क्षेत्र _ n. soil, field; land, place of pilgrimage; geometrical figure; field of activity, the body (as field of the soul). क्षेत्र-ज्ञ _ m. 'knowing the field', farmer; soul. क्षेत्र-पाल _ m. 'guardian of the field/site', a Deity, (esp.). क्षेत्र-सन्न्यास _ m. retiring to an inhabited holy place →वानप्रस्थ.

क्षेत्रिन् _ m. landowner.

क्षेत्री _ {क्षेत्रिन्}.

क्षेपण _ throwing.

क्षेम _ m. safety, peace.

क्षोभ _ m. agitation, emotion.

ख _ n. cavity, empty space, sky, ether. ख-ग _ m. 'moving in the sky', bird.

खड्ग _ m. sword.

खण्ड _ 'broken'; m. piece, fragment; section, chapter (=काण्ड).

खण्डन _ breaking.

खदिर _ (Kattha) m. Khair tree (Catechu, Senegalia catechu) and wood.

√खन् _ खनु अवदारणे 1U dig →खनति.

खनति _ (a verb) {√खन्} he digs. सः भूमिं खनति। He digs the earth.

खनित्र _ n. shovel.

खर _ rough, a स्पर्श; harsh.

खर्जूर _ (Khajur) m. Date palm (Phoenix sylvestris) and fruit.

खलु _ ind. surely, indeed.

√खाद् _ खादृ भक्षणे 1P eat →खादति.

खादति _ (a verb) {√खाद्} he eats. सः भोजनं खादति। He eats food.

खादन _ eating.

खिच्ची _ (Khichdi/Kichari) f. the national dish of India, made from rice and lentils (dal).

खे-चर _ {ख} m. 'moving in the sky', bird; a semi-divine being.

खेदन _ 'piercing', being depressed.

√खेल् _ खेलृ[r] विहारे 1P play →खेलति-खेलसि-खेलामि-खेलन्ति.

खेलति _ (a verb) {√खेल्} he plays.

√ख्या _ ख्या प्रकथने 2P tell; आ. tell; सम्.
  enumerate, analyse →ख्याति.
ख्याति _ (a verb) (1) {√ख्या} he tells. (2) f.
  'declaration', fame, title.
-ग _ »going«, moving.
गगन _ n. sky.
गङ्गा _ f. 'swift-goer', गङ्गा river. गङ्गा-दशमी _
  a festival on ज्यैष्ठ-शुक्ल-दशमी with
  दशहरा. गङ्गा-धर _ m. 'holder of गङ्गा',
  शिव.
गच्छति _ (a verb) {√गम्} he goes. कल्याण-
  कृत् दुर्गतिं न हि गच्छति। One who does
  good never attains misfortune. (भगवद्गीता)
  मनीषिणः अनामयं पदं गच्छन्ति। Wise men
  attain the transcendental ('faultless') abode.
  (भगवद्गीता) सः शान्तिम् अधिगच्छति। He
  attains peace. (भगवद्गीता) शश्वत्-शान्तिं
  निगच्छति। He attains lasting peace.
  (भगवद्गीता).
गज _ m. elephant.
√गण् _ गण सङ्ख्याने 10P count →गणयति.
गण _ m. multitude, group; class of धातु. गण-
  पति _ (=गणेश).
गणना _ f. 'counting', calculation.
गणयति _ (a verb) {√गण्} he counts.
गणित _ n. 'counted', calculation; mathematics
  (comprising arithmetic, algebra and
  geometry) →बौधायन, आर्यभट्ट.
गणेश _ {गण-ईश} m. 'leader of a group' of
  beings, a son of पार्वती. गणेश-चतुर्थी _ a
  festival on भाद्रपद-शुक्ल-चतुर्थी.
गत _ »gone«. गतं न शोच्यम्। The past is not
  to be lamented.
गति _ f. »gait«, motion; course, means; goal.
गद्गदम् _ ind. faltering [voice], indistinct.
गन्तव्य _ 'to be gone to', attained.
गन्ध _ m. aroma, a तन्मात्र, of 9 kinds – इष्ट,
  अनिष्ट, मधुर, कटु, etc.; spice.
गन्धर्व _ m. a celestial musician →गान्धर्व.

√गम् _ गम्लृ गतौ 1P go →गच्छति; अति.
  overpass; अधि. reach; अव. go down,
  understand; आ. come; उप.(सम्.)
  approach; दुर्. go with difficulty; नि. go
  down, attain; वि. go away; सम्.अति.
  completely go over, attain; सम्.आ. come
  together.
गमन _ »going« → (opp.) आगमन.
गम्भीर _ serious.
गरिष्ठ _ 'most गुरु', greatest, best.
गरीयः _ 'more गुरु', greater, better.
गरुड _ m. eagle.
√गर्ज _ गर्ज शब्दे 1P roar →गर्जति.
गर्जति _ (a verb) {√गर्ज} he roars.
  मेघः/शूकरः गर्जति। The cloud/boar roars.
गर्भ _ m. interior, chamber; womb, embryo.
गर्भाधान _ {गर्भ-आधान} n. 'putting the
  embryo'; a संस्कार, marking the intent of a
  couple to have a child; proper time: 4th (or
  better 8th) till 16th night after bleeding, day
  time is prohibited, and also any day of
  religious observance, like चतुर्थी, अष्टमी,
  एकादशी, त्रयोदशी, चतुर्दशी, पूर्णिमा and
  अमावास्या; purpose is to perceive the act of
  impregnation as यज्ञ. "Her lap is the altar,
  her hairs are the कुश grass (which is spread
  over the altar), …"
गर्भोदक _ {गर्भ-उदक} n. 'inner water' of a
  ब्रह्माण्ड, on which विष्णु lies down and
  from His navel sprouts a lotus →हिरण्यगर्भ,
  प्राकृतसर्ग.
गर्व _ m. pride.
गव्य _ {गो} n. 'from a cow', cow product
  →पञ्चगव्य.
गहन _ deep, dense; inexplicable.
गाण्डीव _ n. 'knotty', the bow of अर्जुन.
गात्र _ n. 'instrument of moving', limb of the
  body.
गान्धर्व _ n. 'relating to गन्धर्व', music; love
  marriage, a विवाह where the agreement

between two lovers overrules arrangements of relatives. गान्धर्व-वेद _ m. 'science of music', an उपवेद .

गान्धार _ m. a people and their country (with mod. »Kandahar«) →गान्धर्व ; 3rd स्वर .

गान्धारी _ f. a princess of गान्धार .

गायत्र m. 'song', hymn.

गायत्री _ {गायत्र} f. the गायत्री meter (a triplet of eight syllables each); (esp.) ब्रह्मगायत्री , also called सावित्री (because it addresses सवितृ); any later hymn composed in the गायत्री meter, structured "... विद्महे ... धीमहि । ... तद् नः ... प्रचोदयात् ।" गायत्री-व्रत _ a rite on शुक्ल- चतुर्दशी , worship of सूर्य for health with गायत्री-जप (for 100, 1000, or 10000 times).

गिर् _ f. invocation, praise; language, words.

गिरि _ m. hill, mountain, Russ. »gora«. गिरि-निम्ब _ m. Curry tree (Kadi, Mithi Neem, Murraya koenigii).

गिरीश _ {गिरि-ईश} m. 'mountain- lord', शिव .

गीत _ 'sung', chanted →सङ्गीत .

गीता _ f. a sacred poem; (esp.) भगवद्गीता . गीता-जयन्ती _ f. 'advent of भगवद्गीता ' on मार्गशीर्ष-शुक्ल-एकादशी (827 BCE).

गुग्गुलु _ m. Guggul tree (Commiphora wightii) and resin.

गुड _ m. molasses from sugar-cane →गौड .

गुण _ m. thread, rope; (with numerals: गुण) 'fold', 'times'; subdivision, secondary element →गौण ; quality, good quality → (opp.) विगुण ; a गुण of प्रकृति →त्रिगुण .

गुणमय _ 'made of the गुण ' of प्रकृति .

गुप् _ protecting.

गुप्त _ {गुप्} 'protected', secret; often added to the name of a वैश्य . गुप्त-चर _ m. 'moving secretly', a spy.

गुरु _ 'heavy', »grave«, Lat. »gravis« → (opp.) लघु ; important, respectable; m. an elder,

teacher →चैत्य-, वर्त्म-प्रदर्शक-, शिक्षा-, दीक्षा-गुरु, आचार्य ; बृहस्पति, (hence) Jupiter; a long syllable → (opp.) लघु . गुरु-कुल _ n. 'teacher's family', a domestic school (for 5 months a year, the rest स्वाध्याय and वेदाङ्ग study at home). गुरु-पूर्णिमा _ a festival on आषाढ- पूर्णिमा , आविर्भाव of व्यास , celebrated with व्यासपूजा , recitation of ब्रह्मसूत्र (a work started by व्यास on this day); गुरुपूजा to teachers in general; also honoring Indian academicians; Buddhists worship बुद्ध , Yogis शिव as आदि-गुरु, Jainas महावीर . गुरु-वार _ (=बृहस्पतिवार) m. 'Jupiter-day', Thursday. गुरु-शिष्य _ m. teacher and disciple; their relation was not moneywise (except for a दक्षिणा), because by teaching/studying both pay back their ऋण to sages.

गुरुतर _ 'more गुरु ', heavier, etc.

गुह्य _ n. 'to be covered', secret, mystery.

गृह _ n. house, home. गृह-प्रवेश _ 'entering the [groom's] house'; the welcoming of the bride to her new home by the groom's relatives; with होम , then silence. गृह-स्थ _ m. 'staying at home', householder.

गृहीत _ 'taken', controlled.

गृह्णाति _ (a verb) {√ग्रह्} he takes. नरः नवानि वासांसि गृह्णाति । A person takes new clothes. (भगवद्गीता).

गेह _ (=गृह).

गो _ (declined गौः , ...) m.f. '»go«ing', »cow«, (Pl.) cattle; the earth; m. sense ('going' to sense objects) →गो-चर . गो-कुल _ n. a herd of cows; cow- station; a village near वृन्दावन . गो-कृत _ n. cow-dung. गो-चर _ m. 'cow-/sense-pasture', range for activity, sense object. गो-प _ m. cowherd. गो-पाल _ (=गोप). गो-पुर _ n. town-gate, the ornamented gateway of a temple. गो-मुख _

m. 'cow-faced', a horn. गो-मूत्र _ n. cow-urine. गो-रक्ष _ m. 'cow-protector', cowherd → »Gurkha« (an inhabitant of Nepal). गो-लोक _ m. 'cow-world', the heaven of कृष्ण. गो-वत्स _ m. 'cow-child', calf. गो-वर/गोर्वर _ (Gobar) n. 'cow-gift' (?), (dried) cow-dung. गो-वर्धन _ m. 'cow-prosperity', a celebrated hill near वृन्दावन. गोवर्धन-पूजा _ a festival on कार्तिक-शुक्ल-प्रतिपद् with परिक्रम of गोवर्धन, or preparing a गोवर्धन with cowdung (on the ground) or heaps of cooked food and its worship along with गोपाल (thus this festival is also called अन्न-कूट). गो-विन्द _ m. 'who gives pleasure to गो (earth/cows/senses)', कृष्ण. गो-शाल _ n.f. cow-shed. गो-स्वामी _ m. 'master of cows'; 'master of the senses', the गुरु.

गोतम _ {गो} m. 'best cow', the sage गोतम →गौतम.

गोत्र _ {गो} n. cow-shed, enclosure; family ('enclosed by the hurdle'); lineage (of a गुरु), (esp.) अङ्गिर, कश्यप, भृगु, वसिष्ठ, plus शौनक at नैमिष, भरद्वाज at प्रयाग, व्यास at भद्रिविशाल, अत्रि at चित्रकूट, जमदग्नि, गौतम, विश्वामित्र, अगस्त्य.

गोपन _ {गुप्} protecting, hiding.

गोपी _ f. female गोप. गोपी-चन्दन _ n. a cream-coloured clay from गोपी-सरोवर near द्वारका.

गोल _ m. ball, globe.

गौड _ {गुड} m. 'sugar country', a district in Bengal.

गौण _ 'relating to गुण', secondary. गौण-रस _ m. secondary emotion, 7 kinds – भयानक-बीभत्स-रौद्र- अद्भुत-करुण-वीर-हास्य.

गौतम _ m. 'descendent of गोतम'.

गौर _ white, yellowish.

गौरव _ {गुरु} n. gravity; respect.

ग्रन्थ _ m. 'binding together', composition, book.

ग्रन्थि _ m. knot.

ग्रसन _ n. swallowing.

ग्रस्त _ 'swallowed', influenced by.

√ग्रह _ ग्रह उपादाने 9U take →गृह्लाति; अनु. नि.; दुर्.नि. control with difficulty; नि. control; परि. possess; सम्. collect; control.

ग्रह _ m. »grip«, »grasp«; planet (as 'holder' of destiny) →नवग्रह; eclipse. ग्रह-चिकित्सा _ f. 'planet medicine', psychiatry.

ग्रहण _ n. »grasping«, understanding; eclipse. "The moon (इन्दु) enters the earth- shadow (भू-छाया) in it's own eclipse (स्व-ग्रहण), and the sun[-shine] (भास्कर) in a sun-eclipse (अर्क-ग्रह). ... Coming from the west, चन्द्र hides रवि from below (अधःस्थ) just like a cloud. ... That राहु is not the cause of this, is the real intent of शास्त्र." But there are psychological effects, for which it is recommended to spend that time with जप and greet the sun thereafter with गायत्री.

ग्राम _ m. multitude; village.

ग्राह _ {ग्रह} m. »grasp«, understanding, conception.

ग्रीव _ m. neck.

ग्रीष्म _ m. summer, a ऋतु comprising ज्यैष्ठ- and आषाढ-मास.

ग्लानि _ f. exhaustion, decline.

√घट् _ घट चेष्टायाम् 1A endeavor →घटते.

घट _ m. water-pot.

घटते _ (a verb) {√घट्} he endeavors.

घटना _ f. incident.

घट्ट _ (Ghat) m. quay, steps by a river-side, bathing-place.

घण्टा _ f. a bell or plate of metal struck as a clock; (mod.) hour.

घन _ dense.

घृत _ n. »ghee«.

घोर _ awful, frightful.

घोष _ m. noise, sound.

-घ्न _ killing.

√घ्रा _ घ्रा गन्धोपादाने 1P smell →जिघ्रति.

घ्राण _ n. 'smelling', nose.

च _ ind. and, also.

चक्र _ n. »circle«, Lat. »circus«, wheel; discus, disc; wheel of time (seasons); energetic circle →षट्चक्र; province.
चक्रवत्परिवर्तन्ते दुःखानि च सुखानि च ।
दुःख and सुख revolve like a चक्र . चक्र-व्यूह _ m. a 'circular array' of troops.

चक्षु _ (=चक्षुस्) m. eye.

चक्षुः _ {चक्षुस्}.

चक्षुस् _ n. sight, eye.

चञ्चल _ {चल} moving to and fro, unsteady.

चञ्चलत्व _ n. unsteadiness.

चञ्चला _ f. लक्ष्मी .

चटक _ m. a sparrow.

चण _ m. chick-pea.

चणक _ (Chana) m. Chickpea plant (Chole, Gram, Cicer arietinum).

चतुः-श्लोकी _ {चतुर्-} [the essence] 'in four verses'. चतुः-सन _ m. 'the four सन', sons of ब्रह्मा whose names begin with सन – सनक-सनन्द-सनातन-सनत्कुमार .

चतुर् _ »four«, Lat. »quattuor«, Russ. »četyre« → »quarter«. चतुरङ्ग _ {-अङ्ग} n. 'four limbs' of an army – infantry, cavalry, elephants, chariots; army; the ancient Indian form of chess, Pers. »chatrang«, Arab. »shatranj«. चतुरश्र _ {-अश्र} 'four-cornered', square →त्र्यश्र . चतुरस्त्र _ (=चतुरश्र). चतुर्मास _ n. a season of 'four मास'. चतुर्युग _ (=दिव्ययुग) n. 'four युग'. चतुर्वर्ग _ m. 'four वर्ग', त्रिवर्ग plus मोक्ष . चतुर्वर्ण _ m. 'four वर्ण' →चातुर्वर्ण्य . चतुर्वेद _ m. 'four वेद', त्रिवेद plus अथर्ववेद . चतुर्व्यूह _ m. 'four manifestations' of विष्णु – वासुदेव-सङ्कर्षण-प्रद्युम्न-अनिरुद्ध .

चतुर _ (=चातुर).

चतुर्थ _ »fourth«, Lat. »quartus«.

चतुर्थी _ f. 'fourth [रात्रि]' in both शुक्ल- and कृष्ण-पक्ष . चतुर्थी-कर्म _ a rite on the fourth day, where the first domestic fire is lit, marking the food-related householder life of a new couple.

चतुर्दश _ »fourteen«; »fourteenth«. चतुर्दश-भुवन _ n. 'fourteen worlds', 7 स्वर्ग (upwards) and 7 नरक (downwards), both divided by वैतरणी .

चतुर्दशी _ f. 'fourteenth [रात्रि]' in both शुक्ल- and कृष्ण-पक्ष .

.चन _ (=.चिद्).

चन्द _ m. 'shining, pleasing'; moon (=चन्द्र).

चन्दन _ (Chandan) m. 'pleasing', »sandal«, Sandalwood tree (Santalum album) and wood; sandal paste (prepared by rubbing wood on stone, adding water).

चन्द्र _ {चन्द} m. 'shining', 'pleasing' → »candle«, Lat. »candela«; moon; (in comp.) beautiful →रामचन्द्र . चन्द्र-दर्शन _ n. 'seeing the moon'; when this predicted (just after sunset), then उपवास till moonrise to get the blessings of चन्द्र-देव . चन्द्र-बिन्दु _ m. 'moon-dot'; a nasalization similar to अनुस्वार .

चन्द्रमः _ {चन्द्रमस्}.

चन्द्रमस् _ m. moon.

चन्द्रायण _ {चन्द्र-अयन} n. 'moon- course'.

चपल _ trembling, unsteady.

चमत्- _ (interjection, expressing:) surprise. चमत्कार _ m. 'creating a surprise', astonishment, miracle.

चमर _ m. the bushy tail of the Yak (employed as fan).

चमू _ f. army.

चम्पक _ m. Champa tree (Michelia champaca), wood and flower.

चयन _ collecting.

√चर् _ चर गतौ 1P go, move (act) →चरति; आ. behave, act; वि.अभि. deviate; सम्.आ. behave, perform; सु.दुर्.आ. behave very badly.

चर _ moving → »car«, »chariot«.

चरण _ m. foot.

चरति _ (a verb) {√चर्} he moves. सः उद्याने चरति He roams in the park. केन प्रयुक्तः पूरुषः पापं चरति Impelled by what does a person enacts sin? (भगवद्गीता) यद् यद् श्रेष्ठः आचरति तद् तद् एव इतरः जनः। However the leader behaves, in that same way [behaves] another man. (भगवद्गीता) महा-मत्स्य उभे कूले अनुसञ्चरति। A large fish traverses both banks [of a river]. (बृहद्-आरण्यक-उपनिषद्) भूतानि आत्मनः व्युच्चरन्ति। All beings emanate from the Purusha (Ātmā). (बृहद्-आरण्यक-उपनिषद्).

चरित _ {चर} n. 'moved', practiced.

चरित्र _ {चर} n. practice, deeds, character.

चरु _ m. pot; sweet-rice, an oblation of sweet-rice.

चर्च _ m. consideration, discussion.

चर्पटी _ (Chapati) f. thin bread.

चर्म _ {चर्मन्}.

चर्मन् _ n. hide, skin; shield.

चर्य _ 'to be practiced' →ब्रह्मचर्य.

√चल् _ चल कम्पने 1P tremble (move) →चलति; निर्.(निश्.); वि. move, shake.

चल _ 'moving', unsteady →चञ्चल.

चलति _ (a verb) {√चल्} he moves, trembles. बुद्धिमान् एकेन पादेन चलति एकेन तिष्ठति। The wise man moves with one leg and stands with one. (हितोपदेश).

चलन _ moving.

चलित _ {चल} 'moved', shaken, disturbed.

चातुर _ (=चतुर) clever.

चातुरी _ f. cleverness.

चातुर्मास्य _ n. relating to a season of चतुर्मास. चातुर्मास्य-व्रत _ an observance from आषाढ-शुक्ल-एकादशी to कार्तिक-शुक्ल-द्वादशी, the performer gives up eating शाक in श्रावण-मास, curds in भाद्रपद-मास, milk in आश्विन-मास, and pulses in कार्तिक-मास; on the first day he observes एकादशी-व्रत and सङ्कल्प; in Vedic times there were seasonal यज्ञ called चातुर्मास्य performed on पूर्णिमा of फाल्गुन-, आषाढ-, and कार्तिक-मास.

चातुर्वर्ण्य _ n. the system of चतुर्वर्ण.

चान्द्र _ {चन्द्र} lunar. चान्द्र-मास _ m. 'lunar month' of average 29.5 days →अधिकमास; divided into 30 तिथि (15 in each पक्ष), named after the 12 attendants upon the sun's car – चैत्र, etc.

चान्द्रायण _ {चन्द्रायण} n. observing a fast regulated by चन्द्रायण – beginning with 14 morsels of food and decreasing this by one morsel each day. "During the dark fortnight (कृष्णपक्ष) one should reduce [the food] every day by one morsel (पिण्ड), and during the bright fortnight (शुक्लपक्ष) one should increase it. On the day of the new moon (अमावास्या) one should not eat. This is the चान्द्रायण rule."

चाप _ m. bow.

चापल _ n. fickleness.

चारक _ {चर} m. 'wandering' scholar in search for further education and competition.

चालन _ swinging.

√चि _ चिञ् चयने 5U collect →चिनोति; निर्. ascertain; वि.निर्. ascertain; सु.निर्. ascertain well.

चिकित्सा _ f. medical 'science' (=आयुर्वेद), with texts like चरक-, सुश्रुत-संहिता and अष्टाङ्ग- हृदयम्; several limbs – काय-बाल-जरा-ग्रह- and ऊर्ध्वाङ्ग-चिकित्सा, प्रसूति-

and शल्य-तन्त्र, स्त्री-रोग, रसायन, द्रव्य-गुण, शारीर.

चिकीर्षु _ m. who desires to act.

√चित् _ चिति स्मृत्याम् 10P think, remember →चिन्तयति; अनु. think about; परि. think about.

चित् _ f. 'thinking', consciousness, spirit →चित्त, चिन्ता, चिन्मय, चित्र, चेतः, चैत्य.

चित्त _ {चित्} n. 'thought', consciousness; mind, in अष्टाङ्गयोग incl. मनः and बुद्धि. चित्त-वृत्ति _ f. 'activity of the mind', 5 kinds – knowledge, illusion, विकल्प, निद्रा, स्मृति.

चित्ति _ f. thought, wisdom.

चित्र _ {चित्} excellent, bright; variegated; wonderful; n. wonder; picture. चित्र-रथ _ m. 'excellent chariot', the chief गन्धर्व.

.चिद् _ (=.चन) (an affix, expressing:) any →किश्चिद्, .चन.

चिदानन्द _ {चित्-} 'awareness and bliss'.

चिनोति _ (a verb) {√चि} he collects.

चिन्तयति _ (a verb) {√चित्} he thinks.

चिन्ता _ {चित्} f. 'thought', meditation, anxiety. चिन्ता-मणि _ m. 'thought-gem', a gem yielding desires.

चिन्त्य _ 'to be thought of', conceivable →अचिन्त्य.

चिन्मय _ 'full of चित्', spiritual.

चिर _ lasting; n. delay.

चिरं-जीव _ m. 'who is long-lived'.

चिरम्/चिरात् _ ind. a long time.

चिरेण _ {चिर} ind. 'with delay', slowly.

चिह्न _ n. mark, sign; aim.

चीन _ m. (Pl.) the »Chinese«, Lat. »sina«.

चुम्ब _ m. kissing, kiss.

चुम्बति _ (a verb) {√चुब्} he kisses.

√चुब् _ चुबि वक्त्रसंयोगे 1P kiss →चुम्बति.

√चुर् _ चुर स्तेये 10P steal →चोरयति.

चूडा _ (=शिखा) →चौडा.

चूर्ण _ n. powder.

चूर्णित _ pulverised.

चेतः _ {चेतस्}.

चेतन _ {चित्} n. 'thinking', consciousness.

चेतस् _ {चित्} n. 'thinking', consciousness, mind.

चेद् _ ind. if →यदि.

चेल _ n. cloth.

√चेष्ट् _ चेष्ट चेष्टायाम् 1A endeavor (act) →चेष्टते.

चेष्टते _ (a verb) {√चेष्ट्} he endeavors. ज्ञानवान् अपि स्वस्याः प्रकृतेः सदृशं चेष्टते । Even a man of knowledge (aware of good and bad) acts according to his own nature. (भगवद्गीता).

चेष्टा _ f. 'moving', activity, endeavour; gesture →मुद्रा, a variety of अनुमान.

चैतन्य _ {चेतन} n. consciousness, spirit, soul.

चैत्य _ {चित्} m. 'conscious', soul. चैत्य-गुरु _ m. 'teacher in the heart', god-given intelligence and conscience, परमात्मा.

चैल _ {चेल} n. 'made of cloth', garment.

चोर _ m. thief.

चोरयति _ (a verb) {√चुर्} he steals.

चोल _ m. jacket, bodice; coating for Deities; a people in southern India. चोल-मण्डल _ n. 'चोल territory', »Coromandel« coast.

चौड _ {चूडा} 'rite of चूडा', also called चूडाकरण or चौल; →शिखा.

चौल _ (=चौड).

च्यवते _ (a verb) {√च्यु} he goes. शरीरात् धर्मः च्यवते यथा पर्वतात् सलिलम् । From the body springs Dharma, like water from a mountain. (शङ्ख-स्मृति).

√च्यु _ च्युङ् गतौ 1A go →च्यवते.

छठ-पूजा _ (Chhath) षष्ठीपूजा.

छत्र _ n. shelter; umbrella; mushroom.

√छद् _ छद अपवारणे 10P cover →छदयति.

छदयति _ (a verb) {√छद्} he covers.

छद्म _ {छद्मन्}.

छद्मन् _ n. covering; disguise, pretence.

छन्दः _ {छन्दस्}.

छन्दस् _ n. hymn; poetry governed by a meter; verse meter →वेदाङ्ग .

छन्न _ {छद्} covered.

छात्र _ {छत्र} m. 'under shelter', disciple.

छाया _ f. shade, shadow.

√छिद् _ छिदिर् द्वैधीकरणे 7U divide into two (cut) →छिनत्ति .

छिद _ dividing, 'cutting', »shed«, Lat. »scindere«.

छिद्र _ {छिद्} n. cut, hole.

छिनत्ति _ (a verb) {√छिद्} he divides.

छिन्न _ {छिद्} divided, cut.

√छेद _ छेद द्वैधीकरणे 10P divide into two (cut) →छेदयति .

छेद _ (=छिद्र).

छेदयति _ (a verb) {√छेद} he divides.

-ज _ 'being born', »generated« →जन, जन्तु, जन्म, जाति, निज ; 4 kinds of birth – जीव-आण्ड-उद्भिज्-स्वेद-ज .

जगत् _ n. 'going', world, universe.

जगदीश _ {जगत्-} m. 'world-lord', God.

जगन्नाथ _ {जगत्-} m. 'world-lord', God; a deity of कृष्ण in जगन्नाथ-पुरी → (in English derogatory) »juggernaut«. जगन्नाथ-रथयात्रा _ a festival on आषाढ-शुक्ल-द्वितीया .

जघन्य _ lowest, worst.

जङ्गम _ 'going', movable → (opp.) स्थावर .

जङ्गल _ m. an arid or sterile region → »jungle«.

जटिल _ complicated.

जड _ dull, inanimate.

√जन् _ जनी प्रादुर्भावे 4A be born →जायते ; अभि. be born; उप. be born consequently; प्र. be born, bring forth; सम्. be born.

जन _ {ज} m. »generating«, Lat. »genero« → »gene«, »genius«, »genitalis«, »generator«; living being; man, person; people. जन-लोक _ m. 'world of men', inhabited by

pious men and sons of ब्रह्मा, the 5th heaven →चतुर्दशभुवन .

जनक _ {ज} m. 'giver of birth', father.

जननी _ f. mother, Lat. »genetrix«; →मातृ .

जन्तु _ {जन} m. living being, animal.

जन्म _ {जन्मन्, जन} n. »generation«, birth, Lat. »genesis«; 4 kinds →-ज ; 2 kinds – शौक्र-, ब्रह्म-जन्म . जन्मना जायते शूद्रः । By जन्म [every]one is born a शूद्र . जन्म-अस्तित्व-वृद्धि-विपरिणाम-अपक्षय-नाश _ 6 transformations. जन्म-दिन _ n. birthday. जन्माद्यस्य यतः । {जन्म-आदि अस्य} [ब्रह्म is that] from which there is जन्म, etc., of this [जगत्].

जन्माष्टमी _ {जन्म-अष्टमी} 'birth at अष्टमी' in भाद्र-कृष्ण (18.07. 894 BCE), appearence of कृष्ण ; Celebration: उपवास , पूजा after midnight, जागर at night with music and recitations, पारण at night or in the morning, प्रसाद ; in Maharastra, pots with curds are hang up and later pierced.

√जप् _ जप व्यक्तायां वाचि मानसे च 1P speak (mutter), meditate →जपति .

जप _ m. 'murmuring'; a method of repeating नाम or मन्त्र in a murmuring tone as जपयज्ञ . "One should regularly do जप gently and distinctly, neither quickly nor slowly, neither less nor more." Counting is done on a rosary, called जपमाला . जप-माला _ f. 'prayer-rosary' with generally 108 beads plus the head bead (called मेरु). (Indian astronomy was aware that the sun and the moon were at a distance from the earth of about 108 times their own diameters. The 108 sun diameters distance of the sun from the earth were paralleled by the 108 beads of the rosary for a symbolic spiritual journey of 108 steps from the normal state to one of illumination.) Usually held with the right hand between

अङ्गुष्ठ (gives liberation) and मध्यमा (gives भक्ति and wealth), rarely तर्जनी (destroys enemies) or अनामिका (gives peace). जप-यज्ञ _ m. a व्रत of doing जप a certain daily amount.

जपति _ (a verb) {√जप्} he mutters.

जम्बु/जम्बू _ (Jamun, Jambuka) m./f. Rose Apple tree (Syzygium cumini). जम्बु-द्वीप _ m. 'जम्बु island', Eurasia, divided into 9 वर्ष.

जय _ {√जि} m. conquest, victory.

जयति _ (a verb) {√जि} he conquers.

जयन्ती _ {जय} f. 'victorious' advent, (esp.) जन्माष्टमी and गीताजयन्ती.

जर _ becoming old → Gr. »geron«, »gerontology«.

जरा _ f. old age, a वयः. जरा-चिकित्सा _ f. 'old-age medicine', »geriatrics«.

जल _ n. water; liquid state, a महाभूत.

√जल्प् _ जल्प व्यक्तायां वाचि 1P speak (prattle) →जल्पति.

जल्प _ m. talk, gossip; (in न्याय) inconclusive argument that supports equally the opposite view. जल्प-वितण्डा-वाद _ 3 arguments in न्याय.

जल्पति _ (a verb) {√जल्प्} he prattles.

जहाति _ (a verb) {√हा} he abandons. बुद्धि-युक्तः उभे सुकृत-दुष्कृते जहाति । A Karma-/Buddhi-yogī gives up both good and bad Karma. (भगवद्गीता).

जागर/जागरण _ m. waking, wakefulness.

जागर्ति _ (a verb) {√जागृ} he is awake. या सर्व-भूतानां निशा तस्यां संयमी जागर्ति । Which is night for all beings, in that [sensual 'night', spiritual reality] a self-controlled man wakes. (भगवद्गीता) यस्याम् भूतानि जाग्रति सा पश्यतः मुनेः निशा । In which all beings are awake, that [world of sense objects] is night for the sage who sees. (भगवद्गीता).

√जागृ _ जागृ निद्राक्षये 2P be awake, be watchful →जागर्ति.

जाग्रत् _ m. 'waking', a state of बुद्धि.

जात _ {जन} »generated«, born; belonging to. जात-कर्म _ n. 'birth-rite', a संस्कार; the father welcomes the baby by whispering thrice 'वाक्' into the right ear of the baby, touches the baby's lips with honey and ghee, presents it to the mother for feeding, and prays for मेधाजनन and a long life.

जाति _ f. birth; lineage; species, class → (opp.) व्यक्ति. जाति-फल _ m. Nutmeg tree (Jayaphal, Myristica fragrans) and nut.

जातु _ ind. at any time, ever, sometimes.

जानाति _ (a verb) {√ज्ञा} he knows. ब्रह्म जानाति इति ब्राह्मणः । Who knows the Brahma, he is a Brāhmana. (शास्त्र) अहं क्षत्रियः देहि इति वचनं न जानामि । I am a Kshatriya. The word 'give [me]' I do not know. (महाभारत).

जानु _ n. »knee«, Lat. »genu«.

जाम्बुल _ (=जम्बु).

जायते _ (a verb) {√जन्} he is born. स्त्रीषु दुष्टासु वर्ण-सङ्करः जायते । When women are polluted, confusion of the social orders is generated. (भगवद्गीता) अर्थाः अर्जने दुःखं जनयन्ति । In earning, riches cause suffering. (हितोपदेश) जन्तुः एकः प्रजायते एकः एव प्रलीयते । A living being is born alone, alone it dies. (मनु-संहिता).

जाल _ n. net, snare.

√जि _ जि जये 1P conquer →जयति, जय, जिन; वि. conquer.

जिघांसा _ f. 'desire to destroy', hatred.

जिघ्रति _ (a verb) {√घ्रा} he smells.

जिज्ञासु _ m. 'who desires to know'.

-जित् _ {जिन} winning.

जित _ {जिन} 'won', conquered.

जिन _ m. 'winning', 'victor', a बुद्ध or जैन saint →जय.

जिह्वा _ f. tongue.

जीर/जीरक _ m. cumin.

जीर्ण _ worn out, old.

√जीव् _ जीव प्राणधारणे 1P live →जीवति.

जीव _ m. »living«, Lat. »vivo«, »vivum«, Russ. »živ«, alive; living being, a तत्त्व. जीवस्य मोहो ऽयमहं-ममेति। {अयम् अहम्-} This मोह of a जीव is to think in terms of अहम् and मम. जीवो जीवस्य जीवनम्। One being (जीव) is the subsistence/life (जीवन) of [another] जीव. जीव-आण्ड-उद्भिज्-स्वेद-ज _ 4 kinds of birth. जीव-ज _ 'born alive' as embryo, a birth → -ज. जीव-भूत _ n. »living being«, embodied being → (opp.) ब्रह्मभूत.

जीवति _ (a verb){√जीव्} he lives. इन्द्रिय-आरामः मोघं जीवति। Who delights in the senses, he lives in vain. (भगवद्गीता) भूतानाम् अ-द्रोहेण जीवामि। With no harm towards all creatures I live. (महाभारत) बहवः नराः त्रिदण्ड-व्यपदेशेन जीवन्ति। Many people live by the [false] designation of Sannyāsa. (दक्ष-स्मृति).

जीवन _ n. living, enlivening; life, livelihood.

जीवन्मुक्ति _ {जीवत्-} f. 'liberation while living' in the body.

जीवात्मा _ {जीव-आत्मा} m. 'soul as जीव' → (opp.) विश्वात्मा, परमात्मा.

जीवित _ {जीव} 'lived' through, alive; n. life.

जुगुप्सा _ f. dislike, disgust.

जुष्ट _ liked; served, practiced.

जुहोति _ (a verb) {√हु} he offers in the fire.

जैन _ {जिन} (Jain) m. worshiper of जिन.

-ज्ञ _ »knowing«, Russ. »znat'« →ज्ञान, ज्ञानी.

√ज्ञा _ (1) ज्ञा अवबोधने 9P know →जानाति; अभि. understand; प्र.; प्रति. promise; वि. realize. (2) ज्ञा नियोजने 10P command, direct →ज्ञापयति; अभि.; अव. deride; आ. order.

ज्ञात _ { ज्ञ } »known«.

ज्ञातव्य _ 'to be known'.

ज्ञान _ {ज्ञ} (Gyan) n. »knowing«, »knowledge«, Gr. »gnosis«, Russ. »znanie« → (opp.) अज्ञान; theoretical knowledge → (opp.) विज्ञान; higher knowledge, (esp.) about the soul →ज्ञानयोग. ज्ञान-काण्ड _ n. part of वेद dealing with the soul → (opp.) कर्म-, उपासन-काण्ड. ज्ञान-योग _ m. 'योग through ज्ञान'.

ज्ञानवान् _ {ज्ञानवत्} m. 'with knowledge', a wise person.

ज्ञानिन् _ m. 'who has knowledge', »gnostic«, philosopher.

ज्ञानी _ {ज्ञानिन्}.

ज्ञानेन्द्रिय _ {ज्ञान-इन्द्रिय} n. 'sense of knowledge' – श्रोत्र-त्वक्-चक्षु-जिह्वा-घ्राण; experiencing the तन्मात्र of a महाभूत.

ज्ञापयति _ (a verb) {√ज्ञा} he knows. सः तम् आज्ञापयति। He orders him.

ज्ञेय _ {ज्ञ} 'to be known', the object of knowledge.

ज्यायः _ better; senior.

ज्येष्ठ _ {ज्यायः} best; senior most.

ज्यैष्ठ _ {ज्येष्ठ} a मास (where the पूर्णिमा is in ज्येष्ठ नक्षत्र).

ज्योतिः _ {ज्योतिस्}.

ज्योतिर्- _ {ज्योतिस् in comp.}.

ज्योतिष _ {ज्योतिस्} m. astronomer; n. astronomy, a वेदाङ्ग.

ज्योतिस् _ n. light, brightness (of the sky); (Pl.) planets and stars.

√ज्वर् _ ज्वर रोगे 1P be sick (be hot with fever or passion) →ज्वरति.

ज्वर _ m. fever; mental affliction.

ज्वरति _ (a verb) {√ज्वर्} he is sick.

√ज्वल् _ ज्वल दीप्तौ 1P shine →ज्वलति; अभि.वि..

ज्वल _ m. flame.

ज्वलति _ (a verb) {√ज्वल्} he shines.

झष _ m. fish.

ठक्कुर _ (Thakur, Tagore) m. deity, chief;
  added to names.

तक्र _ n. buttermilk (mixed with water).

तक्षक _ m. 'cutter', carpenter, Lat. »tekton«; a
  नाग king.

तट _ m. slope; shore, bank. तट-स्थ _
  'standing on a bank', marginal.

√तड् _ तड आघाते 10P strike, beat →ताडयति.

तण्डु _ m. an attendant of शिव who taught
  dancing (see ताण्डव).

तण्डुल _ m. grain (after thrashing), esp. rice.

तत _ {तन} 'diffused', pervaded.

ततः _ {तद्} ind. 'from that', after that, then,
  therefore, यतः ... ततः.

तत्कालम् _ {तद्-} ind. 'at that time',
  immediately.

तत्त्व _ {तद्} n. 'of that state', truth, reality;
  principle, element, (esp.) 3 – ब्रह्म-जीव-
  जगत्; (in साङ्ख्य) 24 elements – प्रधान-
  महत्-अहङ्कार-मनः, 10 इन्द्रिय, 5 तन्मात्र, 5
  महाभूत; (in न्याय) 18 – आत्मा, काल, 10
  दिक्, मनः, 5 महाभूत.

तत्त्वतः _ ind. truly.

तत्पर _ {तद्-} 'aiming at that', engaged,
  devoted.

तत्पुरुष _ {तद्-} 'his servant', a समास.

तत्र _ {तद्} ind. 'in that place', there, in that
  case, यत्र ... तत्र.

तथा _ {तद्} ind. 'in that manner', so, thus,
  यथा ... तथा; also, and.

तथावत् _ ind. so, यथावत् ... तथावत्.

तद् _ (a base) →सः, ते; n. that, यद् ... तद्; ind.
  then. तत्त्वमसि। {तद् त्वम् असि} You are
  that (तद्) [same ब्रह्म]. तदनन्तरम् _ ind.
  after that. तदन्य _ other than that. तदर्थम्
  _ ind. for that purpose.

तदा _ {तद्} ind. 'at that time', then, Russ.
  »togda«, यदा ... तदा.

तद्धित _ {तद्-हित} n. 'his welfare'; m. 'good
  for that', an affix; derivative noun.

तद्वत् _ {तद्} ind. 'like that', so,
  यद्वत् ... तद्वत्.

तन _ 'extending', diffusing, weaving.

तनय _ {तन} n. child.

तनु _ {तन} f. body, form.

तन्त्र _ {तन} n. 'weaving', principle, system,
  theory, science; reliance →स्व-, पर-तन्त्र;
  ritual (part of पूजा); 28 works related to
  शिव (=शैवागम); magic.

तन्द्रित _ exhausted.

तन्मात्र _ {तद्-} n. 'its quality', the essence
  (substratum, symptom, cause, active
  principle) of महाभूत – शब्द-स्पर्श-रूप-रस-
  गन्ध; sense object (=इन्द्रियार्थ,
  इन्द्रियगोचर) of ज्ञानेन्द्रिय.

√तप् _ (1) तप सन्तापे 1P heat (burn) →तपति;
  प्र. scorch. (2) तप दाहे ऐश्वर्ये वा 4A burn,
  have power →तप्यते.

तपः _ {तपस्}.

तपति _ (a verb) {√तप्} he burns. विश्वामित्रः
  तपति। Vishvamitra performs Tapasya. अहं
  तपामि। [As sun] I give heat. (भगवद्गीता).

तपस् _ n. 'heat'; affliction; penance
  (=तपस्या), a नियम, asceticism by a
  तपस्वी, (esp.) fasting. "A व्रत taken by a
  doer out of repentance (सन्ताप) is called
  तपः." ... also called प्रायश्चित्त ('thought of
  death') or पश्चात्ताप ('after-pain'), depending
  on factual repentance: "O Yudhiṣthira! By
  तपः, rites (कर्म), and charity (प्रदान) a
  man purifies his sin (पाप), but only if he
  does not commit it again." "All this [world]
  is rooted in तपः, sages say. A fool (मूढ)
  who has not undergone तपः does not
  obtain the fruits of activities." "When first
  well-moistened, thereafter a cloth becomes
  clean by washing. Likewise, for those who
  are self-afflicted by long fasts (उपवास),
  there is later unending happiness (सुख)."

तपस्या _ f. penance.

तपस्विन् _ m. 'who does penance', ascetic.

तपस्वी _ {तपस्विन्}.

तपो-लोक _ {तपस्-} m. 'world of penance',
    inhabited by ascetics, 6th heaven
    →चतुर्दशभुवन .

तप्त _ {तपस्} 'heated', melted; afflicted;
    practiced (as penance).

तप्यते _ (a verb) {√तप्} he burns.

तम् _ {तद्} m. »him«.

.तम _ (an affix, expressing:) most →उत्तम ,
    .तर .

तमः _ {तमस्}.

तमस् _ n. darkness; mental darkness,
    ignorance.

तमालपत्र _ (Tamal) m. Indian Bay Leaf tree
    (Tejpat, Cinnamomum tamala).

तमो-गुण _ {तमस्-} m. 'quality of darkness'
    →गुण .

.तर _ (an affix, expressing:) more →उत्तर ,
    .तम .

तरङ्ग _ {तरम्-ग} m. 'across-goer', wave;
    section of a literary work.

तरण _ 'crossing', swimming.

तरति _ (a verb) {√तृ} he swims/crosses.
    बुद्धिमान् नदीं तरति । A wise man crosses
    the river [of Samsara]. (महाभारत).

तरु _ m. »tree« →दारु , द्रु .

तरुण _ young; m. a youth.

तर्क _ m. argument, logic.

तर्जन _ n. 'threatening', scolding, Germ.
    »drohen«.

तर्जनी _ f. the 'threatening' fore-finger.

तर्पण _ n. 'satiating', pleasing; a libation of
    water during स्नान (only when standing in
    water) – offering 3 अञ्जलि water with joined
    hands and letting the water flow back.

तल _ m. surface; palm of the hand; bottom,
    part underneath.

तव _ {युष्मद्} your.

तस्मात् _ {तद्} ind. 'from that', therefore.

तस्मै _ {तद्} m. to him.

तस्य _ {तद्} m. his. तस्य वाचकः प्रणवः ।
    His (God's) वाचक is ॐ.

.ता _ (an affix forming abstract nouns, =.त्व)
    being, »-ty« → f. समता (=n. समत्व).

ताडन _ beating.

ताडयति _ (a verb) {√तड्} he beats. सः तं
    ताडयति । He beats him.

ताण्डव-नृत्य _ m. 'wild dancing' of शिव .

तात _ m. 'dear one' (an affectionate address to
    a junior or senior) → »dad«, Gr. »tata«;
    (esp.) paternal uncle (तात-गु).

तात्पर्य _ {तत्पर} n. purpose, purport.

तादृक् _ ind. of that kind – यादृक् ... तादृक् .

ताप _ {तपस्} m. heat; pain (mental or
    physical), affliction; (in पञ्चसंस्कार) one
    year of atonements.

तामस _ 'pertaining to तमः ', in तमोगुण ,
    dark, ignorant.

ताम्बूल _ m. betel.

ताम्र _ coppery red color; n. copper.

तारा _ f. star, asterism.

ताल _ {तल} (Taal) m. Palmyra tree
    (Karpaha, Borassus) and fruit; rhythm
    (from clapping).

तावत् _ {तद्} that much, so great,
    यावत् ... तावत् .

तिक्त _ bitter, a रस .

तितिक्षा _ f. tolerance.

तिथि _ m.f. lunar phase /day, the 30th part of
    a चान्द्रमास (15 in each पक्ष). A तिथि lasts
    until the angle between sun and moon has
    increased 12 degrees (and may thus start at
    any time of the day. Its length may fluctuate
    between 19 and 26 hours). Observances
    (like उपवास on एकादशी) are on that day
    whose sunrise falls within the तिथि .

तिमिर _ m. darkness, partial blindness.

तिर्यक् _ horizontal → (opp.) ऊर्ध्व ; m. 'going
    horizontally', animal.

तिल _ (Til) m. Sesame plant (Sesamum indicum) →तैल; any grain or small particle.

तिलक _ {तिल} (=पुण्ड्र) m. a mark on the forehead, compared to तिल; ornament. (1) The वैष्णव तिलक is ऊर्ध्वपुण्ड्र made of clay. It is also called द्वादशतिलक because it is applied to twelve places of the body where विष्णु resides. (2) The शैव पुण्ड्र is त्रिपुण्ड्र made of sacred ash. (3) A बिन्दी between the eyebrows, representing लक्ष्मी, is applied by priests, members of a function and especially women (together with a streak of सिन्दूर or कुङ्कुम in the parting of the hair.) Materials for तिलक and बिन्दि can be चन्दन, गोपीचन्दन, केसरचन्दन, सिन्दूर, अगुरु, कुङ्कुम, कस्तूरी and धूपशेष.

तिष्ठति _ (a verb) {√स्था} he stands. ईश्वरः हृद्-देशे तिष्ठति। The Lord stays in the heart. (भगवद्गीता) सः प्रातः उत्तिष्ठति। He stands up in the morning. सः पुस्तकं कुत्र स्थापयति। Where does he keep the book?

तीक्ष्ण _ sharp, hot; harsh.

तीर _ n. shore, bank.

तीर्थ _ n. bathing-place, pilgrimage site. तीर्थ-यात्रा _ pilgrimage.

तीव्र _ intense, sharp.

तु _ ind. but; and.

तुच्छ _ little, trifling.

तुमुल _ noisy; n. »tumult«, Lat. »tumultus«.

तुरीय _ {चतुर्} n. fourth part; 4th state of बुद्धि in liberation.

तुर्य _ (=तुरीय).

तुल _ {for तुला} m. a राशि, Lat. Libra.

तुलन _ n. weighing.

तुलना _ f. comparison.

तुलसी _ (Tulsi) f. Holy Basil (Basilicum /Ocimum sanctum).

तुला _ {तुलन} f. weight, balance.

तुल्य _ {तुलन} 'to be weighed', equal, alike.

√तुष् _ तुष तुष्यौ 4P be satisfied →तुष्यति; सम्. be completely satisfied.

तुष्यति _ (a verb) {√तुष्} he is satisfied. आत्मानं पश्यन् आत्मनि तुष्यति। Seeing the self one is satisfied in the self. (भगवद्गीता).

तुष्टि _ f. satisfaction →तोष.

तूत _ (Tuti) m. Mulberry tree (Shahtut, Morus indica) and fruit.

तूष्णीम् _ ind. silently, silent.

तृण _ n. grass, straw.

तृतीय _ »third«, Lat. »tertius«, Russ. »tretij«.

√तृप् _ तृप प्रीणने 4/10P please →तृप्यति/तर्पयति.

तृप्त _ satisfied.

तृप्ति _ f. satisfaction, contentment.

तृप्यति/तर्पयति _ (a verb) {√तृप्} he pleases. पादपाः इह मानवान् तर्पयन्ति। In this world, trees please men. (महाभारत).

√तृष् _ जितृषा पिपासायाम् 4P be thirsty, wish →तृष्यति.

तृष्णा _ f. »thirst«, Lat. »sitis«; desire, hankering.

तृष्यति _ (a verb) {√तृष्} he is thirsty.

√तृ _ तृ प्लवनतरणयोः 1P swim; cross; अति. cross; वि.अति. cross; सम्. cross →तरति.

ते _ (1) {तुभ्यम्} 'to you' →नमस्ते. m. (2) {तद्} »they«.

तेजः _ {तेजस्}.

तेजस् _ n. sharpness; radiance, brilliance; prowess; semen.

तेजस्विन् _ 'with तेजः', sharp, radiant, brilliant.

तेजस्वी _ {तेजस्विन्}.

तेजोमय _ (=तेजस्वी) 'full of तेजः'.

तैजस _ (=राजस) 'relating to तेजः', passionate.

तैल _ {तिल} (Tel) n. sesamum oil; oil. तैल-हरिद्रा-आरोपण _ applying oil and turmeric powder to the groom's body from what is left after the bride's body has been so treated.

तोय _ n. water.

तोष _ m. satisfaction, contentment, pleasure →तुष्टि.

त्यक्त _ {त्याग} abandoned.

√त्यज् _ त्यज हानौ 1P abandon →त्यजति; परि. abandon.

त्यजति _ (a verb) {√त्यज्} he abandons. लोभात् मित्राणि त्यजति | Because of greed one abandons friends. (महाभारत).

त्याग _ m. abandoning, loss, renunciation (of कर्मफल) → (opp.) सन्न्यास.

त्यागिन् _ m. renunciant.

त्यागी _ {त्यागिन्}.

त्याज्य _ {त्याग} to be abandoned.

त्र _ (a stem) →त्रि.

.त्र _ (an affix, expressing:) (1) location, 'where' →सर्वत्र. (2) instrument →मन्त्र.

त्रय _ {त्रि} triple; n. triad.

त्रयम्बक _ {for त्र्यम्बक}.

त्रयी _ f. 'threefold [विद्या]', वेद.

त्रयोदश _ »thirteen«; »thirteenth«.

त्रयोदशी _ f. 'thirteenth [रात्रि]' in both शुक्ल- and कृष्ण-पक्ष.

त्रायते _ (a verb) {√त्रै} he protects. धर्मस्य स्वल्पम् अपि भयात् त्रायते | Even a little of Dharma protecs from fear. (भगवद्गीता).

त्रि _ {त्र} »three«, Lat. »tres«, Russ. »tri«. त्रि-कोण _ n. 'three कोण', triangle, Gr. »trigonon« → trigonometry. त्रि-गुण _ n. 'three गुण' – सत्त्व-रजः-तमः; constituting प्रकृति, represented by त्रिमूर्ति and the 3 colors शुक्ल-रक्त-कृष्ण →अन्तरङ्गशक्ति. त्रि-दण्ड _ m. 'three दण्ड', bamboos carried by a वैष्णव-सन्न्यासी. त्रि-दोष _ m. 'three दोष' – कफ-पित्त-वात/वायु. त्रि-पुण्ड्र _ n. 'three [शैव] marks' with horizontal lines. त्रि-भुवन _ (=त्रिलोक) n. three worlds. त्रि-मूर्ति _ God 'with three forms' as विष्णु-ब्रह्मा-

शिव, each one presiding a त्रिगुण. त्रि-लोक _ m. 'three लोक' – भूर्-भुवर्-स्वर् →चतुर्दशभुवन; (or) hell-earth-heaven – पाताल-मर्त्य-स्वर्ग-लोक. त्रि-लोचन _ m. 'with three eyes' (moon, sun and fire), शिव. त्रि-वर्ग _ m. 'three वर्ग', the three goals of human life – धर्म-अर्थ-काम (duty, wealth, gratification) →चतुर्वर्ग. त्रि-वारम् _ ind. three times. त्रि-वेद _ m. 'three वेद' – ऋग्-साम-यजुर्-वेद. त्रि-शूल _ n. a trident, weapon of शिव. त्रि-सन्ध्य _ n. 'three सन्ध्या' of the day – प्रातः-माध्याह्निक-सायं-सन्ध्या.

त्रिंशत् _ »thirty«, Lat. »tricesimus«.

त्रिधा _ ind. threefold.

त्रिपुरारि _ {त्रिपुर-अरि} m. 'enemy of त्रिपुर demon', शिव.

त्रिरात्र-व्रत _ observances for three nights after marriage, like sleeping separately on the ground.

त्रुटि _ f. atomic space of time, a मात्रा; doubt.

त्रेता _ {त्रि} f. the side of a die marked with 'three spots' (2nd in value). त्रेता-युग _ n. the त्रेता age (2nd in value).

√त्रै _ त्रैङ् पालने 1A protect →त्रायते; परि. protect.

त्रैगुण्य _ 'relating to त्रिगुण'.

त्रैलोक्य _ 'relating to त्रिलोक'.

त्रैविद्य _ 'relating to त्रिविद्या (=वेद)'.

त्र्यम्बक _ {त्रि-अम्बक} (=त्रिलोचन) m. 'three-eyed', शिव.

त्र्यश्र _ {त्रि अश्रि} 'three-cornered', triangular.

.त्व _ (an affix forming abstract nouns) being → n. समत्व (=f. समता).

त्वक् _ f. skin.

त्वचन _ covering.

त्वम् _ {युष्मद्} you, »thou«.

.था _ (an affix, expressing manner) 'way' →सर्वथा.

-द _ giving, »donating«, Lat. »do« →दत्त, दान.

दंश _ m. a bite, sting.

दंशक _ m. 'biting', tooth.

दंशन _ biting.

दंष्ट्र _ {दंश} m. large tooth, tusk.

दक्ष _ »dexterous«, Lat. »dexter«, able, expert, clever; right (hand); m. a प्रजापति.

दक्षिण _ {दक्ष} able; right (hand), south (when facing east).

दक्षिणा _ f. an 'able' or prolific cow (as a donation to the priest), on the completion of a ceremony, the यजमान should satisfy the priests with gifts and प्रसाद; any donation (esp.) at समावर्तन; the south.

दक्षिणायन _ {दक्षिण-अयन} n. 'southern course', the progress of the sun to the south of the equator → (opp.) उत्तरायण.

दग्ध _ {दहन} 'burned' to ashes.

√दण्ड _ दण्ड दण्डनिपाते 10P punish, fine, subdue →दण्डयति.

दण्ड _ m. stick, rod →दण्डवत्; a मात्रा (1.8 m, 4 हस्त, 6 ft.); arm span or hight of a man; stick as weapon; scepter as symbol of control and punishment; bamboo carried by a सन्न्यासी →एक-, त्रि-दण्ड; punishment, of 4 kinds – धिग्-वाग्-धन-वध-दण्ड; war (last means in नीति); army; a मात्रा of time (24 min, 12 लघु), also called नाडिका, घटिका, गधि.

दण्डयति _ (a verb) {√दण्ड} he punishes.

दण्डवत् _ ind. 'like a stick', prostrated obeisance →नमस्कार.

दत्त _ {द} given, Lat. »datus« → »date« (letters were closed with the phrase: "given" (»date«) at such and such time), »data«.

ददाति _ (a verb) {√दा} he gives. ब्राह्मणः स्वम् एव ददाति। A Brāhmana gives his own [property as charity]. (महाभारत) पुण्यात् षड्-भागम् आदत्ते। He (the king) takes the sixth part of the virtue [of the citizens]. (याज्ञवल्क्य-स्मृति).

दधाति _ (a verb) {√धा} he holds.

दधि _ (Dahi) n. coagulated milk, curd.

दन्त _ m. »tooth«, Lat. »dens«. दन्त-धावन _ tooth brushing ('cleaning'), reciting the prayer आयुर्बलं यशो वर्चं ... to the tree from which the tooth-stick is taken. One has to take the twig (with its bark) of certain trees (astringent, pungent or bitter in taste), crush the end of the twig with his teeth so as to make a brush of it and then to cleanse his teeth with the brush-like end. The stick should be as thick as the end of one's small finger and 12 अङ्गुल or 1 प्रादेश in length, it should be washed before its use and after use it should not be cast off in an impure place.

दन्त्य _ {दन्त} »dental«.

दम _ m. »tame«, Gr. »daman«, »domination«; sense-control.

दम्भ _ m. deceit, cheating, hypocrisy.

दया _ f. compassion, mercy. दया-राम _ m. someone 'who is the compassion of राम'.

दरिद्र _ poor.

दर्प _ m. pride.

दर्पण _ m. 'causing दर्प', mirror.

दर्शन _ 'showing', viewing, seeing; n. audience; thesis →षड्दर्शन.

दर्शयति _ (a verb) {√दृश्} he shows.

दर्शित _ {दर्शन} shown.

दल _ (Dal) n. fragment, part, Russ. »dolja«; a half → lentils, »dal«; political party; petal, leaf.

दश _ {दशन्}. दश-हरा _ 'destroying ten' [sins], गङ्गा; a व्रत in honor of गङ्गा; acc. to Monier-Williams it is now held as 'Dussehra' in honor of दुर्गा on विजयादशमी in आश्विन- मास. दशहरा-व्रत _ observance on ज्यैष्ठ-शुक्ल-दशमी in celebration of the appearence of गङ्गा on earth.

दशन् _ »ten«, Lat. »decem«, Russ. »desjat'«.

दशम _ »tenth«, Lat. »decimus« →
  »December«.
दशमी _ f. 'tenth [रात्रि]' in both शुक्ल- and
  कृष्ण-पक्ष.
दशा _ f. state or period of life, circumstance.
दशावतार _ {दश-अवतार} m. 'ten अवतार'
  – मत्स्य-कूर्म-वराह-नरसिंह-वामन-
  परशुराम-रामचन्द्र-कृष्ण／बलराम-बुद्ध-
  कल्कि.
√दह् _ दह भस्मीकरणे 1P burn to ashes
  →दहति; परि. burn all over.
दहति _ (a verb) {√दह्} he burns. पावकः एनं
  न दहति। Fire does not burn it (the soul).
  (भगवद्गीता).
दहन _ n. burning.
√दा _ (1) दाण् दाने 1P give →यच्छति. (2)
  डुदाञ् दाने 3U give →ददाति; आ. take; वि.
  hold, make; वि.आ. open wide.
.दा _ (an affix, expressing:) when (time)
  →सर्वदा.
दाक्षिणा _ {दक्षिणा} (Deccan) f. the southern
  country.
दाक्ष्य _ {दक्ष} n. ability, expertness, cleverness.
दाडिम _ (Darim) m. Pomegranate tree (Anar,
  Punica granatum) and fruit.
दातव्य _ {द} to be given.
दाता _ {दातृ}.
दातृ _ {द} m. giver, »donor«, Lat. »dator«,
  Russ. »datel'«.
दान _ {द} n. 'giving', gift, »donation«, Lat.
  »donum«, Russ. »dan'«; charity; bribe,
  tribute, the most effective means in नीति.
  "One should give every day with attention
  liberally something even from a little
  income – this is called charity."
दानव _ m. 'descendent of दनु', demon
  →असुर.
दाम _ {दामन्}.
दामन् _ n. string, rope.

दामोदर _ {दाम-उदर} m. 'having a rope
  around the waist', कृष्ण.
दारु _ n. wood →द्रु, तरु.
दारुमय _ made of wood.
दास _ m. 'servant'. There was no slavery in
  India, but forced service until debts and
  fines were payed back.
दासी _ f. female दास.
दास्य _ {दास} n. servitude, a मुख्यरस.
दाह _ {दहन} m. burning.
दाह्य _ {दहन} to be burnt.
दिक् _ f. point; direction, 10 directions (incl.
  the 2 overhead and underneath); region
  →देश.
दिति _ {दित} f. 'bound', a wife of कश्यप
  →दैत्य, अदिति.
दिन _ n. day, Russ. »den'«.
दिनाङ्क _ {दिन-अङ्क} m. 'number of the day',
  (mod.) date.
दिनेश _ {दिन-ईश} m. 'lord of the day', sun.
दिली-प _ m. 'protector of Delhi' (?), an
  ancestor of राम.
दिव् _ 'shining', 'enjoying' →देव; f. heaven;
  m. day.
दिवस _ m. day; heaven.
दिवा _ {दिव्} ind. by day.
दिव्य _ {दिव्} 'heavenly', »divine«, Lat.
  »divus«. दिव्य-युग _ (=चतुर्युग) n. the 4 युग
  combined. दिव्य-स्नान _ n. an 'ethereal
  bath' in the rain that falls while the sun is
  shining.
√दिश् _ दिश अतिसर्जने 6U give away
  (instruct, narrate) →दिशति; उद्. aim at;
  उप. instruct; निर्. describe; प्र. prescribe,
  ordain.
दिशति _ (a verb) {√दिश्} he gives away.
दिशा _ (=दिक्).
दिष्ट _ {दिक्} 'directed', prescribed.
दीक्षा _ f. initiation; either as उपनयनसंस्कार
  (to upper 3 वर्ण) or पञ्चसंस्कार; यज्ञदीक्षा.

दीक्षा-गुरु _ (=मन्त्र-गुरु) m. initiating
  teacher → (opp.) शिक्षागुरु.
दीक्षित _ {दीक्षा} initiated.
दीन _ depressed, miserable.
√दीप् _ दीपी दीप्तौ 4A shine →दीप्यते; प्र.
  shine, kindle.
दीप _ m. light, lamp.
दीपाली _ {दीप-आली} (Diwali, =दीपावली) f.
  'swarm of lights', a festival with
  illuminations.
दीपावली _ {दीप-आवली} (=दीपाली) f. 'row
  of lights', a festival on अमावास्या, incl. on
  Day 1 नरक-चतुर्दशी with evening
  illumination, celebrating the defeat of
  नरकासुर; Day 2 अमावास्या with उपवास,
  great festivities and kind words (to drive out
  bad fortune), लक्ष्मी-पूजा in the evening,
  illuminations, and प्रसाद; Day 3 कार्तिक-
  शुक्ल-प्रतिपद् (=बलि-प्रतिपद्) with
  worship of बलि, illuminations, decorating
  cows (in the morning) and गोवर्धन-पूजा,
  tying of मार्ग-पाली (in the afternoon), and
  rope pulling; it is (wrongly?) associated
  with the return and coronation of राम in
  अयोध्या, which should be celebrated as
  अयोध्या-सप्तमी on चैत्र-शुक्ल-सप्तमी.
दीपिका _ {दीप} f. light, lamp; 'illuminator' (at
  the end of titles of books).
दीप्त _ {दीप} lit (light).
दीप्ति _ f. light, brightness, shine.
दीप्तिमत् _ 'with light', bright.
दीप्यते _ (a verb) {√दीप्} he shines.
दीर्घ _ long (in space and time), Pers. »dirang«,
  Russ. »dologo«. दीर्घ-फल _ m. San Hemp
  (Taag, Crotalaria juncea).
दुःख _ {दुर्.} uneasy, hard → (opp.) सुख;
  unpleasing, a स्पर्श; n. uneasiness, distress,
  [immediate] suffering (opp. शोक); from 3
  sources – दैहिक-भौतिक-दैविक (=आत्म-
  भूत-देव-हेतु =अध्यात्म-अधिभूत-अधिदैव);

→क्लेश. दुःखम् _ ind. hardly → (opp.)
  सुखम्.
दुग्ध _ (Dudh) n. 'milked', milk.
दुर्. _ (a prefix, expressing:) hard, →दुर्ग; bad,
  »dys-« →दुर्बुद्धि; by सन्धि दुः. →दुःख, दुष्.
  →दुष्कृत.
दुरत्यय _ {दुर्.अति.} hard to pass over.
दुराचार _ {दुर्.} m. bad behavior.
दुर्ग _ {दुर्.} n. 'hard to go or approach',
  fortress.
दुर्गति _ f. 'gone bad', misfortune.
दुर्गा _ f. the 'inaccessible' goddess, with
  different forms, like काली-जगदम्बा-
  अन्नपूर्णा-सर्वमङ्गला-भैरवी-चन्दिका-
  ललिता-भवानी-तारा.
दुर्घटना _ f. 'bad effect', accident.
दुर्जन _ m. 'bad man', villain.
दुर्दैव _ n. misfortune.
दुर्निग्रह _ hard to control.
दुर्बल _ 'bad strength', weak.
दुर्बुद्धि _ 'bad intelligence', evil-minded,
  foolish.
दुर्भग _ 'bad portion', unfortunate.
दुर्भाग्य _ {दुर्भग} n. misfortune.
दुर्मेधः _ {दुर्मेधस्}.
दुर्मेधस् _ 'bad intelligence', stupid.
दुर्लभ _ 'hard to obtain', rare.
दुष्कृत _ {दुर्.} n. 'badly done', evil, sin.
दुष्ट _ bad, wicked.
दुष्पूर _ {दुर्.} 'hard to fill', insatiable.
दुष्प्राप _ {दुर्.} 'hard to obtain'.
दूर _ far.
दूरेण _ {दूर} ind. by far.
दूरात् _ {दूर} ind. from afar.
दूर्वा _ (Durva) f. Bermuda Grass (Cynodon
  dactylon).
दृढ _ firm, »true«. दृढम् _ ind. firmly.
√दृश् _ दृशिर् प्रेक्षणे 1P see →पश्यति,
  दर्शयति; अनु. look at, consider; आ. show;

प्र. see clearly, understand; सम्. look at, consider.

दृष्ट _ seen.

दृष्टवान् _ {दृष्टवत्} m. 'who saw'.

दृष्टि _ f. sight, vision; wisdom.

देव _ {दिव्} m. »divine« being, 10 kinds – विद्याधर-अप्सरः-यक्षः-रक्षः-गन्धर्व-किन्नर-पिशाच-गुह्यक-सिद्ध-भूत →दिव्य, इन्द्र; God, Lat. »deus«, Gr. »theos«, »Zeus« → theism, theology. देव-दत्त _ m. 'given by देव'; a वातदोष that helps relaxation by opening the mouth wide in yawning. देव-दारु _ (Devdar) m. False Ashoka (Polylathia longifolia), see अशोक. देव-नागरी _ m. 'देव script', derived from ब्राह्मी, since the 18th century used for writing Sanskrit all over India. देव-यान _ n. 'way to God', liberation.

देवता _ f. »deity«, देव.

देवन _ playing, lamenting.

देवी _ f. goddess.

देश _ {दिक्} m. direction; region, country, place →विदेश.

देह _ m. 'smearing /mixing' of elements, »dough«, Russ. »deža«; body.

देहात्मा _ (=जीव) m. 'soul in a body' → (opp.) विश्वात्मा.

देहिक _ {देह} bodily.

देहिन् _ m. 'having a body', embodied soul, creature.

देही _ {देहिन्}.

दैत्य _ m. 'descendent of दिति', demon →असुर, (opp.) आदित्य.

दैनिक _ {दिन} daily.

दैन्य _ {दीन} n. depression, poverty.

देव _ {देव} 'godly'; m. a विवाह where the bride is given to a ब्राह्मण; n. 'ordained by देव', destiny, nature; deity (=देवता). देव-हेतु _ 'caused by देव' or nature.

दैविक _ 'relating to दैव' or nature.

दैहिक _ 'relating to देह', bodily.

दोग्धा _ {दोग्धृ}.

दोग्धृ _ m. 'who milks', milkman →दुग्ध.

दोला _ f. swing.

दोष _ m. fault; human error – भ्रम-प्रमाद-विप्रलिप्सा-करणापाटव; alteration; त्रि-दोष.

दौर्बल्य _ {दुर्बल} n. weakness.

द्युति _ f. brightness, lustre, shine.

द्यूत _ n. gambling, (esp.) with dice.

द्रव _ 'flowing'; m. distilling; essence.

द्रवति _ (a verb) {√द्रु} he flows. अम्बु-वेगाः समुद्रम् एव अभिमुखाः द्रवन्ति। Currents of the water flow heading to the ocean alone. (भगवद्गीता).

द्रव्य _ {द्रव} liquid; n. substance, element →तत्त्व, ingredient, object; possession. द्रव्य-गुण _ m. pharmacology.

द्रष्टा _ {द्रष्टृ}.

द्रष्टृ _ m. seer →दृष्ट.

द्राक्षा _ f. Vine /Grapes (Angur, Vitis).

√द्रु _ द्रु गतौ 1P go (flow) →द्रवति.

द्रु _ (=द्रुम, तरु) m. »tree«, Gr. »drys« (oak).

द्रुत _ quick.

द्रुम _ {द्रु} m. »tree«.

द्रोह _ m. 'harming', »treachery«.

द्व _ (a stem) →द्वि.

द्वन्द्व _ {द्व द्व} n. pair, contest; pair of opposites, duality; a समास.

द्वय _ {द्व} twofold, double, Russ. »dvoe«.

द्वयी _ f. pair, both.

द्वादश _ {द्वादशन्}. द्वादश-तिलक _ m. 'तिलक applied to twelve places' of the body where विष्णु resides →ऊर्ध्वपुण्ड्र.

द्वादशन् _ »twelve«; »twelfth«.

द्वादशी _ f. 'twelfth [रात्रि]' in both शुक्ल- and कृष्ण-पक्ष.

द्वापर _ {द्व} m. the side of a die marked with 'two spots' (3rd in value). द्वापर-युग _ n. 'द्वापर age' (3rd in value).

द्वार _ n. »door«, Russ. »dver'«, gate, passage.

द्वारका _ f. 'city with [many] gates', the capital of कृष्ण, (mod.) Dwarka.

द्वि _ {द्व} »two«, Lat. »duo«, Russ. »dva« → »bi-«. द्वि-ज _ m. a 'twice-born', who is 'reborn' through दीक्षा; bird (also born twice). Besides the वैदिकविधि of उपनयनसंस्कार, पाञ्चरात्रिकविधि of पञ्चसंस्कार was open for all. द्वि-वचन _ n. 'speaking of two', dual number → (opp.) एक-, बहु-वचन.

द्विजोत्तम _ {द्विज-उत्तम} m. 'best of द्विज', a ब्राह्मण.

द्वितीय _ second.

द्विधा _ {द्वि} twofold.

द्विधा-करण _ dividing into two.

द्विरुक्ति _ f. 'said twice', repetition.

√द्विष् _ द्विष अप्रीतौ 2U hate, dislike →द्वेषि; प्र. hate.

द्वीप _ {द्वि अप्} m. 'on two sides water', island →सप्तद्वीप.

द्वेष _ m. hatred, quarrel, Germ. »Zwist«; a क्लेश (anger upon frustration of desires).

द्वेषि _ (a verb) {√द्विष्}he hates. सः न द्वेष्टि न काङ्क्षति । He neither hates nor desires. (भगवद्गीता).

द्वेष्य _ 'to be hated'.

द्वैत _ {द्वि} (=भेद) 'twofold', »dual«; n. 'dualism' between ब्रह्म and जीव in regard to quantity, supremacy and individuality (ब्रह्म is विभु परमात्मा and विश्वात्मा, जीव is अणु जीवात्मा and देहात्मा) → (opp.) अद्वैत, केवलाद्वैत; since both द्वैत and अद्वैत views are accepted in शास्त्र (उपनिषद्, वेदान्त, षड्दर्शन, पुराण), the conclusion is द्वैताद्वैत (=भेदाभेद) →नित्यो नित्यानाम्.

द्वैत-वाद _ m. 'thesis of द्वैत'.

द्वैताद्वैत _ n. simultaneous 'द्वैत and अद्वैत'.

द्वैध _ {द्विधा} n. 'twofold', duality, doubt.

द्वैधी-करण _ dividing into two.

धन _ n. wealth. धन-दण्ड _ m. 'wealth-punishment', fine.

धनञ्जय _ {धनम्-} m. 'conquering wealth', अर्जुन; a वातदोष that helps sustenance.

धनिक _ {धन} wealthy.

धनु _ (=धनुस्).

धनुर् _ {धनुस्}. धनुर्धर _ m. 'holding a bow', archer. धनुर्मुष्टि _ 'bow-fist' (the fist with thumb raised), a मात्रा (16 cm). धनुर्वेद _ m. 'science of archery'; military science by भृगु मुनि, an उपवेद.

धनुस् _ n. bow; a राशि, Lat. Sagittarius (hunter).

धन्य _ {धन} wealthy, fortunate. धन्य-वाद _ m. 'wishing fortune', thanks →आशीर्वाद.

धर _ holding.

धरति _ (a verb) {√धृ} he holds.

धर्म _ {धर} m. 'holding' (up), 'which maintains', duty, →त्रिवर्ग. "Because it maintains (धारण) sages call it धर्म. By धर्म the people are maintained. Whatever is connected with maintainance, that is called धर्म – this is the conclusion."; law, justice → justice personified, धर्म-राजा / यम; virtue, morality – सत्य, शौच, दया, तपः → (opp.) अधर्म, पाप; religion. धर्म-राजा _ {-राजन्} m. name of यम, who presides death, worshiped on चैत्र-शुक्ल-दशमी through teaching fearlessness of death. धर्म-शास्त्र _ n. science of law, includes or is synonymous to अर्थ-, नीति-शास्त्र, (esp.) 20 स्मृति like मनुस्मृति.

धर्म्य _ 'according to धर्म', righteous, virtuous.

√धा _ डुधाञ् धारणपोषणयोः 3U hold; nourish →दधाति; अनु. reasearch; अनु.वि. hold; अनु.सम्. meditate; अभि. explain, name; अभि.सम्. hold, aim at; आ. hold, place; नि. hold down; वि. hold, hold, make; प्र. give away, offer; प्र.नि. hold down, prostrate; सम्.आ. hold, concentrate.

धाता _ {धातृ}.

धातु _ {धर} m. 'holding', constituent part, element; chemical element; verbal/word root (√).

धातृ _ {धर} m. 'holder', upholder.

धात्री _ f. 'female धाता', nurse; the earth.

धाना _ f. 'held /conceived by the earth', seed.

धानेय _ {धाना} (Dhania) n. coriander.

धान्य _ {धाना} n. grain; (Dhan) m. Rice plant (Oryza sativa).

धाम _ {धामन्}.

धामन् _ n. »domain«, »domicile«, Lat. »dominium«, abode.

धारण _ {धर} holding.

धारणा _ f. 'holding', uninterrupted remembrance, concentration; 6th limb of अष्टाङ्गयोग, concentration on either a part of the body (हृदय, नासिकाग्र), a syllable /मन्त्र, picture, or God.

धार्मिक _ {धर्म} righteous, virtuous, religious.

√धाव् _ धावु गतिशुद्ध्योः 1U go (run); purify (cleanse) →धावति.

धावति _ (a verb) {√धाव्} he runs. रथः शीघ्रं धावति | The chariot runs fast.

धिक् _ ind. shame!

धिग्दण्ड _ {धिक्-} m. saying 'धिक् as punishment', disapproval.

धी _ f. thought, intelligence.

धीमत् _ 'with intelligence', intelligent.

धीमहि _ we meditate upon.

धीर _ (1) intelligent, wise. (2) sober.

धूप _ m. 'smoke', incense – a paste of cow dung, charcoal dust, sawdust, adhesives, perfumes, spices, fruits, wood (like sandalwood), flowers and oils; this paste is either rolled or applied to a bamboo stick as core (→अगरुवर्ती).

धूप-शेष _ m. 'smoke-remainder', black color made from the soot of a lamp/fire mixed with ghee.

धूम _ m. 'smoke', »fume«, Lat. »fumus«, Russ. »dym«.

धूलि _ f. 'smoke', »dust«.

√धृ _ धृञ् धारणे 1U hold (support) →धरति; उप. hold as, consider.

धृति _ {धर} f. 'holding', determination.

धेनु _ f. 'yielding' milk, cow.

धैर्य _ {धीर} n. 'soberness', patience.

धैवत _ n. 6th स्वर .

ध्याति _ (a verb) {√ध्यै} he meditates. सः ईश्वरं ध्याति | He meditates on God.

ध्यान _ n. 'meditation', Chin. »chan«, Jap. »Zen«, uninterrupted and undivided remembrance; 7th limb of अष्टाङ्गयोग, continued धारणा .

ध्येय _ {ध्यान} 'to be meditated', object of meditation.

√ध्यै _ ध्यै चिन्तायाम् 1P think, meditate →ध्याति.

ध्रुव _ firm, fixed, lasting, sure; m. pole star; a famous king who did तपस् in मधुवन at the यमुना under नारद who gave him the मन्त्र ॐ नमो भगवते वासुदेवाय. ध्रुव-अरुन्धती-दर्शन _ pointing out सप्तर्षि (अरुन्धती) and the pole star (ध्रुव) by going up the back of the 'wagon' of सप्तर्षि five times.

ध्रुवानुस्मृति _ {ध्रुव-अनुस्मृति} f. constant remembrance.

ध्वज _ m. flag.

ध्वनि _ m. sound, thunder.

न _ ind. »no«, »not«, »none«, Lat. »non«, Russ. »ne« →नो .

नक्त _ n. »night«, Germ. »Nacht«. नक्त-व्रत _ n. 'night vow', a fast by eating only once at night.

नक्षत्र _ 'star', 27(+1) constellations (lunar mansions) through which the moon passes, like अश्विनी, भरणी , etc.

नख _ m. »nail«, Germ. »Nagel«, finger-nail, Russ. »nogot'«, toe- nail, claw.

नगर _ n. town, city.

नग्न _ »naked«, Russ. »nagoi«; as in 'Nag(n)a Baba'.

√नट् _ नट नृतौ 1P dance, act →नटति .

नट _ m. actor, dancer. नट-राजा _ m. 'best dancer', शिव .

नटति _ (a verb) {√नट्} he dances.

√नद् _ टुनदि समृद्धौ 1P be glad →नन्दति; अभि. explain, raise.

नदी _ f. river.

नन्द _ m. delight.

नन्दति _ (a verb) {√नद्} he is glad. य: न अभिनन्दति न द्वेष्टि तस्य प्रज्ञा प्रतिष्ठिता । One who neither praises nor hates, his intelligence is steady. (भगवद्गीता).

नन्दन _ m. 'delighting', child.

नन्दिक _ m. Red Cedar tree (Tun, Toona ciliata) and wood.

नन्दिनी _ {नन्दिन्} f. daughter.

नन्दिन् _ m. 'delighting', son; the bull of शिव (as symbol of धर्म).

नन्दी _ {नन्दिन्}.

न-पुंसक _ 'not masculine', neuter. नपुंसक-लिङ्ग _ n. neuter gender → (opp.) पुल्लिङ्ग, स्त्री-लिङ्ग .

नप्ता _ {नप्तृ}.

नप्तृ _ m. grandson → »nephew«.

नप्त्री _ f. granddaughter → »niece«.

नभः _ {नभस्}.

नभस् _ n. mist, Lat. »nebula«; sky, Russ. »nebo«.

√नम् _ नम प्रह्वत्वे शब्दे च 1P bow down →नमति; प्र..

नमः _ {नमस्}. नमो नमः । Repeated नमः .

नमति _ (a verb) {√नम्} he bows down.

नमस् _ n. 'bowing', obeisance, Pers. »namaz«, salute →प्रणाम .

नमस्कार _ m. 'doing नमः', obeisance – either अष्टाङ्ग /दण्डवत् or पञ्चाङ्ग .

नमस्ते _ 'नमः to you!'.

नम्र _ {नमस्} 'bowing', reverential, humble.

नम्रता _ f. humility.

नयति _ (a verb) {√नी} he takes. स: फलं नयति । He takes a fruit.

नयन _ n. 'leading', eye →नीति, नेतृ, नेत्र .

नर _ (=नृ) m. man →नारी; husband; person. नर-सिंह _ (=नृसिंह).

नरक _ m. hell; 7 lower लोक – अतल-वितल-सुतल-तलातल-महातल-रसातल-पाताल .

नराधम _ {नर-अधम} m. 'lowest of men' → (opp.) नरोत्तम .

नरोत्तम _ {नर-उत्तम} m. 'best of men' → (opp.) नराधम .

नर्म _ {नर्मन्}. नर्म-दा _ f. 'pleasure-giving', a river in Gujarat.

नर्मन् _ n. sport, play, pleasure.

नल _ m. reed, pipe, (mod.) tap; water-channel.

नलिका _ {नल} f. tube.

नलिनी _ {नल} f. lotus (because of its stalk).

नव _ (1) {नु} »new«, Germ. »neu«, Russ. »nov«, fresh → »now«. (2) {नवन्} »nine«, Lat. »novem«. नव-ग्रह _ m. 'nine planets' – "सूर्य-सोम-अङ्गारक-बुध-बृहस्पति-शुक्र-शनि-राहु-केतु, these are known as ग्रह ." →सप्ताह .

नव-नीत _ n. 'fresh butter', butter. नव-रत्न _ n. 'nine gems' (related to नवग्रह) – pearl, ruby, topaz, diamond, emerald, lapis lazuli, coral, sapphire, Gomeda. नव-रात्र /-रात्रिक _ n. 'nine nights', celebrated (with विजयादशमी) in different parts of India either with (1) दुर्गा-पूजा (and animal sacrifices), or (2) राम-लीला. नव-वर्ष _ 'New Year' on चैत्र-कृष्ण- प्रतिपद्; celebrated with (1) worship of ब्रह्मा (because His creation started on this तिथि), and (2) होली (North-India).

नवम _ »ninth«, Lat. »nonus« → »November«.

नवमी _ f. 'ninth [रात्रि]' in both शुक्ल- and कृष्ण-पक्ष .

नवीन _ { नव } new.

नव्य _ { नव } newly, new.

√नश् _ नश अदर्शने 4P disappear →नश्यति ; प्र.; वि. destroy.

नश्यति _ (a verb) { √नश् } he disappears. पथि विमूढः नश्यति । One bewildered on the path perishes. (भगवद्गीता) संशय-आत्मा विनश्यति । One who is doubtful is lost. (भगवद्गीता) मे भक्तः न प्रणश्यति । My devotee does not perish. (भगवद्गीता) तस्य अहम् न प्रणश्यामि । For him I do not disappear. (भगवद्गीता).

नष्ट _ { √नश् } destroyed, lost.

नहि _ { न हि } ind. not so, not at all.

नाग _ m. a snake, (esp.) poisoneous snake; a many-hooded snake of the race of कद्रू →शेष , वासुकि , तक्षक ; a वातदोष for opening mouth and eyes. नाग-केसर _ m. Nag Champa tree (Mesua ferrea) and wood.

नाग-पञ्चमी _ a festival on श्रावण-शुक्ल-पञ्चमी (similar to the ancient सर्प-बलि festival on पूर्णिमा) for safety from snake-bites, worshipping images of snakes (or inviting snake charmers) with flowers and presents of curds and food, then distribution of प्रसाद ; images are either from cowdung, clay, or with color (on wooden boards), and are placed on both sides of the entrance.

नागर _ { नगर } 'relating to a city'; clever, cunning; m. a citizen.

नागरी _ f. 'city script' →देवनागरी ; a clever or intriguing woman.

नाटक _ n. drama.

नाट्य _ n. dancing, dramatic art.

नाडी _ f. tube; vein or artery; energy channel, like इडा-पिङ्गला-सुषुम्ना .

नाथ _ m. 'master', lord →जगन्नाथ ; husband.

नाद _ m. sound.

नाना _ ind. in various ways, separately.

नाभि _ f. »navel«, Germ. »Nabe«, »Nabel«.

नाम _ { नामन् }. नाम-करण _ m. 'name-ceremony', a संस्कार ; together with जातकर्म (at least a secret name, like देवदत्त , is given), or performed on the 10th/12th day (on an auspicious तिथि); the baby is bathed and dressed in new garments and the grandmother whispers the name into the baby's ear, then the name is announced.

नाम-धेय _ n. 'name-held/taken', by the name. नाम-सहस्र _ (=विष्णु-सहस्रनाम-स्तोत्र).

नामक _ (=नामन्).

नामन् _ n. »name«, Lat. »nomen« →नामकरण ; good/holy name (हरिनाम), chanting a name of God (esp. जप); a पञ्चसंस्कार where the disciple is given हरि-/राम-नाम (a prayer and a personal name like हरि-/राम-दास); »noun«; ind. »named«, called; indeed.

नायक _ { नयन } m. 'leader', commander, hero.

नारङ्ग _ (Narangi) m. »orange« tree, Ital. »arancia« (Santara, Citrus) and fruit.

नारद _ (Narada Muni) m. a celestial sage and messenger between देव and men.

नारायण _ m. विष्णु .

नारिकेल _ (Nariyal) m. Coconut tree (Cocos nucifera) and fruit.

नारी _ { नर } f. woman.

नाल _ { नल } m. tube.

नाव _ { नौ } m. boat, ship, Lat. »navis«.

नाविक _ belonging to a नाव → »navy«, »navigation«; m. helmsman, pilot, sailor.

नाश _ m. destruction, loss →नष्ट .

नासा _ f. »nose«, Lat. »nasus«, Russ. »nos« →अनुनासिक .

नासिक _ {नासिका or नासिक्य} m. the town Nashik, named after cutting off the 'nose' of शूर्पणखा by लक्ष्मण .

नासिका _ {नासा.क} f. nostril, nose.

नासिकाग्र _ {नासिका-अग्र} n. tip /top of the nose.

नास्ति _ {न अस्ति} ind. 'it is not', non-existent; nothing is beyond →नास्तिक .

नास्तिक _ {नास्ति} m. atheist → (opp.) आस्तिक .

नास्तिकता _ f. atheism.

नि. _ (a prefix, expressing:) down, »nether«, Russ. »niz« →निग्रह .

निःस्पृह _ {निर्.} free from hankering.

निकेत _ m. dwelling.

निगृहीत _ 'held down', suppressed.

निग्रह _ {नि.} m. 'holding down', suppression.

निज _ {-ज} 'inborn', native, own.

नितराम् _ ind. definitely, extremely.

नित्य _ eternal; usual, daily → (opp.) नैमित्तिक; obligatory → (opp.) काम्य . नित्यो नित्यानाम् । [He is the supreme] eternal (नित्य) among the eternal [living beings]. नित्यम् _ ind. eternally, constantly.

नित्यत्व _ n. eternality.

नित्यदा _ ind. always.

नित्यशः _ ind. always.

√निद् _ निदि कुत्सायाम् 1P despise →निन्दति .

निद्रा _ f. sleep.

निधन _ (1) 'no धन', poor. (2) n. 'laying down', end, destruction, death.

निधान _ n. 'laying down', resting place.

निधि _ {नि.} m. 'laying down', store, treasure; the sea.

निन्दति _ (a verb) {√निद्} he despises.

निन्दा _ f. blame, criticism.

निपुण _ clever, skilled.

निबद्ध _ »bound« down, tied.

निबन्ध _ »bondage«.

निमज्जन _ 'sinking down', plunging.

निमन्त्रण _ n. invitation.

निमित्त _ n. sign, omen; motive, reason; cause, instrument. निमित्त-मात्र _ n. just the instrument. निमित्त-माया _ f. 'causal energy', instrumental or efficient cause → (opp.) प्रधानमाया; different causes are named by different schools, like आत्मा, कर्म, गुण, स्वभाव, काम, दैव, काल .

निमिष _ m. twinkling.

निमेष _ {निमिष} m. instant, moment; a मात्रा (0.5 s).

निमेषण _ twinkling.

निम्न _ low, deep.

निम्ब _ m. Neem tree (Azadirachta indica) and wood.

निम्बू / निम्बूक _ (Nimbu) m. »lemon«, Pers. »limu«, Lemon tree (Lime, Citrus) and fruit.

नियत _ {नियम} 'restrained', regular. नियतम् _ ind. regularly, constantly.

नियम _ m. 'restraint', rule; secondary external observances as 2nd limb of अष्टाङ्गयोग . "शौच, सन्तोष, तपः, स्वाध्याय and ईश्वरप्रणिधान are नियम." →क्रियायोग .

नियोजन _ commanding, directing.

नियोजित _ engaged.

निर्. _ (a prefix, expressing:) out →निरस्त; without →निर्जल; by सन्धि निः. →निःस्पृह, निश्. →निश्चल, निष्. →निष्फल .

निरग्नि _ {निर्.} 'without fire'.

निरत _ {नि.} engaged.

निरर्थक _ {निर्.} 'without making sense', nonsense.

निरस्त _ {निर्.} 'cast out', removed.

निरहङ्कार _ 'without अहङ्कार'.

निराकार _ 'without आकार', formless.

निरामय _ {निर्.} 'without illness', healthy.

निराशा _ f. 'without आशा', despair.

निराश्रय _ 'without shelter', destitute.

निराहार _ m. 'without food', fasting.

निरुक्त _ f. 'out-spoken', defined; etymological interpretation of a word, lexicography, a वेदाङ्ग .

निरुक्ति _ (=निरुक्त).

निरुद्ध _ {नि.} 'opposed, confined', controlled.

निरोध _ {नि.} m. 'opposition, confinement', control.

निर्गुण _ 'without गुण ', spiritual.

निर्जल _ 'without जल ', dry; (esp.) उपवास without drinking water.

निर्णय _ {निर्.} m. 'leading out', conclusion, decision.

निर्देश _ m. 'pointing out', description.

निर्देश्य _ to be described.

निर्दोष _ 'without fault', pure.

निर्द्वन्द्व _ 'without duality', absolute.

निर्मम _ 'without mine', without proprietorship.

निर्मल _ 'without dirt', pure.

निर्मलत्व _ n. purity.

निर्मुक्त _ 'released out', liberated.

निर्मूलन _ n. 'rooting out', uprooting.

निर्वाण _ {निर्.} n. 'without blowing', calmness; liberation.

निर्विकार _ 'without alteration'.

निर्विशेष _ 'without difference', unqualified, absolute.

निर्वेद _ 'without despair', indifferent.

निर्वैर _ 'without enmity'.

निवात _ {नि.} 'without wind', calm.

निवास _ m. dwelling.

निवृत्ति _ f. 'without activity', inactivity, renunciation → (opp.) प्रवृत्ति . निवृत्ति-मार्ग _ m. the path of renunciation (=देवयान).

निशा _ f. night.

निश्चय _ {निर्.} m. 'seeking out', ascertainment, conviction.

निश्चल _ {निर्.} 'without motion', steady.

निश्चित _ {निश्चय} ascertained.

निषाद _ m. 7th स्वर .

निषिद्ध _ {निषेध} prohibited.

निषेक _ m. impregnation.

निषेध _ m. 'driving out', prohibition.

निष्कर्म _ {निर्.} 'without कर्म ', free from reaction of work.

निष्कर्ष _ drawing out.

निष्क्रमण _ 'going out' for the first time, in the 4th month (with parents, near family members and friends) to present the baby to the sun and a temple.

निष्ठ _ {नि.स्थ} 'fixed down', firm.

निष्ठा _ f. firmness.

निष्पाप _ {निर्.} 'without sin', sinless.

निष्फल _ {निर्.} 'without fruit', fruitless, useless.

√नी _ नीञ् प्रापणे 1U reach (bring to, lead), take →नयति; आ. bring वि. lead, train.

नीच _ low, Russ. »nic«; mean.

नीति _ {नयन} f. 'leading', guidance; moral conduct (=आचार); policy, 4 means to deal with allies, neutrals, potential enemies and enemies – साम-दान-भेद-दण्ड . नीति-शास्त्र _ n. science of politics (=दण्डनीति, अर्थशास्त्र, धर्मशास्त्र), (esp.) पञ्चतन्त्र and हितोपदेश .

नीर _ n. water.

नीराज् _ (like राजन्) illuminating.

नील _ dark; blue → »lilac«, »Nile«; m. sapphire. नील-कण्ठ _ m. who has a 'dark throat' (due to drinking poison), शिव .

नु _ ind. »now«, Germ. »nun« →नूतन , नूनम् , नव ; indeed.

नूतन _ {नु} new, modern.

नूनम् _ {नु} ind. now, Russ. »nyne«; indeed.

नूपुर _ n. anklet.

नृ _ (=नर). नृ-प _ m. 'protector of men', king. नृ-सिंह _ (=नरसिंह) m. 'man-lion', an अवतार . नृसिंह-चतुर्दशी _ a festival on वैशाख-शुक्ल-चतुर्दशी .

नृत्य _ n. dance.

नेता _ {नेतृ}.

नेतृ _ {नयन} m. leader.

नेत्र _ {नयन} n. 'leading', eye. नेत्र-प्रक्षालन _ rinsing the eyes.

नैमित्तिक _ {निमित्त} occasionally, at ceremonies.

नैमिष _ n. 'twinkling'; name of a town (mod. »Nimsar«), also known as नैमिषारण्य (नैमिष- अरण्य).

नैष्ठिक _ {निष्ठा} m. 'who is firm', a perpetual celibate.

नो _ {न उ} ind. 'not at all', »no«. नो दया मांस-भोजिनः | There is no mercy of a meat-eater.

नौ _ f. ship →नाविक.

नोका _ f. boat.

न्यग्रोध _ (=वट).

न्याय _ {नि.} m. 'coming down' to a universal rule, logic, a प्रमाण (=अनुमान); argument, 3 kinds – जल्प-वितण्डा-वाद; philosophy → (opp.) स्मृति, श्रुति; (esp.) a षड्दर्शन of गौतम, propounding in न्यायसूत्र rules of debate and basic elements.

न्याय्य _ {न्याय} regular, correct.

न्यास _ {नि.} m. 'throwing down', abandoning, renunciation →सन्न्यास; 'placing' words (like नमः, स्वाहा, हुम्/हूम्, वषट्/वौषट्, फट्) or मन्त्र (like 12 names of विष्णु – ॐ केशवाय नमः ...) on hands (कर, →करादि) and various parts (अङ्ग, हृदयादि) of the body.

न्यून _ {नि.ऊन} less → (opp.) अतिरिक्त, अधिक.

न्यूनतम _ 'most less', minimum.

-प _ (1) protecting. (2) drinking.

पक्व _ (pakka) 'cooked', »baked«; digested; ripe; accomplished, perfect →पाक.

पक्ष _ m. wing →पक्षी; one side or half; fortnight →शुक्ल-, कृष्ण-पक्ष; side, party. पक्ष-पात _ m. 'fallen to one side', partiality.

पक्षिन् _ m. 'winged', bird.

पक्षी _ {पक्षिन्}.

पङ्क _ m. mud. पङ्क-ज _ n. 'mud-born', lotus.

पङ्गु _ lame.

√पच् _ डुपचष् पाके 1U cook →पचति.

पचति _ (a verb) {√पच्} he cooks. सः अन्नं पचति | He cooks food. अहम् अन्नं पचामि | I digest food. (भगवद्गीता) ते आत्म-कारणात् पचन्ति | They cook for their own sake, they eat sin. (भगवद्गीता).

पञ्च _ {पञ्चन्}. पञ्च-कन्या _ f. 'five girls' – अहल्या- द्रौपदी-सीता-तारा-मन्दोदरी (the wives of sage गौतम, the पाण्डव, रामचन्द्र, वाली and रावण, resp.); all had supernatural births and suffered great losses. पञ्च-कर्म _ n. 'five treatments' (in आयुर्वेद). पञ्च-गव्य _ n. five cow products – (1) दुग्ध/क्षीर → तक्र, क्षीरज, किलाट, चरु; (2) दधि; (3) नवनीत (plus तक्र) → घृत, पञ्चामृत; (4) शकृत्/गोवर; (5) गोमूत्र → पञ्चगव्य-घृत; esp. a mixture of those (in relation 8-8-4-2-1 plus water). पञ्च-भूत _ n. the five महाभूत. पञ्च-यज्ञ _ m. 'five oblations' to pay back ऋण to देव, ऋषि, पितृ, नृ, भूत through होम, स्वाध्याय, श्राद्ध, आतिथ्य, बलि. पञ्च-रात्र _ m. 'lasting five nights (days)', a class of वैष्णव literature, (esp.) नारदपञ्चरात्र. पञ्च-संस्कार _ 'five sacraments' according to पञ्चरात्र. "ताप, पुण्ड्र, नाम, मन्त्र and याग as fifth – these five संस्कार arouse exclusive devotion."

पञ्चन् _ five, Lat. »quinque«, Russ. »pat'«.

पञ्चम _ fifth, Lat. »quintus«; the 5th स्वर.

पञ्चमी _ f. 'fifth [रात्रि]' in both शुक्ल- and कृष्ण-पक्ष.

पञ्चाङ्ग _ 'five अङ्ग', the Hindu almanac treating तिथि-नक्षत्र-राशि-योग-करण.

पञ्चामृत _ {पञ्च-अमृत} n. the five substances milk, curd, ghee, honey and sugar; a mixture of those.

पटु _ sharp; clever.

√पठ् _ पठ व्यक्तायां वाचि 1P speak (read, study) →पठति.

पठति _ (a verb) {√पठ्} he reads. सः पुस्तकं पठति । He reads the book.

पठन _ n. reading, reciting.

पणव _ m. a small drum.

पण्डित _ learned; m. scholar, »pundit«.

√पत् _ पत्लृ गतौ 1P go (fall) →पतति; प्र.नि. completely fall down; सम्. fall together, clash.

पतङ्ग _ m. flying insect.

पतञ्जलि _ m. a famous grammarian (महाभाष्य) and philosopher (योगसूत्र).

पतति _ (a verb) {√पत्} he falls. एषां पितरः पतन्ति । Their ancestors fall down. (भगवद्गीता).

पति _ m. master, Lat. »potis«; husband.

पतित _ fallen.

पत्त्र _ (=पत्र).

पत्नी _ {पति} f. wife, mistress.

पत्र _ n. wing, feather; leaf, petal; a leaf for writing, document, letter.

पत्रिका _ f. (mod.) journal.

पथ _ m. »path«, Russ. »put'«, course.

पथिन् _ {पथ} m. »path«, course.

√पद् _ पद गतौ 4A go →पद्यते; अनु.प्र. follow; आ. attain; उप. attain, exist; उप. प्रति. सम्. attain; प्र. submit; प्रति. attain; वि.प्रति. go in opposit directions, be perplexed; सम्. attain.

पद _ n. »foot«, Lat. »pes«, »pedis«, »peda«; a मात्रा (30 cm); step, part; position, abode; word →पाद. पद-पाठ _ m. 'word-by-word recitation' (without सन्धि) for understanding → (opp.) क्रमपाठ. पद-यात्रा _ f. pilgrimage by foot.

पद्धति _ m. method, system.

पद्म _ m. lotus. पद्म-लोचन _ m. 'whose eyes are [beautiful] like a lotus'.

पद्मक _ m. Himalayan Cherry tree (Paiyaun, Prunus cerasoides) and gum.

पद्यते _ (a verb) {√पद्} he goes. ये माम् एव प्रपद्यन्ते ते मायां तरन्ति । Those who surrender to me alone they cross Māyā. (भगवद्गीता).

पनस _ m. Jackfruit tree (Kathal, Artocarpus integrifolius), wood and fruit.

पन्थाः _ {पथिन्}.

पयः _ {पयस्}.

पयस् _ n. milk.

पर _ »far«, »fore«, beyond, Gr. »pera«, Russ. »pere-«; other; supreme. पर-तन्त्र _ 'reliant on another', dependent. पर-ब्रह्म _ 'supreme ब्रह्म', the Absolute → (opp.) महद् ब्रह्म (=प्रधान).

परः _ ind. beyond.

परतर _ 'more पर', higher, superior.

परम _ {पर.तम} 'most पर', highest, supreme. परम-हंस _ m. 'supreme swan', a pure soul of the highest order.

परमाणु _ {परम-अणु} m. atom.

परमात्मा _ {परम-आत्मा} m. 'supreme soul', supersoul, God as immanent in all creation; called विष्णु, अन्तर्यामी, पुरुष → (opp.) जीवात्मा.

परमार्थ _ {परम-अर्थ} m. supreme purpose.

परम्परा _ {पर पर} f. 'succession', lineage, tradition.

परस्मै-पद _ n. 'word for another', a form of conjugation (P), → (opp.) आत्मने- (A) and उभय-पद (U).

परशु _ m. axe. परशु-राम _ m. 'राम with the axe', the son of जमदग्नि, an अवतार.

परस्तात् _ ind. beyond.

परस्परम् _ {पर पर} ind. one another, mutually. परस्पर-समीक्षण _ 'looking at each other' at marriage (when a piece of cloth, held between them, is removed at the auspicious moment), reciting मङ्गलाष्टकम्.

परा _ ind. beyond, away; f. a spiritual वाक्, conscience. परा-जय _ m. 'deprived of victory', defeat. परा-जित _ defeated.

परायण _ {पर-अयन} 'supreme path', shelter.

परार्ध _ {पर-अर्ध} m.n. 'latter half', the highest number (100,000 billions), half of the life span of ब्रह्मा.

परि. _ (a prefix, expressing:) around, »peri-« →परिक्रम; fully →परित्याग.

परिक्रम _ m. 'going around', circumambulation.

परिग्रह _ m. 'fully holding', possession, proprietorship.

परिचय _ m. 'search', familiarity.

परिजन _ m. 'people around', attendants.

परिजात _ m. Parijat tree (Night Jasmine, Nyctanthes arbror-tristis) and flower.

परिणाम _ m. 'fully bending', transformation, evolution; result. परिणाम-वाद _ m. 'thesis of evolution' of जगत् (in साङ्ख्य), (esp.) from ब्रह्म (in वेदान्त) →ब्रह्मपरिणामवाद.

परित्याग _ m. 'fully abandoning', renunciation.

परित्राण _ n. 'fully protecting', liberation.

परिप्रश्न _ m. 'fully questioning', enquiry.

परिभाषा _ f. 'fully speeking', definition.

परिमाण _ measuring, weighing.

परिमेय _ 'to be fully measured', measurable →अपरिमेय.

परिवर्तन _ 'turning around', returning, changing.

परिवार _ m. 'fully covering', family.

परिषद् _ f. 'sitting round', community councel for the diffusion of learning and disputation of law.

परिस्थिति _ f. 'situation around', circumstance.

परीक्षा _ {परि.ईक्षा} f. 'looking around', examination.

परोक्ष _ {परः-अक्ष} 'beyond sight', invisible, not witnessed; indirect, by प्रत्यक्ष of others.

पर्जन्य _ m. rain cloud, rain.

पर्ण _ n. feather, wing; leaf.

पर्पट _ (Papad) m. a thin cake made of lentils (dal) baked in oil.

पर्यन्त _ {परि.} m. 'limit around', circumference, limit.

पर्याप्त _ {परि.} 'fully obtained', sufficient. पर्याप्तम् _ ind. sufficiently, enough.

पर्युषित _ {परि.उषित} 'having passed' the night, from the day before.

पर्व _ {पर्वन्}.

पर्वत _ m. mountain, mountain- range →पार्वती.

पर्वन् _ n. joint, division, section (esp. of a book).

पलायन _ n. fleeing, cowerdice.

पलाश _ m. Palash tree (Kimshuka, Parrot Tree, Butea monosperma), wood and flower.

पल्यङ्क _ {पर्यङ्क} (Palang) m. bed, couch → »palanquin«.

पल्लव _ m. sprout, shoot.

पवते _ (a verb) {√पू} he purifies.

पवन _ m. 'purifying', washing; wind.

पवित्र _ n. 'purifying', holy; the sacred thread → उपवीत.

पवित्रारोपण _ {-आरोपण} n. investing a deity with the पवित्र on श्रावण-शुक्ल-द्वादशी.

पशु _ m. domestic animal → (opp.) मृग. पशु-पति _ m. 'lord of animals', शिव.

पश्च _ hinder, later, western.

पश्चात् _ {पश्च} ind. behind, afterwards, westwards. पश्चात्ताप _ {पश्चात्-} m. 'after-pain', atonement; repentance.

पश्चिमा _ {पश्च} f. the west.

पश्यत् _ 'seeing'.

पश्यति _ (a verb) {√दृश्} he sees. कश्चिद् एनम् आश्चर्यवत् पश्यति | Someone sees this

[soul] as wonderful. (भगवद्गीता) तव देहे सर्वान्‍ऋषीन् पश्यामि । In your body I see all sages. (भगवद्गीता) सूरयः विष्णोः पदं पश्यन्ति । The sages see the abode of Vishnu. (ऋग्वेद).

पश्यन्ती _ { पश्यत् } f. a 'seeing' वाक् , concentrated thought, forming mental objects like सुख-दुःख .

√पा _ पा पाने 1P drink →पिबति .

पाक _ m. cooking, »baking«; digestion; ripening →पक्व .

पाखण्ड _ (=पाषण्ड).

पाचक _ m. cook, fire.

पाञ्चरात्रिक _ m. 'according to पञ्चरात्र '. पाञ्चरात्रिक-विधि _ rule of पञ्चरात्र .

पाटव _ { पटु } n. sharpness.

पाठ _ { पठन } m. recitation, 2 modes – पद- and क्रम-पाठ ; lesson.

पाठन _ n. teaching.

पाणि _ m. hand. पाणि-ग्रहण _ taking eachother's hand at marriage near the fire to signify union. पाणि-पाद-वाक्-उपस्थ-पायु _ 5 कर्मेन्द्रिय .

पाण्डव _ m. 'son of पाण्डु ', the 5 पाण्डव – युधिष्ठिर-भीम-अर्जुन-नकुल-सहदेव .

पातक _ n. 'causing to fall', sin.

पाताल _ n. hell, a नरक .

पात्र _ n. cup, any receptacle; a worthy recipient.

पाद _ { पद } m. foot, leg; quarter (as one leg of a quadruped being), quarter verse. पाद-चिह्न _ n. 'foot-print'. पाद-त्राण _ n. 'foot-covering', shoe.

पादुका _ { पाद } f. shoe.

पान _ n. 'drinking', drink, beverage.

पान्थ _ { पथ } m. wanderer, traveller, Russ. »putnik«.

पाप _ n. sin (=अधर्म), mainly 4 – द्यूत-स्त्रीय-सूना-मद → (opp.) पुण्य, धर्म ; crime.

पायु _ m. anus.

पार _ n. 'crossing', further shore.

पारण / पारणा _ { पार } n. 'crossing', accomplishing; conclusion of उपवास , 'break-fast'.

पारिश _ (Paras) m. Portia Tree (Thespesia populnea) and wood.

पारुषक _ m. Phalsa tree (Grewia asiatica) and fruit.

पारुष्य _ n. roughness.

पार्थिव _ { पृथिवी } earthen, terrestrial; m. inhabitant or lord of the earth, king. पार्थिव-स्नान _ n. 'a bath with loose earth'.

पार्वती _ { पर्वत } f. दुर्गा (as daughter of the हिमालय).

पार्श्व _ n. side.

√पाल् _ पाल रक्षणे 10P protect (govern) →पालयति .

पाल _ m. protector, keeper →गोपाल .

पालन _ protecting.

पालयति _ (a verb) { √पाल् } he protects.

पावक _ m. 'purifyer', fire or wind.

पावन _ { पवन } purifying, pure.

पाश _ m. snare, trap.

पाषण्ड _ m. imposter, any one who falsely assumes the characteristics of an orthodox Hindu.

पिङ्गल _ brown, yellow.

पिङ्गला _ f. a नाडी on the right side of the body.

पिचुमर्द _ (=निम्ब).

पिच्छिल _ (=शिंशपा).

पिण्ड _ m. morsel, (esp.) a ball of rice offered at श्राद्ध .

पिता _ { पितृ }. पिता-मह _ m. paternal grandfather, grand-uncle. पिता-मही _ f. paternal grandmother.

पितृ _ m. »father«, Lat. »pater«; (Pl.) ancestors. पितृ-लोक _ m. 'world of ancestors', a heaven. पितृ-ष्वसृ _ { -स्वसृ } 'father's sister', paternal aunt.

पित्त _ n. bile; a दोष which is slightly oily,
  sharp, hot, light, musty, flowing, and liquid.
पित्तल _ n. brass, bell metal.
पिपर्ति/पृणाति _ (a verb) {√पृ} he nourishes.
पिपासा _ f. thirst.
पिप्पल _ m. Pipal tree (अश्वत्थ, बोधिद्रुम,
  Holy Fig, Ficus Religiosa).
पिप्पलि _ f. a vine and its fruit 'long pepper' →
  »pepper«.
पिबति _ (a verb) {√पा} he drinks. सः जलं
  पिबति । He drinks water.
पिशाच _ m. a devil.
पिशुन _ wicked.
√पी _ पीङ् पाने 4A drink →पीयते .
√पीड् _ पीड अवगाहने दुःखक्रियायां च 10P
  press; give pain →पीडयति .
पीडयति _ (a verb) {√पीड्} he gives pain.
  बुभुक्षा मां पीडयति । Hunger pains me.
पीडा _ f. pain, suffering.
पीत _ yellow.
पीयते _ (a verb) {√पी} he drinks.
पीलु _ m. Meswak tree (Jaal, Salvadora
  persica).
पुंस् _ m. man, male being.
पुंसवन _ 'stimulating the living/male being', a
  संस्कार after the third month of pregnancy,
  marking the stage where the baby is
  expected to start moving; celebrated with
  पूजा and the distribution of प्रसाद .
पुङ्गव _ {पुंस्-गव} m. 'male cow', bull; hero.
पुच्छ _ n. tail.
पुण्डरीक _ n. lotus.
पुण्ड्र _ (=तिलक) n. a religious mark on the
  forehead →बिन्दु /Bindi, (esp.) वैष्णव
  ऊर्ध्वपुण्ड्र and शैव त्रिपुण्ड्र markings;
  materials are चन्दन, गोपीचन्दन, कुङ्कुम,
  सिन्दूर, अगुरु, कस्तूरी, धूपशेष ; a
  पञ्चसंस्कार of dedication to God.
पुण्य _ pure, virtuous; n. virtue, merit →
  »Pune«.

पुत्र _ m. child, son →पौत्र .
पुत्रजीवक _ (Putijia) m. Putranjiva tree
  (Putranjiva roxburghii) and wood.
पुत्रिका _ (=पुत्री).
पुत्री _ f. daughter.
पुनः _ {पुनर्} ind. again.
पुनर् _ ind. back, again, moreover. पुनरागम _
  m. 'coming again', return. पुनर्जन्म _ n.
  rebirth.
पुनाति _ (a verb) {√पू} he purifies. तपसा
  पुरुषः पापं पुनाति । By penance a person
  purifies [his] sin. (महाभारत).
पुन्नग _ m. Kath Champa tree (Surpan,
  Calophyllum inophyllum), wood and nut.
पुमान् _ {पुंस्}.
पुर _ n. city, Gr. »polis«, capital, fortress;
  smaller towns are called खेट, any cluster of
  houses ग्राम .
पुरः _ {पुरस्}.
पुरस् _ ind. »pre-«, Lat. »prae«, before, in
  front, eastward.
पुरस्तात् _ ind. before.
पुरा _ {पुरस्} ind. formerly; in the beginning.
पुराण _ {पुरस्} old, ancient; n. ancient
  history, (esp.) 18 महापुराण .
पुरातन _ {पुरा} old → (opp.) नूतन .
पुरी _ {पुर} f. the capital of कलिङ्ग with the
  temple of जगन्नाथ .
पुरु _ m. a son of ययाति (and brother of यदु),
  forefather of कुरु and the पाण्डव .
पुरुष _ m. person, man, human; परमात्मा ; a
  grammatical person – प्रथम-मध्यम-उत्तम-
  पुरुष .
पुरुषार्थ _ {पुरुष-अर्थ} m. 'human pursuit'
  →चतुर्वर्ग .
पुरुषोत्तम _ {पुरुष-उत्तम} m. 'supreme
  person', God.
पुरोहित _ m. priest.
पुलहाश्रम _ m. the अश्रम of sage पुलह .

पुल्लिङ्ग _ {पुंस्-लिङ्ग} n. 'not masculine', neuter [gender] → (opp.) नपुंसक-, स्त्री-लिङ्ग.

√पुष् _ पुष पुष्टौ 1/9P nourish →पोषति/पुष्णाति.

पुष्कर _ n. lotus; the pilgrimage town »Pushkar«.

पुष्कल _ abundant, excellent.

पुष्टि _ f. nourishment, satiation.

पुष्प _ n. flower.

पुष्पाञ्जलि _ {पुष्प-अञ्जलि} m. 'अञ्जलि with flowers', presenting flowers with hollowed hands.

पुष्पित _ {पुष्प} flowery.

पुस्तक _ n. manuscript, book.

पुस्तकालय _ {पुस्तक-आलय} m. 'book-store', library.

√पू _ (1) पूङ् पवने 1A purify →पवते. (2) पूञ् पवने 9U purify →पुनाति.

√पूज् _ पूज पूजायाम् 10P worship, honor →पूजयति.

पूजन _ worshiping.

पूजयति _ (a verb) {√पूज्} he worships.

पूजा _ f. worship; hosting a deity, or important person, as an honored and dearest guest, and receiving their happiness and blessing.

पूज्य _ worshipable.

पूत _ purified, pure.

पूर _ filling.

पूरक _ {पूर} m. 'filling', inhalation, a प्राणायाम; flood. पूरक-रेचक-कुम्भक _ 3 elements of प्राणायाम.

पूरण _ {पूर} filling.

पूरुष _ (=पुरुष).

पूर्ण _ {पूर} 'filled', fulfilled, full, Russ. »polon«; complete, perfect. पूर्णमदः पूर्णमिदम् । That [ब्रह्म] is पूर्ण and this [जगत्] is पूर्ण. पूर्ण-मास _ m. [the night of] full moon. पूर्ण-विराम _ m. full stop ॥.

पूर्णिमा _ (=पूर्णमास).

पूर्णिमान्त _ {पूर्णिमा-अन्त} m. a calender, where each मास begins with कृष्णपक्ष and ends with पूर्णिमा; (opp.) अमान्त.

पूर्त _ {पूर} n. 'fulfilled', rewarding; pious work – like digging tanks, restoring temples, planting trees.

पूर्व _ {पुरस्} »previous«, before, ancient, first, Russ. »perv«; eastern. पूर्वम् _ ind. previously. पूर्व-ज _ 'born before', elder; m. the eldest son or brother. पूर्व-पक्ष _ m. 'first part', the first statement or objection in a discussion.

-पूर्वकम् _ ind. preceded by, with →प्रीतिपूर्वकम्.

पूर्वतरम् _ ind. 'more previous'.

पूर्वा _ f. east.

पृच्छति _ (a verb) {√प्रच्छ्} he asks. तं पुरुषं त्वा पृच्छामि । About that Purusha I ask you. (बृहद्-आरण्यक-उपनिषद्).

पृच्छा _ f. question, inquiry.

पृथक् _ ind. separate, different.

पृथक्त्व _ {.त्व} n. separatedness, difference.

पृथिवी _ (=पृथ्वी). पृथिव्यां त्रीणि रत्नानि जलमन्नं सुभाषितम् । The three jewels on earth (पृथिवी) are जल, अन्न and सुभाषित.

पृथु _ broad, great, abundant; m. the (adopted) son of वेन who greatly improved agriculture and trade.

पृथ्वी _ {पृथु} f. 'wide' world, the earth.

पृष्ठ _ n. the back or top.

पृष्ठतः _ ind. from behind.

√पृ _ पृ पालनपूरणयोः 3/9P protect; nourish /fill →पिपर्ति/पृणाति; आ. fill.

पेषण _ grinding.

पैशाच _ {पिशाच} m. 'devilish', a विवाह after the bride was abducted (asleep or intoxicated).

पैशुन _ {पिशुन} n. wickedness.

पोगण्ड _ m. young boy /girl →पौगण्ड.

पोषण _ n. nourishing, maintaining.
पोषति/पुष्णाति _ (a verb) {√पुष्} he
  nourishes. सर्वाः ओषधीः पुष्णामि। I
  nourish all plants. (भगवद्गीता).
पौगण्ड _ {पोगण्ड} n. boyhood, a वयः.
पौत्र _ {पुत्र} m. 'a son's son', grandson.
पौत्री _ {पुत्री} f. granddaughter.
पौरुष _ {पुरुष} manly, human; n. manhood,
  heroism.
पौर्णमासी _ f. a day/night 'of पूर्णमास'.
पौर्व _ {पूर्व} 'relating to the past or east'.
पौष-पूर्णिमा _ a festival marking the
  beginning of austerities during माघ-मास –
  daily (गङ्गा-/यमुना-)स्नान and दान.
प्र. _ (a prefix, expressing:) before, »pre-«
  →प्राक्; forth, »pro-« →प्राण; full →प्रसाद.
प्रकट _ manifest, clear.
प्रकथन _ telling.
प्रकार _ m. sort, method.
प्रकाश _ m. shine, light.
प्रकाशन _ shining.
प्रकाशक _ m. illuminator; (mod.) publisher.
प्रकृति _ {प्र.} f. 'bringing forth',
  »procreation«; material energy (consisting
  of त्रिगुण), nature →प्राकृतसर्ग; primary
  substance, origin; the uninflected word.
प्रक्रम _ m. 'step', a मात्रा (60 cm, 2 पद).
प्रक्षालन _ n. 'fully washing', cleansing.
प्रगति _ f. 'moving forth', progress.
प्रचुर _ much, abundant → (opp.) अल्प.
प्रचोदयात् _ he shall inspire.
√प्रच्छ् _ प्रच्छ ज्ञीप्सायाम् 6P inquire
  →पृच्छति; परि. ask.
प्रजन _ m. »procreating«.
प्रजा _ f. offspring, »progeny«; race, mankind,
  people. प्रजा-पति _ m. 'master/forefather of
  men', patriarch; (esp.) the first 7 of the 10
  sons of ब्रह्मा – मरीचि (→कश्यप), अत्रि
  (→दुर्वासा), अङ्गिरा (→बृहस्पति), पुलस्त्य,
  पुलह, क्रतु, वसिष्ठ (→पराशर), प्रचेतः/दक्ष,

भृगु (→शुक्राचार्य) and नारद; creator, a
  Deity like सोम or इन्द्र; God.
प्रज्ञा _ {प्र.} f. 'full knowledge', wisdom.
प्रणय _ m. confidence, love.
प्रणव _ m. sound, (esp.) ॐ.
प्रणाम _ {नमस्} (=नमस्कार) m. 'fully
  bowing', obeisance.
प्रणिधान _ m. 'fully laying down', absorption,
  surrender.
प्रणिपात _ m. 'fully falling down', surrender.
प्रताप _ m. 'full heat', power.
प्रतापवत् _ 'with power', powerful.
प्रति. _ (a prefix, expressing:) towards
  →प्रतीक्षा; against, Russ. »protiv«
  →प्रतिकार; each, »per« →प्रतिदिनम्; by
  सन्धि प्रत्य. →प्रत्यक्ष.
प्रतिकार _ m. counteraction, resistance,
  revenge; remedy.
प्रतिकूल _ 'against the bank', adverse,
  unpleasant → (opp.) अनुकूल.
प्रतिग्रह _ m. 'accepting in return' donations →
  (opp.) दान; favour, grace.
प्रतिज्ञा _ f. acknowledgment, promise.
प्रतिदान _ n. giving in return, exchange.
प्रतिदिनम् _ ind. 'each day', daily.
प्रतिध्वनि _ m. 'counter-sound', echo.
प्रतिनिधि _ m. substitution, representative.
प्रतिपक्ष _ m. 'counter-side', opposition.
प्रतिपदम् _ ind. 'each step', on every occasion.
प्रतिबिम्ब _ n. reflection, image, resemblance.
प्रतिमा _ f. image, measure, extent; image of
  God, of 8 kinds – शैल-दारुमय-लौह-लेप्य-
  लेख्य-सैकत-मनोमय-मणिमय; but God can
  be seen in everything – like सूर्य, अग्नि,
  मरुत्, जल, भूमि, ब्राह्मण, गो, सर्वभूत.
प्रतिलोम _ 'against the hair or grain', adverse
  → (opp.) अनुलोम.
प्रतिशतम् _ ind. 'per hundred', (mod.)
  percent.
प्रतिष्ठा _ {स्थ} f. position, foundation.

प्रतिष्ठान _ n. firm standing, foundation.

प्रतिष्ठित _ firmly situated, steady.

प्रतीकार _ (=प्रतिकार).

प्रतीक्ष _ {प्रति.ईक्ष} 'looking forward', waiting, expecting.

प्रतीक्षा _ waiting, expectation.

प्रत्यक्ष _ {प्रति.} 'direct sight', visible → (opp.) परोक्ष; n. perception, a प्रमाण →स्मृति. प्रत्यक्ष-अनुमान-शास्त्र _ 3 प्रमाण.

प्रत्यय _ m. suffix.

प्रत्याहार _ {प्रति.} m. 'withdrawing' the senses from their objects, 5th limb of अष्टाङ्गयोग, making the senses follow the mind (otherwise the mind is prone to follow the unrestricted senses).

प्रत्युत् _ ind. on the other hand, rather.

प्रत्येक _ {प्रति.} 'each one', every one.

प्रथम _ first, »proto-«, Gr. »protos«.

-प्रद _ giving.

प्रदक्षिण _ m. moving 'to the right', circumambulation as worship.

प्रदेश _ m. 'direction', country (as in Uttar-Pradesh); a मात्रा (19 cm, 10 अङ्गुल), 'short span' thumb to forefinger.

प्रदोष _ first part of the night, evening.

प्रद्युम्न _ {प्र.} m. 'very mighty', कामदेव reborn as son of कृष्ण and रुक्मिणी →चतुर्व्यूह.

प्रधान _ {प्र.} n. 'holding forth', chief thing or person; primary matter, substance (=सगुण-/महद् ब्रह्म) →प्राकृतसर्ग. प्रधान-मन्त्री _ m. 'chief-minister', (mod.) prime minister. प्रधान-माया _ f. 'substantial energy', material cause (=उपादान), ingredient; different ingredients are named, like आत्मा, अहङ्कार, प्राण, क्षेत्र.

प्रपन्न _ approached, surrendered.

प्रपितामह _ {प्र.} m. great- grandfather.

प्रपौत्र _ {प्र.} m. great-grandson.

प्रभव _ prominent; m. power, creation.

प्रभा _ {भास्} f. 'shining forth', splendour.

प्रभात _ n. 'shone forth'; dawn.

प्रभाव _ {प्रभव} m. power.

प्रभु _ m. 'having power', master.

प्रमत्त _ {मद} mad, intoxicated.

प्रमर्दन _ crushing.

प्रमाण _ {मा} n. 'measure', standard; 3 kinds of proof – प्रत्यक्ष-अनुमान-शास्त्र.

प्रमाद _ m. madness, intoxication; inattention, a दोष.

प्रमुख _ 'facing', foremost.

प्रमेय _ {मा} 'to be measured', measurable → (opp.) अप्रमेय.

प्रमोद _ {मुद्} m. delight.

प्रयत्न _ m. effort, endeavor.

प्रयाग _ {यजन} m. 'place of sacrifice'; (esp.) a pilgrimage at the confluence of गङ्गा and यमुना, (mod.) Allahabad.

प्रयाण _ n. departure; death.

प्रयास _ m. effort, exertion.

प्रयोग _ m. use, usage, practice.

प्रलय _ m. dissolution, (esp.) destruction of the world at the end of a कल्प; death.

प्रलीन _ {प्रलय} dissolved.

प्रलेपन _ smearing, anointing.

प्रवचन _ n. proclamation, discourse.

प्रवर _ best.

प्रवर्तित _ started.

प्रवाला _ f. sprout, new leaf or branch.

प्रवास _ {प्र.} m. dwelling abroad.

प्रवीण _ {वीणा} skilled.

प्रवृत्ति _ f. 'full activity', progress → (opp.) निवृत्ति. प्रवृत्ति-मार्ग _ m. 'path of (material) progress'.

प्रवृद्ध _ 'fully grown', raised.

प्रवेश _ m. entrance.

प्रवेशन _ entering.

प्रशंसा _ f. praise.

प्रशस्त _ 'praised', auspicious.

प्रशान्त _ pacified.

प्रश्न _ m. question.

प्रसन्न _ {प्रसाद} 'fully settled', calmed,
   satisfied.

प्रसभम् _ ind. forcibly.

प्रसाद _ m. 'fully settling', calmness,
   satisfaction; mercy (as God's satisfaction);
   articles first offered to God and later
   distributed (esp. food).

प्रसिद्ध _ 'accomplished'; well known,
   celebrated.

प्रसूति _ f. procreation. प्रसूति-तन्त्र _ n.
   science of procreation.

प्रसृत _ extended.

प्रस्तावना _ f. introduction.

प्रस्थ _ proceeding, departing →वनप्रस्थ; n.
   'stable' land →इन्द्रप्रस्थ.

प्रहर _ (=याम) (Pahar) m. 'stroke'; stroke on a
   gong; a मात्रा (3 h, 1/8 of the day).

प्रह्लाद _ m. 'full delight', a son of
   हिरण्यकशिपु.

प्राक् _ {प्र.} ind. before →पूर्व.

प्राकृत _ {प्रकृति} 'natural', ordinary, vulgar;
   n. dialect → (opp.) संस्कृत. प्राकृत-सर्ग _ m.
   'natural creation' of matter by God – 1. part
   of ब्रह्म is प्रधान, when agitated by
   काल/दैव, it transforms into 2. प्रकृति,
   which delivers 3. the महत्तत्त्व, giving rise to
   4. अहङ्कार, which manifests 5. मनः, बुद्धि,
   ज्ञानेन्द्रिय, प्राण, कर्मेन्द्रिय, तन्मात्र,
   महाभूत; the above elements (→तत्त्व) form
   6. a कारणसागर, from which विष्णु initiates
   7. unlimited ब्रह्माण्ड and in each of which
   He lays down; from His navel sprouts
   हिरण्यगर्भ, from which 8. ब्रह्मा is born
   (who starts →वैकृतसर्ग). प्राकृत-वैकृत-सर्ग
   _ 2 kinds/stages of सर्ग.

प्राचीन _ eastern; ancient.

प्राजापत्य _ {प्रजा-पति} m. 'from the
   patriarchs', a विवाह (also called क्षात्र)
among क्षत्रिय, where the bride is asked for
   by the groom's relatives.

प्राज्ञ _ {प्रज्ञा} wise.

प्राण _ {प्र.अन} m. 'breathing forth',
   exhalation; breath – प्राण-अपान-व्यान;
   vital energy, 5 gross – प्राण-अपान-व्यान-
   समान-उदान and 5 subtle – नाग-कूर्म-
   कृकर-देवदत्त-धनञ्जय; vital organ – like
   nose, mouth, eyes, ears, and mind; life.

प्राण-अपान-व्यान _ 3 kinds of breath, प्राण.

प्राण-अपान-व्यान-समान-उदान _ 5 kinds of
   gross vital energy, प्राण. प्राण-नाथ _ m.
   'lord of life', lover.

प्राणन _ breathing.

प्राणायाम _ {प्राण-आयाम} m. 'breath-
   control', 4th limb of अष्टाङ्गयोग; (esp.)
   primary exercises – पूरक-रेचक-कुम्भक (to
   clear the नाडी). "Being in that आसन, the
   stoppage of the movements of inhalation
   (श्वास) and exhalation (प्रश्वास) is called
   प्राणायाम." "By practicing प्राणायाम, either
   पूरक-कुम्भक-रेचक or reverse, the path of
   प्राण will be purified, so that the steady
   mind (चित्त) is not flickering. The mind
   (मनस्) of a योगी who has thus conquered
   breathing becomes quickly pure, just as a
   metal like gold gives up its impurity when
   melted ('fanned') with air and fire." Thus he
   becomes fit for concentration. Much later
   injuctions are to mentally recite गायत्री
   during प्राणायाम (plus 3 or 7 व्याहृति, and
   शिरस्, each preceded by ॐ).

प्राणी _ {प्राणिन्, प्राण} m. living being.

प्रातः _ {प्रातर्} ind. in the morning. प्रातः-
   स्नान _ {प्रातर्} n. morning bath. प्रातः-
   स्मरण _ {प्रातर्} n. morning meditation.

प्रातर् _ {प्र.} ind. in the early morning.

प्रादुर्भाव _ {प्र.दुर्.} m. manifestation,
   appearance.

प्राधान्य _ {प्रधान} main.

प्राधान्यतः _ ind. mainly.

प्रापण _ reaching, obtaining, arriving at.

प्राप्त _ obtained.

प्राप्ति _ f. obtainment, gain; a सिद्धि.

प्रामाणिक _ {प्रमाण} authentic.

प्राय _ m. 'going forth', departure, death; anything dominant.

प्रायः _ ind. mostly, generally.

प्रायश्चित्त _ {प्रायः-चित्त} n. 'dominent thought' or 'thought of death', atonement.

प्रारब्ध _ {प्रारम्भ} 'begun', commenced. प्रारब्ध-कर्म _ n. ripe कर्मफल, in 6 forms – जाति-आयुस्-भोग-ऐश्वर्य-श्रुति-श्री.

प्रारम्भ _ m. 'beginning', effort, enterprise.

प्रार्थना _ f. prayer.

प्रिय _ dear, beloved, Russ. »prijatna« →प्रेयस्, प्रेष्ठ; m. friend, lover.

प्रियतम _ 'most dear'.

प्रियतर _ 'more dear'.

प्रिया _ f. beloved woman, wife.

प्रीणन _ pleasing.

प्रीति _ {प्रिय} f. pleasure, love. प्रीति-पूर्वकम् _ ind. with love.

प्रेक्षक-अनुमन्त्रण _ addressing the spectators before a marriage.

प्रेक्षण _ {प्र.ईक्षण} n. observing.

प्रेत _ {प्र.} m. 'departed', dead person, ghost.

प्रेत्य _ ind. in the other world, after death.

प्रेम _ {प्रेमन्, प्रिय} m. love. प्रेम-भक्ति _ (=पर-, उत्तम-, अनन्य-, शुद्ध-भक्ति) f. loving devotion.

प्रेयः _ {प्रेयस्}.

प्रेयस् _ n. 'more प्रिय', dearer; immediate benefit, material pleasure →प्रवृत्तिमार्ग, (opp.) श्रेयः.

प्रेरण _ sending.

प्रेरणा _ f. 'setting in motion', impetus; command.

प्रेष्ठ _ {प्रिय} 'most dear'.

प्रोक्त _ {प्र.उक्त} declared.

प्लक्ष _ m. Pakar tree (Indian Tulip, Ficus lacor) and wood.

प्लव _ m. 'swimming', boat; flood.

प्लवते _ (a verb) {√प्लु} he swims.

प्लवन _ swimming, bathing.

√प्लु _ प्लुङ् गतौ 1A go (jump, fly, float, swim) →प्लवते; सम्. flood.

फट् _ ind. a syllable for मन्त्र.

फल _ (Fal) n. fruit; result (good or bad).

फलोन्मुख _ {फल-उन्मुख} 'facing the fruit', 'ripening' of अप्रारब्धकर्म.

फल्गु _ small, worthless.

√फुल्ल _ फुल्ल विकसने 1P open, blossom →फुल्लति.

फुल्ल _ (Ful) n. 'blown', »flower«, Lat. »florem«.

फुल्लति _ (a verb) {√फुल्ल} he blossoms.

फेन _ m. »foam«, Lat. »pumex«, Russ. »pena«.

बकुल _ (Bakul) m. Bullet Wood tree (Mimusops elengi).

बत _ ind. expressing great sorrow; alas!.

बदरी _ (Ber) f. Jujube tree (Zizyphus mauritiana) and fruit. बदरी-नाथ _ m. a temple at बदरी.

बद्ध _ {बन्ध} »bound«.

√बध् _ बध बन्धने 9P bind →बध्नाति; नि. bind down.

बध्नाति _ (a verb) {√बध्} he binds. सत्त्वं सुख-सङ्गेन ज्ञान-सङ्गेन च बध्नाति । Sattva-Guna binds by attachment to happiness and knowledge. (भगवद्गीता) कर्माणि आत्मवन्तं न निबध्नन्ति । Activities do not bind one who is situated in the self. (भगवद्गीता).

बन्ध _ m. »bond«, Germ. »Band«, »Bund«.

बन्धन _ »binding«.

बन्धु _ m. »bond«, kinsman, friend → (opp.) रिपु.

बर्बर _ m. 'stammering' fool, »barbarian«.

बर्हति _ (a verb) {√बृह} he grows.

बल _ n. »valor«, strength → Russ. »bolshoy« (big); force, army. बल-राम _ m. 'strong राम', a brother of कृष्ण, also called बलदेव, बलभद्र, हलायुध.

बलवान् _ {बलवत्} 'with strength', strong.

बलात् _ ind. forcibly, excessively.

बलि _ m. tribute, tax; oblation; food (to animals); a son of विरोचन (grandson of प्रह्लाद), a विष्णु-भक्त, who surrendered everything to वामन.

बहिः _ {बहिस्} ind. out, beside, except.

बहिर् _ {बहिस्} ind. outside.

बहिरङ्ग _ 'external limb', unessential → (opp.) अन्तरङ्ग.

बहिरङ्ग-शक्ति _ f. external or material energy, its 3 threads are त्रिगुण.

बहु _ much, many. बहु-वचन _ n. 'speaking of many', plural number → (opp.) एक-, द्वि-वचन. बहु-व्रीहि _ m. who has 'much rice', a समास.

बहुधा _ ind. in many ways, variously.

बहुल _ 'containing many', numerous, abundant.

बाण _ m. arrow.

बादाम _ (Badam) m. Indian Almond tree (Terminalia catappa) and wood.

बाधन _ opposing, tormenting.

बान्धव _ {बन्धु} m. kinsman, relative.

बाल _ (1) young; m. child, boy, minor →बाल्य; simpleton. (2) hair (=वाल). बाल-चिकित्सा _ f. 'child medicine', pediatrics.

बालक _ m. boy.

बाला _ f. girl.

बालाग्र _ {बाल-अग्र} n. 'hair-tip'.

बालिका _ (=बाला).

बाल्य _ {बाल} n. boyhood, childhood, a वयः.

बाहु _ m. arm.

बाह्य _ {बहिर्} outside, external.

बिन्दु _ m. drop, dot; colored mark made on the forehead between the eyebrows (of priests, members of a function and women), »Bindi«, representing लक्ष्मी; women wear it with a streak of सिन्दूर or कुङ्कुम in the parting of the hair.

बिभर्ति _ (a verb) {√भृ} he holds. अ-व्ययः ईश्वरः बिभर्ति। The imperishable Lord sustains. (भगवद्गीता).

बिभेति _ (a verb) {√भी} he fears.

बिम्ब _ m. the disk of sun or moon; an image, shadow, reflection.

बिल _ n. cave, hole.

बिल्व _ (Bel) m. the Bael tree (Aegle marmelos) and fruit.

बीज _ n. seed, semen; primary cause. बीज-पूर _ m. Guava tree (Amrud, Psidium guajava) and fruit. बीज-मन्त्र _ n. essential मन्त्र.

बीभत्स _ m. disgust, a गौणरस.

बुद्ध _ 'awakened' or 'learned' → »bode«; m. a wise man or saint, a जिन; (esp.) 'the' बुद्ध (=शक्य- मुनि, सिद्धार्थ, गौतम) →बौद्ध, दशावतार. बुद्ध-पूर्णिमा _ celebration of the birth of बुद्ध in लुम्बिनी on वैशाख-पूर्णिमा (12.04. 563 BCE).

बुद्धि _ f. 'awareness', intelligence (seated in the heart); 5 functions – इष्टानिष्टविपत्तिश्च व्यवसायः समाधिता। संशयः प्रतिपत्तिश्च बुद्धेः पञ्च गुणान्विदुः॥ व्यवसाय, destruction of good and evil thoughts, concentration, doubt, and assertion – these are known as the five qualities of बुद्धि." (महाभारत 12.255.10) ; 3 states – जाग्रत्-स्वप्न-सुषुप्त plus तुरीय; (esp.) resolve →व्यवसायात्मिका बुद्धिः.

बुद्धिमत् _ 'with बुद्धि', intelligent.

बुद्बुद _ n. bubble.

√बुध् _ (1) बुधिर बोधने 1U know →बोधति; अव. know, be awake; नि. know, be awake; प्रति. teach. (2) बुध अवगमने 1P/4A understand →बोधति/बुध्यते; प्रति. teach.

बुध _ (=बुद्ध) m. Mercury (as descendant of सोम), a ग्रह. बुध-वार _ m. 'Mercury-day', Wednesday.

बुभुक्षा _ f. hunger.

√बृह् _ बृह वृद्धौ 1P grow →बर्हति.

बृहत् _ »broad«, Germ. »breit«, large; n. वेद.

बृहस्पति _ {बृहत्-} m. 'lord of वेद', the priest of the gods, regent of Jupiter; Jupiter, a ग्रह. बृहस्पति-वार _ (=गुरुवार).

बोधति _ (a verb) {√बुध्} he knows.

बोधन _ knowing, waking.

बौद्ध _ {बुद्ध} 'Buddhist'. बौद्ध-वाद _ m. 'Buddhist thesis', Buddhism – there is दुःख in समुदय (संसार) and its निरोध (निर्वाण) is on the मार्ग of अहिंसा; what sets Buddhism aside from कर्मवाद of Hinduism is its शून्यवाद.

बौधायन _ m. Indian mathematician who described 600 BCE what became known as 'Pythagoras theorem' and √2.

ब्रवीति _ (a verb) {√ब्रू} he speaks. एतद् ते सत्यं ब्रवीमि। I tell this truly to you. (महाभारत).

ब्रह्म _ {ब्रह्मन्}. ब्रह्म जानातीति ब्राह्मणः। {जानाति इति} ब्राह्मण means, he knows ब्रह्म. ब्रह्म-गायत्री _ f. the गायत्री to सविता/सूर्य-नारायण (repeated at सन्ध्या). ब्रह्म-चर्य _ n. 'practice of ब्रह्म/वेद'; the आश्रम of a ब्रह्मचारी; celibacy, a यम. "By सत्य, तपः, complete ज्ञान, and continence (ब्रह्मचर्य) this self (or the Lord) (आत्मा) is to be obtained eternally." "Death (मरण) is by loosing semen, life (जीवन) by keeping semen." "When a द्विज ब्रह्मचारी spills semen (शुक्र) in sleep without intention, after then taking a bath and worshiping the sun (अर्क), he should mutter thrice the ऋग्वेद verse: 'Let sense power (इन्द्रिय) come back to me (माम्)!" "A wise man who does not know another woman [besides his wife, and this only in her season], he is also a ब्रह्मचारी." ब्रह्म-चारिन् _ m. 'who practices ब्रह्म/वेद'; any disciple living with the teacher; a celibate →नैष्ठिक. ब्रह्म-चारी _ {-चारिन्}. ब्रह्म-जन्म _ n. 'spiritual (or 2nd) birth' as द्विज by दीक्षा → (opp.) शौक्रजन्म. ब्रह्म-परिणाम-वाद _ m. 'thesis of evolution [of जगत्] from ब्रह्म' in वेदान्त →जन्माद्यस्य यतः; its conclusions are ब्रह्मवाद and शक्तिपरिणामवाद. ब्रह्म-भूत _ n. 'spiritual being', unembodied or liberated living being → (opp.) जीवभूत. ब्रह्म-मुहूर्त _ m. 'spiritual मुहूर्त', the 14th of nighttime before dawn. ब्रह्म-रन्ध्र _ n. 'the opening of ब्रह्म' in the crown of the head (where the soul can escape). ब्रह्म-लोक _ (=सत्यलोक) 'world of ब्रह्मा/ब्रह्म'. ब्रह्म-वाद _ m. 'thesis of ब्रह्म', that जगत् is nothing but ब्रह्म, since it comes from ब्रह्म →सर्व खल्विदं ब्रह्म; thus जगत् is as real as ब्रह्म →सत्यं भूतमयं जगत्, (opp.) मायावाद. ब्रह्म सत्यं जगन्मिथ्या जीव ब्रह्मैव न परः। ब्रह्म is real, जगत् is false, and जीव is nothing but ब्रह्म. =मायावाद. ब्रह्म-सूत्र _ (=वेदान्तसूत्र).

ब्रह्मन् _ n. 'great' or 'sound', spirit, the Absolute →ब्रह्मवाद, represented by sounding ॐ; (esp.) the all-pervading impersonal first of 3 features of the Absolute – ब्रह्म-परमात्मा-भगवान्; 2 forms – निर्गुण-पर-ब्रह्म and सगुण-/महद् ब्रह्म (=प्रधान); the self (=आत्मा); वेद (=शब्दब्रह्म); (in comp. also for) m. ब्रह्मा.

ब्रह्मा _ {ब्रह्मन्} m. first created being (from हिरण्यगर्भ →स्वयम्भू) and sub-creator of all beings (भूत) in वैकृतसर्ग; his direct sons are 4 कुमार, 11 रुद्र, 10 प्रजापति, मनु; present mankind/royalty spread from ब्रह्मा mainly in 3 lines – through स्वायम्भुव मनु, मरीचि (सूर्यवंश) and अत्रि (सोमवंश).

ब्रह्माण्ड _ {ब्रह्म-अण्ड} n. 'egg of ब्रह्मा', the unmanifest universe in the shape of an egg, floating on the कारणसागर, containing गर्भोदक; a universe.

ब्रह्मी _ f. 'holy', Brahmi herb (Bacopa monnieri) for memory.

ब्राह्म _ 'relating to ब्रह्म', spiritual, holy; m. a विवाह where the bride is given to a worthy husband. ब्राह्म-तीर्थ _ the root of the thumb, where water is sipped from the palm of the hand (आचमन)

ब्राह्मण _ m. (wrongly »Brahmin«) 'who knows ब्रह्म' (ब्रह्म जानातीति ब्राह्मणः) and embodies आर्जव; member of the first वर्ण – scholar, teacher, priest; his prerogatives are अध्यापन, याजन and प्रतिग्रह for a livelihood; he pays tax only in form of सुकृति; उपासनकाण्ड applied by a गृहस्थ. ब्राह्मण-क्षत्रिय-वैश्य-शूद्र _ 4 social वर्ण.

ब्राह्मी _ f. speech; the goddess of speech, सरस्वती; a script →देवनागरी.

√ब्रू _ ब्रूञ् व्यक्तायां वाचि 2U speak →ब्रवीति; प्र. explain.

भक्त _ {भजन} m. (1) distributed, shared →भाग. (2) 'devoted', devotee, worshiper →भक्ति.

भक्ति _ f. devotion, worship, both as साधन (भजन) and साध्य (प्रेम, at liberation). "O नारद! An activity which is prescribed in scripture and aimed at the satisfaction of God, that is called साधनभक्ति, and by that comes प्रेमभक्ति." भक्त्या मामभिजानाति। {माम्} Through भक्ति one understands Me. भक्ति-योग _ m. 'योग through भक्ति'.

√भक्ष् _ भक्ष भक्षणे 10U eat →भक्षयति.

भक्षण _ n. eating.

भक्षयति _ (a verb) {√भक्ष्} he eats. सः अन्नं भक्षयति। He eats rice.

भग _ m. share, opulence; 6 opulences →शक्ति. "भग is an indication of six [qualities] – complete ऐश्वर्य-वीर्य-यशः-श्री-ज्ञान-वैराग्य."

भगवत् _ 'with भग', opulent, Russ. »bog« →भगवान्.

भगवद्गीता _ {भगवत्-} f. 'hymn of भगवान्', the celebrated dialogue between कृष्ण and अर्जुन.

भगवद्धर्म _ {भगवत्-} (=भक्ति) m. 'duty towards God'.

भगवान् _ {भगवत्} m. title given to God and saints →भागवत.

भगीरथ _ m. a famous king who lead the गङ्गा to the ocean.

भगोः _ ind. respectful address.

भग्न _ {भञ्ज} 'broken', defeated, frustrated.

भञ्ज _ m. breaking; break, breach; hemp.

भङ्गा _ (Bhang) f. Hemp plant (Ganja, Cannabis sativa).

√भज् _ (1) भज सेवायाम् 1U serve →वर्तते. (2) भज विश्राणने 10P impart →भाजयति; प्र.वि. divide.

भजति _ (a verb) {√भज्} he serves. यः मां भजति सः मयि वर्तते। One who worships me, he lives in me. (भगवद्गीता) युक्ततमः मां भजते। The best Yogī worships me. (भगवद्गीता) ये मां प्रपद्यन्ते अहं तान् भजामि। Those who surrender to me, I reward them. (भगवद्गीता) महा-आत्मानः मां भजन्ति। Great souls worship me. (भगवद्गीता) सुकृतिनः जनाः मां भजन्ते। Pious men worship me. (भगवद्गीता).

भजन _ n. (1) distributing, sharing →भाग. (2) worshiping (=साधनभक्ति); (Bhajan) a genre of devotional music, like कीर्तन (Kirtan).

भट्ट _ m. 'lord', a title of respect for a learned man.

भद्र _ fortunate.

भय _ n. fear; danger.

भयङ्कर _ {भयम्-} 'making fear', dreadful.

भयानक _ fearful; m. terror, a गौणरस.

भरण _ supporting.

भरत _ m. (1) the eldest of the 100 sons of ऋषभ, who did तपस् at पुलहाश्रम, but was reborn as a deer and later as जड भरत, instructing King रहूगण; (2) a son of दुष्यन्त in the line of पुरु, after whom the कुरुवंश and the पाण्डव are called भारत; (3) a brother of रामचन्द्र; (4) the famous author of नाट्य-शास्त्र; →भारत

भर्गस् _ n. radiance, lustre.

भर्जन _ roasting, burning.

भर्ता _ {भर्तृ}.

भर्तृ _ m. »bearer«, maintainer →भार.

भर्त्सन _ threatening.

भव _ {√भू} m. »being«, becoming, birth; 'the auspicious one', शिव.

भवति _ (a verb) {√भू} he is/becomes. क्षिप्रं धर्म-आत्मा भवति | Soon he becomes righteous. (भगवद्गीता) अन्नात् भूतानि भवन्ति | All beings are born from food (i.e., its transformations in the form of semen and blood). (भगवद्गीता).

भवान् _ {भवत्} m. »being«, present; You.

भविष्य _ n. 'about to become', future.

भविष्यत् _ n. 'becoming', future. भविष्यत्-काल _ m. future tense.

भस्म _ {भस्मन्}.

भस्मन् _ n. ashes.

भस्मसात् _ ind. into ashes.

√भा _ भा दीप्तौ 2P shine →भाति; प्र. shine.

भाः _ (=भास्).

भाग _ m. part, portion.

भागवत _ m. 'relating to भगवत्', devotee of भगवान्. भागवत-पुराण _ n. a पुराण, also known as श्रीमद्भागवतम्.

भाग्य _ {भाग} fortunate; n. good fortune, destiny.

भाजयति _ (a verb) {√भज्} he imparts.

भाति _ (a verb) {√भा} he shines. भानुः अम्बरे भाति | The sun shines in the sky. (महाभारत).

भाम _ m. passion.

भार _ m. »bearing«, »burden«, load.

भारत _ m. 'descendant of भरत'; India →महाभारत. भारत-वर्ष _ (=भारत, India) m. a वर्ष of जम्बूद्वीप.

भार्या _ {भार} f. »borne«, 'to be maintained', wife.

भाव _ {√भू} m. »being«, »becoming«, existence, any state or manner of being, nature; emotion, love; intention, meaning.

√भाष् _ भाष व्यक्तायां वाचि 1A speak →भाषते; प्र. explain.

भाषते _ (a verb) {√भाष्} he speaks.

भाषा _ f. speech, language.

भाष्य _ n. 'to be spoken', commentary.

√भास् _ भासृ दीप्तौ 1A shine →भासते; आ. shine.

भास् _ f. 'shining', light.

भासते _ (a verb) {√भास्} he shines.

भास्कर _ m. 'creating light', sun.

√भिक्ष् _ भिक्ष याञ्चायाम् 1A beg →भिक्षते.

भिक्षते _ (a verb) {√भिक्ष्} he begs.

भिक्षा _ f. begging, alms.

भिक्षु _ m. beggar, mendicant →सन्न्यासी.

भिन्न _ {भेद} divided.

√भी _ जिभी भये 3P fear →बिभेति.

भी _ f. fear; danger.

भीति _ (=भी).

भीम _ 'fearful', awful; m. the 2nd पाण्डव.

भीष्म _ 'fearful', awful; m. the hero भीष्म. भीष्म-पञ्चक _ a five-day व्रत from कार्तिक-शुक्ल-एकादशी till कार्तिक-पूर्णिमा, celebrated with उपवास (no grains for the whole month and only water the last five days).

भीष्माष्टमी _ {-अष्टमी} death anniversary of भीष्म on माघ-शुक्ल-अष्टमी, celebrated seeking his blessings with उपवास → महाभारत.

भुक्ति _ f. enjoyment.

भुङ्क्ते _ (a verb) {√भुज्} he eats. ब्राह्मणः स्वम् एव भुङ्क्ते । A Brāhmana eats his own [food]. (महाभारत)

√भुज् _ भुज अशने 7A eat →भुङ्क्ते .

भुज _ m. arm; branch.

भुवन _ {√भू} n. world →त्रिभुवन, चतुर्दशभुवन .

भुवनेश्वर _ {भुवन-ईश्वर} 'lord of the world', शिव ; (mod.) Bhubaneswar.

भुवर् _ ind. 'world' of air, atmosphere; a व्याहृति. भुवर्लोक _ m. 'world of atmosphere', inhabited by भूत and प्रेत, 2nd heaven →चतुर्दशभुवन .

√भू _ भू सत्तायाम् 1P »be«, »be«come, exist →भवति; अभि. overcome; प्र. manifest; सम्. be possible, take birth; सम्.उद्. produce →भूत .

भू _ f. place of 'being', the earth (=भूमि). भू-मण्डल _ (=महीतल) n. 'earthly sphere', divided into सप्तद्वीप .

भूत _ n. having »been«, past →भूतकाल, ghost; having »become«, element →महाभूत, being, Russ. »byt'« →जीवभूत, classified in gradation of powers – अ-जीव, प्राण-भृत, स-चित्त, इन्द्रिय-वृत्ति, स्पर्श-विद् (=स्थावर), रस-विद् (=जल-चर), गन्ध-विद् (=कृमि), शब्द-विद्, रूप-विद्, दन्त, बहु-पाद, चतुष्पाद, द्वि-पाद (=मनुष्य), प्रमथ, भूत, प्रेत, पिशाच, यक्ष, राक्षस, गन्धर्व, अप्सरा, सिद्ध, चारण, विद्याधर, किन्नर, असुर, पितृ, सुर, ऋषि, देव, प्रजा-पति, ब्रह्मा. भूत-काल _ m. past tense. भूत-शुद्धि _ f. 'purification of articles' of worship. भूत-हेतु _ 'caused by (other) beings'.

भूतेश _ {भूत-ईश} m. 'lord of beings', शिव .

भूमि _ {√भू} f. the earth, soil; country →मातृभूमि; solid state, a महाभूत .

भूयः _ {√भू} ind. 'becoming', more, further.

भूर् _ ind. the earth; a व्याहृति. भूर्-भुवर्-स्वर् _ 3 लोक, त्रिलोक. भूर्-भुवर्-स्वर्-महर्-जन-तपः- सत्य-लोक _ 7 स्वर्गलोक. भूर्लोक _ (=भूमण्डल) m. 'terrestrial world', inhabited by humans, 1st heaven →चतुर्दशभुवन .

भूरि _ {√भू} ind. much, many →भूयः .

√भूष् _ भूष अलङ्कारे 1P adorn →भूषति.

भूषण _ n. ornament, Russ. »busy«.

भूषति _ (a verb) {√भूष्} he adorns.

√भृ _ डुभृञ् धारणपोषणयोः 3U hold; nourish →बिभर्ति.

भृगु _ m. भृगु मुनि.

-भृत् _ »bearing«, maintaining.

भृत्य _ m. »borne«, 'to be maintained', servant.

भेद _ m. division, difference; dualism (=द्वैत); (in नीति) dividing enemies.

भेदन _ dividing.

भेषज _ n. remedy, medicine.

भैरव _ m. 'frightful', शिव .

भो / भोः _ ind. respectful address.

भोक्ता _ {भोक्तृ}.

भोक्तृ _ m. enjoyer.

भोग _ m. enjoyment, (esp.) food.

भोगिन् _ enjoyer.

भोगी _ {भोगिन्}.

भोजन _ enjoying, eating; n. meal, food.

भौतिक _ 'relating to भूत '.

भौम _ 'relating to भूमि', terrestrial. भौम-स्वर्ग _ m. 'terrestrial heaven' – all नववर्ष of जम्बूद्वीप, except भारतवर्ष; (opp.) दिव्यस्वर्ग, बिलस्वर्ग.

√भ्रंश् _ भ्रंशु अधः पतने 4P fall down →भ्रश्यति; वि. fall down.

भ्रंश _ m. 'falling', decline, ruine.

√भ्रम् _ भ्रमु चलने 1P move (roam about) →भ्रमति; वि. move, roam.

भ्रम _ m. 'wandering', confusion; mistake, a दोष . भ्रम-प्रमाद-विप्रलिप्सा-करणापाटव _ 4 दोष , human error.

भ्रमण _ wandering.

भ्रमति _ (a verb) {√भ्रम्} he roams. मे मनः भ्रमति । My mind is reeling. (भगवद्गीता).

भ्रमर _ m. 'wanderer', bee.

भ्रश्यति _ (a verb) {√भ्रंश्} he falls down.

भ्रष्ट _ {भ्रंश} 'fallen', declined, ruined.

भ्राता _ {भ्रातृ}.

भ्रातृ _ m. »brother«, Russ. »brat«. भ्रातृ-द्वितीया _ a festival on कार्तिक-शुक्ल-द्वितीया on which a sister invites her brother(s) in commemoration of यमुना inviting and worshiping her brother यम ; gifts are made to sisters, or a woman whom one regards as sister.

भ्रू _ f. »brow«, Russ. »brov«, eyebrow.

भ्रूण _ n. embryo. भ्रूण-हा _ {-हन्} m. 'embryo-killer', the worst sinner.

मकर _ m. a sea-monster; a राशि, Lat. Capricorn(us). मकर-सङ्क्रान्ति _ f. 'passage [of the sun from Sagittarius] into the राशी मकर (Capricornus)' around January 14, celebrated as a harvest festival (Lohri, Pongal, Maghi), or in worship of the sun ('उत्तरायण'). Celebration: colorful decorations and kite flying; people invite friends and relatives to their homes for a big feast; food: sweets with peanuts-sesame-jaggery, Halva, खिच्ची with पर्पट , Ghee and Acar (pickles); cattle is decorated with paint, flowers and bells, fed sweet rice and sugar cane. In Tamil Nadu, Jallikattu (bull-taming) contest is a main event. The day before: In Punjab, children go from door to door singing folk songs. They are given sweets, savories and sometimes money. At sunset, bonfires are lit, people sit around it, sing and dance till the fire dies out. Some perform prayer and go around the fire. Some of the colleced items are offered into the fire.

मक्षिका _ f. a fly, Lat. »musca« → »mosquito«.

मग्न _ {मज्जन} »merged«, sunk; sunk into misfortune.

मङ्गल _ n. auspicious (similar to श्रेयः , शिव , भद्र , कल्याण , शुभ , कुशल , क्षेम), good omen; a prayer, amulet; Mars (=अङ्गारक). मङ्गल-घट _ m. 'auspicious pot', installed before a यज्ञ . मङ्गल-वार _ m. 'Mars-day', Tuesday. मङ्गलसूत्र-बन्धन _ tying मङ्गलसूत्र in marriage (a rel. mod. tradition).

मञ्चक _ m. stage; couch.

मज्जति _ (a verb) {√मस्ज्} he purifies.

मज्जन _ n. »merging«, sinking.

मञ्जरी _ f. flower, bud; foliage (as ornament).

मञ्जु/मञ्जुल _ (like मञ्जरी) beautiful, lovely.

मठ _ m. a dwelling as temple or college; a federal type of education, where distant centers of culture and religion are affiliated to a central and common seat of authority at a headquarter.

मणि _ m. jewel. मणि-पूर /-पूरक _ m. 'full of मणि ', a bodice adorned with jewels; navel; n. a षट्चक्र , seat of कुण्डलिनी .

मणिमय _ made of jewels.

मण्डप _ (mod. Pandal) m. an open pavilion, where the यज्ञकुण्ड is situated; the मण्डप is sprinkled with pure water, cleansed with a mixture of cow-dung and water and decorated with designs on the floor, banana trees, leaves, garlands, flags and मङ्गलघट in the eight directions, and the four वेद are installed in pots in the four cardinal directions. मण्डप-करण _ erecting a मण्डप .

मण्डल _ n. disk, sphere →भूमण्डल ; district →व्रजमण्डल ; division of ऋग्वेद .

मण्डूक _ m. frog.

.मत् _ (an affix, expressing possession) having/with →श्रीमत्; becomes .वत् after words ending in -अ →भगवत्.

मत _ {√मन} n. 'thought', »meant«, opinion.

मति _ f. opinion.

मत्त _ {मद} mad; intoxicated, Lat. »mattus«.

मत्तः _ {मद्} ind. from me, than me.

मत्सर _ envious; m. envy.

मत्स्य _ m. fish; an अवतार. मत्स्य-कूर्म-वराह-नरसिंह-वामन-परशुराम-रामचन्द्र-कृष्ण/बलराम-बुद्ध-कल्कि _ 10 अवतार, दशावतार.

मथुरा _ f. the birthplace of कृष्ण on the bank of the यमुना.

मद्- _ my →मदर्थम्.

मद _ m. excitement, madness; intoxication; pride.

मदर्थम् _ {मद्-} ind. for my sake.

मधु _ sweet; n. anything sweet, honey →माधव; »mead«, Germ. »Met«. मधु-पर्क _ a mixture of honey and curd; a reception by offering it; any reception of honorable guests.

मधुक _ m. Mahua wood (Madhuca longifolia) and flower.

मधुर _ sweet; m. sweetness, a रस.

मध्य _ »mid-«, »middle«, Lat. »medius«; n. the »middle«.

मध्यम _ 'most middle', central; 4th स्वर; »medium« → (opp.) कन्य, उत्तम. मध्यम-पुरुष _ m. (in grammar) 2nd ('middle') person.

मध्यमा _ f. 'middle' finger; a 'medium' वाक्, formulated thought.

मध्याह्न _ {मध्य-अहन्} m. midday, noon.

मध्ये _ ind. 'in the middle', amongst.

√मन _ (1) मन ज्ञाने 4A know →मन्यते. (2) मन अवबोधने 8A understand (think) →मनुते (Pass. मन्यते), »meaning«, Russ. »mnit'«, »mnenie« →मनः, मन्त्र, मनु, मुनि.

मनः _ {मनस्}.

मनस् _ {√मन} (=अन्तःकरण) n. 'thinking', »mind«, Lat. »mens«, seated in the heart; मनो व्याकरणात्मकम्। "The मनः consists of discrimination." (महाभारत 12.252.11) 9 functions – कल्प, विकल्प, imagination, argument, inclination, remembrance, धैर्य, क्षमा, quickness; universal मनः →प्राकृतसर्ग; consciousness, incl. अहङ्कार, बुद्धि, चित्त (in अष्टाङ्गयोग studied combinedly as चित्त); heart →मनोहर.

मनीषिन् _ 'thoughtful', wise; m. learned man.

मनीषी _ {मनीषिन्}.

मनु _ {√मन} m. 'thinker', father of men, Germ. »Mannus«, 14 मनु (to one of them मनुसंहिता is ascribed) → »man«, मानव, मन्वन्तर. मनु-संहिता/-स्मृति _ f. 'law-book of मनु'.

मनुते _ (a verb) {√मन} he thinks.

मनुष्य _ m. 'descendent of मनु', »man«, Germ. »Mensch«, human being.

मनो-गत _ {मनस्-} n. 'gone to mind', idea, desire. मनो-रञ्जन _ 'pleasing the mind'. मनो-रथ _ m. 'the mind as chariot', fancy, imagination. मनो-हर _ 'mind-stealing', charming.

मन्तव्य _ 'to be thought', considered.

मनोमय _ 'made of mind', mental.

मन्त्र _ m. 'instrument of thought', advice, counsel; formula, verse; (esp.) hymns for worship; (esp.) with ॐ and words like नमः. मन्त्र-गुरु _ (=दीक्षागुरु) m. teacher who gives a मन्त्र. मन्त्र-मूलं च विजयम्। "विजय roots in counsel." मन्त्र-स्नान _ n. a bath by reciting मन्त्र (and sprinkling oneself with water).

मन्त्रिन् _ m. »mentor«, counsellor; the counsel of a king consisted of 4 ब्राह्मण, 8 क्षत्रिय, 21

वैश्य, 3 शूद्र and 1 सूत; minister, »Mandarin«.

मन्त्री _ {मन्त्रिन्}.

मन्थन _ churning.

मन्द _ slow, dull.

मन्दिर _ n. temple.

मन्दार _ (Mandar) m. Coral Tree (Erythrina) and wood.

मन्यते _ (a verb) {√मन्} he knows; it is thought.

मन्वन्तर _ {मनु-अन्तर} n. ruling 'period of a मनु'.

मम _ {अस्मद्} (=मे) »my«, mine.

.मय _ (an affix, expressing:) full of →मङ्गलमय; made of →गुणमय.

मयूर _ m. peacock.

मरकत _ n. »emerald«, Gr. »smaragdos«.

मरण _ n. 'dying', killing, »murder«; m. death, Lat. »mors« (=मृत्यु).

मरीचि _ m. a sage, father of कश्यप.

मरु _ {मरण} m. wilderness, »moor«, Lat. »mare«; desert.

मरुत् _ m. wind →मारुति.

मर्त्य _ {मरण} »mortal«, Lat. »mortalis«; m. a mortal, man. मर्त्य-लोक _ m. 'world of mortals (men)', the earth (भूर्); भूर्-भुवर्-स्वर् combined, (opp.) 'heaven' from महर्लोक upwards.

मर्दन _ crushing.

मर्म _ {मर्मन्}.

मर्मन् _ n. 'mortal' spot, vital part of the body; heart; the core of anything.

मर्यादा _ f. limit; limit of morality.

मल _ n. dirt, Lat. »malus«.

मलिन _ dirty.

मल्ल _ m. wrestler.

√मस्ज् _ टुमस्जो शुद्धौ 6P purify (bath, immerse) →मज्जति.

मस्तिष्क _ n. brain.

महत् _ »much«, Lat. »magnus«, great; m. (short for) महत्तत्त्व. महत्तत्त्व _ {महत्-} n. 'great principle', universal बुद्धि (a portion of which is individual intellect) of pure सत्त्व; via medium between ब्रह्म and जगत्, wherefrom अहङ्कार binds जीव to जगत् (आत्मा to देह) →प्राकृतसर्ग.

महत्त्व _ {.त्व} n. greatness, importance.

महत्त्व-पूर्ण _ 'full of importance', important.

महर् _ ind. 'great', glorious. महर्लोक _ m. 'world of glory', 4th heaven →चतुर्दशभुवन.

महर्षि _ {महा-ऋषि} m. 'great sage'.

महा- _ {महत् in comp.} →महेश्वर. महाजनो येन गतः स पन्थाः। "The path (पथिन्) is that, by which a महाजन has gone." महा-देव _ m. 'great lord', शिव. महा-पुराण _ 18 prominent पुराण – विष्णु-नारदीय-भागवत-गरुड-वराह-ब्रह्माण्ड-ब्रह्मवैवर्त-मार्कण्डेय-भविष्य-वामन-ब्रह्म-मत्स्य-कूर्म-लिङ्ग-स्कन्द-अग्नि-पुराण. महा-भारत _ n. 'the great narrative of India' with 100,000 verses on भारत and कृष्ण, incl. भगवद्गीता. महा-भूत _ (=पञ्चभूत) n. 'great/gross element' – आकाश-वायु-अग्नि-जल-भूमि; experienced through 5 तन्मात्र by 5 ज्ञानेन्द्रिय; the one material energy is thus perceived by 5 senses as 5 elements. महा-माया _ f. 'great (material) energy' → (opp.) योगमाया; 2 forms – the soul is dragged by निमित्तमाया through प्रधानमाया. महा-वीर _ 'great hero'; m. name of the most celebrated जैन teacher. महा-शिवरात्रि _ f. 'the most important शिवरात्रि' on फाल्गुन-कृष्ण त्रयोदशी-चतुर्दशी, clebrated with उपवास, पूजा and जागर (dance and music).

महात्मा _ {महा-आत्मा} m. 'great soul', saint →माहात्म्य.

महान्त _ {महत्} m. a chief.

महिमा _ (=महत्त्व).

महिला _ f. woman.

मही _ {महत्} f. 'the great' earth. मही-क्षित् _ m. 'earth-ruler', king. मही-तल _ n. 'earth-plane', the earth.

महेन्द्र _ {महा-इन्द्र} m. 'great इन्द्र'.

महेश्वर _ {महा-ईश्वर} m. 'great lord', शिव.

महोत्सव _ {महा-उत्सव} m. great festival.

√मा _ मा माने 2P measure →माति; प्र. measure.

मा _ (1) ind. not, do not. (2) f. mother.

मांस _ n. meat, muscle.

मांसाहारी _ {मांस-आहारी} m. meat-eater → (opp.) शाकाहारी.

माघ-अमावास्या _ a festival celebrated with मौनव्रत and स्नान.

माता _ {मातृ}. माता-मह _ m. 'mother's father', maternal grandfather. माता-मही _ f. 'mother's mother', maternal grandmother.

माति _ (a verb) {√मा} he measures.

मातुल _ m. »maternal« uncle.

मातुलुङ्ग _ m. Citron tree (Galgal, Citrus medica) and fruit.

मातृ _ f. »mother«, Lat. »mater«, Russ. »mat'«; 7 mothers – the own mother; the wives of priest, teacher and king, धात्री, धेनु, पृथिवी. मातृ-ष्वसृ _ f. 'mother's sister (स्वसृ)', maternal aunt.

मातृका _ {मातृ} f. mother, 'divine mother'; particular diagrams (यन्त्र).

मात्र _ {मा} n. 'measure', »meter«, Gr. »metra«; (-मात्र) 'nothing but' →निमित्तमात्र.

मात्रा _ f. 'measure', »meter«; a distance – like अङ्गुल, प्रदेश, वितस्ति, पद, हस्त, दण्ड, क्रोश, योजन; a time unit – like त्रुटि, निमेष, क्षण, मुहूर्त, प्रहर / याम, अहर्, वार / वासर, तिथि, सप्ताह, मास, ऋतु, चतुर्मास, अयन, वर्ष, शताब्द, युग, मन्वन्तर; (in छन्दः) लघु and गुरु.

माधव _ {मधु} m. कृष्ण.

माधुर्य _ {मधुर} n. sweetness; love, a मुख्यरस.

माध्यम _ {मध्यम} »medium«.

मान _ (1) {मा} measuring. (2) {√मन} m. 'thought', »mind«, opinion; regard, honor; pride, anger.

मानव _ 'from मनु', »human«, Lat. »humanus«; m. »man«.

मानस / मानसिक _ 'relating to मनः', »mental«. मानसिक-स्नान _ n. a 'mental bath' by remembering God.

मानित्व _ {मान} n. pride.

माम _ m. 'mine', uncle.

मामक _ {मम} mine.

माया _ {मा} f. 'measuring', art; illusory image, non-reality →मायावाद; supernatural power, God's energy – योग- and महा-माया; (esp.) महामाया. माया-देवी _ f. the goddess of महामाया, दुर्गा. माया-वाद _ m. 'thesis of माया', that जगत् is an illusion →ब्रह्म सत्यं जगन्मिथ्या ।, because its substance is माया → (opp.) ब्रह्मवाद; propounded by शङ्कराचार्य, adopting Buddhist शून्यवाद with original terms of वेदान्त (शून्य →ब्रह्म, निर्वाण →मोक्ष in ब्रह्म).

मार _ {मरण} m. 'death', pestilence, Russ. »mor«.

मारण _ killing.

मारुति _ 'son of मरुत्', हनुमान्.

मार्ग _ m. 'track', path, way. मार्ग-पाली _ f. 'road-protectress', a goddess.

मार्गण _ seeking.

मार्जन _ wiping, cleaning; sprinkling (oneself) with water (by means of कुश grass dipped in water) with 3 verses: आपो हि ष्ठा, etc. "Whatever is doubtful [in its purity] can be sprinkled with water."

मार्जार _ {मार्जन} m. 'which is cleaning itself' (?), cat.

मार्दव _ {मृदु} n. softness, kindness.

मार्ष्टि _ (a verb) {√मृज्} he purifies.

मालती _ f. Chameli tree (Jasminum) and flower.

माला _ f. string of beads, necklace, rosary; flower garland; row, collection.

मालिन् _ {माला} florist, gardener.

मालिन्य _ {मल} n. dirtiness.

माली _ {मालिन्}.

माष _ (=मुद्र).

मास _ m. »moon«; »month«, Lat. »mensis«, Russ. »mesjac«, solar month and lunar month →चान्द्र-, अधिक-मास.

माहात्म्य _ {महात्मा} n. dignity, divinity.

मित _ {मा} »measured«, limited →अमित.

मित्र _ m. friend; name of सूर्य, esp. the morning sun, in वेद worshiped as मित्र-वरुण (day and night, esp. sunrise and sunset); in Persia and later Rome worship as »Mithra«. मित्र-पूर्णिमा _ a festival on आश्विन-पूर्णिमा with worship of मित्र/सूर्य; the next morning is called मित्रप्रभात.

मित्र-प्रभात _ 'morning of मित्र' after मित्र-पूर्णिमा; when a plate with flowers, nuts and fruits is offered to मित्र; children are bathed and dressed in bright red, orange, or yellow silk robes, representing the radiance of the sun; दान is given to the needy.

मित्रता _ f. friendship.

मिथः/मिथो _ ind. together, mutually, secretly.

मिथुन _ {मिथः} m. pair, couple; twins, a राशि, Lat. Gemini.

मिथ्या _ ind. wrongly, to no purpose, false, »myth«, Gr. »mythos«.

√मिल् _ मिल सङ्गे 6P meet →मिलति.

मिलति _ (a verb) {√मिल्} he meets.

मिश्र _ »mixed«, Lat. »miscere«, »mixtura«; (with proper names) accompanied by.

मिश्रण _ mixing.

मिष्ट _ n. a sweetmeat.

मीन _ m. fish, a राशि, Lat. Pisces.

मीमांसा _ {√मन} f. 'deep thought', examination, discussion; a षड्दर्शन of जैमिनि, propounding in पूर्व-मीमांस-सूत्र कर्म and rituals.

मीर _ m. sea, ocean.

मीरा _ f. the poet Mira Bhai.

मुकुट _ m. diadem, crown.

मुक्त _ released, liberated.

मुक्ति _ (=मोक्ष) f. release, liberation →जीवन्मुक्त.

मुख _ n. »mouth«, face; facing, direction; fore part, front; head, best; source, cause.

मुख्य _ {मुख} main, chief. मुख्य-रस _ m. 'main taste', 5 primary emotions – शान्त-दास्य-साख्य-वात्सल्य-माधुर्य/शृङ्गार.

√मुच् _ मुच्लृ मोक्षणे 6U liberate (release) →मुञ्चति; निर्.; प्र. release; वि.; वि.निर्. release.

मुञ्चति _ (a verb) {√मुच्} he releases. कृष्ण-पाद-मूलं न मुञ्चति। He does not give up the sole of the feet of Krishna. (भागवत-पुराण).

मुण्डन _ 'shaving' the head, for the first time in the 3rd year, sometimes repeated with विद्यारम्भ and उपनयन; the same ceremony, only without मन्त्र, was performed for girls also; the tonsure leaves a चूडा/शिखा and is therefore also called चूडाकरण or चौड/चौल.

√मुद् _ मुद हर्षे 1A rejoice →मोदते.

मुद् _ f. delight →मोद.

मुद्र _ m. Mung plant (माष, Golden Gram, Vigna radiata).

मुद्रौदन _ {-ओदन} m. beans and rice (=खिच्ची).

मुद्रा _ f. seal, mark; pass, passport; particular finger-gesture with ritualistic significance.

मुनि _ {√मन} m. 'thinker', sage →मौन.

मुमुक्षु _ 'who desires मुक्ति'.

मुरली _ f. flute.

मुष्क _ {मूष्} m. 'small mouse', testicle → »musk«.

मुष्टि _ {मुष्} m.f. 'stealing', clenched hand, fist; a मात्रा (8 cm).

मुसल _ m. pestle; »mace«, club.

√मुह् _ मुह वैचित्ये 4P lack awareness (be bewildered) →मुह्यति; वि. be bewildered; सम्. be bewildered.

मुहुः / मुहुर् _ ind. time and time again.

मुहूर्त _ m. 'interval', a मात्रा (15 each in daytime and nighttime). Because both the 8th start at local noon /midnight, the 15th cover dusk (with sunset) and dawn (with sunrise). It is a misconception that the 1st starts with sunrise. When day and night are not equal, the length of each मुहूर्त is accordingly calculated, except for dawn and dusk (fixed 48 min, 2 दण्ड). →ब्रह्ममुहूर्त.

मुह्यति _ (a verb) {√मुह्} he is bewildered. योगी न मुह्यति । A Yogī is not bewildered. (भगवद्गीता) अ-ज्ञानेन जन्तवः मुह्यन्ति । By ignorance beings are bewildered. (भगवद्गीता).

मूढ _ 'bewildered', foolish; m. fool.

मूत्र _ n. urine →गोमूत्र.

मूर्ख _ m. fool.

मूर्ति _ f. form, image; statue.

मूर्ध _ {मूर्धन्}. मूर्ध-अभिषेक _ sprinkling water on the head.

मूर्धन् _ m. forehead, head.

मूर्धन्य _ 'towards the head' of the mouth, cerebral (retroflex).

मूल _ n. root; basis, cause; chief. मूल-भूत _ 'being the root', original, basic.

मूलाधार _ {मूल-आधार} n. 'root-support', a षट्चक्र at the base of the spine.

मूल्य _ {मूल} n. value, price.

मूल्यवान् _ {मूल्यवत्} valuable.

मूष् _ m.f. 'thief'; »mouse«, Lat. »mus« →मुष्क.

मूषिक _ {मूष्} m. »mouse«.

√मृ _ मृङ् प्राणत्यागे 6A die →म्रियते.

मृग _ m. wild animal, (esp.) deer → (opp.) पशु. मृग-तृष्णा _ f. 'deer-thirst' (fancying water in a desert), mirage, illusion.

मृगेन्द्र _ {मृग-इन्द्र} m. 'king of animals', lion.

√मृज् _ मृजूष् शुद्धौ 2P purify (cleanse) →मार्ष्टि.

मृत _ {मरण} 'died', dead, »murdered«, Pers. »mat« (as in 'checkmate' – 'the Shah /king is dead' →क्षत्र); n. death →अमृत.

मृत्यु _ {मृत} m. death.

मृत्युञ्जय _ {मृत्युम्-जय} m. 'who overcomes death', शिव.

मृद् _ f. earth, soil. मृदङ्ग _ {मृद्-} m. 'earth-body', made of clay, a drum.

मृदु _ soft, »mild« → (opp.) रूक्ष.

मृषा _ ind. falsely, fruitless.

मेघ _ m. cloud.

मे _ {मम} »my«.

मेधः _ {मेधस्}.

मेधस् _ (=यज्ञ) n. sacrifice; intelligence.

मेधा _ f. intelligence. मेधा-जनन _ development of wisdom.

मेधाविन् _ {मेधा} m. who is intelligent.

मेधावी _ {मेधाविन्}.

मेध्य _ 'fit to be sacrificed', pure.

मेनका _ f. an अप्सरा.

मेन्धी / मेन्धिका _ (Mehandi) f. Henna (Lawsonia inermis) and paste; the marriage feast when the bride's hands and feet are dyed with Henna.

मेरु _ m. mount, seat of ब्रह्मा; the central or prominent bead in a जपमाला.

मेला _ f. assembly.

मेष _ m. sheep; a राशि, Lat. Aries.

मैत्री _ {मित्र} f. friendship, friendliness.

मैथुन _ {मिथुन} 'forming a pair'; n. copulation, marriage.

मोक्ष _ (=मुक्ति) m. 'release', liberation; divorce.

मोक्षण _ releasing, liberating.

मोघम् _ ind. in vain, uselessly.

मोचन _ releasing.

मोद _ {मुद्} m. delight.

मोदक _ m. 'causing delight', sweetmeat.

मोदते _ (a verb) {√मुद्} he rejoices.

मोह _ m. bewilderment, illusion.

मोहन _ bewildering.

मोहित _ bewildered.

मोहिनी _ f. a bewildering /fascinating woman.

मौञ्जि-बन्धन _ the ceremony of 'binding [the girdle of] मुञ्ज grass', उपनयन.

मौन _ {मुनि} m. 'thoughtfulness', silence, 2 kinds – काष्ठ- and आकार-मौन. मौनं सर्वार्थ-साधकम्। मौन is the means to achieve everything. मौन-व्रत _ 'vow of silence', absolute मौन and अहिंसा for 8/6/3/1 or ½ month, 12/6/3, or 1 day.

म्रियते _ (a verb) {√मृ} he dies. मनस्वी कामं म्रियते कार्पण्यं न तु गच्छति। A wise man [rather] dies at will, but weakness he does not attain. (हितोपदेश).

यः _ {यद्} m. he who, यः ... सः.

यक्षः _ {यक्षस्}.

यक्षस् _ m. a class of semi-divine or ghostly beings.

यच्छति _ (a verb) (1) {√दा} he gives. पुष्पम् मे भक्त्या प्रयच्छति। A flower he offers me with devotion. (भगवद्गीता) ये काञ्चनम् प्रयच्छन्ति सर्वान् कामान् प्रयच्छन्ति। Those who gift gold, gift everything desirable. (महाभारत). (2) {√यम्} he restrains.

√यज् _ यज देवपूजासङ्गतिकरण-दानेषु 1U worship, associate, give, sacrifice →यजति/यजते.

यजति/यजते _ (a verb) {√यज्} he worships. ये श्रद्धया यजन्ते ते माम् एव यजन्ति। Those who worship with faith, they worship me alone. (भगवद्गीता).

यजन _ n. sacrificing, worshiping →यज्ञ, (opp.) याजन.

यजमान _ m. the 'sacrificing' institutor of a यज्ञ – the father in a संस्कार, the groom in a विवाह.

यजुर् _ {यजुस्}. यजुर्वेद _ m. 'sacrificial वेद'.

यजुस् _ {यजन} n. worship, sacrifice; sacrificial prayer.

यज्ञ _ {यजन} (Yagya) m. sacrifice, worship; equivalents are याग, सव, अध्वर, सप्ततन्तु, मख and क्रतु; (esp.) fire sacrifice (=अग्निहोत्र, होम); sacrifice personified, विष्णु (यज्ञो वै विष्णुः). A यज्ञ is performed inside a यज्ञशाला or मण्डप (with यज्ञकुण्ड and मङ्गलघट), by a ऋत्विक् on behalf of a यजमान, with the distribution of दक्षिणा and प्रसाद. It plays a central role in weddings, temple ceremonies, community celebrations, and initiations. Any संस्कार, act of renunciation, or व्रत (like जपयज्ञ) is also considered a यज्ञ. यज्ञो वै विष्णुः। यज्ञ is विष्णु. यज्ञ-कुण्ड _ n. 'यज्ञ pit'. In the मण्डप a square pit is built measuring 1 हस्त (45.7 cm) with a 1 मुष्टि (7.6 cm) step on each side. The size of the कुण्ड, according to convenience, may be larger depending upon the area available, the ceremony, number of guests, etc. The pit may be surrounded by one or three step walls. यज्ञ-दीक्षा _ f. initiation of a ब्राह्मण into the performance of यज्ञ (he is then called विप्र). यज्ञ-शाला _ f. sacrifical hall.

यत _ {यम} restrained.

यतः _ {यद्} ind. 'from whom /which', because, यतः ... ततः.

यति _ {यत्न} m. 'who endeavors', an ascetic, सन्न्यासी.

यत्न _ m. endeavor →प्रयत्न.

यत्र _ {यद्} ind. where, यत्र ... तत्र.

यथा _ {यद्} ind. as, यथा ... तथा. यथा राजा तथा प्रजा। As the king, so the population.

यथावत् _ ind. as it is, यथावत् ... तथावत्.

यथोक्त _ {यथा उक्त} 'as said'.

यद् _ (a base) →यः ; n. which, यद्...तद् ; ind. when.

यदा _ {यद्} ind. when (in time), यदा...तदा.

यदि _ {यद्} ind. if, यदि...तर्हि →चेद्.

यदु _ m. a son of ययाति (and brother of पुरु), forefather of कृष्ण.

यदृच्छया _ ind. by accident or chance.

यद्यपि _ {यदि अपि} ind. 'if even', although.

यद्वत् _ {यद्} ind. as, यद्वत्...तद्वत्.

यन्त्र _ {यम} n. instrument, machine; diagram, design →श्रीयन्त्र.

√यम् _ यम उपरमे 1P restrain →यच्छति; उद्. raise; नि. restrain; प्र. restrain, purify; वि.नि. restrain; सम्. restrain; सम्.उद्. raise; सम्.नि. restrain.

यम _ m. 'restraint', rule; primary internal prohibitions as first limb of अष्टाङ्गयोग – "अहिंसा-सत्य-अस्तेय-ब्रह्मचर्य-अपरिग्रह are यम."

यम-राज _ m. King यम, the ruler of destiny.

यमुना _ f. a river which joins the गङ्गा at प्रयाग.

ययाति _ m. a famous king, from whom spread the two lines of सोम-वंश through यदु and पुरु.

यशः _ {यशस्}.

यशस् _ n. fame.

यस्य _ {यद्} m.n. whose.

√या _ या प्राप्तौ 2P attain /reach →याति; उप. attain; प्र. depart; सम्. attain.

याग _ (=यज्ञ).

√याच् _ टुयाचृ याञ्ज्ञायाम् 1U beg →याचति.

याचति _ (a verb) {√याच्} he begs.

याचन _ begging.

याजन _ {यजन} n. sacrificing on behalf of others → (opp.) यजन.

यात _ {यान} f. 'travelled', gone; elapsed.

याति _ (a verb) {√या} he attains. सः मद्-भावं याति । He attains my nature. (भगवद्गीता)

मद्-भक्ताः मां यान्ति । My devotees attain me. (भगवद्गीता).

यात्रा _ {यान} f. travel; pilgrimage →पदयात्रा, procession →रथयात्रा; livelihood.

यात्रिक _ {यात्रा} m. traveller; pilgrim.

यादृक् _ ind. of what kind – यादृक्...तादृक्.

यान _ n. travelling; vehicle, carriage.

याम _ {यान} m. travel, course; period, watch, a मात्रा (8th part of a day, 3 hours) (=प्रहर).

यावत् _ ind. as much, यावत्...तावत्.

युक्त _ {योग} united, engaged, endowed with; restrained; fitted, skilled, moderate; absorbed.

युग _ n. »yoke«, Lat. »iugum«, Russ. »igo«; pair; an age of the world (= 5 संवत्सर), the 4 युग – सत्य-त्रेता-द्वापर कलि →द्वापरयुग.

युग-पत्/-पद् _ ind. 'being in one yoke', together, simultaneously.

युगल _ {युग} n. pair, couple.

युगादि _ {युग-आदि} m. the beginning of a युग, or of the world.

√युज् _ (1) युजिर् योगे 7A join. (2) युज संयमने 10P restrain →योजयति; नि.. (3) युज समाधौ 4A meditate.

युद्ध _ n. 'fought', fight, war. युद्धमुत्तरमुच्यते । युद्ध is the ultimate/last means.

√युध् _ युध सम्प्रहारे 4A fight →युध्यते; प्रति. fight against, attack.

युध् _ f. fight, war.

युधि-ष्ठिर _ m. 'firm in battle', the eldest पाण्डव. युधिष्ठिर-भीम-अर्जुन-नकुल-सहदेव _ the five पाण्डव.

युध्यते _ (a verb) {√युध्} he fights.

युव _ {युवन्}.

युवन् _ »young«, »juvenile«, Lat. »iuvenis«, Russ. »jun«; m. a youth →यौवन, वयः.

युष्मद् _ (a base) →त्वम्, तव.

योग _ {√युज्} m. (1) »yoke«, junction, union; plus → (opp.) वियोग; gain →योगक्षेम;

engagement; (2) restraint, self-control, mind- control →अष्टाङ्गयोग, योगश्चित्त-वृत्ति-निरोधः; (3) meditation; mystic power →योगेश्वर; spiritual अभ्यास, of 3 kinds – कर्म-ज्ञान-भक्ति; an astronomical conjunction between ग्रह, राशि or नक्षत्र. योगश्चित्त-वृत्ति-निरोधः। योग means निरोध of mental activities. योगः कर्मसु कौशलम्। [कर्म] योग is the art in [performing] duties. योग-क्षेम _ m. gain and safety. योग-निद्रा _ f. a state between 'meditation and sleep'; (esp.) the sleep of विष्ण. योग-माया _ f. 'spiritual energy', meditation, spiritual world → (opp.) महामाया.

योगिन् _ m. who practices योग; a mystic.

योगिनी _ f. female योगी.

योगी _ {योगिन्}.

योगेश्वर _ {योग-ईश्वर} m. lord of mystic power.

योग्य _ {युग} 'eligible for the yoke', eligible.

योग्यता _ f. eligibility.

योजन _ {युग} n. 'yoking'; a मात्रा (33 m).

योजना _ f. concentration, plan.

योजयति _ (a verb) {√युज्} he restrains.

योध _ m. fighter, soldier →युद्ध.

योनि _ f. womb, vagina; birth, origin.

यौवन _ {युवन्} n. youth, a वयः.

रक्त _ {रञ्ज} 'colored', reddened, red; n.blood. रक्त-चन्दन _ m. Red Sandalwood tree (Lal Chandan, Pterocarpus santalinus) and wood.

√रक्ष् _ रक्ष पालने 1P protect →रक्षति; अभि. protect fully.

रक्ष _ m. protector.

रक्षः _ {रक्षस्}.

रक्षक _ m. protector, keeper.

रक्षण _ protecting, governing.

रक्षति _ (a verb) {√रक्ष्} he protects. राजा भूमिं रक्षति। The king protects the earth.

प्रजाः परस्परं रक्षन्ति स्म। The people protected each other. (महाभारत).

रक्षस् _ n. 'protecting' treasures, an evil being.

रक्षा _ f. protection. रक्षा-बन्धन _ 'tying रक्षा/रक्षी' on the right wrist on श्रावण-पूर्णिमा as symbol of mutual protection between brother and sister. रक्षा-बन्धन-मन्त्र while tying रक्षा – येन बद्धो बलिराजा दानवेन्द्रो महाबलः। तेन त्वामभिबध्नामि रक्षे मा चल मा चल ॥

रक्षित _ protected.

रक्षी _ (Rakhi) f. 'protector', a thread as amulet.

रङ्ग _ {रञ्जन} m. color, dye.

रङ्गावली _ {रङ्ग-आवली} (Rangoli) auspicious 'colored lines' drawn on the ground or walls.

√रच _ रच प्रतियत्ने 10P make complete (compose) →रचयति.

रचन _ n. creating; arranging.

रचना _ f. creation; arrangement, composition.

रचयति _ (a verb) {√रच} he composes. सः विश्वं रचयति। He creates the world.

रज _ {रञ्जन} m. dust.

रजः _ {रजस्, रज}.

रजति/रज्यति _ (a verb) {√रञ्ज} he is attached.

रजनी _ f. 'dark' night.

रजस् _ n. the 'darkening' गुण of passion →रजोगुण; dust; impurity, (esp.) menstrual discharge.

रजो-गुण _ {रजस्-} m. गुण of passion.

रज्जु _ f. string, rope; a मात्रा (18 m, 10 दण्ड).

√रञ्ज् _ रञ्ज रागे 1/4U dye, be attached to →रजति/रज्यति; अनु. be attracted, love.

रञ्जन _ n. 'coloring' →रङ्ग; pleasing, delighting →मनोरञ्जन.

रञ्जित _ n. 'colored'; delighted.

रण _ m. 'delight', combat, battle. रण-जित _ m. 'who won the battle'.

रत _ {रमण} delighted, fond of.

रति _ f. delight, love, Cupid.

रत्न _ n. 'gift', treasure, jewel →नवरत्न .

रथ _ m. chariot → Lat. »rota« (wheel),
   »rotation«. रथ-यात्रा _ f. procession with a
   chariot.

रन्ध्र _ n. an opening, (esp.) 9 in the body, plus
   ब्रह्मरन्ध्र .

√रभ् _ रभ राभस्ये 1A act rashly (begin, desire)
   →रभते ; आ. begin; प्र.आ.; सम्.आ. begin.

रभते _ (a verb) {√रभ्} he begins.

√रम् _ रमु क्रीडायाम् 1A play (delight) →रमते ;
   अभि. engage; उप. stop, desist.

रमण _ n. pleasing.

रमते _ (a verb) {√रम्} he delights. मनः शब्दे
   रमते | The mind delights in sound.
   (महाभारत) यत्र स्त्रियः पूज्यन्ते तत्र देवताः
   रमन्ते | Where women are adored there the
   [very] gods delight. (महाभारत).

रमा _ f. 'pleasing' woman; लक्ष्मी .

रमेश _ {रमा-ईश} m. 'lord of लक्ष्मी ', विष्णु .

रमेश्वर _ {रमा-ईश्वर} (=रमेश) →रामेश्वर .

रवि _ (=सूर्य) m. sun. रवि-वार _ m. Sunday.
   रवि-सोम-मङ्गल-बुध-गुरु-शुक्र-शनि-वार _
   7 days of the week, स्प्ताह .

रस _ m. sap, juice, essence; taste, a तन्मात्र , of
   6 kinds – मधुर-अम्ल-लवण-कटु-तिक्त-
   कषाय ; emotion (=भाव) – 5 मुख्यरस plus 7
   गौणरस .

रसन _ n. 'tasting', tongue.

रसायन _ {रस-अयन} n. 'fluid- channel',
   medicine prolonging life, rejuvenation.

रस्य _ {रस} juicy, tasty.

रहः _ {रहस्}.

रहस् _ n. solitude.

रहस्य _ {रहस्} n. secret.

रहित _ left alone, wanting.

राका _ f. goddess presiding over the full
   moon.

राकेश _ {राका-ईश} m. शिव .

राक्षस _ {रक्षस्} evil, demoniac; m. demon, of
   3 kinds – followers of कुवेर (यक्ष and रक्षः),
   enemies of the देव (असुर) and evil spirits;
   a विवाह possible among क्षत्रिय where the
   bride is abducted after an open fight.

राग _ {रञ्जन} m. 'color'; feeling, (esp.)
   affection, love →रागद्वेष ; harmony, tune; a
   क्लेश (material enjoyment). राग-द्वेष _ m.
   love and hatred.

रागी _ (Ragi) f. Finger Millet (Eleusine
   coracana).

राज- _ {राजा in comp.} royal. राज-गुह्य _ n.
   royal secret. राज-धानी _ f. 'holding the
   king', capital. राज-नीति _ f. 'royal conduct',
   politics. राज-भोग _ m. royal meal. राज-
   मार्ग _ m. 'royal path', (mod.) highway;
   royal method. राज-वृक्ष _ m. Rajbriksha
   tree (Amaltash, Cassia fistula) and wood.

राज-सूय _ m. royal sacrifice.

राजन् _ 'shining', »radiant«, reigning,
   »radius«, »region«, »regard«, »rule«; m.
   »regent«, king, Lat. »regno«, »rex« →राणा .

राजस _ 'pertaining to रजः ', in रजोगुण ,
   passionate.

राजा _ {राजन्}.

राजिका _ (=सर्षप).

राजीव _ n. blue lotus.

राजेन्द्र _ {राज-इन्द्र} m. 'lord of kings',
   emperor.

राज्ञी _ {राजा} f. Lat. »regina«, queen →राणी .

राज्य _ 'pertaining to a राजा ', »regal«, royal
   →राय ; n. »reign«, »regency«, »regimen«,
   kingship; »region«, kingdom.

राणा _ (=राजा).

राणी _ (=राज्ञी).

रात्र _ (=रात्रि).

रात्रि _ f. night →आरात्रिक .

रात्रौ _ {रात्रि} at night.

राधा _ f. prosperity, success; a celebrated
   गोपी , consort of कृष्ण (राधा-कृष्ण).

राधाष्टमी _ {राधा-} a festival on भाद्रपद-शुक्ल-अष्टमी, celebrating the आविर्भाव of राधा the day before.

राम _ {रमण} m. 'who is pleasing', God; name of 3 अवतार – रामचन्द्र, परशुराम and बलराम. राम-चन्द्र _ m. 'beautiful राम', son of दशरथ; राम is born on 07.04. 1331 BCE (चैत्र-शुक्ल-नवमी), marriage with सीता on 24.05. 1314 (ज्यैष्ठ-शुक्ल-पञ्चमी), exile from 16.03. 1313 (चैत्र-शुक्ल- षष्ठी), kidnapping of सीता by रावण on 08.02. 1300 (माघ-कृष्ण-अष्टमी), march to लङ्का from 25.12. 1300 (पौष-कृष्ण- तृतीया), constructing the bridge within 5 days from 15.01. 1299 (पौष-अधिक-शुक्ल-दशमी), death of रावण on 06.03. 1299 (माघ-अमावास्या), reentering अयोध्या and coronation on 11.04. 1299 (चैत्र-शुक्ल-सप्तमी), ending his life in the river सरयू in 1268. राम-नवमी _ a festival on चैत्र- शुक्ल-नवमी (07.04. 1331 BCE), celebrating the आविर्भाव of रामचन्द्र with उपवास till noon, a मण्डप with भजन and कीर्तन, पूजा at noon, प्रसाद, and रामनाम-लेखन-व्रत. रामनाम-लेखन-व्रत _ writing राम- नाम a lakh of times and पूजा of राम-नाम. राम-राज्य _ 'kingdom of God', justice.

रामायण _ {राम-अयन} n. 'the ways of राम', oldest epos with 24,000 verses on सीता-राम and हनुमान्, by वाल्मीकि.

रामेश्वर _ {राम-ईश्वर} n. 'lord of राम', the town where रामचन्द्र crossed to लङ्का.

राय _ (Roy, =राजा) m. »royal«, king; title of honor.

राशि _ m. 'group', heap; 12 signs of the zodiac through which the sun passes – मेष-वृषभ-मिथुन-कर्क(ट)-सिंह-कन्या-तुला-वृश्चिक-धनु-मकर-कुम्भ-मीन.

राष्ट्र _ {राजा} n. kingdom, nation, province. राष्ट्र-पति _ m. sovereign, president.

राष्ट्रीय _ 'relating to a राष्ट्र', national.

राहु _ m. an eclipse, 8th ग्रह.

रिक्त _ empty.

रिपु _ m. 'deceiver', enemy.

रीति _ f. 'flow', course, manner, practice.

रुक्म _ m. gold.

रुक्मिणी _ f. 'adorned with gold', a queen of कृष्ण.

रुग्न _ sick →रोग.

रुचि _ f. liking, taste.

रुद्र _ m. 'roaring', 11 forms of शिव.

रुद्राक्ष _ {रुद्र-अक्ष} m. 'रुद्र eyed', a berry used for जपमाला; Rudraksh tree (Elaeocarpus).

रुधिर _ »red«, Lat. »rubera« → »ruby«; m. blood.

√रुह् _ रुह जन्मनि प्रादुर्भावे च 1P be born; be manifested →रोहति; आ. ascend; सु.वि. develop very much.

रूक्ष _ dry, hard → (opp.) मृदु; harsh.

रूप _ n. form (incl. color), a तन्मात्र, of 16 kinds – like ह्रस्व, दीर्घ, स्थूल, square, roundish, colors like शुक्ल, कृष्ण, रक्त, पीत, नील, plus impressions; beautiful form, beauty; nature, character; likeness, image.

रूपी _ f. beautiful woman; लक्ष्मी, (hence) money, »Rupee«.

रेखा _ f. scratch, line.

रेचक _ m. 'emptying', exhalation →प्राणायाम.

रेणु _ m. dust.

रोग _ m. 'breaking up' of strength, disease → (opp.) आरोग्य.

रोगिन् _ m. diseased person.

रोगी _ {रोगिन्}.

रोटी _ (=चर्पटी) f. bread.

रोदन _ calling, crying.

रोम _ {रोमन्}. रोम-हर्ष _ m. 'bristling of hair', thrill.

रोमन् _ n. bodily hair.

रोहण _ rising, growing, planting →आरोह.

रोहति _ (a verb) {√रुह्} he is born.

रोहिणी _ {रोहण or रोहित} f. mother of बलराम; a नक्षत्र.

रोहित _ m. 'red', sun.

रौद्र _ {रुद्र} m. anger, a गौणरस.

लक्ष _ (Lakh) m. indication, mark; hundred thousand.

लक्षण _ marking; n. 'indication', mark, sign.

लक्ष्मण _ m. 'having good marks', a brother of राम → »Lucknow«.

लक्ष्मी _ f. 'indication', good sign; fortune, luck, prosperity; goddess of fortune.

लगुड _ m. stick, club.

लघिमन् _ {लघु} m. 'lightness', a सिद्धि.

लघिमा _ {लघिमन्}.

लघु _ »light« (weight), Russ. »legko«, little → (opp.) गुरु; insignificant; (in छन्दः) a short मात्रा; a मात्रा (2 min).

लङ्का _ f. the capital of रावण (probably south of the विन्ध्य mountains), wrongly identified with Sinhala /Ceylon, which was thus renamed Shri-Lanka in 1972.

लज्जा _ f. shame, modesty.

लता _ f. creeper.

लब्ध _ gained →लाभ.

√लभ् _ डुलभष् प्राप्तौ 1A obtain (reach) →लभते; उप. perceive; दुर्. obtain with difficulty; सु.दुर्. obtain with difficulty.

लभते _ (a verb) {√लभ्} he obtains. श्रद्धावान् ज्ञानं लभते I A faithful man obtains [spiritual] knowledge. (भगवद्गीता) ऋषयः ब्रह्म-निर्वाणं लभन्ते I Sages attain liberation (Nirvāna) in the Supreme. (भगवद्गीता).

लम्ब _ 'hanging down', long.

लय _ m. »lying«, resting; melting, dissolution.

√लल् _ लल ईप्सायाम् 10A desire to obtain →लालयते.

लल _ playful →लालन.

ललिता _ f. 'played', (playful) woman.

लव _ small.

लवङ्ग _ (Long) m. Clove tree (Syzygium aromaticum).

लवण _ salty, a रस.

√लष् _ लष कान्तौ 1U desire →लषति.

लषति _ (a verb) {√लष्} he desires.

लाघव _ {लघु} n. lightness, swiftness; insignificance.

लाज-होम _ oblations by the bride.

लाभ _ m. gain.

लालन _ {लल} n. fondling

लालयते _ (a verb) {√लल्} he desires to obtain.

लाल्य _ (Lal) 'to be fondled', darling.

√लिख् _ लिख विलेखने 6P draw, scratch (write) →लिखति.

लिखति _ (a verb) {√लिख्} he writes. सः पत्रं लिखति I He writes a letter.

लिखन _ n. 'scratching', writing.

लिखित _ 'scratched', written.

लिङ्ग _ n. mark, sign (=लक्षण); gender, (esp.) the male organ. लिङ्ग-शरीर _ n. the subtle body.

√लिप् _ लिप उपदेहे 6U anoint, smear →लिम्पति. उप. smear.

लिपि _ f. 'smearing', writing, script.

लिम्पति _ (a verb) {√लिप्} he anoints. कर्माणि मां न लिम्पन्ति I Activities do not stain me. (भगवद्गीता).

लीला _ f. play, sport.

लुप्त _ 'broken', destroyed.

लुब्ध _ greedy →लोभ.

लेखक _ {लिखन} m. writer.

लेखनी _ {लिखन} f. pen, pencil.

लेख्य _ {लिखन} 'to be written' or painted; n. writing, painting.

लेप्य _ {लिपि} 'to be smeared' or modelled (from earth).

√लोक् _ लोकृ दर्शने 1A see →लोकते; अव. see.

लोक _ m. »location«, Lat. »locatio«, region; world →त्रिलोक, चतुर्दशभुवन; people. लोकाः समस्ताः सुखिनो भवन्तु । All लोक shall be happy! लोक-प्रमाण _ n. 'people's standard', traditional usage.

लोकते _ (a verb) {√लोक्} he sees.

लोकोक्ति _ {लोक-उक्ति} (=सुभाषित) f. 'worldly talk', saying, proverb.

लोचन _ n. »looking«, seeing; eye.

लोभ _ m. greed, »love«, Lat. »libido« → Russ. »ljubit'«.

लोह _ m. metal.

लौकिक _ {लोक} worldly.

लौह _ {लोह} made of metal.

वंश _ (Bans) m. Bamboo (Bambusa); genealogy (from its resemblance to the succession of joints in a bamboo).

वंशी _ {वंश} f. bamboo flute.

वक्ति _ (a verb) {√वच्} he speaks.

वक्ता _ (वक्तृ).

वक्तृ _ {वच} m. speaker.

वक्त्र _ {वच} n. 'organ of speech', mouth.

√वच् _ वच परिभाषणे 2P speak →वक्ति; प्र. declare.

वच _ 'speaking', calling, Lat. »voco« → »voice«, »vocal«, »vocabulary«, वाक् .

वचः _ {वचस्}.

वचन _ n. 'speaking', »voicing«, speech; number (singular, etc.).

वचस् _ f. speech, »voice«.

वज्र _ m. thunderbolt, weapon of इन्द्र, Buddhist »dorje«; diamond.

वट _ (Bat) m. Banyan tree (न्यग्रोध, Ficus Benghalensis), the national tree of India. वट-पूर्णिमा _ a festival on ज्यैष्ठ-पूर्णिमा in memory of सावित्री and सत्यवान् (महाभारत, वनपर्व ch. 293-299), celebrated by married women with सावित्री-व्रत for securing long life and health of husband and son.

वणिक् _ (Bania → »Banyan«) m. a merchant, like तिल-, गन्ध-, सुवर्ण-वणिक् →वैश्य.

.वत् _ (an affix, expressing:) (1) having/with →भगवत् (भगवान्). (2) like →दण्डवत्.

वत्स _ m. calf; child, beloved →श्रीवत्स.

वत्सल _ child-loving, tender →वात्सल्य.

√वद् _ (1) वद व्यक्तायां वाचि 1P speak →वदति. (2) वदि अभिवादन-स्तुत्योः 1A offer respects; praise →वन्दते.

वद _ (=वच) speaking.

वदति _ (a verb) {√वद्} he speaks. कश्चिद् एनम् आश्चर्यवत् वदति । Someone describes this [soul] as wonderful. (भगवद्गीता) यद् वेद-विदः अ-क्षरं वदन्ति तद् प्रवक्ष्ये । That which the knowers of the Vedas describe as imperishable, that I will explain. (भगवद्गीता) साङ्ख्य-योगौ पृथक् बालाः प्रवदन्ति । Jnāna-yoga (Sānkhya) and Karma-yoga are different',[thus only] children declare. (भगवद्गीता).

वदन _ n. 'speaking', mouth, face.

वध _ m. slaying, killing. वध-दण्ड _ m. corporal punishment, dealt to an आततायी.

वधू _ f. bride, daughter-in-law. वधू-गृह-आगमन _ the bride- groom's 'coming to the bride's house'. वधू-वर-गुण-परीक्षा _ examining the suitability of bride and bride-groom. वधू-वर-निष्क्रमण _ bride and bride-groom 'coming out' into the Pandal before marriage.

वन _ n. forest →वृन्दावन. वन-प्रस्थ _ n. 'retiring to the forest' as वानप्रस्थ.

वन्दते _ (a verb) {√वद्} he praises.

वन्दन _ n. 'praising', praise; (esp.) नमस्कार or प्रणाम. वन्दे मातरम् । I praise the mother.

वन्दित _ {वन्दन} praised.

वन्द्य _ 'to be praised', venerable.

वपुः _ {वपुस्}.

वपुस् _ n. form, figure; body.

वमन _ vomitting.

वयः _ {वयस्}.

वयस् _ n. vigor, youth; age, period of life (between जन्म and मृत्यु) – बाल्य (till age 5), कौमार (5-15, divided into पौगण्ड with विद्यारम्भ and कैशोर with उपनयन), यौवन (age 15-45), वयोमध्य (age 45-60), जरा (from age 60).

वयस्य _ {वयस्} m. a youth /friend of the same age.

वयो-मध्य _ {वयस्-} n. middle age, a वयः .

वर _ 'choice', »will«, Lat. »velle«, best; m. bride-groom; blessing. वरम् _ ind. eminent, excellent, better. वर-द _ m. 'giving blessings', benefactor. वर-प्रेषण _ 'sending in the name of the bride-groom' persons for the hand of the girl to her father; with वाग्दान settling the marriage (this promise is not a contract; only after सप्तपदी or पाणिग्रहण the marriage is irrevocable).

वरण _ choosing.

वराह _ m. boar; an अवतार .

वरेण्य _ {वर} 'to be choosen', excellent.

वरुण _ m. 'wide sky', an आदित्य presiding over the night (opp. to मित्र) and the waters of atmosphere and ocean.

वर्ग _ m. class, category; 'group' of letters.

वर्जन _ excluding, abandoning.

वर्जम् _ ind. excluding.

वर्जित _ excluded, abandoned.

वर्ण _ m. color; character, class; occupation, guild, social class – ब्राह्मण-क्षत्रिय-वैश्य-शूद्र ; their ratio was and still is 1:10:100:1000 →वर्णाश्रम ; letter, sound – स्वर and व्यञ्जन .
वर्ण-क्रम _ m. 'order of letters', alphabet.
वर्ण-माला _ n. 'row of letters', alphabet.

वर्णाश्रम _ {वर्ण-आश्रम} n. 'class and stage of life', ancient social system. वर्णाश्रम-धर्म _ m. 'duty according to वर्णाश्रम'; Society requires the powers of wisdom (ब्राह्मण), weapons (क्षत्रिय), wealth/land (वैश्य) and labor/skill (शूद्र), which also fit to differences in human nature. If the first three are restricted to only their share of power, they can be balanced. In a degraded society (then called theocracy, aristocracy, plutocracy) these powers have fallen into one hand.

वर्त _ m. 'turning', Germ. »werden«, happening; subsistence, livelihood.

वर्तते _ (a verb) {√वृत्} he happens, acts. यः मां भजति सः मयि वर्तते । One who worships me, he lives in me. (भगवद्गीता) इन्द्रियाणि इन्द्रिय-अर्थेषु वर्तन्ते । The senses are engaged in sense objects. (भगवद्गीता)

वर्तन _ happening, acting.

वर्तमान _ 'happening', present. वर्तमान-काल _ m. present tense.

वर्त्म _ {वर्त्मन्}. वर्त्म-प्रदर्शक _ m. 'showing the way', a गुरु .

वर्त्मन् _ n. way, path, course.

वर्धते _ (a verb) {√वृध्} he grows.

वर्धन _ increasing, growing; m. granter of increase →गोवर्धन .

वर्धयति _ (a verb) {√वृध्} he shines.

वर्म _ {वर्मन्}.

वर्मन् _ n. 'envelope', armor; often added to the name of a क्षत्रिय .

वर्ष _ m. rain; year, either शकाब्द or संवत् , calculated in सूर्यसिद्धान्त with 365.2587 days (today accepted: 365.2596) ; the 9 tracts of जम्बुद्वीप – कुरु-हिरण्मय-रम्यक-केतुमाल-इलावृत-भद्राश्र-हरि-किम्पुरुष-भारत-वर्ष .

वर्षति _ (a verb) {√वृष्} he sprinkles.

वर्षा _ f. rain; 'rainy' season (monsoon), a ऋतु comprising श्रावण- and भाद्रपद-मास .

वल्मी _ f. ant.

वल्मीक _ m.n. ant-hill →वाल्मीकि .

वल्लभ _ beloved, dear.

वश _ m. wish, control.

वश्य _ m. according to wish →अवश्य,
  आवश्यक.
√वस् _ वस निवासे 1P dwell (live) →वसति;
  नि. dwell, live; परि. stay.
वसति _ (a verb) {√वस्} श्रीः दक्षे वसति।
  Fortune resides in activity. (महाभारत)
  सर्वाणि भूतानि परमात्मनि वसन्ति। All
  beings reside in the Supersoul. (विष्णु-
  पुराण) सः नगरे निवसति। He lives in the
  town. यादृशैः सन्निवसति तादृक् पूरुषः
  भवति। Like those with whom he lives
  together, so a person becomes. (महाभारत).
वसन्त _ m. 'shining' spring, Russ. »vesna«, a
  ऋतु comprising चैत्र- and वैशाख-मास.
  वसन्त-ग्रीष्म-वर्षा-शरद्-हेमन्त-शिशिर _ 6
  ऋतु. वसन्त-पञ्चमी _ a festival on माघ-
  शुक्ल-पञ्चमी with सरस्वती-पूजा.
वसु _ 'bright', good; n. wealth; a group of 8
  देव. वसु-देव _ m. the father of कृष्ण
  →वासुदेव. वसु-धा _ f. 'holder of wealth',
  the earth. वसुधैव कुटुम्बकम्। {वसुधा एव}
  The whole वसुधा is [my] family.
वसुन्धरा _ {वसुम्-} (=वसुधा).
वस्तु _ n. 'dwelling' →वास्तु, वास; real object,
  subject-matter →वास्तविक. वस्तु-निर्देश _
  m. description of the subject-matter (of a
  book).
वस्त्र _ n. »wear«, Lat. »vestis«, cloth, garment
  →वास.
√वह् _ वह प्रापणे 1U reach (carry, flow)
  →वहति; आ. carry near; वि. carry away,
  array.
वहति _ (a verb) {√वह्} he carries. सः भारं
  वहति। He carries the burden. अहं योग-
  क्षेमं वहामि। I provide for [their] material
  well-being ('gain and safety'). (भगवद्गीता).
वह्नि _ m. fire.
वा _ ind. or.
वाक् _ {वाच्, वच} f. speech; sound, of 4
  kinds – परा-पश्यन्ती-मध्यमा-वैखरी.

वाक्य _ {वाक्} n. speech, sentence.
वागीश _ {वाक्-} m. 'master of speech', poet.
वाग्दण्ड _ m. 'verbal punishment'.
वाग्दान _ 'gift by word', a promise of a girl in
  marriage.
वाचक _ {वच} 'speaker', messenger;
  expression.
वाच्य _ {वच} 'to be spoken' →अवाच्य.
√वाछ् _ वाछि इच्छायाम् 1P desire →वाञ्छति.
वाञ्छति _ (a verb) {√वाछ्} he desires.
वाञ्छा _ f. »wish«, Germ. »Wunsch«, desire.
वाणिज्य _ {वणिक्} n. trade.
वात _ (=वायु) m. 'blown', »wind«, Lat.
  »ventus«, Russ. »veter«, air; a महाभूत; a
  दोष →प्राण. वात-दोष _ m. the दोष वात,
  said to be dry, light, cold, rough, subtle and
  mobile.
वात्सल्य _ {वत्सल} n. paternal affection.
वाद _ {वद} m. speech, sound; thesis
  →ब्रह्मवाद; (in न्याय) conclusion.
वादी _ {वादिन्, वद} m. 'speaker', who
  declares a thesis.
वाद्य _ {वाद} m. 'to be spoken or sounded',
  musical instrument.
वानप्रस्थ _ {वन-प्रस्थ} m. 'forest- dweller', a
  hermit in the 3rd आश्रम; obligatory for
  ब्राह्मण and क्षत्रिय above the age of 50, but
  open to all; it's mod. equivalent is क्षेत्र-
  सन्न्यास.
वानर _ {वन} m. 'forest-dweller', monkey.
वापी _ (Bavali) f. a large pond, (esp.) stepwell.
वाम _ left (not right); m. left side.
वामन _ m. 'short in stature', dwarf; an
  अवतार.
वायव्य _ 'relating to वायु'. वायव्य-स्नान _ n.
  a bath by contacting air (filled with dust
  raised by cows).
वायु _ (=वात) m. 'blowing', wind; impulse, a
  महाभूत; the god of wind. वायु-मण्डल _ n.
  'wind-sphere', atmosphere.

वार _ m. 'covering'; fixed time, a person's turn; times →त्रि-वारम्; day of the week (=वासर) – रवि-सोम-मङ्गल-बुध-गुरु-शुक्र-शनि-वार →ग्रह, सप्ताह.

वाराणसी _ f. (wrongly written

वाणारसी /Benares) →काशी.

वारि _ n. water.

वारुण _ 'relating to वरुण'; n. water.

वारुण-स्नान _ n. a daily bath in a body of water.

वार्त्ता _ {वृत्ति} f. livelihood, profession; news, talk.

वाल _ (=बाल) m. hair.

वाल्मीकि _ {वल्मीक} m. the author of रामायण.

वास _ m. (1) dwelling (=निवास). (2) cloth, garment = वस्त्र. (3) fragrance → Basmati ('with वास').

वासना _ f. 'dwelling' of the mind, impression from the past.

वासर _ m. 'shining' →वसन्त, वसु; a मात्रा (24 h, 8 प्रहर /याम, 30 मुहूर्त), solar day (=वार, अहोरात्र, दिवस).

वासुकि _ m. a नाग king.

वासुदेव _ m. 'son of वसुदेव', कृष्ण →चतुर्व्यूह.

वास्तविक _ {वस्तु} real, true.

वास्तु _ {वस्तु} n. site of a house. वास्तु-पुरुष _ m. the ideal pattern of a house personified as a deity. वास्तु-शास्त्र _ n. science of वास्तु →स्थापत्य.

वाह _ m. 'carriage', vehicle.

वाहन _ n. 'carrying', vehicle.

वि. _ (a prefix, expressing:) away, without →विगुण; distinct, different →विज्ञान; reverse, bad →विकर्म; by सन्धि व्य्. →व्यर्थ.

विंशति _ »twenty«, Lat. »viginti«.

विकर्म _ {वि.} n. bad कर्म.

विकल्प _ m. 'different notion', option, doubt; diversity.

विकसन _ blossoming, splitting.

विकार _ m. transformation →षड्विकार; alteration.

विकृत _ transformed, altered.

विक्रम _ m. 'distinct step', force.

विक्रान्ति _ f. power, heroism.

विक्षेप _ m. throwing.

विगत _ 'gone away', free from.

विगुण _ 'without गुण', bad.

विग्रह _ m. 'separation', analysis (of a समास); separate form, body, statue; quarrel, war.

विघ्न _ m. 'destroyer', obstacle. विघ्न-विनाश _ destruction of obstacles.

विचार _ m. thought, opinion.

विचारण _ considering.

विचित्र _ wonderful.

√विज् _ ओविजी भयचलनयोः 6A/7P fear; tremble →विजते / विनक्ति; उद्. fear; tremble; सम्. fear; tremble.

विजते / विनक्ति _ (a verb) {√विज्} he trembles.

विजय _ m. conquest, »victory«. विजय-सार _ m. Vijay Shal tree (Pterocarpus marsupium) and wood.

विजया-दशमी _ a festival for welfare and victory, one of the three most auspicious days; (1) worship of अपराजिता-देवी (together with जया and विजया); (2) a yearly ceremony and parade of the king for victory (a great celebration esp. for nobility); (3) celebrating the victory of देवी against महिष-असुर; (4) सरस्वती-पूजा for विद्यारम्भ and all undertakings. (5) The death of रावण should most probably not be celebrated on that day, but on माघ-अमावास्या.

विजित _ conquered.

विज्ञान _ n. 'distinct knowledge', realization → (opp.) ज्ञान; (mod.) science.

वितण्डा _ f. 'striking', perverse argument; (in न्याय) attacking an argument without proving the opposite.

वितर्क _ to conjecture.

वितस्ति _ f. a मात्रा (22.5 cm), 'long span' between thumb and little finger.

वित्त _ n. 'found', wealth.

√विद् _ (1) विद ज्ञाने 2P know →वेत्ति. (2) विद सत्तायाम् 4A be, exist →विद्यते. (3) विद्लृ लाभे 6U obtain →विन्दति.

-विद् _ knowing, »wit«, Celtic »wid«; m. knower →वेद, वेदविद्, Druid (Celtic dru-»wid«).

विदारण _ splitting, breaking.

विदेश _ m. 'different country', abroad.

विदेशिन् _ m. foreigner.

विदेशी _ {विदेशिन्}.

विद्महे _ we know.

विद्यते _ (a verb) {√विद्} he exists. सतः अ-भावः न विद्यते। Of the real [soul] there is no non-existence. (भगवद्गीता).

विद्या _ f. knowledge →वैद्य; education, in 4 steps – श्रवण-ग्रहण-अभ्यास-विज्ञान. विद्या सर्वस्य भूषणम्। Education is an ornament for all.

विद्यारम्भ _ {विद्या-आरम्भ} 'beginning of education', also called अक्षर-स्वीकरण, a संस्कार after बाल्य; on an auspicious day, like विजयादशमी or वसन्तपञ्चमी; after the worship of गणेश, हरि, लक्ष्मी and सरस्वती, the specific विद्या cultivated by the family, and its सूत्रकार, the child is taught at home लिपि (अ-आ- इ-ई), सङ्ख्या and playing a musical instrument; thereafter, teaching is stopped only on the days of अनध्याय.

विद्यार्थी _ {विद्या-अर्थी} m. 'desiring education', student.

विद्यालय _ {विद्या-आलय} m. (mod.) school, college.

विद्युत् _ f. lightning; (mod.) electricity.

विद्वस् _ m. 'who knows', a scholar.

विद्वान् _ {विद्वस्}. विद्वान् सर्वत्र पूज्यते। A scholar is honored everywhere.

विध _ m. division, kind of.

विधान _ piercing.

विधि _ m. rule, method, law, duty.

विधिवत् _ ind. according to precept, properly.

विनय _ {वि.} m. 'leading', training; conduct, modesty.

विनीत _ {विनय} well-behaved, humble.

विना _ ind. without, except.

विनाश _ m. destruction.

विनाशिन् _ destructible.

विनाशी _ {विनाशिन्}.

विनिर्मुक्त _ {वि.निर्.} liberated.

विनिश्चित _ {वि.} ascertained.

विनोद _ m. delight.

विन्दति _ (a verb) {√विद्} he obtains. नरः सिद्धिं विन्दति। A man attains perfection. (भगवद्गीता) पुमान् जायां विन्दते। A man obtains a wife. (व्यास-स्मृति).

विन्ध्याचल _ {विन्ध्य-अचल} m. the विन्ध्य hills.

विपक्ष _ m. 'opposite side', opponent, enemy.

विपद् _ (=आपद्).

विपरिणाम _ m. 'change', transformation, maturing.

विपरीत _ 'reversed', contrary.

विपश्चित् _ m. 'inspired', wise man.

विपिन _ n. forest.

विपुल _ large.

विप्र _ (=विपश्चित्) m. 'inspired, wise', a ब्राह्मण.

विप्रलिप्सा _ {वि.प्र.} f. 'desire for gain'; erring due to preconcepts, a दोष.

विफल _ 'fruitless', useless.

विभक्त _ divided, distributed.

विभक्ति _ f. 'division', a case in declension.

विभाग _ m. division, distribution.

विभाजन _ dividing.

विभीतक _ m. Sabera tree (Beleric, Myrabolan, Terminalia bellirica) and fruit.

विभु _ 'all-pervading', great, mighty → (opp.) अणु.

विभूति _ {विभु} f. might; empowered being; ashes of cow-dung.

विभूतिमत् _ mighty.

विभ्रम _ m. bewilderment.

विभ्रष्ट _ 'fallen', ruined, lost.

विमत्सर _ unenvious.

विमान _ n. 'measuring out', a great celestial car, (mod.) airplane.

विमुक्त _ liberated.

विमूढ _ befooled.

विमोहित _ bewildered.

वियोग _ m. 'disjunction', separation, absence; substraction.

वियोजन _ separating.

विरल _ rare.

विराग _ m. dislike →वैराग्य.

विराज् _ 'shining', ruling; universal पुरुष.

विराट्- _ (=विराज्).

विराम _ m. 'stop', pause; (mod.) holiday; the stop | at the end of a sentence.

विरूपण _ deforming.

विरेचन _ emptying, evacuating.

विरोध _ m. adversity.

विलास _ m. 'shining', play, pleasure.

विलेखन _ drawing; scratching, plowing.

विवर्जित _ abandoned, avoided.

विवर्त _ m. 'turning round', illusion. विवर्त-वाद _ m. 'thesis of विवर्त', that जगत् is an illusion (although its substance is ब्रह्म), because its manifestations are constantly changing and any identification must be wrong → (opp.) मायावाद.

विवर्धन _ n. increasing, growth.

विवस्वान् _ m. a आदित्य son of कश्यप, also called सूर्य.

विवाद _ m. dispute, argument.

विवाह _ m. 'leading away' the bride from her family, the संस्कार of marriage; of 8 kinds – ब्राह्म-दैव-आर्ष-प्राजापत्य-गान्धर्व-आसुर-राक्षस-पैशाच →शुल्क, मोक्ष, सती.

विविक्त _ 'separated', pure.

विविध _ manifold.

विवृत्त _ turned round.

विवेक _ m. 'sifting', separation, discrimination.

√विश् _ विश प्रवेशने 6P enter →विशति; आ. enter; उप. sit down; उप.आ. enter [any state], sit down; उप.आ.; नि. enter; प्र. enter; सम्.नि. enter.

विश् _ f. settlement, Russ. »ves'« →वैश्य.

विशति _ (a verb) {√विश्} he enters. यतयः अ-क्षरं विशन्ति । Sages enter the imperishable. (भगवद्गीता) सः उपविशति He sits down. सुप्तस्य सिंहस्य मुखे मृगाः न हि प्रविशन्ति । Into the mouth of a sleeping lion deer never enter. (हितोपदेश).

विशद _ shining, white; indifferent, a स्पर्श.

विशारद _ experienced, proficient.

विशाल _ large, abundant.

विशिष्ट _ {विशेष} distinct, specific; best.

विशुद्ध _ cleansed, purified; n. a षट्चक्र below the throat.

विशुद्धि _ f. purification.

विशेष _ m. distinction, difference, characteristic.

विशेषण _ 'distinguishing', qualifying; n. the 'qualifier' (adjective) of a विशेष्य.

विशेष्य _ 'to be distinguished'; n. 'to be qualified' by the विशेषण, a noun, substantive.

विश्राम _ m. 'without labor', rest.

विश्लेषण _ n. analysis.

विश्व _ all, Russ. »ves'«, universal; n. world, universe.

विश्वतः _ ind. 'from all' sides, everywhere.

विश्वतो-मुख _ {विश्वतः-} 'facing all sides', universal.

विश्वात्मा _ {विश्व-आत्मा} n. 'soul of the world' (=परमात्मा) → (opp.) जीवात्मा.

विश्वास _ m. 'without (deep) breath', 'breathing freely', faith, trust.

विष _ n. poison. विषादप्यमृतं ग्राह्यम्। अमृत should be taken even from amongst विष.

विषम _ {वि.सम} n. 'unevenness', difficulty.

विषय _ m. sphere; subject matter; sense object.

विषयी _ m. 'sensual', a materialist.

विषाद _ m. 'sinking down', depression.

विष्टर _ m. seat, chair.

विष्णु _ m. 'all-pervader', God →वैष्णव; His शङ्ख is called 'पाञ्चजन्य', the चक्र 'सुदर्शन', गदा 'कौमोदकी', खड्ग 'नन्दक', मणि 'कौस्तुभ', चाप 'शार्ङ्ग', and mark 'श्रीवत्स'.

विष्णु-सहस्रनाम-स्तोत्रम् _ n. a famous 'स्तोत्र with thousand names of विष्णु' from महाभारत – युधिष्ठिर enquired from भीष्म: "In your opinion, what is the highest Divinity (दैवत) in this world, what the highest refuge (परायण), by praising and worshiping whom men will attain what is good (शुभ, i.e., liberation), what is the highest of all धर्म, and reciting what a living being (जन्तु) is freed from the bondage of जन्म-संसार?" भीष्म replied: "In my opinion, the ultimate धर्म of all धर्म is, that one should always with भक्ति worship the lotus-eyed Lord (पुण्डरीक- अक्ष) with prayers (स्तव)." Then he recited the सहस्रनाम.

विसरण _ opening, blossoming.

विसर्ग _ m. 'sending forth', creation; the echo : ḥ.

विस्तर _ extensive.

विस्तार _ m. extension.

विस्तारण _ extending, spreading.

विस्तीर्ण _ extended, broad.

विस्मय _ m. surprise, wonder.

विस्मरण _ n. 'not remembering', forgetting; oblivion.

विस्मित _ {विस्मय} surprised.

विस्मृत _ {विस्मरण} forgotten.

विहार _ m. 'dispersion' → (opp.) संहार; 'walking for pleasure', the campus of a monastery or university; the country मगध, (mod.) Bihar.

विहित _ 'held', prescribed.

विहीन _ 'abandoned', free from.

वीणा _ f. Indian lute (also called Sitar after the Pers. Setar).

वीत _ 'gone away', lost. वीत-राग _ free from passion.

वीर _ m. hero; heroism, a गौणरस.

वीर्य _ n. strength, power, heroism.

वीर्यवान् _ {वीर्यवत्} 'with वीर्य', strong, powerful.

√वृ _ वृञ् वरणे 5U choose (ask for, cover) →वृणोति/वृणुते; अप. uncover; अप.आ. uncover, open; आ. cover; सम्.आ. cover completely.

वृक _ m. »wolf«, Russ. »volk«.

वृक्ष _ m. tree →कल्पवृक्ष.

वृक्षामला _ f. Kokum tree (Biran, Butter Tree, Garcinia indica) and fruit.

वृङ्क्ते/वर्जयति _ (a verb) {√वृज्} he abandons.

√वृज् _ वृजी वर्जने 2A/10P abandon /avoid →वृङ्क्ते/वर्जयति; वि. abandon, avoid.

वृणोति/वृणुते _ (a verb) {√वृ} he chooses. यं एव एषः वृणुते तेन लभ्यः। Only whom He chooses, by him [He] is attained. (कठ-उपनिषद्).

√वृत् _ वृतु वर्तने 1A happen, act →वर्तते; अति. outdo; अनु. act accordingly; अभि.प्र. start to act, be engaged; आ. act reverse, return; नि. stop to act; प्र. start to act, originate; वि.नि. stop to act; to return;

वि.परि. turn; सम्. become; सम्.प्र. start to act.

वृत्ति _ f. activity; livelihood.

वृद्ध _ m. 'grown'; elder, senior.

वृद्धि _ f. growth.

√वृध् _ (1) वृधु वृद्धौ 1A grow →वर्धते. (2) वृधु दीप्त्यर्थः 10P shine →वर्धयति; प्र. grow up, raise; वि. grow.

वृन्द _ n. multitude, a high number, bunch.

वृन्दा _ f. वृन्दा देवी, तुलसी. वृन्दा-वन _ n. the 'forest of वृन्दा' near मथुरा.

वृश्चिक _ m. scorpion; a राशि, Lat. Scorpio.

√वृष् _ वृषु सेचने 1P sprinkle (rain) →वर्षति.

वृषभ _ m. bull; a राशि, Lat. Taurus; chief.

वेग _ m. force, urge; speed.

वेङ्कट _ m. sacred hill and कृष्ण temple of Tirupati.

वेणु _ m. bamboo, reed; flute.

वेत्ता _ {वेत्तृ}.

वेत्ति _ (a verb) {√विद्} he knows. सिद्धानाम् अपि कश्चिद् मां वेत्ति। Even among the perfected (liberated)[only] someone knows me. (भगवद्गीता).

वेत्तृ _ {विद्} m. knower.

वेद _ {विद्} m. »wit«, Lat. »videre«, knowledge; the original वेद; त्रिवेद (=त्रयी) – ऋग्-साम-यजुर्; चतुर्वेद – त्रिवेद plus अथर्ववेद; each वेद has मन्त्र portions (called संहिता) and explanations for priests (ब्राह्मण), hermits (आरण्यक) and mendicants (उपनिषद्). वेद-विद् _ m. knower of वेद.

वेदाङ्ग _ {वेद-अङ्ग} n. 'limb of वेद', 6 preliminary sciences – शिक्षा-छन्दः- व्याकरण-निरुक्त-ज्योतिष-कल्प; studied during कृष्णपक्ष.

वेदान्त _ {वेद-अन्त} m. 'conclusion of वेद', a षड्दर्शन of व्यास, propounding ब्रह्मवाद in वेदान्तसूत्र; elaborated by शङ्कराचार्य as मायावाद in शारीरक-भाष्य. वेदान्त-कृत् _

m. author of वेदान्तसूत्र. वेदान्त-सूत्र _ (=ब्रह्मसूत्र, शारीरक) n. the aphorisms on वेदान्त.

वेद्य _ {विद्} to be known.

वेपथु _ trembling.

वेष _ m. dress.

वै _ ind. verily, truly.

वैकारिक _ {विकार} transforming.

वैकुण्ठ _ m. heaven of विष्णु.

वैकृत _ {विकृत} transforming. वैकृत-सर्ग _ m. 'transforming [secondary] creation' (=विसर्ग, विकल्प) of all beings by ब्रह्मा.

वैखरी _ f. physical वाक्, speech.

वैतरणी _ f. a river between earth and lower regions, which departed souls 'have to cross'.

वैदिक _ {वेद} 'conform with वेद', vedic. वैदिक-विधि _ according to वेद.

वैद्य _ 'versed in विद्या', medical; m. physician.

वैर _ {वीर} m. heroism; enmity.

वैराग्य _ {विराग} n. detachment.

वैरी _ {वैरिन्, वैर} m. hero; enemy.

वैवस्वत _ m. 'son of विवस्वान्', esp. वैवस्वत मनु, the first king of the सूर्य-वंश who ruled आर्यावर्त from अयोध्या.

वैशेषिक _ {विशेष} n. a षड्दर्शन of कणाद, propounding in वैशेषिक-सूत्र the 'distinct' atomic nature of the elements.

वैश्य _ {विश्} m. 'settler', entrepreneur, member of the 3rd वर्ण – क्षेत्री, कृषक, वणिक्.

वैश्वानर _ {विश्वा-नर} m. 'belonging to all men', fire; digestion; sun.

वैष्णव _ m. 'relating to विष्णु', devotee.

व्यक्त _ 'made visible', manifested → (opp.) अव्यक्त.

व्यक्ति _ f. manifestation; an individual, person → (opp.) जाति.

व्यक्ती-करण _ manifesting.

व्यञ्जन _ m. 'manifesting', consonant, a वर्ण →
(opp.) स्वर .

व्यतिरिक्त _ {वि.अति.} excessive.

व्यतीत _ {वि.} 'gone away', passed.

√व्यथ् _ व्यथ दुःखे 1A be unhappy, suffer
→व्यथते ; प्र. be perturbed.

व्यथते _ (a verb) {√व्यथ्} he suffers.

व्यथा _ f. agitation, distress.

व्यय _ {वि.} m. 'going away', changeable →
(opp.) अव्यय ; loss, expense → (opp.) आय .

व्यर्थ _ {वि.} useless.

व्यवसाय _ {वि.अव.} m. 'resolve', endeavor;
(mod.) occupation, business.

व्यवसायात्मिका बुद्धिः । {व्यवसाय-
आत्मिका} बुद्धि means व्यवसाय .

व्यवसायी _ 'who is resolute'; (mod.)
businessman.

व्यवसित _ {व्यवसाय} resolved.

व्यवस्था _ {वि.अव.} f. situation,
arrangement.

व्यवस्थित _ {व्यवस्था} situated, arranged.

व्यवहार _ {वि.अव.} m. practice, conduct.

व्यस्त _ {वि.} 'cast away', scattered, confused;
(mod.) busy.

व्याकरण _ {वि.आ.} n. 'separating', analysis;
grammar.

व्याकुल _ {वि.आ.} 'entirely filled with',
occupied with, troubled.

व्याख्या _ {वि.आ.} f. explanation, definition,
commentary.

व्याघ्र _ m. tiger.

व्याधि _ m. disorder, disease.

व्यान _ {वि.} m. circulation of breath inside
the body, a प्राण .

व्यापार _ m. occupation, business.

व्याप्ति _ {वि.आप्त} f. acquisition; pervasion.

व्यावहारिक _ {व्यवहार} practical, usual.

व्यास _ m. 'compiler', व्यास-देव , the son of
पराशर and father of शुकदेव (also called

कृष्ण for his complexion, द्वैपायन and
बादरायण).

व्याहृति _ f. 'utterance', declaration in a ritual,
like भूर्, भुवर्, स्वर् .

व्युत्पत्ति _ {वि.उद्.} f. derivation, etymology.

व्यूह _ {वि.} m. 'division', military array, like
चक्र-व्यूह ; manifestation, like चतुर्व्यूह .

व्योम _ {व्योमन्} .

व्योमन् _ m. sky, air.

√व्रज् _ व्रज गतौ 1P go →व्रजति .

व्रज _ m. a district around मथुरा . व्रज-मण्डल
_ n. the district of व्रज .

व्रजति _ (a verb) {√व्रज्} he goes.

व्रत _ n. will, resolve; religious vow, practice.

व्रीहि _ m. grain, rice.

√शंस् _ शंसु हिंसायां स्तुतौ च 1P kill /hurt
→शंसति ; praise; प्र. praise.

शंसति _ (a verb) {√शंस्} he praises. कर्मणां
सन्न्यासं शंससि । [First] you praise
renunciation (Sannyāsa) of [all] work.
(भगवद्गीता) अकामेन संवासं मनुः न हि एवं
प्रशंसति । Married life ('living together')
without love Manu does not glorify much.
(महाभारत) वृद्धाः दमं प्रशंसन्ति । The
ancients glorify self-control. (महाभारत).

शंसन _ praising.

शंसा _ f. praise.

√शक् _ (1) शकि शङ्कायाम् 1A doubt →शङ्कते .
(2) शक्लृ शक्तौ 5P be able →शक्नोति .

शक _ m. a people in the north-west of India
around 100 CE.

शकाब्द _ {शक-अब्द} m. a year of the शक
era →वर्ष .

शकुनि _ m. a bird; a brother of गान्धारी .

शकुन्तला _ f. a daughter of मेनका .

शकृत् _ n. excrement, (esp.) cow- dung.

शक्ति _ f. 'ability', energy, power; energy of
God (who is शक्तिमान्) – अन्तरङ्ग-बहिरङ्ग ,
each with 3 threads – बल-ज्ञान-क्रिया . शि

क्त-परिणाम-वाद _ m. 'thesis of evolution through शक्ति' →परिणामवाद .

शक्तिमान् _ {शक्तिमत्} m. 'with शक्ति', God.

शक्त्यावेश _ {शक्ति-आवेश} m. 'entering of शक्ति', an empowered living being →अवतार .

शक्नोति _ (a verb) {√शक्} he is able. सः वक्तुं शक्नोति । He is able to speak.

शक्य _ able, possible.

शङ्कते _ (a verb) {√शक्} he doubts. स्तेनः सर्वतः शङ्कते मृगः इव । A thief fears from all sides, like a deer. (महाभारत).

शङ्कर _ {शम्-कर} m. 'creating fortune', शिव .

शङ्का _ f. fear, doubt.

शङ्ख _ m. »conch«, Lat. »concha«, conch-shell.

शतम् _ n. hundred, Lat. »centum«, Russ. »sto«.

शतशः _ ind. hundreds.

शताब्द _ {शत-अब्द} n. 'hundred years', century.

शत्रु _ m. enemy.

शत्रुत्व _ n. enmity.

शत्रुवत् _ ind. like an enemy.

शनि _ m. 'slow'; Saturn, a ग्रह . शनि-वार _ m. 'Saturn-day', Saturday.

शनैः _ ind. gradually, slowly; little by little.

शनैश्चर _ {शनैः-} (=शनि) m. 'moving slowly'.

शब्द _ m. sound, a तन्मात्र ; word →वाक् ; revelation (=शास्त्र). शब्द-ब्रह्म _ n. 'ब्रह्म in sound', वेद . शब्द-रूप _ n. 'word form', table of declension. शब्द-स्पर्श-रूप-रस-गन्ध _ 5 तन्मात्र, इन्द्रियार्थ .

√शम् _ शमु उपशमे 4P be pacified →शाम्यति; प्र. be pacified.

शम् _ ind. fortune →शङ्कर, शम्भु .

शम _ m. peace, calmness; mind-control →शान्ति .

शमी _ f. Khejri tree (Prosopis cineraria) and wood.

शम्भु _ {शम्} m. 'who exists for fortune', शिव .

शय _ m. 'lying', sleep, rest.

शय्या _ {शय} f. bed, couch.

शर _ m. arrow.

शरण _ n. 'protecting', shelter.

शरणागति _ {शरण-आगति} f. 'approach for protection', taking shelter.

शरद् _ f. autumn (2nd summer), a ऋतु comprising आश्विन- and कार्तिक-मास . शरद्-पूर्णिमा _ a harvest festival on आश्विन-पूर्णिमा celebrated with उपवास .

शरीर _ n. body.

शर्करा _ f. »sugar«, Gr. »sakkharon« → »jaggery«.

शर्म _ {शर्मन्, शरण} n. shelter, house; happiness; often added to the name of a ब्राह्मण .

शलभ _ m. locust.

शलाका _ f. a small stick (for stirring and application of medicine).

शल्मलि _ m. Silk-Cotton tree (Bombax ceiba).

शल्य _ m. a small stick or thorn (lodged in the body). शल्य-तन्त्र _ n. surgery.

शश _ m. hare.

शशाङ्क _ {शश-अङ्क} m. 'hare-marked', moon.

शशि- _ {शशिन् in comp.}.

शशिन् _ (=शशाङ्क) m. moon.

शशी _ {शशिन्}.

शश्वत् _ ind. continuously, permanently, ever.

शस्त्र _ m. 'means for cutting', sword; any weapon, of 4 kinds – पाणि-मुक्त, यन्त्र-मुक्त, मुक्तामुक्त, अ-मुक्त → (from a different धातु) शास्त्र .

शाक _ n. vegetable; 10 kinds – roots, sprouts, stalks, bark, blossom, leaves, flower, fruits, germinated corn and mushroom; the Teak tree (Saigun, Tectona grandis); m. Teak tree (Sagaun, Tectona grandis) and wood.

शाकाहारी _ {शाक-आहारी} m. 'vegetable-eater', vegetarian → (opp.) मांसाहारी .

शाक्त _ m. 'relating to शक्ति'; a worshiper of दुर्गा .

शाखा _ f. branch, subdivision; school of knowledge.

शाटी _ (Sari) f. a strip of cloth.

शान्त _ {शम} 'pacified', calm; n. neutrality, a मुख्यरस . शान्त-दास्य-साख्य-वात्सल्य-माधुर्य / शृङ्गार _ 5 मुख्यरस .

शान्ति _ f. peace; there are various शान्ति rites, like the worship of गणेश as विनायक , or remover of obstacles. शान्तिः शान्तिः शान्तिः । Peace [from 3 kinds of दुःख]!

शाप _ m. curse.

शाम्यति _ (a verb) {√शम्} he is pacified.

शारद _ {शरद्} autumnal.

शारीर _ {शरीर} bodily; n. bodily constitution, anatomy →चिकित्सा .

शाल _ m. Sal tree (Ajakarna, Shorea robusta) and wood. शाल-ग्राम _ m. a village at the गण्डकी river in Nepal.

शाला _ m. »shed«, Germ. »Saal« (hall) →गोशाला .

शावक _ m. cub.

शाश्वत _ {शश्वत्} eternal.

शासन _ n. 'controlling', government.

शास्त्र _ {शासन} n. 'means to control', command; treatise →अर्थशास्त्र ; verbal authority (=आप्तवाक्य); revelation (=श्रुति , शब्द , आम्नाय , आगम).

शिंशपा _ (Shisham) f. Indian Rosewood tree (Sisu, Dalbergia sissoo) and wood.

√शिक्ष् _ शिक्ष विद्योपादाने 1A learn →शिक्षते .

शिक्षक _ m. teacher →शिष्य .

शिक्षते _ (a verb) {√शिक्ष्} he learns.

शिक्षा _ f. learning; teaching; phonetics →वेदाङ्ग . शिक्षा-गुरु _ m. instructing teacher → (opp.) दीक्षागुरु . शिक्षा-छन्दः-व्याकरण-निरुक्त-ज्योतिष-कल्प _ 6 वेदाङ्ग .

शिखर _ n. point, peak, top.

शिखा _ f. tuft of hair 'on top' of the head; any sharp end, point, peak, flame; the head or chief of a class.

शिग _ m. Moringa tree (Sahajan, Drumstick, Moringa oleifera).

शिरः _ {शिरस्}.

शिरस् _ m. head.

शिरीष _ (Shirish) m. East Indian Walnut (Albizia).

शिरो-मणि _ {शिरस्-} m. 'crest- jewel'.

शिला _ f. stone, rock.

शिल्प _ n. manual craft or art →कला .

शिव _ 'auspicious'; m. 'the auspicious one', शिव →शैव ; In this form, for the purpose of material creation, God comes in direct contact with दुर्गा , the personification of material energy (depicted and worshiped as लिङ्ग inside a योनि). "These offspring (प्रजा) of दुर्गा (महेश्वरी) [i.e., all created beings] are born from the principles of लिङ्ग and योनि . शिव (महेश्वर), embodying the लिङ्ग , is that same all-mighty God (पुरुष)." He is depicted with white color, matted hair with a moon, sitting on elephant skin, wearing leopard skin and snakes as ornaments, sometimes riding on नन्दी , and holding त्रिशूल . One of His expansions is the रुद्र principle, which first manifested as anger from between the eyebrows of lord ब्रह्मा . Thus शिव is said to be presiding over तमोगुण or annihilation by His ताण्डवनृत्य , just as ब्रह्मा presides of रजोगुण or creation, and विष्णु over सत्त्वगुण or preservation. His other names are आशुतोष , उमापति , गङ्गाधर , गिरीश , त्रिपुरारि , त्रिलोचन , त्र्यम्बक , नटराजा , नीलकण्ठ , पशुपति , भव , भूतेश , भैरव , महादेव , महेश्वर , मृत्युञ्जय , शङ्कर , शम्भु and हर . In India there are 12 ज्योतिर्लिङ्ग . In वैष्णव pilgrimages शिव is installed as क्षेत्रपाल. शिवरात्रि is the festival of His appearance, celebrated on माघ-कृष्ण-चतुर्दशी. शिव-रात्रि _ f. 'night of शिव', a शैव observance every चतुर्दशी.

शिशिर _ m. 'cold' winter, a ऋतु comprising माघ- and फाल्गुन-मास.

शिशु _ m. child, baby.

√शिष् _ शिष असर्वोपयोगे 10P leave a residuos →शेषति/शेषयति; अव. leave remaining; उद्. leave remaining; वि. excel.

शिष्ट _ (1) 'left', remaining →शेष. (2) 'taught', learned →शिक्षा, शिष्य.

शिष्टाचार _ {शिष्ट-आचार} m. 'learned conduct', good behavior.

शिष्य _ m. 'to be taught', pupil, disciple →»Sikh« religion, शिक्षक.

√शी _ शीङ् स्वप्ने 2A sleep (lie down) →शेते; सम्. sleep, lie down.

शीघ्रम् _ ind. quickly.

शीत _ cold → (opp.) उष्ण. शीत-काल _ m. 'cold season', winter.

शीतल _ cold.

शीर्ष _ {शीर्षन्}.

शीर्षन् _ {शिरस्} n. head.

शीर्षासन _ {शीर्ष-आसन} n. headstand

शील _ n. 'practice', habit, conduct; character →सुशील.

शुक _ m. parrot; शुक-देव, the son of व्यास.

शुक्र _ m. 'bright'; Venus, a ग्रह; a son of भृगु and preceptor of the दैत्य; n. 'brightness'; semen. शुक्र-वार _ m. 'Venus-day', Friday.

शुक्राचार्य _ {शुक्र-आचार्य} m. 'seminal' or hereditary family priest; title of शुक्र.

शुक्ल _ bright, light; white; pure. शुक्ल-पक्ष _ m. 'bright part', bright fortnight, waxing moon →चान्द्रमास.

√शुच् _ शुच शोके 1P regret, lament →शोचति; अनु. lament for.

शुचि _ bright; clean, pure →शौच.

शुद्ध _ 'purified', pure; unmixed → (opp.) मिश्र.

शुद्धि _ f. purity, 11 means – काल, वायु, अग्नि, जल, मृद्, कर्म, तपः, निराहार, पश्चात्ताप, मनः, ज्ञान; →शौच.

√शुध् _ शुध शौचे 4P wash (purify) →शुध्यति; वि. wash, purify; सम्. wash, purify.

शुध्यति _ (a verb) {√शुध्} he purifies. अग्रतः समुन्नं वस्त्रं शुध्यति। When first well-moistened, a cloth becomes clean. (महाभारत).

√शुभ् _ शुभ दीप्तौ 1A shine →शोभते.

शुभ _ beautiful, pleasant; auspicious; n. beauty, fortune.

शुल्क _ m. price; tax; dowry, a honorable gift to the bride from either side as her स्त्रीधन; when it is given to purchase the bride from her relatives, the विवाह is called आसुर; (mod.) the bride's side has to pay Dahej (from Arab. Jahez).

शुश्रूषु _ m. 'who desires to hear'.

√शुष् _ शुष शोषणे 4P dry →शुष्यति; उद्. dry up; परि. dry completely.

शुष्क _ dried, dry.

शुष्यति _ (a verb) {√शुष्} he dries.

शूद्र _ m. member of the 4th वर्ण – anyone who does work for payment.

शून्य _ 'empty'; n. void; »zero«, Arab. »sifr« → »cipher«. शून्य-वाद _ m. Buddhist 'thesis of void', that neither ब्रह्म, जीव, जगत् are real; atheism →नास्ति.

शूर _ strong, heroic; m. hero.

शूल _ m. spike, lance, trident →त्रिशूल.

शृगाल _ m. »jackal«.

शृङ्ग _ n. horn of an animal. शृङ्ग-वेर _ n. »ginger«, Lat. »zingiberi« →आर्द्रक.

शृङ्गाटक _ m. Singhara plant (Paniphal, Water Caltrop, Trapa bispinosa) and vegetable; n. a pastry (Samosa), Pers. »sanbosag«.

शृङ्गार _ m. love, a मुख्यरस.

शृणोति _ (a verb) {√श्रु} he hears कश्चिद् एनम्
  आश्चर्यवत् शृणोति । Someone hears of this
  [soul] as wonderful. (भगवद्गीता).

शेखर _ {शिखर} m. top, crown; chief.

शेते _ (a verb) {√शी} he lies down. पुरुषः
  जीवेन पुरेषु शेते । The Lord resides ('lies') in
  [all] bodies together with the Jīva. (भागवत-
  पुराण).

शेष _ m. remainder, rest →शिष्ट; a नाग king
  →अनन्त.

शेषति/शेषयति _ (a verb) {√शिष्} he leaves
  remaining.

शैल _ {शिला} 'made of stone', stone-like.

शैलेन्द्र _ m. Gum Arabic tree (Babul,
  Vachellia nilotica) and wood.

शैव _ 'relating to शिव'; m. a worshiper of
  शिव.

शैवागम _ {शैव-आगम} m. works related to
  शिव →तन्त्र.

शोक _ m. sorrow, lamentation, [consequent]
  distress and depression (opp. दुःख).

शोचति _ (a verb) {√शुच्} he laments. यदा
  जामयः शोचन्ति तदा कुलं न अस्ति । When
  the daughters-in-law lament, then the
  family perishes. (महाभारत).

शोच्य _ {शोक} lamentable.

शोधन _ purifying.

शोभते _ (a verb) {√शुभ्} he shines.

शोभा _ {शुभ} f. beauty, loveliness.

शोषण _ drying.

शोष्य _ to be dried up.

शौक्र _ {शुक्र} 'seminal', hereditary. शौक्र-
  जन्म _ n. 'seminal (or first) birth' through
  mother and father →ब्रह्मजन्म.

शौच _ {शुचि} m. cleanness, purity, a नियम; 2
  kinds – बाह्य-अभ्यन्तर; (esp.) शौच refers
  more to बाह्य/'toilet' (→शौचालय) and शुद्धि
  more to अभ्यन्तर/'purification'. "शौच is of
  two kinds – external (बाह्य) and internal
(अभ्यन्तर). बाह्य is with earth (मृद्) and
water (जल), अभ्यन्तर is शौच of thought
(भाव). Better than impurity is बाह्य, better
than that is अभ्यन्तर. [But only] one who is
pure (शुचि) by both [means] is actually
pure (शुचि), no one else."

शौचालय _ {शौच-आलय} m. (mod.) toilet.

शौर्य _ {शूर} m. prowess, heroism.

श्मशान _ n. burial-place.

श्याम _ black, dark; m. कृष्ण.

श्याल _ स्याल.

श्रद्धा _ {श्रद्-धा} f. 'holding the truth', faith
  →श्राद्ध; faith in God (=आस्तिक्य)
  (aroused by पुण्य).

श्रद्धावान् _ {श्रद्धावत्} m. 'with faith'.

श्रम _ m. hard labor (in vain), exhaustion.

श्रमण _ m. 'laboring', 'who mortifies himself',
  an ascetic, »shaman«; "Naked sages (मुनि)
  who are ascetic (श्रमण), celibate, peaceful
  (शान्त), renounced (सन्न्यासिन्), and pure,
  attain the abode called ब्रह्म." The Buddhists
  were one of the श्रमण sects.

श्रयति _ (a verb) {√श्रि} he resorts to.

श्रवण _ n. 'hearing', learning.

श्राद्ध _ {श्रद्धा} n. offering 'with faith'
  oblations in the name and for the benefit of
  dead relatives, performed esp. by the son.
  "Because a son can deliver the father [by
  श्राद्ध even] from hell (called पुत्), therefore
  he is called 'पुत्र' (from 'पुत्-त्र') by ब्रह्मा
  (स्वयम्भू) himself."

√श्रि _ श्रिञ् सेवायाम् 1U serve (resort to)
  →श्रयति; आ. take shelter; अति.उद्. raise
  much; उप.आ. take shelter; वि.अप.आ.
  take shelter; सम्. take shelter; सम्.उप.आ.
  completely take shelter.

श्रित _ 'sheltered' →आश्रय.

श्री _ f. fortune, (esp.) beauty; लक्ष्मी; holiness
  (prefixed to deities, persons and works), as
  in श्री-कृष्ण. श्री-चक्र _ n. 'auspicious चक्र'

inside the श्रीयन्त्र, 9 triangles representing शक्ति. श्री-निवास _ (=श्रीवास). श्री-/लक्ष्मी-पञ्चमी _ a festival on चैत्र-शुक्ल-पञ्चमी. श्री-मूर्ति-दर्शन _ seeing the auspicious मूर्ति of God in a temple. श्री-यन्त्र _ n. 'auspicious design', a particular diagram depicting creation. श्री-रङ्ग _ m. 'love of लक्ष्मी', विष्णु; a place and temple. श्री-लङ्का _ (=लङ्का). श्री-वत्स _ m. 'beloved of श्री', a mark of विष्णु. श्री-वल्ली _ f. Soap-Pod tree (Shikakai, Acacia concinna) and leaves. श्री-वास _ m. 'dwelling of श्री', विष्णु.

श्रीमत् _ 'with श्री', holy.

श्रील _ (=श्रीमत्).

√श्रु _ श्रु श्रवणे 1P hear (obey) →शृणोति; अनु. hear in trradition, learn.

श्रुत _ n. 'heard', education.

श्रुति _ f. revelation (=शास्त्र, आम्नाय, आगम), like वेद and उपनिषद् → (opp.) स्मृति, न्याय; a quarter tone.

श्रेणि _ f. series, multitude.

श्रेयः _ {श्रेयस्}.

श्रेयस् _ n. 'more श्री', better; ultimate benefit, liberation →निवृत्तिमार्ग, (opp.) प्रेयः.

श्रेष्ठ _ 'most श्री', best.

श्रोत्र _ n. 'organ of hearing', ear.

श्लक्ष्ण _ soft, tender, small.

श्लेषण _ embracing, adhering.

श्लोक _ m. sound, voice; praise; verse, (esp.) in अनुष्टुप्.

श्व _ {श्वन्}.

श्वः _ ind. tomorrow.

श्वन् _ m. dog.

श्वशुर _ m. father-in-law.

श्वश्रू _ f. mother-in-law.

√श्वस् _ श्वस प्राणने 2P breath →श्वसिति; आ. breath freely.

श्वसिति _ (a verb) {√श्वस्} he breathes.

श्वास _ m. (deep) breath →विश्वास.

श्वेत _ »white«, bright, Russ. »svet«.

षट्_ {षष्} »six«, Lat. »sex«, Russ. »šest'«. षट्-चक्र _ n. »six circles« of bodily energy – मूलाधार-स्वाधिष्ठान-मणिपूर-अनाहत-विशुद्ध-आज्ञा plus सहस्रार. षट्-चक्र-योग _ m. 'योग by raising प्राण through षट्चक्र'.

षड्-ज _ {षट्-} m. 1st स्वर, 'born of six' organs – tongue, teeth, palate, nose, throat and chest. षड्-दर्शन _ {षट्-} n. six philosophies – न्याय-वैशेषिक-साङ्ख्य-योग-मीमांसा-वेदान्त or उत्तर-मीमांसा. षड्-विकार _ m. 'six transformations' of matter /bodies – जन्म-अस्तित्व-वृद्धि-विपरिणाम-अपक्षय-नाश.

षष्ठ _ {षष्, षट्} »sixth«, Lat. »sextus«.

षष्ठी _ f. 'sixth [रात्रि]' in both शुक्ल- and कृष्ण-पक्ष. षष्ठी-पूजा _ ('छठ'/Chhath) सूर्य-पूजा on कार्तिक-शुक्ल-षष्ठी. This festival is described even in ऋग्वेद, रामायण (performed by राम after His return to अयोध्या) and महाभारत (performed by द्रौपदी). It is the only festival without a पण्डित. Once a family starts this festival it is continued, except for a year in which a family member dies. The worshiper (व्रती) sleeps on the floor on a single blanket. 1st day (चतुर्थी) – river-bath, taking water home to clean the house, lunch (Kichri) as only meal that day; 2nd day (पञ्चमी) – उपवास (निर्जल), after sunset offering of Khir-Chapati-fruits to सोम and गङ्गा, dinner with that प्रसाद; 3rd day (षष्ठी, main festival day) – निर्जलव्रत continued, सन्ध्या-अर्घ्य (offering) of sweets and fruits on a river bank, सूर्य-नमस्कार to the setting sun; 4th day (सप्तमी) – उषा-अर्घ्य and सूर्य-नमस्कार to the rising sun, then पारण.

स- _ ind. with, Russ. »s« →सह.

संयत _ {सम्.} restrained.

संयमन _ restraining.

संयुक्त _ endowed.

संयोग _ m. union, combination.

संवत् _ {संवत्सर} ind. a year of the विक्रम era →वर्ष.

संवत्सर _ m. 'complete year', year; revolution (of any ग्रह).

संवरण _ covering.

संवाद _ m. conversation; agreement.

संविग्न _ 'shaken', agitated, terrified.

संवेदन _ thinking, perceiving.

संशय _ m. 'rest', irresolution, doubt.

संशुद्ध _ purified.

संशुद्धि _ purity.

संश्रित _ sheltered.

संसद् _ f. 'sitting together', assembly, multitude.

संसार _ m. 'flowing', wandering; transmigration; material existence.

संसिद्ध _ perfected.

संसिद्धि _ perfection.

संस्कार _ m. 'making perfect', 'refine', purify, consecrate; preparation for a certain purpose. (1) mental impression (like वासना), temperament; (2) »sacrament«, ritual, there are lists of 48 (अग्नि-पुराण 166.9ff.) and 40 (गौतम-स्मृति ch.8), like गर्भाधान, जातकर्म, नामकरण, अन्नप्राशन, विद्यारम्भ, उपनयन, समावर्तन and विवाह. "One who has these forty-eight संस्कार, is a ब्राह्मण."

संस्कृत _ 'made perfect', consecrated; m. the »Sanskrit« language → (opp.) प्राकृत.

संस्कृति _ f. culture.

संस्तुति _ f. praise.

संस्था _ f. »institute«, foundation.

संस्थापक _ m. founder.

संस्थापन _ n. founding.

संस्पर्श _ mutual contact; perception, realization.

संहार _ m. 'collection', contraction →विहार; universal destruction.

संहित _ 'held together', joined, composed.

संहिता _ f. literary composition; the मन्त्र portion of वेद, कर्मकाण्ड memorized by a ब्रह्मचारी.

सः _ {तद्} m. he, यः ... सः. सः अस्ति । He is. सो ऽहम् । {सः अहम्} I am He.

स-कृत् _ ind. 'acting at once', once, suddenly, immediately.

सक्त _ {सञ्ज्} 'attached', engaged.

सक्ति _ f. attachment.

सखा / सखि _ m. friend, Lat. »socius«.

सखी _ f. female friend.

सख्य _ n. friendship; a साधन (attending the deity like a friend).

स-गुण _ 'with गुण', virtuous; 'with the गुण [of प्रकृति]', material.

सङ्कट _ n. danger.

सङ्कर _ {सम्.} m. 'putting together', mixture, (esp.) of वर्ण.

सङ्कर्षण _ {सम्.} n. 'drawing' a child to the womb of another mother; m. बलराम, elder brother of कृष्ण (who was transferred from देवकी to रोहिणी) →चतुर्व्यूह.

सङ्कल्प _ {सम्.} m. 'complete idea', resolution; (in the morning of a व्रत or ritual) declaring its purpose and vowing the completion on a certain तिथि. सङ्कल्प-विकल्प _ m. 'resolution and doubt', functions of the mind.

सङ्केत _ m. agreement; hint.

सङ्कोच _ m. contracting, diminution.

सङ्क्रान्ति _ f. 'passage' of the sun into the next राशि →मकरसङ्क्रान्ति. सङ्क्रान्ति-व्रत _ consisting of (गङ्गा-) स्नान, एकभक्त, दान.

सङ्ख्य _ 'naming together', summing up; n. battle, battlefield.

सङ्ख्या _ f. calculation →साङ्ख्य; numeral, number – like शून्य-एक-द्वि-त्रि-चतुर्-पञ्च-

षट्-सप्त-अष्ट-नव-दश-शत-सहस्र . सङ्ख्या-वाचक _ n. 'number expression', cardinal → (opp.) क्रम-वाचक .

सङ्ख्यान _ counting, calculating.

सङ्ग _ m. (1) contact, association (=सङ्गम) →सत्सङ्ग . (2) attachment →सक्त .

सङ्गम _ {सम्.} m. 'going together', meeting; confluence (of rivers or of a river with the ocean).

सङ्गीत _ {सम्.} n. 'sung together', chorus; the art of music (with instruments and dance).

सङ्ग्रह _ {सम्.} m. 'holding together', summary, collection, compendium.

सङ्ग्राम _ m. 'multitude' of people; battle.

सङ्घ _ {सम्.} m. 'crushing together', congregation; councel (=परिषद्).

सङ्घर्ष _ m. 'friction', rivalry, struggle.

सङ्घात _ {सङ्घ} m. 'crushed together', put together, battle; aggregate, (esp.) of matter; the body.

सच्चिदानन्द _ {सत्-चित्-} m. 'eternal life, awareness and bliss'.

सज्जन _ {सत्-} m. a virtuous man.

सञ्चय _ {सम्.} m. collection, heap.

सञ्जय _ {सम्.} 'complete victory'.

सञ्जीवन _ {सम्.} m. 'reviving', an elixir.

सञ्ज्ञा _ {सम्.} f. 'knowing together or completely'; agreement, harmony; understanding, definition.

सञ्ज्ञित _ {सञ्ज्ञा} named, defined.

सत् _ 'being', existing, real; being good, true; n. a being or good being, »saint« (from Pl. सन्तः) →सती .

सततम् _ {स-तत} (=सन्ततम्) ind. constantly, always.

सती _ {सत्} f. 'female saint'; a daughter of दक्ष , consort of शिव , who burned herself; »suttee«, a wife who enters the puneral fire of her husband; any faithful wife.

सतीश _ {सती-ईश} m. 'lord of सती ', शिव .

सत्कार _ {सत्-} m. kind treatment, hospitality.

सत्तम _ {सत्} 'most good', best.

सत्ता _ (=सत्त्व).

सत्त्व _ {सत्} n. existence, strength, matter; goodness →त्रिगुण . सत्त्वं यद् ब्रह्म-दर्शनम् । सत्त्वगुण reveals ब्रह्म . सत्त्व-गुण _ m. 'गुण of goodness'. सत्त्व-रजः-तमः _ 3 गुण .

सत्य _ {सत्} real, true; good, virtuous; n. reality; truth, truthfulness, a यम ; promise; goodness. सत्यं वद । Speak the truth! सत्यं ब्रूयात्प्रियं ब्रूयात् । One should speak what is सत्य and प्रिय . सत्यमेव जयते । He (a योगी) attains that Absolute Reality (सत्य).

सत्यम् _ ind. truly, indeed. सत्य-त्रेता-द्वापर कलि _ 4 युग . सत्य-नारायण-व्रत _ n. worship of सत्यनारायण (विष्णु) on occasions like पूर्णिमा and विवाह , with उपवास , हरि-कथा , पूजा , स्नान and pious activities like दान . सत्य-युग _ (=कृतयुग) n. 'age of सत्य '. सत्य-लोक _ (=ब्रह्मलोक) m. 'world of सत्य ', inhabited by ब्रह्मा and almost liberated souls.

सत्सङ्ग _ {सत्-} m. association with a saint.

सदन _ n. »sitting«, Lat. »sedeo«; dwelling.

सदस् _ n. »seat«, Lat. »sedes«; seat in an assembly.

सदसत् _ सत् and असत् .

सदस्य _ {सदस्} m. member of an assembly.

सदा _ {स-.दा} ind. always.

सदृशम् _ ind. similarly.

सद्धर्म _ {सत्-} m. true धर्म .

सद्यः _ {स-द्यु} ind. 'same day', immediately.

सन _ old, Lat. »senior«, ancient; m. 'who is ancient' →चतुःसन .

सनक _ {सन} m. 'who is ancient', Lat. »Seneca«, a चतुःसन .

सनत् _ {सन} ind. ancient, eternally.

सनत्कुमार _ m. 'eternally child', a चतुःसन .

स-नन्द _ m. 'who delights', a चतुःसन .

सनात् _ {सन} ind. 'from old', ancient,
   eternally.
सनातन _ {सनात्} ancient, eternal; n. a
   चतुःसन. सनातन-धर्म _ m. 'eternal धर्म'.
सन्तः _ {सत् in Pl.} m. »saint«.
सन्ततम् _ {सम्.} (=सततम्) ind. constantly,
   always.
सन्ताप _ {सम्.} m. 'complete heat', affliction.
सन्ति _ {√अस्} are. ते सन्ति। They are. सर्वत्र
   क्षत्रियाः सन्ति। Everywhere there are
   [good]rulers. (महाभारत).
सन्तुष्ट _ {सन्तोष} satisfied.
सन्तोष _ {सम्.} m. satisfaction, contentment,
   a नियम. सन्तोष-तुल्यं धनमस्ति नान्यत्।
   There is no धन equal to सन्तोष.
सन्दर्भ _ {सम्.} m. 'binding together', arrange;
   context, reference book.
सन्दीपन _ kindling.
सन्देश _ {सम्.} m. 'direction', message.
सन्देह _ {सम्.} m. 'mixing together', doubt.
सन्धि _ {सम्.} m. 'holding together', junction
   →सन्ध्या; (in व्याकरण) junction of sounds;
   (in नीति) alliance (=साम). सन्धि-विग्रह _
   m. separation of सन्धि; peace and war.
सन्ध्या _ {सन्धि} f. juncture, (esp.) of the day;
   (short for:) सन्ध्यावन्दन. सन्ध्या-वन्दन _ n.
   salute [to the sun] at सन्ध्या, the oldest
   extant liturgy in world religion; prescribed
   at त्रिसन्ध्य, but generally observed only
   twice (covering the rising and setting of the
   sun, or 24 min after).
सन्न्यास _ {सम्.न्यास} m. 'completely
   throwing down', renunciation of all activity
   → (opp.) त्याग; 4th आश्रम, the highest
   stages are called हंस and परमहंस.
सन्न्यासी _ m. 'renunciant', wandering
   mendicant, member of the 4th आश्रम;
   external symptoms are saffron clothes and
   दण्ड; A सन्न्यासी is traditionally helt in high
   esteem because of his renunciation: "After

seeing a सन्न्यासी (यति) with his triple staff,
who is an image of the gods (i.e.,
representing them), if someone does not
offer नमस्कार, he is purified by fasting
(उपवास)." "The mendicant rather than the
resident community of monks has been the
Indian ideal." "ध्यान, शौच, भिक्षा, and
always living in solitude are the four duties
of a सन्न्यासी (भिक्षु); there is no fifth." "He
should not make disciples (शिष्य), study
many books (ग्रन्थ), undertake discourses
(व्याख्या) [as a means of livelihood], and
attempt enterprises (आरम्भ) in any way."
"Without sacrificial fire or fixed dwelling
(अनिकेत), he should enter a village (ग्राम)
only for food." "He should only eat so
much food that the body can function.
Taking from each only a little, the sage
(मुनि) should practice the occupation of a
bee, thus not harming the household
(गृह)." "Many people live by the
designation of सन्न्यास (त्रिदण्ड). One who
does not know the Supreme (ब्रह्म), he is
certainly not worth of सन्न्यास."
सपीतक _ (Sapota) m. Chiku tree (Manilkara
zapota) and fruit.
सप्त _ {सप्तन्}. सप्त-द्वीप _ 'seven islands'
   or continents of भूमण्डल – जम्बू-प्लक्ष-
   शाल्मली-कुश-क्रौञ्च-शक-पुष्कर-द्वीप.
सप्त-पदी _ taking seven steps together
   during विवाह (to the north of the fire),
   representing the legal part of Hindu
   marriage; each step includes a promise to
   each other before the fire as witness;
   sometimes a piece of clothing or sashes
   worn by the bride and groom are tied
   together for this ceremony. "At the seventh
   step, after marriage, a woman (नारी) is
   divorced from the tradition of her own
   family (स्व-गोत्र). Then all rituals like

charity (दान) and श्राद्ध (पिण्ड-उदक)
should be done by the tradition of the
husband's family."

सप्तन् _ »seven«, Lat. »septem«.

सप्तम _ »seventh«, Lat. »septimus« →
»September«.

सप्तमी _ f. 'seventh [रात्रि]' in both शुक्ल- and
कृष्ण-पक्ष .

सप्तर्षि _ {सप्त-ऋषि} m. seven sages;
(astron.) the seven stars comprising the Big
Dipper ('big spoon' or wagon).

सप्ताङ्ग _ {सप्त-अङ्ग} n. 'seven limbs' of
government (राज्य) – स्वामी-अमात्य-पुर-
राष्ट्र-कोश-दाण्ड-सुहृद् (in the order of
importance).

सप्ताश्व _ {सप्त-अश्व} m. having 'seven
horses', sun.

सप्ताह _ {सप्त-अह} m. 'seven days', week, a
मात्रा →वार .

स-फल _ 'with fruit', fruitful, successful.

सफलता _ f. fruitfulness, success.

सभा _ f. assembly, Germ. »Sippe«,
congregation.

सभ्य _ {सभा} 'fit for an assembly', civilized.

सम् . _ {सम} (a prefix, expressing:) together
→समवेत; complete, perfect →समर्चा; by
सन्धि सं. →संस्कृत, सङ्. →सङ्ख्या, सञ्.
→सञ्जय, सन् . →सन्धि.

सम _ {स-} 'together', »sum«, »some«;
»same«, Lat. »similis«, equal, even. समम् _
ind. with, once, equally.

समक्ष _ {सम्.} 'before the eyes', presence.
समक्षम् _ ind. in front of.

समग्र _ {सम्.} all, whole.

समञ्जन _ anointing.

समता _ (=समत्व).

समत्व _ {सम} n. 'sameness', equality.

समन्त _ {सम्.} complete.

समन्ततः _ ind. all around, completely.

समय _ m. time.

समर्चा _ {सम्.} f. worship.

समर्थ _ {सम्.} 'desiring or preparing', able,
strong.

समर्पण _ {सम्.} n. offering.

समस्त _ {समास} 'thrown together',
combined, all.

समा _ {सम} f. year.

समागत _ {सम्.} assembled.

समाज _ {सम्.} m. 'bringing together',
meeting, society.

समाधि _ {सम्.आ.} m. 'completely holding
up', concentration, absorption; 8th limb of
अष्टाङ्गयोग ; sanctuary of a saint.

समान _ (1) (सम) same, equal, common. (2)
(सम्.) m. a वातदोष for digestion. (3) (स-)
with honor or anger.

समाप्त _ obtained, completed.

समारम्भ _ m. undertaking, endeavor.

समावर्तन _ n. 'returning' home after study,
graduation, a संस्कार with a final स्नान (for
which the graduate is called स्नातक till
marriage), wearing new garments and two
ear-rings; since Vedic study is nowadays
mostly not done, समावर्तन takes place soon
after उपनयन as a mere formality.

समाविष्ट _ 'entered', filled with.

समावृत _ covered.

समाश्रित _ 'sheltered', resting.

समास _ {सम्.} m. 'throwing together',
compound; compound word; summary
→समस्त .

समासतः _ ind. summarily.

समिति _ {सम्.} f. 'gone together', assembly.

समिद्ध _ {सम्.} 'kindled', blazing.

समीप _ near; n. nearness.

समीपम्/समीपे _ ind. near, in one's presence.

समीर _ m. wind.

समुत्थ _ {सम्.} risen.

समुदय _ m. 'aggregate' of elements, material
existence.

समुद्भव _ m. production, origin.

समुद्यम _ m. effort.

समुद्र _ {सम्.} m. 'mass of water', ocean.

समूह _ {सम्.} m. 'sweeping together', multitude, group.

समृद्ध _ {सम्.} flourishing.

सम्पत्ति _ {सम्पद्} f. wealth, fortune.

सम्पद् _ {सम्.} f. 'falling together', obtaining; wealth.

सम्पन्न _ {सम्पद्} 'obtained', endowed with.

सम्पर्क _ m. 'mixing together', mixture; touch, contact.

सम्पूर्ण _ 'completely filled', complete.

सम्बन्ध _ m. 'binding together', connection, relation.

सम्बन्धिन् _ m. a relative.

सम्बन्धी _ {सम्बन्धिन्}.

सम्बोधन _ 'addressing'.

सम्भव _ m. 'becoming', creation; probability, a variety of अनुमान .

सम्भाष _ m. 'speaking together', conversation.

सम्भाषण _ n. 'conversing', conversation.

सम्भूत _ created.

सम्भोग _ m. enjoyment; sexual pleasure.

सम्भ्रम _ m. confusion, hurry.

सम्मान _ m. honor.

सम्मूढ _ befooled.

सम्मोह _ bewilderment.

सम्यक् _ ind. truly, perfectly; totally, completely.

सरः _ {सरस्}.

स-रथ _ with /on the chariot.

सरल _ 'running', easy, straight.

सरस् _ n. 'running', water; pond.

सरस्वती _ {सरस्} f. 'abounding with water', a river; a goddess (also identified with speech and wisdom). सरस्वती-पूजा _ a festival on वसन्त-पञ्चमी .

सरित् _ {सरस्} f. river.

सरोवर _ {सरस्-वर} n. 'best water', lake.

सर्ग _ m. 'sending', creation → (opp.) स्थिति, प्रलय ; 2 kinds/stages – प्राकृत-वैकृत-सर्ग (also called सर्ग-विसर्ग, or कल्प-विकल्प).

सर्प _ m. 'crawling', »serpent«, Lat. »serpens«.

सर्पति _ (a verb) {√सृप्} he creeps. अप्सु पतितः तैल-बिन्दुः प्रसर्पति । Fallen on water, a drop of oil spreads. (बृहस्पति-स्मृति).

सर्पिः _ {सर्पिस्}.

सर्पिस् _ n. ghee.

सर्व _ all, whole, Lat. »salvus«. सर्वं खल्विदं ब्रह्म । {खलु इदम्} All this [जगत्] indeed is ब्रह्म. सर्व-देवमयो हरिः । [Worship of] हरि includes all देव . सर्व-भूत _ n. all beings. सर्व-शक्त _ almighty.

सर्वतः _ ind. wholly.

सर्वतो-भद्र-चक्र _ n. 'all-auspicious', a square diagram in astrology.

सर्वत्र _ ind. everywhere.

सर्वथा _ ind. every way.

सर्वदा _ ind. every time, always, Russ. »vsegda«.

सर्वशः _ ind. wholly.

सर्षप _ (Sarso) m. Brown Mustard plant (Rai, Brassica juncea) and seed.

सविता _ {सवितृ}.

सवितृ _ m. 'stimulator /progenitor', the sun-deity सूर्य →सावित्री , गायत्री .

सव्य _ (=वाम).

सस्य _ n. grain.

√सह _ सह/षह मर्षणे 1A/10P tolerate →सहते/साहयति ; उद्. tolerate.

सह _ {स-} ind. with, along, together. सह-ज _ 'born together', innate, natural →निज .

सहते /साहयति _ (a verb) {√सह /षह} he tolerates.

सहन _ n. enduring, forgiving; overcoming.

सहस् _ {सहन} n. strength.

सहसा _ {सहस्} ind. 'with strength', forcibly; suddenly.

सहस्र _ n. thousand.
सहस्रार _ {सहस्र-अर} m. 'thousand spokes', a षट्चक्र at the crown of the head.
सहाय _ m. helper, friend.
सहायक _ (=सहाय).
स-हित _ (=संहित). स-हितम् _ ind. along with.
सहिष्णु _ {सहस्} enduring, patient.
साक्ष _ {स-अक्ष} 'with [one's own] eyes'.
साक्षात् _ {साक्ष} ind. visibly, directly, really.
साक्षात्कार _ m. realizing, realization.
साक्षी _ {साक्षिन्, साक्ष} m. witness.
साख्य _ {सखि} (=सख्य) n. friendship, a मुख्यरस.
सागर _ m. ocean, named after King सगर.
साङ्ख्य _ {सङ्ख्या} n. 'calculating', analysis; (esp.) a षड्दर्शन of कपिल, propounding in साङ्ख्य-सूत्र the evolution of 24 elements (→तत्त्व).
सात्त्विक _ 'related to सत्त्व', 'in सत्त्वगुण', good. सात्त्विक-पुराण _ "The auspicious विष्णु-, नारदीय-, भागवत-, गरुड-, पद्म-, and वराह-पुराण are to be understood as सात्त्विक-पुराण."
साधक _ m. 'who perfects' or practices; worshiper.
साधन _ n. 'perfecting', practice, means →साध्य, साधक, साधु, सिद्धि. साधन-भक्ति _ (=भजन) f. 'भक्ति in practice'.
साधर्म्य _ {स-धर्म} 'of the same nature'.
साधु _ {साधन} 'perfect', good; m. saint. साधवः साधु-भूषणाः । Saints (साधु) are ornamented with all good (साधु-) qualities. साधु-सङ्ग _ m. 'association with a saint'.
साध्य _ {साधन} n. 'to be perfected', perfection, goal.
साम _ {सामन्}. साम-दान-भेद-दण्ड _ 4 नीति, political means. साम-वेद _ m. 'वेद of hymns'.
सामग्री _ f. 'totality', collection of materials.

सामन् _ n. pacifying, conciliation; praise; hymn, (esp.) of the सामवेद.
सामर्थ्य _ {समर्थ} n. ability.
सामान्य _ {समान, सम} general, usual.
साम्य _ {सम} n. 'sameness', equality.
सायंकाल _ {सायम्-} evening-time.
सायम् _ ind. at twilight, at dusk, in the evening.
सार _ m. substance, essence; nectar.
सारथि _ {स-रथ} m. charioteer, driver.
सावित्री _ f. (1) a मन्त्र 'to सविता/सूर्य' (=ब्रह्मगायत्री); (2) name of a celebrated woman (→वट-पूर्णिमा). सावित्री-व्रत _ a vow by women (esp.) on वट-पूर्णिमा in honor of (2) सावित्री, with उपवास, sprinkling water at the root of a Banyan (वट), winding a white thread seven times around the tree, and praying to सावित्री.
साहस _ {सहस्} n. boldness.
साहित्य _ {स-हित} (=संहिता) n. union, literary composition.
सिंह _ m. lion; title as hero or king, (mod.) »Singh« (added also to the name of a Sikh); a राशि, Lat. Leo. सिंह-पुर _ n. name of a city, (mod.) »Singapore«.
सिंहासन _ {सिंह-आसन} n. 'lion- seat', throne.
सित _ white.
सिद्ध _ {साधन} 'perfected'.
सिद्धान्त _ {सिद्ध-अन्त} m. 'perfect end', conclusion of an argument (after refuting पूर्वपक्ष), axiom.
सिद्धार्थ _ {सिद्ध-अर्थ} m. 'who has accomplished an aim'.
सिद्धि _ {सिद्ध} f. 'perfection', achievement, success; mystic power, (esp.) 8, like अणिमा, लघिमा, प्राप्ति; liberation.
√सिध् _ सिधु/षिधु संराद्धौ 4P accomplish →सिध्यति; प्र. succeed; सम्. succeed.

सिध्यति _ (a verb) {√सिध्/पिध्} he accomplishes.

सिन्दूर _ n. vermilion from red lead or sulphur and potash; used as चोल for the deities of हनुमान् and गणेश.

सिन्धु _ m. 'river', सिन्धु river, »Indus« → »India«, »Hindu«, »Hindi«; ocean.

सीता _ f. furrow; consort of रामचन्द्र (born from a furrow). सीता-नवमी _ a festival on वैशाख-शुक्ल-नवमी celebrating the आविर्भाव of सीता देवी.

सीता-राम _ m. सीता and राम.

सीमन्/सीमा/सीमन्त/सीमान्त _ (like सीता) border; 'parting line' of the hair.

सीमन्त-/सीमान्त-उन्नयन _ 'drawing the parting line of the hair', a संस्कार for a pregnant woman in the eighth month, when baby and mother are said to be in a safe phase; nowadays mostly observed as Godh Bharai ('filling the lap'), a women gathering with presents, esp. of food, to cheer the mother-to-be.

सु. _ (a prefix, expressing:) well →सुकृति; beautiful →सुकन्या; very →सुसुखम्; by सन्धि स्व्. →स्वल्प.

सुकन्या _ f. beautiful girl.

सुकृत _ n. 'well done'.

सुकृति _ (=पुण्य) f. virtuous act → (opp.) दुष्कृति, 2 kinds – पूर्त-इष्ट; merit.

सुख _ easy, happy → (opp.) दुःख; pleasing, a स्पर्श; n. easiness, happiness. सुखम् _ ind. easily, happily. सुख-दुःख _ n. सुख and दुःख.

सुगन्ध _ m. 'beautiful aroma', fragrance.

सुगन्धि _ 'fragrant', virtuous; m. God.

सुघोष _ m. pleasant sound.

सुदर्शन _ m. 'beautiful audience', a son of अग्नि. सुदर्शन-चक्र _ n. 'सुदर्शन disc', sun-disc, the चक्र weapon of विष्णु, depicted as wheel with flames (simplified as स्वस्तिक).

सुदुर्लभ _ {सु.दुर्.} 'very difficult to obtain', very rare.

सुदुष्कर _ {सु.दुर्.} very difficult to do.

सुधा _ {सु.} f. 'good drink', nectar, a beverage of the gods.

सुधी _ {सु.} f. 'good sense', intelligence.

सुनिश्चितम् _ {सु.} ind. 'well- ascertained', certainly.

सुनील _ very blue.

सुनीत _ well led or guided.

सुनीति _ f. good conduct or policy.

सुन्दर _ beautiful.

सुप्त _ {स्वप्न} n. 'slept', sleep.

सुप्रभात _ {सु.} n. 'beautifully illuminated' by dawn, daybreak; morning prayer.

सुभाषित _ n. 'well said', saying, proverb.

सुमनस् _ 'good-minded', gracious, cheerful, wise; m. a wise man; f. flower.

सुमित्र _ m. good friend.

सुमेधः _ {सुमेधस्}.

सुमेधस् _ 'good intelligence', wise.

सुर _ m. a god → (opp.) असुर.

सुरक्षित _ 'well-protected', safe.

सुरभि _ {सु.} f. 'sweet-smelling', a heavenly cow.

सुरारि _ {सुर-अरि} (=असुर) m. 'enemy of gods'.

सुरेन्द्र _ {सुर-इन्द्र} m. 'king of gods', इन्द्र.

सुलभ _ 'easy to be obtained', feasible.

सुवर्ण _ (=स्वर्ण) m. 'beautiful color', gold.

सुशील _ 'of good character', well- behaved.

सुषुप्त _ {सु.सुप्त} n. 'deep sleep' without dreaming, a state of बुद्धि.

सुषुप्ति _ (=सुषुप्त).

सुषुम्ना _ f. a नाडी between इडा and पिङ्गला.

सुसुखम् _ ind. very easily, happily.

सुहृद् _ {सु.} m. 'good heart', friend, ally.

सूक्त _ {सु.उक्त} n. 'well said', hymn.

सूक्ष्म _ small, subtle → (opp.) स्थूल.

सूचना _ f. 'pointing out', indication, information.

सूची _ f. 'pointing', needle; (mod.) list, table.

सूत्र _ n. 'thread'; rule, aphorism; text book, सूत्र literature →वेदान्त-, योग-सूत्र. सूत्र-कार _ m. author.

सूनु _ m. 'born', »son«, Germ. »Sohn«, Russ. »syn«, child.

सूर _ m. sun; wise man.

सूर्य _ {सूर} m. sun, a ग्रह ; deity of the sun (charioteer of the sun is अरुण). सूर्य-वंश _ m. 'solar dynasty' from मरीचि (with रामचन्द्र). सूर्य-सोम-अङ्गारक-बुध-बृहस्पति-शुक्र-शनि-राहु-केतु _ 9 ग्रह .

सूर्यास्त _ {सूर्य-अस्त} m. sunset.

सूर्योदय _ {सूर्य-उदय} n. sunrise.

√सृज् _ सृज विसर्गे 4A/6P let loose (leave, create) →सृजति; उद्. let loose, create; वि. let loose.

सृजति _ (a verb) {√सृज्} he creates. प्रभुः लोकस्य कर्तृत्वं न सृजति । The Lord does not create the doership of people. (भगवद्गीता) ऊर्ण-नाभिः सृजते गृह्णते च । A spider sends forth and draws in [its web]. (मुण्डक-उपनिषद्) अहम् आत्मानं सृजामि । I manifest myself. (भगवद्गीता).

सृति _ f. 'run', path.

√सृप् _ सृप्लृ गतौ 1P go (creep) →सर्पति .

सृष्ट _ 'released', created.

सृष्टि _ f. creation.

सेचन _ sprinkling.

सेतु _ m. 'binding', bond; dam, bridge. सेतु-बन्ध _ m. 'binding a bridge', (esp.) the ridge to लङ्का built by हनुमान् for राम , on पौष-अधिक-शुक्ल-दशमी (15.01. 1299 BCE), wrongly celebrated on ज्यैष्ठ-शुक्ल-दशमी .

सेना _ f. army.

√सेव् _ सेवृ/षेवृ सेवने 1A serve →कल्पते; उप. serve.

सेव _ (Seb) m. Apple tree (Malus domestica) and fruit.

सेवक _ m. »servant«.

सेवते _ (a verb) {√सेव्} he serves. यः मां सेवते सः ब्रह्म-भूयाय कल्पते । One who worships me, he is eligible for the state of Brahma (spiritual existence). (भगवद्गीता).

सेवन _ n. »serving«.

सेवा _ f. »service«; worship.

सैकत _ made of sand.

सैनिक _ {सेना} m. soldier, army group.

सोम _ m. 'extract', juice; juice of the सोम plant; सोम plant; moon (because the juice was extracted by moon light), a ग्रह . सोम-रस _ m. सोम juice. सोम-वंश _ m. 'solar dynasty' from अत्रि (with कृष्ण). सोम-वार _ m. 'moon-day', Monday.

सौन्दर्य _ {सुन्दर} n. beauty.

सौम्य _ 'resembling सोम ', cool, mild; gentle.

सौर _ 'relating to सूर / सूर्य ', solar; m. worship of the sun.

स्कन्द _ m. कार्तिकेय .

स्कन्ध _ m. shoulder; trunk of a tree, branch.

स्तन _ m. breast.

स्तब्ध _ {स्तम्भ} »stopped«; stubborn, proud.

स्तम्भ _ m. »stopping«, fixing; »stem«, »stump«; pillar; »stop«, »stoppage«, obstruction.

स्तर _ {स्त्रि} (=तारा) m. scattering or »strewing« light, »star«, Lat. »stella«.

स्तव _ (=स्तुति).

स्ताव _ (=स्तुति).

√स्तु _ स्तुञ्/ष्टुञ् स्तुतौ 2U praise →स्तौति .

स्तुति _ f. praise, hymn.

स्तूप _ m. crest, top; Buddhist dome-like monument.

स्तेन _ m. thief.

स्तेय _ n. »stealing«, theft.

स्तोत्र _ (=स्तुति).

स्तोम _ (=स्तुति).

स्तौति _ (a verb) {√स्तु} he praises. महर्षि-सिद्ध-सङ्घाः त्वां स्तुवन्ति । Hosts of great sages and Siddhas praise you. (भगवद्गीता).

स्त्रि _ »strew«, scatter, spread; m. »star« ('scattered' in the sky, or 'spreading' light).

स्त्री _ f. woman, wife. स्त्री-धन _ n. 'wife's property' from शुल्क and gifts. स्त्री-रोग _ m. 'women-disease', gynecology. स्त्री-लिङ्ग _ n. feminine gender → (opp.) पुल्लिङ्ग , नपुंसक-लिङ्ग .

स्त्रीय _ desiring a woman, womanizing.

-स्थ _ »standing«, Lat. »stare«; »staying«, being »situated« →स्थान, स्थित, स्थिर . स्थ-पति _ m. 'place-official'; architect.

स्थल _ {स्थ} m. standing »still«, dry land, ground. स्थल-पद्म _ m. Hibiscus plant (Sthalkamal, Hibiscus mutabilis).

√स्था _ √स्था / ष्ठा गतिनिवृत्तौ 1P stay, stand →तिष्ठति; अनु. follow; अधि. preside over; अभि.उद्. stand up; अव. stand down, stay; आ. attain, resort; उद्. stand up; नि. stay down; परि.अव. be steady; प्रति. stand firmly; वि. be situated; वि.अव. stay; सम्.अव. stay; सम्.उद्. stand up; सम्.उप. stand near, attain; सम्.प्रति. stand firmly; सु.अनु. follow well.

स्थाणु _ {स्थ} »stationary«.

स्थान _ {स्थ} n. »state« → Rajasthan, Afghanistan, etc.; place, department of a university or आश्रम – अग्नि-स्थान for यज्ञ , ब्रह्म- for वेद , विष्णु- for नीति and वार्त्ता , विवस्वत- for astronomy, सोम- for botany.

स्थापत्य _ {स्थ-पति} m. architecture. स्थापत्य-वेद _ m. 'science of architecture', an उपवेद →वास्तु .

स्थायी _ {स्थायिन्, स्थ} »staying«, permanent.

स्थावर _ {स्थ} »standing« fixed, immovable → (opp.) जङ्गम .

स्थाली _ {स्थल / स्था} (Thali) »standing« firm, any vessel, pot, plate.

स्थित _ {स्थ} »situated« → »institute«, »sitting«.

स्थिति _ f. »situation«, »position«; maintenance.

स्थिर _ {स्थ} »stern«, steady. स्थिर-सुखमासनम् । आसन means [sitting] steadily and easily.

स्थूल _ large, thick; gross → (opp.) सूक्ष्म .

स्थैर्य _ {स्थिर} n. »steadiness«.

√स्ना _ स्ना शौचे 2P bath →स्नाति .

स्नातक _ {स्नान} m. 'who has bathed' during समावर्तन-संस्कार , a graduate.

स्नाति _ (a verb) {√स्ना} he bathes. सः नद्यां स्नाति । He bathes in the river.

स्नान _ n. 'bathing', washing; bath, sacred bath; either मुख्य (as वारुण-स्नान) or गौण (पार्थिव-आग्नेय-वायव्य-दिव्य-मन्त्र-मानसिक-स्नान); either नित्य-नैमित्तिक-काम्य .

स्नायु _ f.n. »sinew«.

स्निग्ध _ {स्नेह} 'sticked', oily; smooth, a स्पर्श; attached, lovely.

स्नेह _ m. 'sticking', oil, salve; attachment, love.

स्नेहन _ loving.

स्पर्श _ {स्पृश्} m. touch, a तन्मात्र, of 11 kinds – उष्ण-शीत-सुख-दुःख-स्निग्ध-विशद-खर-मृदु-रूक्ष-लघु-गुरु; sense perception.

स्पर्शन _ n. 'touching', sense of touch.

स्पष्ट _ 'seen', perceived; clear.

-स्पृक् _ {स्पृश्} touching.

स्पृष्ट _ {स्पृश्} 'touched'.

स्पृहा _ f. 'eagerness', desire, longing.

स्म _ ind. indeed; after a verb in present tense it gives a past sense.

स्मय _ m. »smile« →स्मित; wonder; pride.

स्मयते _ (a verb) {√स्मि} he smiles.

स्मरण _ n. 'remembering' → »memory«, Lat. »memor« →स्मृति, 5 stages (corresponding to अष्टाङ्गयोग) – अनुसन्धान-धारणा-ध्यान-ध्रुवानुस्मृति-समाधि.

स्मरति _ (a verb) {√स्मृ} he remembers. सः देवं स्मरति । He remembers God. सः तद् विस्मरति । He forgets it.

स्मार्त _ m. 'based on स्मृति'; an orthodox ब्राह्मण.

√स्मि _ स्मिङ् ईषद्धसने 1A smile →स्मयते; वि. smile, be surprised.

स्मित _ {स्मय} »smiled«, smiling.

√स्मृ _ √स्मृ आध्याने चिन्तायां वा 1P long for; think of →स्मरति; वि. forget.

स्मृत _ {स्मरण} »remembered«, recorded.

स्मृति _ f. memory; recorded tradition – वेदाङ्ग, पुराण, इतिहास, नीति (based on प्रत्यक्ष) → (opp.) श्रुति, न्याय; (esp.) law-books →मनुस्मृति.

स्याल _ m. brother-in-law.

स्याली _ f. sister-in-law.

स्योनाक _ m. Indian Caper (Sonapatha, Oroxylum indicum), see हिंस्र.

स्रवण _ flowing.

स्रोतः _ {स्रोतस्}.

स्रोतस् _ n. 'flowing', current, »stream«, Germ. »Strom«, river.

स्व _ own, »self«, Lat. »se«, Russ. »svoj«. स्व-जन _ m. 'own man', kinsman. स्व-तन्त्र _ 'self-reliant', independent. स्व-धर्म _ m. 'own duty', (esp.) in वर्णाश्रम. स्व-भाव _ m. 'own nature', character. स्व-रूप _ n. 'own form', inner /real nature. स्व-स्थ _ 'own state', well, healthy.

स्वकीय _ {स्व} own.

स्वच्छ _ {सु.अच्छ} 'very clear', clean, pure.

√स्वप् _ जिस्वप्/जिष्वप् शये 2P lie down (sleep) →स्वपिति.

स्वपिति _ (a verb) {√स्वप्/ष्वप्} he sleeps. सः रात्रौ स्वपिति । He sleeps at night.

स्वप्न _ m. sleep, a state of बुद्धि; dream.

स्वयम् _ ind. oneself, personally; on its own accord, spontaneously.

स्वयम्-भू _ m. 'self-existing', name of ब्रह्मा.

स्वर् _ ind. heaven, a व्याहृति →स्वर्ग.

स्वर _ m. sound; vowel, a वर्ण → (opp.) व्यञ्जन; the 7 notes – षड्ज-ऋषभ-गान्धार-मध्यम-पञ्चम-धैवत-निषाद (mod. Sa-Re-Ga-Ma-Pa-Da-Ni) plus कोमल and तीव्र variants, via Persia (do-re-mi-fa-so-le-ci) to Europe (do-re-mi-fa-sol-la-si).

स्वर्ग _ {सु.वर्ग} m. heaven; 7 लोक upwards, beginning with earth – भूर्-भुवर्-स्वर्-महर्-जन-तपः-सत्य-लोक; (esp.) स्वर्, the दिव्य-स्वर्ग, or 'celestial heaven' of इन्द्र → (opp.) भौम-, बिल-स्वर्ग. स्वर्ग-लोक _ m. 'world of heaven', 3rd heaven →चतुर्दशभुवन.

स्वर्ग्य _ 'relating to स्वर्ग', heavenly, leading to heaven.

स्वर्ण _ {सु. वर्ण} m. gold.

स्वल्प _ {सु.अल्प} very little, very small.

स्वसा _ {स्वसृ}.

स्वसृ _ f. »sister«, Germ. »Schwester«.

स्वस्ति _ {सु.अस्ति} ind. 'well- being', expression of auspiciousness, fortune, hail! स्वस्ति-वाचन _ the performer of a rite honors all guests and requests with folded hands: "May you declare the day to be auspicious for this ceremony of ... which I ... am about to perform.", they reply with three times ॐ स्वस्ति.

स्वस्तिक _ {स्वस्ति} m. 'creating fortune', auspicious solar symbol (curtailing the सुदर्शनचक्र).

स्वागत _ {सु.आगत} n. 'well come', welcome.

स्वातन्त्र्य _ {स्व-तन्त्र} n. independence.

√स्वाद् _ स्वाद आस्वादने 1A taste (be pleasing, like) →स्वादते.

स्वाद _ m. 'tasting well', »sweet«, Lat. »suavis«, taste; charm.

स्वादते _ (a verb) {√स्वाद्} he tastes.

स्वादिष्ट _ most delicious.

स्वादु _ delicious.

स्वाधिष्ठान _ {स्व-अधिष्ठान} n. 'own place', organ; a षट्चक्र .

स्वाध्याय _ {स्व-अध्याय} m. 'own study', reciting texts to oneself, repetition of parts already studied (in this there are no forbidden days) →अध्याय); (esp.) study of the वेद , a नियम .

स्वाभाविक _ {स्व-भाव} inherent, natural.

स्वामी _ {स्वामिन्, स्व} m. 'owner', master; title of a king, गुरु or सन्न्यासी . स्वामी-अमात्य-पुर-राष्ट्र-कोश-दाण्ड-सुहृद् _ 7 limbs of government, सप्ताङ्ग .

स्वायम्भुव _ m. 'son of स्वयम्भू / ब्रह्मा', the first मनु .

स्वार _ {स्वर} m. sound, tone.

स्वार्थ _ {स्व-अर्थ} m. self-interest.

स्वास्थ्य _ {स्व-स्थ} n. health.

स्वाहा _ {सु.आहा} f. 'blessing', expression for giving oblations; an oblation, oblation personified (as consort of अग्नि , presiding over fire in यज्ञ).

स्वी- _ {स्व in comp.}. स्वी-करण / -कार _ m. 'making one's own', accepting, acquiring.

स्वेद _ m. »sweat«, moisture. स्वेद-ज _ 'born through स्वेद (heat and moisture)', said of germs → - ज .

ह / हे / हो _ ind. address.

हंस _ m. »goose«, Germ. »Gans«; symbol of the migratory and pure soul →परमहंस ; swan.

हठ _ m. force. हठ-प्रदीपिका _ m. 'light on हठयोग ' by स्वात्मराम . हठ-योग _ m. 'forced योग' through प्रत्याहार by आसन and प्राणायाम , propounded in हठप्रदीपिका ; many mod. forms of अष्टाङ्गयोग are based on it – Shivananda Yoga by Swami Shivananda, Kundalini Yoga by Yogi Bhajan, Vini Yoga by Krishnamacarya, Iyangar Yoga by Iyangar, Bikram Yoga by Bikram Choudhury, Vipassana Yoga by Goenka.

हत _ {हन्} »hit«, hurt, killed → -हा .

हताश _ {हत-आश} 'killed hope', hopeless.

हत्या _ {हत} f. 'killing', murder.

√हन् _ हन हिंसागत्योः 2P kill, hurt; go →हन्ति ; अभि. strike at, sound an instrument; उप. strike at, harm; नि. strike down, kill.

हनु _ f. chin, Gr. »genus«, jaw.

हनुमज्जयन्ती _ {हनुमत्-} a festival on चैत्र-पूर्णिमा celebrating the आविर्भाव of हनुमान् .

हनुमान् _ {हनुमत्} m. 'with (large) jaws', a chief of monkey-like beings and servant of रामचन्द्र .

हन्त _ ind. expressing grief ('Oh, no!') or joy ('Oh, yes!').

हन्ता _ {हन्तृ}.

हन्ति _ (a verb) {√हन्} he hurts. चन्द्रः तमः हन्ति । The moon destroys darkness. (हितोपदेश).

हन्तृ _ m. killer →(?) »hunter«.

हय _ m. horse.

हर _ m. 'taking', destroyer, शिव .

हरण _ {हर} n. taking, destroying.

हरति _ (a verb) {√हृ} he takes. यद् मनः अनुविधीयते तद् अस्य प्रज्ञां हरति । That [sense] on which the mind is placed, that takes away his intelligence. (भगवद्गीता).

हरि _ {हर} m. 'taking', विष्णु /God. हरिः ओम् । God is addressed with ॐ . हरि-दास _ m. 'servant of God'. हरि-वासर _ m.n. 'day of the Lord', एकादशी . हरि-द्वार _ n. gate of विष्णु . हरि-नाम _ n. 'name of God', chanting a name of God.

हरिद्रा _ (=हलदी).

हरीतकी _ f. Haritaki tree (Terminalia chebula) and fruit.

हरे कृष्ण _ {हरि} "O हरि, o कृष्ण !"

हर्ष _ m. 'bristling' of the hair in delight;
   delight.
हल _ m. plough.
हलदी _ (Haldi) f. Turmeric (Curcuma,
   Curcuma long) →कुङ्कुम.
हविर् _ n. an oblation into fire, anything
   offered as an oblation (like ghee and grains).
√हस् _ हसे हसने 1P laugh →हसति; प्र. smile.
हस _ m. laughter.
हसति _ (a verb) {√हस्} he laughs. सः किमर्थं
   हसति। Why does he laugh?
हसन _ laughing.
हस्त _ m. hand; fore-arm, a मात्रा (45 cm, 2
   वितस्ति), 'cubit', elbow to finger tips; an
   elephant's trunk.
हस्तिन् _ m. 'having हस्त', elephant.
हस्ती _ {हस्तिन्}.
√हा _ √ओहाक् त्यागे 3P _ abandon →जहाति;
   प्र. abandon completely; वि. abandon.
-हा _ {हन्} 'killing', killer.
हानि _ {हन्} f. loss.
हास्य _ {हस} n. 'laughable', laughter, a
   गौणरस.
हि _ ind. indeed; because.
हिंसा _ f. harm, violence. "हिंसा means
   causing anxiety, pain, injury, blood and
   misery, or obstructing something beneficial,
   breaking the heart, denying happiness,
   confining and killing – thus it is tenfold."
हिंस्र _ m. Caper bush (Kabra, Capparis
   spinosa) and fruit, see स्योनाक.
हिङ्गु _ (Hing) m. asafetida.
हित _ {धर} 'held', arranged, beneficial; n.
   benefit. हित-कारी _ m. 'who does benefit',
   friend.
हितोपदेश _ {हित-उपदेश} m. 'beneficial
   advice'; a work in the line of पञ्चतन्त्र, 4
   chapters – मित्र-लाभ, सुहृद्भेद, विग्रह,
   सन्धि (dealing with दान-भेद-दण्ड-साम)
   →नीति.

हिनस्ति / हिंसयति _ (a verb) {√हिस्} he
   harms. आक्रोश-परिवादाभ्याम् अबुधाः
   बुधान् विहिंसन्ति। By abuse and accusation
   the ignorant harm the wise. (महाभारत).
हिम _ m. cold, snow; winter, Russ. »zima«.
हिमाचल _ {हिम-अचल} m. 'snow-
   mountain'.
हिमाद्रि _ (=हिमाचल).
हिमालय _ {हिम-आलय} m. 'snow- region'
   →हिमाचल, हिमाद्रि.
हिरण्य _ n. gold. हिरण्य-कशिपु _ m. 'having
   a golden cushion /clothing', a दैत्य son of
   कश्यप, famous for his son प्रह्लाद for whom
   नृसिंह appeared. हिरण्य-गर्भ _ m. 'golden
   fetus', a lotus which sprouts from the navel
   of विष्णु (गर्भोदक), in its stem चतुर्दशभुवन
   (incl. त्रिलोक); ब्रह्मा, who takes birth from
   that lotus.
√हिस् _ हिसि हिंसायाम् 7/10P kill, harm
   →हिनस्ति / हिंसयति.
हिहि _ ind. expressing laughing.
हीन _ {हानि} abandoned, wanting.
हीरा _ m. diamond.
हुत _ 'offered as oblation'; n. oblation →होत्र,
   होम.
हुताश _ {हुत-आश} m. 'oblation eater', fire.
√ह _ हञ् हरणे 1U carry, remove →हरति;
   अप. take away; आ. carry near; उद्. carry
   up; उद्.आ. set up, declare, illustrate; उप.
   carry near, offer; परि. carry round, leave; प्र.
   carry forward, throw; वि.आ. pronounce;
   सम्. withdraw; सम्.आ. withdraw, destroy;
   सम्.उद्. extricate.
हृत _ {हर} 'taken', bereft of.
हृद् _ n. »heart«; region of the heart, seat of
   the soul; the essential /best /dearest /most
   secret part of anything.
हृदय _ (=हृद्). हृदय-स्पर्श _ 'touching the
   heart' of the bride with a मन्त्र.
हृद्य _ {हृद्} »hearty«, pleasing.

√हृष् _ हृष तुष्टौ 4P be satisfied →हृष्यति; प्र. rejoice.

हृष्यति _ (a verb) {√हृष्} he is satisfied.

√हु _ √हु वह्लौ दाने 3P offer in the fire, sacrifice →जुहोति.

हे _ ind. oh!

हेतु _ m. 'sending forth', impulse; motive, reason, cause.

हेतुमत् _ 'with reason', reasonable.

हेम _ {हेमन्}.

हेमन् _ n. gold.

हेमन्त _ {हिम} m. [pre-]winters, a ऋतु comprising मार्गशीर्ष- and पौष-मास.

होत्र _ {हुत} n. 'offering oblation', fire-sacrifice →अग्निहोत्र, यज्ञ.

होम _ (=होत्र).

होलिका / होलाका _ f. (1) a demoness who deceived प्रह्लाद into a fire, but was burned herself; (2) a राक्षसी who could only be expelled by great noise →होली. होलिका-दहन _ 'burning [a doll of] होलिका' →होली.

होली _ f. a very ancient spring- festival of victory of प्रह्लाद over होलिका, or good over evil; Celebration: (1) होलिकादहन on फाल्गुन-पूर्णिमा evening, (2) festival of colors on चैत्र-कृष्ण-प्रतिपद् (=नववर्ष in North-India).

ह्यः _ ind. »yester«day, Lat. »hesternus«.

ह्रस्व _ short (metrically) → (opp.) दीर्घ.

ह्री _ f. shame, shyness, modesty.

√ह्लाद् _ ह्लादी अव्यक्ते शब्दे सुखे च 1A sound; be happy →ह्लादते.

ह्लाद _ m. »gladden«, delight.

ह्लादते _ (a verb) {√ह्लाद्} he delights. पुत्रं प्रेक्ष्य जनिता ह्लादते । Seeing the child the father rejoices. (महाभारत).

ह्लादिनी _ f. »gladdening«, delighting.

"Land of ancient India! Cradle of Humanity. Hail! Hail revered motherland whom centuries of brutal invasions have not yet buried under the dust of oblivion. Hail, Fatherland of faith, of love, of poetry and of science, may we hail a revival of thy past in our Western future." (Louis Francois Jacolliot, French judge in India and writer, 1837-1890)

"A time must come when the Indian mind will shake off the darkness that has fallen upon it, cease to think or hold opinions at second and third hand and reassert its right to judge and enquire in a perfect freedom into the meaning of its scriptures." (Sri Aurobindo, Indian philosopher, 1872-1950)

"It is already becoming clear that a chapter which had a Western beginning will have to have an Indian ending if it is not to end in self-destruction of the human race. At this supremely dangerous moment in human history, the only way of salvation is the ancient Hindu way. Here we have the attitude and spirit that can make it possible for the human race to grow together in to a single family." (Arnold Joseph Toynbee, British historian, 1889-1975)

"So now we turn to India. This spiritual gift, that makes a man human, is still alive in Indian souls. Go on giving the world Indian examples of it. Nothing else can do so much to help mankind to save itself from destruction." (Arnold Joseph Toynbee, British historian, 1889-1975)

"What is happening in India is a new historical awakening. ... Indian intellectuals, who want to be secure in their liberal beliefs, may not understand what is going on. But every other Indian knows precisely what is happening: deep down he knows that a larger response is emerging even if at times this response appears in his eyes to be threatening." (Sir Vidyadhar Surajprasad Naipaul, Trinidad-born British Nobel Laureate)

FSC
www.fsc.org
MIX
Papier aus ver-
antwortungsvollen
Quellen
Paper from
responsible sources
FSC® C105338